EAST COAST WINERIES

EAST COAST WINERIES

A COMPLETE GUIDE FROM MAINE TO VIRGINIA

CARLO DE VITO

RUTGERS UNIVERSITY PRESS
New Brunswick, New Jersey, and London

Library of Congress Cataloging-in-Publication Data

De Vito, Carlo.
East coast wineries : a complete guide from Maine to Virginia / Carlo De Vito.
     p.   cm.
   ISBN 0-8135-3312-0 (pbk. : alk. paper)
   1. Wine and wine making—East (U.S.) 2. Wineries—East (U.S.)—Guidebooks.
 I. Title.
   TP557.D435 2004
   641.2'2'0974—dc22
      2003015885

British Cataloging-in-Publication information is available from the British Library.

The publication program of Rutgers University Press is supported by the Board of Governors of Rutgers, The State University of New Jersey.

Manufactured in the United States of America

This book is dedicated to my two boys,
Dawson Cordell De Vito and Dylan Charles De Vito.
They are of a special and fine vintage that I hope
will someday blossom into a *grand cru* nonpareil.

It is also dedicated to all those individuals who
pioneered winemaking in this region and those
who followed in their footsteps. Thank you.

And of course to my wife. She is my wine cellar.
She is a storehouse of all the qualities I find
so admirable. She has the deep character of a complex
Cabernet, the sophistication of a smooth Merlot,
the delicate qualities of a delightful stainless-steel
Chardonnay, the youthful sweetness of a late-harvest
Riesling, and the effervescence of a fine sparkling wine.

CONTENTS

ACKNOWLEDGMENTS ▪ ix

INTRODUCTION ▪ xi

WINE FESTIVALS ON THE EAST COAST ▪ xv

A NOTE ON THE ENTRIES ▪ xix

CONNECTICUT   1

DELAWARE   11

MAINE   13

MARYLAND   20

MASSACHUSETTS   33

NEW HAMPSHIRE   44

NEW JERSEY   48

NEW YORK   68

PENNSYLVANIA   206

RHODE ISLAND   250

VERMONT   257

VIRGINIA   264

WEST VIRGINIA   318

ACKNOWLEDGMENTS

First, I must acknowledge and commend Mr. Howard G. Goldberg for his advice, thoughts, and good conversation. As one of the forerunners in the appreciation of East Coast wines, Mr. Goldberg has been sounding the clarion call for a great many of us. Some are finally listening.

Second, there is Tom Amibile. The vintner of Cream Ridge Winery answered question after question. Despite my repeated visits, he has always been patient and knowledgeable. He is the epitome of the East Coast winemaker—friendly, open, and available. Thank you.

Third, there are Willie and Fred Frank. They were always more than happy to talk about East Coast winemaking and about world winemaking in general. They were helpful and generous to a fault. In addition, special thanks to Susan Sampson of Sakonnet for her advice and friendly conversation. And finally, to a whole host of winemakers from Maine to Virginia that I pestered with questions—thank you for your time and patience.

Any author of such an effort also owes a huge debt of gratitude to those who went before him. Several writers' works have proved invaluable to me. The writings of About.com's East Coast wine guide Lisa Shea were extremely valuable. They were entertaining in their quirkiness and personal charm, and her reviews were telling and informative. I am indebted to the late Leon D. Adams for *The Wines of America* and Kevin M. Atticks for numerous volumes on wine throughout the United States. My copy of Marguerite Thomas's *Wineries of the Eastern United States* is dog-eared. Jan Aaron's *Wine Routes of America*, and Peter M. Gianotti's remarkable writings on Long Island, are also excellent works. And there are many others too numerous to name.

I would also like to thank the many journalists who cover the wineries on a regular basis. *Wine Spectator* and *Wine Enthusiast* were consulted almost daily. Obviously, *Food & Wine*, *Gourmet*, and *Bon Appétit* were invaluable sources of information, as were the nearly 350 articles from newspapers, magazines, and publicity offices that went into the making of this book. I thank all these writers and sources for bringing the wine industry to life for those of us who cannot be there every day.

I would also like to thank Mr. Stuart Teacher, publisher of Running Press Book Publishers, for allowing me to pursue this project despite my obligations and responsibilities to him and our staff in Philadelphia. He is an avid wine collector who downplays his own considerable and experienced knowledge. Without his cheerful assent, this opportunity would have passed beyond my reach.

I owe a debt of special thanks to Greg Moore and Gilbert King for their ear and opinions, and to Matt Hannifan for his advice and editorial help. I would also like to thank the numerous family and friends that I have plied with good, disappointing, and exquisite wines from up and down the eastern seaboard. Thank you for your forbearance and good humor.

I would of course like to thank my editor, Helen Hsu, who acquired the book, and Audra Wolfe, who edited and managed me. Were it not for Audra's excitement and enthusiasm, I might have given up at any time under the massive weight of such an undertaking. She was cheerleader, fan, and tough-love coach, as well as a forgiving and understanding friend. I thank her for this opportunity as well as Adi Hovav and all those at Rutgers University Press who helped make this book a reality. Also, special thanks to Will Hively and Suzanne Kellam who worked tirelessly and unceasingly, and tried to keep my mistakes to a minimum . . . the thirteenth labor, no doubt.

And finally I would like to thank my wife, Dominique. She is a real trouper. She has weathered, withstood, and been intrigued by my general love of wine, and has shared in that passion. I have dragged her to wineries all over the world, from Spain and France to Chile, California, Maine, and Virginia. She was friend, counselor, secretary, expert, confidante, and pillar during the writing of this book. She helped transcribe reviews, exchange e-mail, and follow up with various and sundry items. My successes in my job and work are a result of her effort, love, and understanding. She makes my failures and disappointments seem inconsequential. We have shared many secrets, successes, and disappointments over countless glasses of wine. She is my sounding board, my conscience, and my confessor.

INTRODUCTION

The East Coast is a major winemaking region—and it has arrived! Those who would speak against that fact would have to be oblivious to the more than 250 wineries to be found between Maine and Virginia. The fact that so many wineries are thriving is testament to a new movement in winemaking.

And to those in the know, including such magazines and newspapers as *Wine Enthusiast*, *Wine Spectator*, the *New York Times*, the *Los Angeles Times*, *Food & Wine*, *Gourmet*, *Bon Appétit*, and other major publications, the reputations of the wines being made are sparkling.

The *Los Angeles Times* published an article in March 2001 titled "Who Makes the Best Riesling? New York, Baby!"—this from the state with the wine capital of the United States (Napa Valley). In this article, the *Wine & Spirits* magazine writer Rod Smith claimed, "In only the last ten years or so has the Finger Lakes wine community begun to attract world wide attention with Riesling, Pinot Noir, and sparkling wines that can stand with the world's best." Looking ahead, Robb Walsh wrote an article for *American Way* magazine asking the question, "The Next Napa? The Fabulous Future of New York's Finger Lakes Wine Region."

Renowned *Food & Wine* writer Lettie Teague also chimed in on the phenomenon of Finger Lakes success with her August 2002 article titled "New York State of Mind." In it Teague admitted to never having tasted an upstate wine. But on her first pilgrimage to the region she was impressed with the Riesling and the Gewürztraminer. Speaking of Riesling, she wrote, "It's the one Finger Lakes wine that has gotten some attention from the rest of the world." Her intention on making her journey had been to find an excellent Riesling. "But like a character in a Jane Austen novel," she confessed, "I ended up falling in love with another: Gewürztraminer."

Howard G. Goldberg, wine writer for the *New York Times* and columnist for *Decanter* magazine, has written more than any other newspaper or magazine writer on the East Coast wines. For his newspaper he has covered New York State (including Long Island, the Finger Lakes, and the Hudson Valley), Connecticut, Rhode Island, Maryland, and New Jersey. Goldberg can easily extol the virtues of any of those regions quickly, succinctly, and happily. Writing in the *New York Times* about New Jersey wines, for example, he led with a sober truth: "New Jersey wine is hardly a top priority of the state's wine drinkers." But he went on to extol the virtues of the state's recent winner of the Governor's Cup, a prize awarded in each state for the best wine entered for that year. In his weekly column, Goldberg has championed Chardonnays, blushes, rosés, Rieslings, Gewürztraminers, dessert wines, Merlots, Cabernet Sauvignons, and more from all these states. He is one of the great prophets of East Coast winemaking.

Two other evangelists must be mentioned as well. One is Marguerite Thomas, whose *Wineries of the Eastern United States* sits dog-eared on my shelf. She was the first to attempt to put some kind of order to the eastern wineries and help establish the region. Her book is the standard by which all others will be judged. The second evangelist is Lisa Shea. As a guide on About.com, she has reviewed as many eastern wineries, especially in New England, as anyone else. Her friendly, cheerful, and quirky reviews have guided thousands to the wonderful treasures of the Northeast. She has certainly been a guidepost to this tourist and author.

Long Island is another story. *Wine Spectator* magazine regularly awards wines from New York scores of 80 and above—some as high as the low 90s. From the toughest of wine critics, these reviews are tantamount to a profession of respect, if not love. Meanwhile the *New York Times* has vigilantly chronicled the many successes of Long Island in too many articles to begin recounting them here.

"In the late seventies and the early eighties . . . Virginia became one of the . . . most dynamic wine regions on the East Coast," wrote Karen MacNeil in *The Wine Bible*. Just how dynamic might that be? World-renowned winemaker Warren Winiarski of Stags Leap (and former president of the International Wine and Spirits Competition) wrote this assessment in an introduction to Felicia Warburg Rogan's *Virginia Wines & Wineries*: "I have suggested that many of Virginia's wineries have their wines judged at an international level. . . . it was my impression . . . that many wines had transcended their regional virtues and could be judged on a world stage."

Regionwide, the same story is being repeated. The Beverage Testing Institute and *Wine Enthusiast Magazine* have awarded scores in the 80s and 90s to wines from all over the East Coast. Today, wines from these states regularly appear in food magazines rated alongside wines from not only California but around the world. *Food & Wine*, *Gourmet*, *Bon Appétit*, and others recommend them among their "Top Ten" and "Highly Recommended" lists.

Many major wine regions begin by establishing themselves in a particular type of wine. It was the same with microbreweries a decade ago. They didn't make the same pilsners you could buy from a major brewery; they established themselves by creating or reviving small-niche beers. So, too, the East Coast wineries first established an ability for making quality wines that were not part of the mainstream; now they are branching out to more recognized varietals. But some of the esoteric wines that were made first have also gone on to establish themselves as quality wines.

THE NEW WINES

In the United States, Chardonnay and Cabernet Sauvignon are the hallmarks of California. In that region, superior whites matured before the reds.

The whites of the East matured faster too. East Coast winemakers now turn out some excellent white wines. Some notable Chardonnays are from Millbrook (N.Y.), Chaddsford (Pa.), Piedmont Vineyards and Winery (Va.), Catoctin (Md.), and Sakonnet (R.I.), as well as a host of Long Island wineries. There are excellent sparkling wines of Westport Rivers (Mass.), Hermann J. Wiemer (N.Y.), and Chateau Frank (N.Y.).

However, the East has introduced the wine-drinking public to other, lesser-known whites. Unionville Vineyards (N.J.) and Sakonnet Vineyards (R.I.) both make excellent Seyval Blancs and Vidal Blancs. And Chateau Morrisette (Va.) makes a sweet light blend called Our Blue Dog that is delightful, and the perfect pairing for summer soups and salads. Penn Shore's (Pa.) Reflections of Lake Erie, the white wines of Dr. Konstantin Frank (N.Y.), and the joint venture between Tomasello and Sylvin Vineyards (both N.J.) all rate highly.

One of the most prized titles the East Coast can now boast about is that of an exceptional maker of Rieslings and Gewürztraminers. Hermann J. Wiemer (N.Y.), Dr. Konstantin Frank (N.Y.), and Standing Stone (N.Y.) rate among the world's best producers of those styles, easily outranking California, Oregon, and Washington in those categories. Even Unionville Vineyards (N.J.) makes a nice Riesling.

Fruit wines and dessert wines (which should not be confused with one another) have flourished here. From the exceptional ice wines of Elk Run (Md.) and Hunt Country (N.Y.), to Duck Walk's Aphrodite (Late Harvest Gewürztraminer) (N.Y.) and Pindar's Late Harvest Gewürztraminer (N.Y.) and Wolffer's Late Harvest Chardonnay (N.Y.), to the exciting fruit wines of Bartlett (Maine), to the exquisite Red Raspberry wine of Alba Vineyards (N.J.), the East Coast has brought forth a cornucopia of new wines.

MEADS AND CIDERS

The East Coast has also seen a rise in the making of meads and sophisticated French- and English-style ciders. Wonderful meads are being made at The Meadery at Greenwich (N.Y.) and Earle Estates (N.Y.) among others. And wonderful ciders are being produced by such establishments as Farnum Hill (N.H.) and Hudson Valley Draft Cider Company (N.Y.). Frank Browning wrote in *Food & Wine* magazine that they "make a drink as sophisticated as champagne." These are not inexpensive quaffing ciders but world-class dry and off-dry handcrafted ciders that call out for sophisticated dishes and gourmet treatment. Any decent wine cellar should have two or three.

There have even been some real strides in the making of red wines on the East Coast. The Pinot Noirs of Dr. Konstantin Frank (N.Y.) and Chaddsford (Pa.), the red blend of Blue Mountain (Pa.), the Italian-style reds of Basignani (Md.) and Villa Appalachia (Va.), and the Merlots of Long Island, like Macari's Bergen Road and Pellegrini's Merlot—among others—are drinkable, savory, sophisticated dry red wines that pair nicely with all kinds of food. Shockingly, one of the most interesting dry reds we tasted was Bartlett's Blueberry Dry (Maine), an Italian-style red wine made solely from blueberries . . . and you wouldn't know it.

Yes, there are some horrible wines out there. But any wine taster could tell you the same about West Coast wines—or those of any region. And yes, the East Coast, which for more than a century has been the home of Concord wines, has been known for the purply, sweet concoctions one critic infamously derided as "grape juice with a shot of booze in it." Those days are gone, and the people who use that quote are the ones who are going to miss all the fun.

Serious wine fans are rightfully collecting these wines. Some are meant to be drunk fresh, as some European wines are meant to be, and some are meant to be aged. Either way, they are meant to be savored—and deserve to be. Indeed, many wines cited herein have been on the wine lists of nationally rated restaurants up and down the seaboard, including several famous New York City restaurants.

But the greatest testament to the region is the fact that many wineries that have gone on the market have been bought for more than it took their creators to establish them. Wineries and winemakers from all over the world are getting a foothold in this new world. As you will see inside, winemakers from as far away as Australia, Europe, and California have all come here in search of new fertile ground. Wineries and grape growers such as Robert Young Vineyards and Villa Banfi have bought vineyards or wineries here. The East Coast wine business has become a multibillion-dollar industry. And this is only the beginning.

The thing to keep in mind is to keep an open mind. The wineries in this region have been making wonderful fruit wines, dessert wines, meads, and ciders, as well as classic red and white wines. Try everything. There were many wines I wrinkled my nose at the thought of that actually brought a pleased smile to my lips. And I believe they will have the same effect on you. Thousands of people in this region's industry (from around the world) are betting millions of dollars on the same thing. They can't all be wrong—and they aren't. Enjoy!

WINE FESTIVALS ON THE EAST COAST

The major difference between East Coast wineries and their Left Coast brethren is that the East Coast business models place greater emphasis on selling directly to the consumer. Therefore the wineries featured in this book rely on festive events and other tourist attractions to lure additional retail traffic. Jazz, bluegrass, and blues festivals are popular. So are art exhibits. Always popular is the classy café or cozy restaurant attached to a winery.

Wine festivals are also a popular way to gain new customers and bring back old ones. Pennsylvania, Virginia, Maryland, and New York all host yearly events, and individual wineries in those states have events almost every weekend. At the state events, many winemakers gather in one place, allowing people to sample wines from wineries that would otherwise take weeks or months to get to individually. Virginia's and Maryland's are among the nicest events. The Finger Lakes festivals and Pennsylvania's are also very nice. All these events offer a tremendous number of wines to taste, gourmet foods to eat, music, and arts and crafts.

While the idea of drinking so much wine all in one weekend might seem daunting, the idea of spitting wines out instead of swallowing them after tasting suddenly makes sense to even the most inexperienced of festival goers. Professional tasters spit out wines for exactly that reason. No one can drink the amount of samples that are available without getting a little loopy. Several tips include:

- Drink lots of water or other nonalcoholic beverages during the course of the day.
- Drink early, leaving the later portions of the day to visit the crafts stalls and giving you time to walk off any ill effects of drinking too much.
- Eat at the festival.
- Spit out the wine after tasting it instead of swallowing all the wines—especially those you don't like (but don't be rude or sloppy).
- Use the guides provided to taste the award-winning wines first; then use your remaining time experimenting with lesser-known wines.
- Don't drink and drive. Most festivals are surrounded by law enforcement officers, looking for drivers who might be leaving the premises under the influence.

Another nice thing about wine festivals is that most offer to have your wine sent to pickup areas, where your purchases will be held until you are ready to leave. Make sure to take advantage of this. It may seem like a nuisance to have to go pick up your wine after already having purchased it, but carrying it around is cumbersome.

With these tips in mind, the question now becomes which festivals to go to. Yes, there are a great many wine-tasting events in the region from Boston to New York to Washington, D.C., but the list I have compiled is a bit more myopic. The idea is that the events noted below are the easiest way to experience the greatest variety of wines being made with the least amount of travel.

There is no substitute for going to a vineyard and experiencing the wonders of each winemaker's home. However, it's also difficult to cover the wineries one might like to visit in states as large as Pennsylvania, Maryland, Virginia, and New York, or the wineries as remote as some in West Virginia or Maine. Thus wine (or food and wine) festivals that feature local wines are listed below.

This is not a complete list, and by all means you are entreated to search the web by region to find other festivals that might feature a good selection of wines from various East Coast makers.

MAINE

Maine has a series of fairs and festivals where local wines can be had. The Yarmouth Clam Festival (mid-July) and The Maine Lobster Festival (late July) are among the most popular in the state.

MARYLAND

Maryland Wine Festival (mid-September). The state's entire list of winemakers is on hand for two days of gourmet food and excellent wine. Small but extremely well organized, and the wine is good!

Mid-Atlantic Wine Festival (mid-September), Annapolis. Wines from the region, food, art, and recording artists. Phone 410-280-3306.

MASSACHUSETTS

While Massachusetts hosts excellent wine festivals such as The Boston Wine Expo and the Nantucket Food & Wine Festival, the state still lacks a gathering that focuses just on local winemakers.

NEW JERSEY

In spite of a thriving local wine industry (with almost as many wineries as Maryland), New Jersey still lacks an official state wine festival. However, a number of events feature local wine, and there are three excellent little festivals that suffice: Blues & Wine at Waterloo (Memorial Day weekend), at Waterloo Village in Stanhope, the Belmar Seafood Festival (early June) in Belmar, and Harvest Wine Festival at Alba Vineyards (early October).

NEW YORK

As one of the major wine-producing regions in North America, New York State offers numerous wine festivals, the most notable of which is the Finger Lakes Wine Festival.

Wine & Herb Festival (early May), Cayuga Wine Trail. A fabulous food and wine experience, filled with wild dishes and lots of good wines to complement them.

Finger Lakes Wine Festival (mid-July), Watkins Glen. Winemakers from over sixty local wineries pour their best wines. Phone 607-535-2481.

Long Island Wine Tasting (September). The crowds converge in the crisp autumn air to sample flavorful Cabernets and Chardonnays offered by Long Island vineyards and local wine dealers.

Harvest Weekend (late September), Lake Ontario Wine Trail. Includes wineries from the Lake Erie and Lake Ontario region. Phone 315-594-2502.

Wine, Wreaths and Ornaments (early November), Chautauqua Wine Trail. Each guest receives a grapevine wreath, a special ornament from each winery, and a recipe book featuring the food and wine pairing served at each winery.

PENNSYLVANIA

Pennsylvania Wine Festival (early June). Winemakers from all over the state attend this exciting and well-organized festival. One of the larger ones on the East Coast.

North East Wine Festival (late September), in the town of North East on Lake Erie. Also called the Wine Country Harvest Festival, it's a popular weekend celebration of music, arts, crafts, and the fruits of the vine! Phone 814-725-4262. www.nechamber.org/winefest.

VIRGINIA

Vintage Virginia Wine Festival (early June). One of the largest single wine fairs in the country, and one of the best. Extremely well organized and civilized. Lots of fun.

WEST VIRGINIA

Uniquely West Virginia (April), Berkeley Springs. A food and wine festival featuring some of the state's best wineries.

West Virginia Wine Festival (late May), Glen View. A collection of winemakers from all over the state converge at the spacious Daniel Vineyards.

A NOTE ON THE ENTRIES

I tasted every wine noted in these pages. Wines that I especially liked are sometimes reviewed more thoroughly than the wines the makers are known for. The reason is quite simple. I felt it important not to expose myself as a reviewer to owners and winemakers, so that I could get a visitor's perspective. Many times, well-known critics or reviewers have tasted wines and vintages made available to them that the wineries cannot make available to every patron. In my quest to make this guide as useful as possible, I did not review many wines that would not be made available to the average consumer.

Regardless of whether they knew my purpose, I found most East Coast winery owners, winemakers, and others involved in the industry to be very open about what they do, why they do it, and most important, how they do it. I can't even begin to estimate how many times at wineries or wine festivals it was easy to talk to any of these people, and how available they made themselves to the "average Joe." I found this both unique and refreshing, as it is not the norm at many other wineries throughout the United States, or around the world.

My wife Dominique and I have traveled to many wineries throughout the world, including California, Canada, the East Coast, France, Chile, and Spain. Using that wider world as a basis of comparison, I have included ratings of the exceptional wineries and wines in my book to give the newcomer a head start in understanding the quality of wine available to the consumer, and where to start looking for top quality in any corner of the region. This is meant to be a starting point—a point of departure.

RATINGS

WINES

- ♥ A good wine. We bought it and drink it at home and have or would buy it again.
- ♥ ♥ A very good wine. We serve it to guests at dinner parties.
- ♥ ♥ ♥ An excellent wine. Compares with any wine of the type from anywhere.

WINERIES

✧ A good winery on the East Coast.

✧✧ A good winery no matter where you are in the world.

✧✧✧ One of the better wineries anywhere.

PRICES

$ $10 and less

$$ $10–$20

$$$ $20 or more

NOTES

Dry—No hint of sugar or sweetness noticeable to the palate.

Off-dry—Only a slight hint of sweetness.

Semisweet—More toward the sweeter range in wines.

Sweet—Generally reserved for dessert wines and port-like wines.

Nice—A good wine worth tasting and buying.

Comes through—Wineries advertise flavors. Confirms winery's assertions.

EAST COAST WINERIES

CONNECTICUT

Bishop Farms & Winery

500 S. Meriden Rd., Cheshire, CT 06410 • Phone 203-272-8243

A 200-year-old working farm, Bishop Farms makes cider and has a fruit winery. Other attractions include farm animals, antiques, gifts, a Christmas shop, and a dried-flower shop. Bishop's offers hayrides through the apple orchards as well as samplings of their fruit wines and apple cider. There is also a children's farm to visit.

Wines: $–$$

HOURS AND DIRECTIONS Wed.–Sun. 10 a.m.–5 p.m., June–July; daily 10 a.m.–5 p.m., Aug.–Dec. ■ On Rte. 70 (Meriden Rd.) about 3 miles east of the Rtes. 10 and 70 intersection in downtown Cheshire.

Chamard Vineyards ✿ ✿ ✿

115 Cow Hill Rd., Clinton, CT 06143 • Phone 860-664-0299 •
Fax 860-664-0297 • www.chamard.com • chamard@cshore.com

Owned by Tiffany & Company chairman William R. Chaney, Chamard produces fine, classic wines that have won raves from the critics. Hugh Johnson called Chamard Connecticut's top winery in the 2002 edition of his *Pocket Wine Book*; *Wine Spectator* called it "a gem of a vineyard"; and *Connecticut Magazine* voted it the state's best winery in 1998, 1999, 2000, and 2001. Set in the beautiful, rolling Connecticut countryside, the winery's 20-plus acres are primarily planted with Chardonnay (70%), with the remaining 6 acres producing Merlot (12%), Cabernet Sauvignon (6%), Cabernet Franc (6%), and Pinot Noir (4%). The first rootstocks were planted in 1983, the first wine was sold in 1988, and since then both vines and winery have flourished. In Connecticut, Chamard wines are sold in more than four hundred wine shops and one hundred restaurants, and in Manhattan Mr. Chaney has placed his bottles on the wine lists of restaurants such as La Cote Basque and Le Cirque 2000.

Wines: $–$$$

White Wines

Chardonnay—Citrus and oak flavors, well balanced, with a nice finish. ♥

Estate Reserve Chardonnay—Tropical fruits, soft taste, buttery, with a dry finish.

Red Wines

Cabernet Sauvignon—A deep, dry red wine. Berries and oak come through.

Estate Reserve Cabernet Franc—A deep, spicy red with a beautiful ruby color. Dry.

Estate Reserve Cabernet Sauvignon—A thick, chewy Cabernet Sauvignon blended with 15% Cabernet Franc and 10% Merlot.

Estate Reserve Merlot—A soft, silky, garnet gem.

Merlot—Full bodied.

REVIEWS AND AWARDS

"Top Chardonnay!"   —*Hugh Johnson's Pocket Wine Book 2002*

"[In the 1998 Chardonnay] concentrated fruit that's rich and almost sweet is balanced by tangy mineral flavors. . . . An immense bargain."

—Jonathan Alsop, *In Vino Veritas* (February 2000)

"[The 1999 Estate Reserve Chardonnay] is a classic, well-balanced wine with overtones of toasty peach and ripe apricots. . . . [The 1997 Estate Pinot Noir is] a light-styled red with a crisp, acidic backbone."

—Bob Chaplin, *Hartford Courant* (February 10, 2002)

"[The 1997 Cabernet Sauvignon] has a ripe-fruit bouquet, pretty dark-fruit flavors, with black currant standing out. . . . smooth."

—Howard G. Goldberg, *New York Times* (November 21, 1999)

HOURS AND DIRECTIONS Tasting Room open Wed.–Sat. 11 a.m.–4 p.m. year-round for tasting, tours, and retail sales. ■ Take exit 63 off I-95. Turn left onto Rte. 81 north. Just past the outlet stores, turn left onto Walnut Hill Rd. and continue 0.8 mile. It will merge into Cow Hill Rd., and you will see the vineyard on your left.

DiGrazia Vineyards

131 Tower Rd., Brookfield, CT 06804 • Phone 203-775-1616 • Fax 203-775-3195 • www.digrazia.com • wine@prodigy.net

Nestled among lush, rolling hills just north of Danbury, DiGrazia is a fabulous stopping-off point for folks making a day's drive through the western Connecticut countryside. Dr. Paul DiGrazia and his wife, Barbara, planted 45 acres of vineyards here in 1978 with the intention of eventually founding a winery. Their first four wines were made available six years later, and by 1994 DiGrazia wines had the distinction of being served to President Bill Clinton. Today, DiGrazia produces more than 7,000 cases annually, with twenty-eight different brands—one of the largest selections of any small vineyard in the region. Dr. DiGrazia, an attending physician at Danbury Hospital, is one of the nicest vineyard owners you may ever meet.

Wines: $$

White Wines

Autumn Spice—One of the most distinctive wines in all New England, made from honey, sugar pumpkins, and white grapes, seasoned with cinnamon, ginger, cloves, and nutmeg. Excellent. Perfect for the holidays. ♥

Vintage Festival Wine—A dry Seyval Blanc.

Wind Ridge—A semidry Seyval Blanc. Light, lively, and very tasty.

Winners Cup—A dry, smooth, full-bodied Seyval Blanc.

Red Wines

Fieldstone Reserve—A Rhône-style blend of reds. Dry and smooth.

Harvest Spice—A medium-dry spiced wine made from red grapes, sugar pumpkin, and real spices.

Blush Wines

Anastasia's Blush—A blend of Seyval and Vidal, blushed with red grape. Delightful.

Dessert Wines

Berrywood—A grape wine fermented with raspberry and honey.

Honey Blush—Full bodied, with no detectable sulfites (less than 10 parts per million) and honey used in place of preservatives.

Winterberry—A grape wine fermented with black currant, raspberry, honey, and orange spirits.

Yankee Frost—Made from frozen grapes. Sweet and delicious, and not as thick or concentrated as many Vidal ice wines.

Port Wines

Blacksmith—A medal-winning, ruby-style port. Wood matured.

Evangelico—A blend of pear, black walnut, and aged grape brandy.

Terra Virgo—A blend of white grapes, orange spirits, and aged brandy.

White Magnolia—A light, white port. Apricot flavors definitely come through.

REVIEWS AND AWARDS

Blacksmith—Gold medal, 1998 American Wine Society National Competition.

"Charming, tasty, imaginative, even entertaining."
—Howard G. Goldberg, *New York Times* (May 23, 1999)

"Hands down . . . the most intense, enlightening and enjoyable vineyard experience." —Kathy O'Connell, *Hartford Advocate* (autumn 1998, special section)

HOURS AND DIRECTIONS Open Wed.–Sun. 11 a.m.–5 p.m. year-round or by appointment. ■ Take exit 9 off I-84, follow Rte. 25 north to Brookfield Center, turn right onto Rte. 133 east, and follow the blue Wine Trail signs. DiGrazia is the first left on Tower Rd. off Rte. 133.

Haight Vineyards

29 Chestnut Hill Rd., Litchfield, CT 06759 • Phone 203-572-1978 • www.haightvineyards.com

In 1974, gentleman-farmer Sherman Haight read an article in the *Wall Street Journal* about Ukrainian-born Dr. Konstantin Frank, the legendary pioneer of New York State *Vitis vinifera* cultivation (i.e., the growing of noble European varieties such as Chardonnay and Cabernet). Inspired, Haight flew to Rochester to meet Frank, and in 1975 became the first to plant vines in Connecticut—and in historic Litchfield County, no less, some of the most beautiful countryside in the state. Haight and his staff weathered some difficult winters and summers in the harsh New England climate, but went on to create some of the state's best wines, including the local favorite Covertside White.

Wines: $–$$

White Wines

Chardonnay—A dry white. Delicate fruit character is preserved through cold fermentation.

Covertside White—An off-dry blend of Seyval Blanc from several estate vineyards. Fruity, fresh, and deservedly popular.

Honey Nut Apple—From Haight's Mystic Winery. Flavored with pure honey. An award winner.

Riesling—A popular German grape. Of all of the Haight wines, we liked this one best. ♥

Summer Breeze—A Seyval Blanc artfully flavored with honey and a hint of lemon. Different and refreshing.

Blush Wines

Barely Blush—A popular blush wine fermented at low temperature and stopped with a hint of sweetness.

REVIEWS AND AWARDS

"Chardonnay appears, by a short head, to be his best wine, followed by a Germanic style Riesling which has some slight residual sugar."   —Wineontheweb.com

"Haight's signature white, Covertside . . . is clean and bright, with hints of citrus."
        —Kathy O'Connell, *Hartford Advocate* (autumn 1998, special section)

"The Riesling is fruity, with a light apple flavor."
        —Lisa Shea, About.com (August 2000)

HOURS AND DIRECTIONS Tastings and tours offered Mon.–Sat. 10:30 a.m.–5 p.m., Sun. noon–5 p.m., year-round. ■ Look for Wine Trail signs at the intersection of Rtes. 8 and 118 or Rtes. 202 and 118. The winery is located 1 mile from the village of Litchfield, just off Rte. 118 on Chestnut Hill Rd.

Haight Vineyards has a second location at Olde Mistick Village, Coogan Blvd., Mystic, CT 06355 (phone 860-572-1978). Tours and tastings are available Mon.–Sat. 10 a.m.–6 p.m. and Sun. noon–5 p.m. year-round • Take exit 90 off I-95. Follow signs to New Mystic Aquarium and Wine Trail signs. The winery is across the parking area from the aquarium.

Heritage Trail Vineyards

291 N. Burnham Hwy., Lisbon, CT 06351 • Phone 860-376-0659 •
Fax 860-376-6478 • www.heritagetrail.com • vintner@heritagetrail.com

Having won several awards for home winemaking, Heritage Trail owner Diane Powell is working to establish a small presence in the world of commercial winemaking. And when we say small, we mean small. Even by northeastern standards, this operation is tiny. Every grape is grown, selected, picked, and crushed carefully, and case quantities are very small. Each wine is a personal statement, as is the winery itself, which looks more like an inviting little general store. Its sign reads simply "Wine Bar, Light Foods." Far from the madding crowd, Heritage Trail's beautifully maintained grounds are eminently strollable, dotted with gardens, a fountain, and a pond.

Wines: $–$$$

White Wines

Estate-Bottled Chardonnay—Aged in glass. Achieves its full, buttery flavor through malolactic fermentation. An award winner.

Heritage Sweet Reserve White Table Wine—Delightfully sweet, but light and without as much sugar as you'd think; 100% Vignoles Blanc.

Quinebaug White—An off-dry white with slightly sweet overtones. Made from Vignoles Blanc grapes.

Red Wines

Heritage Trail Cabernet Franc—A nice blend of Cabernet Franc, Pinot Noir, and Merlot, aged in French oak *barriques* 2 years. Let it age in your cellar some.

Shetucket Red—Unique French-American hybrid blend of Baco Noir and Buffalo, aged several months in American oak.

REVIEWS AND AWARDS

Estate-Bottled Chardonnay—Bronze medal, 1995 and 1996 Amenti del Vino statewide amateur winemakers' competition.

"[The Quinebaug White] is a spicy, light white with a great finish, perfect with fish or salads."   —Lisa Shea, About.com (August 2000)

HOURS AND DIRECTIONS Open Fri.–Sun. 11 a.m.–5 p.m., May–Dec. ■ From New Haven, take I-95 north to I-395 north to exit 83A (Lisbon), then turn left onto Rte. 169. Heritage Trail will be approximately 3 miles on your left. ■ From the Boston area, take I-395 south to exit 87 to Rte. 12; go south on Rte. 12 to a sign for Rte. 169 (about 4 miles); turn right on Butt's Bridge Rd. and go to Rte. 169 (2 miles); turn left onto Rte. 169. The winery is 2 miles down the road.

Hopkins Vineyard

25 Hopkins Rd., New Preston, CT 06777 • Phone 860-868-7954 • Fax 860-868-1768 • www.hopkinsvineyard.com

Set in the Connecticut hills, Hopkins Farm was founded in 1787 by Revolutionary War veteran Elijah Hopkins and in the course of time has seen almost every imaginable kind of agribusiness: sheep, race horses, grain, tobacco, dairy, and now—since 1979—wine. Owners Bill and Judy Hopkins (descendants of Elijah) have converted the farm's nineteenth-century red barn into a winery, tasting room, and instant step-back-in-time experience. It looks especially lovely in summer and autumn, surrounded by thick, striking vegetation. While the winery is as pretty as it gets, you don't get the full experience unless you sample some of offerings with dinner at the wonderful Hopkins Inn, right next door.

Wines: $–$$$

White Wines

Chardonnay Estate Bottled—100% barrel fermented and aged in French and American oak. Dry, buttery.

Seyval Blanc Estate Bottled—Crisp and clean, with fruit overtones.

Vidal Blanc—A gold, sweet nectar. Very nice. Not cloying.

Westwind—A semisweet white. Refreshing.

Red Wines

Cabernet Franc Estate Bottled—A dry, deep red with blackberry overtones.

Highland Estate—A medium-bodied dry red blended from select French-American hybrid grapes.

Blush Wines

Sachem's Picnic—A deep, ruby-colored blush wine. Semisweet.

Sparkling Wines

Sparkling Wine Gold Label—A traditional *méthode champenoise* blend of barrel-aged Chardonnay and Pinot Noir.

Sparkling Wine Silver Label—Crafted in the traditional Champagne method, each bottle is 3 years in the making.

Ciders

Cider—Their "authentic farmhouse version" of New England cider. Clean, crisp, but with some tannins. Nice!

REVIEWS AND AWARDS

Chardonnay Estate Bottled 1997: "Score: 82"   *—Wine Spectator*

"Their seyval blanc and cabernet franc . . . are delicious, the former crisp and dry with a citrusy finish, the latter berry-rich but not heavy."
    —Kathy O'Connell, *Hartford Advocate* (autumn 1998, special section)

HOURS AND DIRECTIONS Open Mon.–Fri. 10 a.m.–5 p.m., Sat. 10 a.m.–6 p.m., Sun. 11 a.m.–6 p.m., year-round. Guided tours Sat. and Sun. at 2 p.m. ■ From New York City, take the Saw Mill or Henry Hudson Parkway to I-684 north to I-84 east to Rte. 7 north to Rte. 202 east to Rte. 45 north (New Preston). ■ From Hartford, take I-84 west to Rte. 4 west (Farmington) to Rte. 118 west to Rte. 202 west to Rte. 45 north. ■ From Boston, take I-90 (Mass. Pike) west to I-84 west to Hartford; then follow the directions from Hartford.

McLaughlin Vineyards

Albert's Hill Rd., Sandy Hook, CT 06482 • Phone 203-426-1533 •
Fax 203-270-8722 • mclaughlinwine@snet.net

This third-generation 160-acre farm and winery, owned and operated by the McLaughlin family since the early 1940s, didn't start growing grapes until 1979 and didn't release a wine of its own making until the early 1990s, but it has quickly gained a reputation as one of the better wineries in the state, a real up-and-comer. Only 15 acres of the land is actually planted in grapes, accounting for about 60% of the annual wine production (about 5,000 gallons). The remainder of the fruit is contracted from growers in New York's Finger Lakes region and the North Fork of Long Island. Russell Hearn, the Australian-born winemaker at Pellegrini Vineyards—one of Long Island's most progressive estates—has consulted for owner Morgan McLaughlin Smith, and the house style shows his influence.

Wines: $–$$

White Wines

Chardonnay—A straw-colored dry white wine. Citrus ending.

Lees Flour—A light white blend.

Riesling—A light, off-dry German-style wine.

Seyval Blanc—A dry, light white wine. Granny Smith apples come through.

Red Wines

Coyote—Light, semisweet red.

Merlot—A deep, rich, dry red wine. Smooth.

Red Table Wine—A medium-bodied dry red.

Blush Wines

Bell Rosé—A light, semisweet blush wine.

REVIEWS AND AWARDS
"Lees Flour [is] a great tasting, crisp, semi-sweet white."

—Karen Forrest, Acorn-online.com

HOURS AND DIRECTIONS Tastings daily 11 a.m.–5 p.m., June–Dec.; Sat.–Sun. only, Jan.–May. Winery tours by appointment only. ■ From I-84, take exit 10 and turn right at end of ramp (if coming from Danbury) or left (if coming from Waterbury). Take the first left onto Walnut Tree Hill Rd. Continue 2 miles to an island and bear left onto Albert's Hill Rd. The entrance is 100 yards ahead on the right.

Nutmeg Vineyards

800 Bunker Hill Rd., Coventry, CT 06238 • Phone 860-742-8402

Anthony Maulucci did not buy farmland in 1968. Instead, he did it the hard way, carving three small vineyards out of the thick woodlands around Andover and planting them with Chardonnay, Baco Noir, Seyval, and other grape varieties. Since then he has slowly built up one of the smallest and most hidden winery gems in the state. A unique little property with its own bass-filled pond, the winery is a one-man operation and serves as Maulucci's completely self-sufficient home as well, with solar panels providing electricity and cordwood stacked at hand to stoke the stove.

Wines: $–$$

White Wines

Chardonnay—Light, more fruity than dry. Very nice.

Seyval Blanc—Tart, light, crisp. A rough but wonderfully idiosyncratic Seyval.

Red Wines

Red Table Wine—Mostly Baco Noir.

Dessert Wines

The Angel Wings—A dessert wine made from Chardonnay.

REVIEWS AND AWARDS

"The Chardonnay [is] light, fruity, and gentle. A great wine for sipping on its own, as well as one that would go well with light cheese or other appetizers. . . . The red table wine . . . is rich and gamey, with a smooth, non-tannic flavor. Great with wild game or rich meats."   —Lisa Shea, About.com (August 2000)

HOURS AND DIRECTIONS Tours and tastings Sat.–Sun. 11 a.m.–5 p.m. year-round. ■ Take Rte. 6 from Hartford toward Andover. Bunker Hill Rd., a dirt road, is right off Rte. 6.

Sharpe Hill Vineyards

108 Wade Rd., Pomfret, CT 06258 • Phone 860-974-3549 •
Fax 860-974-1503 • www.sharpehill.com • sharpehill@snet.net

One of the brightest up-and-coming wineries on the entire East Coast, Sharpe Hill has been giving Connecticut stablemates Chamard and Stonington a run for their money since the late 1990s, and in 1999 was praised by *New York Times* local wine critic Howard G. Goldberg, who noted that their wines show "a playful, populist bent."

Situated on a 700-foot hill that offers views of Massachusetts and Rhode Island, the winery is owned by Steven and Catherine Vollweiler, who planted their first grapevines in 1992. The two have work tirelessly, and today the vineyard consists of

20 acres planted with Chardonnay, Melon de Bourgogne, Pinot Blanc, and Vignoles for white wines; and Cabernet Franc, Carmine, and St. Croix for red. Beyond the core winery business, Catherine spends a great deal of time directing the property's two excellent restaurants: The Wine Garden, a small French-style entertaining garden situated at the base of the vineyards, and the Fireside Tavern, a replica of an old-fashioned New England tavern. Both serve wonderful fare.

Wines: $–$$

White Wines

American Chardonnay—Barrel fermented, with well-balanced fruit and oak.

Ballet of Angels—A crisp, clean, semidry white with strong fruit. Their greatest award winner, and one can see why. ♥

French Chardonnay—A lightly oaked Chard, fermented in French oak barrels. ♥

Reserve Chardonnay—French Burgundy style, with heavier oak, longer aging. ♥ ♥

Red Wines

Cabernet Franc—Bordeaux style. Smooth and dry.

Red Seraph—A dry red table wine made from mostly St. Croix grapes.

Select Late Harvest—Made entirely from estate-grown, handpicked botrytised Vignoles. Excellent mouth feel and nice balance, with just the right amount of alcohol and acidity. Very nice.

St. Croix—Rhône-style red made from 100% St. Croix and barrel fermented 18 months. Dry.

REVIEWS AND AWARDS

American Chardonnay—Silver medal, Los Angeles County Fair Wine Competition.

St. Croix—Gold medal, 2000, 2001, and 2002 Tasters Guild International Wine Competition.

Ballet of Angels—29 medals in competition, "reminiscent of candied apple, honeydew, mint. Score: 82 (tasted on March 31, 1997). . . . Faint aroma of pear and melon follow through on a medium-bodied palate with forward fruit and clean, off-dry finish. . . . Score: 81 (tasted in March 2002)."
—Beverage Testing Institute

"The Reserve Chardonnay . . . is their topmost white. It's a well-crafted Burgundian-style wine, elegant and soft on the finish."
—Bob Chaplin, *Hartford Courant* (February 10, 2002)

"The Reserve and French Chardonnays were both very good . . . balanced with classic chardonnay fruit flavor and a nice touch of oak. Both of these wines could give similarly priced California Chards a run for their money. . . . [The Cabernet Franc was] my personal favorite. The nose was classic cabernet with complex spicy aromas of white pepper . . . medium bodied and well balanced with a lean fruit style similar to Bordeaux reds."   —Chris Pedersen, Oxfordwineroom.com

"Sharpe Hill's Cab Franc has always been a favorite of ours, and this year was no exception. The 1998 was lighter than the 1997s we'd had before, and of course younger. It was peppery, fruity, with hints of cinnamon and wet leather in the aroma. A nice spicy finish, with a peaty aspect. Quite tasty."
—Lisa Shea, About.com (December 2000)

"Perhaps the most fascinating wine sampled was a hefty, tannic, enjoyable Rhône-like red from Sharpe Hill, made from St. Croix grape, a virtually unknown French hybrid."   —Howard G. Goldberg, *New York Times* (May 23, 1999)

HOURS AND DIRECTIONS Tours and tastings Fri.–Sun. 11 a.m.–5 p.m. year-round. ∎

From I-395, take exit 93. Head west on Rte. 101 (which becomes Rte. 44) for 7 miles to Rte. 97. At the junction of the Rtes. 44 and 97 (Rucki's General Store), go south on Rte. 97 for exactly 4 miles and turn left onto Kimball Hill Rd. The winery will be 1.8 miles on your right. ■ From I-84, take exit 69. Head east on Rte. 74 to the end. At the junction of Rtes. 74 and 44, head east. Stay on 44 to the junction with Rte. 97 (Rucki's General Store); then follow directions as above.

Stonington Vineyards   ✪ ✪

523 Taugwonk Rd., Stonington, CT 06378 • Phone 860-536-1222 • Fax 860-535-2182 • www.stoningtonvineyards.com • stoningtn@aol.com

Just minutes from Mystic Seaport, where the Long Island Sound meets the Atlantic, the town of Stonington is an unlikely place for any winery, much less one of the best in New England. Former international banker Nick Smith and his wife Happy established the winery in 1987, using 58 acres of rich Connecticut farm country, and together with general manager and winemaker Mike McAndrew have produced wines that have garnered praise from the *New York Times,* the *Boston Globe,* the *Hartford Courant, Wine Spectator,* and others. Best known for its barrel-fermented Burgundy-style Chardonnays, Stonington also produces Pinot Noir, Riesling, and Vidal, as well as two proprietary blends, Seaport White and Seaport Blush.

Wines: $–$$

White Wines

Chardonnay—Fermented and aged in both French and American oak barrels. Nice. ♥

Fumé Vidal Blanc—What a great idea! This wine is finished 7 to 8 months in older oak barrels to give it just a light touch of oak. Slight citrus taste. Very nice.

Gewürztraminer—Complex, slightly sweet, with a nice finish.

Seaport White—Stonington's most popular wine, a delicious off-dry Vidal/Chardonnay blend that's light, crisp, and clean.

Red Wines

Cabernet Franc—Dry, Bordeaux-style red, with a deep ruby color.

Blush Wines

Seaport Blush—Very nice, and not as sweet as we expected.

REVIEWS AND AWARDS

"Perhaps the best Chardonnay in New England."   —*Boston Globe*

"[In his 2000 Chardonnay,] winemaker Mike McAndrew has crafted yet another elegant, minerally wine . . . and his creamy 1999 Fumé Vidal Blanc is . . . similar to a top Italian Pinot Grigio. A steal at $10.99."
—Bob Chaplin, *Hartford Courant* (February 10, 2002)

"Seaport White—maybe the best inexpensive wine in Connecticut."
—*Connecticut Magazine*

HOURS AND DIRECTIONS Open daily 11 a.m.–5 p.m. year-round. Tours daily at 2 p.m. ■ From Mystic, New York, and points west, take I-95 to exit 91. At the end of the ramp turn left onto Taugwonk Rd. and go 2.4 miles. The winery is on the left. ■ From Providence, Boston, and Down East, use the same directions but make a right at end of ramp. ■ From Norwich, Hartford, and the north, take Rte. 2 south past the casino to the North Stonington traffic circle. Turn right onto Rte. 184 (west) and go 2.3 miles. Turn left (south) at the blinking light onto Taugwonk Rd. The vineyard is 0.6 miles on the right.

OTHER CONNECTICUT WINERIES

Jerram Winery: 535 Town Hill Rd. (State Rd. 219), New Hartford, CT 06057 •
Phone 860-379-8749 • jerramfarm@freewwweb.com

Jonathan Edwards Winery: 74 Chester Maine Rd., North Stonington, CT 06359 •
Phone 860-535-0202 • Fax 860-535-2662

Priam Vineyards: 11 Shailor Hill Rd., Colchester, CT 06415 • Phone 860-267-8520

Vineyard at Strawberry Ridge: 23 Strawberry Ridge Rd., Warren, CT 06754 •
Phone 860-868-0730

DELAWARE

Nassau Valley Vineyards

36 Nassau Commons, Lewes, DE 19958 • Phone 302-645-9463

Until not very long ago, Delaware state law prevented any single business from grow-ing grapes, making wine, and selling and distributing its own product—but that was before Peggy Raley came along. In the late 1980s, Peggy and her farmer dad conceived the idea of building the state's first winery, and by 1990, after giving her political savvy and diplomacy a good workout, Peggy succeeded in having the law changed. Ten years later, Nassau Valley's wines are being compared favorably with some far more visible labels: a 2001 article by Beth Miller in the *News Journal Prime Life Magazine* (Delaware) described a tasting in which Raley's limited-bottling Clifford Brown White (named for the late Wilmington jazz trumpeter) beat out a Louis Jadot Pouilly-Fuisse and a Kendall-Jackson Chardonnay.

Physically, this is a beautiful and entertaining little winery, set in the gently rolling green hills of Delaware not far from the state's beaches. Visitors enjoy a complimen-tary tasting as well as a five-gallery tour of the history of winemaking. An attached art gallery features the work of local artists.

Wines: $-$$

White Wines
Chardonnay—Aged in French oak.
Clifford Brown White—A light white blend.
Meadow's Edge—Part Seyval Blanc and part Villard Blanc. Slightly sweet, with a
   beautiful scent of honey sweetness up front.

Red Wines
Cabernet Sauvignon—100% Cabernet Sauvignon, aged in oak.
Clifford Brown Red—A light red blend. ♥
Laurel's Red—Their "user-friendly red," meant to go with food. A solid 100%
   Chambourcin. Not aged in oak.

Blush Wines
Cape Rosé—A semisweet blush wine.

REVIEWS AND AWARDS
"[Nassau Valley's Chardonnay is] delicate yet well balanced . . . aged in French oak."
                    —Gail A. Sisolak, *News Journal Prime Life Magazine* (May 2001)

"At $7.50, the Meadow's Edge white, a semi-sweet blend of Seyval Blanc and Villard Blanc, is a steal of a summer pâté-on-the-porch wine, even more than the light and easy $8 all-Chambourcin Laurel's Red or the $10 dry Cape Rosé."
—Washington Post (May 26, 2000)

"Laurel's Red . . . has a light and fruity taste. . . . No matter what your taste in wine, most people enjoy it." —Stephan Hengst, *CAMP Rehobeth* (July 17, 1998)

HOURS AND DIRECTIONS Tours and free tastings offered year-round, Tues.–Sat. 11 a.m.–5 p.m., Sun. noon–5 p.m. ▪ Take Rte. 1 north to Rte. 9 toward Georgetown and follow the signs. Or look for the winery just off Rtes. 9 and 404 about 1 mile west of Five Points.

OTHER DELAWARE WINERIES

Felton Crest Vineyards: 1671 Peach Basket Rd., Felton, DE 19943 • Phone 302-284-9463

MAINE

Bartlett Maine Estate Winery ✿

U.S. Hwy. 1 (RR 1 Box 598), Gouldsboro, ME 04607 • Phone 207-546-2408

Maine's first winery (founded in 1982), Bartlett has quickly become one of the best boutique fruit-wine makers in the United States, if not in the entire Western Hemisphere, producing 16,000 gallons annually. The winery is the creation of food lovers Kathe and Bob Bartlett, who opted to produce their wines from locally grown fruit rather than attempt grape cultivation in Maine's harsh climate. It hasn't always been an easy sell. The Beverage Testing Institute ranks Bartlett as one of the top three fruit-wine makers in the United States, and its Reserve Blueberry as one of the forty best red wines *in the world*, but among the public at large, fruit wine is still perceived as either "country wine" or, worse, as the kind you drink out of a paper sack. "The hard part [is] getting people to try it," Bob Bartlett told the *Wineman*. "We get people in the wine-tasting room who are grape wine connoisseurs. [Once they taste it, though] you can see in their face that they are impressed."

Wines: $–$$$

Fruit Wines

Blueberry Dry—A dry red wine with extraordinary grace. If the label didn't say so, you wouldn't know it was made from blueberries. Nice fruit. Nice dry finish. ♥ ♥

Coastal Apple & Pear—Light, crisp, fruity, but not cloying.

Mead—Traditional honey-based wine. An excellent example of this varietal.

Nouveau Blueberry—The Beaujolais Nouveau of fruit wines, made in much the same way and (in some circles) awaited with the same anticipation each holiday season.

Peach Wine—Semidry. An excellent sipping wine.

Pear Reserve French Oak—Won a medal, and generally considered their best wine. ♥

Sweet Raspberry Wine—A great dessert wine, excellent with chocolate desserts, especially chocolate-covered fruits.

Other Wines

Apple, *Blueberry* (semisweet), *Coastal*, *Pear*, and *Strawberry*

REVIEWS AND AWARDS

Pear Reserve French Oak—Bronze medal for pear wine, 1999 International Eastern Wine Competition.

Beverage Testing Institute Ratings: Sweet Raspberry Wine ranked as one of the best U.S. dessert wines (rating: 91); Coastal Apple & Pear rated 87; Peach Wine rated 85.

"The Blueberry French Oak Reserve . . . [is] a genuine revelation."
—Michael Uhl, *Exploring Maine on Country Roads and Byways*

HOURS AND DIRECTIONS Open June 2–Oct. 15. Tours and tastings Tues.–Sat. 10 a.m.– 5 p.m., Sun. noon–5 p.m. ■ Whether coming from the north or south, you need to get onto Rte. 1 (the Coastal Route) and be east of Ellsworth by about 22 to 23 miles. The winery is located near Fred Ashe Brook and Fred Ashe Rd.

Blacksmiths Winery ✪

967 Quaker Ridge Rd., South Casco, ME 04077 • Phone 207-655-3292

Located near Sebago Lake, Blacksmiths is named for William Watkins, a mid-nineteenth-century smith who had his home and shop in the building that now houses the winery. This lends the physical space of the winery a nice historical ambience, but owners David Ulrich and Steve Linne also know their wine: their wine brokerage, Cellars of Maine, has over the years been responsible for introducing scores of Pacific Northwest wines to the Maine market.

Despite a difficult start in 1999 (including a government thumbs-down on their first wine formula, which included maple syrup), Blacksmiths was still able to produce six wines of 1999 vintage, and production has risen steadily since: from 1,000 cases in 2000 to 3,000 in 2001, with plans calling for 5,000 cases in 2002. Ulrich and Linne use their Cellars of Maine contacts to purchase the very finest grapes and juice from New York and the Pacific Northwest, storing the wines in a new cellar they created below the winery. Maine blueberries find their way into the fun port Roughshod, which is 85% blueberry wine and 15% Oregon brandy. The winery is hoping one day to use grapes from its own burgeoning vineyard, but for now will refer to those plantings only as test vineyards.

Wherever the derivation of the grapes, I'll be going back for more. Linne and Ulrich are savvy merchants who understand marketing and presentation and want to increase the volume and prestige of their brand, but they also understand fine food and wine. This is a winery to watch out for.

Wines: $–$$$

White Wines
Chardonnay—A smooth, creamy, dry white with tart finish.
Seyval Blanc—Dry, green-appley white wine. Nice.
Vidal Blanc—A light white wine with great midpalate and nice finish. ♥

Red Wines
Blueberry (dry)—A reddish-colored fruit wine. Deep fruit. Nice dry finish. Reminds one of a nice Italian-style wine. Surprisingly nice. ♥
Cabernet Sauvignon—A deep, dry red with nice fruit and tart ending.
Casco Bay Port—A light red port. Nice sweetness. Nice balance. ♥
Chambourcin—A deep, dry red. Smooth. Tart finish. ♥
Roughshod—A blueberry port. Nice sweetness with just the right amount of balance. Not overly sweet.

REVIEWS AND AWARDS

"I went for their Roughshod Blueberry Port. Oh my God—I'd found heaven on earth!! It was truly delightful, and next trip over I'm gonna stock up. Not cloyingly sweet or too fruity—rich & mellow & just right."
—*Barleycorn Press* (December 2000)

"[The Vidal Blanc is a] crisp, fruity-tasting white wine that would go well with seafood. It was the clear favorite among the small group of tasters . . . [and] won a bronze medal at the 25th annual International Eastern Wine Competition in Corning, New York."   —*Portland Press Herald* (September 30, 2001)

HOURS AND DIRECTIONS Open May–Dec. daily, 11 a.m.–6 p.m.; winter, Thurs.–Mon. 11 a.m.–5 p.m. ■ The winery is located at the intersection of Rte. 302 and Quaker Ridge Rd. in South Casco.

Cask & Hive Winery

155 Norris Hill Rd., Monmouth, ME 04259 • Phone 207-933-9463

Many Maine wineries use their pastoral, agrarian setting as a marketing tool, but with Cask & Hive one gets the sense that it's the real deal, as close to homegrown as it gets. And it gets good. The winery is in fact part of an orchard complex whose main business is fruits and vegetables. In season, piles of pumpkins are scattered about, and the atmosphere is very low key.

Like other Maine wineries, Cask & Hive focuses on fruit and honey wines, including several different cysers—white wines made from different apple combinations. Chickadee, for example, is made from McIntosh and Red Delicious. There's also the slightly more powerful Chickadee Barrel Select, aged 4 months in old wooden casks that have been used only once to ferment bourbon. Served chilled (about the same temperature as champagne), these wines are light, fruity, and crisp. Other wines are made with blueberry, elderberry, and other fruits. Their mead, made from Maine raspberry blossom honey, is heavy bodied, simple, and dry rather than sweet, much like a Chenin Blanc. All these wines are fermented and aged in oak barrels that you can see through a glass partition in the tasting room. All Cask & Hive wines are sulfite free.

Wines: $–$$

Fruit and Honey Wines

Arthur's Ambrosia—An excellent wine sold like a Riesling or late-harvest dessert wine, in a small, thin bottle.

Chickadee—McIntosh and Red Delicious blend. Touch of honey. Nice apple flavor. Off-dry. Sparkling and tart. ♥

Chickadee Barrel Select—Sparkling cider. Less sweet than Chickadee.

REVIEWS AND AWARDS

"A pleasant stopping point for anyone driving through the area admiring the landscape, and looking for something refreshing to drink!"
—Lisa Shea, About.com (September 1999)

"The mead . . . was truly incredible! . . . Semi-dry (or semi-sweet depending on your personal tastes), full bodied, and has a very nice oak aroma and flavor that balances the honey character well."
—Geoffrey A. McNally, *Mead Lover's Digest* #625, ed. Dick Dunn.

HOURS AND DIRECTIONS Call for hours. ■ From I-495 (near Lewiston) take exit 12 (U.S. 202/Maine 4/Maine 100) toward Farmington/Rumford/Rangeley/Mechanic Falls, driving about 0.5 mile. Keep left at the fork in the ramp, then turn left onto U.S. 202 east and go about 21.5 miles. At Maine 132, turn right for the winery.

Cellardoor Winery / Cyder Valley Farm

367 Youngtown Rd., Lincolnville, ME 04849 • Phone 207-763-4478 or 887-899-0196 • cyder@midcoast.com

Stephanie and John Clapp have worked hard to create this idyllic winery and bed-and-breakfast in rural Maine's rolling hills, a setting perfect for both brief visits and longer, more relaxed stays. Their rustic 1790 house offers two guest rooms with private baths and queen-size beds, while their eighteenth-century barn is now the tasting room. And the grounds always look spectacular. Both Stephanie and John have green thumbs, and spend all summer cultivating vegetables and hundreds of flower varieties. One year, they decided to grow grapes.

"In the spring of 1998 we planted 2,000 grapevines," says John, and today the grounds are covered with vinifera and numerous new hybrids, including Niagara, Cayuga White, Valiant, Elvira, Foch, Beta, Horizon, Traminette, Frontenac, DeChaunac, Chardonel, Concord, Concord S'less, Blue-Black, Canadice, Leon Millot, Swenson Red, St. Croix, St. Pepin, Riesling, Lacrosse, and several others. A number of their wines are also made from fruit, and like other Maine wineries they also use some grape juice bought from New York.

Wines: $–$$$

White Wines

Cayuga White—Dry, crisp, smoky, and full of complex flavors. The oak-barrel treatment is unusual for this variety.

Chardonnay—Made in the Burgundy tradition, fermented in small French and American oak barrels and aged *sur lie* (on the sediment). Smooth and buttery.

Riesling—A wonderful wine! Off-dry, with a floral and spicy aroma.

Red Wines

DeChaunac—Light red table wine.

Marechal Foch—Tuscan-style dry red wine. Barrel fermented.

Fruit Wines

Apple—Made from Maine-grown apples and fermented slowly in medium-toasted American oak barrels at cool cellar temperature.

Dessert Wines

Pear—A delightful coppery yellow dessert wine.

HOURS AND DIRECTIONS Open year-round Fri–Sun. 1–5 p.m. or by appointment. ■ Located just under 6 miles from Camden off Rte. 52. ■ From the south, the drive from Camden takes just a few minutes and is one of the most beautiful drives in Maine. From Rte. 1 north, turn left at the Camden Library onto Rte. 52 (Mountain St.). Go 5 miles past the lake and turn right onto Youngtown Rd. (just before the Youngtown Inn). The winery is 1 mile up, on the left. ■ From the north, going south on Rte. 1, turn right onto Rte. 173, drive 1 mile, then turn left on Youngtown Rd. The winery is 2 miles up.

Parson's Family Winery

60 Brixham Rd., York, ME 03909 • Phone 207-363-3332 •
Fax 207-363-3334 • parsonswinery@cybertours.com

In some senses, the operative word at Parson's is *tradition*. The winery's owners can date their Maine roots back 300 years, and their farmland was first settled over 200 years ago by ancestor Zebulon Preble, a veteran of the Battle of Louisburg. Four generations of Parsons call the winery home today, including brothers Joe and John, who often play host in the tasting room. In another sense, though, the winery is all new, having been established only in September 1996. In that short time, their wines have garnered high praise.

The winery specializes in apple wine, offering four varieties made from several different apple types—New England natives Baldwin, Cortland, and Northern Spy, plus McIntosh, all bought from local Maine orchards. The Baldwin wine is exceptional, more reminiscent of a fine white than of what one normally expects from fruit wines. Other Parson's wines include Peach, Pear, Raspberry, and Blueberry (some created with juice brought from the West Coast), plus a hard cider that harks back to old Maine tradition.

Visit for Maine crafts and gifts, for the tours (which are more like storytelling sessions), or for the folk and bluegrass festival the winery holds each August.

Wines: $$

Apple Wines

Baldwin—Dry, somewhere between Sauvignon Blanc and Chardonnay.

Cortland—A fresh, off-dry white wine, made with a hint of apples.

McIntosh—A semisweet fruit wine.

Northern Spy—Off-dry, somewhere between a Riesling and a Gewürztraminer.

Other Fruit Wines

Blueberry—Light and not cloyingly sweet.

Peach—Fresh with the taste of ripe peaches.

Pear—Not tasted.

Raspberry—Fresh and tart.

REVIEWS AND AWARDS

"Drink [the Northern Spy] for a taste of spices and rich apple. If you enjoy German Riesling then this is the wine for you. . . . [The Baldwin Wine is] very dry and aromatic. The taste is light oak and resembles a French white wine."

—Rita Cook, Lodging.com

"The Baldwin is aged in oak barrels. It is dry, with a delicious flavor and smooth finish. The Cortland . . . is our favorite. This is a light, spicy wine, like a Riesling, with only a hint of apple flavor. . . . The pear was light and delicate . . . delicious with a salad or light meal. . . . The raspberry was very good—not a syrupy sweet dessert wine. Would hold up well against chocolate."   —Lisa Shea, About.com

HOURS AND DIRECTIONS Open for free tastings and tours year-round, Mon.–Sat. 10 a.m.–5 p.m., Sun. noon–5 p.m. ■ Find Rte. 1 in York, Maine. If you are traveling northward, make a left onto Brixham Rd. after first passing Smelt Brook. ■ If you are traveling south on Rte. 1 toward Brixham Rd., you'll probably first pass the junction with Rte. 236 before turning left onto Brixham. Once on Brixham, continue to the winery on your right, not far from Mall Rd. in Kittery.

The Sow's Ear

Rte. 176, Brookville, ME 04617 • Phone 207-326-4649

The Sow's Ear is Maine's only totally organic winery, producing wines made from local, organically grown apples, rhubarb, and blueberries, made with natural yeasts and no sulfates, and allowed to ferment naturally in oak barrels, a process that sometimes takes 2 years. The wines are coarsely filtered, allowing continued development in the bottle, with sediment accruing with age.

As if this weren't pleasantly crunchy enough, the Sow's Ear is also home to local artisan Gail Disney, whose weaving studio and showroom is located upstairs from the tasting room. Her handwoven rag rugs are part folk art, part functional, and make for a nicely out-of-the-blue bonus you don't get at your average winery.

Wines: $–$$

Fruit Wines and Ciders

Blueberry—Made from wild, unsprayed lowbush Maine blueberries.

Cider—Drier than one might expect, and very tasty. Made from the juice of wild, unsprayed apples and fermented slowly at cool temperatures.

Rhubarb—Maine, they say, is an excellent climate in which to grow rhubarb, so why not rhubarb wine? This one's a light and somewhat fruity white.

Sparkling Cider—Not too heavy or cloying. Refreshing and, yes, crisp. Made from unsprayed apples in the traditional *méthode champenoise*, undergoing a second fermentation in the bottle.

REVIEWS AND AWARDS

"Be sure to take home a bottle of cider or one of the more exotic local varieties like the blueberry or rhubarb wine (both of which are delicious)."
—Alicia Mayes, *News Herald* (March 22, 1998)

HOURS AND DIRECTIONS The tasting room is open year-round Tues.–Sat., 10 a.m.–5 p.m.
■ Take Rte. 176 east out of Brookville. The winery is not far from Herrick Rd.

Winterport Winery

279 S. Main St., Winterport, ME 04496 • Phone and Fax 207-223-4500 •
www.winterportwinery.com

In 1972, as the story goes, Michael Anderson was a contractor and accountant, and his new wife Joan was a nurse. For their first Christmas together, Joan wanted to get her new husband a gift he'd remember forever, so she bought him a winemaking kit. Thirty years later, with that kit expanded to eight 1,000-liter tanks and a bevy of oak aging barrels imported from France, it's a safe bet that he remembers.

Par for the course in Maine, Winterport wines are made from locally grown fruits. "I have to be very careful with the fruit," Michael told Kristen Adresen for her article "Time in a Bottle" (*Bangor News*, November 28, 2001). "Wine is such a unique thing— the flavors and the aromas—you have to be right on the money."

The tasting room is painted crème and maroon, and the floors are cork. Wine racks line the walls, and there is a small oak bar. It's a friendly and comfortable place, which is exactly the effect the Andersons were looking for. "I want people to come back here because they like the place and because the wine was good, too," Michael told Adresen. "We're not a bar. Wine is a food. It's part of life."

Wines: $–$$

Fruit Wines

Apple—A pronounced grapefruit-and-lemon flavor followed by the apples' mild sweetness. Made from a variety of apples.

Blueberry (demi)—A light-bodied table red.

Blueberry (dry)—A Chianti-like dry red wine.

Pear (demi)—A semisweet light white, with a smooth finish.

Pear (dry)—A Chardonnay-like dry white wine. Nice fruit. Dry finish.

Spring Fever—An apple-strawberry wine with a citrus component, created to celebrate the arrival of spring after the long Maine winter.

Strawberry—Dark and chewy, with an attempt at dryness.

Blush Wines

Orchard Blush—An interesting new idea: an 80/20 combination of light apple and darker blueberry wines—a kind of fruit-wine rosé.

Dessert Wines

Raspberry Rain—Easily their most enjoyable wine, and their most popular as well. Like the strawberry, goes well with chocolates and cigars.

REVIEWS AND AWARDS

"Strawberry Wine—Unbelievable nose, good mouth feel, full, like an older Tawny Port. . . . Pear Wine (both demi- and dry)—very fruity, good legs, and a long finish from front to back of the tongue. Hints of citrus."   —Allamericanwine.com

HOURS AND DIRECTIONS Open the first weekend in April through the last weekend in December, Tues.–Thurs. 11 a.m.–5 p.m., Fri.–Sat. 11 a.m.–7 p.m., or by appointment. Closed Sundays and holidays. ■ From Bangor, drive 17 miles south on Rte. 1A to downtown Winterport. The winery is on the right at the intersection of Rtes. 1A and 69. ■ From I-95 (north or south), take exit 43 (Carmel/Winterport) to Rte. 69 east and go all the way to the end, 11.9 miles. The winery is on the right.

MARYLAND

Basignani Winery ✡ ✡ ✡

15722 Falls Rd., Sparks, MD 21152 • Phone 410-472-0703 •
Fax 410-433-2536 • www.basignani.com • bert@basignaniwinery.com

Bert Basignani's grandparents made their own wine when he was a child, and the memory must have been inspiring. In 1972, while still a student at Towson State, he bought 10 acres 20 minutes outside Baltimore with the specific intent of one day planting a vineyard. Two years later he married his wife, Lynn, and immediately planted six different varieties of grape and read every book on winemaking he could find. In 1986, the winery was opened to the public, and today self-taught Bert is president of the Association of Maryland Wineries. The secret of his success? "The vineyard, the growing of the grapes, is the most important part," he said in *Where Baltimore* magazine. "If you don't have a good ripe fruit, you're not going to make good wine."

And make good wine they do. Of all the East Coast wineries, Basignani is one of the few that delivers high quality in all of its varietals and can compare favorably with Washington and Oregon wineries—and even some in California. In 2000, *Baltimore Magazine* rated them the number-one winery in Maryland, and *The New Sotheby's Wine Encyclopedia* said they were "among the very best producers, vineyards and wines in the author's experience." Several of their wines are named for Bert and Lynn's children, all of whom work at the winery.

Wines: $–$$$

White Wines

Chardonnay—Aged in small French barrels.

Elena—A dry, Pinot Grigio–like wine made from Seyval (85%) and other hybrid grapes (15%).

Riesling—Crisp white with fruit overtones.

Seyval—A very nice, mature wine, aged in oak. ♥

Vidal—A semisweet German-style white, sweeter than the Riesling. Very nice. ♥

Red Wines

Cabernet Sauvignon—A deep mouthful of berry, with a dry finish.

Lorenzino Reserve—A blend of Cabernet Sauvignon, Cabernet Franc, and Merlot. An exceptional wine for any winery. ♥ ♥

Marisa—A blend of Cabernet Sauvignon, Chancellor, Chambourcin, Foch, and Cabernet Franc. ♥

Blush Wines

Blush—A nice blush wine. Sweet.

REVIEWS AND AWARDS

Cabernet Sauvignon 1998 and *1999*—Bronze medal, 2003 Los Angeles County Fair
Wine Competition.

Lorenzino Reserve 1999—Silver medal, 2003 Los Angeles County Fair Wine
Competition.

"[The 1997 Lorenzino Reserve] possesses an enthralling nose of blackberry jam,
fresh herbs, and spices. It is well structured . . . with well ripened tannins. . . .
Score: 88."
—Pierre Rovani, *Wine Advocate*

"Basignani makes good Cabernet Sauvignon, Chardonnay [and] Seyval."
—*Hugh Johnson's Pocket Wine Book 2002*

"[Basignani Marisa is] an inexpensive blend . . . consistently a delicious red."
—Best of Baltimore, *Baltimore Magazine* (September 2000)

HOURS AND DIRECTIONS Tasting and tours year-round Wed.–Sat. 11:30 a.m.–5:30 p.m.,
Sun. noon–5 p.m. ■ From Baltimore, take I-83 north to Shawan Rd. west (exit 20B).
Go 3 miles to Falls Rd. and turn right. Go approximately 6 miles north, passing Black-
wood Rd. (Rte. 88). Look for the winery entrance on the left, after the bridge. ■ From
Washington, D.C., take I-195 north to I-695 west toward Towson; then take I-83 north.
From there, directions are the same as from Baltimore.

Boordy Vineyards

12820 Long Green Pike, Hydes, MD 21082 • Phone 410-592-5015 •
Fax 410-592-5385 • www.Boordy.com • wine-info@boordy.com

Boordy is one of the most important wineries in the history of North American viticulture. It was founded by Philip Wagner, a 1930s London correspondent and later edi-

tor of the *Baltimore Sun*, who through his
experiments with French rootstocks in the
1940s introduced French hybrids to the U.S.
wine industry. Today, these hybrids are the
dominant rootstocks used in the creation of
American fine wines.

Wagner authored the classic books *Grapes
into Wine* and *A Wine Grower's Guide* and
presided over Boordy Vineyards for 35
years, finally selling the Boordy name in
1980 to Robert Deford III, whose family had
worked for him as grape growers. Deford
relocated Boordy to his family farm, where
the winery now occupies a totally charming
nineteenth-century barn—so charming that in 1998 it hosted a James Beard Foundation Dinner where Boordy wines were served alongside French, California, and Washington varietals.

Despite the ownership change, Boordy has been operating continuously for 51
years, making it one of the oldest labels in the United States. Beautiful and memorable,
it makes a wonderful day trip, just minutes from Baltimore.

Wines: $–$$$

White Wines

Blanc de Blanc—Boordy has always been known for their sparkling wines. This is a nice bottle of bubbly, one of the best on the East Coast.

Boordy White—A nice, dry table white.

Chardonnay—Clean and crisp, with a lovely finish.

Seyval Blanc Reserve—Clean and crisp, with complex flavors and fruit overtones. Dry finish. Delicious. ♥

Vidal—Fruit overtones, like Granny Smith. Crisp and refreshing.

Red Wines

Boordy Red—A light blend of reds. Nice, Rhône-like style. Good with pasta, hamburgers, or pizza. Very drinkable.

Cabernet Franc—A deep, dry wine.

Cabernet Sauvignon—Another dry, deep red.

Blush Wines

Blush—A drinkable version of the popular favorite.

Dessert Wines

Eisling—Sweet and smooth.

REVIEWS AND AWARDS

Chardonnay 2001—Silver medal, 2003 Grand Harvest Awards.

Eisling 2001—Silver medal, 2003 Grand Harvest Awards.

"[Boordy Chardonnay has] pleasant green apple and floral notes, with a hint of toast. Light, slightly crisp finish. Drink now. . . . 83 Points."

—Wine Spectator (May 2002)

Boordy Eisling 2000: "Dessert wine of the year."

—Cellar Notes, WYPR Radio (Maryland)

Boordy White: "One of the best wines for $10 or less."

—Barbara Ensrud, *Best Wine Buys for $10 or Less*

HOURS AND DIRECTIONS Tastings and tours Mon.–Sat. 10 a.m.–5 p.m., Sun. 1 p.m.–5 p.m. ■ From the north on I-95, take exit 74 west (Rte. 152, Mountain Rd.) to Rte. 147 (Harford Rd.) and drive south 3.1 miles to the stoplight in Fork. Turn right onto Fork Rd. Continue 2.6 miles to the stop in Baldwin. Turn left onto Long Green Pike and continue 1.3 miles to Boordy's entrance, on right. ■ From the west on I-695, take exit 29 (Cromwell Bridge Rd.) and go left 2.9 miles. Make a sharp left over the bridge onto Glen Arm Rd. and continue 3.2 miles to stop. Turn left onto Long Green Pike and go 2 miles to Boordy's entrance, on left.

Catoctin Winery ✫ ✫

805 Greenbridge Rd., Brookeville, MD 20833 • Phone and Fax 410-774-2310

We can't recommend this little treasure of a winery enough! While centrally located—almost equidistant from Frederick, Baltimore, and Washington, D.C.—it has remained one of those small, out-of-the-way places that those in the know keep quiet about, saving it for themselves.

The vines were originally planted in 1975, and the winery opened in 1983 under the leadership of winemaker Bob Lyons. A graduate of U.C. Davis and Chateau Montelena, Lyons set out to prove that good grapes can be grown and good, collectible wines made and sold on this side of the continent. He's succeeded, offering well-crafted classic wines that are reasonably priced, considering their quality.

Wines: $$–$$$

White Wines

Chardonnay—Made in stainless steel and aged in French barrels, this light, crisp, delicate wine has citrus flavors and other soft notes. Every bit as good as any other Chardonnay made anywhere else in the world, and a great personal favorite. ♥ ♥ ♥

Chardonnay (oak fermented)—Spends a little longer in the barrel and the cellar before it's released. A nice wine. ♥

Johannisberg Riesling—A slightly sweetish flavor up front, but ends with a slightly dry pop on the palate. Grapefruit.

Mariage—A nice, off-dry Riesling blend.

Red Wines

Cabernet Sauvignon—A deep ruby version of the classic red, done in a Bordeaux style. Lots of fruit, and a dry finish.

Chambourcin—A lighter red than many other houses in the East attempt. A good pasta wine.

Blush Wines

Eye of the Oriole—A semisweet sipping wine.

Dessert Wines

Apple Dew—A *frizzante* apple wine. Very nice for dessert or with cheeses. Makes for a nice aperitif.

Persian Apple—Made from peaches.

REVIEWS AND AWARDS

Chardonnay 1997—Bronze medal, 1999 International Eastern Wine Competition (no small feat, since every winery has a Chardonnay).

"Recommended wines: Cabernet Sauvignon (Reserve), Chardonnay (Oak Fermented), Johannisberg Riesling."   —*The New Sotheby's Wine Encyclopedia*

HOURS AND DIRECTIONS Tours and tastings year-round Sat.–Sun. noon–5 p.m., Mon–Fri. sales only; tours by appointment. ■ From Baltimore, take I-95 south to Rte. 198 west. Turn right on Hampshire Ave.; then make another right onto Greenbridge Rd. The winery is on the left. ■ From Washington on I-495, take the Hampshire Rd. exit north of Washington onto Hampshire Ave.; then turn right onto Greenbridge Rd. The winery is on the left.

Cygnus Wine Cellars

3130 Long Ln., Manchester, MD 21102 • Phone 410-374-6395 • www.cygnuswinecellars.com • cygnus@cygnuswinecellars.com

Cygnus did not celebrate its "first crush" until 1995, and wasn't officially licensed until 1996, but its wines have developed a fast and steady fan base. Because some bottlings remain limited, wines often sell out quickly—the first sign of a good winery.

The winery is one of a growing breed, buying its grapes from prime growers all over Maryland—a strategy by which owner Ray Brasfield seeks out the very best microclimate and most loving growers for each grape variety. Brasfield takes his winemaking seriously, but he's also a quirky fellow, sporting a veritable mane of a mustache. His winery—housed in a 60-year-old former slaughterhouse that's been going through some lengthy renovations—is as quirky as he is. The results, however, are moo-ving.

Wines: $–$$$

White Wines

Chardonnay—A nice, dry Chardonnay grown by Hidden Spring Farm Vineyard in Frederick County. Production is very limited, and it goes fast due to its popularity.

Late Harvest Vidal—A solid addition to the late-harvest ranks. Slight citrus and melon flavors. Smooth finish.

Manchester Hall—A semidry 100% Vidal Blanc, made in the tradition of French Muscadet and German *Kabinett/Spätlese* Riesling. A crisp mouthful of fruit with a sweet ending.

Sauvignon Blanc—Clean and dry.

Red Wines

Cabernet Sauvignon—A big, dry version of the popular French Bordeaux-style wines.

Julian—Cygnus's version of a Meritage wine. Made from Cabernet Franc (23%) and Cabernet Sauvignon (77%), this is a reserve red.

Maryland Red—Another solid red blend made from Chancellor (85%), Cabernet Sauvignon (10%), and Cabernet Franc (5%) and created using a combination of traditional vat fermentation, barrel fermentation, and barrel aging. Big, soft, smooth, dry. New and used American oak barrels help lend a roundness and steadfastness to the wine.

Millers Time—A blend of Chancellor and Seyval, this light red is an excellent burger, pizza, and pasta wine.

Nouveau—A light red sipping wine, slightly off-dry.

Blush Wines

Hampton Cuvée Brut Rosé—Blended from red and white grapes and then tinged with dry red wine in the final stages. A mouthful of fruit, but a dry finish. Very nice.

Sparkling Wines

Blanc—A solid version of the French classic using old-world methods.

Cuvée de Chardonnay—Made from 100% Chardonnay grapes.

Dessert Wines

Port of Manchester—Made from a blend of Chancellor (48%), Cabernet Sauvignon (25%), and Cabernet Franc (27%). A rich red dessert wine.

REVIEWS AND AWARDS

"Ray Brasfield at Cygnus Wine Cellars . . . makes a killer Vidal called Manchester Hall . . . gentle flavors of green melon and peach."   —*Baltimore Magazine* (2001)

HOURS AND DIRECTIONS Tours and tastings year-round Sat.–Sun. noon–5 p.m. All other times by appointment only. ■ Cygnus is located in the center of Manchester at 3130 Long Ln., one block east of Main St. behind the Maple Grove Business Center. ■ From Baltimore and points east, take the Baltimore Beltway (I-695) to I-795 north to exit 9; take Rte. 30 north to Manchester; just as you enter the town, turn right onto Beaver St. and then left onto Long Ln.; the winery is about 2 blocks down, on the right. ■ From Washington, D.C., and northern Virginia, take the D.C. Beltway (I-495 or I-95/495) to Rte. 97 north to Westminster; turn left onto Rte. 140 and exit onto Rte. 27 north to Manchester; at Manchester, turn right (south) onto Rte. 30 (Main St.); go approximately 2 blocks to the traffic light; turn left onto York St. and then right onto Long Ln.; the winery is about 2 blocks down, on the left.

Deep Creek Winery

177 Frazee Ridge Rd., Friendsville, MD 21531 • Phone 301-746-4349 • www.deepcreekwinery.com • deepwine@qcol.net

A relatively new winery, begun by Paul and Nadine Roberts in 1997, with 8 acres of vines, Deep Creek has two major distinctions: its grapes, grown at 2,100 feet above sea level, are some of the highest plantings in all North America, and its winemaking employs many organic methods. Wines are made from grapes harvested from the winery's two properties, as well as some from other Maryland and Pennsylvania grape growers.

A rustic outpost in the remote rural countryside of Maryland, Deep Creek makes for a lovely day's visit. And while you're tasting and buying, be sure to pick up a copy of Paul's book, *From This Hill,* which tells his wine story—from his early interest in wine while growing up in Missouri, to his California wine apprenticeship, to his planting of a Cynthiana vineyard in the East. For those who dream of owning their own winery or just want to know what makes these people tick, it's a wonderful read.

Wines: $–$$

White Wines

Yellow Jacket White—A light, sweet white wine. Excellent for sipping. Great with fruits and cheese, salads, or desserts.

Red Wines

Artisan Red—A deep berry taste with dry finish. A great pasta wine.

Blue Dolce—Sweet blueberry vintage made from locally grown blueberries. Surprisingly nice.

Summer Claret—A deep blush wine. Surprisingly dry. Nice.

Watershed Red Reserve—A medium-bodied blend of Cabernet Franc and Cabernet Sauvignon, with Grenache, Carignane, and Zinfandel added in for balance and panache.

HOURS AND DIRECTIONS Tours and tastings Wed.–Sat. 11 a.m.–6 p.m.; other times by appointment. Closed Dec. 15–Apr. 15. ■ Located near Deep Creek Lake in western Maryland. ■ From Baltimore, take I-70 west from the Beltway to I-68 west near Hancock, to exit 4 (Friendsville). From there, take Maryland Rte. 42 6.5 miles north to Frazee Ridge Rd., where you'll see the winery. ■ From Washington, D.C., take I-270 west from the Beltway to I-70 west at Frederick, to I-68 west near Hancock, to exit 4 (Friendsville); then follow directions from Baltimore.

Elk Run Vineyards

15113 Liberty Rd., Mount Airy, MD 21771 • Phone 410-775-2513 or 410-875-2009 • elk_run@msn.com

The Elk Run vineyards sit on an historic 1750s estate in the rolling hills of Mt. Airy, an unlikely little hamlet that's also home to the Linganore and Loew wineries (listed below). It's one of the prettiest of the East Coast's small wineries and one of our favorites, its small brick-and-gingerbread farmhouse looking like something out of a children's fairy tale and its wines proving just as otherworldly.

Fred and Carol Wilson founded the winery in 1983, and Fred, who studied with Dr. Konstantin Frank of Vinifera Wine Cellars in New York, has been the winemaker ever since. He's definitely doing something right: Elk Run was chosen as one of the top wineries on the East Coast by *Vineyard & Winery Management* magazine and has received a rave review from *The New Sotheby's Wine Encyclopedia*.

Wines: $-$$$

White Wines

Chardonnay: Cold Friday Vineyard—Dry, soft, clean. Slight vanilla and apple. ♥

Chardonnay: Liberty Tavern Vineyard—Aged longer in oak. Softer, buttery, and slight mineral taste.

Gewürztraminer—Slightly sweet, with some touch of grapefruit. Very drinkable. ♥

Johannisberg Riesling—A slightly sweet version of the popular German style.

Red Wines

Cabernet Franc—A well-crafted red with a deep ruby color.

Cabernet Sauvignon—A deep, soft, big red. Great color.

Port—A nice, spicy attempt at the classic fortified wine, with flavors of berries, currants, and raisins.

Blush Wines

Annapolis Sunset—A blush slightly sweeter than the Chesapeake Bay version.

Chesapeake Bay Sunset—A blush wine that is a blend of Seyval and Cabernet. Not too sweet. Nice.

Sparkling Wines

Champagne—In the fashion of the French brut style. Nice.

Dessert Wines

Sweet Katherine—A deep, thick red dessert wine. Really should be considered a port, but it isn't mixed with wine from another vintage. Made from Cabernet Sauvignon. Excellent. ♥

Vin de Jus Glacé—This award-winning Riesling ice wine is one of the best ice wines on the entire East Coast, including Canada. Tremendous taste and value! ♥ ♥

REVIEWS AND AWARDS

Cabernet Franc 2001—Silver medal, 2003 Los Angeles County Fair Wine Competition.

Cold Friday Chardonnay—Silver medal, 2003 Jerry Mead New World International Wine Competition; silver medal, 2003 Atlanta Wine Summit.

Vin de Jus Glacé—1977 and 1978 winner of Maryland's Governor's Cup.

"[The 2000 Vin de Jus Glacé has a] brilliant yellow straw hue . . . aromas of canned peaches and honey. Follows through with a thick, full bodied palate displaying lush forward peach fruit. . . . Finishes with generous sweetness. . . . Score: 85."
—Beverage Testing Institute

"Elk Run Chardonnay 1998 scores 86—an excellent value [offering] appealing toast and dense white fruit aromas. Medium- to full-bodied, thick, oily-textured, plump wine packed with ripe pear and subtle smoke."
—Robert M. Parker, Jr., *Wine Advocate* (December 1999)

"[The Elk Run Millennium Champagne is] a marvelous wine—a 50/50 blend of Chardonnay and Pinot Noir, it is broad, rich and deep with nutty, nutmeg flavors complemented by a smooth creamy texture. A treat!"
—Al Spoler, *Baltimore's Style Magazine* (December 1999)

Cabernet Franc Maryland 2000: "Score: 81."   —*Wine Spectator* (May 2002)

"Elk Run has quietly earned the envy of every Pinot Noir–producing winery in California and Oregon by making Pinot Noir that bears a striking resemblance to really good red Burgundy." —*Baltimore Magazine* (August 2001)

HOURS AND DIRECTIONS Open year-round Tues.–Sat. 10 a.m.–5 p.m., Sun. 1 p.m.–5 p.m. Other days by appointment. ■ From Baltimore, take I-70 to Mt. Airy. Go right on Rte. 27 north, proceed 8 miles to Taylorsville; then turn left on Rte. 26. Elk Run is 2.5 miles on the right. ■ From Washington, D.C., take I-270 to Father Hurley Blvd., turn right onto Rte. 27 north; then follow directions from Baltimore.

Fiore Winery

3026 Whiteford Rd., Pylesville, MD 21132 • Phone 410-879-4007 or 410-836-7605 • www.fiorewinery.com • Eric.Fiore@FioreWinery.com

Fiore has always been one of our favorite red producers in the East, making wines that were the first that we really found comparable to others we knew and drank. Their innovative Zinnavo is one of the best reds in the region. Right up there with the quality of their wines, though, is the quality of the overall winery experience, intimate and family-style, presided over by Mike Fiore, his wife Rose, and their family.

Mike (a.k.a. Michele Fiore Melacrinis) was born in Calabria, Italy, where his family's winemaking roots date back some 400 years. In the New World, Fiore family tradition holds that Thomas Jefferson, anxious to produce wines at Monticello, asked ancestor Philip Mazzei to establish a vineyard. Today, Mike will stand at the tasting bar and talk wine with you all day if you would like. We liked.

Fiore produces more than 15,000 gallons of wine a year, and its rustic grounds are full of picnic spots where you can enjoy a lunch among the vines. (There's also a large hall that's available for weddings and other events, if you're so inspired.)

Wines: $–$$

White Wines

Chardonnay—Fermented and aged in French oak barrels. Dry, crisp, not too overly oaked. Nice.

L'Ombra—Semidry Vidal/Seyval white blend. Slight oak. Nice finish. The name comes from the Italian word for shade.

Riesling—A semidry white. Minerally. Slight grapefruit finish.

Vidal Blanc—Slightly off-dry white with citrus overtones. Very nice.

Vignoles—Semidry white. Crisp. Clean.

Red Wines

Cabernet Franc—Estate grown. Smooth and silky with a dry finish. You can definitely taste the plums.

Cabernet Sauvignon—A dry red, aged for 2.5 years in a combination of French and American oak barrels.

Caronte—A blend of Merlot (60%), Cabernet Sauvignon (30%), and Sangiovese (10%). Big, fruity, and lush, with a dry finish.

Chambourcin—A deep, dark ruby wine. Full bodied. Dry. One of our favorite Chambourcins. ♥

Zinnavo—Maryland Cabernet Sauvignon and Cabernet Franc blended with California Zinfandel grapes, touted as "Maryland's first bi-coastal proprietary wine." ♥

Blush Wines

Blush of Bel Air—A semidry rosé. Very popular.

Scarlette—Sweet wine made from Concord and white wine. A popular wine.

Dessert Wines

Late Harvest Vidal Blanc—A lovely, smooth version of this popular new classic dessert wine.

REVIEWS AND AWARDS

Cabernet Sauvignon 1999—Gold medal, 2003 International Eastern Wine Competition.

Vidal Blanc 2002—Gold medal, 2003 San Diego National Wine Competition.

Zinnavo 2000—Gold medal, 2003 International Eastern Wine Competition.

"Fiore's Chambourcin is interesting."   —*Hugh Johnson's Pocket Wine Book 2002*

HOURS AND DIRECTIONS Tours and tastings year-round Wed.–Sat. 10 a.m.–5 p.m., Sun. noon–5 p.m. Mon.-Tues. by appointment only. ■ From East Baltimore, Annapolis, and Washington, D.C., take I-95 north to exit 74 (Fallston-Joppatowne). Turn left at the light onto Rte. 152 and continue to Rte. 165. Turn right onto Rte. 165 and continue to Rte. 24. Turn left on Rte. 24 and continue to Rte. 136, Whiteford Rd. Turn right and continue for 1 mile. The winery is on the right. ■ From West Baltimore, Towson, and western Maryland, take I-695 to exit 27B (Dulaney Valley Dr., Rte. 146). Follow Rte. 146 north to Rte. 23. Turn right on Rte. 23, continue to Rte. 165 and turn left; then follow the local directions.

Linganore Wine Cellars / Berrywine Plantations

13601 Glissans Mill Rd., Mt. Airy, MD 21771 • Phone 410-795-6432 or 301-831-5889 • Fax 301-829-1970 • www.linganore-wine.com • lucia@linganore-wine.com

Located in beautiful, rural Mt. Airy, this unique winery produces two wonderful labels. Linganore is a classic boutique winery, creating some wines that emulate old-world traditions using classic vinifera and others that employ new blends. Berrywine Plantations is a label that represents the winery's commitment to fruit wines, created mostly from Maryland-grown fresh produce. These tend to be on the fruity side, but that can be to your advantage: they're fantastic for making sweet desserts, a process that the staff will be happy to explain to you.

The combined Linganore/Berrywine operation is fairly large, with state-of-the-art wine presses and other winemaking equipment, and a tasting room that's one of the most opulent on the East Coast. Outside, there are plenty of places within the vineyards where you can take your wine and a picnic lunch. A wonderful treat.

Wines: $–$$

Linganore White Wines

Chardonel—Barrel fermented followed by malolactic fermentation, and aged *sur lie*. Full bodied and dry.

Chessie's Legend—Dry, crisp, delicate white.

Melody—Semisweet German-style white. Rich, luscious apricot flavors come through.

Mountain White—A blend of native American grape varieties, this light, semisweet white is fruity and tasty.

Skipjack—A semisweet white wine, medium bodied. Done in oak, so it has body.

Terrapin White—Made in the classic German Johannisberg Riesling style. Aged in stainless steel. Nice.

Traminette—A white done in the classic *Auslese* Gewürztraminer style.

White Raven—An off-dry white. Big fruit taste without being sweet. Well balanced.

Linganore Red Wines

Bacioni—A blended red dinner wine. Aged in oak. The name is Italian for "hugs and kisses."

Black Raven—A red table wine done in the Beaujolais style. Big fruit, mostly dry. A great pasta wine.

Cabernet Sauvignon—A French-style red.

Chambourcin—Produced in the Bordeaux style. Berry comes through.

Millennium Nouveau 2001—A fruity, low-tannin, blended red. Meant to be drunk young. Nice.

Linganore Blush Wines

Fox Hunt Blush—Popular blush blend. Light and crisp.

Mountain Pink—A semisweet blush. Very nice.

Linganore Dessert Wines

May Wine—A slightly sweet wine made with woodruff herb. This wine is traditionally served over fresh strawberries—try it yourself. A wonderful spring or midsummer wine.

Spicy Regatta—A semisweet red wine spiced with cinnamon cloves. Serve heated with slices of orange and apples for fall and winter entertaining.

Steeple Chase Red—A semisweet red. Good with chocolate desserts.

Sweet Chessie—Dessert in a bottle. Sold in imported Italian bottles and hand dipped in wax. Very nice.

Berrywine Fruit Wines

Blackberry—A light- to medium-bodied pure fruit wine.

Blueberry—Light to medium bodied.

Currant & Apple—Made from 50% of each.

Dandelion—Berrywine has been producing this delightful semisweet (weedy) wine since 1978. Light in body. Very floral bouquet.

Medieval Mead—A solid rendition of the Noble Honey Wines of the Middle Ages. Slight cinnamon touch is different.

Peach—A slightly sweet fruit wine. Light to medium bodied. Wonderful as a dessert wine.

Plum—A pure fruit wine

Raspberry—Medium bodied.

Spiced Apple—Made from Maryland apples. A semisweet wine spiced with cinnamon and clove. Serve chilled or warm in a mug with a stick of cinnamon.

Tej—A pale, dry, Ethiopian-style honey wine with natural flavors. An original idea to be sure.

REVIEWS AND AWARDS

"I found a local winery that produces a mead that is drinkable. . . . That winery is Berrywine Plantations."

—Gordon Cassells, *Mead Lover's Digest* #483, ed. Dick Dunn

HOURS AND DIRECTIONS Tours and tastings year-round Mon.–Fri. 10 a.m.–5 p.m., Sat. 10 a.m.–6 p.m., Sun. noon–6 p.m. ■ From the north, take I-95 toward Baltimore.

When you see the tunnel sign, get into the right lane to *avoid* the tunnel. Get off at the right lane exit for I-695 west. Pass Towson and follow I-70 and Frederick signs. Take I-70 west to exit 62 for New Market. Turn right onto Rte. 75 north for about 5 miles, then turn right on Glissans Mill Rd.; continue 4 miles to winery. ■ From Baltimore, take I-70 west to exit 62 (Libertytown/New Market), 10 miles before Frederick. Turn right onto Rte. 75 north; then follow the local directions above. ■ From Washington, D.C., take I-270 north to exit 22 (Hyattstown). Turn left onto Rte, 109, left again onto Rte. 355, right onto Rte. 75 north for 13 miles. Turn right on Glissans Mill Rd. and continue 4 miles to winery.

Loew Vineyards

14001 Liberty Rd., Mt. Airy, MD 21771 • Phone 301-831-5464 •
Fax 301-831-5464 • www.loewvineyards.net • loewvineyards@erols.com

Bill Loew hails from Galicia, a region that was once part of the Austro-Hungarian Empire and is now divided between Ukraine and Poland. There, his family had begun making honey wine in the mid–nineteenth century, running a business whose product was distributed throughout the European continent. The winery operated until the war broke out in 1939, and at the end of the war Bill emigrated to the United States, where he became an engineer, married the lovely Lois Hendrickson, and raised three beautiful daughters. But wine was still in his blood. In March of 1982, Bill and Lois bought 37 acres in the Maryland countryside and began transforming the land into a vineyard. They sold their first bottle in 1986 and have subsequently established an excellent reputation and won numerous awards. Enjoy the wines or stroll the vineyards to drink in 150 years of family winemaking tradition.

Wines: $$

White Wines

Chardonnay Reserve—Fermented in the barrel for complexity and a rich, full body.

Harvest Gold—A blend of Seyval Blanc and Chardonnay aged in oak. Clean and crisp. Fruit comes through.

Johannisberg Riesling—European-style varietal. Fruit in the bouquet. Just slightly sweet. Nice.

Serendipity—A unique wine made from Reliance grapes. Fruity. Pineapple.

Twilight—A blend of Seyval and Riesling. Nice for sipping or with light salads or summer soups.

Red Wines

Cabernet Sauvignon—This garnet-colored Cab is aged in French oak barrels. Lots of fruit. Smooth.

Classic Red—Using a Beaujolais style of fermentation, this blend of Marechal Foch, Leon Millot, and Cabernet Franc produces a very drinkable red. A nice pasta wine.

Harvest Red—A nice blend of Cabernet Franc, Cabernet Sauvignon, and Chancellor, aged in oak.

Blush Wines

Celebration—Light, blush-style wine.

Fruit Wines

Apples & Honey—A special blend of apple cider and clover honey. Nice.

Blueberry—Made from local blueberries. Fermented in the skins.

Honey & Grape—A very nice blend of white grapes with local honey.

Raspberry in Grape—A light blend of Vidal Blanc and raspberries.

HOURS AND DIRECTIONS Tours and tastings Sat. 10 a.m.–5 p.m., Sun. 1 p.m.–5 p.m. ■ From Bethesda or Washington, D.C., take I-270 north to exit 16 (Father Hurley Blvd.), which becomes Rte. 27 toward Damascus. Proceed through Damascus and Mt. Airy and continue for another 7 miles or so. Turn left at the intersection with Rte. 26 (Liberty Rd.), where you'll see gas stations and a traffic light. Proceed 5 miles, slowing down (but not turning) when you see the sign for Albaugh Rd. The winery entrance is 0.1 mile from that point, on the left. ■ From Baltimore, drive west (toward Frederick) on Rte. 70. Exit at Mt. Airy, bearing right. Continue about 7 miles to the intersection with Rte, 26. Follow the local directions (above) from this point.

Woodhall Wine Cellars

17912 York Rd., Parkton, MD 21120 • Phone 410-357-8644 • Fax 410-467-1990 • www.woodhallwinecellars.com • woodhall83@hotmail.com

Woodhall Wine Cellars is on the antiques route between Cockeysville, Md., and southern Pennsylvania, and was established by co-owners Al Copp and former pilot Chris Lang and his wife Patricia in 1983. Since then they have seen steady growth, going from an initial offering of only five varieties to today's substantially longer list, which includes some dessert wines and some extremely limited-run, high-quality wines. Winemaker Chris Kent sticks primarily to classic European-style wines, many of them tending to be on the dry side.

In 2001, Woodhall added a production house with state-of-the-art equipment, increasing their capability and their quality. Tastings and other events are held in a beautifully renovated pole barn that dates back to the nineteenth century. A deck off the back overlooks the vineyards, and a small herb garden is laid out near the front doorway. On a nice day, a stroll around the grounds is a real treat.

Wines: $–$$$

White Wines

Angler White—A Vidal Blanc. Nice, semisweet table wine.

Chardonnay—Big fruit up front, subtle oak. Complex with nice finish.

Riesling—Off-dry Riesling with a nice finish.

Seyval—A nice off-dry varietal. Tropical fruit, some oak.

Vidal Blanc/Riesling—Clean, crisp, no oak.

Red Wines

Angler Red—A light, sweet red blend. Fans of blush wines will like this one

Cabernet Sauvignon—Barrel aged.

Chambourcin—A medium-bodied version of this popular eastern varietal.

Duet—A blend of Cabernet Sauvignon and Cabernet Franc.

Merlot—A deep garnet-colored wine. Soft, with a nice finish.

Parkton Prestige 1997—A blend of Cabernet Sauvignon (70%), Merlot (25%), and Cabernet Franc (5%). Nice finish.

Simply Red—A red blend that's great with pasta.

Blush Wines

Cabernet Blanc—A dry pink rosé. Very interesting.

Dessert Wines

Late Harvest Vidal—Very flavorful. Nice balance between sweetness and acidity.

REVIEWS AND AWARDS

Seyval and Cabernet Sauvignon: "Recommended."

—Hugh Johnson's Pocket Wine Book 2002

HOURS AND DIRECTIONS Tours and tastings year-round Tues.–Sun. noon–5 p.m. ■ The winery is located immediately north of the Gunpowder River, within minutes of I-83, 11 miles south of the Pennsylvania border. ■ Take I-83 to exit 27 (Mt. Carmel Rd.), travel east on Mt. Carmel a short distance to York Rd., turn left onto York, and proceed to the winery.

OTHER MARYLAND WINERIES

Copernica Vineyards: 1116 E. Deep Run Rd., Westminster, MD 21158 • Phone 410-848-7577 • www.copernicavineyards.com • Jack@copernicavineyards.com

North Lake Vineyards: 805 Greenbridge Rd., Brookeville, MD 20833 • Phone 410-774-2310

Provenza Vineyards: 805 Greenbridge Rd., Brookeville, MD 20729 • Phone 301-774-2310

MASSACHUSETTS

Cape Cod Winery

681 Sandwich Rd., East Falmouth, MA 02536 • Phone 508-457-5592 •
Fax 781-235-4946 • www.capecodwinery.com • capewinery@aol.com

Most people travel to Cape Cod for the ocean breezes, but many who have gone there recently have been lured by the local wineries, among them the wonderful Cape Cod Winery, located in the seaside resort of Falmouth.

Brazilian émigré Dr. Antonio Lazzari and his microbiologist wife, Kristina, started the 6-acre winery in 1994, and today they produce 1,800 cases of wine annually. While some might not think the Cape would be such a good place for a vineyard, the sandy gravel soil and gentle slopes are ideal for wine-grape growing. According to the Lazzaris, conditions at their small vineyard parallel those at the great vineyards of southern France and northern Italy.

Wines: $$

White Wines

Cranberry Chardonnay—A blend of Chardonnay tinged with cranberry makes this an excellent sipping wine. Refreshing. Highly recommended with roasted turkey or chicken.

Nobska Cranberry Blush—Seyval white with a splash of Cape Cod cranberry juice. Wonderful light color with a unique, lingering cranberry finish.

Nobska White—A blanc de blanc–style blend of Seyval and Vidal grapes. Citrus and honey flavors come through.

Pinot Grigio—This Pinot includes definite pear and citrus. A nice surprise.

Red Wines

Nobska Red—Blend of Cabernet Sauvignon and Cabernet Franc. Aged in oak barrels 12–18 months.

Merlot—Smooth and complex. Aged in oak barrels.

Dessert Wines

Regatta—Seyval with a splash of Concord and peaches. Very nice.

REVIEWS AND AWARDS

Nobska Red—Bronze medal, International Eastern Wine Competition.

"[Their Pinot Grigio has] a delicious, citrusy aroma to it. Definitely one of the best, if not the best, whites I have tasted around."

—Lisa Shea, About.com (March 1999)

HOURS AND DIRECTIONS Open Memorial Day–Thanksgiving for wine tasting and sales. June 13–Aug. 31, Wed.–Sun. noon–4 p.m.; Sept. 1–Dec. 1, Sat.–Sun. noon–4 p.m. ■ Take I-495 south (from the Boston area) or I-195 west (from Providence) to Bourne Bridge over the Cape Cod Canal. Stay on Rte. 28 toward Falmouth. Exit at Rte. 151. Bear right toward Mashpee to the light (3 miles). Turn right onto Sandwich Rd. The winery and vineyard are 2 miles on the left.

Chicama Vineyards

Stoney Hill Rd., West Tisbury, MA 02575 • Phone 888-CHICAMA or 508-693-0309 • Fax 508-693-5628 • www.chicamavineyards.com • info@chicamavineyards.com

George and Catherine Mathiesen founded Chicama Vineyards in 1971, which makes it the first bonded winery in the state. Today, the six Mathiesen children all help out in one way or another. For instance, daughter Lynn (who worked at Chandon in California years ago) makes the surprisingly stunning champagne.

Chicama is located 5 miles out into the Atlantic Ocean on the island of Martha's Vineyard, near the town of West Tisbury. The 35-acre vineyard—and the island in general—offers breathtaking views, and the gray-shingled barn that houses the winery is so wonderfully New Englandy that visitors never want to leave. The wine may also have something to do with this.

Wines: $–$$

White Wines

Cape White—An off-dry white. Crisp, clean.

Chenin Blanc—Fruity, off-dry white. Light and refreshing.

Hurricane Chardonnay—Big fruit, but dry.

Ondine—Made from 100% Viognier grapes. Pear and apricot come through as advertised. Very nice.

Semillon—Citrusy, dry white wine. One of the few vineyards on the entire East Coast that makes a classic dry, white Semillon.

Red Wines

Merlot—A full-bodied Merlot.

Shiraz—Ground pepper and plum flavors come through.

Summer Island Red—Light red, fruity, off-dry Zinfandel.

Zinfandel—Plummy, dry red wine.

Sparkling Wines

Sea Mist—100% Chardonnay grapes using the French *méthode champenoise*. Brut. Nicely dry . . . not cloying.

Dessert Wines

Cranberry Satin—Pink, delicious dessert wine. Sweet but tart.

REVIEWS AND AWARDS

Cited as a great day trip on Martha's Vineyard. —*USA Today* (May 2002)

HOURS AND DIRECTIONS Tastings Jan. to mid-May, Sat. 1–4 p.m.; late May, Mon.-Sat. 1–4 p.m.; June–Sept., Mon.–Sat. 11 a.m.–5 p.m., Sun. 1–5 p.m. (tours at noon, 2 p.m., and 4 p.m.; no noon tour on Sun.); Oct. to mid-Nov., Mon.–Sat. 1–4 p.m.; mid-Nov. through Dec., Mon.–Sat. 11 a.m.–4 p.m., Sun. 1–4 p.m. Other hours by appointment only. ■ Transportation to Martha's Vineyard is by ferryboat from Woods Hole, docking at Vineyard Haven. (Call The Steamship Authority at 508-693-8600 for more information.) Leave Vineyard Haven on State Rd., following the signs toward West Tisbury and Gay Head. Go 2.5 miles; you'll see the green-and-white winery sign on your left. Turn left here and follow the dirt road 1 mile to the winery.

Church Street Winery & Via Vineyards

513 Church St., Raynham, MA 02767 • Phone 508-822-7775 • Fax 508-824-7999 • www.capecodcranberrywine.com • webmaster@capecodcranberrywine.com

Located not far from the beautiful Taunton River, Church Street Winery & Via Vineyards is owned and operated by the gregarious Pumberto DiCroce, who carries on his family winemaking tradition with the aid of Hungarian-born winemaker Matyas Vogel, who grew up on vineyards still in his family's hands today. Inside, the winery has some wonderful touches, from its gleaming new Italian-made stainless steel tanks to the wonderfully old and rustic wooden door set in a classic heavy stone archway. Throughout, the vineyard's European staff is on hand to explain the winemaking process.

Wines: $$

White Wines

Cape Cod Dry—A straw-colored wine, with bold fruit. A versatile food wine that can stand up to strong flavors.

Cape Cod Semi-Dry—A white semidry blend. Rich fruit flavors. Serve cold.

Cranberry Delight—A blush-type wine, and one of the winery's most popular. Serve cold. Use it to make wine spritzers, coolers, and sangrias, or mix with 33% champagne for a refreshing summer cooler.

Red Wines

Cape Cod Red—Made from California grapes and aged in oak.

Dessert Wines

Cape Cod Raspberry Rave—Made from Cayuga White grapes and native New England raspberries. A nice dessert wine.

REVIEWS AND AWARDS

Cape Cod Semi-Dry—Gold medal, 1998 Tasters Guild International Wine Competition.

"[Church Street's Cape Cod Dry] is worthy of winning medals."
—Donald Breed, *Providence Journal*

HOURS AND DIRECTIONS Call for hours. ■ From I-495 (north or south), get off at the Rte. 44 exit, going west. Drive about 15 minutes. Winery will be on your left. ■ From Rte. 24 (north or south), get off at Rte. 44 going east. Drive for about 15 minutes. Winery will be on the right. ■ From Taunton, take Rte. 44 east. Pass Rte. 24 and continue driving for about 15 minutes. Winery will be on the right.

Mellea Winery

108 Old Southbridge Rd., P.O. Box 1328, Dudley, MA 01571 • Phone 508-943-5166 • Fax 508-949-2539 • www.melleawinery.com • melleawinery@melleawinery.com

If you're a sucker for family-run businesses, you'll love Mellea vineyards. The winery was begun around 1990 by Joe and Allie Compagnone; was named for Joe's mother,

Rosina Mellea (pronounced Mal-LAY-ah), and is now run by Joe and Allie's niece Anita and her daughter—though Uncle Joe's long arm is still strong and influencing. This is a family affair.

The current winery sits on the former site of the Haven Farm, and the vineyards stretch out from the windows of the tasting room. Those vineyards produce mostly French-American hybrids, but the Mellea wines also use grapes and fruit from neighboring growers and from California.

Wines: $–$$

White Wines

Brookside White—A blend of Seyval, Vidal, and Cayuga grapes. Sweet.

Chardonnay—Pale gold color. Aged in oak 7 months.

Cranberry Classic—A blend of French Colombard and a hint of cranberry. Sweet and tart. Their most popular wine.

Seyval Blanc—Light, tart, and crisp. Slightly oaked.

Red Wines

Cabernet Sauvignon—A full-bodied, deep red aged in oak.

Raspberry—Almost a blush color. Sweet.

Blush Wines

First Blush—A rosé. A blend of French Colombard tinged with Cabernet. Off-dry. Very popular.

Rosina Rosé—A blend of French Colombard and Pinot Noir, with a light ruby color.

REVIEWS AND AWARDS

"The Cabernet Sauvignon is one of my favorites, and is oaky and fruity, again with a cherry flavor to it."
—Lisa Shea, About.com (July 1999)

HOURS AND DIRECTIONS Call for hours. ■ From I-395, take exit 2 (Webster/Douglas). Follow Rte. 16 west to Rte. 197, cross the Connecticut state line, then turn right onto Rte. 131. Look for the Mellea sign on left, about 0.5 mile.

Nantucket Vineyard

5 Bartlett Farm Rd., Nantucket, MA 02584 • Phone 508-228-9235 • Fax 508-325-5145 • www.NantucketVineyard.com • ackwine@nantucket.net

Founded in 1986 by Dean and Melissa Long, Nantucket Vineyard is located on a 7-acre spread 30 miles offshore from Cape Cod, near a beach and surrounded by 90 acres of flower and vegetable gardens. As Dean admitted to Thomas Matthews of *Wine Spectator* in 1997, "Grape growing is an uphill battle around here. . . . Especially because I didn't know anything when we started." He has apparently learned. Today, the Longs manage the vineyard and do all the winemaking themselves, employing a traditional French method and working from Pinot Blanc, Riesling, and Merlot grapes, with some Cabernet and Pinot Noir used to make blush wines. Some grapes are purchased from the mainland. The pressed grapes are aged in oak barrels, racked instead of filtered, and minimal additives are used.

Nantucket offers a range of red, rosé, white, and sparkling wines as well as hard cider. All their wines are grape wines and include Nantucket Sleighride, Pinot Blanc, Riesling, and Sauvignon Blanc.

Wines: $–$$

REVIEWS AND AWARDS
"[The Chardonnay is] their best local wine."
—Thomas Matthews, *Wine Spectator* (July 1997)

HOURS AND DIRECTIONS Open summers, tours and tastings Mon.–Sat. 10 a.m.–6 p.m., Sun. 11 a.m.–5 p.m. Phone ahead for days and hours other times of year. ■ The vineyard is located 5 miles from town: take Main St. to Milk St. to Hummock Pond Rd. to Bartlett Farm Rd.

Nashoba Valley Winery & Brewery

100 Wattaquadoc Hill Rd., Bolton, MA 01740 • Phone 800-286-5521 or 978-779-5521 • Fax 978-779-5523 • www.nashobawinery.com • email@nashobawinery.com

Located just 40 minutes west of Boston, Nashoba Valley Winery and Brewery is set amid more than 55 beautiful acres and is known for its festivals, picnics, private functions, and weddings. Its orchard was revived in 1983 and new owners took over the operation in 1995, bringing it back to top form and adding twenty-seven new medals to the approximately fifty the winery had already garnered in national and international competition.

Nashoba Valley has had great success in competition with their Cranberry Apple, Azule, and particularly their Peach wines (see reviews and awards below). Its products have also received accolades from *Food & Wine*, *Wine Enthusiast*, and *Boston Magazine*, but if you have a family outing in mind, there's more than just good wine here. Nashoba Valley was named "Best Place to Pick Apples" by the *Boston Parents' Paper*, and for a meal after your picking, there's a wonderful little rustic farmhouse restaurant on the property called J's, which is very pleasant.

Wines: $–$$$

White Wines

Vidal Blanc—Light white varietal. Nice.

Vignoles—A nice wine with big citrus and apricot flavors.

Fruit Wines

Baldwin—A light, dry apple wine. Refreshing, not cloying.

Chardonnay—Apples and pears come through, and oak adds smoothness.

Cherry—Blush wine with intense fruit flavors.

Chrysleton—Light red with berry overtones and a definite taste of apples.

Cranberry Apple—Tart apple wine tinged with cranberries.

Cyser—Apple wine with apple and pear flavors. Very refreshing when served cold.

Dry Blueberry—Surprisingly dry, with big fruit flavors. Interesting.

Dry Pear—A nice pear wine. Not cloyingly sweet, but dry. A versatile wine, very good when served cold.

Golden Russet—Golden straw-colored wine made from heirloom apple varieties.

Gravenstein—Crisp, light apple wine. Refreshing.

Maiden's Blush—A blush made from apple and elderberry wine. Named after the Maiden's Blush apple, one of over eighty "antique" apple varieties grown in the winery's own orchard.

Semi-Sweet Blueberry—Big berry flavor. Rich.

Strawberry Rhubarb—Like a nice, tart strawberry rhubarb pie, but without the crust. Fun.

Sparkling Wines

Sparkling Apple Brut—An apple wine made into a full-bodied sparkling wine using the traditional *méthode champenoise*. Delightful.

Dessert Wines

After Dinner Peach—Golden peach wine. Rich. ♥

Amora—Red dessert wine with raspberry and blackberry flavors.

Azule—An intense berry wine.

Dessert Plum—A ruby dessert wine with deep flavors. Almost port-like.

New English Cider—A mild sweetness does not overpower the fine, tiny bubbles. Crisp and fine. Very nice. ♥

Perry—Light bodied, a little more refined.

Plum—A light blush dessert wine made from plums.

Raspberry—Tartness surprises. Not as sweet as you might expect. Pleasant.

REVIEWS AND AWARDS

Azule—Gold medal, 1997 World Wine Championships.

Cranberry Apple—Seven medals dating back as far as 1983 and as recently as 1996.

Peach—Eleven medals between 1983 and 1997, including four golds.

Azule 2001: 86 points, "Highly Recommended."　　　—Beverage Testing Institute

Dry Pear 2001: 80 points, "Recommended."　　　—Beverage Testing Institute

HOURS AND DIRECTIONS Open year-round 11 a.m.–5 p.m. daily. Tours every half hour on weekends, beginning at 11:30 a.m. Last tour starts at 4 p.m. Group tours on weekdays by reservation only. ■ Located less than 1 hour from Boston and Worcester. ■ From Boston, take either Rte. 2 west to I-495 south (from the northern suburbs) or I-90 (Mass. Pike) west to I-495 north (from the southern suburbs). From I-495, follow Rte. 117 west (exit 27) 1 mile to Bolton Center. Turn left onto Wattaquadoc Hill Rd. at the blinking light immediately before a Mobil gas station. Stay on this road about 0.3 mile to the winery, which is on the left. ■ From Worcester, take I-290 east to I-495 north; then follow the directions from Boston.

Plymouth Bay Winery

114 Water St. Rear, Plymouth, MA 02360 • Phone 877-683-5463 or 508-746-2100 • www.plymouthbaywinery.com • plymouthbaywinery@aol.com

Many people go to Plymouth for historical sightseeing, but few know there's a wonderful little family-owned winery there too, overlooking historic Plymouth Bay. It is located not far from Plymouth Rock and the somewhat less historic Ocean Spray Cranberry World. Since it sits smack-dab in the heart of America's cranberry capital, it should be no surprise that Plymouth Bay produces cranberry wine, as well as other delightful fruit wines.

Wines: $–$$

White Wines

Drydock White—A light, citrusy white wine, made in the classic Chablis style.

Widow's Walk—A light, semidry white. Spicy enough to stand up to numerous dishes. One of the winery's most popular wines.

Fruit Wines

Cranberry Bay—Ruby-red cranberry wine.

Cranberry Blush—A blush wine made from white grapes and cranberry. A nice summer sipping wine.

Peach Bay—A good sipping wine made from fresh peaches. Sweet.

Dessert Wines

Blueberry Bay—A rich, purple dessert wine that tastes like your grandmother's blueberry pie filling.

Raspberry Bay—A deep red raspberry dessert wine.

HOURS AND DIRECTIONS Call for hours. ■ From the Boston area and points north, take I-93 south to Rte. 3 south. Plymouth is located just off Rte. 3 at exit 6A. Follow Rte. 44 east (Samoset St.). Go straight through the intersection and lights. (You'll see a Gulf station and a Mobil station, and you'll cross over Rte. 3A.) At the small rotary, take a right onto Water St. The winery is right after Isaac's Restaurant, in a white building toward the back of the parking lot. ■ From Connecticut and points south, take I-95 north through Providence to I-495 south. Take exit 6 onto Rte. 44 east to Plymouth; then follow the local directions above. ■ From western Massachusetts, take the Mass. Pike (I-90) or Rte. 2 east to I-495 south; take exit 6 onto Rte. 44 east and follow the local directions.

Plymouth Colony Winery

Pinewood Rd., Plymouth, MA 02360 • Phone 508-747-3334

Like most wineries in America's cranberry basket, this little place produces cranberry wines, but it has the distinction of having been the first place in town to do so, with operations dating back to 1983. Located in the middle of a 10-acre cranberry bog, the winery is a former cranberry screening house, circa 1890. Everything here is about homegrown cranberries, which winemaker John Lebeck turns into straight cranberry wine or mixes with other local fruits or imported grapes to create a small but interesting array of blends. The Cranberry Grande and Cranberry Raspberry have both won awards.

Wines: $–$$

Fruit and Blush Wines

Cranberry—Wonderfully strong, but not overpowering or cloyingly sweet. Very nice.

Blueberry—Strong blueberry flavor. Sweet.

Blush—A blend of grape and cranberry.

REVIEWS AND AWARDS

"The Cranberry wine is some of the best I've ever tasted—a good, strong flavor, but not too tart." —Lisa Shea, About.com (July 2001)

HOURS AND DIRECTIONS Open Apr.–Dec., Mon.–Sat. 10 a.m.–5 p.m., Sun. noon–5 p.m.; Mar., Sat.–Sun. noon–4 p.m.; closed Jan.–Feb. ■ To reach the winery, take Rte. 3 to exit 6 onto Rte. 44. Go west 3 miles and turn left onto Pinewood Rd.

Truro Vineyards of Cape Cod

Route 6A, North Truro, MA 02652 • Phone 508-487-6200 • Fax 508-487-4248

It's hard to miss the little Truro Vineyards winery. Above the roof, its huge tower proffers a giant, nineteenth-century wine cask 50 feet over your head. Owned by Judy

Wimer and Kathleen Gregrow, the historic 1830s farmstead on which Truro Vineyards is located has been in continuous operation for over 160 years and remains one of the last working farms on Cape Cod. In 1992 they established a vineyard with plantings of Chardonnay, Cabernet Franc, and Merlot, among others. They also restored a wonderful little cottage that acts as a charming B & B.

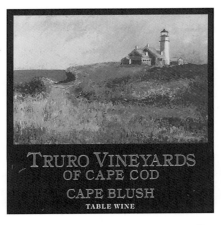

"This is Cape Cod's first vinifera vineyard," according to *Yankee Magazine*'s 2002 *Travel Guide to New England.* "Inside the 1836 white Federal farmhouse, the vineyard owners have amassed a museum-quality collection of wine-making artifacts, including a 150-year-old wine press." Outside, the temperate maritime climate works its magic on the vinifera. "Cape Cod's warm ocean breezes, well drained sandy soils and extended growing season combine to produce grapes with intense flavor and lush varietal character" ("Toasting Cape Cod," *Cape Cod Today*, August 28, 2001).

Truro celebrated its first release in 1996, issuing a barrel-fermented Chardonnay that received favorable reviews. Then they released their first red, a Cabernet, in the summer of 1997. Another hit! Visit there and you won't be disappointed.

Wines: $$

White Wines

Barrel Fermented Chardonnay—A nice Chardonnay. Clean, citrusy.

Red Wines

Cabernet Franc—A deep red wine. Berries and currants abundant. Dry finish.

Merlot—Another deep ruby offering. Smooth. Lots of fruit.

Blush Wines

Cape Blush—A semisweet blush wine that has a slight *frizzante* touch. A wonderful sipping wine. Serve chilled. ♥

REVIEWS AND AWARDS

"I just came back from the Cape and discovered Truro Vineyards, making super Cabernet Franc and estate Chardonnay!"
—Bill Bradley, executive chef, Bricco Ristorante & Enoteca, Boston, in *Beverage Business* (October 2001)

HOURS AND DIRECTIONS Tasting room open daily mid-May through Oct., 12–5 p.m.; Nov–Dec., Fri–Sun. only, noon–5 p.m. ■ Take Rte. 3 south, cross the Sagamore Bridge, and follow Rte. 6 to the exit for North Truro. Turn left onto Rte. 6A and go 0.2 mile to the vineyard, on the right.

West County Winery & Ciders

Pine Hill Orchard, Colrain-Shelburne Rd., Colrain, MA 01340 •
Phone 413-624-3481• www.westcountycider.com •
info@westcountycider.com

Terry and Judith Maloney moved from northern California to Colrain in 1972 and made their first stab at winemaking—an attempt that failed when they could not get the quality or quantity of grapes they needed. However, they soon became enamored of the hard ciders being made by their neighbors and decided to give it a try themselves. The rest is history.

The Maloneys produced their first commercial hard cider in 1984. In subsequent years, experimenting with various apples, yeasts, and fermentation processes, they began to grow their understanding and repertoire of fine ciders. Today they offer many varieties, made with apples grown in the eleven towns of the northern Berkshires that comprise "West County," the western half of Franklin County. Their own orchard comprises about 1,000 English, French, and American cider-apple trees, from which they harvest and sort between 36,000 and 60,000 pounds annually. They rely on other growers for more popular types such a McIntosh, Northern Spy, and Baldwin.

Cidermaking at West County Cider is a family affair. Terry is in charge of fermenting; Judith does most of the selling and tastings; and their son Field helps with the tasting and blending. If you're a fine-cider enthusiast you'll love this place, and if you're a wine snob, give everyone (including yourself) a break and take a trial taste.

Ciders: $–$$

Still Ciders

Baldwin—Made from Baldwin apples grown in hillside orchards in the northern Berkshires. Off-dry with big fruit flavors.

Cidre Doux—Made in the classic French tradition. Slightly tangy. Very nice.

Dry Baldwin—A drier version the regular Baldwin.

Kingston Black—An unblended cider in the classic English tradition, made from English cider apples.

West County—A unique cider made from several varieties of heirloom apples.

West County Dry—A dry cider made with acidic apples such as Reine de Pomme, Catamount, and Russets, balanced with sweeter, more aromatic apples like McIntosh and Northern Spy.

Sparkling Ciders

Catamount Hill Orchard—A blend of Reine de Pomme, Baldwin, McIntosh, and Roxbury Russet apples. (The name comes from the fact that, in 1812, the first U.S. flag ever raised over a public school went up at the schoolhouse on Colrain's Catamount Hill.)

Crown—A fine hard cider in the French tradition. Dry. Goes well with fowl and fish.

Extra Dry—Another French-tradition hard cider. Extremely dry. Wonderful with seafood. ♥

Farm Cider—Made from fresh-pressed apples, with nothing added but yeast for fermentation. No sulfites.

Redfield—A blend of McIntosh, Northern Spy, and the rare Redfield, an American cider apple with red flesh. Off-dry, tart, and blush colored.

Reine de Pomme—Made from Reine de Pomme, "Queen of the Apples," a tannic and fruity archaic French cider apple. ♥

Trembletts—A Trembletts Bitter, Golden, and Roxbury Russets blend. Very dry. Fine bubbles.

HOURS AND DIRECTIONS Open May–June, Sat.–Sun. 11 a.m.–5 p.m.; June–Dec., Thurs.-Sun. 11 a.m.–5 p.m. Closed Jan.–Apr. ■ From eastern Massachusetts, take either Rte. 2 west (which funnels you onto I-91 at Greenfield) or the Mass. Pike (I-90) west to I-91; get off I-91 at exit 26 and continue on Rte. 2 west for 3.7 miles. Turn right on Colrain-Shelburne Rd. West County is about 3 miles up on the right. ■ From western Massachusetts, go east on Rte. 2 until you get to Shelburne Falls. Go past the Rte. 112 north turnoff and drive about 4.9 miles to Colrain-Shelburne Rd. on the left. Follow that road 3 miles to West County. ■ From Connecticut or farther south, take I-91 north to exit 26 and follow the local directions above.

Westport Rivers Vineyard & Winery ✫✫✫

417 Hixbridge Rd., Westport, MA 02790 • Phone 800-396-9463 or 508-636-3423 • Fax 508-636-4133 • www.westportrivers.com

Unlike many of the winery excursions described in this book, a visit to Westport Rivers isn't just a day trip; it's a mission. If you live on the East Coast and like wine, you *must* make a pilgrimage here.

Bob and Carol Russell founded Westport Rivers in 1982 after Bob, a Harvard M.B.A., realized he was putting in 80-hour weeks at his metals-manufacturing company. The couple had grown vines in their backyard in the past and Carol's father had owned a winery before Prohibition, so they decided to get out of metals and go into wine. They initially purchased a 100-acre section of the famed Smith Long Acre Farm, which had been cultivated for more than 250 years, first by the Wamsutta Indians, then by the White, Macomber, and Smith families. In 1996 the Russells increased their holdings to 190 acres, 76 of which are now planted with vines.

In less than 20 years, the Russells have turned their winery into one of the most renowned in the eastern half of North America, making more than 8,500 cases per year using their own grapes and a small percentage purchased from Long Island. Their wines have won a list of medals as long as your arm and have been roundly praised in the wine media: *Wine Spectator* reviews their wines regularly, giving them scores in the 80s, and *Hugh Johnson's Pocket Wine Book 2002* raves about their "good chardonnay and elegant sparkling [wines]." They're listed as a recommended winery in *The New Sotheby's Wine Encyclopedia* and are among the Beverage Testing Institute's fifteen "recommended" American sparkling wine producers.

The Russells are passionate about food too, and so founded Long Acre House, a culinary school where chef Kerry Romaniello teaches cooking and the proper pairing of food and wine. A graduate of the New England Culinary Institute in Montpelier, Vt., she also attended the Beringer School for American Chefs under the direction of famed chef and cookbook writer Madeleine Kamman. The winery's website lists numerous one-day events, many taught by notable visiting chefs.

Wines: $$–$$$

White Wines

Chardonnay: Estate Classic—Lots of fruit in the mouth, but finished in oak for a well-balanced flavor. ♥

Johannisberg Riesling—Citrusy. Not too sweet, very clean.

Riversong—A white blend in the French Chenin Blanc tradition.

Red Wines

Signature Reserve—A transparent ruby-red color. Lots of fruit. Nice tannins.

Blush Wines

Rosé of Pinot Noir—A Pinot Noir rosé. Off-dry makes this excellent with light fare like salads or meals of fish or fowl. Very nice.

Sparkling Wines

Cuvée Maximilian (a.k.a. *MAX*)—This is a magnum of their best champagne-style sparkling wine. Each bottle comes individually packed in a custom wooden box. Makes a wonderful gift. ♥

Westport Blanc de Blancs—A brassy-colored bombshell of a wine. Fine, tiny bubbles leave a string of beautiful pearls through a champagne flute. Drink them up as quickly as you can! ♥ ♥

Westport Brut Cuvée RJR—A golden-colored elixir. Fine bubbles and a well-balanced mouthful. ♥

Westport Imperial Sec—A golden, flaxen blend of grapes. Very citrusy, with an ever so light touch of sweetness because it's made from Riesling. Not to be missed. ♥

REVIEWS AND AWARDS

Chardonnay 1998: "87 points."   —*Wine Spectator's Ultimate Guide to Tasting Wines*

"[The 1997 Chardonnay has a] bright yellow-straw hue. Crisp citrus aromas. . . . Taut pure clean style. . . . 86 points."

—Beverage Testing Institute, *Buying Guide to Wines of North America*

"[Westport] made the short list of 5 in the tastings, which featured more than 35 California sparklers."   —*Quarterly Review of Wines* (winter 2000)

HOURS AND DIRECTIONS Tastings daily year-round 11 a.m.–5 p.m. Tours Sat.–Sun. 1–3 p.m. ■ From Boston, go south on the southeast expressway (I-93) to Rte. 128 north. Exit onto Rte. 24 south. Follow Rte. 24 south to I-195 east. Take exit 10 (Westport/Horseneck Beach/Rte. 88 south). Take a left at the fourth stoplight onto Hixbridge Rd. Westport Rivers is 1.3 miles down Hixbridge on the right. ■ From Cape Cod, leave the Cape on the Bourne Bridge. Follow signs onto I-195 west, take exit 10, and follow the local directions above. ■ From Providence, take I-195 east to exit 10 and follow the local directions. ■ From Newport, take Rte. 24 north to I-195 east. Take Exit 10 and follow the local directions.

OTHER MASSACHUSETTS WINERIES

Goodale Orchards Winery: 143 Argilla Rd., Ipswich, MA 01938 • Phone 508-356-5366

NEW HAMPSHIRE

Farnum Hill Ciders (at Poverty Lane Orchards) ✪ ✪

98 Poverty Ln., Lebanon, NH 03766 • Phone 603-448-1511 •
Fax 603-448-7326 • www.farnumhillciders.com • info@farnumhillciders.com

Stephen Wood and Louisa Spencer founded Farnum Hill at Poverty Lane Orchards with the idea of making world-class ciders equal to the French, British, and Belgian classics—and they have. These are exquisite ciders, definitely worth serving to friends and family, and even to distinguished gourmets—all will thank you for the experience. The winery is a great place to visit too.

Ciders: $–$$

Extra-Dry—Dry, pale gold cider. Champagne-like and creamy. No sweetness. Big apples on the nose and the midpalate. Like a fine, dry, white, slightly *frizzante* apple wine. ♥ ♥

Extra-Dry Still—A dry golden apple cider. No fizz. Has a complex, wine-like quality.

Farmhouse—Light, yellow-golden cider. Nice bubbles. Slightly sweet but with some tanginess. Clean, crisp, and refreshing. A nice drinking cider.

Semi-Dry—Great nose bursting with apples. Golden, with nice, fine bubbles. Some sweetness but a more refined cider than the Farmhouse. More acidity and balance. Very nice. ♥ ♥

Semi-Dry Still—Clean, straw-colored still cider. Wonderful nose. Slight sweetness.

REVIEWS AND AWARDS

"Farnum Hill Ciders stand alone."   —Amanda Hesser, *New York Times*

"Subtle, often surprising aromas that recall vanilla, mango, pineapple, and even leather. . . . These ciders . . . must be appreciated in their own right. They are American classics."

—Thomas Christopher, *Martha Stewart Living* (October 2001)

"Most Farnum Hill ciders are dry and lightly tannic with complex undertones, not only of apple but of raspberry, mango, oak, and general autumn muskiness. That combination of flavors and aromas marks great ciders wherever they're produced."

—Frank Browning, *Food & Wine* (2001)

"The Sparkling Semi-Dry has a waft of citrus blossoms and pear that travels up to your nose. It is dry and crisp, with a gentle warming quality, like a scotch. . . . Extra Dry has the same kind of vibrancy with an aroma of cherries and melon that seems to leap from the glass. It is dry and distinct with a pleasant sharpness reminiscent of bitter oranges. . . . Terrific."   —Amanda Hesser, *New York Times*

HOURS AND DIRECTIONS Open seasonally. Call for hours. ■ Located near exit 19 off I-89 in New Hampshire, minutes from the junction of I-91 and I-89 in the Upper Connecticut River Valley. ■ From I-89 (north or south) take exit 19. Turn west onto Rte. 4 from the off-ramp. At the first light, turn left (uphill) onto Poverty Ln. ■ From I-91, take I-89 south across the Connecticut River to reach exit 19.

Flag Hill Winery

297 N. River Rd., Lee, NH 03824 • Phone 603-659-2949 • Fax 603-659-5107 • www.flaghillwinery.com • wine@flaghillwinery.com

In our opinion, attending a tasting in Flag Hill Winery's 1794 barn, overlooking more than 20 acres of French hybrid vineyards, is one of the best things you can do in the state of New Hampshire. The barn is beautifully redone, transformed into a wonderful Yankee tasting room complete with local wine trinkets and New England folk art, and on a sunny day there's no finer place to buy a bottle of wine, stroll the vineyards, and find a spot to settle down and picnic.

The farmland itself has been in the same family since 1950, when the total 200 acres was purchased for a mere $6,000. Frank Reinhold, Sr., and his family ran it as a dairy farm then, but when the next generation took over they traded in cows for grapes. The first vines were planted in 1990, the first harvest was in 1995, and the winery opened to the public two years later, after that wine had aged and fermented. More vines have been planted every year since, and today the winery produces 2,500 cases a year, with plans to bottle more in the future. Everything made here is pure 100% New Hampshire, including their Heritage Dessert wines, which are made with New Hampshire maple syrup.

One of the best times to visit is during the harvest, when as many as 3,000 visitors show up to help bring in the crop (though only about 500 actually get to do the work). It's a big party, a family-oriented day that's also practical for the winery: "I mean," said owner Frank Reinhold, Jr., in the *Exeter News-Letter* (July 23, 2000), "where do you find people to pick 19 acres of grapes?"

Wines: $–$$

White Wines

Cayuga—A semisweet white.

Niagara—A light, semisweet white.

Seyval Blanc—A light, off-dry white wine.

Vignoles—A light, semisweet wine.

Red Wines

DeChaunac—A medium-bodied red.

Leon Millot—A medium-bodied table red.

Maiden's Blush—Tart, with a dry finish, and not as sweet as you'd expect.

Marechal Foch—A medium-bodied red table wine.

Ports

North River Port—A nice port. Deep and sweet.

Other Wines

Red Dessert and *White Dessert*

REVIEWS AND AWARDS

"[The Niagara White] would be delicious with a warm apple pie . . . [and the Cayuga White] had a dry, smooth flavor. It has a light, almost effervescent aspect to it."

—Lisa Shea, About.com

"Tour the vineyards and taste wines that will make the Napa Valley stand up and take notice." —*Yankee Magazine* (2002, special fall issue)

HOURS AND DIRECTIONS Jan.–Mar., Sat.–.Sun. 11 a.m.–5 p.m.; Apr.–Dec., Wed.–Sun. 11 a.m.–5 p.m. ■ From the Boston area, take I-95 north; exit onto Rte. 101 west, toward Exeter. Travel about 6 miles to the town of Epping and exit onto Rte. 125 north. Travel 4 miles and turn right onto Rte. 155. Drive 0.3 mile to the winery and vineyard, on the right. ■ From the Manchester/Nashua area, take Rte. 101 south east to Epping and exit onto Rte. 125 north; then follow the local directions above.

Jewell Towne Vineyards

65 Jewell St., South Hampton, NH 03827 • Phone 603-394-0600 • jewelvin@nh.ultranet.com

When you drive up to Jewell Towne Vineyards, the first thing that strikes you is the marvelous gray-and-white clapboard New England barn wherein the tasting and wine-making are housed. Topped with its towering cupola, the sight is heartwarming right off—and it's a reproduction.

The 12 acres of farmland were purchased by emergency room physician Peter D. Oldak and his wife Brenda in 1977. They planted their first six vines in 1982 and subsequently planted more than sixty different varieties of grapes, searching for those that would do best in the local soil. By 1990 Dr. Oldak had narrowed his choices to twenty varieties, and by 1992 his South Hampton White had won a gold medal and his Alden a silver at the American Wine Society's National Competition. Until 1996 the Oldaks made their wines in the basement of their home, but as production needed to increase to keep up with demand, something needed to be done. That's when the Oldaks built their marvelous barn. The post-and-beam building is a reproduction of those built in the area in the eighteenth century, and is as historically accurate as possible.

The winery is still a family-run operation. Brenda, a nurse and an artist, creates the labels, and their children Tenley and Trevor help in the day-to-day operation of the winery. For the doctor, the winery is a welcome enterprise: "Everybody hates doctors and the hospital frightens people," he told the *Eagle Tribune* in September 2000. "The winery is happy and upbeat. It's an excellent way to see the other side of the public."

Wines: $–$$

White Wines

Aurore—Clean, clear, and crisp. Chablis-like.

Canadice—Interesting off-dry white. Definitely taste the grapefruit.

Cayuga—Nice off-dry white. Slight taste of peach.

Chardonnay—Light, smooth.

Chardonnay Private Reserve—More full bodied, with a touch of oak.

Melody—A fruity blend. Very tasty.

Riesling—A nice white with a taste of apricot.

Seyval—The winery's most popular white, off-dry and full bodied.

Red Wines

Baco Noir—A light, dry red.

Chancellor—Full-bodied red. Rich and deep.

Landot Noir—Medium-bodied red. Won a gold medal.

Leon Millot—Light, clear, ruby red.

Marechal Foch Private Reserve—A light, dry red in the style of a Beaujolais.

Suffolk Red—Refreshing.

Blush Wines

Alden—Clean, crisp, rosé-type wine, almost a light red.

Steuben—Semisweet blush.

Dessert Wines

South Hampton White—A blend of muscat and Gewürztraminer. An excellent, award-winning dessert or sipping wine.

Vidal—German-style Vidal. Crisp, clean, slightly citrus.

Vidal Ice Wine—A surprisingly nice version of the dessert classic.

Vignoles—Sweet dessert wine. Not cloying, slightly lemony. Tasty.

REVIEWS AND AWARDS

Alden—Silver medal, American Wine Society National Competition.

Landot Noir—Gold medal, 2000 American Wine Society Commercial Wine Competition.

South Hampton White 1992—Gold medal, American Wine Society National Competition.

"Chardonnay is considered the winery's signature wine."
—Anita Perkins, *Eagle-Tribune* (September 2000)

"[Their Seyval] was really lovely, slightly dry . . . a wonderful choice for a beautiful summer day. It's nice to have a local winery that makes a good glass of vino."
—*Union Leader and New Hampshire Sunday News* (March 2001)

HOURS AND DIRECTIONS Tastings and tours May–Dec., Sat.-Sun. 1–5 p.m. ■ From the south (Boston area), take I-95 north to (Mass.) exit 58 west (Rte. 110/Amesbury). Turn right at first light onto Elm St. Continue to rotary (center of Amesbury) and turn right at the Provident Bank onto Rte. 150. Proceed approximately 0.5 mile until the road forks. Bear left (107A). Proceed 2.5 miles and turn left onto Jewell St. Continue down the hill and take the first left onto Whitehall Rd. The vineyard entrance is 100 yards down on the left. ■ From the northeast (I-95 heading south), take (N.H.) exit 1 (Rte. 107 west). Proceed past the Seabrook Race Track to Rte. 150 intersection. Turn left and proceed south approximately 2 miles to the Fern Ave. intersection. Turn right and continue to the end of Fern. Turn right onto Rte. 107A. Proceed approximately 1.5 miles to Jewell St., turn left onto it, and take the first left onto Whitehall Rd. to the vineyard.

OTHER NEW HAMPSHIRE WINERIES

New Hampshire Winery: 38 Flanders Rd., Henniker, NH 03242 • Phone and Fax 603-428-9463

NEW JERSEY

Alba Vineyards ✪ ✪

269 Rte. 627, Finesville, NJ 08848 • Phone 908-995-7800 • Fax 908-995-7155 •
www.albavineyard.com • albavineyard@enter.net

Founded in 1983, Alba Vineyards is co-owned by winemaker Rudy Marchesi, who
wants Alba to become a cultural arts center, and marketer Tom Sharko, who's president
of the Garden State Wine Growers Association and has a wicked sense of humor. "New
Jersey grapes," he told *New Jersey Monthly* in August 2001, "are one of the few crops
that can compete with New Jersey's biggest crop: center-hall colonials."

Arts and architecture aside, what's clear is that Alba is evolving into a premier winery. In 20 short years, it has raised the profile not only of New Jersey wine but of East
Coast wine in general. The winery's Red Raspberry
won gold medals at the 1998 World Wine Championships in Chicago, the Tasters Guild International
Wine Competition in Florida, and the fourth Wine
Lovers Consumer Wine Competition and Conven-
tion in Washington, D.C., and was named one of the
top ten dessert wines in North America by the Beverage Testing Institute. The BTI also gave the winery an
overall "recommended" rating for its fruit wines,
while in May 1999 *New York Times* weekend wine
critic Howard G. Goldberg made note of their New
Jersey Blush, Vidal Blanc, and Riesling.

Alba is also a beautiful winery, so a visit is well
worth the time. An historic 1805 wood and fieldstone barn houses the winery and beautifully appointed tasting room, as well as the Musconetcong
Art Gallery—proof that Rudy Marchesi isn't kidding
with that cultural center idea.

Wines: $–$$

White Wines

Chardonnay Barrel Reserve—A solid Chardonnay,
aged *sur lie* in oak barrels.

Chardonnay Finger Lakes—Sourced from several East Coast vineyards, each contributing to the crisp, clean, bright apple character. Aged in French and American oak.

Dry Riesling—Rich and complex bouquet, dry finish. Versatile food wine.

Mainsl White—One of Alba's most popular wines, blended from Vidal Blanc, Cayuga White, and a little Riesling. Light. At the winery they call it the "Wednesday Night White" because it goes with just about any dish and fits the midweek dinner budget. ♥

Riesling—Complex, off-dry white with citrus and other fruits.

Vidal Blanc—A light, clean, crisp, off-dry version of this classic French grape.

Viognier—A limited-production (around 1,200 bottles) off-dry white with complex bouquet and palate.

Red Wines

Heritage New Jersey Red Table Wine—The winery's high-end red. Thick, deep, and chewy.

Old Mill Red—A blend of Marechal Foch and Chambourcin with small amounts of Merlot, Cabernet Franc, and Cabernet Sauvignon, all fermented and aged separately until blending, then matured in small American oak barrels 8–10 months. Rich fruit character.

Blush Wines

New Jersey Blush—A semisweet blend of Foch with Cayuga White. Strawberry and peach flavors come through.

Dessert Wines

Alba Apple—A semisweet white made from locally pressed apple cider. Nice, not cloying. Lovely with hot apple or pumpkin pie.

Blueberry—A straight blueberry made from Jersey produce. Very nice.

Moscato Carlitu—An intense and delicious dessert wine made from Muscat Canelli grapes. Named after the winemaker's grandfather, Carlo "Carlitu" Marchesi.

Red Raspberry—Wonderful, chewy, thick, and sweet without being cloying. A perfect accent to any chocolate dessert, and also makes for a wonderful Kir when added to white wines or a Kir Royale when added to champagne. My wife and I have served this at many dinner parties, where it's always a hit. Definitely one of the premier wines of the region. ♥ ♥ ♥

Ports

Vintage Port—A port made in the classic method from Marechal Foch. Big, big fruit.

REVIEWS AND AWARDS

Bluebery—Gold medal, 2003 New Jersey Wine Competition.

Alba also won five siver medals and six bronze medals, 2003 New Jersey Wine Competiton.

Red Raspberry: "Luscious . . . Sweet and tart, it captures the fruit's essence. A dollop in Bourgogne aligoté wine makes a nifty kir. It is also a dessert in itself and lovely with chocolate."　　　—Howard G. Goldberg, *New York Times* (April 27, 2003)

"[Alba's Red Raspberry has a] light ruby-garnet cast. Full acidity. Highly extracted. Pleasantly aromatic, with a wave of pure raspberry flavors. Dried herbs, red fruits. Rather unusual aromatics lead lighter-styled palate feel, with extremely tart finish. . . . 91 points."　　　—Beverage Testing Institute

"This vineyard . . . is best for rich, sweet, plummy port-styled wines."
　　　—*The New Sotheby's Wine Encyclopedia*

"Alba Riesling and Vidal Reserve: Best Buys."

—Barbara Ensrud, *Best Wine Buys for $10 or Less*

HOURS AND DIRECTIONS Open year-round Wed.–Thurs. noon–5 p.m., Fri. noon–7 p.m., Sat. 11 a.m.–6 p.m., Sun. noon–5 p.m. ■ From the New York metropolitan area and points west, take I-78 west to exit 7 (Bloomsbury). Bear right off the ramp onto Rte. 173 west. At 1.3 miles bear left at the fork and follow the sign pointing toward Riegelsville, onto Rte. 639 west. Go 2.8 miles to the stop sign and bear left onto Rte. 519 south. The road will turn into 627 south, and the winery is about 2 miles ahead on the right. ■ From Philadelphia, take I-276 (Pa. Turnpike) to exit 27 (Willow Grove/Rte. 611). Take 611 north into Riegelsville. Turn right at the light (following sign pointing to business district), cross a small one-lane bridge over the canal, then cross the bridge into N.J. Bear right off the bridge, cross the train tracks, and continue straight onto Rte. 627 north. The winery is 2 miles up on the left.

Amalthea Cellars

267A Hayes Mill Rd., Atco, NJ 08004 • Phone 609-768-8585

Amalthea Cellars was founded in 1981 by Lou Caracciolo, who named his new business for a Jersey-size moon that was discovered orbiting Jupiter while he was setting up shop. One of New Jersey's smallest wineries, producing only about 3,000 cases annually, Amalthea has not yet joined the ranks of New Jersey's best-known fine wine-makers, but it's not for lack of trying: Lou, a food scientist, is a bit of a mad professor in the cellar, constantly seeking the formula for the next great wine. And he has, in fact, designed some wonderful wines, intending them to be cellared rather than consumed immediately. Lou's wife, Gini, estimated that their reds would keep for five years and the whites for three.

Amalthea's wine cellar and tasting room are set on a nice piece of property not far from the Caracciolos' house. All in all, it's a homey little find of a winery. Go see.

Wines: $–$$

White Wines

Chardonnay—A clean, citrusy mouthful of fruit.

Chardonnay Reserve—Made in the classic French style in oak, *sur lie*.

Elara Blanc—A dry Chardonnay and Riesling blend.

Metis—Off-dry white blend.

Red Wines

Chancellor Reserve—A deep, dry red.

HOURS AND DIRECTIONS Open year-round Sat.–Sun. 11 a.m.–5 p.m. ■ From New York City, take the N.J. Turnpike to Rte. 73. Follow it south until you get to Milford Rd. (Rte. 30). Take Rte. 30 south and turn right on Vineyard Rd. The winery is on right. ■ From Philadelphia, take Rte. 168 north to Rte. 73. Turn right on Vineyard Rd. The winery is on the right.

Amwell Valley Vineyards

80 Old York Rd., Ringoes, NJ 08551 • Phone 908-788-5852 • Fax 908-788-1030 • www.amwellvalleyvineyard.com • jeffreyfisher@usa.net

Established in 1978 by scientist Michael Fisher and his wife Elsa, Amwell Valley was the first New Jersey winery licensed under the Farm Winery Act of 1981, a law Michael himself helped bring into being. Today, the couple's son Jeff is helping make the winery a successful venture, with the help of his wife Debra. The winery and the family homestead both sit on a 30-acre parcel that is as bucolic and wonderful as the New Jersey countryside can get. Inside the picturesque buildings, the winemaking equipment and new bottling machinery sparkle, testament to the winery's hard-won success.

Wines: $-$$

White Wines

Chardonnay—Soft and clean. Aged in Nevers oak.

Johannisberg Riesling—A sweet version of the classic German wine. Light, refreshing, and not too cloying.

Rayon d'Or—Off-dry and light, with lots of fruit. Made from the most widely grown hybrid grape in France and most of central Europe.

Seyval Blanc—Crisp, dryish white wine from the French-American hybrid.

Seyval Blanc Proprietor's Reserve—A limited-production run of Seyval aged in American oak. Nice.

Vidal—A dry white aged in American oak.

Red Wines

Cabernet Sauvignon—A dry red made in the classic Bordeaux manner. Aged in Limousin oak.

Landot Noir—Light red made in the Beaujolais style from a French-American hybrid of the Gamay variety. Aged in American oak.

Marechal Foch—Another Beaujolais-style red made from a French-American hybrid, aged in American oak. Soft. Not too heavy.

Blush Wines

Pleasant Ridge Blush—A semisweet blend of wines including Seyval Blanc, Aurore, Ravat, and Landot Noir. Light and fruity.

Sparkling Wines

Blanc de Blancs—Individually fermented in the bottle using the *méthode champenoise*. Finished brut.

Blanc de Noir—A semisweet rosé sparkling wine made from Marechal Foch.

Dry Riesling—Fermented using the *méthode champenoise*, with Riesling as the base white wine. Dry. Interesting.

Ports

Ruby Port—Made from Marechal Foch grapes. ♥

Dessert Wines

Late Harvest Seyval Blanc Special Reserve—Made in the classic Sauternes fashion, where the grapes take on the great "noble rot." Interesting and not overpowering.

Plum Limited Reserve—Made from a combination of classic plum varieties. Tart. Nice.

Ravat Special Reserve—Clean and crisp. Not too heavy.

Other Wines

Aurore, Peach, Pear, and *Vignoles*

REVIEWS AND AWARDS

Ruby Port 1995—Gold medal, Best of Show, 2000 New Jersey Commercial Wine Competition.

[The 1999 Ruby Port] "Most Notable Wine in New Jersey" —*USA Today* (June 28, 2002)

"The winery makes two of the best New Jersey wines I've tried: a soft, rich, age-worthy red from the marshal foch grape . . . and a surprisingly good sparkling wine made from Germany's Riesling grape . . . made in the champagne style."

—T. J. Foderaro, *Newark Star Ledger*

HOURS AND DIRECTIONS Open Sat.–Sun. 1–5 p.m. year-round for tours, tasting, and retail sales. ■ Located 5 miles south of the Flemington circle on Rte. 202/31 at Rte. 514 east (Reaville exit).

Balic Winery

Rte. 40, Mays Landing, NJ 08330 • Phone 609-625-2166

Balic Winery is named for its owner, Savo Balic, an alternately witty, charming, and irascible gentleman of eastern European descent who crafts unassuming, quality wines and sells them for much less than he probably could. They're a steal.

The winery—a large, gray, cinder-block building that's also Mr. Balic's home—is surrounded by lush vines on three sides and is impossible to miss: if the huge green sign doesn't catch your eye, the six large American flags flying out front will. Inside, the gift shop is cool and filled with the sounds of soft classical music, which makes the process of choosing a wine so much more pleasant.

Wines: $

White Wines
Chablis—A dry, light white.
Chenin Blanc—A light white.
Classic White—An interesting semisweet blend with a nice finish.
Vidal Blanc—Off-dry.

Red Wines
Chancellor—A deep red mouthful of berries.
Country Red—A blend of red varieties. A good pasta red.

Blush Wines
Blush—A semisweet, pinkish wine. One of Balic's most popular.
Rosé Supreme—A nice semisweet blush wine.

HOURS AND DIRECTIONS Open Mon.–Sat. 9:30 a.m.–5:30 p.m. ■ Located not too far from Atlantic City. From Philadelphia, take Rte. 40 east to Mays Landing. The winery is on the left.

Cape May Winery & Vineyard

709 Townbank Rd., Cape May, NJ 08204 • Phone 609-884-1169 • Fax 609-884-5131 • www.capemaywinery.com

Cape May Winery was established in 1995 by Joan and Bill Hayes just outside its historic and popular namesake beach-resort town, with its many wonderful restaurants and scenic streets lined with immaculately restored Victorian houses. Originally a home winemaker, Bill worked for Frank Salek of Sylvin Farms for some time before going on his own. For the first few years the Hayeses bottled about 1,000 cases annually in the basement of their home, with nearly the entire run going to a few local liquor stores and restaurants (Oyster Bay Steak and Seafood, the Peter Shields Inn, and Godmother's Italian Restaurant). In the summer of 2001, however, they decided to take their winery to the next level, increasing their volume to keep up with demand and opening a tasting room to appease the countless wine tourists who were constantly calling to ask about tastings and tours.

Since opening in 1995, the winery has been awarded twenty-five medals. Its most popular wines are summer whites—understandable considering the seasonal character of this seaside town.

Wines: $–$$

White Wines

Chardonnay—Clean and citrusy.

Chardonnay Barrel Fermented—A varietal done in the classic French tradition. Nice.

Red Wines

Cabernet Franc—Deep color. Lots of fruit, dry finish. Very drinkable.

Cabernet Sauvignon—A deep red, well done.

Cabernet Sauvignon Barrel Reserve—You can taste the difference the oak makes.

Merlot—A nice deep red.

Blush Wines

Victorian Blush—Their most popular wine, with good reason. Semisweet but not cloying. Very nice. ♥

REVIEWS AND AWARDS

Pinot Grigio 2002—Gold medal, 2003 New Jersey Wine Competition.

Eight bronze medals, 2003 New Jersey Wine Competition.

"Worth consumers' attention . . . a '97 chardonnay reserve and '96 cabernet sauvignon, both from a promising newcomer."
—Howard G. Goldberg, *New York Times* (May 23, 1999)

"Bursting with exuberant flavor—Beaujolais bounce and Loire fruitiness—[the 1998 Cabernet Franc] was my favorite."
—Howard G. Goldberg, *New York Times* (August 27, 2000)

HOURS AND DIRECTIONS Tours and tastings June-Sept., Fri.–Sat. 11 a.m.–5 p.m. ■ From New York City, take the Garden State Pkwy. south to Rte. 109 west, then take Rte. 9 south. Turn right at Seashore Rd., then left at the next light, onto Townbank Rd. The winery will be on your right. ■ From Cape May, take Rte. 9 north. Turn left onto Rte. 644, right onto Rte. 648, then turn right. The winery will be on your left.

Cream Ridge Winery

145 Rte. 539, P.O. Box 98, Cream Ridge, NJ 08514 •
Phone 609-259-9797 • creamridgewinery.com

Family-run Cream Ridge Winery is located in the beautiful countryside of Cream Ridge, N.J., not far from Six Flags Great Adventure amusement park. Tom Amabile bought the land 10 years before he retired and began making wines, eventually coming to specialize in premium fruit wines made with all–New Jersey fruit. These can range from dry to intoxicatingly sweet, with the fruits easily tasted on the tip of the tongue. He opened the winery officially in 1988 and quickly started winning awards, walking away with five consecutive Governor's Cups (the highest award given to a wine in the state of New Jersey) for his cherry, plum, and cranberry wines.

The winery is known locally for the wonderful bluegrass festival it sponsors every summer. The winery and grounds can be rented for events and receptions.

Wines: $–$$

White Wines
Chardonnay—Dry. Aged in oak.

Eastern White—Made from Niagara and Catawba grapes. Semisweet, fruity.

Riesling—Delicately sweet.

Red Wines
Black Malvoisie—A light red, Beaujolais-style spring wine.

Cabernet Sauvignon—Dry. Aged in oak.

Merlot—Dry. Aged in oak.

A Perfect Blend—60% Cabernet Sauvignon, 20% Merlot, 20% Cabernet Franc.

Raley's Red—Winemaker's blend of grapes and berries.

Blush Wines
Country Blush—Similar to a White Zinfandel. Semisweet.

Fruit Wines
After Dinner—Apricot wine sweetened with honey. Similar to ice wine. Limited edition, sold in 375-ml bottles (half-size).

Almondberry—Raspberry and white wine with almonds.

Blackberry—Lightly sweet, made with 100% blackberries.

Ciliegia Amabile—Award winner. Barely sweet. Tastes like you're drinking a cherry pie. ♥

Cranberry—Made from dry-harvested cranberries. Another award winner. ♥

Cream Rossare—Cherry and white wine with vanilla bean.

Dry Cherry—Oak-aged cherry wine.

Sparkling Wines
Champagne—Off-dry.

REVIEWS AND AWARDS
A Perfect Blend—Gold medal, 2003 New Jersey Wine Competition.

Twelve bronze medals, 2003 New Jersey Wine Competition.

Ciliegia Amabile—2000 Governor's Cup winner. Also *USA Today* and *New York Times* choice.

Cranberry—1999 Governor's Cup winner.

"Like a genie that materialized from an open bottle, ready to do one's bidding, a delicious raspberry aroma filled the dining room at dinner and then lingered on until morning. . . . Every time I open a Cream Ridge Winery fruit wine, the genie appears in different guises."

—Howard G. Goldberg, *New York Times*

HOURS AND DIRECTIONS Open year-round Mon.–Sat. 10 a.m.–6 p.m., Sun. 11 a.m.–5 p.m. ■ From north or south on the N.J. Turnpike, get off at exit 7A. Bear right onto I-195 east toward Six Flags. Get off at exit 17B onto Rte. 539 south to Allentown. In Allentown you will pass the Black Forest Restaurant, located in the Old Mill on the right. After crossing the bridge, 539 makes a sharp left, where it becomes High Street. The winery is exactly 3 miles on the right. ■ From the east and shore points, take I-195 west toward Trenton; get off at exit 16 onto Rte. 537 west toward Six Flags. At the first traffic light turn right onto Rte. 539 north toward Allentown. The winery is the first building on the left past the Cream Ridge Golf Course.

The Four Sisters Winery

10 Doe Hollow Ln., Belvedere, NJ 07823 • Phone 908-475-3671 •
Fax 908-475-3555 • www.matarazzo.com/winery.html • rjm@interactive.net

Set against the green hills and gentle swells of lush farmland in Warren County, N.J., is a picturesque winery called Four Sisters, established in 1981 by Matty and Laurie Matarazzo as part of a 392-acre produce farm. The Matarazzos stress farming as well as tasting to help educate consumers about fine wine and great food. Four Sisters has won over twenty regional, national, and international awards for its red, white, rosé, and fruit wines.

Wines: $–$$

White Wines

Cayuga—An excellent semidry, tart white wine.
Cedar Hill White—Semisweet golden white wine. Lots of fruit. Tart finish.
Chardonel—A crisp, dry white wine from a Chardonnay parent.
Niagara—Semisweet native American grape.
Seyval Blanc—A delicately dry, smooth varietal of French origin.
Seyval Reserve—Oak aged, with a very dry finish.
Vidal Blanc—A dry, well-balanced white.
Warren Hills White—Semisweet, with a flowery nose.

Red Wines

Beaver Creek Red—Sweet, almost port-like. Made from Concord grapes.
Chambourcin—A dry red.
Holiday Seasoned—Spicy and sweet. A good all-occasion table wine.
Leon Millot—Dry and solid.
Papa's Red—Medium-bodied red. Tart. Made with Baco Noir grapes.
Warren Hills Red—A blended, dry pasta wine.

Blush Wines

Autumn Rouge—A semisweet rosé.
Cedar Hill Rose—Semisweet. Made from Niagara grapes.
Merrill Blush—A light blush. Not cloying. Slightly tart.

Fruit Wines

Cherry Melissa—A blend of tart cherry and English sweet cherry juices. A nice dessert wine.
Robin's Raspberry—A nice raspberry wine. Not too dark. Limited quantity.
Sadie's Apple—Made from late-harvest apples. Light gold. Semisweet. Crisp.
Spicy Sister—A semisweet, spiced apple wine.
Strawberry Serena—Like a big mouthful of strawberries. Tart finish.

Sparkling Wines

Maggie's Magic—A semisweet sparkling wine made in the classic *méthode champenoise* tradition. Lots of fruit. Smooth finish.

HOURS AND DIRECTIONS Open daily 9 a.m.–6 p.m. (but closed Tues.–Wed. during Jan.–Mar.). ■ Located on County Rte. 519 just 3 miles north of Rte. 46 and 6 miles south of I-80 exit 12, in Belvedere.

King's Road Winery

Rte. 579, Asbury, NJ 08802 • Phone 800-479-6479 or 908-479-6611 •
www.kingsroad.com • nicolaas@kingsroad.com

You pretty much have to like any winery where the tasting room is the hayloft of an old dairy barn. Granted, the place looks new from the outside, but inside it's all character, and the surrounding grounds are among the loveliest in all of New Jersey.

King's Road was founded in 1980 by KRV Inc. and is overseen by winemaker Nicolaas Opdam and his wife Lorraine, both of whom obsess about their business. The result? Some nice wines.

Wines: $-$$

White Wines

Beach Sand Blanc—A light, semisweet wine.

Chardonnay—Dry, classic varietal.

Chardonnay Reserve—Dry, classic, aged in French oak.

Ensemble—Semisweet white.

Lieblich Fruchtig—Semidry Riesling. Translated, the name means "Lovely Fruit."

Seyval Blanc—Crisp, with pleasant fruit.

Weekend White—A semidry blend of Chardonnay and Seyval Blanc. Crisp and tart.

Red Wines

Cabernet Sauvignon—Made in the tradition of Burgundian table wine. Aged in French oak.

Blush Wines

Royal Blush—Semisweet.

Sunburn Blush—Lighter and fruitier than Royal Blush.

Sparkling Wines

Champagne Brut—Traditional champagne-style wine, 100% Chardonnay.

Champagne Extra Dry—Off-dry sparkling wine with a touch of sweetness at the end.

Champagne Reserve Rosé—Off-dry rosé sparkling wine.

Specialty Wines

Late Harvest Riesling—A perennial gold medal winner. Great mouth feel, excellent fruit, smooth finish.

Marcato—A semidry made from Cabernet and Merlot.

Pinot Noir—Lots of fruit. Dry finish.

Queen's Gold Honey Wine—Sweet, 100% pure mead.

Regal Red—Sweet red.

Royal Raspberry—A sweet red raspberry wine.

St. Nicks Cider—A sweet, spiced apple wine.

Sunset Red—A light, semisweet red.

REVIEWS AND AWARDS

Riesling 1997—Silver medal, 1999 New Jersey Commercial Wine Competition.

HOURS AND DIRECTIONS Open Wed.–Sun. noon–5 p.m. year-round. ■ From the New York area, take the George Washington Bridge to I-95 south. Continue to I-78 west to exit 11 (Pattenburg). Bear left as you leave the exit and follow the signs for Pattenburg. Go straight through the traffic light on the Rte. 78 overpass, which will put you on Rte. 614 (not marked). Continue about 3 miles to the junction of Rtes. 614 and 579. Turn right onto 579. The winery is just down the road on the left. ■ From the Trenton area, take Rte. 31 north to the Rtes. 202 and 31 intersection, in Ringoes. Continue north on Rte. 202/31 into Flemington, where the roads split. Take Rte. 31 into Clinton, to I-78. Take I-78 west to exit 11 (Pattenburg) and follow the local directions above.

LaFollette Vineyard and Winery

64 Harlingen Rd., Belle Mead, NJ 08502 • Phone 908-359-9234 •
www.lafollettewinery.com • grapes@lafollettewinery.com

LaFollette Vineyard and Winery is located in the rolling hills of central New Jersey, minutes from the Princeton University campus. The family-owned and -operated winery produces small batches of Seyval Blanc white wine with pride and care. The wines can be bought at the winery or at two restaurants in Princeton: Nassau Street Seafood and Mrs. Chou's Chinese Restaurant.

Mimi LaFollette Summerskill is a prolific author, traveler, and activist. The mother of five children, Mimi still lives at the winery and helps oversee its operation. One of her books, *Daughter of the Vine: A Vintner's Tale*, tells the entire story of the LaFollette Vineyard and Winery. Richard LaFollette Wright, Mimi's eldest son, is the current manager. The winery has been in the family for over 20 years.

Wines: $–$$

White Wines

Seyval Blanc—Crisp, semidry, light white. Melon and apple flavors come through nicely.

REVIEWS AND AWARDS

"Over the years, the reputation of the winery has grown due to the excellence of the product."   —Louise Handelman, *Princeton Packet* (September 29, 1999)

HOURS AND DIRECTIONS Open weekends May–Sept. Please call ahead before visiting. ■ From New York City, take I-78 west to exit 29 (I-287 south). Take I-287 south to exit 17 for Rte. 206 (follow signs for Rte. 206 to Princeton; you will catch Rte. 206 in a roundabout). Drive south on 206 approximately 10 miles until you reach Harlingen Rd. (there is a Gulf gas station at the corner), and turn left onto Harlingen. The vineyard is 0.3 mile down the road on the left. ■ From Philadelphia, drive north on I-95 into New Jersey. Take exit 7B to Rte. 206 north. Continue approximately 12 miles on 206 (you will have to make a left turn in downtown Princeton to stay on it) until you reach Harlingen Rd. (there is a Gulf gas station at the corner). Turn right onto Harlingen. The vineyard is 0.3 mile down the road on the left.

Poor Richard's Winery

220 Ridge Rd., Frenchtown, NJ 08825 • Phone 908-996-6480 •
www.intac.com/~poorrich • poorrich@ptd.net

Poor Richard's is possibly the most unimpressive winery you might ever come across, housed in what looks like the foundation of an incomplete house. You could, of course, call this a wine cellar, but that implies more charm than you'll find here. You might even want to turn right around and leave once you step through the door and catch sight of disheveled winemaker "Poor" Richard Dilts (who looks a bit like some part-time caretaker), but take a minute, because while Richard and his odd cinder-block cave aren't at all impressive, the wines are.

Richard is actually a kind of mad genius, a classic cellar rat who's constantly busy handcrafting his wines, talking to himself, practicing some variety of wonderful alchemy. The Chancellor and the Chambourcin in particular are worth sticking around for, and the Copper Penny's a wonderful treat too.

In a nod to atmosphere, the view from the observation deck is actually quite nice, looking out over the 15-acre vineyard—full mainly of winter-hardy French hybrids (including Chambourcin, Chancellor, Boca Noir, Leon Millot, Vidal, and Seyval) plus small amounts of Ravat and Melody.

Wines: $–$$$

White Wines
Barrel Seyval—Aged in French and American oak barrels.

Frenchtown White—A nice, light table white.

Seyval Blanc—Dry white wine.

Vidal Blanc—An off-dry white.

Red Wines
Chambourcin—Fermented on the skins and aged in oak. Deep red color. Dry finish. ♥

Chancellor—A well-rounded, oaked deep red. ♥

Frenchtown Red—A nice, dry blend.

Vineyard Red Reserve—A Chambourcin and Chancellor blend made in very limited amounts, fermented with skin contact and aged in oak.

Blush Wines
Sunglo—A blush wine made from a blend of grapes.

Sparkling Wines
Judith—A dry Vidal sparkling wine with lots of tiny bubbles and big fruit. Very popular.

Dessert Wines
Copper Penny—A copper-colored semisweet wine. More of a wine than a straight-out dessert. Nice.

REVIEWS AND AWARDS
Barrel Seyval—Silver medal, 1993 New Jersey State Wine Competition.

Chambourcin—Gold medal, 1991 American Wine Society National Competition; bronze, 1991 New Jersey State Wine Competition; silver, 1993 American Wine Society National Competition; silver, 1993 New Jersey State Wine Competition; bronze, 1999 New Jersey Commercial Wine Competition.

Chancellor—Bronze medal, 1991 and 1993 New Jersey State Wine Competition.

HOURS AND DIRECTIONS Open year-round for tastings Thurs.–Sun. noon–6 p.m. ■ Located in Frenchtown, New Jersey, the winery is only a few miles from the Delaware River. ■ From I-78, take exit 15, then head south on Rte. 513 to Frenchtown. Turn left onto Rte. 12, then left onto Ridge Rd. (the third left). Go 2 miles and turn right into the winery. ■ From Flemington, take Rte. 12 west. At the second traffic light, turn right onto Rte. 519, then left onto Ridge Rd. Go 1.5 miles and turn left into the winery. ■ From I-95, take exit 1 and go north on Rte. 29 to Frenchtown, then turn right onto Rte. 12, then left onto Ridge Rd. (the third left). Go 2 miles and turn right into the winery.

Renault Winery

72 N. Breman Ave., Egg Harbor City, NJ 08215 • Phone 609-965-2111 •
www.renaultwinery.com • wine@renaultwinery.com

NEW JERSEY

Renault is one of those places people don't believe exists. Founded by master vintner Louis Nicholas Renault in 1864 (a year before the Civil War ended), it's the country's longest-operating winery and was once its largest distributor of champagne, pumping out more than a million gallons annually when it was in its prime. Joseph Milza bought the operation in 1977, by which point the winery's glory days were a distant memory. Run-down and rickety, it was considered something of a joke among local residents.

Today, you'd never know. The gourmet restaurant Milza opened on the property is often cited by regional magazines and newspapers as one of the most romantic in southern New Jersey, with an absolutely fabulous collection of wineglasses on display, dating back hundreds of years. Outside, the country club surroundings continue the glassware theme with a pair of cement champagne bottles that tower 24 feet into the sky, one marking the entrance to the winery. Built in 1939, when Renault was in its heyday, they've recently been declared eligible for inclusion on New Jersey's Register of Historic Places. Similar bottles were manufactured as advertising for Renault and can still be found dotted all over the country.

And finally, there is the wine—more than 40,000 cases of the stuff every year. It's drunk mostly by patrons who come for dinner or for the acclaimed brunch, but some is also sold in the tasting room, which has a separate entrance. Go for a meal: try the brunch—it's less expensive than a dinner and just as good.

Wines: $–$$$

White Wines
Chablis—A dry and fruity white wine.
Chardonnay—Their premium dry white wine.
Chenin Blanc—A light, dry white wine.
French Colombard—Made in the French style. A dry white.
Fumé Blanc—Light, dry Sauvignon Blanc. Citrusy.
Johannisberg Riesling—German-style, semidry light white wine.
May Wine—Made with a sweet strawberry flavoring.
Sauvignon Blanc—Dry white table wine.

Red Wines
Burgundy—Rich and mellow dry red.
Cabernet Sauvignon—Their premium dry red wine.
Merlot—Another premium dry red. Smooth.
Sangria—Semisweet red fruit wine.

Blush Wines
Blush—Semisweet blush blend.
Pink Lady—A sweet rosé.
White Zinfandel—Light and refreshing blush wine.

Sparkling Wines
American Champagne—Dry and fruity.
Blueberry Champagne—Semisweet sparkling wine.

Premium Champagne—Hand-fermented dry champagne.

Spumante—Semisweet sparkler.

REVIEWS AND AWARDS

Brut Champagne NV—Best Sparkling/silver medal, 2003 New Jersey Wine Competition.

"Best Romantic Restaurant"

—*Atlantic City Magazine* "Best of the Shore" issue (1997 and 1998)

"Best Winery" —*Daily Journal* Readers Choice Award (1997)

HOURS AND DIRECTIONS Tours and wine tastings year-round Mon.–Fri. 11 a.m.–4 p.m., Sat. 11 a.m.–8 p.m., Sun. noon–4 p.m. ■ From Philadelphia, take the Atlantic City Expwy. to exit 17 (Egg Harbor). Turn left onto Rte. 50 north, then right onto Rte. 30, then left onto Bremen Ave. Continue 2.25 miles to Renault. ■ From North Jersey, take the Garden State Pkwy. south to exit 44. Make a sharp right onto Moss Mill Rd. (Alt. Rte. 561) and continue 5 miles to Bremen Ave. Turn right and drive 0.3 mile to the winery. ■ From Atlantic City, take Rte. 30 west approximately 16 miles to Bremen Ave. Turn right onto Bremen (at the Renault bottle) and drive 2.25 miles to the winery. ■ From South Jersey, take the Garden State Pkwy. north. Exit at the food and fuel service area, mile marker 41. Proceed to the north end of the service area. From there, follow signs to Jimmy Leeds Rd. At the traffic light, turn left. At the fork, bear right and continue on Rte. 561 to Bremen Ave. Turn right onto Bremen and drive 1.5 miles to Renault.

Sylvin Farms

24 N. Vienna Ave., Germania, NJ 08215 • Phone 609-965-1548 • Fax 973-778-9165

Founded as a winery in 1985 by Franklin and Sylvia Salek, Sylvin Farms is one of the smallest wineries in New Jersey but has acquired a unique reputation by devoting its energies exclusively to the production of vinifera (European) grape varieties. Its location has something to do with this:

the moderating influences of the Atlantic Ocean and the Mullica and Great Harbor Rivers (which flow on either side of the property) couple with the vineyard's gravelly loam soil to produce growing conditions similar to those of the most famous grape-producing regions of Europe.

Dr. Salek claims to have introduced to the United States the most widely grown white grape in Russia, which he uses jointly with Tomasello Winery to produce a Rkatziteli (pronounced ar-kat-si-TEL-ee), a sparkling wine with a Riesling-like character, finished slightly sweet. Salek has personally grafted all of his vines onto phylloxera-resistant rootstock, and his efforts have paid off with six New Jersey Governor's Cup wins.

Wines: $–$$

White Wines

Chardonnay—A dry version in the classic French tradition.

Riesling—A dry, light white.

Red Wines

Cabernet Franc—Slightly lighter than the Sauvignon, and very nice.

Cabernet Sauvignon—A deep, dry red.

Merlot—A soft finish on a mouthful of fruit.

Pinot Noir—A nice, light red.

Sparkling Wines

Blanc de Noirs—A dry sparkling wine of great presence. Beautiful brassy color, with fine trails of bubbles and a dry finish. ♥

Sparkling Rkatziteli—Joint effort with Tomasello Winery. A wonderful wine. Inventive, off-dry, and exquisite. Delicate. The only Sparkling Rkatziteli in the United States. ♥ ♥

REVIEWS AND AWARDS

Cabernet Franc 1995—1999 New Jersey Governor's Cup.

Sparkling Muscat Ottonel (NV)—1998 New Jersey Governor's Cup.

HOURS AND DIRECTIONS Open weekends by appointment only. ■ From New York City, take the Garden State Pkwy. to exit 44. Turn right onto Alt. Rte. 561 (Moss Mill Rd.), then right onto Vienna Ave. Follow to winery. ■ From Philadelphia, take the Atlantic City Expwy. to exit 17 (Egg Harbor) and Rte. 50 north. Turn right on Rte. 30. Turn left onto Vienna Ave. and continue to winery.

Tomasello Winery

225 White Horse Pike, Hammonton, NJ 08037 • Phone 800-666-WINE or 609-561-0567 • Fax 609-561-8617 • www.tomasellowinery.com • info@tomasellowinery.com

Tomasello Winery was founded in 1933 by Frank Tomasello, who made it a success despite such events as the Great Depression and World War II. Now, 70 years later, his grandsons Jack and Charles have brought the 70-acre winery to new levels. It's the largest winery in New Jersey by a huge margin (producing fully half the wine made in the state), and its distribution is incredible, especially for an East Coast winery. Not only can Tomasello wines be found in most liquor stores throughout Jersey and neighboring

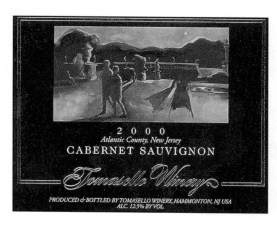

states, but some have reached international fame as well.

This presence works both for and against them. Tomasello offers one of the biggest wine lists on the eastern seaboard—more than thirty different varieties, from inexpensive table wines to more prestigious vintages. Unfortunately, many wine snobs see only the ubiquitous low-end brands, and thus miss out on experiencing the wonderful fine wines. We can remember when a friend told a group that Tomasello Cabernet Sauvignon had just received an excellent notice in the *New York Times*. Several people practically gagged, and lamented the great paper's demise.

But the simple fact is, Tomasello makes good wines, and year after year continues to collect awards. Their dessert wines are especially prized, and have found audiences as far away as Japan and other Asian countries. Reviewers for the *New York Times*, Hugh Johnson, Robert Parker, Sotheby's, and many other wine critics have lauded the winery's innovative, entrepreneurial approach, which includes alliances with respected boutique wineries such as Sylvin Farms, known in wine circles as one of New Jersey's finest.

The winery has a large dining facility they use to cater to bus crowds, weddings, and corporate events. The food is excellent, and the wines . . . well! Go visit, and see what we're talking about.

Wines: $–$$$

White Wines
Atlantic County Chardonnay—A dry, light Chardonnay. Citrus flavors.
Atlantic County Niagara—Semisweet white wine.
Atlantic County Riesling—Crisp and clean. Not sweet.
Atlantic County Rkatziteli—Celebrated, popular, semisweet white with flavors of melon and slight citrus. Very nice. Sells out quickly.
Atlantic County Vidal Blanc—Green apple. Citrus. Not cloyingly sweet.
Nevers Oak Chardonnay—Chardonnay aged 7 months in Nevers oak casks.
Traminette—A Gewürztraminer-style white. Fruity and crisp. Tangy.
Veneto Pinot Grigio—Citrus flavors. Tart.

Red Wines
Atlantic County Cabernet Franc—Dark garnet wine. Big fruit. Dry finish. ♥
Atlantic County Cabernet Sauvignon—The winery's best red. Aged in new American oak 7 months. Dried berries. Plum. Dry finish. ♥
Atlantic County Chambourcin—A dry red wine made in a fruity Beaujolais style.
Atlantic County Villard Noir—A lighter-style red.

Blush Wines
Atlantic County Steuben—An off-dry rosé made from French hybrid Steuben grapes.

Sparkling Wines
Blanc de Blanc Brut—Same *cuvée* as the Blanc de Blanc Natural sparkler, but not quite as dry.
Blanc de Blanc Extra Dry—Semisweet sparkling wine.
Blanc de Blanc Natural—A blend of Seyval Blanc, Villard Blanc, and Vidal Blanc grapes.
Pink Champagne—A blush sparkling wine made with Steuben. Strawberry flavors come through.
Sparkling Burgundy—A light plum-colored sparkling wine. Sweet.
Sparkling Rkatziteli—Joint effort with Sylvin Farms. A wonderful wine. Inventive, off-dry, and exquisite. Delicate. The only Sparkling Rkatziteli in the United States. ♥ ♥
Spumante—The sweetest white sparkling wine from this winery.

Dessert Wines
American Almonique—A white wine with natural almond and vanilla flavors added.
Blackberry—Made from 100% Marion blackberries. Cassis comes through. Sweet.
Blueberry—A pure 100% blueberry wine from cultivated highbush blueberries grown

by New Jersey's Atlantic Blueberry Company, the largest single-family blueberry farm in the world. Semisweet. A mouthful of blueberries.

Cranberry—A light, ruby red, 100% cranberry wine. Sweet but not cloying. Great with chocolate desserts.

Epilogue 2001—A dessert Riesling made in the fashion of the German *Eiswein*. A very nice version. Sweet but well balanced. Not overpowering.

Mulled Spice—A recipe wine made with the native American Concord grapes. Sweet, with cinnamon and clove flavor.

Tomasello Red Raspberry—A 100% raspberry wine. Sweet up front. Some acidity but not too tart. Great with chocolate. ♥

Other Wines

American Merlot, Burgundy, Cape May Red, Cape May White, Claret, French Colombard, Oak Reserve Chardonnay, Ranier Red, Ranier Rosé, Ranier White, and *White Zinfandel*

REVIEWS AND AWARDS

Chambourciin 2001—Governor's Cup/gold medal/Best Estate Wine/Best Hybrid, 2003 New Jersey Wine Competition.

"Blanc de Noirs: Recommended." —*The New Sotheby's Wine Encyclopedia*

"Good Chambourcin. Promising Cabernet Sauvignon and Merlot." —*Hugh Johnson's Pocket Wine Book 2002*

"New Jersey has come a long way, with more than a dozen wineries, one of the most serious, being Tomasello. . . . The 1996 Atlantic County Chardonnay Oak Reserve is oaky indeed, in the manner of a Robert Mondavi chardonnay." —Diane Nottle, *New York Times* (January 1998)

"Charles and Jack Tomasello are producing a great array of wines from the native concord as well as hybrids. Don't miss the Beaujolais-like Chambourcin and the noteworthy Cabernet Sauvignon." —Marguerite Thomas, *Wine News* (June/July 1997)

"[Tomasello Chambourcin] appears to be emerging as the Philadelphia area's most consistently superior red wine." —Deborah Scoblionkov, *Philadelphia Inquirer*

"I have had several delightful Chardonnays from Tomasello Winery." —Robert M. Parker, Jr., *Parker's Wine Buyer's Guide*

HOURS AND DIRECTIONS Open year-round Mon.–Sat. 9 a.m.–8 p.m., Sun. 11 a.m.–6 p.m. ■ From Pennsylvania, take Walt Whitman Bridge to New Jersey. Follow signs for Rte. 42 south to Atlantic City Expwy. south. Take the expressway to exit 28 (Hammonton). Bear left off the exit ramp onto Rte. 54 north. Follow this road 3 to 4 miles through downtown Hammonton until you reach a split in the road. Follow the road on the right and look for the Silver Coin Diner. The traffic light here is the intersection of Rtes. 30 (White Horse Pike) and 206. Turn left onto Rte. 30 west and go to the next light. The winery is on the right. ■ From the Jersey Shore, travel west on Rte. 30 (White Horse Pike) You will stay on Rte. 30 all the way to the winery. In Hammonton look for DiDonato's Bowling Alley on the right. Approximately 0.5 mile past this landmark there will be a traffic light (Kessler Memorial Hospital on the left). Continue west on Rte. 30, going through three more lights about 0.5 mile apart. At the third light you'll see the Silver Coin Diner on your left. (This intersection is Rte. 30 and 206.) Continue through this intersection to the next light (fourth light) and you'll see Tomasello on the right.

Unionville Vineyards ✫ ✫

9 Rocktown Rd., P.O. Box 104, Ringoes, NJ 08551 • Phone 908-788-0400 • Fax 908-806-4692 • www.unionvillevineyards.com • uvineyard@aol.com

NEW JERSEY

One nice thing about wine tasting is that you get to gush about your favorites, and we'll admit an extreme prejudice in favor of Unionville Vineyards. It's easily one of our favorites on the East Coast.

Founded in 1993 by Kris Nielson and Patricia Galloway, the winery is nestled into the rolling hills of Hunterdon County, in a converted dairy barn that makes for a classic country setting. Inside, you can walk downstairs to the wine cellar on a self-guided tour or wander around the beautifully appointed shop, buying wine accessories or bric-a-brac with hunt-country themes. Hunterdon County is big horse country, so it's not at all uncommon to hear customers and vineyard workers split their talk between horses and wines, a dual theme that's reflected on the winery's labels.

Australian winemaker Keith Brown has done a wonderful job on the selections, making a slew of lovely whites (from dry to dessert wines) that we've served at numerous dinner parties. Guests are never disappointed. The reds are making big strides, too: The 2000 Nielson Estate Proprietor's Reserve took the Governor's Cup in the seventeenth annual New Jersey State Wine Competition.

Wines: $–$$$

White Wines

Chardonnay—A soft white wine, barrel fermented in the finest quality American oak *barriques*. Aged *sur lie* 11 months. Well rounded with citrus notes and hints of vanilla. Buttery.

Hunter's White—An off-dry blend of Vidal Blanc and Cayuga grapes. Fermented in stainless steel tanks. Fruity but not cloying.

Hunter's White Reserve—A wonderful Vidal Blanc. Crisp, clean, and tart. Cool fermentation, then aged 8 months in small oak *barriques*. ♥ ♥

Riesling—Named for the Windfall Vineyards, where the grapes are grown. A crisp, clean, tart Riesling with a hint of sweetness. ♥

Windfall Vineyard Seyval Blanc—A 100% Seyval Blanc. Fermented in new oak barrels and aged *sur lie*. Dry and clean. The oak lends buttery and vanilla flavors that come through. ♥

Red Wines

Cabernet Sauvignon—A 100% Cabernet Sauvignon. Handcrafted and aged 15 months in small oak *barriques*.

Chambourcin—Fermented on the skins 14 days and barrel aged 12 months.

Hunter's Red—A light table wine made from Marechal Foch grapes. A nice pasta wine.

Hunter's Red Reserve Meritage—A blend of Cabernet Franc and Merlot grapes, aged 14 months in small oak barrels.

Nielson Estates Proprietor Reserve—A blend of Cabernet Franc (95%) and Chambourcin (5%) aged 12 months in American oak.

Blush Wines

Fields of Fire—A semisweet blush wine made from Cayuga and Chambourcin grapes. Refreshing.

Fruit Wines

Hunter's Gold—A well-crafted, light golden-colored wine made from locally pressed apple cider. A wonderful sipping wine, in summer or winter. Great before dinner or with dessert. Also goes nicely with salads or spring soups. ♥

Ports

Port VAT 7—Dark, heavy dessert wine made in the classic port tradition.

Dessert Wines

Cool Foxy Lady—Pressed from frozen Vidal Blanc grapes. A thick, golden honey-colored wine of great substance. Acidity balances out the sugar, so the sweetness is not overpowering. Tropical flavors come through. And a good bargain at such a price, compared to other ice wines.♥ ♥

REVIEWS AND AWARDS

Chardonnay—Gold medal, 2003 New Jersey State Wine Competition; gold medal, 2001 New Jersey State Wine Competition.

Hunter's Red—Silver medal, *Dallas Morning News*.

Hunter's Red Reserve 2001—Gold medal, 2003 New Jersey State Wine Competition.

Hunter's White Reserve—Gold medal, 2003 New Jersey State Wine Competition; silver medal, *Dallas Morning News*.

Four silver medals and five bronze medals, 2003 New Jersey State Wine Competition.

"One of New Jersey's newest and fastest-rising wineries."
—*The New Sotheby's Wine Encyclopedia*

"One of New Jersey's best wineries. . . . Lovely Riesling, French-American hybrids elevated to near-vinifera status."   —*Hugh Johnson's Pocket Wine Book 2002*

"This New Jersey Riesling [1997] is a lot of fun. Relatively light (11.5% alcohol), it is off-dry and flowery in a German style . . . surprisingly good on the mid-palate. Pleasing and charming. I liked it. . . . 85 points."
—Mark Squires, *E-Zine on Wine* (July/August 1998)

HOURS AND DIRECTIONS Open year-round Thurs.–Sun. 11 a.m.–4 p.m. ■ From New York, take the N.J. Turnpike south to exit 14. Take I-78 west for approximately 25 miles to I-287 south toward Somerville. Take the exit for U.S. 202/206 toward Princeton/Flemington and continue south on 202 to Flemington (approximately 13 miles). Continue south on 202/31 for 6 miles to Wertsville Rd. (Ringoes). Take the jug-handle crossover onto Wertsville Rd. and drive 1.8 miles to the second right (Rocktown Rd.). The winery is the first driveway on left. ■ From Philadelphia, take I-95 north across Scudder Falls Bridge to New Jersey. Take the first exit (at end of bridge) onto Rte. 29 north, toward Lambertville. Proceed through Lambertville to U.S. 202. Go north on 202 for approximately 6 miles to Wertsville Rd. Turn right. Go approximately 1.3 miles and make the second right onto Rocktown Rd. ■ From Princeton, drive north on U.S. 206 toward Rocky Hill to Rte. 518. Turn left onto 518 toward Hopewell, then right in downtown Hopewell on Greenwood Ave. (County Rd. 907). Drive approximately 5.5 miles to the T intersection with Wertsville Rd. Turn left and go approximately 1.5 miles to the second left, Rocktown Rd. ■ From Trenton, take Rte. 31 north to U.S. 202. Go north on 202 for 0.3 mile to the first light (Wertsville Rd.), where you'll turn right. Go 1.3 miles to the second right (Rocktown Rd.) and turn right again.

Valenzano Winery

340 Forked Neck Rd., Shamong, NJ 08088 • Phone 609-268-6731 • Fax 609-859-8014 • www.valenzanowine.com • tony@valenzanowine.com

Valenzano Winery was founded in 1998 by self-taught vintner Anthony Valenzano at his family farm, where he'd been growing grapes for more than 12 years, bottling his first home wine in 1990. Starting with just a few varieties on 3 planted acres, he now has vines on more than 30 (including a new vineyard planted with Chambourcin and Cynthiana) and has partnered with his sons Anthony, Jr., and Mark to make wines that cost less than $10 and are getting better all the time. Get in while the gettin's good.

Located in the heart of New Jersey's Pine Barrens, Valenzano is an unassuming winery and sometimes looks closed, but it's not. Since it's run out of the family home, there's always someone there. However, plans call for a new tasting room to be opened in the new vineyards. It will have more constant hours and be open for business regularly. Just to be on the safe side, call before you drive over.

Wines: $–$$

White Wines

Chardonnay—Oak-fermented golden white, finished in American oak. Lemony, with buttery overtones.

Riesling—Off-dry, crisp white with tropical flavors. Pears come through.

Vidal Blanc—Light, off-dry white with a tart finish.

Red Wines

Cabernet Franc/Merlot—A blend of Cabernet Franc, Merlot, and Chambourcin wines.

Chambourcin—An oak-aged dry red.

Cynthiana—A complex, silky red made from Cynthiana (Norton) grapes. Full bouquet and light tannins. At this point, Valenzano is the only winery in New Jersey (and one of the few on the East Coast) making wine with Cynthiana. The result is worth the effort, but you've got to be quick: They only produce 60 cases annually.

Labrusca—Semisweet red, made from 100% labrusca (native) grapes. Purplish color along with a fruity, semisweet taste.

Merlot—Dry red aged in American oak. Limited supply.

Shamong Red—A rich, sweet table red made from Concord grapes. One of the better sweet Concord wines around.

Blush Wines

Pinelands Blush—A semisweet blush made from 100% red Concord grapes.

Fruit Wines

Blueberry—Sweet purplish wine, made from fresh, locally grown New Jersey blueberries. A nice dessert wine.

Cranberry—Sweet red made from locally grown cranberries. Tart.

Raspberry—A red, sweet dessert wine, made from 100% fresh red raspberries. Nice complement to chocolate desserts.

REVIEWS AND AWARDS

Chambourcin 2001—Silver medal, 2003 New Jersey State Wine Competition.

HOURS AND DIRECTIONS Tours and tastings Mon.–Sat. 10 a.m.–5 p.m., Sun. noon–4 p.m. Hours may change seasonally, so call ahead. ■ From the Philadelphia area, cross the Walt Whitman Bridge (I-76) and take I-295 north to Rte. 70 east. Follow 70 to Rte. 206 south (at the Red Lion Circle) and continue on 206 about 7 miles. At 0.5 mile past the Shamong Diner is Forked Neck Rd., a small side street. Turn left onto Forked Neck and continue 1 mile around the bend. The winery is on the right. ■ From North Jersey, follow the N.J. Turnpike south to exit 7. Take Rte. 206 south past Rte. 70 (at the Red Lion Circle); then follow the local directions above.

OTHER NEW JERSEY WINERIES

Bellview Winery: 150 Atlantic St., Landisville, NJ 08236 • Phone 856-697-7172 • www.bellviewwinery.com • bellview@aol.com

Heritage Vineyards of Richwood: 480 Mullica Rd. (Rte 322), Richwood, NJ 08074 • Phone 856-589-4474 • Fax 856-218-8144 • www.heritagestationfruit.com • heritagestation@snip.net

Silver Decoy Winery: 610 Perrineville Rd., Robbinsville, NJ 08691 • www.silverdecoywinery.com

Tamuzza Vineyards: 1526 Dutch Mill Rd., Franklinville, NJ 08322 • Phone 800-362-0309 • www.tamuzzavineyards.com • winemaker@tamuzzavineyards.com

Westfall Winery: 141 Clove Rd., Montague, NJ 07827 • Phone 973-293-3428 • www.westfallwinery.com

NEW YORK

New York State has well over two hundred wineries. Although scattered over a large area, they tend to cluster in regions with distinct characteristics. This chapter reflects that natural organization: it is divided into regions. Within each region, wineries are listed alphabetically, and all are within easy day-tripping distance of one another. To find out which region you are in as you thumb through the chapter, look in the margin of any right-hand page. The regions are also listed below, in the roughly east-west order you will find them.

- New York City
- Long Island
- Hudson River Valley
- Central New York and Lake Ontario
- Finger Lakes: Cayuga
- Finger Lakes: Seneca
- Finger Lakes: Keuka
- Finger Lakes: Canandaigua
- Lake Erie

NEW YORK CITY

Crown Regal Wine Cellars / Joseph Zakon Winery

586 Montgomery St., Brooklyn, NY 11225 • Phone 718-604-1430 • ywine@hotmail.com

Joseph Zakon founded his Brooklyn winery in 1981 and made 600 cases in his first year. He was just out of school. An Orthodox Jew, Zakon was repulsed by the numerous ultrasweet kosher wines he'd tasted in his life and thought the problem lay more in bad winemaking than in religious orthodoxy. Not only did he turn out to be right, but he also discovered that sweet kosher wines are a uniquely American invention—so why not make a change?

Since the winery was established, Zakon has gone on to become a well-known if still somewhat small producer of better kosher wines, currently selling more than 3,000 cases annually in seven states and throughout Europe and Canada, bottling under the Kesser and Joseph Zakon Winery labels.

Wines: $–$$

White Wines

Chardonnay—A dry white, lightly oaked.

Niagara Blanc—An off-dry wine.

Riesling—A dry version of this classic German wine.

Seyval—Surprisingly dry.

Red Wines

Kesser Concord—A sweet Concord for those that won't give up on the usual kosher taste. The winery makes a dry version as well.

Dessert Wines

Joseph Zakon Muscatini—A sweet red dessert wine made from Muscat grapes grown in California's southern San Joaquin region. A flat-out good wine, kosher or not. We have several bottles in our cellar.

HOURS AND DIRECTIONS By appointment only. Call for directions.

Schapiro Wines Company

126 Rivington St., New York, NY 10002 • Phone 800-830-9108 or 212-674-4404 • Fax 212-420-7240

Founded in 1899 by Samuel Schapiro, who immigrated to this country from Galitzia, Austria, Schapiro Wines was (according to the company) Manhattan's first winery, and is still run by his family today from a storefront operation on in the old Jewish Lower East Side. Schapiro's was one of the first wineries to make the kind of thick, sweet kosher wines with which Jews have been celebrating religious holidays for more than 100 years. "The cherished taste of Passover since 1899," says the company slogan. Talk about tradition!

Wines: $–$$

Traditional Wines

Extra Heavy Concord—Classic, sweet.

Light Sweet Tokay—Has the nutlike sweetness characteristic of Hungarian raisin wine.

Malaga—Extrasweet holiday favorite.

Naturally Sweet Concord—No sugar added. Half the sweetness of the original.

Sauternes—Luscious taste and rich golden color. A hint of sweetness.

Table Wines

Blanc de Blanc—A superior blend of premium white grapes.

Burgundy—Classic dry red, with a rich color.

Chablis—Crisp and fruity.

Vin Rosé—The wine that goes with everything.

Cream Blended Wines

Cream Pink Concord—Sweeter than cream white, with the same velvet texture.

Cream Red Concord—The sweetest cream. Rich ruby color.

Cream White Concord—Medium sweet and velvety smooth.

HOURS AND DIRECTIONS Sun.–Thurs. 10 a.m.–6 p.m., Fri. 10 a.m.–3 p.m., year-round.

■ In Lower Manhattan, head east on Houston St., turn right onto Sussex, then right again onto Rivington. The winery is 2 blocks up.

Vintage New York

482 Broome St., New York, NY 10013 • Phone 212-226-9463 •
www.vintagenewyork.com • info@vintagenewyork.com

One of the best stops in New York City, Vintage New York was an immediate hit when it opened in 2000, offering more than fifty wines from twenty other fine New York State wineries, as well as their own, all in one easy-to-find SoHo location. The exciting part is that all its wines are available for sampling at a large, comfortable bar at the back of the large, attractive store. The people behind the counter are very knowledge-able and friendly, and happy to help you find the right wines for you. Along with won-derful wines, you can find an array of New York food products from artisanal and boutique producers as well as a large assortment of wine accessories and other gour-met lifestyle products.

A second Vintage New York store is set to open soon at 2492 Broadway, at 93rd St.

Wines: $–$$$

REVIEWS AND AWARDS

"Vintage New York's selection represents a tour d'horizon of grapes and wines,
simple through sophisticated."   —Howard G. Goldberg, *New York Times*

"New York wines, long overshadowed by their West Coast brethren,
are getting new respect."   —Ryan Isaac, *Wine Spectator* (July 1999)

"Fresh and inviting."   —*New York* magazine

"Vintage New York is an act of regional patriotism in a city not known
for its love of the local vineyards."
                    —Matthew DeBord, *Wine Spectator* (April 2001)

HOURS AND DIRECTIONS Open Mon.–Sat. 11 a.m.–9 p.m., Sun. noon–9 p.m., year-round. ■ In Lower Manhattan, follow Broadway south and turn right onto Broome St. The winery is a little over 2 blocks down.

OTHER NEW YORK CITY WINERIES

Delmonico's Winery: 182 15th St., Brooklyn, NY 11215 • Phone 718-768-7020 •
Fax 718-768-8825

Pebble Ridge Vineyards and Wine Estates: 152 W. 57th St., 17th floor,
New York, NY 10019 • Phone 212-586-4333 • DBova@aol.com

Transamerica Wine Corp.: Bldg. 120, Brooklyn Navy Yard, Brooklyn, NY 11205 •
Phone 718-625-0990

LONG ISLAND

Abarbanel Wine Co.

100 Cedarhurst Ave., Cedarhurst, NY 11516 • Phone 888-691-9463 or
631-374-2240 • Fax 631-374-2565 • howbarb@idt.net

Abarbanel is co-owned by Alex Haruni and Howard Abarbanel. The company features small, handcrafted kosher wines from around the world. Abarbanel wines are made here in the States from mostly California-grown grapes. The Dalton brand, which is owned by the English-born Haruni, goes onto wines that are made in Israel. Both companies pride themselves on the excellence of their wines and the strict standards they observe regarding the kosher laws. All of their products are supervised by the foremost rabbis in their respective winemaking regions—strictly Orthodox and Haredi *mashgichim* who are uncompromising in their standards. To them, kosher wine is a process, not an appellation.

The following labels, distributed by Abarbanel are award-winning wines that have also garnered good press; they are some of the better kosher wines available in the marketplace today.

- Australian: Beckett's Flat
- Bordeaux: Chateau Peroudier Bergerac Blanc, Layla Vineyards, Le Rabault Sancerre Rouge, Premium Petits Chateaux Wines
- Chilean: Layla Malbec
- Israeli: Dalton Estate Vineyards; Streit's Premium Israeli Kiddush Wine
- South African: Kleine Draken

Wines: $$-$$$

White Wines
Chardonnay—Nice fruit up front. Creamy, dry finish.
Gewürztraminer—A nice, German-style fruity wine.
Riesling—Fruity up front with a citrus ending. Nice.

Red Wines
Beaujolais Villages—A light, fresh, fruity red with dry finish.
Beaujolais Villages Nouveau—A lively, light, dry red.
Cabernet Sauvignon—A big, fruity red with a dry finish.
Merlot—A soft, round, big, deep red.
Premium Barrel Cabernet Sauvignon—Plums and berries give way to a dry and satisfying finish.
Premium Barrel Reserve Merlot—Deep, dark fruit. Nicely oaked. Dry finish.
Syrah—A peppery, dark red with a dry finish.

Sparkling Wines
Brut Cremant D'Alsace—A dry, sparkling wine with creamy texture.

REVIEWS AND AWARDS
Abarbanel Riesling Alsace Mevushal 1999: "Score: 87."
—*Wine Spectator* (October 2001)

Brut Cremant D'Alsace NV: "The Best of Year 2000," 86 points.
—*Wine Enthusiast* (January 2001)

Gewürztraminer 1997: "One of America's Top Kosher Wines."   —*Bon Appétit*

"This estate bottled wine [Riesling, Vin d'Alsace, France] has lovely aromas of apples and citrus blossoms. The well balanced texture has dry, crisp flavors of apples, oranges and peaches. Wonderful acidity and concentration typical of fine wines from Alsace." —Dave DeSimone, *Pittsburgh Post-Gazette* (March 2001)

HOURS AND DIRECTIONS No tastings available. Can be found in many liquor stores. Call for the nearest retailer.

Banfi Vintners

111 Cedar Swamp Rd., Old Brookville, NY 11545 • Phone 800-645-6511 or
516-626-9200 • Fax 516-626-9085 • www.banfi.com • bwhiting@banfi.com

Old Brookville Chardonnay is named for the bucolic village in which the grapes are grown. The 127-acre estate of vineyards, manicured lawns, and trimmed woods complements a 60-room Elizabethan manor, which also serves as world headquarters of Banfi Vintners, a major U.S. wine importer and a major producer of premium varietal wines in Tuscany and Piedmont, Italy. Fredrick Frank, of Dr. Konstantin Frank, established Old Brookville Chardonnay before going back to his family's winery.

Banfi Products Corp. is a family-owned and operated firm founded in New York in 1919 by John Mariani, Sr. He named it for an aunt, Teodolinda Banfi. Today his sons, John F. Mariani, chairman and chief executive officer, and Harry F. Mariani, president and chief operating officer, have expanded on the empire he founded. Castello Banfi is the Mariani family's vineyard estate in Montalcino, Tuscany, and Vigne Regali is the name of the family's sparkling wine cellars in Strevi, Piedmont. They also import many major labels including Concha y Toro of Chile, Riunite of Italy, and Walnut Crest of Chile.

Wines: $$

White Wines

Old Brookville Chardonnay—Medium-bodied white wine. Nice tropical fruit leads to creamy midpalate and nice, dry finish. Very nice. ♥

REVIEWS AND AWARDS—OLD BROOKVILLE CHARDONNAY 2000

"Medium-bodied, versatile wine, barrel-fermented and buttery, but comparatively light on the oak. The wine boasts good fruit, and a hint of pear."
—Peter M. Gianotti, *Newsday* (October 2001)

"Classy, polished. The aroma is honey-like and floral; the spicy, buttery flavor is redolent of pears, apples, tropical fruits and butterscotch; the texture is smooth; the acidity, refreshing; the aftertaste, long; the overall effect, round and pretty. On the standard 100-point scale, it's an 88."
—Howard G. Goldberg, *New York Times* (October 2001)

HOURS AND DIRECTIONS Not open to the public. Call for the nearest retailer.

Bedell Cellars ✿ ✿ ✿

36225 Main Rd. (Rte. 25), Cutchogue, NY 11935 • Phone 631-734-7537 •
Fax 631-734-5788 • www.bedellcellars.com

"Winemaker Kip Bedell makes Long Island's best red wines," wrote Thomas Matthews, senior editor at *Wine Spectator* (June 30, 1999). And if that wasn't high enough praise, Hugh Johnson of the *Encyclopedia of Wine* wrote, "Bedell . . . has become synonymous with world-class Merlot, the varietal that is the region's strongest suit." And Karen MacNeil rates Bedell as one of the "top Long Island wineries" in *The Wine Bible*. What else can one say? The raves go on and on.

Kip and Susan Bedell established the 32-acre (7 then) vineyard and winery in 1980. On August 10, 2000, Michael Lynne, president of New Line Cinemas, became the new owner of Bedell Cellars. Mr. Lynne now works with Kip Bedell, who has remained as the winemaker. Considerable kudos must also be given to vineyard manager Dave

Thompson and his staff in nurturing the fruit that goes into these exquisite wines. Bedell Cellars is definitely one of the leaders on the East Coast.

Wines: $$-$$$

White Wines

Chardonnay—Slightly oaked, crisp white. Pineapple and tropical fruit come through. Nice finish.

Chardonnay Reserve—Vanilla comes through. Aged 10 months in oak. Smooth. ♥

Gewürztraminer—Alsatian style. Floral nose and citrus taste. Very nice.

Main Road White—A blend of Chardonnay, Riesling, and Gewürztraminer. Nice.

Viognier—Aged in French oak, floral nose. Peach and pear come through. Clean finish.

Red Wines

Cabernet Sauvignon—Blended with a hint of Merlot. Cherries and raspberries come through. Nice tannins. Nice, dry finish. ♥

Cupola—A Bordeaux-style blend of Cabernet Sauvignon, Cabernet Franc, and Merlot. Full bodied, chewy red. Spicy, with deep, rich fruit and nice, dry finish. ♥

Main Road Red—A blend of Merlot, Cabernet Sauvignon, and Foch. Spicy.

Merlot—Aged 14 months in American and French oak. Cherry and raspberry come through. The mouth feel is smooth and spicy. Nice, dry finish. ♥

Merlot Reserve—Comes from 2-acre plot known as "C-block south." Smokier and richer than previous Merlot. Very nice.

Dessert Wines

Late Harvest Riesling—75% Riesling, 20% Sauvignon Blanc, and 5% Gewürztraminer. Rich, golden dessert wine. Peach, pear, and mango come through. ♥ ♥

Raspberry—Chambord-like red wine fortified with 190-proof grape neutral spirits. Very fun. Often sells out, and you can see why. ♥ ♥

REVIEWS AND AWARDS

"Of the East End's established producers, only a handful have earned real brand recognition. . . . The league leader is Bedell's Merlot, both regular and reserve, which sets the pace for the East End's signature grape and are a match for the top versions from anywhere." —Howard G. Goldberg, *New York Times* (June 30, 2002)

HOURS AND DIRECTIONS Open daily 11 a.m.–5 p.m. except Christmas, Thanksgiving, and Easter. ■ From New York City, take the Long Island Expwy. (I-495) east to exit 73 (last exit). Go about 14 miles east on County Rte. 58, which becomes Rte. 25 after the traffic circle in Riverhead. Bedell Cellars is 1.5 miles on the left after the light in the center of Cutchogue village.

Bidwell Vineyards

Rte. 48, Cutchogue, NY 11935 • Phone 631-734-5200 • Fax 631-734-6763

This 30-acre vineyard in Cutchogue produces more than 8,000 cases of wine each year. The winery was founded by Bob, Jim, and Kerry Bidwell. The small tasting room showcases handmade wines that are nurtured and cared for by the founders. Their love shows.

Wines: $$-$$$

White Wines

Chardonnay—A barrel-fermented Chardonnay. Pear and vanilla come through.

Sauvignon Blanc—Light white wine. Barrel fermented and aged *sur lie* for several months. Floral nose. Crisp, clean finish.

Red Wines

Cabernet Sauvignon—A rich, full-bodied red. Currants and plums come through. Smooth on the midpalate. Nice finish.

REVIEWS AND AWARDS

"Steadily fine Riesling."   —*The New Sotheby's Wine Encyclopedia*

HOURS AND DIRECTIONS Open daily 11 a.m.–5 p.m. year-round. ■ Call for directions.

Castello di Borghese / Hargrave Vineyard

Rte. 48 (Sound Ave.) and Alvah's Ln., Cutchogue, NY 11935 •
Phone 631-734-5111 • Fax 631-734-5485 • http://castellodiborghese.com •
info@castellodiborghese.com

Castello di Borghese/Hargrave Vineyard is owned by Ann Marie and Marco Borghese, who purchased the vineyard in the fall of 1999. Their purchase was news in the wine industry that signaled the ascent of East Coast winemaking. Hargrave Vineyards, as it was known then, was established by Alec and Louisa Hargrave in 1973, when they settled on this patch of land after looking for land in California, Oregon, and Long Island. They were pioneers in this region, and certainly as important to Long Island as Dr. Frank was to the Finger Lakes. When the Hargraves sold their 75,000-gallon-capacity, 10,000-case winery, which had been selling its wines since 1975, it was national news, appearing in not only the top industry magazines but also newspapers like the *New York Times* and other national publications.

Castello di Borghese continues the fine traditions the Hargraves established but is attempting now to compete with the plethora of newer wineries in the region. And they are doing well. Vineyard manager and winemaker Mark Terry continues to craft delicious wines amid the beautiful surroundings in this 84-acre estate.

Wines: $$–$$$

White Wines

Chardonnay—Stainless steel fermented, then oak aged in French barrels. Lemon and butter come through. Creamy midpalate. Nice, dry finish.

Chardonnay Reserve—French Burgundian-style white wine. Full bodied.

Chardonette—Stainless-steel-fermented light white. Fresh, citrusy. Nice finish.

Pinot Blanc—Light white. Clean, crisp, and dry finish.

Sauvignon Blanc—A light white. Lemony. Good finish. Aged in French oak. Very nice. ♥

Red Wines

Borghese Meritage Red—A Bordeaux blend of 65% Cabernet Sauvignon, 21% Merlot, and 14% Cabernet Franc. The company's premier red. Not tasted.

Cabernet Franc—Peppery, deep red wine. Nice fruit. Dry finish

Cabernet Sauvignon Reserve—Smoky and peppery.

Merlot—Aged in French oak. Nice fruit. Peppery. Nice finish. Very good.

Merlot Reserve—Aged 18 months in French oak. Complex and deep. Well balanced. ♥

Petit Chateau—A Bordeaux blend of Merlot and Cabernet Franc. Good fruit and nice tannins. Dry finish.

Pinot Noir—Cherry and berry come through. Deeper than you might expect. Nice, dry finish.

Blush Wines

Fleurette—A salmon-colored Pinot Blanc. A dry rosé in the French tradition. Nice.

REVIEWS AND AWARDS

Cabernet Franc: "impressive with immediate appeal" —Gerald Asher, *Gourmet*

Chardonnay: "truly first rate." —Frank J. Prial, *New York Times*

Chardonette: "like a village-level Chablis." —*New York Times*

Chardonette: "charming...a delightful gulping wine." —*Wall Street Journal*

Merlot: "elegant and seductive." —Thomas Matthews, *Wine Spectator*

Merlot: "beautifully textured flavors and [a] clean, rich finish suggested by one of Bordeaux's finest St. Juliens." —Robert Parker, *The Wine Advocate*

Pinot Noir: "this is what California and Oregon ought to be making."
—Paul Marks, *Boston Globe*

HOURS AND DIRECTIONS Open daily 11 a.m.–6 p.m. year-round. ■ From New York City, take I-495 east (Long Island Expwy.) to exit 71 (Calverton). Turn left off the exit ramp onto Edwards Ave. and go 3.8 miles north to Sound Ave. Turn right onto Sound Ave. (Rte. 48) and go east 11 miles. Castello di Borghese is 3 miles from the start of the double lanes on the south side of Rte. 48.

Channing Daughters Winery

1427 Scuttlehole Rd., Bridgehampton, NY 11932 • Phone 631-537-7224 • Fax 631-537-7243 • www.channingdaughters.com

The Channing Winery is the home of venture capitalist and sculptor Walter Channing, Jr., who is renowned for his evocative wooden masterpieces. The estate is beautiful and is tastefully studded with Channing's work. It is the home of the Channing family as well. The winery was named for his four daughters. The family is very conscious of man's place in the universe and the consequences that human impact has on Long Island's fellow inhabitants. The 127-acre Channing Farm is the largest unbroken tract on the South Fork, and in conjunction with The Peconic Land Trust, the Channings hope to leave the farm, winery, and land intact.

They also happen to make very nice wine. Larry Perrine, the managing partner of the winery and the winemaker, is one of the most recognized and experienced winemakers on the island. And the reviews show it. One of the better wineries located on the South Fork, Channing Daughters gets a lot of attention; their wines have been reviewed in numerous magazines.

Wines: $$–$$$

White Wines

Brick Kiln Vineyard Chardonnay—Burgundian-style, complex, dry white. Pears come though. ♥

Mudd Vineyard Sauvignon Blanc—Lemony, dry white. Refreshing. Very nice.

Sculpture Garden Chardonnay—Fermented in French oak. Dry. Apple comes through.

Scuttlehole Vineyard Chardonnay—Citrusy, dry white. Very nice.

Red Wines

Fresh Red Merlot—90% Merlot and 10% Cabernet Franc. Raspberry and cherry come through. Nice, dry finish.

Mudd Vineyard Cabernet Sauvignon—Deep, dry red. (Not tasted.)

Novello D'Hamptons—100% Merlot. Medium-bodied, light red.

Sculpture Garden Vineyard Merlot—Deep, plummy red. Dry finish.

Blush Wines

Mudd Vineyard Fleur de la Terre Rosé—Dry rosé in the best French tradition.

Fruit Wines

Mudd Vineyard Cuvée Tropical—Semisweet, fruity light white.

REVIEWS AND AWARDS

"The first noticeable feature [of the 2000 Fresh Red Merlot] is the jammy aroma; the second is the velvet texture; then, confectionery flavors come across as a compote of strawberries and raspberries . . . sumptuous."
—Howard G. Goldberg, *New York Times* (August 12, 2001)

Sculpture Garden Vineyard Merlot 1998: "Score: 85. Plum, black cherry and mineral flavors are concentrated and balanced in this round red. Yet it's still fresh and balanced." —*Wine Spectator* (August 2001)

HOURS AND DIRECTIONS Open daily 11 a.m.–5 p.m. year-round. ▪ From New York City, take the Long Island Expwy. (I-495) to exit 70. Follow County Rte. 111 south to Montauk Hwy. (Rte. 27), through Southampton's commercial district to Watermill. Continue 0.5 mile heading east on Rte. 27. Turn left onto Scuttlehole Rd. The winery is approximately 3.5 miles from Rte. 27; watch for the sign, shaped like a totem pole, at the entrance on the right-hand side of road.

Corey Creek Vineyards ✡

45470 Main Rd. (Rte. 25), P.O. Box 921, Southold, NY 11971 • Phone 631-765-4168 • Fax 631-765-1845 • www.coreycreek.com • info@coreycreek.com

"This is a fairly new outfit and they seem to be off to a good start," wrote wine critic Mitch Kornfeld for the *Union Square Journal* in a rave review of the winery's 1998 Merlot. Corey Creek Vineyards is owned by Michael Lynne, who is also owner of Bedell Cellars. Lynne bought this vineyard in 1999.

Corey Creek, which is located on the North Fork, was established in 1981 by Joel and Peggy Lauber. They were grape growers who eventually decided to make wine as well. The 30-acre vineyard is planted to only classic vinifera. They produce a limited number of quality wines. They are a well-respected winery. The winery is attractive. The tasting room has a lovely view of the vineyards. There is also a deck that makes loitering kind of nice and easy.

Wines: $$–$$$

White Wines

Chardonnay—Fermented in 100% French oak *barriques*. Crisp and complex. Nice.

Reserve Chardonnay—100% French oak barrel fermentation and aging. Creamy. Vanilla comes through. Very nice. ♥

Red Wines

Merlot—A blend of 88% Merlot and 12% Cabernet Franc. Aged in French oak. Cherries come through. Nice.

Blush Wines

Domaines CC Rosé—Dry, crisp, French-style rosé. Cherry comes through. Nice finish. ♥

REVIEWS AND AWARDS

Estate Chardonnay 1998: "Score: 83."   —*Wine Spectator*

Reserve Chardonnay 1998: "Score: 88."   —*Wine Spectator*

Reserve Chardonnay 1999: "Recommended."

                                            —*Food & Wine* magazine *Wine Guide 2002*

"Bull's-eye. [The 1998 Estate Chardonnay is] an exact specimen of the food-oriented genre. Simple, light-bodied, snappy, alive with fresh apple acidity, its life is incomplete at the table without, say, a rotisserie chicken for company."

                          —Howard G. Goldberg, *New York Times* (March 19, 2000)

"[The 1998 Domaines CC Rosé is] a delightfully dry wine with considerable body and lovely color . . . fashioned in the style of Tavel, the best of Rosé in the Rhone Valley."   —Peter Gianotti, *Newsday*

HOURS AND DIRECTIONS Open year-round Sun.–Fri. 11 a.m.–5 p.m., Sat. 11:30 a.m.–6 p.m. ■ From New York City, take the Long Island Expwy. (I-495) east to the end, exit 73. Proceed farther east on County Rte. 58, which becomes Rte. 25, for about 18 miles.

Diliberto Winery

250 Manor Ln., Jamesport, NY 11947 • Phone 631-722-3416

This winery only received its farm winery license in early 2002. It is the longtime dream of Sal Diliberto and his wife Maryann. Sal has been a home winemaker for more than 17 years, buying his grapes from Peconic Bay Winery. The Hollis Hills, Queens, attorney and his wife fell in love with Long Island's North Fork and bought a parcel of land on Manor Lane. Since purchasing the property, they have built a new house and restored the barn, which will house the winery and tasting room. And the first 2 acres of vines were planted in 1997. The total acres planted to vines numbers 8, including many vinifera grapes, and they hope to add another 10–15.

At the time of this writing, the wine list was not yet available.

HOURS AND DIRECTIONS Call for hours and directions.

Duck Walk Vineyards   ✿ ✿

231 Montauk Hwy. (Rte. 27A), Water Mill, NY 11976 • Phone 631-726-7555 • Fax 631-726-4395 • www.duckwalk.com • staff@duckwalk.com

Dr. Herodotus "Dan" Damianos bought the 86-acre Duck Walk Vineyards when they went bankrupt in 1994. It was the chateau-style winery's second failure. Originally it was called Le Reve Winery and then the Southampton Winery. Damianos, a Stony Brook physician who also owns Pindar, began replanting the vineyards and added to the company's holdings by buying more vineyards in 1996 in Mattituck.

While Dr. Dan managed the operations and finances, Pindar winemaker Mark Friszolowski began turning around the wines. The winery is now extremely successful and popular. Dr. Dan's son Jason, a University of California, Fresno, enology grad, is now the winemaker under the doctor's and Mark's watchful eyes. While the reds have recently been gaining awards due to the desire to expand the winery's line, the flagship wines have been their dessert wines, which continue to excel.

Duck Walk Vineyards is well worth a visit.

Wines: $$–$$$

White Wines

Chardonnay—Pear and apple come through. Nice, dry finish. ♥

Chardonnay Reserve—Aged in oak. Creamy, complex white, with dry finish.

Red Wines

Cabernet Sauvignon—Nice, big fruit with velvet midpalate and dry finish.

Merlot—Full-bodied dry red. Currant and blackberry come through.

Merlot (Reserve)—Unfiltered, big, dry red. Plum comes through. Velvety. Dry finish.

Pinot Meunier—A medium-bodied red. Nice, dry finish.

Dessert Wines and Ports

Aphrodite—A light, golden dessert wine. Delicate, with apricot and honey flavors and aromas made from Late Harvest Gewürztraminer. One of the best dessert wines available in the United States. And very affordable. ♥ ♥ ♥

Blueberry Port—A thick, rich, purple dessert wine made from Maine blueberries and aged in French oak 1 year. Their most popular wine. ♥ ♥

Boysenberry—Rich, deep dessert wine. Not tasted.

Other Wines

Southampton White, Windmill Blush, Windmill Red, Windmill White

REVIEWS AND AWARDS

Late Harvest Gewürztraminer Aphrodite 1999—Double gold medal, 2003 New York Tasters Guild International Wine Competition.

Pinot Noir 1998—Double gold medal, 2001 New York Wine and Food Classic.

Cabernet Sauvignon North Fork of Long Island Reserve 1998: "Score: 87."
                                                                                                     —*Wine Spectator*

Blueberry Port 1996: "87 points"   —*Wine Enthusiast*

"When you're heading to that next holiday party how about bringing a bottle of port that will arouse the interest of your friends and family! We recommend a Long Island Duck Walk Vineyards 2000 Blueberry Port."   —*LongIsland.com*

HOURS AND DIRECTIONS Open daily 11 a.m.–6 p.m. year-round. ■ Located in Water Mill on Montauk Hwy. just past Mecox Bay.

Galluccio Estate Vineyards / Gristina Vineyards

24385 Main Rd. (Rte. 25), Cutchogue, NY 11935 • Phone 631-734-7089 • Fax 631-734-7114 • www.gristinawines.com • gristinaV@aol.com

Galluccio Estate Vineyards/Gristina Vineyards has gone through many changes since late 2000. New methods were employed in the vineyards, new French oak barrels were brought in, a new 1,500-gallon fermenter and additional land were bought. And Charles Girard was named the new winemaker. This new infusion of excitement and ideas was brought in by Vincent and Judy Galluccio when they bought Gristina Vineyards in August of 2000.

Gristina was founded in 1983 by Jerry Gristina, M.D., and his wife. Longtime wine aficionados, the Gristinas, along with their son Peter, who ran the business, were among the pioneers in the region, not far from Hargrave (as it was known then). Gristina, especially in the late 1990s, scored some impressive numbers with its reds in magazines like *Wine Spectator* and *Wine Enthusiast*. Vincent Galluccio, a successful international businessman, hired Pomerol-based wine consultant Michel Roland to take the winery to the next level. With another 40 acres planted, they have big plans.

Given the changes they've wrought and the plans they have, this will be a winery to watch in the next few years.

Wines: $$–$$$

White Wines

Andy's Field Reserve Chardonnay—Straw-colored, medium-bodied white. Complex. Good fruit. Dry. One of their most popular wines, and deservedly so.

Avalon—A slightly sweet Riesling blend. Apple and peach come through. Crisp.

Estate Chardonnay—Creamy, full-bodied, dry white. Nice oak. Mineral finish.

Point House Chardonnay—Citrusy steel tank Chardonnay. Clean. Crisp. ♥

Red Wines

Andy's Field Reserve Cabernet Sauvignon—Plum and black cherry come through. Nice.

Andy's Field Reserve Merlot—Blackberry comes through. Smoky. Dry finish.

Estate Cabernet Franc—Medium-bodied, dry red. Soft.

Estate Cabernet Sauvignon—Medium-bodied red. Plum comes through. Nice.

Estate Merlot—Medium-bodied red. Aged 12 months in oak. 15% Cabernet Sauvignon.

Blush Wines

Rosé of Cabernet Sauvignon—An off-dry rosé. Refreshing. Excellent. ♥

REVIEWS AND AWARDS

Andy's Field Reserve Cabernet Sauvignon 1995: "Score: 86." Estate Cabernet Franc 1997: "Score: 86." —*Wine Spectator*

Cru George Allaire: "Its cabernet sauvignon effect—cassis, beet, a little tobacco, a sprinkle of herbs—came through vividly. The wine is juicy, vibrant, and pleasing, and I was sorry when the bottle was finished." —Howard G. Goldberg, *New York Times* (April 6, 2003)

Estate Cabernet Franc 1997: "87 points." —*Wine Enthusiast*

Rosé of Cabernet Sauvignon 2000—"Like an Oscar Wilde epigram, the mouth-filling 2000 rosé . . . delivers a serious message lightly. A flirtatious salmon-coral in color, the wine is a savory aperitif." —Howard G. Goldberg, *New York Times*

Rosé of Cabernet Sauvignon 2000—"Firm blackberries, fruit and a stiff spine. The best we've come across in ages." —AlcoholReviews.com

Rosé of Cabernet Sauvignon 2000—"Except for the pink color. There's nothing frivolous about this very good wine made from Cabernet Sauvignon." —*Food & Wine* magazine *Wine Guide 2002*

"[The 2000 Point House Chardonnay] has a fresh-apple bouquet and a lightly fruity flavor; its near-weightlessness stands out; it has crisp, tangy appetite-whetting acidity and a long finish." —Howard G. Goldberg, *New York Times* (December 2, 2001)

"[The 1998 Estate Cabernet Franc is] lush and smooth with sweet berry fruit and complex flavors of smoke, oak and spice. 88." —*San Jose Mercury News*

HOURS AND DIRECTIONS Open year-round Mon.–Fri. 11 a.m.–5 p.m., Sat.–Sun. 11 a.m.–6 p.m. ■ From New York City, take the Long Island Expwy. (I-495) east to exit 73 (last exit). Go about 5 miles east on County Rte. 58; it then becomes Rte. 25 at the large, highway-like intersection with Rte. 105. Continue east on Rte. 25 approximately 8 miles. Once you are in Cutchogue, look for the large Galluccio Estate Vineyards signs on the left.

Jamesport Vineyards

Main Rd. (Rte. 25), Jamesport, NY 11947 • Phone 631-722-5256 •
Fax 631-921-4607 • www.jamesportvineyards.com •
jamesportvineyards@email.msn.com

Jamesport Vineyards is located in a renovated 150-year-old barn that contains the winery and tasting room. There are touches of both the new and old. Jamesport Vineyards is the brainchild of Ron Goerler, Sr., and Ron Jr. They began by selling fruit from their 60-acre farm in Cutchogue. The vines were originally planted in 1981, the barn was bought in 1986, and they began selling wines in Jamesport in 1989.

Today more than 48 acres of their farm is planted to vines, and they make 5,000 cases of wine each year. This is one of the few estate wineries in the North Fork, as they supply all their own grapes from their own vineyards. California winemaker Sean Capiaux made the wines from 1997 to 2000, and now the winemaker is Keith Bodine. Jamesport's wines have been highly rated by such magazines as *Wine Spectator* and the *Wine Advocate*.

Wines: $$–$$$

White Wines

Chardonnay—Peach and pear come through. Nice, minerally flavor.

Riesling Estate—Off-dry Riesling with honey and peach coming through. Nice acidity.

Sauvignon Blanc Estate—Unique wine: 50% was aged in oak barrels and aged 7 months *sur lie*; 20% of that wine was fermented using the natural yeast from the vineyard. The other 50% was fermented in stainless steel. A dry, refreshing, crisp light white. ♥

Red Wines

Cabernet Franc—Dark, dry, ruby red wine. Cedar and cherries come through. Dry ending.

Mélange de Trois—46% Cabernet Franc, 47% Cabernet Sauvignon, and 9% Merlot. Deep, dry red. Very nice.

Merlot—Aged in French *barriques*. Blend of 80% Merlot, 16% Cabernet Sauvignon, and 4% Cabernet Franc. Smoky. Deep, dry red.

Pinot Noir—Light-bodied red. Cherry and cola flavors come through. Dry finish.

Dessert Wines

Riesling Late Harvest Estate—Apple, honey, and vanilla come through. Nice. ♥ ♥

Semi-Glacé Estate—Unique Semillon ice wine. Pineapple, peach, and honey flavors.

Other Wines

Island Blanc, Island Rosé, Island Rouge

REVIEWS AND AWARDS

Riesling Late Harvest Estate 1998—Gold medal, *Dallas Morning News* Wine Competition.

Merlot 1997: "87 points." —*Wine Advocate*

Merlot 1997: "Score: 86." —*Wine Spectator*

HOURS AND DIRECTIONS Open daily 10 a.m.–6 p.m. year-round. ■ Located on Rte. 25 (Main Rd.) in Jamesport, 7 miles east of the Riverhead traffic circle. The winery is on the north side of the road behind a large white house. Watch for the sign.

Jason's Vineyard

Main Rd. (Rte. 25), Jamesport, NY 11947 • Phone 631-298-6358 •
Fax 631-726-4395 • jasonsvineyards@aol.com or jasond@duckwalk.com

Jason's Vineyard is a brand-new 20-acre vineyard not yet open at the time of this writing. It is run by Jason Damianos, who is the son of Pindar founder and Duck Walk owner Herodotus Damianos. Jason was newly named the winemaker at Duck Walk. He received his B.S. degree in business at the University of Hartford, then pursued a course in enology and viticulture at the University of California, Fresno, leading to his second bachelor's degree. He also studied at the University of Bordeaux for 2 years. Located in Jamesport on the North Fork, Jason's will be dedicated to wine styles in the Bordeaux tradition. The wines will be produced and bottled by Jason at Duck Walk.

HOURS AND DIRECTIONS Call for hours and directions.

Laurel Lake Vineyards ✠

3165 Main Rd. (Rte. 25), Laurel, NY 11948 • Phone 631-298-1420 •
Fax 631-298-1405 • www.llwines.com • info@llwines.com

Laurel Lake Vineyards is owned by a conglomeration of Chilean wine entrepreneurs including Francisco Gillmore, Alejandro Parot, Ricardo Poblete, Juan Esteban Sepulveda, Cesar Baeza, and Joseph DePietto. Baeza is the owner of Brotherhood Winery, the oldest in America. Laurel Lake's original 17 acres were planted in 1980, making it one of the oldest vineyards in the North Fork. The winery was founded in 1994 by Michael McGoldrick, and the 6,000-square-foot fermenting facility was opened in 1997. Under new ownership more land was added to the operation as well as a new nursery. Rolf Achterberg is the new winemaker. Laurel Lake is a winery that will be growing in reputation and size in the coming years. Watch out.

Wines: $–$$$

White Wines

Chardonnay—Steel tank, light Chardonnay. Tropical fruits come through. Citrusy. ♥
Chardonnay Estate Bottled Reserve—Creamy, oaked Chardonnay. Very nice. ♥ ♥
Riesling—An off-dry Riesling with tropical fruits and slightly citrus finish.
Wind Song White—A semisweet, light white wine.

Red Wines

Cabernet Sauvignon—Full-bodied, deep red. Smooth.
Cabernet Sauvignon Reserve—Deep red. Big fruit followed by nice tannins.
Merlot—A smooth, full-bodied, deep red. Smoky. Nice fruit. Dry finish.
Syrah—Oak aged 18 months. Plummy, deep red. Pepper too. Nice.
Wind Song Red—A light and fruity dry wine. Good cheese and pasta wine.

Blush Wines

Lake Rosé—Cabernet Sauvignon rosé. Nice fruit but puckery ending. Refreshing. ♥ ♥
Wind Song Blush—Semisweet, pink blush wine. Nice.

Sparkling Wines

Moscato Sparkling—A nice, rich dessert wine, slightly *frizzante*. Nice acidity.

REVIEWS AND AWARDS

Chardonnay Estate Bottled Reserve 1999: "Score: 86." Chardonnay Estate Bottled
     Reserve 1997: "Score: 85."   *—Wine Spectator*

"[The 1998 Lake Rosé is] one of Long Island's best wines."
—*Wall Street Journal* (September 4, 1998)

"[The 2000 Lake Rosé is] amiable, tasty and dry."
—Howard G. Goldberg, *New York Times* (February 11, 2001)

HOURS AND DIRECTIONS Open Jan.–Mar. daily, 11 a.m.–5 p.m.; Apr.–Dec. daily, 11 a.m.–6 p.m. ■ From New York City, take the Long Island Expwy. (I-495) to the end. Follow signs to Orient and Greenport. Laurel Lake Vineyards is 9.5 miles east on County Rte. 58 (Main Rd.), on left side of the road after Jamesport.

Lenz Winery ✻ ✻ ✻

Main Rd. (Rte. 25), Peconic, NY 11958 • Phone 800-974-9899 or
631-734-6010 • Fax 631-734-6069 • www.lenzwine.com • pc@lenzwine.com

Lenz Winery is one of the oldest and most respected wineries on Long Island. They have always been at the forefront of what is going on in wine. The wines are extremely good right across the board, making Lenz one of the best wineries on the East Coast. Hugh Johnson rated Lenz with three stars in 2002, scribbling, "Classy winery of North Fork. . . . Fine austere Chardonnay in the Chablis mode, also Gewürztraminer, Merlot and sparkling wine."

Restaurateurs Peter and Patricia Lenz (A Moveable Feast) first established this winery in 1978. In 1988 English-born Peter Carroll and his wife Debbie, who already had a vineyard in Mattituck, took over the winery. The first thing they did was to hire Mondavi winemaker Eric Fry. Fry and vineyard manager Sam McCullough have turned Lenz into a world-class operation. *The New Sotheby's Wine Encyclopedia* by Thomas Stevenson awarded Lenz a full star. And Karen MacNeil included Lenz in her "top Long Island wineries." Most telling was Peter Kaminisky's piece in *New York* magazine with Eberhard Müller, chef-owner of Lutece in New York City. "Lenz champagne won Müller's blind tasting over Veuve Cliquot; and he puts the [Lenz] winery's barrel-fermented Chardonnays ahead of Grand Cru Montrachets. 'In a tremendous upset,'" he later recalled for Kaminisky, "'we voted the Lenz '95 Merlot ahead of [Chateau] Pétrus!'"

Enough said. Don't miss this winery . . . period.

Wines: $$–$$$

White Wines

Gewürztraminer—Alsatian-style white. Nice tropical fruits with citrusy ending. Nice. ♥ ♥
Gold Label Chardonnay—Fermented in small oak barrels. Rich, full-bodied, creamy. ♥
Pinot Gris—A light, dry white wine. Clear and crisp. Refreshing. ♥
Silver Label Chardonnay—Slightly oaked Chardonnay. Nice acidity, slightly creamy texture.
White Label Chardonnay—Stainless steel Chardonnay. Clean, crisp, citrusy. Very nice. ♥

Red Wines

Estate Bottled Cabernet Sauvignon—Dry red with nice fruit up front and dry finish.
Estate Bottled Merlot—Deep, inky red. Rich, full bodied. Cherries and plums. Smooth. ♥ ♥ ♥
Estate Bottled Pinot Noir—Medium-bodied, dry red. Cherry comes through.
Reserve Merlot—Dry red with nice fruit and good tannins.
Vineyard Selection Merlot—Deep, dry red. More plummy than the Reserve Merlot. Smooth. Nice tannins.

Sparkling Wines

Cuvée—Made with 70% Pinot Noir and 30% Chardonnay using *méthode champenoise*. Fine bubbles. Toasty. Elegant. Dry.

Cuvée RD—Using the late-finishing method of *récemment dégorgé* (inverted first, then recently disgorged). Not tasted.

REVIEWS AND AWARDS

"Surprisingly few first-rate dry gewürztraminers are made in America—most tend towards sweetness. Lenz's version has always been one of the best."
—Howard G. Goldberg, *New York Times* (April 1, 2001)

Chardonnay: "Recommended." —*The New Sotheby's Wine Encyclopedia*

"[The 1996 Gold Label Chardonnay is] well-crafted, medium-bodied, silky-textured . . . [with] complex hazelnut, yeast, and toast aromatics. . . . 86 Points." —Pierre Antoine Rovani, *Wine Advocate*

"[The 1995 Merlot] reveals excellent ripeness, with loads of chocolate and mocha-imbued red and black cherries that are found throughout its flavor profile and long finish. Presently luscious, creamy, and verging on opulent. . . . 88 points." —Pierre Antoine Rovani, *Wine Advocate*

"[The Lenz 1994 Cuvée] starts out with aromas of toast, strawberries and citrus. Tart and dry and very fresh. . . . Editor's Choice: 90 Points."
—Joe Czerwinski, *Wine Enthusiast*

"[The Lenz 1997 Estate Bottled Merlot] is a big, dense wine pumped full of black cherries and capped off by hints of cedar and coffee. . . . Cellar Selection: 91 Points." —Joe Czerwinski, *Wine Enthusiast*

HOURS AND DIRECTIONS Open daily 10 a.m.–6 p.m. year-round. ▪ From New York City, follow the Long Island Expwy. (I-495) east to exit 73. Take County Rte. 58 east to Rte. 25 east and keep going until you get to Peconic. Lenz Winery is on the left.

Lieb Cellars ✪

14990 Oregon Rd., Cutchogue, NY 11935 • Phone 631-734-1100 • Fax 631-734-1113 • www.liebcellars.com • info@liebcellars.com

Mark and Kathy Lieb live in a house set among their vineyards with their two children, Garrett and Brett. Lieb Cellars' 50-acre estate was first established in 1992 when the Liebs bought their first parcel of land. Since then they've added to that holding several times. Mark Lieb was an investment banker and now owns a money-management firm. Kathy was a vice president at Salomon Brothers. Jin Eller is the general manager, who has years of North Fork experience. Kathy runs the tasting room, sales, and marketing, while Mark oversees the vineyards with Ray Hines, the vineyard manager.

Their 13 acres of Pinot Blanc date back to 1983. The vines are from the French Alsace region. Originally planted by Steve Mudd of Mudd Vineyards, one of the premier growers on the East Coast, they were maintained by Sam McCullough, now at Lenz Winery. The vineyards are operated in an "environmentally friendly" way, meaning they are as organic as they can be. The wines are actually made at PWG (Premium Wine Group) on Long Island, a custom winery that sells no wines of its own but makes the wines for many of Long Island's vineyards.

The Liebs make quality wines that are served in such New York City restaurants as Gramercy Tavern, Grand Central Oyster Bar, and the Metropolitan Museum of Art Cafe and Restaurant. The Liebs' awarding-winning wines have appeared in such newspapers and magazines as the *New York Times, Hamptons Magazine* and others. The Liebs just opened a new wine-tasting center at PWG in May of 2001. Go there and have fun!

Wines: $$–$$$

White Wines

Chardonnay Reserve—Made from first-run juice only. 100% barrel fermented in French oak. Pears and apples come through. Vanilla too. Dry ending. Nice.

Pinot Blanc—Clean, crisp, acidic white wine. Light, dry, elegant. Excellent.♥ ♥ ♥

Red Wines

Merlot Reserve—Merlot blended with Cabernet Franc and Cabernet Sauvignon. Deep red color with cherry and plum coming through. Nice dry finish.♥

Sparkling Wines

Blanc de Blanc—A *méthode champenoise* sparkling wine. Made with 100% Pinot Blanc. Citrusy with nice fruit and real pucker. Nice.

REVIEWS AND AWARDS

"[The Pinot Blanc is] crisp in the Alsace style with pear and pineapple hints in the bouquet, and flavor that tastes best served lightly cool with food."
—Howard G. Goldberg, *New York Times* (February 10, 2002)

"Pinot Blanc is disarmingly fresh and engaging and Lieb Cellars is very good."
—*Hamptons Magazine*

"The '98 Lieb Pinot Blanc opens with a silky, sandalwood nose leading to a flavor of cedar and orange, and finishes with an elegant balance of fruit and acid."
—*East Hampton Star*

"[The Merlot has a] delectable bouquet, concentrated fruit and a measure of grape. It is decidedly Bordeaux style."
—Howard G. Goldberg, *New York Times* (August 12, 2001)

HOURS AND DIRECTIONS Open daily 11 a.m.–6 p.m. year-round ■ For tastings at PWG, take Rte. 48 to 35 Cox Neck Rd. Phone 631-298-1942.

Loughlin Vineyards

S. Main St., Sayville, NY 11782 • Phone and Fax 631-589-0027

Bernard Loughlin got out of the army in 1946. That year he bought 11.5 acres in Sayville, Long Island, a half mile from Great South Bay. Loughlin then opened and operated until recently a successful print shop in Sayville. It took him another 37 years to plant vines in 1983, on Memorial Day. The lovable Irishman had spent much time in the North Fork wineries with his late wife but was told he couldn't grow grapes on his land. That was that, and 1,900 vines went into the ground. The labels feature in drawings and photos a donkey named Pinky, who was a family member for 41 years.

Since then, this out-of-the-way winery has been producing wines that are quite drinkable at a clip of 1,000 cases per year. Friends and family help Bernard handpick the grapes. The wines are made at Peconic Bay and sold at the Loughlin Vineyards tasting room as well as at shops in and around Sayville. They are worth a try.

Wines: $–$$

White Wines

Chardonnay Reserve—A nice, dry white wine.

Red Wines

Cabernet Sauvignon—A deep, ruby red, dry wine.

Merlot—A medium-bodied red wine.

Blush Wines

South Bay Breeze—A semisweet blush wine.

HOURS AND DIRECTIONS Open Memorial Day–Election Day, Sat.–Sun. noon–5 p.m. ■ Call for directions.

Macari Vineyards ✫ ✫

150 Bergen Ave., Mattituck, NY 11952 • Phone 631-298-0100 •
Fax 631-298-8373 • www.macariwines.com • macari@peconic.net

The Macari family, headed by Joseph Macari, Sr., has the largest landholdings of any family on the North Fork, with more than 370 acres, much of which is planted to vines. While the Macaris have owned land in this region for 40 years, the winery itself is relatively new. The operations are headed by Joseph Macari, Jr., and his wife Alexandra. The winery sits on the former site of Mattituck Hills Winery. This new Tuscanstyle winery, established in 1995, had an excellent debut and immediately became well known for its Bergen Road Bordeaux blended red and its dessert wine Essencia. Macari wines have been served at the White House and have gained good reviews and impressive awards, both nationally and internationally.

The secret to great wine, the family insists, is in the grapes. And Macari pampers its vines and fruit to the utmost. Vineyard care is the no. 1 cry at Macari. It doesn't hurt that José Antonio Montilla is the winemaker either. This is certainly one of the wineries to be watching out for in the future.

Wines: $$–$$$

White Wines

Estate Chardonnay—Brightly colored white wine. Apples come through. Clean. Crisp.

Reserve Barrel Fermented Chardonnay—Golden white. Creamy. Dry.

Sauvignon Blanc—Refreshing, crisp, minerally white wine. Nice.♥ ♥

Red Wines

Bergen Road—A Bordeaux blend of 55% Cabernet Sauvignon, 25% Merlot, 16% Cabernet Franc, and 4% Malbec. Aged 20 months in *barriques*. Inky-colored wine. Nice plum comes through. Deep, dry finish.♥ ♥

Cabernet Franc—75% Cabernet Franc and 25% Cabernet Sauvignon. Cherry comes through. Nice.

Merlot—Full-bodied, deep red. Cherries come through. Deep, dry finish.

Blush Wines

Rosé d'une Nuit—Light, salmon-colored, fruity wine. Berries come through.

Dessert Wines

Essencia—Ice wine made from Viognier, Chardonnay, and Sauvignon Blanc. Deep, golden, honey-colored wine. Honey, apples, and pears come through. Nice acidity.♥

Sparkling Wines

Méthode Champenoise—A sparkling white wine. Clean and crisp. More extradry than brut.

Other Wines

Collina 48 Red, Collina 48 White

REVIEWS AND AWARDS

Bergen Road 1997—Best of Show and Best Red Blend, 2002 New York Food and Wine Classic; silver medal, 2000 International Wine and Spirits Competition.

Cabernet Franc 1997—Silver medal, International Wine and Spirits Competition.

Bergen Road 1997: "Score: 88."
                                                                    —*Wine Spectator*

"[The 2000 Sauvignon Blanc is] by far the finest Long Island sauvignon blanc—and thus one of the best New York State whites—I have tasted. . . . It is world-class, a knockout, the equal of splendid sauvignon blancs from the Loire, New Zealand and California."

                          —Howard G. Goldberg, *New York Times* (May 27, 2001)

HOURS AND DIRECTIONS Open daily 11 a.m.–5 p.m. year-round. ■ From New York City, take the Long Island Expwy. (I-495) east to exit 71 (Edwards Ave.). Turn left, heading north. At Sound Ave., which is called North Rd., turn right and head east to the vineyards.

Martha Clara Vineyards

6025 Sound Ave., Jamesport, NY 11947 • Phone 631-298-0075 • Fax 631-298-5502 • www.marthaclaravineyards.com • info@marthaclaravineyards.com

On the East Coast the Entenmann name is associated with fine baked products. Today, while the company thrives, the descendants of the founders have moved on to wine. Originally based in Long Island, Entenmann's Bakery was sold by the family in 1978. The 112-acre Entenmann family farm was used to breed and raise thoroughbred race-horses. Polo fields and horse paddocks were plowed under in 1995 to make way for 87 acres of classic European vinifera. The winery is named in honor of Robert Entenmann's mother.

The Entenmanns are going all out. By 2002 they grew their business to a 10,000-case operation. The wines were originally made by PWG. A new winery is under way, and a new tasting room was opened on Sound Avenue. Although newly established, Martha Clara has garnered good early press. Noted wine critic Peter M. Gianotti of *Newsday*, one of the authorities on Long Island wines, wrote, "Martha Clara Vineyards has built an early reputation for good white wines. They've done it with red, too." He's right. Go and enjoy.

Wines: $$–$$$

White Wines

Chardonnay—Dry white wine, aged *sur lie* in French oak.

Estate Reserve Chardonnay—Dry white, with pear and oak. Dry finish.

Gewürztraminer—Floral nose. Tropical fruits. Lively white wine.

Riesling—Off-dry German-style Riesling. Light. Refreshing.

Sauvignon Blanc—Dry, light white. Citrusy and minerally. Nice.

Semillon—Light white wine. Melon comes through. Citrus too. Nice, dry finish.

Viognier—Off-dry, light white wine. Apples and pears come through.

Red Wines

Merlot—Deep purple/red wine. Berries and cassis come through. Dry finish.

Syrah—Dry red/violet wine. Berries come through. Spicy. Deep.

Other Wines
Glaciers End Chardonnay, Glaciers End White

REVIEWS AND AWARDS

"This year's most interesting new release that I've tasted is Martha Clara's
nonvintage brut." —Howard G. Goldberg, *New York Times* (June 29, 2003)

"[Their Semillon is] an intensely lemony wine that folds in some pear aromatics.
Quite full on the palate and yet very fresh, clean and citrusy; tailor-made for the
region's shellfish." —*Wine Enthusiast* (April 2001)

"Martha Clara's 1999 Viognier and Gewürztraminer are superb."
—Dr. Michael Apstein, noted wine writer for the
Boston Globe and *Southampton Press*

"Martha Clara Vineyards continues its delightful debut with a vibrant
1999 Riesling." —Peter Gianotti, *Newsday*

"In my ideal world, I could sidle up to a bar and have a glass of '98 Martha
Clara Viognier." —Leonard Barkan, *East Hampton Star*

HOURS AND DIRECTIONS Open year-round Mon.–Sat. 11 a.m.–5 p.m., Sun. 11:30 a.m.–
5 p.m. ■ From New York City, take the Long Island Expwy. (I-495) east to exit 71. Turn
left onto Edwards Ave. and continue straight until it ends. Turn right onto Sound Ave.
and head east approximately 10 miles. Martha Clara will be on your right.

Osprey's Dominion Vineyards ✚ ✚

44075 Main Rd. (Rte. 25), Peconic, NY 11958 • Phone 631-765-6188 •
Fax 631-765-1903 • www.ospreysdominion.com • inemkr@ospreysdominion.com

Bud Koehler and Bill Tyree founded Osprey's Dominion in 1983. The 90 acres of vineyards feature some of the oldest vines on the island. The winery is named for the elegant hawks that make their home on this part of Long Island. Osprey's Dominion
started out selling grapes to winemakers in 1986, and didn't start making wines until
1993. The winery makes a wide range of wonderful wines, but it is noted for its excellent Chardonnays. Along with winemaker Peter Silverberg and the rest of the team at
Osprey's Dominion, the winery will continue to excel. The setting is very dramatic,
with the view of the vineyards and the beautifully manicured lawns. Your visit will be
a real treat to yourself.

Wines: $$–$$$

White Wines

Bayman's Harvest—Dry, white, Chard-heavy blend. Light, crisp, and refreshing.

Chardonnay—100% barrel fermented. Pineapple and apricot come through.
Refreshing, full-bodied white. Dry finish. ♥ ♥

Johannisberg Riesling—Floral nose. Tropical fruits. Mineral end. Nice.

Regina Maris Chardonnay—40% barrel fermented, 60% stainless steel fermented.
Nice fruit. Creamy midpalate. Refreshing, crisp end. Named for a Long Island
tall ship. ♥

Reserve Chardonnay—Tropical fruits come through. Full bodied. Nice acidity. ♥

Sauvignon Blanc—Stainless-steel-fermented, light white wine. Aromatic. Light fruits
on midpalate. Honey too. And a refreshing, crisp, clean ending. ♥ ♥

Red Wines

Cabernet Franc—85% Cabernet Franc, 15% Merlot. Cherry comes through. Dry.

Cabernet Sauvignon—85% Cabernet Sauvignon, 10% Merlot, 5% Cabernet Franc. Aged 2 years in French and American oak barrels. Blackberry and chocolate notes. Nice.

Flight-Meritage—50% Merlot, 45% Cabernet Sauvignon, 5% Cabernet Franc. Very deep garnet color. Blackberry comes through in this smoky, dry red.

Merlot—Cherry and plum come through. Smooth. Nice tannins. Dry finish.

Pinot Noir—Medium-bodied, dry, smoky red. Cherry comes through.

Richmond Creek Red—A red blend. Medium bodied. Dry. Nice.

Blush Wines

Twilight Blush—A semisweet blush from Cabernet Franc. Refreshing.

Sparkling Wines

Champagne—Fresh bread nose. Creamy middle. Nice bubbles. Dry ending. Nice.

Dessert Wines and Ports

Peach—A thick, luscious glass of peaches.

Port—100% Cabernet Sauvignon. Unfined and unfiltered. Very nice.

Spice—Cinnamon, nutmeg, and clove make this a wonderful winter warmer.

Strawberry—A lovely, tart version of a 100% strawberry wine.

REVIEWS AND AWARDS

"Osprey's [1999] Sauvignon Blanc belongs in the winner's circle. . . . [It's] heavily aromatic, mouth-filling and drenches the palate with subtle flavors, among them honeydew melon. It's as light as a soufflé and seemingly minutes long."
—Howard G. Goldberg, *New York Times* (January 27, 2002)

"Leaner than a California Cabernet, with more exotic black-cherry and blackberry fruit than a Bordeaux, this polished [1999 Cabernet Sauvignon] from the North Fork of Long Island stakes out new territory for a familiar red grape."
—*Food & Wine* (May 2002)

Sauvignon Blanc North Fork of Long Island 2002: "Score: 83."
—*Wine Spectator* (August 31, 2002)

"[The Regina Maris Chardonnay is] probably the greatest value in Long Island: crisp, dry, fruity, yet with real chardonnay taste. Much better than more expensive chardonnays from both Long Island and California."
—*Wall Street Journal* (September 4, 1998)

HOURS AND DIRECTIONS Open year-round Mon.–Sat. 11 a.m.–5 p.m., Sun. noon–5 p.m. ■ From New York City, take the Long Island Expwy. (I-495) to the last exit. This brings you to County Rte. 58 (and the Tanger Mall); continue heading east through the Riverhead traffic circle. You are now on Rte. 25; continue 17 miles to the winery.

Palmer Vineyards

108 Rte. 48, Aquebogue, NY 11931 • Phone 631-722-WINE •
Fax 631-722-5364 • www.palmervineyards.com

Palmer Vineyards is one of the most celebrated wineries on Long Island or in New York State. Established in 1986 by former advertising executive Robert Palmer, Palmer Vineyards has won numerous gold medals over the years. Karen MacNeil included Palmer in her list of "top Long Island wineries." And Hugh Johnson in his *Pocket Wine Book 2002* rated Palmer with three stars, writing, "Superior Long Island producer and byword in Darwinian metropolitan market. . . . Tasty chardonnay, Sauvignon Blanc and Chinon-like Cabernet." And *The New Sotheby's Wine Encyclopedia* also praised Palmer, awarding it one star and claiming that Palmer "quickly started producing attention-grabbing wines. The reds in particular, simply have more richness than other New York wineries can manage."

What else can one add? Wine from the 125-acre vineyards (formerly potato and pumpkin fields) is poured in half the states in the United States and in five countries including Canada and China. One of the secrets to Palmer's success is its long relationship with winemaker Tom Drozd. He gives Palmer the ammunition it needs to extend itself in the press. The tasting room is made to look like an old-style British pub.

Wines: $$–$$$

White Wines

Estate Pinot Blanc—Aged in French oak. Vanilla comes through.

Gewürztraminer—Award-winning light white. Tropical flavors and citrus finish. Nice.

North Fork Chardonnay—50% stainless steel fermented and 50% barrel fermented. Apple and pear come through. Nice acidity. Crisp. Clean. ♥

Pinot Blanc—Nice fruit up front on this light white. Oak comes through. Nice.

Reserve Chardonnay—Burgundian-style white. Nice fruit. Creamy. Dry finish.

Riesling—Fruity Riesling with tropical flavors and nose. Crisp finish.

Sauvignon Blanc—Grassy nose. Grapefruit comes though. Nice acidity.

Select Reserve White—55% Chardonnay, 20% Sauvignon Blanc, 10% Pinot Blanc, and 15% Gewürztraminer. Light and refreshing. Complex. Very nice. ♥

Red Wines

Cabernet Franc—A lighter-style Franc. Cherry comes through. Dry finish.

Merlot—Smoky red with lots of fruit and dry finish.

N41 W72 Merlot Cuvée—Named for the North Fork's geographical latitude and longitude. Aged 2 years in *barriques* and casks. Deep fruit. Big tannins. ♥

Select Reserve Red—71% Cabernet Sauvignon, 26% Cabernet Franc, and 3% Merlot. Deep, rich, full-bodied wine. Black cherries and berries come through. Pepper too.

Other Wines

Lighthouse Red, Lighthouse Rosé, Lighthouse White

REVIEWS AND AWARDS

Gewürztraminer 1999—Gold medal, 2002 New York Wine and Food Classic; gold medal, 2002 San Diego National Wine Competition.

Reserve Chardonnay 1998: "86 Points—Highly Recommended."
—Beverage Testing Institute

Pinot Blanc 2000: "Score: 85. Highly Recommended. Best Buy."
—Beverage Testing Institute

"[The Select Reserve White] is quite possibly the most exciting white wine made on Long Island." —Karen MacNeil, *The Wine Bible*

N41 W72 Merlot Cuvée 1998: "86 Points—Best Buy." —Beverage Testing Institute

HOURS AND DIRECTIONS Open daily 11 a.m.–6 p.m. year-round ■ From New York City, take the Long Island Expwy. (I-495) to the last exit (73). Continue east on County Rte. 58 to Osborne Ave. Turn left. Drive to the end. Turn right onto Sound Ave. (Rte. 48). Drive 6 miles to Palmer Vineyards, on the left.

Paumanok Vineyards ✫ ✫ ✫

1074 Main Rd. (Rte. 25), Aquebogue, NY 11931 • Phone 631-722-8800 • Fax 631-722-5110 • www.paumanok.com • info@paumanok.com

"Rising fine Long Island winery," claims *Hugh Johnson's Pocket Wine Book 2002*. "Promising Cabernet, Merlot, Riesling, Chardonnay, outstanding Chenin Blanc, savoury late-harvest Sauvignon Blanc," he went on to write while rating the winery with three stars. Their wines have also been reviewed in the *New York Times* and *Food & Wine* magazine. They have been included in *Bon Appétit*'s annual "Best of the Year" issue for 5 years in a row. They make around 8,000 cases per year. The cedar barn with white trim is classic Long Island and beautifully set against a clear blue summer sky.

Paumanok is the Native American name for Long Island. The 52-acre winery, established in 1983, is owned by Charles and Ursula Massoud. Former IBM executive Charles, of Lebanese descent, comes from a family of hoteliers, while Ursula's family actually owns vineyards in Germany. Charles and winemaker Ryan Leeman make award-winning European-style wines that have garnered the winery excellent press. So much so that *Wine Spectator* awarded the 1998 Cabernet Franc 88 points and their "Critics Choice." Paumanok wines have been served at the White House and in numerous notable New York City restaurants. Go and see what all the excitement is about.

Wines: $$-$$$

White Wines
Barrel Fermented Chardonnay—A clean, smooth, crisp white. Pears come through. ♥
Chenin Blanc—Flowery nose. Hint of honey. Slightly spritzy. Citrus ending. ♥ ♥
Riesling Dry—Light, dry, and slightly *frizzante*. Refreshing. ♥
Semi Dry Riesling—Peach comes through. Slightly *frizzante*. Refreshing. ♥

Red Wines
Cabernet Franc—A medium-bodied, dry red. Nice fruit. Nice, dry ending.
Cabernet Sauvignon—A deep red. Plum and currant come through. Very nice.
Merlot—Plum comes through. Smooth red. Nice.

Blush Wines
Vin Rosé—A fruity, off-dry blush wine. Tart and nicely balanced.

Dessert Wines
Riesling Late Harvest—Orange and honey come through. Very nicely balanced.
Sauvignon Blanc Late Harvest—A nicely balanced golden dessert wine. Very nice.

Other Wines
Assemblage, Cabernet Sauvignon Grand Vintage, Chardonnay Grand Vintage, Festival Chardonnay, Festival Red, Merlot Grand Vintage

REVIEWS AND AWARDS
Chardonnay North Fork of Long Island Barrel Fermented 2000: "Score: 87."
—*Wine Spectator* (August 2002)

"The zesty 2000 Chenin Blanc is a winner." —Howard G. Goldberg, *New York Times*

"Massoud makes Grand Vintage bottlings of Merlot and Cabernet Sauvignon that can be among the region's best." —Joe Czerwinski, *Wine Enthusiast* (April 2001)

Tuthills Lane Vineyard Cabernet Sauvignon 1995: "Score: 89+." 1998 Late Harvest Sauvignon Blanc: "Score: 89+." —*Wine Advocate* (January 2000)

"[The 2000 Riesling Dry] is a relatively simple wine, but it delivers lovely fruit flavors and the crisp acidity to balance them. . . . Recommended."
—*Food & Wine* magazine *Wine Guide 2002*

"[The 2000 Chenin Blanc has] gentle aromas of citrus and pear; delicate but deep flavors." —Eric Asimov, *New York Times* (April 11, 2001)

HOURS AND DIRECTIONS Open year-round Mon.–Sat. 11 a.m.–6 p.m., Sun. noon–6 p.m. ■ From New York City, the Midtown Tunnel leads directly to the Long Island Expwy.; take it to the last exit (73). The exit ramp will bring you onto County Rte. 58 eastbound. Stay on this road, which will turn into Rte. 25 (or Main Rd.). From the Long Island Expwy. to Paumanok is exactly 6 miles. It is on the left side of the road.

Peconic Bay Winery ✪

31320 Main Rd. (Rte. 25), Peconic, NY 11958 • Phone 631-734-7361 • Fax 631-734-5867 • www.peconicbaywinery.com

Ursula and Paul Lowerre bought Peconic Bay Vineyards in January of 1999. It was among the many sales in the Long Island region. The Lowerres brought in a new team including Matt Gillies (general manager), Greg Gove (winemaker), and Charlie Hargrave (viticulturist).

The winery was originally established by Ray Blum in 1980. Blum's first purchase of land was 30 acres, but today Peconic Bay numbers more than 200 acres. The Lowerres are determined to set Peconic Bay apart from other wineries. And with their new team and the wines so far, it seems like this Long Island winery is ready to make the jump.

Wines: $$–$$$

White Wines

La Barrique Chardonnay—Pear and apple come through. Nicely oaked. ♥

Riesling—Refreshing, off-dry Riesling. Tropical fruits and citrusy finish. ♥

Vin de L'Ile Blanc—Light, semisweet white. Honeysuckle and pear come through.

Red Wines

Cabernet Franc—Soft, spicy, medium red. Cherry and plum come through.

Cabernet Sauvignon—Deep red. Cherry and currant come through. Dry finish.

Blush Wines

Rosé of Merlot—Rosé from Merlot. Lively. Refreshing. Dry finish. ♥

Other Wines

Local Flavor Red, Local Flavor White

REVIEWS AND AWARDS

La Barrique Chardonnay—Double gold medal for best Chardonnay, 2000 New York Wine and Food Classic.

Steel Fermented Chardonnay 2001—Gold medal, 2003 Finger Lakes International Wine Competition.

"[The 1999 Rosé of Merlot is] pinkish-salmon in color . . . sleek, piquant and upbeat, captures the character of traditional rosé."
—Howard G. Goldberg, *New York Times* (July 2, 2000)

Rosé of Merlot 1999: "While California marketers push sweet-and-a-bit-stupid White Merlot on the masses, folks on Long Island are making a rosé worth drinking. . . . Recommended." —*Food & Wine* magazine *Wine Guide 2002*

"[The 2000 Riesling is] spirited. . . . There's good acidity and a touch of sweetness." —Peter M. Gianotti, *Newsday*

HOURS AND DIRECTIONS Open year-round Mon.–Thurs. 11 a.m.–5 p.m., Fri.–Sun. 11 a.m.–6 p.m. ■ Take Rte. 25 from Aquebogue toward Orient. Peconic Bay is on your left just after you pass Depot Ln. and Sterling Ln., which is just outside of Cutchogue downtown.

Pellegrini Vineyards

23005 Main Rd. (Rte. 25), Cutchogue, NY 00935 • Phone 631-734-4111 •
Fax 631-734-4159 • www.pellegrinivineyards.com

"Long Island's most enchantingly designed winery. . . . Opulent Merlot, stylish Chard, Bordeaux-like Cab. Inspired winemaking. Exceptionally flavorful wines," says *Hugh Johnson's Pocket Wine Book 2002*. And Peter M. Gianotti of *Newsday* wrote, "Pellegrini Vineyards makes some of the best wines on Long Island . . . satisfying, well-priced wines" (February 2000). And *The New Sotheby's Wine Encyclopedia* raves, "Pellegrini is one of the most promising North Fork producers."

Former graphic designer Bob Pellegrini and his wife Joyce, a retired schoolteacher, purchased what used to be known as Island Vineyards in 1991. Together with Russell Hearn, their Australian winemaker, they have made the wines of Pellegrini Vineyards classic in tone. "Australian-born Russell Hearn is arguably Long Island's most gifted winemaker," claimed *Wine & Spirits* (April 1999). "Virtually everything he touches surges with flavor and stylishness, most notably his cabernet franc and the Bordeaux-style blend labeled [Vintner's Pride] Encore."

The winery itself is beautiful, and Pellegrini's design background influences everything. You should go for yourself first, the wine second, and the beautiful winery third. But don't miss it, whatever you do.

Wines: $$–$$$

White Wines

Chardonnay—Pear and apple come through. Creamy. Nice, dry finish.

Vintner's Pride Chardonnay—Big fruit up front. Pears and apples. Some spices. Dry.

Red Wines

Cabernet Franc—A nice, dry red. Smooth and soft.

Cabernet Sauvignon—Inky deep, dry red. Berries and chocolate come through. ♥

Merlot—Deeply colored dark, dry red. Plum comes through. Nice.

Vintner's Pride Encore—Currant, cherry, and plum come through. A smoky tinge
  somewhere. Nice tannins. Nice, dry ending. ♥

Vintner's Pride Merlot—Deep ruby color. Big fruit up front. Plums and currants. Smooth.

Blush Wines

Rosé of Cabernet—100% Cabernet Sauvignon. Dry, fruity. Nice acidity. Very good. ♥ ♥

Dessert Wines

Vintner's Pride Finale—Golden apricot, peach, and honey flavors. Luscious
  dessert wine.

Other Wines

East End Select Chardonnay, East End Select Merlot

REVIEWS AND AWARDS

Rosé: "At most, a choice rosé should aspire to be a charming trifle, a bauble, a liquid
  entertainment. Pellegrini's easily meets that simple standard."
                    —Howard G. Goldberg, *New York Times* (April 27, 2003)

"[The 1995 Vintner's Pride Encore] hits the bull's-eye. . . . It merits a place in
  serious wine drinkers' bins. . . . It is a beautifully balanced and supple wine,
  richly grapy, meaty and complex."
                    —Howard G. Goldberg, *New York Times* (October 2, 2001)

Merlot 1997: "Score: 90."   —*Wine Spectator* (June 2000)

Cabernet Franc 1998: "Dry, medium-bodied, full tannin, medium-acidity, chocolaty flavor with hints of black cherry and coffee."

—*Food & Wine* magazine *Wine Guide 2002*

HOURS AND DIRECTIONS Open daily 11 a.m.–5 p.m. year-round. ■ From New York City, take the Long Island Expwy. (I-495) east to the last exit (73). Go 14 miles on County Rte. 58 east (it becomes Rte. 25 a few miles after you leave the Long Island Expwy.). As you approach Cutchogue, look for Pellegrini Vineyards on the left.

Pindar Vineyards

Main Rd. (Rte. 25), Peconic, NY 11958 • Phone 631-734-6200 •
Fax 631-734-6205 • www.pindar.net • staff@pindar.net

Pindar winery was established by Long Island wine icon Dr. Herodotus "Dan" Damianos in the North Fork in 1979. He built the winery in 1982. "Long Island's largest producer, and one of its best," raves *The New Sotheby's Wine Encyclopedia*. "Large 287-acre operation on North Fork," reports *Hugh Johnson's Pocket Wine Book 2002*, awarding the winery two stars. Pindar is one of the most popular wine destinations on Long Island.

The vineyard is named for Pindar, a great Hellenic poet from Sparta who lived circa 500 B.C. The vineyards were planted on what had been a potato farm as far back as 1840. During the tours, you can visit the old potato cellar, which is now the wine cellar. The winery has grown since Hugh Johnson's 2002 review to more than 550 acres, making it the largest on the island. The winery itself is wonderful and inviting, and the wines are fun. Winemaker Mark Friszolowski (who also makes wines for Duck Walk) is easily one of the best dessert winemakers in the country, and Pindar is worth the visit for only that—but he makes other nice wines too. In fact, Pindar has one of the largest lists of offerings on the island.

Wines: $$–$$$

White Wines

Reserve Chardonnay—100% barrel fermented. Apple comes through.

2000 Chardonnay Sunflowers Special Reserve—Special-site Chardonnay. Creamy.

Red Wines

Mythology—Award-winning Bordeaux-like blend. Deep, dark, full-bodied red. Nice fruit. Good tannins. Nice, dry end. Very nice. ♥

Pythagoras—Nonvintage red blend. Cabernet Sauvignon, Cabernet Franc, Merlot, Petit Verdot, and Malbec. Dry, complex. ♥

Reserve Cabernet Sauvignon—A big, meaty red. Nice fruit. Big flavors. Dry ending. Powerful. ♥

Dessert Wines

Johannisberg Riesling Ice Wine—A thick, rich, sweet nectar. Honey and apricot come through. Just the right amount of acidity and tartness. Wonderful flavors. ♥ ♥

Late Harvest Gewürztraminer—A rich, sweet dessert wine. Apricot, peach, and tropical fruits come through. Nice acidity. Slightly tart. Truly excellent! ♥ ♥ ♥

Other Wines

Autumn Gold, Beaujolais, Cabernet Port, Chardonnay Peacock Label, Cuvée Rare Champagne, Johannisberg Riesling, Merlot, Spring Splendor, Summer Blush, Sweet Scarlet, Syrah, Viognier, Winter White

REVIEWS AND AWARDS

Cabernet Port 1999—Gold medal, 2003 Finger Lakes International Wine Competition.

Johannisberg Riesling Ice Wine 2000—"Best of the East" (Top Ten Wines), 2003 Annual Wineries Unlimited Seminar and Trade Show; double gold medal, 2003 Tasters Guild International Wine Competition.

Late Harvest Gewürtzaminer 2000—"Best of the East" (Top Ten Wines), 2003 Annual Wineries Unlimited Seminar and Trade Show.

"[Mythology is an] especially good Bordeaux-type red blend."
—Hugh Johnson's Pocket Wine Book 2002

"[The 1997 Mythology is] a very complex Bordeaux wine from a vintage year. Class in a glass, the best red wine from L.I."
—Howard G. Goldberg, *New York Times* (December 1997)

Mythology: "One of the top 50 wines of the world."   *—Bon Appétit* (January 1997)

Mythology: "The best red wine from Bordeaux to California."   *—Grapevine Magazine*

"[The 1995 Reserve Cabernet Sauvignon is] a macho steakhouse red if ever there was one. . . . smooth-textured . . . black currant (cassis) flavor."
—Howard G. Goldberg, *New York Times*

HOURS AND DIRECTIONS Open daily 11 a.m.–6 p.m. year-round. ■ From New York City, take the Long Island Expwy. (I-495) east to exit 73 (County Rte. 58), which becomes Rte. 25. Continue east approximately 12 miles to Peconic. Pindar Vineyards is on your left.

Pugliese Vineyards

Main Rd. (Rte. 25), Cutchogue, NY 11935 • Phone 631-734-4057 • Fax 631-734-5668 • www.pugliesevineyards.com

Pat and Ralph Pugliese founded their winery in 1980. This 36-acre vineyard and winery has been their home since. Ralph is a retired plasterer and union leader. His family is from Italy, and they made wine in his home when he was a child. He was ten when he first started to help making wine, and he is the winemaker now. The winery specializes in bubbly wines and also makes a few different, unique wines. It's all good fun.

Pugliese is one of the smaller vineyards, and they don't intend to change that for the time being. Ralph makes the wines, Pat runs the wine shop, son Ralph, Jr.'s landscape photography lines the walls, and daughter Dominica's homemade condiments and salad oils line the shelves.

Wines: $$–$$$

White Wines

Chardonnay Gold—Creamy, buttery Chardonnay. Soft.

Chardonnay Reserve—Barrel fermented. Crisp. Citrusy. Nice.

Red Wines

Cabernet Sauvignon Reserve—Deep, rich, velvety red. Nice tannins.

Blush Wines

Blush—Merlot and Niagara blend. Semisweet and tangy. Nice.

Sparkling Wines

Blanc de Blanc Brut—Chardonnay sparkling wine. Dry, toasty, and delicate.

Pinot Noir "Nature" Champagne—Completely dry. Salmon-colored.

Sparkling Merlot—Something different. Very nice. Semisweet. Serve cold. Good! ♥

Ports

Port Bello—Cabernet Sauvignon port. Rich, sweet, dark.

Raffaello White Port—A thick, rich, white dessert wine. Something different. Nice. ♥

REVIEWS AND AWARDS

Blanc de Blanc Brut 1996—Millennium Award, 1999 Los Angeles County Fair Wine
Competition; gold medal, 1999 Tasters Guild International Wine Competition;
silver medal, 1999 Grand Harvest Awards; silver medal, 1999 Jerry Mead New
World International Wine Competition.

Blanc de Noir 1996—Millennium Award, 1999 Los Angeles County Fair Wine
Competition; bronze medal, 1999 National Orange Show Pacific Rim; bronze
medal, 1999 Riverside International Wine Competition.

Raffaello White Port 1997—Bronze medal, 1999 Grand Harvest Awards.

Sparkling Merlot 1996—Millennium Award, 1999 Los Angeles County Fair Wine
Competition; bronze medal, 1999 National Orange Show Pacific Rim; bronze
medal, 1999 San Diego National Wine Competition.

Blanc de Blanc Brut and Blanc de Noir: "Sparklers from this family-run North Fork
winery have always been a personal favorite."

—Howard G. Goldberg, New York Times (June 29, 2003)

HOURS AND DIRECTIONS Open daily 10 a.m.–5 p.m. year-round. ■ From New York
City, take the Queens Midtown Tunnel onto the Long Island Expwy. (I-495) and go
east 69.7 miles to the last exit. Bear right off the exit ramp and go east 0.4 mile. Continue on County Rte. 58, Old Country Rd., and go east 2.3 miles. Continue around the
traffic circle on Old Country Rd. and go east another 1.3 miles. Continue on Rte. 25
(Main Rd.) northeast 11.9 miles to Pugliese Vineyards.

Raphael ✪

39390 Main Rd. (Rte. 25), P.O. Box 17, Peconic, NY 11958 •
Phone 631-765-1100 • Fax 631-298-1389 • www.raphaelwine.com •
info@raphaelwine.com

Raphael, a 60-acre estate winery, was established in 1996. It is the dream come true
of Ronkonkama, Long Island, builder John Petrocelli and his wife Joan, who named
the winery after John's father. The winery is quite impressive from the road: a
Mediterranean villa complete with red tiled roof and beige stucco walls in a grand
tradition. However, it's not just about looks at Raphael. They have a very lofty goal.
Petrocelli and general manager/winemaker Richard Olsen-Harbich are attempting
something no one on the East Coast has yet dared try. Inspired by the great Bordeaux houses, Raphael will make only one wine in quantity (a big red made mostly
from Merlot), and two smaller-quantity wines to round out the list (a second Merlot and a Sauvignon Blanc). Raphael counts on the advice of consultant and general manager Paul Pontallier of Chateau Margaux in France. Raphael wants its
premier wine to be a world-class red, and they are certainly on their way to making it soon.

Wines: $$–$$$

White Wines

Raphael Sauvignon Blanc—In keeping with the chateau tradition, Raphael produces a
small quantity of white wine. A nice, dry, light white wine.

95

Red Wines

Raphael Merlot—The premier wine of the winery. Always 80% Merlot, the wine also contains small amounts of Cabernet Franc, Cabernet Sauvignon, Malbec, or Petit Verdot.

Raphael Second Label Merlot—A Merlot blended wine. Includes grapes from young vines and those not chosen that year for the house's main wine.

REVIEWS AND AWARDS

"This is a strong recommendation to buy a wine that you should not drink. The 1999 Raphael Merlot is at a very early stage of what should be a long life . . . a remarkable, tres French vin, as might be expected with Paul Pontallier of Chateau Margaux as Raphael's consultant." —Peter M. Gianotti, *Newsday* (June 30, 2002)

"Raphael's 1999 merlot, recently released and easy to confuse with a fine Pomerol. . . . The bouquet, hinting at the red's intricacies, is winning. . . . Everything in the scent turned up in the flavor and in the seamless, elegant structure. I give it a 94 on a 100-point scale." —Howard G. Goldberg, *New York Times* (June 2, 2002)

HOURS AND DIRECTIONS Open for tastings Mar.–Aug. Call for hours. ■ From New York City, take the Long Island Expwy. (I-495) east to exit 73; follow County Rte. 58 east to Rte. 25 east. Raphael is located on the south side of Main Rd. (Rte. 25). just east of the village of Cutchogue, in the hamlet of Peconic.

Schneider Vineyards

2248 Roanoke Ave., Riverhead, NY 11901 • Phone 631-727-3334 • Fax 631-727-3242 • www.schneidervineyards.com

Bruce and Christiane Baker-Schneider's 22-acre estate was founded in 1994. However, it's difficult to say what they founded. They had no vineyards and no winery. They bought grapes from local growers and had the wines made at two different Long Island wineries. All that, and they still made some very nice wines. However, in 2000 the Schneiders bought 22 acres and have planted mostly Cabernet Franc as well as some other varieties. The goal is to be able to make 2,000 cases of wine a year. The Cabernet Franc was featured in *Time* magazine.

Bruce's family has long been in the wine business, importing wine for three generations. Together with Sean Capiaux (former winemaker at Peter Michael Winery in Calistoga, California), the Schneiders have made quite a statement already. Their award-wining wines have also been met with nice reviews from the critics. And they are deserved. They make lovely, food-oriented wines that are tasty and easy to drink.

Wines: $$–$$$

White Wines

Potato Barn White—Chardonnay and Pinot Blanc blend. Apricot and minerally. Clean and crisp. Nice.

Schneider Chardonnay—Clean, crisp, creamy, dry Chardonnay. Very nice. ♥

Red Wines

Cabernet Franc Schneider—Big berry flavor and nose. Soft and smooth. Spicy. ♥

Merlot Schneider—Deep, ruby/purple, rich, smoky Merlot. Plum comes through. Nice.

Potato Barn Red—Cabernet Franc and Merlot blend. Deep ruby color. Smoky. Nice.

Blush Wines

Potato Barn Rosé—Made from Cabernet Franc and Merlot. Cherry comes through. Dry finish. Refreshing. ♥

REVIEWS AND AWARDS

Cabernet Franc 2000: "Dark, brooding, stern, meaty, nuanced, and complicated, the 2000 is, as the French might say a *vin de garde*—a wine for keeping."
—Howard G. Goldberg, *New York Times* (April 20, 2003)

"[Schneider Chardonnay is on] the cutting edge of food-oriented East End lightness." —Howard G. Goldberg, *New York Times* (February 20, 2000)

Merlot Schneider: "Rated one of the world's best Merlots."
—Matthew DeBord, *Wine Spectator* (October 2001)

Cabernet Franc Schneider: "Full, rich, smooth mouth feel, and a long, silky finish tinged with tobacco and chocolate. . . . 90 points." —*Wine Enthusiast*

HOURS AND DIRECTIONS Call for hours. ■ From New York City, take the Long Island Expwy. (I-495) east to exit 73. Follow County Rte. 58 east for 2.4 miles to a rotary and go three-fourths of the way around onto Roanoke Ave. Schneider Vineyards is 2.4 miles on the right. Wines can also be tried at The Tasting Room, listed under Other Long Island Wineries at the end of this section.

Sherwood House Vineyards

2600 Oregon Rd., Mattituck, NY 11952 • Phone 631-298-2157 •
Fax 212-752-5822 • info@sherwoodhousevineyards.com

Dr. Charles Sherwood Smithen, a highly regarded cardiologist in New York City as well as a faculty member at Cornell Medical School, along with his wife Barbara, founded Sherwood House Vineyards. Smithen discovered good wine in the 1960s in London while there for medical studies. The Smithens planted Chardonnay vines from Burgundian clones in 1996, under the supervision of legendary Long Island vineyard manager Steve Mudd. Merlot, Cabernet Sauvignon, Cabernet Franc, and Petit Verdot have also been planted on Sherwood House's 38 acres of former corn and potato fields.

Wines: $$$

White Wines

Chardonnay—Full-bodied, Burgundy-style white. Dry, complex, creamy. Slight minerally flavor. Some citrus. Crisp and refreshing. ♥ ♥ ♥

REVIEWS AND AWARDS

Chardonnay 1999: "89 points." —Beverage Testing Institute

"Burgundian in style, the '99 Sherwood House chardonnay offers an aromatic bouquet, applelike crispness and intense flavor. It debuts with a 91 rating on my 100-point scale." —Howard G. Goldberg, *New York Times* (June 10, 2001)

"The 2000 chardonnay from tiny, virtually unknown Sherwood House Vineyards, was lovely." —Howard G. Goldberg, *New York Times* (May 5, 2002)

HOURS AND DIRECTIONS Call for hours and directions. Wines are also available at The Tasting Room, listed under Other Long Island Wineries.

Ternhaven Cellars

331 Front St., Greenport, NY 11944 • Phone and Fax 631-477-8737 •
hwesleyw@aol.com

Ternhaven Cellars has to be one of the smallest wineries on the entire island. A tiny, 5-acre estate, Ternhaven makes only reds. Established in 1994, they did not open until 1998. The idea is to release Bordeaux-style reds in small batches. With an annual output of 700 to 1,000 cases, Ternhaven is the ultimate boutique winery, just perfectly made for *garagistes!*

The wines are complex and handcrafted. Owner Harold Watts is excited about his small but award-winning winery and wines. And there's good reason to be. Several of his 1997 wines medaled in New York State wine competitions. Good things are coming out of Ternhaven.

Wines: $$–$$$

Red Wines

Cabernet Sauvignon—A deep, dry red. Blackberries and cherries. Dry finish.
Claret D'Alvah—Not tasted.
Merlot—A deep, dry red. Big fruit. Plums and currants. Nice dry finish.

Blush Wines

Harbor Rosé—Semisweet.

HOURS AND DIRECTIONS Open Apr.–Dec. Fri.–Sun. noon–5 p.m. (later in summer), and by appointment. ■ Call for directions.

Wolffer Estates / Sagpond Vineyards

139 Sagg Rd., Sagaponack, NY 11962 • Phone 631-537-5106 •
Fax 631-537-5107 • www.wolffer.com

Wolffer Estates "has come of age with modish Chardonnay, Merlot and sparkling from German-born winemaker. Proof that good wine can be made on Long Island's South Fork," raves *Hugh Johnson's Pocket Wine Book 2002*, while giving the winery three stars. Wolffer Estates is owned by Christian Wolffer. Originally the land served as a weekend getaway for the world traveler. (Wolffer's career encompasses investment banking, venture capital, real estate, agriculture, and entertainment parks.) His estate, originally purchased in 1978 and continually added upon since then, is connected to a state-of-the-art horse park, Sagpond Stables. The 55 acres planted to vines were originally called Sagpond Vineyards, but in 1997 the winery name was changed, although the vineyards continue to be called by their original name.

Wolffer's is a sprawling estate that has the look and feel of a European winery. And why not? The German winemaker, Roman Roth, is as well traveled and experienced as any great winemaker can be. Together with vineyard manager Richard Pisacano, Roth makes sophisticated and polished wines that have won numerous awards and solid critical praise. Their Rosé is dry and elegant, one of the best in the world—bar none. Just ask the *New York Times*, *Food & Wine* magazine, and others.

Wines: $$–$$$

White Wines

Estate Selection Chardonnay—Made in the best Burgundian tradition. Full bodied. Apples and pears come through. Creamy texture. Nice.
Late Harvest Chardonnay—A late-harvest Chard? Yep. And it's very good. Honey-colored with tropical fruits and honey coming through. But nice balance of acidity and tangy finish. An excellent dessert wine! ♥ ♥ ♥
Reserve Chardonnay—Complex, full-bodied, dry Chardonnay.

Red Wines

Cabernet Franc—A nice, dry red wine with nice fruit and solid tannins.

Reserve Merlot—Dark ruby. Berries come through. Nice tannins. Nice, dry finish.

Verjus—Acidic "green" juice used by chefs and serious cooks as a vinegar and lemon juice substitute. One of the only wineries on the East Coast to offer verjuice. Serious cooks should buy this when it's available. ♥

Blush Wines

Rosé—Salmon-colored rosé made from Merlot and Chardonnay. Big fruit up front but an elegant, dry finish. ♥ ♥ ♥

Sparkling Wines

Cuvée Sparkling Wine Brut—Made *méthode champenoise*. Crisp and clean and dry.

Other Wines

La Ferme Martin Chardonnay, La Ferme Martin Merlot, Wolffer Pinot Noir

REVIEWS AND AWARDS

"[The 2000 Rosé is] pale salmon in color, with a delicate aroma of citrus and candied cherry. Packs more punch than its 11.5 percent alcohol level suggests. . . . A Top-Ten Rosé."   *—Food & Wine* (August 1, 2001)

"The '00 is Mr. Roth's richest, tastiest rosé to date. At $10.50, it's a nifty buy. The wine is as dry as ever—superdry, some might say. The familiar, pretty salmon pink and coral color is still present. In addition to the flavor, what's noticeably heightened this time is the smooth texture."   —Howard G. Goldberg, *New York Times* (June 17, 2001)

HOURS AND DIRECTIONS Open daily 11 a.m.–6 p.m. year-round. ■ Take the Montauk Hwy. (Rte. 27) east past Bridgehampton toward Sagaponack. Pass the monument and school in Bridgehampton and turn right onto Sagg Rd./Main St. Wolffer Estates is 200 yards ahead on the right-hand side.

OTHER LONG ISLAND WINERIES

Broadfields: North Fork, Long Island • proprietors@broadfields.com

Dzugas Vineyards: 4200 North Rd., Southold, NY 11971 • Phone 631-765-3692

The Old Fields Vineyard: P.O. Box 726, Southold, NY 11971 • Phone 631-765-2465

The Tasting Room: 2885 Peconic Lane, Peconic, NY 11958 • Phone 631-765-6404 • thetastingroom@earthlink.net

Wine Services, Inc.: 1825 Cross River Dr., Riverhead, NY 11901 • Phone 631-722-3800 • Fax 631-722-8770

HUDSON RIVER VALLEY

Adair Vineyards

52 Allhusen Rd., New Paltz, NY 12561 • Phone 845-255-1377 • adairwines@aol.com

Adair Vineyards has been making and selling estate-grown wines since 1987. It is not only a winery but also a nationally registered landmark that thousands have visited. The farm was founded by French Huguenots in the seventeenth century. The winery was originally founded in 1984 by Jim and Gloria Adair. It is housed in a 200-year-old barn constructed in the Dutch fashion that bears a plaque signifying its importance as a landmark.

Marc Vincent Stopkie and his wife Lorie bought the winery in 1997. They have continued to use the 10 acres of vines planted to grapes as the source for their wines. The atmosphere is informal and friendly—a very worthwhile visit.

Wines: $–$$

White Wines

Chardonnay—A dry, clean, crisp, Chardonnay with tropical fruits and creamy texture.
Seyval—A dry, crisp white wine.
Vignoles—A light white wine.

Red Wines

Landmark Red—A dry red blend of Marechal Foch and Millot.
Picnic Red—Light-bodied, dry red wine. Nice.

Dessert Wines

Mountain Mist—A late-harvest dessert wine made with Vignoles.

HOURS AND DIRECTIONS Open June–Oct. daily 11 a.m.–6 p.m.; Dec.–May Fri.–Sun. 11 a.m.–5 p.m.; closed Nov. ■ Located on Rte. 94 just north of Rte. 17A.

Alison Wines & Vineyards

231 Pitcher Ln., Red Hook, NY 12571 • Phone 845-758-6335 • Fax 845-758-5073 • www.alisonwines.com • vintner@idsi.net

Alison wines sold its first vintage in 1999. Richard and Alison Lewit founded the winery in 1998 with former dairy farmer Norman Greig. A former Gannett-Westchester newspaper reporter, Lewit left the giant media company to manage Millbrook Vineyards. After that he moved to Oregon to work for Ponzi. Greig was determined to sell his dairy herd, and the Lewits convinced him that winemaking would keep the Greig family farm as a productive agriculture fixture. The barns and outbuildings were renovated, and the Lewits moved back to New York State. The Greig Farm Market is still in operation right across the road, so you can pick up fresh produce and food specialties.

The 1999 Pinot Noir was an award winner, and it will be the winery's flagship wine. The first vines were planted in 2001, so for now the winery is making wine with grapes grown at other vineyards. The Lewits and Greig are determined to make a success of their wines, and Richard is dedicated to his craft. This will be a vineyard to watch out for.

Wines: $–$$

White Wines

Chardonnay—Dry white wine, lightly oaked. Nice finish. Lemon comes through. Clean.
Reserve Chardonnay—Apple and pear come through. Made in the spirit of a fine French Chablis. Nice.

Red Wines

Pinot Noir—Black cherry comes through. Nice mouth feel. Dry finish. Very nice. ♥

REVIEWS AND AWARDS

Pinot Noir 1999—Silver medal, 25th Annual (2000) International Eastern Wine Competition.

HOURS AND DIRECTIONS Open year-round Tues.–Fri. noon–6 p.m., Sat.–Sun. 11 a.m.–6 p.m. ■ From the N.Y. Thruway take exit 19, follow signs for Rhinecliff Bridge (Rtes. 209/199), and cross the bridge. At the second traffic light, turn left onto Rte. 9G, go north 2.8 miles to Kelly Rd. (second light), turn right onto Kelly, go to the stop sign, and turn left onto Budds Corners Rd.; then make the next right onto Pitcher Ln. ■ From the Taconic Pkwy. take the exit for Rte. 199/Red Hook/Pine Plains. Go 8 miles west on Rte. 199 to the second traffic light in the village of Red Hook. Turn right onto Rte. 9, go north 3 miles, then left onto Pitcher Ln.

Applewood Winery

82 Four Corners Rd., Warwick, NY 10990 • Phone 845-988-9292 • www.applewoodorchardsandwinery.com

Applewood is a small, family-owned winery. Donald Hull, a physician, bought the farm in 1949 for his son David, who dreamed of being a fruit grower. Dave and his wife Elaine turned the place, over the course of the years, into a regional powerhouse with pick-your-own promotions that set the standard in the region. David's son Jonathan, and Jonathan's wife Michele, founded the winery with grandfather Donald's help in 1993.

Jonathan, who is both owner and winemaker, can often be found in the winery's cellar, concocting their newest offering. Michele is well known for her food and wine parties that she hosts at the winery. Applewood makes wines from classic vinifera and from hybrids, makes cider from apples grown it its own orchards, and makes sophisticated fruit wines. It is a real working farm in the heart of the Hudson Valley.

Wines: $–$$$

White Wines

Autumn Mist—Sweet white wine

Seyval/Chardonnay—A dry, crisp white blend. Very nice.

Seyval/Chardonnay Reserve—Aged in American oak. Nice, buttery texture. Good finish.

Summer Fields—Semidry, light white wine. Refreshing.

Wawayanda White—Semidry, light white.

Red Wines

Cabernet Franc—Dry red. Berries come through. Nice finish.

Country Road Red—A dry, medium-bodied red.

International Red—Off-dry, light red.

Merlot—Dry, sophisticated red.

Obr—Means oak barrel reserve. Dry red aged in oak. Nice fruit. Earthy.

Fruit Wines, Ciders, and Dessert Wines

Apple Blossom Blush—Semisweet blush wine made from apples and grapes. Nice. Refreshing.

Cherry—Semisweet red wine made from cherries. Nice.

McIntosh—Off-dry apple wine. Very nice. Refreshing.

Ruby's Kiss—Sweet red dessert wine. Big fruit, nice balance.

Stone Fence Hard Cider—Semisweet sparkling cider. Honey comes through.

HOURS AND DIRECTIONS Open year-round Fri.–Sun. 11 a.m.–5 p.m. ■ From New York City or Albany, take the N.Y. Thruway (I-87) to exit 16 Harriman (Woodbury Commons). Then take Rte. 17 west to exit 127 (Greycourt Rd.); follow signs to Sugar Loaf, then Warwick, on either County Rte. 13 or 13A; also look for the grape cluster wine trail signs. Continuing on Rte. 13 or 13A for 3 miles past Sugar Loaf, turn right on Four Corners Rd. Go 1 mile; Applewood is on the right down a long dirt road.

Baldwin Vineyards

176 Hardenburgh Rd., Pine Bush, NY 12566 • Phone 845-744-2226 • Fax 845-741-6321 • www.baldwinvineyards.com

Though Jack and Pat Baldwin established their winery in 1982, the farm itself is much older. The original estate, known as the Hardenburgh Estate, dated back to 1786. Since the Baldwins entered the winemaking business, they have gone on to great success, winning numerous awards including many gold medals.

Jack, a former pharmaceutical executive, and his wife fell in love with wine after a trip to wine country in France in 1974. They followed that trip with the purchase of a wine cellar and then this farm and winery. Come in and they will tell you their story and let you taste their wines, which have received raves from reviewers as well established as *Wine Spectator*. Their strawberry wine is well regarded, and has been recommended several times by *New York Times* wine writer Howard G. Goldberg.

Wines: $–$$

White Wines
Chardonnay—Full-bodied, rich, classic-style Chardonnay.
Illusions—Off-dry white wine. Refreshing.
Mist di Greco—Full-bodied, crisp white wine.

Red Wines
Cabernet Sauvignon—A deep, dry red. Cherries come through.
Merlot—A medium-bodied red wine.
Pinot Noir—Medium-bodied dry red. Spicy. Nice finish.

Sparkling Wines
Anthony's Vintage—A *frizzante* wine with a hint of raspberry. Very nice.
Memories—Brut sparkling wine made in the *méthode champenoise*.

Dessert Wines
Late Harvest Riesling—Elegant dessert wine, in the classical tradition
Late Harvest Vignoles—Full-bodied, rich dessert wine. Nice balance.
Raspberry—Made from black raspberries. Nicely balanced.
Strawberry—Made from 100% fresh strawberries. Very nice. One of the best strawberry wines we tasted. Also one of their most popular wines. ♥
Visions—A rich, golden dessert wine.

Other Wines
Cherry, *Embers*, and *Joseph's Vintage*

REVIEWS AND AWARDS
"The Baldwins are noted for their Gold-medal Chardonnay and Johannisberg Rieslings, but the family's pride and joy is a very popular Strawberry Wine."   *—Star-Ledger*

"[The Strawberry wine] . . . tastes like the concentrated essence of strawberry."   *—Wine Tidings*

Strawberry: "The nose leaps and dances. Great Value. Extraordinary (rated 89 of 100)"   *—Wine Access*

"[The Strawberry is] . . . the most outstanding of the lot. . . . grab it." *—Wine Spectator*

"A strawberry jewel, tasting of pure strawberry." *—Toronto Sun*

Raspberry: "Splendid." *—New York Times*

HOURS AND DIRECTIONS Apr.–June and Nov.–Dec. Fri.–Mon 11:30 a.m.–5 p.m.; July–Oct., daily 11:30 a.m.–5:30 p.m.; Jan.–Mar. Sat.–Sun. 11:30 a.m.–4:30 p.m. ■ From New York City take the Tappan Zee Bridge (I-87) to Rte. 17 west to exit 119 to Rte. 302 north to Pine Bush. Then follow the signs. ■ From New Jersey take Rte. 17 north to Rte. 17 west and follow the directions above ■ From Connecticut take I-84 west across the Newburgh/Beacon Bridge to exit 8 and Rte. 52 west to Pine Bush. Then follow the signs.

Benmarl Vineyards & Winery ✠

156 Highland Ave., Marlboro, NY 12542 • Phone 845-236-4265 • Fax 845-236-7271 • info@benmarl.com

Benmarl is one of the country's oldest wineries. Mark Miller, the current owner and founder, a former Hollywood costume designer and magazine illustrator, purchased the winery and its original vines in 1956 with his late wife Dene. Miller lived in Burgundy, France, for many years, and the former Oklahoman is quite enamored of the region's culture and wine, to the consumer's benefit. Miller's goal is to make a world-class wine comparable to French wines. He is highly regarded in both American and French wine circles. And his winemaker, Anne Reagan, is a catch!

Benmarl has an art gallery where visitors can see Miller's work and buy prints as well as wines. Miller was one of those instrumental in getting the Farm Winery Act passed. Benmarl holds N.Y. State Farm Winery license no. 1. He is also the proud father of Eric Miller, who went on to found the highly acclaimed Chaddsford Winery in Pennsylvania. Benmarl produces approximately 6,000 cases of wine each year. A wonderful and enchanting visit is in store at this lovely winery.

Wines: $–$$$

White Wines

Chardonnay—Fermented in French and American oak *sur lie.*

Chardonnay Clare's Cuvée—A dry white blend of Chardonnay and Seyval. Very nice. Dry, crisp, clean, and no oak. Very nice.

Estate Seyval Blanc—Steel fermented, then sent through malolactic fermentation and barrel aged.

Red Wines

Barbera—A dry red wine. More smooth than what you'd expect from Barbera.

Cabernet Sauvignon—Big berry flavor up front. Clean finish.

Coast to Coast—Baco blended with West Coast Zin. Peppery. Very good. ♥

DeChaunac—A deep, hearty red.

Estate Baco Noir—Big berry flavor. Nice body. Good mouth feel. Nice finish.

Merlot—Big fruit up front. Nice mouth feel. Nice finish.

Syrah—A nice berry, peppery, Rhône-styled red.

Zinfandel—Deep, dry red.

Dessert Wines

Escapade—A late-harvest Vignoles. Pineapple and apricot come through. Nice balance.

REVIEWS AND AWARDS

Cabernet Sauvignon 2000—Bronze medal, 2001 American Wine Society Commercial Wine Competition.

Merlot 2000—Bronze medal, 2001 American Wine Society Commercial Wine Competition.

Zinfandel 1997—Best U.S. red wine, 2000 Atlanta Wine Summit.

"Mark Miller experimented with vinifera, but devoted his efforts to hybrids. His reds are intense and complex and he is particularly proud of some of his older vintages. They can, in fact, rival some of the best viniferas."

—Frank J. Prial, *New York Times*

"The curving sweep of his vines, the ripeness of his wines, make the outing worthwhile. You come home happy."

—Howard G. Goldberg, *New York Times*

HOURS AND DIRECTIONS Open Apr.–Dec. daily, noon–5 p.m.; Jan.–Mar. Wed.–Mon. noon–4 p.m. Tasting and tour $5; includes parking, winery tour, wine tasting, art gallery, and use of picnic area. ■ From Rte. 9W in Marlboro, take Western Ave. west, turning left on Highland Ave. Watch for the Benmarl sign in about 0.5 mile.

Brimstone Hill Vineyards

61 Brimstone Hill Rd., Pine Bush, NY 12566 • Phone 845-744-2231 • www.brimstonehillwine.com • bhvwine@frontiernet.net

Like many other East Coast wineries, Brimstone Hill Vineyards is a family-operated winery. The vineyard was started in 1969 with an experimental planting of several French hybrid varieties by Valerie and Richard Eldridge, the founders. Since then they have gone on to produce a number of award-winning wines that have been served by both Governor Mario Cuomo and President Reagan.

The Eldridges sold their first two wines, Vin Rouge and Vin Blanc, in 1979. Today they have more than 13 acres planted to grapevines and offer a wide range of wines. Every one of their wines has won one kind of award or another by this time. And the winery has been expanded to accommodate 150 people comfortably in their banquet room, which can be rented for weddings and other celebrations.

Wines: $–$$

White Wines

Cayuga White—Semisweet, light wine.

Chardonnay—An oak-aged, dry white. Nice.

Riesling—Semisweet, light white wine.

Seyval Blanc—A dry version of this light white wine.

Vin Blanc—A dry white blend.

Red Wines

Cabernet Franc—A deep, dry red.

Vin Rouge—An off-dry red blend.

Other Wines

Domaine Bourmont (sparkling wine), *Nouveau*, and *Vidal*

REVIEWS AND AWARDS

Cabernet Franc 2000—Bronze medal, New York State Fair Wine Competition.

HOURS AND DIRECTIONS Open July–Oct. Thurs.–Mon. 11:30 a.m.–5:30 p.m.; Nov.–Dec. and May–June Fri.–Mon. 11:30 a.m.–5:30 p.m.; Jan.–Apr. Sat.–Sun. 11:30 a.m.–5:30 p.m. ■ From the N.Y. Thruway, going either north or south, take exit 16 toward Harriman/Rte. 17. Turn onto Rte. 17 west; take exit 119 (Rte. 302) toward Pine Bush. Turn right onto Rte. 302, which becomes Maple Ave. Turn left onto Rte. 52, then right onto County Rte. 7/New Prospect Rd. Then follow signs to the winery.

Brotherhood Winery ✫

35 North St., Washingtonville, NY 10992 • Phone 845-496-9101 •
Fax 845-496-8720 • www.brotherhoodnywines.com

Brotherhood is "America's Oldest Winery" and has been making wine since 1837. The first commercial winery in the Hudson Valley, it was then named Jacques Brothers Winery. They made mostly altar wine. However, in 1885–1886 the winery changed hands and was renamed Brotherhood Winery by new owners Jesse Emerson and his son. The Farrell family owned the winery from 1921 to 1987. In 1987 Cesar Baeza, an internationally acclaimed vintner, bought the winery, and he is attempting to elevate Brotherhood to new heights. Regardless, it is the nation's oldest continuously operated winery. Brotherhood also has the largest wine cellars in the United States, which are fun to see on the tour.

Wines: $–$$$

White Wines
Chardonnay—Dry and buttery.
Johannisberg Riesling—Sweet version of the German classic. Their best-selling wine.
May Wine—Light white wine with strawberry juice and woodruff. A signature wine for Brotherhood.
Seyval Blanc—Dry, crisp white table wine.

Red Wines
Chelois—Young, light, dry red wine.
Holiday—Famous, traditional, spiced red wine.
Mariage—75% Cabernet Sauvignon and 25% Chardonnay. A barrel-aged red wine. Limited collector's edition. This prizewinning wine deserves accolades. ♥
Merlot—Dark, ruby red color. Dry, full bodied, yet soft to the palate.
Pinot Noir—Light, soft, dry red wine.

Sparkling Wines
Grand Monarque—Produced in the *méthode champenoise*. A nice sparkling wine. Clean, dry.

Dessert Wines
Ginseng Black—"Blend of the finest quality Ginseng Root and premium New York State dessert wine." Not tasted.
Late Harvest, Eiswein Johannisberg Riesling—Rich, luscious dessert wine. Tangy. ♥ ♥
Sheba Tej Honey—Ethiopian-style honey wine.

Other Wines
Cream Sherry, Melody Lodge Cabernet Sauvignon, New York Blush Chablis, New York Burgundy, New York Chablis, Rosario, Ruby Port, Sauterne, and *White Zinfandel*

REVIEWS AND AWARDS

"It's the winery's *eiswein*, a sweet wine made from grapes left on the vine until the winter cold freezes them, that continues to make converts."

—Karen MacNeil, *The Wine Bible*

HOURS AND DIRECTIONS Open May–Oct. daily, noon–5 p.m.; Nov.–Apr. Sat.–Sun. noon–5 p.m. Adults $4, ages 15–20 $2, children under 15 free. ■ From the N.Y. Thruway (I-87) going either north or south, take exit 16 (Harriman) onto Rte. 17W, then exit 130 onto Rte. 208 north; continue approximately 7 miles to Washingtonville. In the center of town, turn onto Rte. 94 east; turn left at Brotherhood Plaza.

Cascade Mountain Winery and Restaurant

835 Cascade Mountain Rd., Amenia, NY 12501 • Phone 845-373-9021 • Fax 845-373-7869 • www.cascademt.com • cascademt@mohawk.net

Cascade Mountain Winery and Restaurant was established in 1972 by New York City novelist William Wetmore. He and his family were among the first to plant a vineyard and make premium wines on the east side of the Hudson River. Bill, his wife Margaret, and their three children Charles, Michael, and Joan planted the vineyard in 1972 on their more than 70-acre spread. Bill and his son Charles, who was then a high school senior, built the winery in 1977 as part of Charles's project. In 1985 they added the restaurant. The restaurant offers such regional specialties as goat's milk cheese, smoked trout, salmon mousse, duck pâtés, and locally raised fowl and vegetables in season on its luncheon menu. The more formal dinner menu features several courses and matching wines. Cascade Mountain is a wonderful day trip destination, and the restaurant a wonderful gastronomic treat.

Wines: $–$$

White Wines

Private Reserve White—A Chardonnay/Seyval Blanc aged in oak. Nice.

Seyval Blanc—A dry white blend of Seyval Blanc and Chardonnay aged in stainless steel. Crisp and clean.

Summertide—An off-dry blend of Seyval and Vidal. Light and refreshing.

Red Wines

Coueur de Lion—Light-bodied red made Beaujolais style with Cabernet Sauvignon. Nice. ♥

Private Reserve Red—A full-bodied red blend aged in oak. Not tasted.

Blush Wines

Harvest Rose—A fresh, fruity, lively blush made from Chancellor. Crisp. Clean.

Dessert Wines

Heavenly Daze—Red spiced wine includes cinnamon, lemon zest, vanilla beans.

Vignoles—A golden, sweet white dessert wine. Rich. Honey comes through.

HOURS AND DIRECTIONS Open daily 10 a.m.–6 p.m. year-round, but reservations are suggested for the restaurant, which is on Flint Hill Rd. ■ From Amenia go 3 miles north on Rte. 22. Turn left on Webutuck School Rd. and follow the signs.

Clinton Vineyards

212 Schultzville Rd., Clinton Corners, NY 12514 • Phone 845-266-5372 • Fax 845-266-3395 • www.clintonvineyards.com • info@clintonvineyards.com

Founder and winemaker Ben Feder, a former graphic designer in the New York City publishing world, produces a series of excellent white wines, both dry and sweet— from sparkling wine to Seyval Blanc to Riesling. Along with his wife Phyllis, he founded the winery in 1976. The current winery is housed in a charming nineteenth-century dairy barn.

Clinton's award-winning wines have been served at the Democratic National Conventions in New York City and Chicago and were served at the White House as well as at the Clinton-Yeltsin summit meeting at Hyde Park, N.Y.

Wines: $-$$$

White Wines

Tribute, Seyval Blanc—Harvested on September 11, 2001, this release is named to commemorate that day. Crisp, bright, and clean.

Sparkling Wines

Jubilee—A brut edition of the Seyval Naturel. Very nice.

Peach Gala—A blend of citrus and peach flavors in a sparkling wine. Nice.

Seyval Naturel—A 100% Seyval Blanc sparkling wine made in the classic *méthode champenoise*. Different. Very nice.

Dessert Wines

Desire—Rich wine made from organically grown blackberries. Delicious.

Duet—A blend of rhubarb and strawberries. Tastes like pie in a bottle.

Embrace—Made from organically grown raspberries. Big berry flavor. Deep and rich.

Rhapsody—Almost port-like blueberry dessert wine.

Romance—Fresh and focused late-harvest, port-style Seyval. Pear and peach come through.

Liqueurs

Cassis—A cassis (made from black currants) in the classic style. Very nice.

HOURS AND DIRECTIONS Open year-round Fri.–Sun. 11 a.m.–5 p.m. ■ Located midway between New York City and Albany, Clinton Vineyards is only 7 minutes from the Taconic Pkwy. Take the Salt Point exit, proceed east on Salt Point Rd., and follow the signs to the vineyard, which is on Schultzville Rd.

Demarest Hill Winery

Grand St./81 Pine Island Tpke., Warwick, NY 10990 • Phone 845-986-4723 • Fax 201-384-0027 • www.demaresthillwinery.com

Francesco Ciummo and his wife Orietta own the beautiful Demarest Hill Winery, which sits high atop the hill of the same name in Warwick. The 137-acre family winery is one of Orange County's newest and largest. Francesco is the winemaster. He learned his winemaking skills at his father's side in Molise, Italy. Francesco worked as a laborer all over the world and saved enough money after decades of toil to buy this tract of land in the early 1990s. The reward for Francesco and Orietta came in 1994, when the winery sold its first wines. The atmosphere is both welcoming and informal. They'll make you feel like family here. Go along. It's fun and it's tasty.

Wines: $-$$

White Wines

Chardonnay Supreme—Aged 2 years in oak. A full-bodied white. Vanilla comes through.

Chenin Blanc—A nice, light, dry white wine.

Red Wines

Cabernet Sauvignon—A full-bodied red. Rich and deep.

Red Bouchet—A rare grape with a French heritage. Full bodied, fruity red.

Red Classico—A blend of California grapes. Nice pasta wine.

Red Zinfandel—Robust red varietal. A deep, rich pasta wine.

Victoria Merlot—Made from grapes from Lodi Valley, California, the wine is soft and well balanced.

HOURS AND DIRECTIONS Open Nov.–May 11 a.m.–5 p.m.; June–Oct. 11 a.m.–6 p.m. ■ Coming from the north or south on the N.Y. Thruway, take exit 16 (U.S. 6/Rte. 17) toward Harriman. Merge onto U.S. 6 west. Take exit 17 (Greycourt Rd.) toward Sugar Loaf/Warwick. Merge onto Leigh Ave., which becomes Kings Hwy. Turn right onto Rte. 17A. Turn left onto Grand St., which becomes Pine Island Tpke. Then follow the signs approximately 1–2 miles to the winery.

El Paso Winery

742 Broadway, Ulster Park, NY 12487 • Phone 845-331-8642

The El Paso Winery was begun in 1977 by Felipe Beltra and sold its first wines in 1981. Beltra is from Uruguay, and his family there makes wine as well. His Spanish-style wines are very popular and are usually sold out within the year. The winery is housed in a small, rustically renovated barn more than 150 years old. Ernest Herzog, owner of Royal Kedem Winery, helped Beltra purchase the barn, which was sitting idle on the company's property. El Paso offers over fifteen different varieties of wine, all very moderately priced, and many are available in larger bottles.

Wines: $–$$

White Wines

Cream Niagara—A classic cream. Native grape blend. Very drinkable.

Seyval Blanc—A dry Spanish-style white. Very nice.

Red Wines

Concord—The classic regional grape.

Chianti—A dry, deep red. Full bodied.

HOURS AND DIRECTIONS Open Apr.–Dec. Wed.–Mon. 11 a.m.–6 p.m. ■ El Paso is found on Rte. 9W, 4 miles south of Kingston.

Elk Hill Winery

225 Prim Ln., Berne, NY 12023 • Phone 518-872-2314 • Fax 518-872-9587 • www.elkhillwinery.com • sales@elkhillwinery.com

Elk Hill Winery is nestled in the Heldeberg Mountains, approximately 20 minutes' driving time from Albany. It was founded by Joe Primiano and his family. In their own words, "It's a no nonsense winery." The tasting room is rustic and charming, if not opulent. And the wines are simple and very tastefully done. The Primianos aren't pretentious about wine and make the wine-tasting experience fun and unintimidating. A great stop for wine lovers of all levels.

Wines: $

White Wines

Chardonnay—California-grown grapes, aged in American oak. Crisp and dry.

French Colombard—California-grown grapes. Dry, full-bodied white. Nice.

Jeme—A dry white blend. Silky mouth feel. Nicely balanced.

Red Wines

Cabernet Sauvignon—Dark velvet wine. Blend of 80% Cabernet and 20% Merlot. Rich, dry, nice finish.

Carignane—(pronounced kare-in-YAWN) Fruity, light red wine. A lovely pasta wine.

HOURS AND DIRECTIONS Open May–Dec. Fri.–Sun. noon–6 p.m. ■ Call for directions.

Hudson Valley Draft Cider Company

200 Centre Rd., Staatsburg, NY 12580 • Phone 845-266-3979 • www.hudsonvalleycider.com • ciderdraft@aol.com

Hudson Valley Draft Cider is located at Breezy Hill Orchard and Cider Mill. Husband and wife Peter Zimmerman and Elizabeth Ryan bought Breezy Hill Orchard and Cider Mill in 1984. A family farm, Breezy Hill had been known since 1949 for growing an unusually wide range of high-quality fruits, including forty-five varieties of apples, eight varieties of pears, and 20 acres of organic vegetables. The orchard had been planted in 1949. However, the farm was dilapidated when the new owners took it over. Since then, it's been a tough but successful struggle. First they strengthened their fruit business, then began making specialty foods, pies, etcetera. All Breezy Hill preserves, jams, and chutneys are produced in small batches and are absolutely wonderful.

Elizabeth Ryan cofounded Hudson Valley Draft Cider with Hillary Baum, a marketing consultant, through a private stock offering. Elizabeth is a press maven. She's appeared on Charles Kuralt's *Dateline: America*, Martha Stewart, TV Food Network, the Lifetime network, and National Public Radio, to name just a few. And newspapers and magazines flock to sing the praises of the company's cider—including, among others, the *New York Times*, the *San Francisco Chronicle*, and *Food & Wine*. The praise is well deserved.

Ciders: $

Hudson Valley Farmhouse Cider—Handcrafted in small batches. Rich, fruity apple cider. Nice finish. ♥

Hudson Valley Farmhouse Perry—Cider from pears—traditionally called "Perry"— is much valued because of its rarity. Made from Beurré Bosc and Williams Bon Chrétien (Bartlett) among others. A nice, dry cider with just a touch of sweetness. Delicious! ♥

Maeve's Draft Cider—Named for Celtic goddess Queen Maeve. A delicate, dry, and appley cider. Refreshing without being cloying. Very nice. ♥ ♥

REVIEWS AND AWARDS—MAEVE'S DRAFT CIDER

"Fragrant stylishly dry and delicate"   —*San Francisco Chronicle*

"Delicate apple fragrance with a lingering winy flavor."   —*New York Times*

"Light, clean and dry."   —*Wine Spectator* (October 1997)

"Dry, complex and earthy."   —*Food & Wine*

HOURS AND DIRECTIONS Open daily 10 a.m.–5 p.m. ■ From the N.Y. Thruway heading north, take exit 18 (New Paltz). Cross the Mid-Hudson Bridge to Poughkeepsie. Take Rte. 9 north to Hyde Park. Turn right onto either Rte. 40A or 41. Proceed approximately 1

mile and turn left onto Rte. 9G north; continue to the light in East Park (Mobil station on right, Stewart's on left). Proceed through the light on 9G approximately 4–5 miles. Directly after 9G Garden Center, turn right onto Hollow Rd. (County Rte. 14). Go approximately 4 miles to the first stop sign. Turn left onto Centre Rd. (County Rte. 18). Go 0.9 mile; Breezy Hill Orchard is on the right. ■ From the N.Y. Thruway heading south, take exit 19 (Kingston) and follow signs for the Kingston-Rhinecliff Bridge. Cross the bridge, proceed to Rte. 9G south, and turn right onto it. Turn left onto Slate Quarry Rd. (County Rte. 19) and go approximately 4 miles. At the sign for Schultzville and Clinton Corners, turn right onto Centre Rd. (County Rte. 18). Proceed 2.4 miles to the Schultzville stop signs and go straight on Centre Rd. for another 1.5 miles; Breezy Hill Orchard is on the left.

Johnston's Winery

5140 Bliss Rd., Ballston Spa, New York 12020 • Phone 518-882-6310 •
Fax 518-882-5551 • www.johnstonwinery.com • webmaster@johnstonswinery.com

Johnston's Winery, owned by Kurt Johnston, is located just north of Albany in what is really considered Galway, despite the address. They sell inexpensive, simple, and tasteful wines made by Kurt, as well as a host of other specialty food products for which they are regionally known. Their list of jams and preserves is just as mouthwatering as their wines, and includes blueberry, raspberry, and strawberry jams, hot and mild salsas, a marinara sauce, sweet pickled beans, bread and butter pickles, cranberry sauce (very good), and assorted vinegars.

Wines: $

Red Wines
Pinot Noir—Light, dry red. Cherry flavors come through.

Fruit Wines
Blackberry—Semisweet fruit wine.
Blueberry—A off-dry red wine.
Cherry—Rich, heavy, sweet red dessert wine. Nicely balanced.
McIntosh—Apple and honey blend. Dry. Nice finish.
Raspberry—Semisweet raspberry wine. Nice.

HOURS AND DIRECTIONS Open year-round Sat. 11 a.m.–6 p.m., Sun. noon–6 p.m., or by appointment. Call for expanded hours late summer and fall. ■ Call for directions.

Larry's Vineyard & Winery

3001 Furbeck Rd., Altamont, NY 12009 • Phone 518-355-7365 •
v1945p@juno.com

Larry's Vineyard & Winery, located in beautiful Altamont, is believed to be the only winery in the capital region of Albany. The wine sold at Larry's is called Grossi Hill Wines—named for Larry Grossi, who uses an old-world approach to making these award-winning wines in the traditions of his native Tuscany. He offers nine varieties.

Wines: $–$$

White Wines
Cayuga—A light, sweet white wine made from this native American standard-bearer.
Edelweiss White—Mildly fruity and similar to a Chablis.
Seyval Blanc—A light, dry white wine. Nice fruit. Good finish.

St. Papin—A German-style wine made from the St. Papin grape. Fruity with a touch of sweetness.

Star White—A Cayuga White variety. Dry, like a light Chardonnay.

Red Wines

Foch—A medium-bodied red wine.

DeChaunac—A medium-bodied red wine.

Northern Red—An award-winning wine made entirely from DeChaunac. Aged in oak or stainless steel, the wine is similar to Cabernet Sauvignon. Nice.

HOURS AND DIRECTIONS Open mid-Mar.–Dec. Wed.–Sat. 10 a.m.–5 p.m., Sun. noon–5 p.m. ■ Call for directions.

Magnanini Farm Winery & Restaurant ✺

172 Strawridge Rd., Wallkill, NY 12589 • Phone 914-895-2767 • Fax 914-895-9458

Magnanini Farm Winery & Restaurant, located in Wallkill (Ulster County), has been owned by Galba and Eileen Magnanini since 1954. It is very popular. The restaurant offers dancing for romantic couples who are enticed by live accordion music. It also offers a prix fixe northern Italian dinner along with wines made on the premises. Magnanini produces six country wines and four hybrids. They are made by Richard Magnanini, who is chief, cook, and bottle washer, with his wife Rachel.

Magnanini's has been recommended as one of the best stops along the Hudson Valley Wine Trail by the *New York Times*. The winery and restaurant are set amid a beautiful landscape. Reservations are necessary to get a table for the single seating the restaurant offers.

Wines: $–$$

White Wines

Seyval Blanc—A light, dry white wine. Wonderful food wine.

Red Wines

DeChaunac—A medium-bodied red wine. Nice fruit. Nice finish.

REVIEWS AND AWARDS

"Bottles of friendly, rustic nonvintage wines like Bianco Amabile and Rosso Da Tavola cost extra. Talk about a cottage industry!"
                                                                —Howard G. Goldberg, *New York Times*

HOURS AND DIRECTIONS Restaurant open Apr.–Dec. Sat. 7 p.m., Sun. 1 p.m. (reservations required). Wine tasting only, at the tasting room, Sat.–Sun. 10 a.m.–6 p.m. ■ From Wallkill, take Rte. 300 east 1 mile, turn right on Plains Rd., and right again on Strawridge Rd. to Magnanini Farm.

The Meadery at Greenwich

RR 4 Box 4070, Meader Rd., Greenwich, NY 12834 • Phone 1-800-MEADERY or 518-692-9669

The Meadery at Greenwich, America's oldest meadery, is located on the Hudson River in a country area between the Adirondack Mountains of New York and the Green Mountains of Vermont. The area is absolutely spectacular and is extremely popular during the fall, when thousands of New Yorkers drive northward to watch the breathtaking fall foliage.

The Meadery at Greenwich is owned by BetterBee Inc., one of North America's largest and most well-known beekeeping equipment wholesalers. They offer an entire catalog of all the things beekeepers need to raise and propagate bees. And the man in charge is Robert A. Stevens, who won a grant from the USDA recently for his company's advancement in developing microencapsulated medicines to protect honeybees.

They haven't made mead in about 3 years, but enthusiasts still talk about their mead, and they are a well-known supplier in the industry, worth noting here.

HOURS AND DIRECTIONS Mon.–Sat. 9 a.m.–5 p.m. year-round. ■ Call for directions or catalog.

Millbrook Vineyards & Winery ✬ ✬ ✬

Wing and Shunpike Rds., Millbrook, NY 12545 • Phone 800-662-9463 or 845-677-8383 • Fax 845-677-6186 • www.millbrookwine.com • shudson@millbrookwine.com

Without question, Millbrook Vineyards & Winery is the best winery in the Hudson River Valley. It has been called "the Hudson Valley's flagship winery" by the *New York Times* and "a great place to visit" by the *Wall Street Journal.* Hugh Johnson wrote: "Top Hudson River region winery. Dedicated viticulture and savvy marketing has lifted spiffy whitewashed Millbrook in big old barn into NY's firmament. Burgundian Chardonnays: splendid; Cabernet Franc can be delicious."

Karen MacNeil claimed in *The Wine Bible,* "Perhaps the most avant-garde winery in the region." They were also recommended by Felicia Sherbert in *The Unofficial Guide to Selecting Wine,* and their Chardonnays were recommended by Ed McCarthy and Mary Ewing-Mulligan in *White Wine for Dummies.* Millbrook's Cabernet Franc was featured in *Time* magazine in 2003.

Millbrook was established by former New York State commissioner of agriculture John Dyson. He established the 70 acres of vineyards (on the 170-acre estate) and the large barn that houses the operation in 1981. Dyson and his wife Kathe also own Pebble Ridge Vineyards and Estates, which is a holding company that operates a half-dozen wineries around the world. At Millbrook, Dyson grows about twenty-five varieties of European grapes, more than any other winery in the state. John Graziano, the winemaker, has done a wonderful job here since the winery opened.

If you travel to this region and can go only to one winery, go to this one. It's beautiful and it's delicious—simply the best.

Wines: $$–$$$

White Wines

Arneis Central Coast, California—A light and crisp Italian white wine. Delicious.
Castle Hill Chardonnay—A dry, full-bodied Chardonnay. Nice fruit, clean finish. ♥
Chardonnay New York State—Well balanced. Clean, crisp. ♥
Chardonnay Proprietor's Special Reserve—A rich Chardonnay. Creamy mouth feel. Citrusy ending. Very nice. ♥ ♥
Pinot Grigio Central Coast, California—Light, dry white wine. Peach and tangerine come through.
Tocai Friulano Hudson River Region, Estate Bottled—Citrus flavors and tropical fruits. Nice finish. ♥

Viognier Central Coast, California—A full-bodied white wine. Aromatic nose. Tropical fruits come through. Very nice.

Red Wines

Cabernet Franc—Big fruit up front. Plum comes through. Dry finish. ♥

Cabernet Franc Proprietor's Special Reserve—Blended with 15% Merlot and 5% Cabernet Sauvignon. Very nice. Recently featured in *Time* magazine. ♥

Hunt Country Red—A blend of Cabernet Franc, Cabernet Sauvignon, and Merlot. ♥

Pinot Noir—Smoky, medium-bodied red. Cherry comes through. Dry finish. ♥

Blush Wines

Hunt Country Rosé—Chardonnay, Pinot Noir, and Gamay Noir blend. A refreshingly dry, crisp rosé. Very nice.

REVIEWS AND AWARDS

Tocai Friulano Hudson River Region, Estate Bottled 2000: "The bright, savory 2000 edition of this Dutchess County white, made from a grape that thrives in Friuli, is a treat. It is herbal, mouth filling and reminiscent of New Zealand sauvignon blancs." —Howard G. Goldberg, *New York Times* (July 29, 2001)

"Perhaps the most avant-garde winery in the region." —Karen MacNeil, *The Wine Bible*

HOURS AND DIRECTIONS Open daily noon–5 p.m. year-round. ■ From the Taconic Pkwy., take Rte. 44 east to Rte. 82 north; proceed 3.5 miles to Shunpike Rd. Turn right; the winery is another 3 miles.

North Salem Vineyard

441 Hardscrabble Rd., N. Salem, NY 10560 • Phone 914-669-5518 • Fax 914-669-5079 • www.northsalemwine.com • naumburg@aya.yale.edu

North Salem Vineyard is the closest suburban winery to Manhattan. It was founded by Dr. George Naumburg, a practicing physician in New York, and his wife Michelle. The good doctor and his family bought the property, an old dairy farm, in 1964. They began growing grapes the next year. In 1979 the vineyards were replanted in some spots; grapes that did not perform well were weeded out. The Naumburgs renovated the barn in 1979, wherein the winery and tasting room are housed. Visitors can also use the deck to look over the beautiful and very nicely kept 18 acres of vineyards. Dr. Naumburg has been making his own wine for more than 33 years, so this winery is a labor of love. The Naumburgs make wine in stainless steel, and their wines tend to be clean and crisp. If you are in Manhattan, they are approximately an hour and fifteen minutes from Columbus Circle. What a nice little trip—and well worth it.

Wines: $–$$$

White Wines

Seyval Blanc—A dry white wine. Clean, crisp, and refreshing. Nice. ♥

Red Wines

Merlot—A dry red wine made from Long Island grapes.

Sweet Red—A sweet red wine of Foch, DeChaunac, and Chancellor.

Blush Wines

Doc's Own—A sweet, light blush wine. Nice.

HOURS AND DIRECTIONS Open Sat.–Sun. 1–5 p.m. year-round. ■ Take exit 8 off I-684 and turn right onto Hardscrabble Rd. The winery is at the intersection of rural Rte. 2, about 2.5 miles away.

Pazdar Winery / DBA Pazdar Winery

6 Laddie Rd., Scotchtown, NY 10941 • Phone and Fax 845-695-1903 • pazdar@warwick.net

David and Tracy Pazdar established the Pazdar Winery in 1995. They released their first wines in 1996. David received a B.S. in chemistry with an emphasis on winemaking from the University of Connecticut in 1984. He got his M.B.A. 10 years later and worked in the beverage industry for more than 10 years. In that time he has been a winemaker and worked for brandy distillers and juice companies.

Pazdar Winery is located in a residential area. As part of their agreement with the Town of Wallkill, David and Tracy agreed not to have a tasting room. However, on weekends during the late summer and fall months, one of them is usually at a farm market or a local liquor store where their wines can be tasted and bought. Their website keeps current lists of where their wines can be bought. Call for more information.

Wines: $-$$

White Wines

Chardonnay—Crisp white, lightly oaked. Butter and vanilla come through.
Gewürztraminer—A dry, fruity wine made in the traditional Alsace style.
Riesling—Off-dry, spicy white. Fruity. Peaches and apricots come through.

Red Wines

Chambourcin—Dry red wine. Raspberry and cherry come through.

Blush and Specialty Wines

Dragon Fire—Off-dry wine made with hot peppers! Made with habeneros from Burd Farm not far away. Interesting. Different.
Rendezvous Rosé—Fruity, off-dry blush.

Dessert and Fruit Wines

Attitude—A port made from peaches. Different. Interesting. Very sweet and rich.
Attitude II—A cherry port. Rich, sweet, thick.
Eden's Pleasure—A blend of white wines. Sweet dessert wine.
Forbidden Fruit—An off-dry spiced apple wine. Cinnamon comes through.
Seduce—A cream sherry. Aged 5 years in oak. Light, sweet, and nutty.

HOURS AND DIRECTIONS The winery is not open to the public. The wines can be found at many food and wine festivals throughout the state, in some liquor stores, and at farm markets. They are worth searching out.

Prospero Winery

134 Marble Ave., Pleasantville, NY 10570 • Phone 914-769-6870 • Fax 914-769-6832 • www.prosperowinery.qpg.com • antonellap@aol.com

Prospero Winery is one of New York's newer wineries. They produce nine different types of wine. The winery was started in 1997. Their recently opened tasting room is attractively appointed, and the staff is friendly.

Wines: $

White and Blush Wines

Chardonnay—A dry, simple white table wine.
White Zinfandel—An off-dry blush wine.

Red Wines

Merlot—A dark-cherry-colored, light dry red.

HOURS AND DIRECTIONS Open year-round Mon.–Sat. 11 a.m.–7 p.m.; Sun. noon–5 p.m. ■ Call for directions.

Regent Champagne Cellars

200 Blue Point Rd., Highland, NY • Phone 914-691-7296 • Fax 914-691-7298

Regent Champagne Cellars is the Hudson Valley's second-oldest winery. There is history here too. The winery itself is located on a rocky overlook used by the Continental Army as its second line of defense after West Point during the Revolutionary War. And the view from the winery is one of the most spectacular in the state, with beautiful vistas of the river and valley.

Regent was founded in 1904 as the Hudson Valley Wine Company. It was established by an investment banker named Alphonso Bolognesi. The current owner, Herbert Feinberg, bought the company in 1969 and renamed it in 1987. The winery's stone buildings, courtyard, clock tower, and house are arranged in the style of an Italian manor. It's really quite something to see—very picturesque.

Wines: $–$$

Fruit Wines

Almond—This is something different. Definitely worth the try, especially if you are an Amaretto lover.

Blueberry—Made from New York State blueberries.

Peach—A sweet mouthful of peaches.

Raspberry—A nice, sweet yet tart wine.

Strawberry—Sweet but not cloying. Nice tartness.

Sparkling Wines

Brut Champagne—Dry sparkling wine. Toasty. Nice finish.

HOURS AND DIRECTIONS Open weekdays, but groups may arrange weekend visits. Call for hours. Closed mid-Dec.–spring. ■ Starting from Highland, take Rte. 9W about 2 miles south and turn east onto Blue Point Rd. Follow signs to the winery.

Rivendell Winery

714 Albany Post Rd., New Paltz, NY 12561 • Phone 845-255-2494 • Fax 845-255-2290 • www.rivendellwine.com

Rivendell is a wonderful, 55-acre winery located about halfway between New York City and Albany. It has been one of the most awarded wineries in the country, with an unprecedented number of medals (more than five hundred) in national and international competitions. "If you can visit only ONE Hudson Valley Winery, make it Rivendell," declared *Time Out New York*. *Wine Spectator* agreed, declaring, "New York continues to show progress, and the wines of Rivendell show well. Highly Recommended and Best Buy!"

Whether tasting the exceptional wines, touring the facilities, walking the grounds, browsing the extensive gourmet gift shop, or tasting more than fifty other New York State wines in the newly redesigned tasting room, there is plenty to do at Rivendell. The winery was originally established in 1970 as the Gardiner Vineyard and Farms.

The Ransom family bought the vineyard in 1987. The winery is now owned and operated by Robert Ransom and Susan Wine, former owner of the legendary Quilted Giraffe, a four-star restaurant in New York City. Rivendell has two labels: Rivendell and the new line of popular wines called Libertyville Cellars.

Rivendell is a leader and a forward-thinking operation. They established in New York City a wine store named Vintage New York that carries many of the best-tasting wines from all over New York State. It is one of the most exciting visits one can make in the state. Vintage New York carries many hard-to-find brands.

Wines: $–$$$

White Wines

Chardonnay—A full-bodied white wine. Nice fruit. Rich and creamy. ♥

Dry Riesling—Made in classic German style. Fruity but nice, dry finish.

Northern Lights—Semisweet, fruity blend. Light. Excellent with summer soups or light salads. Very nice. ♥ ♥

Sarabande—Barrel-fermented Seyval Blanc and Vignoles. Crisp, dry, light.

Seyval Blanc—Cold fermentation in stainless steel and full malolactic makes this a wonderful wine. Crisp and clean. Very nice. ♥

Red Wines

Bistro Red—Semisweet red. Nice burger wine.

Merlot—100% Merlot from the North Fork of Long Island. Medium bodied, lightly oaked. Big fruit up front. Dry finish.

Southern Nights—A sweet blend of red wines. Big berry and jam flavors.

Blush Wines

Interlude Blush—Salmon-colored blush. Apples and strawberries come through.

Fruit Wines

Cranboise—A grape and cranberry blend. Light, sweet. Nice.

Dessert Wines

Apres . . . —100% Vignoles. Light, sweet dessert wine. Pears and apples come through. ♥

Late Harvest Tear of the Clouds—A late-harvest-style dessert wine. Intense fruit flavor. Apricots and honey come through. Nice acidity. Nice balance. Excellent. ♥ ♥

Other Wines

Elfen Red (a mulled Christmas wine), *Sangria, SoHo Cellars Chardonnay, SoHo Cellars Riesling, Vampire's Blood* (red wine made at midnight)

REVIEWS AND AWARDS

Dry Riesling—Gold medal, 2001 New York Wine and Food Classic.

Late Harvest Tear of the Clouds—Gold medal 3 years in a row (1990s), New York Wine and Food Classic.

"Some of the best come from Rivendell!" —Frank Prial, *New York Times*

"One of America's 26 Most Reliable Chardonnay Producers." —*Wine & Spirits*

"Outstanding." —Howard G. Goldberg, *New York Times*

HOURS AND DIRECTIONS Open daily 10 a.m.–6 p.m. year-round. ■ From New York City or Albany, take the N.Y. Thruway (I-87) to exit 18 (New Paltz). At the light off the exit turn left onto Rte. 299. Follow it all the way through the town of New Paltz, over a small bridge, and make your first left 0.5 mile past the bridge onto Libertyville/Albany Post Rd. Continue for 5 miles; the winery will be on your right.

Riverview Winery

1338 Rte. 9W, Marlboro-on-Hudson, NY 12542 • Phone 845-236-3260

Riverview, a small winery on the west side of the Hudson River, offers a wonderful view from that side of the valley. It was originally owned by the Charbot family; Tim Biancalana was the winemaker. Although the winery has gone through its ups and downs, it still has a reputation for fine sparkling wines.

Wines: $–$$

White Wines
Chardonnay—Clean, crisp version of the classic-style Chardonnay.

Red Wines
Pinot Noir—A light, medium-bodied red. Finishes dry.

Sparkling Wines
Méthode Champenoise—A dry sparkling white wine, made in the French tradition from Pinot Noir and Chardonnay. Nice.

HOURS AND DIRECTIONS Open Sat.–Sun. noon–5 p.m. year-round. ■ Call to confirm hours and directions.

Royal Kedem Winery / Royal Wine Corporation

1519 Rte. 9W, Marlboro, NY 12542 • Phone 845-236-4000 (Marlboro) or 914-795-2240 (Milton) • Fax 845-236-4370 • www.royalwine.com • service@royalwines.com

Royal Kedem Winery is owned and operated by the Royal Wine Corporation, which produces and sells wines from all over the world, including Italy, Israel, France, Scotland, Chile, Hungary, and the United States. Royal Kedem is owned and operated by the Herzog family. Founded in Czechoslovakia, the Herzogs' original corporation was the sole supplier of wine to Emperor Franz Josef I of Austria. Eugene Herzog and his family fled Germany in 1948. Eugene came to the United States and worked for the Royal Wine Company in that same year as winemaker, truck driver, and salesman. In 1958 Eugene and his son Ernest bought the company. They added the word Kedem, which in Yiddish means "forward" or "renew our days as before."

Today, Eugene's grandson Michael is winemaker and manager. Royal Kedem produces more than twenty-five kosher wines, made from local hybrid and native American grapes in varieties ranging from dry to sweet. Royal Kedem offers two sites for visiting. Marlboro-on-Hudson is where the grapes are grown and the wine is produced. The Milton operation tasting room and shop operate inside a 130-year-old train station overlooking the Hudson River.

Royal Kedem also makes or imports Alfasi, Barkan, Baron Rothschild, Bartenura, Binyamina, Carmel, Charles Lafitte, Chateau De Paraza, Chateau Giscours, Gamla, Givon, Herzog Selections, Kesser, Langer Reserves, Laurent Perrier Nicolas Feuillatte, Rashi, Rodrigues, Teal Lake, Weinstock, Zakon, and many others.

Wines: $–$$$

White Wines
Chablis—A dry, smooth white wine. Nice.
Sauterne—Medium-bodied, semisweet white wine.

Red Wines

Burgundy—A dry red wine. Nice body.

Concord Grape—A fruity and hearty, extraheavy wine.

Blush and Sweet Wines

Blush Concord—Soft, mellow, and sweet, with low alcohol.

Concord Kal—Sweet, fruity, and hearty, with low alcohol.

Malaga—A rich, full-bodied, extrasweet wine.

Marsala—Rich, full-bodied cooking and sipping wine.

Dessert Wines

Cream Sherry—A sweet wine with creamy texture and golden hue.

50th Anniversary Port—An oak-aged and blended, heavy wine.

New York State Port—Dark and thick port. Nice.

Plum—A semisweet wine with the luscious taste of plums.

Sherry—A full-bodied, rich, moderately sweet, amber wine.

Tokay—A full-bodied, sweet wine.

Other Wines

144 Blanc, 144 Blush, 144 Peach, 144 Rouge, Concord, Cream Catawba, Cream Malaga, Cream Niagara, Cream Pink, Cream Red, Cream Rosé, Cream White, and *Rouge Soft.*
Also makes Kedem Estates: *Blush Chablis, Classic Red, Classic White, Red Chablis*

HOURS AND DIRECTIONS The Marlboro facility is open year-round Fri. and Sun. 10 a.m.–5 p.m. The Milton facility is open daily, except Fri., 10 a.m.–5 p.m. ■ The Marlboro facility is on Rte. 9W a little over 1 mile north of town. Call for directions to the second location in Milton.

Warwick Valley Winery

114 Little York Rd., Warwick, NY 10990 • Phone 845-258-4858 •
Fax 845-258-4461 • www.wvwinery.com • wvwinery@warwick.com

Warwick Valley's 100-acre orchards are appropriately nestled between Mount Adam and Mount Eve. Owner Joe Grizzanti's romantic renovated post-and-beam barn now holds the tasting room and overlooks a goose pond and the orchards. In the winter months the mood is made cozier by the sight and warmth of a glowing wood-burning stove, some mulled wine, and hot chocolate. The winery and farm also holds a real, working horse stable as well. The winery was founded in 1989 and was opened to the public in 1993. Last year Warwick Valley Winery was the proud recipient of a New York State agricultural grant to create a fruit distillery industry in the state.

Warwick, like some of its upstate cousins, offers a wide range of fresh farm produce (including pick your own) and gourmet food specialties. Besides wine you'll find stocks of jams, preserves, and fruit spreads, gift baskets, and select dry goods. During the warm months graduate chefs from the nearby Culinary Institute of America produce a delicious selection of fruit pies, turnovers, and cakes. All this makes for a wonderful day trip that the whole family can enjoy.

Wines: $–$$$

White Wines

Chardonnay—Buttery mouth feel. Vanilla comes through. Nice. ♥

Riesling—Tropical fruit up front with dry finish.

Red Wines

Black Dirt Classic—Baco Noir. Medium-bodied, dry red.

Cabernet Franc—Aged in French and American oak 8–9 months. Currants and blackberries come through. Perry. Nice finish.

Pinot Noir—Oak aged in a blend of French and American oak 8–9 months. Black cherry and raspberry come through.

Dessert and Fruit Wines

Doc's Draft Hard Apple Cider—A crisp, clean hard cider. Very good. ♥ ♥ ♥

Doc's Strawberry Fields—Cider is refermented with strawberries. Very original. Very nice. ♥

New York State Red Port—Aged in French oak. Rich, deep, sweet red. Nice.

New York State White Port—A thick, sweet dessert wine.

Raspberry Serenade—A 100% raspberry wine. Wonderful dessert wine.

HOURS AND DIRECTIONS Summers Fri.–Sun. 11 a.m.–6 p.m.; Sept.–Oct. daily, 11 a.m.–6 p.m.; winter and spring Sat.–Sun. 11 a.m.–6 p.m. ■ From the New York City area heading north on the N.Y. Thruway (I-87), get off at exit 15A (Sloatsburg) and turn left onto Rte. 17. Go north 7 miles and turn left onto Rte. 17A; continue approximately 17 miles into Warwick. At the intersection of Rtes. 17A and 94, turn left onto 94 south. Proceed on 94 for 0.3 mile and turn right onto Rte. 1A. Travel west approximately 6 miles and turn right onto Little York Rd. The winery is 1 mile down on the right.

West Park Wine Cellars

Rte. 9W, West Park, NY 12493 • Phone 914-384-6709

Owners Louis Fiore and Nelda Gerner purchased a former dairy farm operated by the Christian Brothers Order from Ireland and turned it into a winery. When they founded West Park Wine Cellars in 1983, their idea was to establish a wine estate for the exclusive production of vintage-dated Chardonnay wines. And that's all they do, but they do it well. On site, they also have a self-guided tour that starts with a 10-minute video that illustrates all phases of grape growing and winemaking. The gift shop is nicely appointed and offers a wide range of imaginative items.

Wines: $–$$

White Wines

Chardonnay—A nice, dry white wine with tropical fruits up front and a clean, dry finish.

Chardonnay Barrel Reserve—A full-bodied white wine with vanilla. Creamy mouth feel with dry finish. Nice.

HOURS AND DIRECTIONS Apr. 1–Dec. 1 Sat.–Sun. 10:30 a.m.–5 p.m. ■ From New York City or Albany, take the N.Y. Thruway (I-87) to New Paltz (exit 18), turn right (east) onto Rte. 299, and go approximately 5 miles to Rte. 9W. Turn left (north) onto 9W and go approximately 2.8 miles to the winery, located south of the town of West Park.

Whitecliff Vineyard & Winery

331 McKinstry Rd., Gardiner, NY 12525 • Phone 845-255-4613 • Fax 845-255-0628 • www.whitecliffwine.com

The 70-acre Whitecliff Vineyard & Winery, just 60-miles from New York City, is one of the newest vineyards in the Hudson Valley region. Opposite the Shawangunk Cliffs, the vineyards offer spectacular vistas of the valley and cliffs. From the tasting deck, all one can do is look in awe. The cliffs also share their name with the Shawangunk Wine Trail (of which this winery is a part), which includes a small section of the Hudson Valley.

Michael Migliore bought this property in 1979 while he was still a college student at SUNY–New Paltz and knew he wanted to grow grapes. A few years later he met his wife Yancey Stanforth, who shared in that dream. A former engineer at IBM, Michael is now the winemaker and manager. Today, they have 27 acres planted to vines.

Michael and Yancey's vineyard and winery has been featured on the cover of *Hudson Valley* magazine and in *Country Living* magazine. The winery also exhibits local artists' works. A visit to this lovely place is a treat, both to the eye and to the senses. The gift shop is fun and inviting, and the wines are tasty. You can also sometimes find Michael and Yancey exhibiting at farmers' markets around the state.

Wines: $–$$

White Wines

Awosting White—80% Seyval blended with Riesling and Vignoles. A nice, light white with nice fruit and dry finish. Nice.

Chardonnay—Dry, full-bodied Chardonnay. Barrel fermented, aged *sur lie*. Nice vanilla and butterscotch flavors. Nice dry finish.

Riesling—Sweet up-front flavors end in pucker. Very nice.

Red Wines

Cabernet Franc—Rich red wine with deep color. Nice tannins. Dry finish.

Merlot—90% Merlot, 10% Cabernet Franc. Full-bodied, deep red wine. Nice fruit. Cherries come through. Dry finish.

Blush Wines

Rosé—100% Gamay Noir. Traditional French-style rosé. Dry, clean, crisp.

REVIEWS AND AWARDS

"On the west side of the Hudson you'll find the Shawangunk Wine Trail . . . the trail's best winery is its newest, Whitecliff Vineyard."

—AAA Automobile Club of New York

"Open since 1999, this is the youngest of the wineries in the area. Still, husband-and-wife team Yancey Stanforth-Migliore and Michael Migliore know what they're doing." —Carole Braden, *Time Out New York*

HOURS AND DIRECTIONS Open Memorial Day weekend through Oct. Thurs.–Fri. and Sun. noon–5 p.m., Sat. 11:30 a.m.–6 p.m. Open weekends Nov.–Dec. and Apr. 20–Memorial Day. ■ From New York City or Albany, take the N.Y. Thruway to exit 18 (New Paltz). Turn left onto Rte. 299. Drive through the town, across the Wallkill River, and bear left onto Libertyville Rd. (Rte. 7) at the fork just past Wallkill View Farm. Stay on Libertyville Rd. for 6 miles to the junction with Rtes. 44 and 55, where it becomes Bruynswick Rd. Continue another 1.9 miles and turn left onto McKinstry Rd. Whitecliff Vineyard is 0.8 mile along on the right-hand side.

Windsor Vineyards

26 Western Ave., Marlboro, NY 12542 • Phone 845-236-4233

No longer an operating winery, this is now a shop for Windsor Vineyards' California wines. However, while the wines are not from New York State, Windsor Vineyards made a name for itself in a time when few wineries relied on tourist trade or walk-in traffic. Despite its enormous popularity, its distribution remains largely intact—Windsor still relies on selling directly to the consumer as the base of its business.

The company was founded in 1959 by famed vintner and entrepreneur Rodney Strong, who began the business by selling his wines right there in the building where he made them. And the business grew. Windsor was the nation's first mail-order winery. The Klein family bought the winery in 1989 and raised the profile of the company tremendously. The company is now owned by Beringer Blass Worldwide. They were voted America's no. 1 winery in 1998, 1999, and 2000. And their wines consistently receive high ratings from numerous magazines, including *Wine Enthusiast*.

The wines are excellent. They include Blanc de Noir Champagne, Brut Champagne, Cabernet Sauvignon, Carignane, Chardonnay, Chenin Blanc, Extra Dry Champagne, French Colombard, Fumé Blanc, Gewürztraminer, Grenache Rosé, Johannisberg Riesling, Meritage, Merlot, Muscat Canelli Late Harvest, Nonalcoholic Champagne, Petite Syrah, Pinot Noir, Port, Rosé du Soleil, Semillon, Sherry, Shiraz, Syrah, White Zinfandel, and Zinfandel.

Wines: $$–$$$

Recommended Wines

Cabernet Sauvignon, Paso Robles
Cabernet Sauvignon, Sonoma County, Signature Series
Chardonnay, North Coast
Chardonnay, Russian River Valley, Vintner's Reserve, Private Reserve
Fumé Blanc, Mendocino County, Vintner's Reserve
Merlot, Dry Creek Valley, 40th Anniversary Reserve
Muscat Canelli, Late Harvest, Murphy Ranch, Private Reserve

REVIEWS AND AWARDS

Carignane 1996: 89 points — *Wine Enthusiast*
Merlot 1995, Shelton Signature Series: 90 points — *Wine Enthusiast*
Preston Ranch 1996, Private Reserve: 86 points — *Wine Enthusiast*

HOURS AND DIRECTIONS Open year-round Mon.–Sat. 10 a.m.–5 p.m., Sun. noon–5 p.m.
■ Call for directions.

OTHER HUDSON RIVER VALLEY WINERIES

Allied Wine Corp.: 121 Main St. S., Fallsburg, NY 12779 • Phone 914-434-3746

Ashkol Wine Co.: 33-49 Mulberry St., Middletown, NY 10940 •
Phone 914-344-0090 • Fax 914-341-1270

Cagnasso Winery: Rte. 9W, Marlboro, NY 12542 • Phone 914-236-4630

Galenwood Estates: 232 Church Rd., Putnam Valley, NY 10579 •
Phone 212-526-9469 • costello1@mindspring.com

CENTRAL NEW YORK
AND LAKE ONTARIO

Ashley Lynn Winery / Leon's Farm Market and Hurlbut Orchards

4142 Rte. 104, Mexico, NY 13114 • Phone 315-963-3262 • lhurlbut@excite.com

Ashley Lynn Winery is owned and operated by Leroy and Pat Hurlbut. The Hurlbut family has been making apple wines for family and friends for more than 40 years. Hurlbut Apple Orchards is located on the southeastern shore of Lake Ontario in the small town of New Haven. Established in 1928, on 130 acres of rolling farmland, Hurlbut Orchards has been a premier producer of McIntosh and Cortland apples. The winery is named for Leroy and Pat's granddaughter. It's a family-run farm; sons Leon and Craig are partners on the winery, which was established in 1999.

Leon's Farm Market is the home of the Ashley Lynn Winery. The wine is pressed, aged, blended, and bottled at this location. All the apples used are grown locally. Wine tasting is conducted daily. The farm market also sells flowers, home and garden products, and gift baskets. It's a fun and wonderful visit, and a great visit during the fall foliage time of year—it's so wonderful you think places like this don't exist any more.

Wines: $–$$

Apple Wines

Apple—A dry, light white wine. Refreshing.

Apple Cherry—A apple/cherry blend. A nice dessert wine.

Apple Cranberry—Blend of apple wine with a hint of cranberry. Very nice.

Apple Grape—A refreshing, sweet blend.

Apple White Grape—A light, sweet apple/grape wine. Nice.

REVIEWS AND AWARDS

Apple Cranberry—Silver medal, New York State Fair Wine Competition.

Apple Grape—Silver medal, New York State Fair Wine Competition.

Apple White Grape—Silver medal, New York State Fair Wine Competition.

HOURS AND DIRECTIONS Open daily May–Dec. 10 a.m.–6 p.m. ■ Leon's Farm Market is located 5 miles from the farm on Rte. 104 between the town of Mexico and Oswego.

Bear Pond Winery

2515 Rte. 28, Oneonta, NY 13820 • Phone 607-643-0294 •
Fax 607-643-0219 • www.bearpondwines.com

Bear Pond was founded by Joan and Hank Nicols. Hank provides systems support at Bassett Hospital in Cooperstown. Bear Pond likes to brag that they are midway between the Baseball Hall of Fame in Cooperstown and the Soccer Hall of Fame in Oneonta, which makes it a convenient stop as well as a great destination. The winery was founded in 1999, and some wines from its original release were made at Brotherhood Winery while its grapevines were still maturing.

"The first wines we made onsite to sell sold out almost immediately," Hank told Doug Blackburn of the *Albany Times Union* (June 28, 2000). "Our production probably will never be able to keep up with demand." The Nicolses have winemaking in their blood. The family's history of winemaking goes back more than six generations. Great-grandfather Hans Barth earned his living making wine in Weinsberg, Germany, in the shadow of the Castle Weibertreu, for whom the Castle Collection is now named.

They make three different sets of wines. The Bear Pond Winery line of wines is made up of wines made from native American grapes and hybrids. The Castle Collection is a cross of wines of German traditional style and some French traditional style. And the sporting wines tend to be a combination of hybrids and vinifera. Go and sample some—it's worth the trip.

Wines: $–$$

The Bear Family Selection

Baby Bear—Made from Chelois grapes. A young, light, dry red wine.

Goldilocks Favorite—Alcohol-free, light blend of Concord and Niagara grape juice.

Grizzly Red—A hearty, Burgundy-style, dry red.

Polar White—A Sauterne-style Niagara-grape dessert wine. Nice balance.

The Castle Collection

Castle Cabernet—A dry, deep Cabernet aged in oak 2 years.

Hohenzolleren Pinot Noir—A medium-bodied, dry red wine.

Neushawanstein White—A semidry blush. Fruity and crisp.

Weibertreu White—An off-dry Johannisberg Riesling white wine. Very nice.

Sporting Wines

Baseball Red—Dry, full-bodied ruby red.

Goal—A dry, clean, crisp Seyval Blanc.

Grand Slam Champagne—Off-dry sparkling wine.

Soccer Ball White—A dry, white blend of Chardonnay and Seyval Blanc. Crisp. Nice.

HOURS AND DIRECTIONS Open daily Memorial Day–Labor Day, noon–7 p.m.; open Sept.–Oct. and Apr.–May Sat.–Sun. noon–6 p.m. ■ From points east (New England), take I-90 west (N.Y. Thruway) past Albany. Take exit 25A onto I-88 west, then exit 17 to Rte. 28 north. Proceed 3.3 miles to Bear Pond Winery on your left. ■ From points south (New York City, New Jersey), take I-87 (N.Y. Thruway) north, which becomes I-90 west near Albany; then follow the directions above. ■ From western New York State and beyond, take I-90 east to exit 28 (Herkimer) to Rte. 28 south through Cooperstown; continue 12 miles to Bear Pond Winery on your right.

Behling's Spookhill Farms

12139 U.S. 11, Adams Center, NY 13606 • Phone 315-583-6181 • Fax 315-583-6441 • behling@gisco.net

The Behling family has harvested apples and other produce from its 200-acre farm for generations. And it still operates as a working farm. In the fall they offer hayrides, wagon tours around the farm to the pumpkin fields, carnival rides, a fantasy land with clowns, a living maze, and a Saturday night haunted hayride, among other things.

And they make wine. They offer fourteen different varieties of fruit wines. The gift shop also has fresh produce, jams, and other food specialties like gourmet cheeses, and local crafts.

Wines: $–$$

Fruit Wines

Apple—Like a bite of a fresh apple. Off-dry. Nice.

Strawberry—Nice mouth feel. Fresh strawberries come through. Nice.

HOURS AND DIRECTIONS Winery tours available May 1–Dec. 25. Call for directions.

Charlotte's Vineyard

301 Hubble Hollow Rd., Cooperstown, NY 13326 • Phone 607-547-2412 • www.charlottesvineyard.com

Ed Olsen's mother's name was Charlotte. And Charlotte always wanted to turn the family's land into a winery. Ed and his wife Lennie made that dream come true, but the dream was realized too late, as the winery finally blossomed after she passed on. And so they named it in honor of her. If you are going to Cooperstown to see the Hall of Fame, you must definitely stop by and see Charlotte's Vineyard. The little red house, barn, and outbuildings, trimmed in white and set against the beautiful rolling New York countryside, and the small pond that reflects the clear blue sky—all transport you back to a Norman Rockwell or Winslow Homer painting. It's about as American as one can get.

Ed, Lennie, and Ed's dad all work hard on this labor of love, and it's worth the visit. The wines are tasty, and it's a fun way to cap off the day. In the summertime especially, Cooperstown, a small place, can get somewhat congested. This is a great way to blow off a little steam and reenergize away from the maddening crowds.

Charlotte's Vineyard makes nice red and white table wines at affordable prices.

Wines: $

HOURS AND DIRECTIONS Apr. 27–May 26 Sat.–Sun. noon–6 p.m.; May 27–fall Thurs.–Sun. noon–5 p.m. ■ From downtown Cooperstown and the Baseball Hall of Fame, starting from Main St. at the stop light, turn left onto Chestnut St. (Rte. 28). Turn left onto Susquehanna Ave. (County Rte. 52). Continue on Susquehanna about 1 mile past the Clark Sports Center on your right. Cross the small bridge to your right and then bear left to continue on County Rte. 52, up and over Murphy Hill to the intersection of County Rte. 52 and Rte. 166. Turning left onto Rte. 166, drive approximately 4 miles to Hubble Hollow Rd. on your left. Turn left onto it, and Charlotte's Vineyard will be on your left after approximately 1 mile.

Giancarelli Brothers Winery

10252 Shortcut Rd., Weedsport, NY 13166 • Phone 315-626-2830 • Fax 315-626-2650

Giancarelli Brothers Winery produces small batches of first-quality dessert wines using fruits and berries grown by SG&S Farms. SG&S Farms was established in 1937. Since SG&S is a working farm, they offer fruits and vegetables for sale as well as offering a "U-Pick" program, which is fun for family outings.

The winery uses fruits grown on the SG&S Farms as well as fruits and grapes from neighboring farms. The farm offers a wonderful shop filled with produce and food treats. The brand-new tasting room is now also open.

Wines: $–$$

Fruit Wines

Blueberry—Dessert wine made from fresh-picked blueberries.

Elderberry—A sweet wine, lighter than the rest. Nice version of classic wine.

Raspberry—Dessert wine made from raspberries. Nice.

Strawberry—Dessert wine made from strawberries.

HOURS AND DIRECTIONS Open June–Sept. daily 8 a.m.–8 p.m.; Oct.–May Thurs.–Sun. 1–4 p.m. ■ Call for directions.

Johnson Estate Winery

8419 W. Main Rd., Westfield, NY 14787 • Phone 716-326-2191 • Fax 716-326-2131 • www.johnsonwinery.com • jwinery@cecomet.net

Currently, Johnson Estate Winery is the oldest continuing exclusively estate winery in New York. It was established in 1961. The winery likes to point out that all the grapes used to make their wines are grown within 3,000 feet of the winery itself.

The winery was founded by Fred Johnson, Jr., Tony Johnson, and Lilla Behm. Winemaker Mark R. Lancaster and vineyard manager Charles Miller work hard to make handcrafted wines from this 130-acre, 90,000-gallon-capacity estate.

Wines: $–$$$

White Wines

Chautauqua Blanc—Semisweet white wine. Refreshing.

Seyval Blanc—A crisp, fruity, dry white table wine.

Vidal Blanc—Off-dry, light white wine.

Red Wines

Chambourcin—A velvety, deep, dry red wine.

Chancellor Noir—Medium-bodied, dark red wine. Raspberries and elderberries come through.

Chautauqua Rouge—Light-bodied, off-dry, Beaujolais-style red wine.

Ives Noir—A semisweet red wine.

Blush Wines

Dry Rosé—A dry blush in the best French tradition.

Dessert Wines

Liebestropfchen—Means "Little Love Drops." A rich, fruity dessert wine.

Vidal Ice Wine "Sweet Dreams"—A rich, complex dessert wine. Honey and apricots come through. ♥

HOURS AND DIRECTIONS Open daily 10 a.m.–6 p.m. year-round. ■ Located 2 miles west of the village of Westfield on Rte. 20. Visitors using I-90 should take exit 60, turning left onto Rte. 394 toward Westfield/Mayville. At the traffic light in Westfield, turn right (west) onto Rte. 20. The winery is 3 miles from the light on the south side of the road.

Martin's Honey Farm and Meadery

14699 Center Rd., Sterling, NY 13156 • Phone 315-947-5965 • Fax 315-947-6235 • martinhf@zlink.net

George Martin has been handling bees for 30 years. A maker of honey, he and his sons Ed and Bill established the meadery in August of 1999. They take good care of their bees—very good care. Every fall, as winter begins to set in, George and his sons fill a tractor trailer with more than two thousand beehives and transport them down to

Florida: they go south in November and come back in April. Talk about pampered. George says he's been taking bees south for the winter since 1988, and it's stood him in good stead. They put the same kind of care into their award-winning wines and meads. They take it all very seriously, and you'll taste the difference.

Wines: $–$$

White Wines

Seyval Blanc—A nice version of a Seyval Blanc.

Red Wines

Dry Chancellor—Full-bodied, dry red wine.

Blush Wines

Lake Effect Blush—A cranberry/apple blush. Refreshing. Nice. ♥

Fruit and Honey Wines

Cranberry Harvest—Tart, 100% cranberry wine made from New York State cranberries.

Golden Delicious Apple—Golden Delicious apples. Great nose. Nice, refreshing.

Johnny Apple Mead—An apple/honey wine blend. Very nice. Made for desserts. Great for mulling. Very nice. ♥

Just Peachy—Apricots and peaches come through. Not cloying. Nice balance.

Pear Perfection—Bartlett pear wine. Big pears up front, nice finish.

Plum Passion—Sweet 40% plum and 60% honey wine. Different. Interesting.

Semi-Sweet Honey—A wine with strong tones of honey. Nice.

Strawberry Sunset—Nice nose. Tart strawberries. Nice.

Traditional Dry Honey—A dry, crisp wine. Honey and citrus come through.

Traditional Sweet Honey—A warm, sweet honey wine. Great mouth feel. Nice.

HOURS AND DIRECTIONS Open mid-Apr.–Dec. Fri.–Sun. 11 a.m.–6 p.m. (till 8 p.m. July–Aug.). ■ Call for directions.

Montezuma Winery

2981 Auburn Rd., Seneca Falls, NY 13148 • Phone 315-568-8190 • Fax 315-568-8607

This is a boutique winery, the only winery in Seneca Falls. They recently showed at the New York Finger Lakes Wine Festival. The wine shop offers all kinds of trinkets and other products from local makers, including the Vineyard Series of handcrafted pottery from Kim Marie Fine Pottery.

Wines: $

White Wines

Seyval Blanc—An off-dry white. Vanilla bean and melon come through.

Red Wines

Chancellor—Full-bodied, dry red wine.

Fruit and Honey Wines

Cherry—A tart cherry wine.

Blueberry—Not tasted.

Mead—A dry, crisp wine. Floral nose. Melon comes through.

REVIEWS AND AWARDS

Blueberry—Silver medal, 2002 Finger Lakes International Wine Competition.

HOURS AND DIRECTIONS Call for hours and directions.

North Country Apple Winery

10583 Slaght Rd., Wolcott, NY 14590 • Phone 315-594-2248

Linda and Mason Yancy's North Country Apple Winery is affiliated with North Huron Cider Mills. They have been blending different apple juices for over 70 years through two generations. An environmentally friendly operation, they are conscious of their agricultural legacy to subsequent generations. Their ciders are available not only at the winery but also at the Syracuse farmers' market, where North Country Apple Winery shares a booth with North Huron Cider Mills. Whether you go to the winery or the farmers' market, you won't be disappointed.

Wines: $

Apple Wines

Cherry Apple—A tart blush made from apples and cherries. Nice. ♥

Cran Apple—Semisweet apple wine. Tart. Nice.

Grandma's Hard Cider—This is some of that "Ol' time farm beverage." Aged in rum barrels for a smooth presentation. Nice.

Grape Apple—Semisweet, light wine.

HOURS AND DIRECTIONS Open Sat.–Sun. 11 a.m.–6 p.m. year-round. ■ From the Geneva exit off the N.Y. Thruway, go north on Rte. 14 until you reach Rte. 104. Cross over Rte. 104 into Alton. (You will remain on Rte. 14 only 1 block in Alton). Turn right at your first light/stop sign in Alton onto Ridge Rd. Remain on Old Ridge Rd. about 5–7 miles. Turn left onto ∗. Huron Rd. Go through one stop sign and look for Slaght Rd. about 2 miles past the stop sign. Turn right onto Slaght Rd. North Country Apple Winery will be about 100 yards up this road on your left.

Onondaga Winery, Inc.

8697 Brewerton Rd. (U.S. 11), Cicero, NY 13039 • Phone 315-698-0855

Oneida's not a Finger Lake, but fourteen New York wines are created in Cicero at Onondaga Winery. Sip a few samples and smile. Browse through a gift shop stocked with wine-related gift items and made-to-order gift baskets. Twice a week, Onondaga Winery's bottling process is on display. It's fascinating if you can catch it, but there's no set schedule. Onondaga Winery imports all its grapes from New York State. They offer a wide range of wines, from fruit wines to native American grapes to hybrids and classic vinifera. All their wines are pure 100% New York.

Wines: $–$$

White Wines

Chardonnay—Clean, crisp, with hint of apples.

Seyval—A dry, clean, crisp white wine.

Vignoles—A light, sweet white wine.

Red Wines

Baco Noir—A soft, medium-bodied red.

Pinot Noir—Medium-bodied, light, dry red.

Blush and Dessert Wines

Café—Semisweet blush wine. Nice.

Cherry—A deep, sweet mouthful of cherries.

HOURS AND DIRECTIONS Call for hours. ■ One mile north of Cicero on Rte. 11.

St. Benedict Wines

701 Rte. 79, Windsor, NY 13865 • Phone 607-655-2366

Located 15 miles southeast of Binghamton in Windsor, St. Benedict Wines is Broome County's first winery. It is nestled in the Susquehanna River Valley in the beautiful southern tier of New York State. St. Benedict Wines is operated by the Benedictine nuns of Transfiguration Monastery; they got into the wine business after their home-made raspberry wine became such a hit with the locals. The wine shop offers small gifts and books as well as the wonderful—dare we say heavenly?—wines. St. Benedict is one of the little, hidden gems of New York Sate winemaking.

Wines: $

White Wines

White Table Wine—A light, semisweet white wine. Clean, refreshing.

Red Wines

Red Table Wine—Full-bodied, dry red wine.

Sherries and Fruit Wines

Monastery Reserve Cherry—A cherry/grape blend. Refreshing.

St. Placid Raspberry—A refreshing mouthful of sweet raspberries.

Susquehanna Gold Peach—A luxurious peach wine. Sweet but nicely balanced. One of the best peach wines we've had. ♥ ♥

HOURS AND DIRECTIONS Call for hours and directions.

Stone Age Winery

1013 Tulip St., Liverpool, NY 13088 • Phone 315-457-6718 • www.stoneagewinery.com

Stone Age Winery currently stands where another winery once stood. The vines are 100 years old and continue to produce beautiful fruit. Robert Mattuci founded his vineyard on April 1, 1999. He called the winery Stone Age because he uses simple, old-time methods that were used by his grandfather and great-grandfathers. Mattuci's philosophy is to create the tastiest wine in the most natural way possible.

The winery currently does not take visitors, as it is not yet set up with a tasting room, etcetera. However, Mattuci sells his wines, like other makers, at the Syracuse farmers' market as well as other locations, including the Finger Lakes Wine Festival, where we first found them.

Wines: $

White Wines

Wedding—Pink Catawba/Cayuga light white. Nice.

Red Wines

Cabernet Franc—A medium-bodied, dry red.

Cabernet Franc–Chambourcin—A deep, dry red wine. Full bodied. Nice.

Rougeon-DeChaunac—A nice, deep, off-dry red. Probably the only off-dry red we keep cellared at our home. Suggest decanting 3–6 hours before serving for maximum flavor. ♥

REVIEWS AND AWARDS

Cabernet Franc–Chambourcin—Bronze medal, Indiana State Fair Indy International Wine Competition.

HOURS AND DIRECTIONS Stone Age wines are available Saturday mornings at the farmers' market in Syracuse.

Thorpe Vineyard, Inc.

8150 Chimney Heights Blvd., Wolcott, NY 14590 • Phone 315-594-2502

Thorpe Vineyard is Wayne County's only farm winery on Lake Ontario. It is also Lake Ontario's oldest winery; the first vintage was in 1988. Fumie and Jack Thorpe produce a wide selection of wines, from classic European varieties to innovative New World blends, and they sell it from their wine shop, which overlooks Lake Ontario.

Thorpe Vineyard is located less than a mile from the incredibly beautiful Chimney Bluffs State Park, after which the Thorpes have named a series of wines. It a beautiful part of the world. I especially recommend visiting this part of the country during harvest and fall foliage time. The cider is good, the wines are wonderful, and the air is intoxicating.

Wines: $–$$

White Wines

Cayuga White—A light, sweet white wine. Nice.

Chardonnay—Dry and not oaked. A fruity, lighter style. Clean, crisp. Very nice.

Riesling—An off-dry version of the classic German grape.

Vidal—Crisp, refreshing, and dry.

Red Wines

Baco Noir—A medium-bodied red wine, tinged with Pinot Noir. Nice.

Chancellor—Ruby red dry wine.

Marechal Foch—A light red wine, off-dry.

Pinot Noir—Lightly oaked, medium-bodied red.

Blush Wines

Evening Glow—A dry, oaked rosé blend of Chardonnay and Pinot Noir.

Fialka—Sweet blush wine.

Fruit Wines

Harvest Moon—A tart apple wine. Clean, refreshing.

HOURS AND DIRECTIONS Open May–June and Sept.–Oct. Fri.–Sun. noon–6 p.m.; July–Aug. Thurs.–Sun. noon–6 p.m.; Nov.–Dec. Sat.–Sun. noon–5 p.m. ■ Call for directions.

OTHER CENTRAL NEW YORK WINERIES

Black Bear Farm Winery: 248 County Rte. 1, Chenango Forks, NY 13746 • Phone 607-656-9863

Colebrook Country Wines: 562 Colebrook Rd., Gansevoort, NY 12831

Hemp Wine America: 56 Walnut St., Binghamton, NY 13905 • Phone 888-520-9463 • Fax 607-766-0222 • info@hempwine.com

FINGER LAKES: CAYUGA

Americana Vineyards

4367 E. Covert Rd., Interlaken, NY 14847 • Phone 607-387-6801 •
Fax 607-387-3852 • pricklysoft.com/americana • Wineinny@aol.com

Founded in 1981 by James and MaryAnne Treble, and now owned by former computer programmer Joseph Gober, Jr., Americana Vineyards is the second-oldest winery on Lake Cayuga, and produces about 52,000 bottles a year—but quietly. One of the least self-promotional wineries, Americana sells its wines only at the winery itself, amid a rustic and rural setting that features an Adirondack-style gazebo built of fieldstone—a lovely place to picnic while visiting.

You can visit the winery's fermentation room and tasting room, and browse a number of local products at the small gift shop. The winery also sponsors events year-round and is a regular participant in Ithaca's Cayuga Wine Trail Wine and Herb Festival. Their contribution in 2002—a salad of fresh greens topped with a summer vinaigrette made with their Americana Indian Summer wine—was a big hit!

Wines: $-$$

White Wines

Americana White—A Catawba white wine. Citrus overtones. Nice.

Cayuga White—A light, semidry white.

Chardonnay—Fermented and aged in European oak. Pear and butter flavors come through.

Finger Lakes Chablis—A blend of Chardonnay and Cayuga. Light, dry, and tasty. Nice citrus. ♥

Red Wines

Baco Noir—Baco Noir made in the best Burgundy tradition. Big berries. Smooth finish. Nice.

Crystal Lake—Niagara red wine. Sweet. They say it's "Grape juice with a kick." Serve cold.

Indian Summer—Semisweet Baco Noir–Catawba red wine.

November Harvest—A fruity sipping red made at the end of the season from a variety of grapes. They call it their "Monday Night Football Wine." Good with pizza and burgers.

Revolutionary Red—Semidry red blend. Cherry and cranberry come through.

Blush Wines

Americana Blush—A light blush wine with the color and taste of peaches. Different, and very nice.

Dessert Wines

Sweet Rosie—A strawberry-like dessert wine made with the Ives grape. Different. Nice.

HOURS AND DIRECTIONS Open daily Mar.–Dec., Mon.–Sat. 10 a.m.–5:30 p.m., Sun. noon–5:30 p.m.; Jan.–Mar. open Sat. 10 a.m.–5:30 p.m., Sun. noon–5:30 p.m. ■ Take Rte. 89 north out of Ithaca and turn left onto E. Covert Rd. a few miles past Taughannock Falls. There will be a Cayuga Wine Trail sign for Americana Vineyards. It's a mile up E. Covert Rd. on the right.

Bellwether Hard Cider

1609 Trumansburg Rd. (Rte. 96), Ithaca, NY 14850 • Phone 607-27-CIDER • www.cidery.com

Bill and Cheryl Barton's Bellwether Hard Cider Company, located smack in the middle of the Cayuga Wine Trail just outside Ithaca, creates a number of highly regarded ciders that are served in numerous restaurants, including the famed vegetarian Moosewood Restaurant.

Ciders: $–$$

Cherry St.—A light, salmon-pink, bubbling cider. Slightly sweet and made with New York State cherries. Delicious. Almost like a dessert wine. ♥

Liberty Spy Hard Cider—Handcrafted cider made from Liberty Spy apples. Crisp, sparkling, and refreshing.

Original Hard Cider—Pale, golden, medium-bodied cider. Slightly sparkling, bone dry, and sophisticated, with fine bubbles and a slight tanginess. ♥

HOURS AND DIRECTIONS Fri.–Sun. noon–6 p.m. year-round and by appointment. ■ Call for directions.

Cayuga Ridge Estate Winery

6800 Rte. 89, Ovid, NY 14521 • Phone 607-869-5158 • Fax 607-869-3412 • www.cayugaridge.com • crew@cayugaridge.com

Inhabiting a pair of old-fashioned working farm barns, Cayuga Ridge is a bit on the plain side, presentationwise, but the same cannot be said of their wines, all handcrafted by owner/winemaker Tom Challen, formerly of Paul Masson. You can taste the care.

Tom and his wife Susie bought Cayuga Ridge in 1991 from former Clarkson University president Robert Plane and his wife Mary (who'd opened it in 1980 as the Planes Cayuga Vineyard). In addition to making their own wines, Tom and Susie also rent out vines (in lots of 10, 20, or 30) to visitors who tend, prune, and harvest their own grapes for home winemaking purposes. The winery offers seminars on pruning, tying, thinning, and harvesting, and at the end of the year you can either take the grapes home and make your own wine or have the winery create a special microbatch vintage from your grapes. It's a really great idea and has attracted quite a bit of interest. We wish we lived closer!

Wines: $–$$$

White Wines

Barrel-Fermented Chardonnay—The most popular of their whites. Made in the classic Burgundy tradition. Nice fruits. Vanilla.

Cranberry Essence—A crisp white blended with a refreshing cranberry essence. Semisweet, but refreshing.

Duet—A surprising, semisweet blend of Cayuga White and Vignoles. Nice.

Riesling—Off-dry and crisp, with a nice bouquet and a clean finish.

Stainless Steel Chardonnay—Fermented and kept only in stainless steel, with no barrel aging. This results in a full, fresh, clean, crisp wine.

Red Wines

Cabernet Franc—A dry, oak-aged red. Mature.

Chancellor Reserve—A dry red aged in American oak.

Pinot Noir—A light, dry red with some cherry flavor. Soft, with a nice balance and a
    dry finish.

Blush Wines

Trio—An off-dry rosé blend. Light and refreshing, with some sweetness. Nice.

Dessert Wines

Late Harvest Solo—Rich, sweet dessert wine. Apricots and honey. Very nice.

REVIEWS AND AWARDS

Cayuga White—Gold medal, 2000 Grand Harvest Awards.

Chancellor Reserve—Bronze medal, 2000 Grand Harvest Awards.

HOURS AND DIRECTIONS Open daily 11 a.m.–5 p.m. mid-May–mid-Nov.; Sat.–Sun.
noon–4 p.m. mid-Nov.–mid-May. ■ Located approximately midway up Rte. 89, which
runs along the bank of Lake Cayuga. ■ From Ithaca, take Rte. 89 north. The winery
will be on your right about 10–15 minutes after you pass the town of Sheldrake. ■
From Seneca, take Rte. 89 south. The winery will be on your left. (If you come to the
town of Sheldrake, you've gone too far.)

Frontenac Point Vineyard

9501 Rte. 89, Trumansburg, NY 14886 • Phone 607-387-9619 •
www.frontenacpoint.com • contactus@frontenacpoint.com

Jim and Carol Doolittle planted the first Frontenac Point vines in 1978 and sold their
first wines to the public 4 years later. Twenty-some years later, it's impossible to think
of them as anything but winemakers—a view their younger selves must have shared.
A former New York State Department of Agriculture employee, Jim knew that excellent
fruit was the basis for all good and prosperous winemaking, and was intimately
involved in the passage of New York State's Farm Winery Act of 1976. On the other
side, Carol edited the journal of the American Wine Society. Now that's a team! Don't
you just want to buy wine from them already?

Frontenac is known for making barrel-fermented dry red wines, which account for
more than half of their production.

Wines: $–$$$

White Wines

Chardonnay—A dry Chardonnay aged in new oak. Tropical fruits. Dry finish. Very nice.

Frontenac White—An off-dry blend of whites, featuring Seyval. Fruity, with citrus
    flavors.

Riesling—A dry white in the classic Alsatian tradition. Delicate. Nice.

Vidal Blanc—A light, off-dry white. Apples and melons come through.

Red Wines

Chambourcin—A nice, deep red wine with fruit and a dry finish.

Chelois Noir—Light-bodied red. Aged 2 years in oak and 2 years in the bottle. Nice
    fruit, dry finish.

Frontenac Red—A proprietary blend of four grapes and two vintages. Black cherries
    come through.

Pinot Noir—A nice, dry red with a deep garnet color.

Proprietor's Reserve—A blend of three grapes, highlighted by Pinot Noir. Aged 22
    months in oak. Big fruit; blackberries come through. Dry finish.

Blush Wines

Chateau Doolittle—An off-dry rosé with the Doolittle family crest on the label.

HOURS AND DIRECTIONS Fri.–Sat. 10 a.m.–4 p.m., Sun. noon–4 p.m., May–Nov. ■ From the north, take the N.Y. Thruway to exit 41; pick up Rte. 318 to Rte. 89 south. Take the gravel road to the winery when you see the sign ■ From the south, take I-81 from Binghamton to the Whitney Point exit. Take Rte. 79 into Ithaca and pick up Rte. 89 north. Take the gravel road to the winery when you see the sign.

Goose Watch Winery　　　　　　　　　　✿

5480 Rte. 89, Romulus, NY 14541 • Phone 315-549-2599 •
Fax 315-549-2596 • www.goosewatch.com • goosewatch@flare.net

On Lake Cayuga, Goose Watch is a picture-perfect little winery with a beautiful century-old gray and white barn set just right to offer a view of the vineyards from its deck. There's also a breathtaking chestnut grove that you can walk through, and even a trout farm. You won't want to leave, especially after you taste the wines inside.

The brainchild of Dick and Cindy Peterson, Goose Watch is an exciting winery offering uncommon varieties such as Pinot Gris, Pinot Noir Brut Rosé Champagne, Traminette, and Diamond in addition to classic vinifera.

Wines: $–$$$

White Wines

Bartlett Pear—Made from 100% locally grown Bartlett pears. You can almost feel the juices run down your chin. Semisweet to sweet, but does has some crispness. Great dessert wine, also wonderful with foie gras or summer soups or salads. ♥

Diamond—One of the best white wine grapes grown in New York. Semisweet.

Melody—Crisp semidry wine made from a newer premium grape developed at the New York State Agricultural Experiment Station. Citrusy and very nice. ♥

Pinot Gris—Widely grown in Oregon, Alsace, and Italy, Pinot Gris is a rare find in the Finger Lakes. Light, with crisp tart palate.

Pinot Gris Barrel Reserve—Fermented in French oak, with malolactic fermentation and *sur lie* aging.

Traminette—Made from a new premium wine grape developed by Cornell University. Dry, spicy finish.

Villard Blanc—New York's only Villard Blanc, very dry with hints of citrus and herbs.

Viognier—A dry white, with tropical fruit.

Red Wines

Cabernet Sauvignon—An inky, barrel-aged Cabernet, big on fruit and with a peppery kick.

Lemberger—A varietal rarely found outside Germany and Austria. Light and dry, but with a pucker at the end.

Merlot –Big fruit. Lots of pepper. A very nice red.

Renaissance Red—A semisweet red that's only tinged with sugar. Big fruit. Still some pucker, though. A nice pasta wine for those that like it sweet.

Strawberry Splendor—Grape wine sweetened and flavored with strawberry juice and natural strawberry flavors.

Blush Wines

Bayside Blush—Semidry blush. Crisp and refreshing.

Rose of Isabella—A semisweet blush made from one of the first grapes ever planted in the Finger Lakes, back as early as 1819. Boysenberry-like aromas and flavors.

Sparkling Wines

Blanc de Noir Champagne—Made from lightly pressed Pinot Noir, aged in the bottle more than 2 years. Dry, elegant, toasty. Very nice!

Golden Spumante Champagne—A semisweet sparkling wine in the best Italian tradition. Effervescent and fruity. A multiple gold medal winner.

Pinot Noir Brut Rosé Champagne—A sparkling wine made from Pinot Noir. Crisp and light, with whiffs of cherry. ♥ ♥

REVIEWS AND AWARDS

Bartlett Pear—Gold medal, 2000 Tasters Guild International Wine Competition.

Bayside Blush—Gold medal, 1999 Los Angeles County Fair Wine Competition.

Blanc de Noir 1998—Gold medal, 2003 Jerry Mead New World International Wine Competition.

Brut Rosé NV—Gold medal, 2003 Los Angeles County Fair Wine Competition.

Diamond—Double gold medal, 2000 Great Lakes Wine Competition; gold medal, 2000 Riverside International Wine Competition; gold medal, 2003 Jerry Mead New World International Wine Competition; silver medal, 2000 Tasters Guild International Wine Competition.

Pinot Noir Brut Rosé NV—Gold medal, 2003 Great Lakes Wine Competition.

"[Their Merlot is] bright violet red with a luminous cast. Bright, sweet juicy aromas show violets and raspberries. . . . Very vibrant, fresh and youthful with zesty appeal. . . . 86 Points."   —Beverage Testing Institute

HOURS AND DIRECTIONS Open daily 10 a.m.–6 p.m. year-round. Tram Tours weekends 1 p.m. and 3 p.m. Memorial Day–Oct. ■ Goose Watch is located on the Cayuga Wine Trail, just 40 minutes north of Ithaca, 15 minutes south of Seneca Falls. ■ From Rochester or Syracuse, take the N.Y. Thruway (I-90) to exit 41. Follow Rte. 414 south to Ogden Rd. (County Rte. 124), then turn left onto Rte. 89 south and continue 2.5 miles. ■ By boat, the winery is 0.5 mile north of Dean's Cove and has docking available.

Hosmer Winery

6999 Rte. 89, Ovid, NY 14521 • Phone 888-467-9463 or 607-869-3393 • Fax 607-869-9409 • www.hosmerwinery.com • info@hosmerwinery.com

Maren and Cameron "Tunker" Hosmer founded this wonderful little winery in 1985. Located not far from the lake, its tasting room is wide open and beautifully appointed, and its gift shop has lots of lovely things to offer as well as foodstuffs to go with your wine—all the fixings for a picnic out in the vineyard.

The Hosmers offer a range of wines that are all quite nice, but they have always been known for their whites.

Wines: $–$$

White Wines

Alpine White—A dry white blend of Chardonnay and Seyval, aged in American oak. Innovative. Tropical flavors, with slight vanilla.

Cayuga White—Off-dry, with rich apricot and pineapple flavors.

Chardonnay—Chardonnay aged in oak. Fruity. Creamy. Dry finish.

House White—Inexpensive dry, light, crisp blend of predominantly Seyval, with Chardonnay. Aged in oak.

Johannisberg Riesling—Semisweet light white wine. Pears and apricots come through. Tart finish.

Late Harvest Riesling—Rich, golden dessert wine. Apricot and honey. Not too sweet. Nice balance.

Limited-Release Chardonnay—Chardonnay aged in oak. Solid fruit, tinged with oakiness. Vanilla comes through. Dry finish.

Pinot Gris—Dry, rich white table wine. Pear and citrus flavors. Versatile.

Raspberry Rhapsody—Sweet white wine infused with fresh raspberries. Intensely rich aroma and flavor.

Riesling—Light, off-dry white. Pears and peaches come through. Clean, citrusy finish. ♥ ♥

Seyval—Semidry, with citrus and apple flavors. Clean, refreshing finish.

Red Wines

Cabernet Franc—A dry, medium-bodied red, aged in oak.

Fireside Red—A light, semisweet red.

House Red—Dry, versatile, everyday red. A nice pasta wine.

Pinot Noir—Dry, light, oak-aged red. Black cherry comes through.

Sangria—A blended red wine with lemons, oranges, and limes.

Blush Wines

Carousel Blush—Semisweet blend of Cayuga White and Catawba.

Sparkling Wines

Brut Sparkling Wine—Sparkling white wine made from 100% Cayuga White in the *méthode champenoise*. Off-dry.

REVIEWS AND AWARDS

Chardonnay 1999—Gold medal, 2001 Finger Lakes International Wine Competition.

Dry Riesling 2001—2002 Governor's Cup winner; double gold medal, 2002 New York Wine and Food Classic.

Raspberry Royale—Double gold medal, 2003 Finger Lakes International Wine Competition.

Riesling 1998—Silver medal, 1999 Los Angeles County Fair Wine Competition.

Riesling 2002—Gold medal, 2003 Great Lakes Wine Competition.

Sangria—Silver medal, 1999 New York Wine and Food Classic.

"Their most popular wine is Raspberry Rhapsody, a semisweet white infused with fresh raspberries, at $8.50 a bottle. The Rieslings, at $10, are very good indeed." —Vera Vida, *Boston Globe* (August 20, 2000)

HOURS AND DIRECTIONS Call to see if they are open. ■ Located on the west side of Rte. 89. ■ From Ithaca, take Rte. 89 north past Sheldrake. Fifteen minutes after Sheldrake, the winery will be on your left. ■ From Seneca Falls, take Rte. 89 south; the winery will be on your right about 5–10 minutes after you pass Cayuga Ridge Estate Winery.

King Ferry Winery / Treleaven Wines

658 Lake Rd., King Ferry, NY 13081 • Phone 800-439-5271 or 315-364-5100 • Fax 315-364-8078 • www.treleavenwines.com • treleaven@aol.com

The land on which King Ferry Winery sits has been in the Stonstall family ever since the current owner's father quit his job as a Cornell University agriculture professor, bought 700 acres, and turned himself into a successful farmer. Most of the land was sold when he eventually passed away; however, a small parcel named Treleaven Farm (named for the family the land had been purchased from) was kept in the fam-

ily and is now home to King Ferry's 22-acre vineyard and winery, founded in 1984. The first vintages were released in 1989, and owner/winemaker Peter Stonstall now produces approximately 8,000 cases per year based on his philosophy of quality over quantity. The winery is slowly building a dedicated and happy following, especially in Boston, where the wines are sold in more than a dozen shops.

In addition to grapes from its own fields, King Ferry also purchases another 10 acres' worth of fruit from the North Fork of Long Island.

Wines: $–$$$

White Wines

Chardonnay—Chardonnays are the shining star of King Ferry. Aged in French oak. Nice acidity. ♥

Dry Riesling—Light white with tropical flavors. Tart finish, but with a touch of sweetness.

Gewürztraminer—Light, off-dry white with a tart finish.

Reserve Chardonnay—Crisp, clean. Aged in oak.

Semidry Riesling—A light, fruity, off-dry white.

Silver Lining Chardonnay—Fermented in stainless steel tanks. Very clean. ♥

Red Wines

Mélange—A Pinot Noir/Merlot blend with just a touch of sweetness. Sold by the winery as "our red wine for the white wine drinker."

Merlot—Plums and raspberries come through.

Pinot Noir—Light red, lightly oaked.

Reserve Mélange—Big fruit. Cherry comes through. Softer than the regular Mélange.

Saumon—A semidry Merlot and Vidal blend.

Fruit Wines

Apple Mystique—Off-dry apple wine. Nice flavors.

REVIEWS AND AWARDS

Chardonnay 1999—Silver medal, 2002 Jerry Mead New World International Wine Competition; silver medal, 2002 Hilton Head Spring Fest Wine Weekend.

Reserve Chardonnay 1999—Silver medal, 2002 Tasters Guild International Wine Competition; silver medal, 2002 Hilton Head Spring Fest Wine Weekend.

Chardonnay 1999: "Recommended . . . 84 Points"
—2002 Beverage Testing Institute Championships.

Merlot 1999: "Recommended . . . 84 Points"
—Beverage Testing Institute Championships 2002.

Reserve Chardonnay 1999: "Highly Recommended . . . 86 Points"
—Beverage Testing Institute Championships 2002.

"Recommended Gewürztraminer and Chenin Blanc. . . . Recommended U.S. Chardonnay Producer. . . . [The 1997 Chardonnay has] interesting, spicy, nutty aromas . . . smooth texture and crisp apple flavors showing interesting spice through the finish. Rather distinctive. . . . 89 Points."
—Beverage Testing Institute, *Buying Guide to Wines of North America*

HOURS AND DIRECTIONS Open daily Apr.–Dec.; weekends only Feb.–Mar.; closed Jan. Call for hours. ■ From Rochester, Buffalo, and points west, take the N.Y. Thruway (I-90) east to exit 41. Turn right at the exit and go to Rte. 318 east, left on Rtes. 5 and 20 east, then right onto Rte. 90 south. Follow 90 past Aurora; watch for the winery sign at Lake Rd. Go 1 mile south on Lake to the winery at the intersection with Center Rd. ■ From Boston and points east, take the Mass. Pike (I-90) to the N.Y. Thruway. Take exit 40 to Weedsport. Go south on Rte. 34 through Auburn. Turn right onto Rte. 34B in Fleming and continue to the village of King Ferry and a short distance to Center Rd., where you'll turn right and drive 1 mile to the winery. ■ From Binghamton and points south, take I-81 north to Whitney Point (exit 8); follow Rte. 79 west to Ithaca. In Ithaca turn right onto Rte. 13 north, exit to Rte. 34 north, and go approximately 6 miles to Rte. 34B north. Take 34B approximately 10 miles; watch for the NYSEG power station on the left. Lake Rd. is 0.3 mile past the power station; turn left on Lake Rd. to the winery at the intersection with Center Rd. Or continue on 34B until you see the winery sign and turn left onto Center Rd. to the winery.

Knapp Vineyards Winery ✡

2770 County Rte. 128/Ernsberger Rd., Romulus, NY 14541 •
Phone 800-869-9271 or 607-869-9271 • Fax 607-869-3212 •
www.knappwine.com • winery@knappwine.com

Set on the shore of Lake Cayuga, Knapp Vineyards Winery was established in 1982 by Doug and Suzie Knapp and has been garnering praise ever since. *Hugh Johnson's Pocket Wine Book 2002* gave the winery two stars; Karen MacNeil's *Wine Bible* cites Knapp as one of the "rising stars" of the region; and *The New Sotheby's Wine Encyclopedia* gives them a half-star, recommending their Cabernet Sauvignon and Chardonnay and noting that they produce "one of the state's best Seyval Blancs." The winery and carefully planted rows of grapevines let onto wonderful views of the countryside and lake, whose 400-foot-deep waters help create a nourishing microclimate for the grapes.

Attached to the winery is a wonderful little restaurant cited by the *New York Times* as "a fine example of what dining can and should be." Outside seating under their pergola is a romantic and enjoyable treat.

Wines: $–$$$

White Wines

Barrel Reserve Chardonnay—Aged in oak. Dry. ♥

Cayuga Lake Chardonnay—No oak fermentation, light and fruity.

Dry Riesling—Peach-like aromas that complement a crisp finish. A nice dry Riesling.

Dutchmans Breeches—Sweet in the beginning, tart in the finish. One of their best-selling wines.

Ladys Slipper—Fruity with crisp and bright flavors.

Seashore White—Flavors of light green apple and a hint of citrus. Semidry.

Semi Dry Riesling—Bright and flavorful, with lots of fruit.

Vignoles—Bright, bracing tropical fruit flavors.

Red Wines

Cabernet Franc—Medium bodied, with red berry fruit. Very nice.

Cabernet Sauvignon—Hearty fruit, black pepper spice, medium oak. Very nice.

Merlot—Rich in Merlot fruit, with earthiness and oak. Very nice.

Pasta Red—Berry flavors with subtle sweetness.

Pinot Noir—Ripe Pinot fruit with subtle oak. ♥

Prism—A light classic Bordeaux blend.

Sangiovese—Northern Italian classic. Rare for this part of the world.

Dessert Wines

Vintners Select Vignoles—Intense sweetness with an abundance of fruit. A golden nectar.

Fruit Wines

Jammin' Strawberry—Fresh summer strawberries.

Mon Cherry—Full wild cherry flavors.

Sparkling Wines

Blanc de Blanc Champagne—Slightly off-dry.

Brandy, Cordials, and Ports

Brandy—Golden, medium-bodied brandy.

Cherry Aviñac—Distilled wild cherry.

Grappa—Unaged Italian brandy.

Limoncello—An absolutely delightful after-meal sipper modeled after the popular Italian lemon liquor.

Peach Aviñac—A sweet, subtle peach cordial.

Ruby Port—Ruby red port.

Strawberry Grappa—This cordial has intense strawberry flavor. Excellent served well chilled.

REVIEWS AND AWARDS

"Now in its third vintage, the Sangiovese showed bright cherry aromas and flavors and was quite enjoyable, though at $18, it's also one of Knapp's priciest wines." —Dana Nigro, *Wine Spectator* (February 2000)

"Tasty Bordeaux-style blend, Cabernet Sauvignon, Riesling [and] sparkling Brut." —*Hugh Johnson's Pocket Wine Book 2002*

"The Knapps . . . make brandies and a delicious Cherry Aviñac, a distilled cherry wine, that we bought to serve back home when we had a special dinner party." —Vera Vida, *Boston Globe* (August 20, 2000)

HOURS AND DIRECTIONS Open Mon.–Sat. 10 a.m.–5:30 p.m., Sun. 11:30 a.m.–5:30 p.m., Apr.–Dec. Restaurant open daily 11 a.m.–3:30 p.m. year-round. ■ From Seneca Falls, take Rte. 89 south. You'll go a third of the way down the west side of the lake. After passing County Rte. 124, turn right onto County Rte. 128 (Ernsberger Rd.). The winery will be on your left. ■ From Ithaca, take Rte. 89 north halfway up the west side of the lake, passing Vineyard Rd. Turn left onto County Rte. 128 (Ernsberger Rd.). The winery will be on your left.

Lakeshore Winery

5132 Rte. 89, Romulus, NY 14541 • Phone 315-549-7075 •
Fax 315-549-7102 • www.lakeshorewinery.com • info@lakeshorewinery.com

Bill and Doris Brown established Lakeshore Winery in 1978, planting Riesling, Chardonnay, Gewürztraminer, and Cabernet Sauvignon rootstock on farmland whose history dates to 1825. (The founder of Cornell University's College of Agriculture, Isaac Philips Roberts, was born on the property in 1833.) The first vintage was in 1981, and they opened for selling in 1982. Today, Lakeshore is owned and operated by John and Annie Bachman, who purchased the vineyards in June of 1994 and have maintained the fun, relaxed, and educational tasting room experience established by the previous owners, as well as the quality and variety of wines. They have won numerous awards.

The winery's vineyards slope down to Lake Cayuga, where there's a dock for visiting boaters.

Wines: $–$$

White Wines

Aunt Clara—Semisweet blend featuring Catawba.

Cayuga White—Semidry and lightly oaked. Their best-selling wine. Very nice.

Chardonnay—A dry dinner wine made in the French tradition, aged in oak barrels. Dry. Ripe apple and toast. ♥

Dry Riesling—Made in the old German style, dry and aged in oak. Tart finish. ♥

Semi-Dry Riesling—Flavors of grapefruit and apricots. Tart but sweet.

Red Wines

Baco Noir—Dry red dinner wine. Their most popular red.

Cabernet Franc—Dry red with lots of tannin. Completely fermented on the skins, then aged in oak barrels for nearly a year. One of their most popular reds.

Cabernet Sauvignon—A dry, full-bodied, Bordeaux-style dinner wine.

Country Claret—Based on the Baco Noir grape. A light red pasta wine.

Nouveau—Available in November. Fresh, fruity, and dry.

Pinot Noir—The classic Burgundy-style dinner red. Robust, strong, smoky.

Rocking Chair Red—A semisweet red.

Blush Wines

Country Blush—Sweet and fruity.

Uncle Charlie—Less sweet than most blush wines.

REVIEWS AND AWARDS

Aunt Clara—Silver medal, 2002 New York Wine and Food Classic.

Country Claret—Silver medal, 2002 New York Wine and Food Classic.

Pinot Noir 1997—Silver medal, 2001 New York Wine and Food Classic.

HOURS AND DIRECTIONS Open Mon.–Sat. 10:30 a.m.– 5 p.m., Sun. noon–5 p.m., May–Dec.; Sat.–Sun. noon–5 p.m. Jan.–Mar.; Fri.–Sun. noon–5 p.m. Apr. ■ From the west via the N.Y. Thruway, use exit 41 (Waterloo). Turn south on Rte. 414, then east on Rte. 318 until it ends at the intersection with Rtes. 5, 20, and 89. Jog left on 5 and 20, then immediately turn right (south) on Rte. 89. Go about 13 miles; watch for Lakeshore on your right, just past Cobblestone Farm. ■ From the east via the N.Y. Thruway, use exit 40 (Weedsport). Go south on Rte. 34, then west on Rte. 31 through Port Byron. Rte. 31 makes a right turn here, so watch for the sign. Turn left (south) onto Rte. 90, right onto Rtes. 5 and 20, then left onto Rte. 89. Go about 13 miles; watch for Lakeshore on your right just past Cobblestone Farm. ■ From the southeast via Ithaca, watch for signs for Rte. 89 north upon entering Ithaca. Follow 89 north for about 30 miles. Lakeshore is on your left just after the small settlement of East Varick.

Long Point Winery

1485 Lake Rd., Aurora, NY 13026 • Phone 315-364-6990 • Fax 315-364-6713 • www.longpointwinery.com • gjb@longpointwinery.com

Over the course of 23 years, home winemaker Gary Barletta accumulated more than sixty awards and medals, specializing in making dry red wines. Since opening Long Point with his wife Rosemary in 2000, he's added to his collection with awards in both national and international competitions: his first four Long Point wines collected seven medals.

The family-run winery is located at the midpoint of Lake Cayuga, on the eastern shore, and enjoys breathtaking lake views from its big red barn and vineyards, which produce more than 5,000 gallons annually. The wine shop offers an array of wonderful treats, including gifts made by area craftspeople.

Wines: $–$$

White Wines

Chardonnay—A barrel-fermented white. Pear and honey come through. Buttery. Very drinkable. ♥

Chardonnay Reserve (Barrel Select)—A dry white wine aged in French and Hungarian oak.

Sauvignon Blanc—A crisp, dry white with flavors of grapefruit, lemon-lime, and passion fruit.

Vidal Blanc—Delicately sweet and light. Nice.

Red Wines

Cabernet Sauvignon—A dry, rich ruby red. Blackberries.

Cambrie—A 100% Grenache wine done in the Beaujolais tradition. Nice.

Merlot—A dry red wine aged in oak. Raspberry and plum come through. My wife thought it a "very romantic wine." Good mouth feel.

Merlot Reserve—More mature than the regular Merlot. More polished.

Moon Puppy—A semisweet red wine. Fruity.

Syrah—A big-fruit, big-oak, deep red. Strong initial pop in the mouth.

Zinfandel—A deep garnet, dry red. Peppery. Spicy. Enjoyed this very much! ♥

Zinfandel Reserve (Barrel Select)—Aged in Hungarian and French oak. Jamminess of plums and cherries comes through.

Blush Wines

Ciera—A blend of Vidal (75%) and Grenache (25%). Off-dry. Nice.

REVIEWS AND AWARDS

Cabernet Sauvignon—Bronze medal, 2001 New York State Fair Wine Competition.

Cambrie—Bronze medal, 2001 Indiana State Fair Indy International Wine Competition; bronze medal, 2001 New York State Fair Wine Competition.

Merlot Reserve—Silver medal, 2001 New York State Fair Wine Competition; bronze medal, 2001 Indiana State Fair Indy International Wine Competition.

Syrah—Double gold medal, 2001 New York State Fair Wine Competition; gold medal, 2001 Eastern International Wine Competition.

Zinfandel—Silver medal, 2002 Eastern International Wine Competition.

HOURS AND DIRECTIONS Open Mon.–Thurs. noon–5 p.m., Fri.–Sat. 10 a.m.–6 p.m., Sun. 11 a.m.–5:30 p.m., year-round. ■ From Rochester, Buffalo, and points west, take the N.Y. Thruway (I-90) east to exit 41. Turn right at the exit and go to Rte. 318 east. Turn left onto Rtes. 5 and 20 east, then right onto Rte. 90 south. Follow Rte. 90 past Aurora, and after approximately 2 miles watch for the winery sign at Lake Rd. ■ From points east (Boston), take the Mass. Pike to the N.Y. Thruway (I-90). Take exit 40 to Weedsport. Go south on Rte. 34 through Auburn. Turn right onto Rte. 34B in Fleming, and keep making a continuous right turn onto Rte. 90 and go approximately 2 miles. Watch for Lake Rd. and the winery sign on the left. ■ From Binghamton and points south, take I-81 north to Whitney Point (exit 8) and follow Rte. 79 west to Ithaca. In Ithaca, go right on Rte. 13 north, exit to Rte. 34 north, and go approximately 6 miles to Rte. 34B north. Take 34B approximately 12 miles to King Ferry. Turn left onto Rte. 90 and travel approximately 5 miles (past diner). Watch for Lake Rd. and the winery sign on the left.

Lucas Vineyards

3862 County Rte. 150, Interlaken, NY 14847 • Phone 800-682-WINE or 607-532-4825 • Fax 607-532-8580 • www.lucasvineyards.com • lucaswyn@epix.net

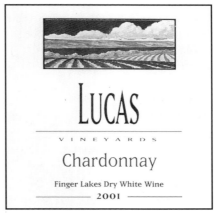

The story behind Lucas Vineyards actually begins in New York City's Bronx borough, where Bill Lucas worked on tugboats after spates as a summer farmworker and a bus driver in New York's Finger Lakes region. In 1974, after working his way up to captain, Bill convinced his city-girl wife Ruth to move, and by 1975 the Lucases had planted their first vines. Five years later they opened their winery—the first on Cayuga Lake—and their debut vintage of 400 cases won gold and silver medals at the New York State Fair Wine Competition.

It was the beginning of a long chain of national and international medals and awards.

And guess who made these wonderful wines? Not the tugboat captain (nor daughter Stephanie nor son-in-law Jeff, who also work on the property), but the young woman who gave her country-loving husband such a hard time. Ruth's touch tends to be light, producing about 12,000 cases of tasty and delicate wines annually. My wife and I often serve them at dinner parties, and friends are always delighted.

Wines: $–$$

White Wines

Blues—A blend of Seyval and Cayuga White. Light. Refreshing.

Cayuga White—A semidry Cayuga white. A nice sipping wine. Refreshing.

Chardonnay Private Reserve—A dry Chardonnay partially aged in oak. Nice creamy taste followed by tart green apple. ♥

Dry Riesling—A light, dry version of this German wine. Good! ♥

Evening Tide—Off-dry blend of Cayuga white and oak-fermented Vidal grapes. Named after one of the tugs that Captain Lucas piloted. Crisp and refreshing.

Gewürztraminer—This off-dry wine is very nice. Lovely flavors, with some citrus ending. ♥

Harbor Moon—A semidry blend of Vidal, oak-aged Vidal, and Cayuga. Citrus and tropical fruit come through. Crisp.

Riesling—Semidry, light Johannisberg-style Riesling. Peach comes through. Crisp finish. Very nice. ♥

Seyval Blanc—A dry, crisp white. Very nice

Tug Boat White—A semidry blend of Cayuga white and Vignoles. Light, fruity, but not too sweet. Nice.

Red Wines

Cabernet Franc—Classic vinifera aged in new oak barrels. Rich, smooth, and pleasant. Blackberries come through.

Dry Dock—Oak-aged red blend. Big fruit up front. Dry, smooth finish.

Meritage—Bordeaux-style blend, aged in oak. Not tasted.

Tug Boat Red—Intensely fruity, semisweet light red.

Blush Wines

Captain's Belle—A blend of four whites and one red. Very nice.

Sparkling Wines

Blanc de Blancs Champagne—100% Chardonnay sparkling wine. Very nice.

Brut Champagne—Made in the classic French style, from a Chardonnay–Pinot Noir blend. Finishes dry. Nice.

Extra Dry Champagne—Made using the *méthode champenoise*. Fruit flavors and toasty. Very nice.

Dessert Wines

Vignoles—Rich, golden, fruity dessert wine.

REVIEWS AND AWARDS

Blanc de Blancs Champagne—Silver medal, 2002 Grand Harvest Awards.

Dry Dock 1999—Gold and silver medals, 2002 New York Wine and Food Classic.

Harbor Moon 2000—Silver medal, 2002 Grand Harvest Awards.

Seyval 1997—Gold medal, 2002 New York Wine and Food Classic.

Seyval Blanc—Silver medal, 2002 Grand Harvest Awards.

"We preferred the dry Riesling, which has a subtle peach flavor."
—Vera Vida, *Boston Globe* (August 20, 2000)

HOURS AND DIRECTIONS Open Mon.–Sat. 10:30 a.m.–5:30 p.m., Sun. noon–5:30 p.m., May–Dec.; Sat. 10:30 a.m.–5:30 p.m., Sun. noon–5:30 p.m., Jan.–Apr. ■ Located halfway between Rtes. 96 and 89. ■ From Ithaca:, take Rte. 89 north to Interlaken, approximately 17 miles. Turn left onto County Rte. 150 and follow the signs. The winery is located on the left. ■ From Geneva, Waterloo, and Seneca Falls, take Rtes. 5 and 20 east to Rte. 89. Head south on Rte. 89 to Interlaken, approximately 20 miles. Turn right onto County Rte. 150 and follow the signs. The winery is located on the left. ■ From Watkins Glen, take Rte. 414 north to Lodi; then turn right onto Rte. 96A. Follow

96A to Interlaken, approximately 5 miles. Turn left onto Rte. 96 north and continue through town. Turn right onto County Rte. 150 and follow the signs. The winery is located on the right. ■ From the N.Y. Thruway (I-90), take exit 41. Head briefly south on Rte. 414 to Rte. 318. Follow 318 to Rte. 89 and then follow local directions from Geneva, above.

Sheldrake Point Vineyard and Cafe

7448 County Rte. 153, Ovid, NY 14521 • Phone 607-532-9401 •
Fax 607-532-8967 • www.sheldrakepoint.com • finewine@sheldrakepoint.com

Sheldrake Point is the most prominent point on the west coast of Lake Cayuga. It was once home to a large population of Cayuga Indians who hunted and fished its coves, streams, and woods and farmed the surrounding hillsides. Due to those same coves, and because it is the midpoint of the lake, it became a natural port, and so by the early 1800s was a popular ferry stop. By the late 1800s it had become an extremely popular summer resort.

The 160 lakeshore acres now occupied by Sheldrake Point Vineyard (with 40 of those acres planted to vines) were an orchard and dairy farm from 1850 to the mid-1900s. Sheldrake Point cofounder Bob Madill purchased the property from dairy owner Sy Diamond in 1997 and planted the property with premium vinifera grapes: Cabernet Franc, Riesling, Pinot Noir, Pinot Gris, Gamay, Merlot, Gewürztraminer, and Chardonnay. The first wine made from their vines was sold in 1999.

Sheldrake Point also has a café, nestled into beautiful manicured gardens overlooking the lake and offering appetizers, tapas, sandwiches, and other light fare, and seasonal entrées. The reviews of the restaurant have been unanimously wonderful.

Wines: $–$$$

White Wines

Dry Riesling—An off-dry, light white with peach and apricot followed with a citrus finish.

Sheldrake Spring Riesling—Semidry white tinged with fruits. Has a little tartness at the end.

Summer White—A semidry blend of Cayuga White and Vidal. Light and refreshing.

Waterfall Chardonnay—A dry, barrel-fermented white. Citrus flavors, but mellowed with nice finish.

Red Wines

Cabernet Franc—Classic red aged in American oak. Plum comes through. Deeper than it looks. Nice.

Gamay—Dry, medium-body red. Jammy in a nice way.

Luckystone Red—Dry red blend. Berries come through. A nice pasta wine.

Merlot—A dry red. Cherry comes through.

Pinot Noir—A light, dry red. Berry and smoky oak.

Blush Wines

Petite Dry Rosé—A dry, European-style rosé. Very nice.

Dessert Wines

Barrel-Reserve Cabernet Franc—Full-bodied dry red wine. Berry, oak, and vanilla. All very nice.

Barrel-Reserve Chardonnay—Big bouquet. Good fruit. Nice oak.

Barrel-Reserve Merlot—Made in the classic French Bordeaux style. Cherry comes through.

Barrel-Reserve Pinot Noir—A nice light red. Dry but with big fruit.

Merganser Meritage—A nice blend. Rich, bold flavors.

Raspberry Splash—Rich, sweet wine. Not too overpowering.

Riesling Ice Wine—Rich, golden dessert wine produced in the traditional German style. Luxurious.

REVIEWS AND AWARDS

Spring Riesling 1999—Bronze medal, 2001 Los Angeles County Fair Wine Competition.

"The rustic backdrop of barns and informal gardens inspires Chef Douglas Leach toward vegetarian fare and tapas, but he also embraces French, American and Caribbean cooking. . . . Leach's approach to food is almost a spiritual experience."
—Lorraine Smorol, *Syracuse New Times* (Autumn 2000)

HOURS AND DIRECTIONS Open daily 11 a.m.–6 p.m. Apr.–Nov.; Sat.–Sun. noon–5 p.m. Dec.–Mar. ■ Sheldrake Point is located on the western shore of Cayuga Lake, 20 miles south of Geneva/Seneca Falls and 20 miles north of Ithaca. ■ Follow Rte. 89 north from Ithaca or south from Seneca Falls. Look for signs directing you down County Rte. 139 to Sheldrake; then turn right at the little four-way stop onto County Rte. 153. The winery is a few hundred yards down on the right. ■ From Geneva, take Rte. 96A south toward Ithaca. A few miles south of the blinking red light in Ovid, look for the green Cayuga Wine Trail signs directing you left onto County Rte. 138. This will take you down to Rte. 89. Turn right, look for the signs directing you to Sheldrake, and follow the directions above.

Signore Winery

153 White Church Rd., Brooktondale, NY 14817 • Phone 607-539-7935

This small winery is located about 5 miles southeast of Ithaca. Owned and operated by Donato Signore, it's known for making very drinkable table wines. The hours of the winery are somewhat spotty, but the wines themselves can be found in most area liquor stores.

Wines: $–$$

White Wines

Chardonnay—Not too dry.

Riesling—A light, off-dry rendition of the German favorite.

Red Wines

Baco Noir—A smoky red.

Chambourcin—A deep red.

Classic Red—A blend of Baco Noir, Cabernet Sauvignon, and Carmine.

Pinot Noir—Light, with lots of fruit.

HOURS AND DIRECTIONS Open Sat.–Sun. noon–5 p.m. Apr.–Dec., and by appointment. ■ Take Rte. 79 south out of Ithaca. Go about 5 miles. Turn right onto White Church Rd. You are there.

Six Mile Creek Vineyard

1553 Slaterville Rd. (Rte. 79E), Ithaca, NY 14850 • Phone 607-272-WINE • Fax 607-277-7344 • www.sixmilecreek.com • smc@lightlink.com

Ithaca's only winery, Six Mile Creek is a family-owned boutique enterprise housed in a beautifully restored, century-old, Dutch reform–style barn, with a pre–Civil War cemetery and stagecoach stop out on the property. Owned and managed by Roger and Nancy Battistella, the winery commands incredible views of gorgeous meadows spotted with small stands of evergreens and hardwoods. Hiking and cross-country ski trails network throughout the property, offering numerous opportunities for wonderful meditative nature walks.

Winemaker Roger, a Cornell University professor, likes to make his wines dry, with a few sweet vintages mixed in to keep things lively.

Wines: $–$$

White Wines

Cascadilla White—A sweet, light white. Lots of fruit.

Chardonnay—A light, dry white. Pears comes through, with nice acidity. Clean and crisp.

Chardonnay Reserve—Aged in French oak. Honeydew melon flavors come through. Creamy, but with dry finish. Nice.

Ithaca White—Semidry white table wine. Light and refreshing.

Pasa Tiempo—A light white blend. Crisp finish.

Riesling—Floral nose. Tart finish. Nice.

Vignoles—A semisweet white. Nice.

Red Wines

Cabernet Franc—A garnet-colored, medium-bodied red. Smooth and dry.

Escapade—A Cabernet with some sweetness, and big cherry flavors.

Ithaca Red—A garnet blend, dry and mature.

Pinot Noir—A sapphire-colored wine. Cherry comes through. Dry.

Quintessence—A light Bordeaux blend. Dry finish.

Blush Wines

Odyssey—Strawberry and raspberry flavors.

Dessert Wines

Dolce Vita—Sweet.

REVIEWS AND AWARDS

"We particularly liked the [Ithaca] red."   —Vera Vida, *Boston Globe* (August 20, 2000)

HOURS AND DIRECTIONS Open daily noon–5:30 p.m. year-round or by appointment. Call during winter-month weekdays. ■ The winery is located in close proximity to Cornell University and Ithaca College. From downtown Ithaca, follow Rte. 79 east. The winery and vineyards are only 2 miles from the city limits. Look for the landmark post-and-beam barn. There are signs as you approach.

Swedish Hill Vineyard

4565 Rte. 414, Romulus, NY 14541 • Phone 888-549-WINE or 315-549-8477 • www.swedishhill.com • swedhill@flare.net

Dick and Cindy Peterson started small, crushing their first grapes in 1985 and opening a year later with only 1,300 cases. Today, however, Swedish Hill is one of the region's largest wineries, producing more than 40,000 cases annually and winning more than seventy-eight medals since 1996. Still family owned and operated, it is one of the top award-winning wineries in New York State. Dick and Cindy Peterson also founded Goose Watch Winery.

Wines: $–$$

White Wines

Cayuga White—Crisp, semidry white. Citrusy.

Delaware Glenside Vineyards/Old Vine Reserve—One of the few wines made from the Delaware grape. Floral aromas. Fruity. Interesting!

Dry Riesling—A Riesling in the classic style. Floral. Tart. ♥

Just Peachy—Semisweet peach wine. Rich. Not overly sweet. Nice balance.

Reserve Chardonnay—100% barrel fermented with 100% malolactic fermentation. Dry, buttery.

Riesling—Off-dry version of the German classic wine. Fruity. ♥

Surfside Chardonnay—Offers subtle aromas of apples combined with a distinctive nutty aroma (from aging in French oak).

Svenska White—A semisweet table white.

Vidal Blanc—Semidry varietal. Fruity. Clean.

Vignoles—A semisweet white varietal. Big fruit up front. Peaches. Finishes tart and sweet.

Vignoles Late Harvest—Honey and apricot come across to the nose and on the palate. Very nice! ♥

Viking White—A blend of Cayuga, Chardonnay, and Vidal. Crisp, slightly fruity. Apple.

Red Wines

Cabernet Franc—Done in the classic Bordeaux style. Oak aged and dry.

Country Concord—A deep, velvety purple, semisweet wine.

Glogg Wine—A spicy and aromatic red made with special Swedish extract containing cinnamon, cloves, cardamom, and ginger. Makes for a nice wassail, heated up with fruit.

Marechal Foch—Made in a light red, Beaujolais style. A nice pasta wine.

Optimize—A blend of Cabernet Sauvignon, Merlot, and Cabernet Franc, in the classic Bordeaux style. Aged in oak. Their most ambitious red.

Radical Raspberry—Sweet red wine that shouts "raspberries!" A nice dessert wine.

Svenska Red—A semisweet red blend, aged in oak.

Viking Red—A dry red blend. A nice table wine.

Blush Wines

Svenska Blush—The winery's most popular. Refreshing.

Sparkling Wines

Blanc de Blanc—Semidry.

Brut—A dry sparkling wine, blended from 35% Chardonnay and 65% Pinot Noir and aged on the yeast for 2.5 years. Bottle-fermented in the *méthode champenoise* tradition.

Naturel—Dry sparkling wine blended from Chardonnay and Pinot Noir, the classic champagne varieties.

Riesling Cuvée Champagne—A sparkling wine using Riesling. Finishes off-dry. Very nice.

Spumante Blush—A fruity blush style of sparkling wine.

Ports

Cynthia Marie Port—Oak-aged port made from a blend of 1995–2000 vintages. Named after co-owner Cynthia Marie Peterson. Not tasted.

REVIEWS AND AWARDS

Chardonnay 2001—Gold medal, 2003 Jerry Mead New World International Wine Competition.

Concord NV—Gold medal, 2003 Great Lakes Wine Competition.

Dry Riesling 2002—Gold medal, 2003 Los Angeles County Fair Wine Competition.

Svenska Red 2001—Gold medal, 2003 Great Lakes Wine Competition.

Vidal Blanc—Gold medal, 2000 Pacific Rim International Wine Competition; gold medal, 1999 Long Beach Grand Cru.

Vignoles Late Harvest—Double gold medal, 2000 Great Lakes Wine Competition; Double gold medal, 1999 San Francisco International Wine Competition; gold medal, best of class, and sweepstakes award for best dessert wine, 1999 Long Beach Grand Cru.

"[Their Riesling] shouldn't be missed"   —Karen MacNeil, *The Wine Bible*

HOURS AND DIRECTIONS Open daily 9 a.m.–6 p.m. year-round. Tours are available May–Oct. at 1 and 3 p.m. weekdays and at noon, 2, and 4 p.m. weekends. ■ The winery is located in central New York, 8 miles south of Seneca Falls or 35 miles north of Ithaca on Rte. 414.

FINGER LAKES: SENECA

Amberg Wine Cellars

2200 Rtes. 5 and 20, Flint, NY 14561 • Phone 585-526-6742 •
Fax 315-462-6512 • www.ambergwine.com

As one of the region's premier grape growers and grape care experts, the Amberg family's Grafted Grape Vine Nursery is among the most well-known viticultural horticulturists around, but it took more than 20 years—and an explosion of interest in regional wineries—before they decided to make and sell their own wines. A dozen years later, their enterprise is well established in a beautiful new barn with real old-world charm.

Herman Amberg, an expert in grapevine management, is in charge of the vineyards, and has been instrumental in testing Traminette, selling it as a blend in his Pearl and Gypsy wines. His son, Eric Amberg, is the winemaker, and uses his California-to-Germany education and experience to blend tradition and innovation. Mother Ute and daughter-in-law Debbie maintain the other operations throughout the winery.

Wines: $–$$

White Wines

Barrel Select Chardonnay—Made in the Burgundian tradition, and aged in oak.

Bianca—A barrel-aged white. Not tasted.

Dry Riesling—Crisp white wine. Fruity and clean.

Gypsy—A semisweet blend of Traminette and Riesling.

Pearl—A blend of Traminette and Riesling. Not tasted.

Semi-Dry Chardonnay —Fruity version of the classic grape, tinged with oak.

Semi-Dry Riesling—Off-dry version in the Johannisberg tradition. Very nice.

Traminette—A new variety developed by Cornell University. Off-dry and light, with a floral nose. Very clean, very nice.

Red Wines

Burgundy—A dry red blend in the Rhône style. Nice.

Cabernet Sauvignon—Oak-aged Cabernet in the Bordeaux tradition.

Claret—Classic Bordeaux style. Deep fruit. Nice.

Pinot Noir—A light, dry red in the French Burgundy tradition. Subtle up front, but late explosion of taste comes from the back of the mouth. Interesting.

Red Baron—A rich, sweet, fruity red.

Red Panda—A semisweet blend of Cabernet Franc and Merlot created to honor the small, endangered cousin of the giant panda.

Blush Wines

Blush—A Semisweet mouthful of berries.

Dessert Wines

Pegasus—A rich, sweet dessert-style white with a flowery aroma and rich, fruity flavor. Smells like freesia. ♥

HOURS AND DIRECTIONS Open June–Oct. Mon.–Sat. 10 a.m.–6 p.m., Sun. noon–6 p.m.; Nov.–Dec. and Feb.–May Mon.–Sat. 10 a.m.–5 p.m., Sun. noon–5 p.m.; Jan. Fri.–Sat. 10 a.m.–5 p.m., Sun. noon–5 p.m. ■ Located on Rtes. 5 and 20 between Geneva and Canandaigua, on the north side of the road a few minutes after you pass the intersection with Rte. 14A. An easy drive from Geneva.

Anthony Road Wine Company

1225 Anthony Rd., Penn Yan, NY 14527 • Phone 800-559-2182 or 315-536-2182 • Fax 315-536-5851 • www.anthonyroadwine.com • anthonyroad@flare.net

John Martini is a former president of the New York Wine Grape Growers Association. Derek Wilbur is a former winemaker for Finger Lakes Wine Cellars. In 1989, they teamed up and, along with their wives Ann and Donna, opened Anthony Road Wine Company in a gorgeous new plantation-style home. Their latest endeavor involves the development of more than 100 acres of Finger Lakes wine-growing land in association with Robert Young Estate Winery, makers of one of California's best Chardonnays.

Wines: $–$$

White Wines

Chardonnay—A dry white, fermented and aged in both stainless steel and small oak barrels. Very nice.

Dry Riesling—A dry white with a dry finish. Peas and apricots come through.

Semi-Dry Riesling—Off-dry. Apple and pear come through.

Semi-Dry Vignoles—This golden white is semisweet up front, but with nice balance.

Seyval Blanc—A dry white. Citrusy. Nice.

Solstice—Off-dry, barrel-aged Cayuga and Vidal.

Red Wines

Cabernet Franc—Dry medium-bodied red. Green pepper and blackberry flavors come through.

Tony's Red—An inexpensive, semisweet red blend.

Vintner's Red—An inexpensive red blend aged in oak. Dry.

Blush Wines

Poulet Rouge—A semisweet wine, light salmon-pink in color.

Vintner's Blush—Semisweet blend of rosé and white wine.

Dessert Wines

Late Harvest Vignoles—Rich, gold, sweet dessert wine. Nice acidity balances it out.

REVIEWS AND AWARDS

Late Harvest Vignoles—Silver medal, 2000 Grand Harvest Awards.

Semi-Dry Riesling—Double gold medals, 2000 New York Wine and Food Classic.

Riesling Finger Lakes Dry 2001: "Score 87."   —*Wine Spectator* (October 2002)

Vignoles Finger Lakes Veritas Trockenbeeren 2000: "Score 87."
                                                —*Wine Spectator* (October 2002)

HOURS AND DIRECTIONS Open Apr.–Dec. Mon.–Sat. 10 a.m.–5 p.m., Sun. noon–5 p.m.; Jan.–Mar. by appointment only. ■ From Seneca, take Rte. 14 approximately 7 miles south. Pass the intersection with Rte. 16, and the winery will be less than a mile up on the east side of the road. ■ From Watkins Glen, take Rte. 14 north about 20 miles up the west side of Lake Seneca. After you pass the intersection with Rte. 54 (near Dresden), begin looking for the winery on your right. It's about 3 miles up.

Arcadian Estate Vineyards

4184 Rte. 14, Rock Stream, NY 14878 • Phone 800-298-1346 or 607-535-2068 • Fax 607-535-4692 • www.arcadianwine.com • arcadian@exotrope.net

Arcadian Estate Vineyards was founded back in 1979 by Mike and Vera Giasi, who renovated the farmland into a proper winery. It's now owned by Mike and Joanne Hastrich, who bring the winery's three-story, 170-year-old wooden barn to life with ghost stories about a Civil War veteran who likes to roam its creaky planks. It's a friendly, easygoing place, with a colorful and artistic flavor evident not only in the winery barn (whose periwinkle blue and sunflower yellow highlights are total eye candy) but also in its wild labels, each of which is as unique as the wine it announces.

Wines: $–$$

White Wines

Sail Away Chardonnay/Cayuga—An off-dry light white blend.

Snowy Evening Chardonnay/Lakemont—A light white blend.

Starry Night Riesling—Tropical flavors with a citrusy ending. Nice.

Two Roads Chardonnay—Lightly oaked, with some tropical flavors.

Red Wines

Family Reserve Cabernet Sauvignon—A rich, dry red.

Flora de la Noche DeChaunac—A medium-bodied red.

Silver Series Pinot Noir—Medium-bodied red.

Watkins Red—A solid, off-dry pasta-and-burger wine.

Blush Wines

Watkins Way Cool Blush—A blush that delivers strawberries and peaches.

Dessert and Fruit Wines

Cherry Fantasy—A mouthful of cherries.

Shining on Me Pear—Nice nose. Sweet, with flavors of soft ripe pears. Crisp finish.
   A simple pleasure. ♥

Take My Time Black Raspberry—Sweet, rich, and full.

Where Does the Time Go Strawberry—Light, sweet, and different. Nice.

HOURS AND DIRECTIONS Open Apr.–Nov. Mon.–Sat. 10 a.m.–6 p.m., Sun. noon–6 p.m.; Dec.–Mar. Fri.–Sun. noon–6 p.m. ■ Located 15 minutes north of Watkins Glen on the western side of Seneca Lake. ■ From Watkins Glen, drive about 10 miles north on Rte. 14. The winery is on the east side of the road around near Rock Stream. If you get to Rte. 46, you've gone too far. ■ From Geneva, take Rte. 14 south about 20 miles. After you pass Lakemort, keep an eye out for Rte. 46. Stay on 14 and pass the Rte. 46 intersection. Arcadian is on the east side of the road, on your left.

Atwater Estate Vineyards

5055 Rte. 414, Hector, NY 14841 • Phone 607-546-8463 • Fax 607-546-8464 • www.atwatervineyards.com • info@atwatervineyards.com

Seven miles north of Watkins Glen is Atwater Estate, a small, charming winery owned and operated since 1999 by Ted Marks and award-winning winemaker Phil Hazlitt, a sixth-generation Finger Lakes resident and owner of Hazlitt 1852 Vineyards, located just 4.5 miles to the north. The Atwater vineyards originally belonged to Ed and Joanne Grow, who ran the property in the 1980s as Rolling Vineyards.

The winery produces approximately 6,000 cases per year, focusing on the vinifera families—classic dry reds and whites and traditional old-world-style dessert wines, all produced from the winery's 60 acres and vines grown on the Hazlitts' other properties. It's a small, classy list that's starting to show promise.

Wines: $–$$

White Wines

Chardonnay—A rich, full-bodied white from 20-year-old vines. Aged in oak barrels in the French tradition. Creamy. Dry finish.

Estate White—A light white blend of Chardonnay, Seyval, Cayuga, and Vidal. Clean and dry.

Riesling—Full-bodied Alsatian-style Riesling. Their best-selling wine.

Vidal Blanc—Cold fermented, clean, and crisp. Nice.

Red Wines

Estate Red—A medium- to light-bodied red blend made from Foch, Chelois, and Pinot Noir. A nice pasta wine.

Meritage—Bordeaux-style blend of Cabernet Sauvignon, Cabernet Franc, and Merlot. Fermented and aged in French oak barrels. Full-bodied and dry.

Reserve Red—Medium-bodied dry Marechal Foch fermented in American oak barrels.

Blush Wines

Estate Blush—Fruity blush from Catawba grapes.

Dessert Wines

Late Harvest Vignoles—Golden, rich dessert wine with nice acidic balance.

Vidal Blanc Ice Wine—Golden, thick, rich, sweet dessert wine.

REVIEWS AND AWARDS

Gewürztraminer 2001—Gold medal, 2003 Finger Lakes International Wine Competition; silver medal, 2002 Finger Lakes International Wine Competition.

Late Harvest Vignoles 1999—Gold medal, 2001 New York Wine and Food Classic.

Late Harvest Vignoles 2000—Double gold medal, 2003 Tasters Guild International Wine Competition.

"[The 2001 Riesling] was a delightfully refreshing, fairly dry wine (.5 percent residual sugar)."   —Jeff Richards, *Star-Gazette* (May 2, 2002)

HOURS AND DIRECTIONS Open Mon.–Sat. 10 a.m.–5 p.m., Sun. noon–5 p.m., year-round. ■ From Watkins Glen, take Rte. 414 north along Lake Seneca's western shore. Go 7 miles. Atwater is on your left just after Chateau Lafayette Reneau Winery.

Billsboro Winery

4760 W. Lake Rd., Geneva, NY 14456 • Phone 315-789-9571 • rmp2@cornell.edu

Dr. Robert M. "Bob" Pool, professor of viticulture at Cornell University's New York State Agricultural Experiment Station, is a very important man in the Finger Lakes wine world: according to Cornell, he's "in charge of vine management research for the state." In his spare time, he teaches at Hobart and William Smith Colleges and, with Jennifer Morris, runs this boutique winery, producing high-end, high-quality wines in small amounts for discerning buyers. They established the winery in 2000.

Wines: $–$$

White Wines
Chardonnay—Not tasted.
Viognier—Not tasted.

Red Wines
Cabernet Franc—Not tasted.
Petite Syrah—Not tasted.
Pinot Noir—Not tasted.

HOURS AND DIRECTIONS Open May–Oct. weekends, no set hours; Jan.–Apr. by appointment only. ■ From Geneva, take Rte. 14 south. The winery is on the west side of the road about 10 minutes out of town. If you get to Earl's Hill Rd., you've gone too far. ■ From Watkins Glen, take Rte. 14 north all the way up the west side of Lake Seneca. The winery lies a few minutes beyond Earl's Hill Rd., on your left.

Cascata Winery at the Professors' Inn

3651 Rte. 14N, Watkins Glen, NY 14891 • Phone 607-535-8000 • www.cascatawinery.com • cascata@cascatawinery.com

Cascata Winery is a little bit of everything, beginning as a combination bookstore/gallery/café/antique shop and in 1995 a tasting bar was added. In 2000 it moved to its current home, a beautiful old Victorian in which husband and wife David Hannie and Coralee Burch opened the Professors' Inn—part charming B & B, part winery, part all of the above, where they also offer weekend workshop packages on topics ranging from communication skills to art. Coralee, a former radio personality and professor, creates the winery's imaginative labels and is the finest B & B hostess you'll ever meet, while David, a former university president and chemistry professor, takes care of the administrative details.

Since 1995, Cascata has increased its award-wining wine offerings from one to twelve, including sweet native grape blends, raspberry mead, dry Riesling, and barrel-fermented

Chardonnay, all made to the couple's specifications by several different regional wineries. To round out the Cascata experience, savor a meal at the Professors' Place Restaurant, in a separate location on Franklin St.

Wines: $–$$

White Wines

Cascade Riesling—Off-dry Riesling. Tropical fruits come through. One of the more pleasant Rieslings offered in the Finger Lakes—and that's saying something. ♥

Chardonnay—A lightly oaked Chardonnay. Apples, pears, and oak come through.

Fireside Chardonnay—Old-world Chardonnay of the oldest tradition. French oaked, with deep forest.

Riesling—A dry Riesling. Notes of peach and apricot. Dry finish.

Red Wines

Awakening—Labrusca (a native American grape) wine.

Celebration Iris—Semisweet light wine from Delaware grapes. Slightly *frizzante*.

Luna Rossa—A dry red blend of Lemberger and Pinot Noir.

Pinot Noir—A Beaujolais-style dry red.

Professors' Classics: Cabernet Franc—Intense dry red.

Red Bouquet—A full-bodied Baco Noir. Forward cherry. Dry finish. ♥

Regatta Red—An unusual blend of native grapes and Baco Noir.

Sweet Iris—An award-winning Delaware with a light, fruity taste and a floral aroma.

Blush Wines

Morning Blush—Semisweet blush made from Cayuga grapes.

Sparkling Wines

Blushing Flamingo Spumante—An off-dry bubbly made with Catawba.

Fruit Wines

Elderberry—Fermented fresh elderberries. Sweet, with incredible flavor.

REVIEWS AND AWARDS

Professors' Classics: Riesling 2000—First prize, 2001 Whale Watch.

HOURS AND DIRECTIONS Open summer and fall 11 a.m.–5 p.m. Call other months. ■ Located not even 5 minutes from downtown Watkins Glenn. Take Rte. 14 north going out of town. It will be on your right, between the lake and Rte. 14. Follow the signs.

Castel Grisch Estate Winery

3380 County Rte. 28, Watkins Glen, NY 14891 • Phone 607-535-9614 • Fax 607-535-2994 • www.fingerlakes-ny.com/CastelGrisch • castelgrisch@aol.com

Castel Grisch Estate is one of the more unique wineries in the Finger Lakes region, a combination hotel, restaurant, winery, vineyard, and tasting room/gift boutique, all run with a European flavor instilled by its original owners. Alois and Michelle Baggenstoss started the business here in 1982 because of its beautiful location, whose scenic hillside site and panoramic views of Seneca Lake reminded them of their native Switzerland. Tom and Barbara Malina bought the 135-acre operation in 1992 and have maintained the Baggenstosses' traditions, operating out of the winery/hotel/restaurant, which looks like a Swiss chalet or an English Tudor house and offers wonderful accommodations and cuisine with a German, Swiss, and eastern European focus (think sauerbraten, fondue, goulash, and spätzle) plus basic steak, chicken, and pasta.

Wines: $–$$$

White Wines

Cayuga White—Off-dry light white. Lively fruit flavors. Refreshing.

Chablis Grand Cru—A light, off-dry blend.

Chardonnay—Toast and almond flavors. Butternut finish comes through. Clean.

Chardonnay Reserve—Limited production. Not tasted.

Gewürztraminer—Not tasted.

Johannisberg Riesling—Floral nose. Tropical fruits. Citrus finish. Clean. Crisp. Nice.

Riesling Ice Wine—Not tasted.

Seneca Dream White—A Niagara/Delaware blend. Sweet and light.

Vidal Blanc—Light white with peach nose. Nice fruit. Crisp finish.

Vidal Blanc Ice Wine—Not tasted.

Red Wines

Baco Noir—Medium-bodied dry red. Blackberry fruit. Spicy.

Estate Reserve Burgundy—A dry red blend. Medium bodied. Nice fruit.

Seneca Dream Red—Rose petal aromas with great fruit flavors. Clean, crisp finish.

Blush Wines

Seneca Blush—Semisweet. Clean, fruity, and crisp.

HOURS AND DIRECTIONS Open daily 10 a.m.–5 p.m. year-round. Restaurant open for lunch and dinner. ■ The winery is located 2 miles above Watkins Glen. Take County Rte. 409 to County Rte. 28.

Chateau Lafayette Reneau

P.O. Box 238, Hector, NY 14841 • Phone 800-4NY-WINE or
607-546-2062 • www.clrwine.com • CLRWINE@aol.com

Known for its fine Chardonnays and Rieslings, Chateau Lafayette Reneau was founded by Richard and Elizabeth Reno in 1985 on 140 acres that are now dotted with vineyards, ponds, meadows, woodlands, and an old brick house and renovated barn winery. The 26-by-60-foot deck attached to the tasting room affords an absolutely fabulous panoramic view of Seneca Lake. Succeeding winemakers Rob Thomas and David Whiting (who now owns Red Newt Cellars) both made some excellent wines here, winning the Governor's Cup in 1998 and 2000, and in 2002 sharing the Tasters Guild International Winery of the Year award with Gloria Ferrer Champagne Caves of Sonoma.

The charming, Craftsman-style Inn at Chateau Lafayette Reneau was built in 1911 as the home of fruit farmer George Cortin, and is now a romantic little getaway with a bright, cheerful, and warm early-American farmhouse atmosphere. Each of the ten lovely guest rooms is named after one of the winery's labels (Chardonnay, Riesling, Owner's Reserve) and offers wonderful views of the lake and vineyards. Several have Jacuzzis.

Wines: $–$$

White Wines

Barrel Fermented Chardonnay—Oak, vanilla, and cinnamon come through. Lemony finish. Clean and crisp. Good. ♥

Dry Riesling—A fizzy Riesling? Yes! Peach and other fruits come through. A nice citrus finish. More off-dry than dry. Very nice. ♥ ♥

Johannisberg Riesling—A Semisweet light white. Peaches come through. Very nice.

Niagara Mist—Sweet light white.

Proprietor's Reserve Chardonnay—Chardonnay aged 10 months in new oak barrels. Pear, apples, oak, and butterscotch come through. Full bodied, well rounded, and very much worth the price. ♥

Seyval-Chardonnay—Fruity with apples coming through. Crisp. Clean. Nice.

Red Wines

Cabernet Sauvignon—A Cabernet aged in oak. Fruity. Cherries come through. Good tannins.

Cuvée Rouge—A semisweet blend of vinifera and French-American hybrid grapes. Light and lively. Smooth.

Merlot—Not tasted.

Owner's Reserve Cabernet Sauvignon—Black cherry and plum come through. A full-bodied and well-balanced red.

Pinot Noir—A light red. Cherries and currants come through.

Blush Wines

Meadow Mist—Semisweet blush blend of native American and French-American hybrid grapes. Fruity.

Pinot Noir Blanc—Off-dry blush.

Sparkling Wines

Blanc de Blancs—Sparkling Chardonnay made in the traditional *méthode champenoise* style. A rich and elegant wine.

REVIEWS AND AWARDS

Johannisberg Riesling 2001—"Best of the East" (Top Ten Wines), 2003 Annual Wineries Unlimited Seminar and Trade Show.

Late Harvest Riesling 2002—Double gold medal, 2003 Tasters Guild International Wine Competition.

Chateau Lafayette Reneau racked up ten gold medals between 1997 and 2000, with their Chardonnays winning at least one gold each year.

"Wineries such as . . . Chateau Lafayette Reneau . . . are consistently producing Rieslings that can compete with the world's best."

—Rod Smith, *Los Angeles Times* (March 28, 2001)

HOURS AND DIRECTIONS Open Apr.–Oct. Mon.–Sat. 10 a.m.–6 p.m., Sun. 11 a.m.–6 p.m.; Nov.–Mar. Mon.–Sat. 10 a.m.–5 p.m., Sun. 11 a.m.–5 p.m. ■ Take Rte. 414 12 miles north from Watkins Glen. You will pass the Finger Lakes Champagne House on your right. Chateau Lafayette Reneau will be on your right.

Earle Estates Winery & Meadery

3586 Rte. 14, Himrod, NY 14842 • Phone 607-243-9011 • Fax 315-536-1239 • www.meadery.com • meadery@hotmail.com

Founded in 1993, Earle Estates is a leader in the mead and fruit wine categories, recognized by *Wine Enthusiast* magazine in 1996, 1997, and 1998 and recommended in the Beverage Testing Institute's *Buying Guide to Wines of North America*.

John and Esther Earle bought their first colony of honeybees in 1980, which eventually led to both honey production and mead- and winemaking. Their meadery is one of only three in New York State, employing old-world secrets to make their elegant Honey Mead Traditional and a new process to make their lighter "Contemporary" variety. All told, Earle Estates offers more than twenty-five different wines, including numerous fruit wines (all from New York–grown fruits) and grape wines. In 1999, they expanded by opening the Torrey Ridge Winery 3 miles down Rte. 14, producing Earle Estates mead and fruit wines (see review in this chapter). Both the Torrey Ridge and Earle Estates operations are family run, with son Marty in charge of the Earle tasting rooms. An observational beehive there allows you to see honey-making in progress.

Wines: $–$$

White Wines

Cayuga White—A light, refreshing white.

Chardonnay—A lightly oaked wine with fruit up front and a dry finish.

Niagara—A crisp, dry white.

Riesling—A dry, fruity white. Nice.

Seyval—A crisp, dry white.

Red Wines

Cardinal Red—A light red made from a DeChaunac grape.

Blush Wines

Starlight Blush—Light.

Fruit and Honey Wines

Apple Cyser—A good, very delicate apple-honey blend.

Apple Enchantment—A nice apple wine. Not too sweet.

Autumn Harvest—Blend of 30% raspberry wine, 30% pear wine, and 40% honey wine.

Black Jewel—Semisweet black raspberry wine.

Blueberry—Rich blueberry wine.

Blueberry Bounty—Blueberry and honey. Fun.

Candlelight Blush—A blend of 35% Concord wine and 65% honey wine.

Cherry Charisma—Full cherry and honey aroma and taste.

Crimson Blush—A blend of apples and cranberries. Refreshing and unique. Really very nice.

Cruisin' Cranberry—A blend of 70% cranberry wine and 30% honey wine.

Honey Mead Contemporary Dry—Subtle honey and grape tones. Comparable to a Chardonnay.

Honey Mead Contemporary Semi-Sweet—Honey aroma with grape and apricot overtones.

Honey Mead Traditional—Honey with grape overtones. Comparable to a late-harvest Riesling.

Peach Perfection—Semisweet peach wine. Very nice.

Pear Mead—Sweeter than the Pear Wine, with both honey and pear tones.

Pear—A light pear table wine.

Raspberry Reflections—A dessert wine with raspberry and honey flavors. Very nice.

Strawberry Shadows—Strawberry and honey aroma and taste.

REVIEWS AND AWARDS

"[The Blueberry Wine is] bright ruby purple. . . . Exotically flavorful in the mouth, with vibrant acidity that lends a sense of balance to the sweetness in the finish. . . . 86 points. . . . [The Peach Perfection has a] bright straw cast . . . sweet and round on the palate, with well-defined flavors. Spritzy acidity maintains a sense of balance and keeps the finish refreshing. . . . 86 points."

—Beverage Testing Institute, *Buying Guide to Wines of North America*

HOURS AND DIRECTIONS Open May–Dec. Mon.–Sat. 10 a.m.–5:30 p.m., Sun. 11:30 a.m.–5:30 p.m.; Jan.–Apr. Thurs.–Mon. noon–5 p.m. ■ Located on the west side of Seneca Lake, halfway between Watkins Glen and Geneva. ■ From Syracuse/Albany and Rochester/Buffalo, take the N.Y. Thruway to exit 42, then Rte. 14 north. ■ From Binghamton, take Rte. 17 to Elmira, then Rte. 14 north. ■ From Corning, take Rte. 22 to Rte. 414, then Rte. 14 north in Watkins Glen.

Finger Lakes Champagne House

6075 Rte. 414, Hector, NY 14841 • Phone 607-546-5115 •
Fax 315-549-8477 • www.swedishhill.com/tastingrooms/flch.html •
www.goosewatch.com/tastingrooms/flch.html • swedhill@flare.net

Dick and Cindy Peterson of Swedish Hill and Goose Watch wineries are at it again, setting up this small champagne house on Lake Seneca, just 12 miles north of Watkins Glen and not too far from their two Lake Cayuga wineries. The only "exclusively champagne" tasting room in the Finger Lakes, it offers Swedish Hill's and Goose Watch's champagnes and makes for a nice little stop, especially if you aren't going to be visiting the other wineries. The tasting room is an inviting little space in a light gray barn with wonderful views of Seneca Lake and some of the region's premier vineyards.

Wines: $$–$$$

Sparkling Wines

Goose Watch Golden Spumante—Semisweet. Fruity and refreshing.

Goose Watch Pinot Noir Brut Rosé—A brut rosé. Dry and crisp.

Swedish Hill Blanc de Blanc—An off-dry, light, fruity sparkling wine.

Swedish Hill Brut—Dry classic blend of Pinot Noir and Chardonnay, produced and aged in the bottle on the yeast up to 4 years. Toasty. Nice finish.

Swedish Hill Naturel—A lighter, crisp, dry Chardonnay and Pinot Noir blend.

Swedish Hill Spumante Blush—Semisweet and fruity blush sparkling wine. Refreshing. Nice.

HOURS AND DIRECTIONS Open May–Oct. Mon.–Sat. 10:30 a.m.–5:30 p.m., Sun. noon–5:30 p.m.; Nov.–Apr. Sat. 10:30 a.m.–5:30 p.m., Sun. noon–5:30 p.m. ■ Located 12 miles north of Watkins Glen on Rte. 414. The winery is on the right-hand side.

Four Chimneys Farm Winery

211 Hall Rd., P.O. Box 11, Himrod, NY 14842 • Phone 607-243-7502 •
Fax 607-243-8156 • fourchim@linkny.com

Located in a Civil War–period Victorian estate on Seneca Lake's western shore, along Yates County's Hall Rd. Scenic Corridor, Four Chimneys was the first organic winery in North America. The operation was founded by former Russian studies professor and Macmillan Publishing editor Walter Pederson, who planted his first vines in 1976 and sold his first bottle of wine in 1980. The huge pegged-construction barn, originally erected in 1860, has monstrous oak timbers that rise 36 feet, but the real story here is that the winery farms using only natural elements, or finds ingenious ways to circumvent problems—using sticky flypaper with scent attractors, for example, instead of insecticides, and using extensive filtration in lieu of chemicals to weed out harmful bacteria in their wines.

Four Chimneys has been recognized by NOFA (Northeast Organic Farming Association) for efforts like these, and takes the organic approach a step further by avoiding the use of animal products in their wines, including FDA-approved additives such as bull's blood, gelatin, and egg whites.

Wines: $–$$$

White Wines
Day Spring—A light, aromatic, and fruity white. Nice.

Kingdom White—A dry, mildly oaked Aurore wine. Fruity, smooth.

Reserve White—A blend of Chardonnay and Aurore. Dry, oak-fermented, finished with malolactic fermentation. Full bodied and buttery.

Red Wines
Kingdom Red—A dry red blend, barrel aged.

Reserve Red—A robust, deep, full-bodied red.

Blush Wines
Eye of the Dove—Dry, Provençal-style rosé.

Golden Crown—A semisweet blush wine. Floral nose and lots of fruit.

Sparkling Wines
Coronation Brut Champagne—Organic sparkling wine made in the traditional fermented-in-the-bottle *méthode champenoise*.

Dessert and Fruit Wines
Blueberry Skies—Made from locally grown organic blueberries and grapes.

Celestial Peach—A blend of organically grown peaches and grapes. All fresh peaches are used, no artificial flavorings or concentrates. Very nice.

Dry Blueberry—Dry berry wine, oaked for balance. A pleasant surprise.

Eye of the Bee—Rosé-colored, rich, sweet grape and honey wine. Just the right amount of acidity. Very nice!

Honeydew Moon—An unusual melon and grape wine. Interesting.

Kyrie Dessert—A rich, golden, late-harvest-style dessert wine. Nice balance between acidity and sweetness.

Raspberry Sunrise—Made from organically grown raspberries. Fruity, sweet, tart.

Shingle Point Red—A rich, sweet, port-style wine aged in oak.

Strawberry Meadows—Rich, sweet dessert wine made from organically grown strawberries.

Wild Blue Yonder—Rich, sweet dessert wine made from 100% wild blueberries.

REVIEWS AND AWARDS
Kingdom Red 2002—Gold medal, 2003 Finger Lakes International Wine Competition.

"The most picturesque winery in the Finger Lakes."   *—National Geographic*

HOURS AND DIRECTIONS Open Mon.–Sat. 10 a.m.–5 p.m., Sun. noon–5 p.m., year-round. ■ Located 15 miles north of Watkins Glen on Rte. 14. Turn right onto Hall Rd. Look for signs.

Fox Run Vineyards

670 Rte. 14, Penn Yan, NY 14527 • Phone 800-636-9786 or 315-536-4616 • www.foxrunvineyards.com • info@foxrunvineyards.com

Now one of the top wineries on the East Coast, Fox Run was founded in 1990 by a retiree who sold the business 3 years later after the workload proved too great. The buyer, Scott Osborn, is a man with long experience in the wine trade, beginning as a labeler and climbing all the way up to general manager of Pindar on Long Island. He's a man with ideas, and has surrounded himself with capable people, including vineyard manager John Kaiser, vice president Andy Hale, and master winemaker Peter Bell. Together, they've created a beautiful and exciting winery whose award-winning wines have been recommended by every major journal. Their Pinot Noir won the New York Wine and Food Classic Governor's Cup in 1997, and was noted by former Windows on the World beverage director Andrea Immer as "a great wine."

Located in the hills of Penn Yan on the shores of Seneca Lake, Fox Run is one of those wineries that people visit and then go home wanting to own. Out in the fields, almost 60 acres are planted to vines, with 15 more slowly coming into production, while the winery itself is housed in a gray New England–like barn with large windows that bring gorgeous views right into the tasting room. Beautiful views are also to be had from the patios, the gift shop, and the new Café at Fox Run, which serves delicious gourmet soups, exotic salads, and specialty sandwiches, all made from local farmers' produce and ingredients.

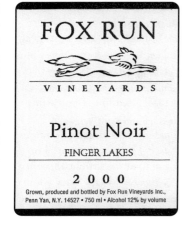

In recent years, Fox Run has produced as many as 18,000 cases per year, with almost half that total dedicated to Chardonnay and Riesling. Their goal is 25,000 cases, and based on their success till now, we don't doubt that they'll reach it.

Wines: $–$$$

White Wines

Arctic Fox—Off-dry light white blend. Refreshing.

Chardonnay—A clean, crisp, light Chardonnay. Pears and apples come through. ♥

Dry Riesling—Light, with apricot and citrus flavors. ♥

Gewürztraminer—Highly distinctive, with a floral bouquet and a richness of fruits midpalate. Dry finish. Very nice.

Reserve Chardonnay—Complex and creamy. Peaches and lemon come through. Nice.

Riesling—Off-dry version of the light German-style wine. Nice. ♥

Red Wines

Cabernet Franc—Rich red, aged in oak, with a mouthful of berries and a dry finish.

Cabernet Sauvignon—A Cabernet done in the classic French style. Berries come through. Nice spiciness to it.

Lemberger—Full-bodied, moderately tannic dry red. Not tasted.

Meritage—A deep, dry red blend aged in oak.

Merlot—Dark fruits and smokiness lead to a rich wine with dry finish. Nice.

Pinot Noir—Not quite off-dry, but a Pinot with a slight twinge of sweetness. Very drinkable. A wonderful pasta or burger wine. Especially nice with grilled foods. ♥ ♥

Reserve Pinot Noir—A very nice Pinot. Floral nose leads to berries and cherry. Smooth. Dry.

Sable—Off-dry, soft red.

Blush Wines

Ruby Vixen—Semisweet blush. Strawberries come through.

Ports

Vintage Character Port—Not tasted.

REVIEWS AND AWARDS

"[The 1998 Cabernet Franc] just blew us away. We are extremely stingy with five
    stars, but this one really stood out." —F. Paul Pacult, *Sky* magazine (February 2001)

"[A] good example of the new generation of Finger Lakes winemaking; some of
    the region's best Chardonnay, Riesling, Pinot Noir and Bordeaux-style red. . . .
    Three stars."   —*Hugh Johnson's Pocket Wine Book 2002*

"A rising star. [Their Riesling] shouldn't be missed." — Karen MacNeil, *The Wine Bible*

"Fox Run Vineyards is gaining a reputation for producing not only some of the
    best wines in New York State, but wines on a world class level as well."
    —Scott Gunerman, *Wine Brats* (October 15, 2001)

"[Winemaker Peter] Bell continues to make outstanding dry and off-dry Finger
    Lakes Riesling. Fox Run Rieslings have beautiful fruit and, more important,
    a clear underlying stoniness."   —Rod Smith, *Los Angeles Times* (March 28, 2001)

Chardonnay 1999: "Best Buy. . . . Score—86 points." —*Wine Enthusiast* (March 2002)

Dry Riesling 1999: "One of the top 25 Rieslings." —*Vines Magazine* (May–June 2002)

Dry Riesling 2000: "One of the 10 perfect BBQ White Wines."
    —F. Paul Pacult and Susan Woodley, *Spirit Journal*

Reserve Pinot Noir 1999: "Four stars. . . . Among the finest U.S. Pinots."
    —*Food & Wine* magazine *Wine Guide 2002*

Riesling 1999: "[One of the best wines for] sipping on the porch."
    —*Bon Appétit* (August 2001)

HOURS AND DIRECTIONS Open Mon.–Sat. 10 a.m.–6 p.m., Sun. 11 a.m.–6 p.m., year-round. Café open daily 11 a.m.–5 p.m. ■ The winery is at 670 Rte. 14, just 8 miles south of Geneva on the west side of Seneca Lake. From Watkins Glen, Geneva, Ithaca, or Rochester it's an unhurried, scenic ride along the Seneca Lake Wine Trail.

Fulkerson Winery & Juice Plant

5576 Rte. 14, Dundee, NY 14837 • Phone 607-243-7883 • Fax 607-243-8337

Home winemakers can make up to 200 gallons of wine per year for their own personal consumption, but since most don't have the space to grow their own grapes, they have to buy them elsewhere. They have two options: go to a grape grower, who will sell them fresh fruit, or get pressed grape juice. Nancy and Sayre Fulkerson offer both, plus numerous other supplies, running one of the most successful home-winemaking supply companies on the East Coast. Since 1990, they've also made wine on a piece of land that's been active as a farm since 1805—and the awards just keep coming in. In addition to tasting the wines, visitors can also check out a whole raft of fun wine-making accoutrements. It's quite an education!

Wines: $–$$

White Wines

Bailey Bridge White—An off-dry blended white.

Chardonnay—A buttery, full-bodied, dry white with toasty oak and vanilla aromas.
    Nice.

Delaware—Rich, fruity white wine.

Diamond—An off-dry wine made from Diamond grapes, developed in Brighton, N.Y., in 1870.

Dry Riesling—Light, dry white with tropical fruits and a grapefruit finish.

Gewürztraminer—Light, off-dry white, with up-front tropical-like flavors. Puckers at the end.

Johannisberg Riesling—Light and fruity.

Traminette—Light, off-dry white, spicy with pear, apples, and honey. Nice.

Red Wines

Bailey Bridge Red—Semisweet red with a big strawberry nose.

Cabernet Franc—Dry, full-bodied red in the Bordeaux style. Berries and plums. Dry finish.

Cabernet Sauvignon—Deep, full-bodied red with a nice round taste and a dry finish.

Merlot—Made from grapes grown in Long Island. Black cherries and oak come through. Dry.

Pinot Noir—Medium bodied, with balanced oak and fruit.

Red Zeppelin—Semisweet red blend.

Reserve Red—A light, off-dry Baco and Chelois blend aged in oak.

Vincent—Light, dry red with lots of fruit. Big blackberries. Dry finish. Nice.

Blush Wines

Sunset Blush—A light, Catawba-based blush.

Dessert and Fruit Wines

Matinee—A light, sweet white. Kiwi comes through.

Ravat 51 Vignoles—Late-harvest German-style dessert wine. Golden color. Rich, fruity, and well balanced. Very nice.

Vidal Ice Wine—Thick, rich, golden dessert wine aged in oak. Very sweet but not cloying. Honey, peaches, and pears come through.

REVIEWS AND AWARDS

Delaware 1999—Bronze medal, 2000 International Eastern Wine Competition.

Pinot Noir 1997—Bronze medal, 2000 Grand Harvest Awards.

Ravat 51 Vignoles 1997—Gold medal, 2002 New York Food and Wine Classic; gold medal, 2001 Grand Harvest Awards.

Traminette 2000—Silver medal, 2001 New York State Fair Wine Competition.

Vincent 1999—Bronze medal, 2000 Grand Harvest Awards.

HOURS AND DIRECTIONS Open May–Dec. Mon.–Sat. 10 a.m.–5 p.m., Sun. noon–5 p.m.; Jan.–Apr. Sat.–Sun. noon–5 p.m. ■ Located 8 miles north of Watkins Glen on Rte. 14, just after Arcadian Estate Vineyards.

Glenora Wine Cellars

5435 Rte. 14, Dundee, NY 14837 • Phone 800-243-5513 or 607-243-5511 • Fax 607-243-5514 • www.glenora.com

Named as "one of the region's most famous historic wineries" in Karen MacNeil's *Wine Bible*, Glenora was founded in 1976 by Ted Griesinger, who later sold to Gene Pierce, Ed Dalrymple, and Scott Welliver. It has become well known for Chardonnays and seasonal wines, and was noted as one of the "great U.S. sparkling wine producers" by the Beverage Testing Institute's *Buying Guide to Wines of North America*, alongside such well-established names as Domaine Chandon, Gloria Ferrer, Mumm Cuvée Napa, and Piper-Sonoma.

Glenora's vineyards stretch from the winery down toward the lake's shore and, along with grapes purchased from other New York vineyards, produces more than 40,000 cases per year. On the property, the Inn at Glenora Wine Cellars offers thirty spacious guest rooms elegantly furnished with Stickley furniture and a complimentary bottle of Glenora wine. Ten "Vintner's Select" guest rooms come with Jacuzzis. Veraisons Restaurant, a gorgeous room trimmed in cherry wood, features regional fusion cuisine with a French classical influence, along with beautiful views of the lake and vineyards. The chef works closely with local farmers to get the freshest produce.

Wines: $–$$$

White Wines

Barrel-Fermented Chardonnay—Creamy, full-bodied Chardonnay with melon and tropical fruits. Aged in oak.

Barrel-Fermented Pinot Blanc—A dry white aged in oak. Pear and citrus flavors come through. A nice finish.

Chardonnay—A dry, classic white, lightly oaked. Melon and other fruits come through.

Dry Riesling—Dry, light white. Tropical fruit flavors. Crisp. Clean. Very nice.

Glenora Alpine White—An inexpensive, semisweet blend of Chardonnay and Cayuga.

Glenora Cayuga White—An inexpensive, semisweet, light white wine.

Glenora's Niagara—Inexpensive, semisweet wine.

Riesling—Semisweet, light white wine. Honey and tropical flavors come through.

Seyval Blanc—A light, refreshing, off-dry white. Melon comes through.

Red Wines

Glenora Bobsled Red—A good pizza or burger wine created as a fund-raiser for rebuilding the historic bobsled run at Lake Placid, site of the 1932 and 1980 Winter Olympic games.

Lodi Cabernet Sauvignon—Dry red, aged in small oak barrels. Raspberries come through.

Merlot—Dry, deep, rich, elegant red. Currant and berry flavors come through. Good.

Syrah—A rich red wine with shades of black cherry, peppery spice, and French oak.

Vintner's Select Cabernet Franc—A dry, oak-aged, full-bodied red. Blackberry comes through.

Vintner's Select Meritage—A blend of Cabernet Franc (62%), Cabernet Sauvignon (32%), and Merlot (6%) made in the classic Bordeaux style. Big raspberry and blackberry flavors. Dry finish.

Vintner's Select Pinot Noir—Deep plum and black cherry aromas with French oak.

Blush Wines

Glenora's Baco Noir Rosé—Semisweet and different.

Glenora Classic Blush—An inexpensive, semisweet rosé.

Sparkling Wines

Blanc de Blancs, Méthode Champenoise—Dry, 100% Chardonnay sparkling wine.

Brut, Méthode Champenoise—Made from Pinot Noir and Chardonnay. Dry, full bodied, and creamy. ♥

Glenora Spumante—A light, white, semisweet sparkling wine in the Italian tradition.

Peach Spumante—Sweet peach/grape sparkling wine, fermented in the bottle. ♥ ♥

25th Anniversary Cuvée—Dry white sparkler aged *en tirage* more than 5 years.

Ports

Port—Produced from Cabernet Sauvignon, Baco Noir, Syrah, and Merlot grapes, then aged in French oak barrels.

Fruit Wines and Blends

Glenora Jammin' Red—A sweet blend of wine and natural fruit flavor.

Peach Orchard Farms Blueberry Breeze—Light white wine and blueberry juice.

Peach Orchard Farms Cranberry Chablis—A sweet Cayuga/cranberry blend.

Peach Orchard Farms Peach Passion—Semisweet, light white table wine enhanced with peach nectar.

Peach Orchard Farms Raspberry Rosé—A nice, semilight sipping white touched with raspberry juice.

REVIEWS AND AWARDS

Blanc de Blancs 1998—"Best of Class" and "Best New World Sparkling Wine," 2002 Jerry Mead New World International Wine Competition.

Brut 1998—Double gold medal, 2001 New York State Fair Wine Competition.

Riesling, Vintner's Select 2000—Double gold medal, 2001 New York Wine and Food Classic.

"Highly recommended New York Chardonnay. . . . In the top ten."
—Beverage Testing Institute, *Buying Guide to Wines of North America*

Johannisberg Riesling Finger Lakes 1995: "84 points."
—*Wine Spectator's Ultimate Guide to Tasting Wines*

Riesling Finger Lakes Vintner's Select 2000: "Score: 87."
—*Wine Spectator* (October 2002)

HOURS AND DIRECTIONS Open May–June daily, 10 a.m.–6 p.m.; July–Aug. daily, 10 a.m.–8 p.m.; Sept.–Oct. daily, 10 a.m.–6 p.m.; Nov.–Apr. Mon.–Sat. 10 a.m.–5 p.m., Sun. noon–5 p.m. Veraisons Restaurant is open for breakfast (8–10 a.m.), lunch (11:30 a.m.–3 p.m.), and dinner (Sun.–Thurs. 5–9 p.m., Fri.–Sat. 5–10 p.m.). ■ From Buffalo, take the N.Y. Thruway east to exit 42 (Rte. 14). Take 14 south approximately 35 miles to Glenora. The winery will be on the left. ■ From Watkins Glen, follow Rte. 14 north 8.5 miles. The winery will be on the right.

Hazlitt 1852 Vineyards ✿ ✿

5712 Rte. 414, Hector, NY 14841 • Phone 888-750-0494 or 607-546-9463 • Fax 607-546-5712 • www.hazlitt1852.com • hazlitt@lightlink.com

Hazlitt's had been growing tree fruit and grapes on this farm for over 130 years before Jerry and Elaine Hazlitt founded their winery in 1984, building the most relaxed, casual tasting room in the Finger Lakes, staffed with fifth- and sixth-generation Hazlitts for a total family winery experience. Munch on popcorn, learn about the Seneca Indians through all kinds of artifacts, browse a collection of antique tools, or just enjoy the wide range of award-winning wines, with several to suit any palate.

In 2001 the winery won fifty-four medals, ten of them gold, and in 2002 their run of 1999 Cabernet Sauvignon, Merlot, and Cabernet Franc won a slew of golds, signaling a shift from sweet, casual wines to drier varieties and raising their profile among serious wine drinkers. While my wife and I liked their dry reds (our usual taste), we also bought the Schooner White, a multiple-award winner that's become one of our favorites. It's named for the family's tall ship *Chatney*, which is available for charter on Lake Seneca.

Wines: $–$$

White Wines

Chardonnay—Full bodied, with tropical fruits and creamy mouth feel. Fermented in small oak casks.

Gewürztraminer—Light white with nice citrus and tropical fruits. Crisp and clean.

Pinot Gris—A rich, dry white. Pleasant fruit. Spicy.

Riesling—Off-dry white. Pears and apples come through. Crisp and clean.

Schooner White—An off-dry white blend. Not too fruity. Very nice. ♥ ♥

Spyder Bite—A semisweet white made from Spy and Spygold apples. One of their more popular wines. ♥

White Stag—A sweet blend of Cayuga, Ravat, and Vidal. Fruity.

Red Wines

Bramble Berry—A sweet blend of red and blackberry essence with grape wine.

Merlot—Dry, deep red with currants and cherries. Nice finish.

Schooner Red—An off-dry blend of Baco Noir, Cabernet Franc, Cabernet Sauvignon, and Merlot. Just tinged with sweetness. ♥

Blush Wines

Cabin Fever—A semisweet blush blend of Catawba and Cayuga. Nice.

Sparkling Wines

Lame Duck—Sweet sparkling wine made from a blend of native American grapes.

Other Wines

Cabernet Franc, Cabernet Sauvignon, Ravat-51 (their first late-harvest dessert wine), *Red Cat*

REVIEWS AND AWARDS

Cabernet Franc 1999—Double gold medal, 2001 New York State Fair Wine Competition; gold medal and best of class, 2001 Jerry Mead New World International Wine Competition; gold medal, 2001 Indiana State Fair Indy International Wine Competition; gold medal, 2001 Tasters Guild International Wine Competition; 2001 Jefferson Cup finalist.

Cabernet Sauvignon 1999—Gold medal and best of class, 2001 New York Wine and Food Classic; gold and best of class, 2001 New York State Fair Wine Competition; gold medal, 2001 Tasters Guild International Wine Competition.

Chardonnay 1999—Gold medal, 2001 Tasters Guild International Wine Competition; silver medal, 2001 Finger Lakes International Wine Competition; silver medal, 2001 Great Lakes Wine Competition.

Merlot 1999—Gold medal and best of class, 2001 New York State Fair Wine Competition; gold medal, 2001 Great Lakes Wine Competition.

Riesling 2000—Gold medal, 2001 New York Wine and Food Classic; gold medal, 2001 International Eastern Wine Competition; 2001 Jefferson Cup finalist; silver medal, 2001 New York State Fair Wine Competition.

HOURS AND DIRECTIONS Open year-round Mon.–Sat. 10 a.m.–5 p.m., Sun. noon–5 p.m. ■ From Watkins Glen, take Rte. 414 north approximately 10 miles. Go through the town of Hector. After you pass Leidenfrost Vineyards, Hazlitt 1852 Vineyards will be on your right. If you reach Valois, you've gone too far.

Hermann J. Wiemer Vineyard ✡ ✡ ✡

Rte. 14, Box 38, Dundee, NY 14837 • Phone 800-371-7971 • Fax 607-243-7983 • www.wiemer.com • wiemer@linkny.com

The first time I tasted a Hermann J. Wiemer Vineyard wine was at the New York State Wine Festival, and I was a novice, traveling with my wife and a friend. We came upon their unassuming stand, looked at the unassuming labels, and shrugged. We'd never heard of them, but why not take a taste? We weren't expecting much, but we were waylaid. There wasn't a wine we didn't like. I look back on those tasting notes with a sense of humor. Why? Because Hermann J. Wiemer is probably the most celebrated living winemaker on the entire East Coast, called one of the pioneering visionaries of American wine by *Food & Wine*, praised by every other major food and wine magazine, and rated with two-to-three stars in *Hugh Johnson's Pocket Wine Book 2002*.

Wiemer was raised in Germany's Moselle Valley, where his family had been involved in the winemaking business for more than 300 years—his father was one of those responsible for replanting Germany's wine regions after World War II. Hermann came to the United States in 1968 and became winemaker at Bully Hill, where he worked from 1968 to 1980 and won numerous awards for wines made from hybrids and native American grape stocks. In 1973, however, he began planting his own vines, concentrating only on vinifera—the first such grapes planted in the Seneca Lake region. By 1979 he was able to produce one barrel, by 1980 he had opened his doors to the public, and by 1989 his wines were being served to first-class passengers on American Airlines and to patrons at Manhattan's poshest restaurants, including Lutece. *Food & Wine*'s *Wine Guide 2002* rated three of Wiemer's wines—the Reserve Johannisberg Riesling and the 1997 and 1998 Chardonnays—among the top ten from New York State, and *Wine Spectator*'s 1998 *Guide to Great Wine Values* numbered his Rieslings among the "Most Reliable Values," alongside Chateau St. Michelle and Dr. Konstantin Frank.

Surrounded by vineyards, the 140-acre winery is as beautiful as its wines, and today produces more than 12,000 cases per year. A separate and highly successful nursery supplies other vineyards throughout North America.

Wines: $–$$$

White Wines

Chardonnay—Classic full-bodied white with tangerines, apples, toast, and minerals. ♥

Dry Johannisberg Riesling—A crisp dry Johannisberg Riesling in the classic German *Mosel Kabinett* style. Fruity nose with well-balanced fruit flavors and a dry finish. ♥

Estate White—A blend of Rieslings, Chardonnay, and Pinot Gris. A nice, light, off-dry sipping wine.

Gewürztraminer—Off-dry version of the German classic grape. Apples and melons come through, as well as a touch of citrus at the end. Very nice. ♥

Late-Harvest Johannisberg Riesling—An Alsatian-style late-harvest wine. Apricots and honey flavors come through. Very nice balance.

Reserve Johannisberg Riesling—A very dry Riesling with beautiful structure and acid balance. Apples and pears come through. Great mouth feel. Lively. Dry finish. ♥

Semi-Dry Johannisberg Riesling—Semisweet, light white wine. Very fruity but with nice acidity. Very nice. ♥ ♥

Red Wines

Estate Red—A light red blend of Pinot Noir, Gamay, and Dornfelder (a classic German variety). Dry finish.

Merlot—A deep, full-bodied red with soft round edges. Cherry and plum come through. Dry finish.

Pinot Noir, old vines—A smooth, medium-bodied, dry wine, garnet red in color, with flavors and aroma of black cherries and French oak.

Blush Wines

Dry Rosé—A full-bodied blend of Pinot Noir and Gamay Noir.

Sparkling Wines

Blanc de Blanc—Made in the *méthode champenoise* tradition. More extradry than brut. Slightly softer. Nice balance. ♥ ♥

Cuvée Brut—A classic, full-bodied blend of Pinot Noir and Chardonnay grapes in the *méthode champenoise* tradition. Lively fruit flavors. Dry finish. ♥ ♥

Dessert Wines

Select Late-Harvest Ice Wine—Thick, rich, golden dessert wine. Apricots, honey, and tropical fruits come through. Very nice balance.

REVIEWS AND AWARDS

"Perhaps the second most significant winemaker to change the course of Finger Lakes wine is German-born Hermann Wiemer."

— Jeff Morgan, *Wine Spectator* (September 1995)

Blanc de Blanc 1998: "Score: 82."   —*Wine Spectator* (December 2001)

Late-Harvest Johannisberg Riesling 1997: "Score: 86."

—*Wine Spectator* (December 1998)

HOURS AND DIRECTIONS Open year-round Mon.–Fri. 10 a.m.–5 p.m.; additionally, Apr.–Nov. Sat. 10 a.m.–5 p.m., Sun. 11 a.m.–5 p.m. ■ Hermann J. Wiemer Vineyard is located on the west side of Seneca Lake, 14 miles north of Watkins Glen and approximately 20 miles south of the center of Geneva. ■ From the N.Y. Thruway (I-90), take exit 42 to Rte. 14 south. ■ If coming from the south via Rte. 17 westbound, take exit 52N (Horseheads) to Rte. 14 north. ■ If coming from Rte. 17 eastbound, take exit 46 in Corning to Rte. 414 north; follow 414 to Watkins Glen, and then take Rte. 14 north.

Lakewood Vineyards

4024 Rte. 14, Watkins Glen, NY 14891 • Phone 607-535-9252 •
Fax 607-535-6656 • www.lakewoodvineyards.com • lwoodwine@aol.com

The Stamp family had been growing grapes near Reading Center as far back as 1918, planting their first vineyards on Lakewood Farm in 1952. From then until the mid-1980s the Stamps sold grapes to winemakers, then opened their own winery in 1988. Currently, Monty and Beverly Stamp and their sons David and Christopher have more than 65 acres of vineyards under cultivation. In 1997, they were named Grower of the Year, Wine Family of the Year, and Winemaker of the Year, and in 1999 they were named Winegrape Grower of the Year. Among their offerings, the Glaciovinum is a standout, a unique and wonderful blend of Delaware and Concord that was noted by John Schreiner in his critically acclaimed book *Ice Wine: The Complete Story.*

Wines: $–$$$

White Wines

Carpe Vinum—A crisp, fruity Cayuga white.

Chardonnay—Burgundian-style Chardonnay with 40% malolactic fermentation and 100% barrel fermented in small French and American oak cooperage. Full bodied with tropical fruits and dry finish. Nice.

Dry Riesling—Crisp and fruity, with a dry finish.

Long Stem White—German-style white. Light and crisp, with a hint of sweetness.

Niagara—A fruity wine.

Semi-Dry Riesling—Peach and pears come through. Crisp. Clean.

Vignoles—Light, fruity white. Apples and apricots come through. Nice. ♥

White Catawba—Semisweet Catawba.

Red Wines

Cabernet Franc—Deep, rich red. Black raspberry comes through.

Crianza—Off-dry Cabernet Sauvignon. Cherry pie comes through.

Crystallus—A full-bodied blend of 61% Cabernet Sauvignon and 39% Cabernet Franc. Very nice.

Long Stem Red—An earthy, medium-red blend of Baco Noir, Foch, and Leon Millot. Dry finish.

Pinot Noir—Deep ruby red. Cherries and plums come through.

Blush Wines

Abby Rosé—Semisweet ruby blush.

Delaware—A ruby blush blend.

Honey Wines

Wildflower Mystic Mead—A blend of wildflower and orange blossom honeys.

Dessert Wines and Ports

Borealis Ice Wine—Made from Concord grapes. Sweet, rich, and fruity.

Glaciovinum—A lovely ice wine. Tropical fruits flow over the palate. Orange and vanilla overtones. Nice finish. Very good. ♥ ♥

Port—Made from 100% late-harvest Baco Noir grapes.

REVIEWS AND AWARDS

Crystallus—Silver medal, 2002 New York Wine and Food Competition.

Glaciovinum 1999—Gold medal, 2001 Los Angeles County Fair Wine Competition; gold medal, 2002 Riverside International Wine Competition.

Pinot Noir—Gold medal, 2002 New York Wine and Food Competition.

"With classic Old World aromas of minerals, petrol, green apples and roses, this [1998 Dry Riesling] has a rich, complex palate perfect for Thai curry."
—Debra E. Meiburg, *Rochester Magazine* (September/October 2000)

Riesling Finger Lakes 2001: "Score: 86."   —*Wine Spectator* (December 2002)

HOURS AND DIRECTIONS Open Mon.–Sat. 10 a.m.–5 p.m., Sun. noon–5 p.m.; closed Easter, Thanksgiving, Christmas, and New Year's Day. ■ Take Rte. 14 north 5 miles out of Watkins Glen. The winery is located just before Rte. 14A deviates from Rte. 14, on the right side.

Lamoreaux Landing Wine Cellars   ✫ ✫

9224 Rte. 414, Lodi, NY 14860 • Phone 607-582-6011 • Fax 607-582-6010 • www.lamoreauxwine.com • llwc@epix.net

Bar none, Lamoreaux Landing has the most striking tasting room on the East Coast, and even gives some established West Coast wineries a run for their money. The striking neo–Greek Revival structure towers over the landscape, rising along a river valley like some Greek temple out of Fritz Lang's *Metropolis*. Inside, it's just as tasteful, with wood-paneled walls.

The winery was established by Mark Wagner, who grew up in a grape-growing family. Winemaker Samuel Alexandre presides over creation of the award-winning wines.

Wines: $–$$$

White Wines

Chardonnay (barrel fermented)—Apple, pineapple, and citrus come through. Lightly oaked. Clean, crisp, and light. Nice. ♥

Chardonnay Reserve (barrel fermented)—Full bodied, rich, and mellow. Nice.

Dry Riesling—Citrus, pineapple, and peach flavors come through.

Estate White (barrel fermented)—A blend of Chardonnay and Riesling. Flavors of apples and pears, with a citrusy ending. Clean and crisp. ♥

Gewürztraminer—Tropical fruits come through. Clean, crisp.

Semi-Dry Riesling—Semisweet white. Floral nose. Tropical fruits come through.

Red Wines

Cabernet Franc—A fruit-forward, barrel-aged red with a very dry finish. ♥

Estate Red—A medium-red blend of Pinot Noir and Cabernet Franc.

Merlot—A full-bodied, barrel-aged, dry red with flavors of blackberries and currants.

Pinot Noir—A bright, dry, barrel-aged red. Berries and spiciness come through.

LAMOREAUX
LANDING

FINGER LAKES
Cabernet Franc

Sparkling Wines

Brut—Classic blend of Chardonnay and Pinot Noir. Toasted almond and citrus. Nice.

REVIEWS AND AWARDS

Cabernet Franc 2000—Gold medal, 2003 Great Lakes Wine Competition.

Chardonnay Reserve 2000—Silver medal, 2001 New York Wine and Food Classic.

Gewürztraminer 2000—Gold medal, 2003 Great Lakes Wine Competition; gold medal, 2001 New York Wine and Food Classic.

Gewürztraminer 2001—Gold medal, 2003 Great Lakes Wine Competition; gold medal, 2003 Jerry Mead New World International Wine Competition.

Merlot 1999—Gold medal, 2001 New York State Fair Wine Competition.

Semi-Dry Riesling 2000—Silver medal, 2001 New York Wine and Food Classic.

"The winery's sheer originality defies you to pass by . . . and the wines are equally arresting."   —Jeff Morgan, *Wine Spectator* (September 1995)

"This is a serious winery—with its Greek Revival style, it even feels a bit like a temple—and there's not a single labrusca or hybrid varietal on the 11-wine list. . . . [the Gewürztraminer was] so heady it was hard to pull my nose away from it."   —Dana Nigri, *Wine Spectator* (February 2000)

"Nothing symbolizes the improvements in Finger Lakes winemaking better than this three-year-old winery." —Howard G. Goldberg, *New York Times* (September 17, 1995)

HOURS AND DIRECTIONS Open year-round Mon.–Sat. 10 a.m.–5 p.m., Sun. noon–5 p.m. ■ From the N.Y. Thruway (I-90), take exit 41 (Rte. 414) south to Seneca Falls. In Seneca Falls take Rtes. 414 and 5 and 20 east to Rte. 414 south. ■ From Corning, take Rte. 17 (new I-86) to exit 47 to Rte. 414 north. ■ From Ithaca, take Rte. 13 (Meadow St.) to Rte. 96 north to Interlaken; turn left onto Rte. 96A to Lodi, then left onto Rte. 414 south, 3 miles to the winery. ■ From Elmira, take Rte. 17 (new I-86) to exit 52N to Rte. 14 north to Watkins Glen, then 414 north.

Leidenfrost Vineyards

5677 Rte. 414, Hector, NY 14841 • Phone 607-546-2800

The Leidenfrost family has been growing produce on this parcel of land since 1947, and today John Leidenfrost, Jr., son of a home winemaker, runs an interesting little vineyard and winery, known for its reds.

White Wines

Chardonnay—Clean and crisp.

Gewürztraminer—A light white in the best Alsatian tradition.

Log Cabin White—A light, off-dry white.

Riesling—A light, off-dry edition of the German classic.

Red Wines

Baco Beaujolais—A light, fruity red with a tart finish.

Baco Noir—Medium bodied.

Cabernet Sauvignon—Full bodied and dry.

Catawba—A semisweet sipping wine.

Log Cabin Red—An off-dry red.

Merlot—A deep red with a dry finish.

Pinot Noir—A light- to medium-bodied red.

Blush Wines

Seneca Rosé—A light, fruity blush.

HOURS AND DIRECTIONS Open June–Nov. daily, noon–5 p.m.; Dec.–May Fri.–Sun. noon–5 p.m., and by appointment. ■ From Watkins Glen, take route 414 north. Go through Hector. After the town, you'll pass signs for Red Newt Cellars. Leidenfrost will be on your left.

Logan Ridge Estates Winery ✡

3800 Ball Diamond Rd., Hector, NY 14841 • Phone 866-546-6486 or
607-546-6600 • www.loganridge.com • gene@loganridge.com

This is one of Lake Seneca's newest wineries, creating award-winning Chardonnays, Rieslings, Cabernet Francs, Cabernet Sauvignons, Merlots, and Pinot Blancs. Both the winery and restaurant, Petioles, offer spectacular hilltop views from under an airy cathedral ceiling, accented by a towering fireplace and chimney. With seating for more than 225 people, the restaurant is perfect for special occasions.

Wines: $–$$$

White Wines

Chardonnay—Straw colored, clean, crisp, and refreshing.
Pinot Blanc—Light, clean, and dry. Pear comes through. Very good. ♥
Reserve Chardonnay—Apples and pears come through. Medium bodied. Tangy. Crisp. ♥
Riesling—Semisweet light white. Apricot comes through. Citrusy finish.

Red Wines

Cabernet Franc—Light- to medium-bodied dry red. Cherry comes through.
Merlot—Blackberry and plum come through. Deep red color. Nice, dry finish. ♥
Pinot Noir—Medium-bodied dry red. Cherries and plums come through.

Blush Wines

Rosé of Sangiovese—A Sangiovese off-dry blush wine. Raspberry comes through.

HOURS AND DIRECTIONS Winery open daily year-round, 11 a.m.–5 p.m. Lunch daily 11 a.m.–3 p.m.; dinner Sun.–Thurs. 5–8 p.m., Fri.–Sat. 5–9 p.m. ■ From Watkins Glen, take Rte. 414 north to Ball Diamond Rd., between Hector and Valois. Logan Ridge Estates will be on your right. Watch for the sign.

Nagy's New Land Vineyards

623 Lerch Rd., Geneva, NY 14456 • Phone 315-585-4432 •
Fax 315-585-9981 • info@nagyswines.com

Founded by Nancy Newland and her former husband, New Land Vineyards debuted in 1982 as one of the first wineries opened under New York State's Farm Winery laws. Dale J. Nagy, whose family has made wine for generations, bought the property in September 2001 and now uses all of its grapes for wine, rather than selling a large percentage of them.

New Land has always had a reputation for small output and good ratings. Their Pinot Noir once rated as high as 86 in *Wine Spectator*, and in October 1992 the *Ithaca Journal* called their varietals "nothing short of extraordinary."

Wines: $–$$

White Wines

Chardonnay—Slightly off-dry. Oak aged. Clean and crisp.
Dry Gewürztraminer—Dry Alsatian-style white. Aromatic, with a nice finish.
Dry Riesling—Medium bodied, crisp, fruity, and dry, with a clean finish.
Gewürztraminer—Semisweet and very spicy. Nice nose.
Riesling—Off-dry white. Pears and apricots come through.
Sauvignon Blanc—Dry, clean, and crisp. The only Sauvignon Blanc grown and
    produced in the Finger Lakes region.

Red Wines

Nagy's Red—Fruity, semisweet blend of Delaware and Pinot Noir.

Pinot Noir—Black cherries come through. Aged in new American oak. In the past, the winery's signature wine.

Blush Wines

Pinot Noir Blanc—Off-dry blush.

Dessert Wines

Late-Harvest Riesling—Thick and rich, with a nice balance.

Other Wines

Late Harvest Sauvignon Blanc, Raspberry Riesling, Cabernet Sauvignon, Merlot, Merlot/Cabernet Blend

HOURS AND DIRECTIONS Open year-round Mon.–Fri. noon–5 p.m., Sat.–Sun. 11 a.m.–5 p.m. ■ Take Rte. 96A south out of Geneva, through the town of Rose Hill. Turn right on Lerch Rd. and drive till you get there.

Poplar Ridge Vineyards

9782 Rte. 414, Valois, NY 14888 • Phone 607-582-6421

Founded by David Bagley, a well-seasoned winemaking professional formerly of Wagner Vineyards and Bully Hill Vineyards (where he was cellar foreman), Poplar Ridge is dedicated to making good wines at reasonable prices. Their antisnobbish motto, displayed on the wine labels, says it all: "Wine Without Bull."

Wines: $–$$

White Wines

Bagley's Brut Sparkling Chardonnay—Pale, straw colored, and clean, with a dry finish.

Cayuga White—Light, sweet, and yet crisp. Nice.

Ravat 51—Sweet, light white made from the Ravat 51 grape variety.

Riesling—Cobalt blue bottle, with a silkscreen image of Sarah Bernhardt. Nice.

Vidal Blanc VSR—Light bodied and sweet.

Red Wines

Baco Noir—Medium-dry red.

Cabernet Sauvignon—Not tasted.

Chelois—Made from a hybrid grape variety rare for New York State. Almost tastes like Merlot.

One-Eyed Cat—A Catawba, crisp and refreshing.

Valois Rouge—Carmine grapes sweetened with Seyval juice.

Blush Wines

Queen Of Diamonds—A sweet blend of Cayuga and Concord.

HOURS AND DIRECTIONS Open May–Oct. Mon.–Sat. 10 a.m.–5 p.m., Sun. noon–5 p.m.; Nov.–Apr. Sat.–Sun. noon–5 p.m. ■ From Watkins Glen, take Rte. 414 north through Hector and Valois. You'll pass Standing Stone Vineyards on your left, followed shortly by Poplar Ridge on the same side.

Prejean Winery

2634 Rte. 14, Penn Yan, NY 14527 • Phone 315-536-7524 • Fax 315-536-7635 • www.prejeanwinery.com • wine@prejeanwinery.com

Prejean was founded in 1986 by Elizabeth (Libby) Prejean and her late husband James, who planted Merlot, Chardonnay, Riesling, Gewürztraminer, Marechal Foch, Cayuga White, and Vignoles on their 38 acres. Today, under the guiding hand of Libby and her talented and affable winemaker, Jim Zimar, the winery's output has grown to 25,000 gallons per year, with a new addition added to the facility in 1997.

Wines: $-$$

White Wines

Cayuga White—A light, semisweet wine.

Chardonnay—Apples and pears come through. Crisp and clean. Dry finish. ♥

Dry Gewürztraminer—A light, dry white with a citrusy ending. Nice.

Dry Riesling—Peaches and pears come though. Crisp, dry finish.

Semi-Dry Gewürztraminer—Pears, cinnamon, clove, and tropical fruits. Nice.

Semi-Dry Riesling—Floral nose. Peaches come through. A clean finish. Nice.

Vintner's Reserve Chardonnay—Barrel fermented in French oak and aged *sur lie*. Pears and apples come through. Creamy mouth feel.

Red Wines

Cabernet Sauvignon—A dry red wine. Cherry and berry flavors come through. Nice.

Marechal Foch—A hearty, dry red with flavors of blackberry and prune.

Merlot—A rich, dry, deep garnet wine. Blackberry, raspberry, and plum come through strong.

Proprietor's Red—An off-dry, medium-bodied red. Strawberries come through.

Dessert Wines and Ports

Late Harvest Chardonnay—Rich, golden dessert wine. Tropical fruit and butter rum.

Other Wines

Bird of Paradise (Chardonnay port), *Cabernet Franc*, *Late Harvest Vignoles*, *Tiger Lily*

REVIEWS AND AWARDS

Dry Riesling 1999—Gold medal, Great Lakes Wine Competition; gold medal, San Francisco International Wine Competition.

Late Harvest Chardonnay 1999—Gold medal, 2001 Jerry Mead New World International Wine Competition; Gold medal, New York Wine and Food Classic; Gold medal, New York State Fair Wine Competition.

HOURS AND DIRECTIONS Open year-round Mon.–Sat. 10 a.m.–5 p.m., Sun. 11 a.m.–5 p.m. ■ Located about an hour southeast of Rochester, 1.5 hours southwest of Syracuse, 1.5 hours northwest of Binghamton. ■ From Buffalo or Albany, take the N.Y. Thruway (I-90) east to exit 42 (Geneva). Take Rte. 14 about 17 miles south to the winery, which is on the right side. ■ From south of Geneva, take Rte. 17 to Elmira and then Rte. 14 north. The winery is about 18 miles north of Watkins Glen on the left-hand side.

Rasta Ranch Vineyards & Nursery

5882 Rte. 414, Valois, NY 14888 • Phone 607-546-2974

Just south of Valois on Lake Seneca's western shore, 30 acres and a partially renovated 1960s barn houses Rasta Ranch Vineyards & Nursery, a large, operating farm that produces both wine grapes and other produce. During summer and early fall, they also sell seasonal produce, tree fruit, grapes, herbs, flowers, greenhouse and nursery plants, preserves, and specialty foods.

Despite the name, the theme here is not Caribbean (though the Rasta philosophy comes through in the organic growing process) but is slightly hippie, with rock music from the 1960s and 1970s playing in the background and all the wines named for tunes by Jimi Hendrix, Janis Joplin, the Grateful Dead, and others. The inside of the barn is cool, low-lit, and stark, with bracelets, leather jackets, and miscellaneous trinkets for sale and hanging on the walls.

Wines: $

White Wines

Niagara—A light, fruity white with a tart kick at the end.

Blush Wines

Ja Maca Me Blush—A sangria-type wine.

Fruit Wines

Arlo's Apple—Sweet, light wine made from fresh New York State apples.

HOURS AND DIRECTIONS Open spring and summer daily, noon–5 p.m.; fall, Sat.–Sun. noon–5 p.m.; closed Jan.–Mar. Call in advance to make sure they are there. ■ From Watkins Glen take Rte. 414 north past Hector. Go past Hazlitt 1852 Vineyards on your right to Rasta Ranch.

Red Newt Cellars

3675 Tichenor Rd., Hector, NY 14841 • Phone 607-546-4100 • Fax 607-546-4101 • www.rednewt.com • info@rednewt.com

When Red Newt's owner/winemaker David Whiting got out of college, he backpacked through California's wine country, eventually started working in the wine industry, and later brought what he'd learned back to New York, where he worked for numerous Finger Lake wineries, becoming one of the most talented winemakers on the East Coast. With his wife Debra, he founded Red Newt in 1998, and only three years later won the coveted Governor's Cup with his 2000 Riesling. My wife and I were introduced to Red Newt (and David) for the first time at our first New York State Wine Festival, where we began tasting with no expectations but walked out with a half case of wine and two T-shirts. We've been hooked ever since.

Many of the wines are pointedly food oriented, so it's no surprise that the on-site bistro is every bit as good as the winery. Chef Debra Whiting has crafted a wonderful

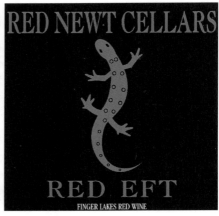

menu that really complements her husband's classy wines. Besides the fabulous pork, beef, fish, and vegetarian entrées, there's also a four-course prix fixe menu.

Wines: $-$$$

White Wines

Chardonnay—Barrel fermented and aged *sur lie*. Nice fruit. Crisp. Clean. Very nice.

Gewürztraminer—Dry, full bodied, and complex. Very good. ♥

Red Newt White—A semidry, exquisitely fruity blend of Vidal Blanc and Cayuga White. Very nice.

Riesling—Tangerine, apricot, and citrus come through. Crisp and clean. Very nice. ♥ ♥

Red Wines

Red Eft—A deep, very drinkable blend of Cabernet Franc, Merlot, Cabernet Sauvignon, and Pinot Noir. Dry and full bodied, with big fruit. ♥ ♥

Syrah—A bright, medium-bodied red. Lots of fruit, but with a dry finish. Nice.

Syrah–Cabernet Franc—A deep red blend of 68% Syrah and 32% Cabernet Franc. Plum comes through.

Viridescens—A red blend of 37% Cabernet Franc, 36% Merlot, and 27% Cabernet Sauvignon. Cranberry and raspberry come through, as does some pepper. Dry finish. Nice.

REVIEWS AND AWARDS

Riesling 2000—2001 New York Wine and Food Classic Governor's Cup (best in show).

Viridescens 1999—Gold medal and "Best New York State Red," 2001 International Eastern Wine Competition.

"If you're looking for a fabulous gourmet lunch along with a wine tasting, look no further than Red Newt Cellars."   —*The Scoop* (September 2000)

"Dining here is an exquisite experience, whether seated in the large dining room or on the outdoor covered deck overlooking Seneca Lake's valley. The menu, which changes every two weeks, always has pleasant surprises."
     —Lorraine Smorol, *Syracuse New Times* (Autumn 2000)

"Dave Whiting, winemaker and owner, took the Governor's Cup last year for his 2000 Riesling, and I think [the 2001] is even better. Harmonious and beautifully balanced, this luscious wine will show you how good a Riesling can be."
     —Rae Burchfiel, *Democrat and Chronicle* (July 9, 2002)

"Full-bodied and spicy with terrific, mouthwatering acidity and long finish, [the 2000 Gewürztraminer] was like a great Alsace Gewürz without being too sweet (as many Alsace wines are today)."
     —Lettie Teague, *Food & Wine* (August 2002)

Gewürztraminer Finger Lakes Reserve 2001: "Score: 89."
     —*Wine Spectator* (December 2002)

Riesling Finger Lakes Reserve 2001: "Score: 89."   —*Wine Spectator* (December 2002)

HOURS AND DIRECTIONS Winery open year-round Mon.–Sat. 10 a.m.–5 p.m., Sun. noon–5 p.m.; bistro open Thurs.–Sun. noon–4 p.m. for lunch, 4–9 p.m. for dinner. ■ Located on the east side of Seneca Lake just off Rte. 414, about 10 miles north of Watkins Glen (just after Atwater Estate Vineyards). Follow the signs and turn right on Tichenor Rd. The winery is on the left.

Seneca Shore Wine Cellars / DeMarco Vineyards

Rte. 14 and Davy Rd., Penn Yan, NY 14527 • Phone 800-588-VINO or 315-536-0882

Seneca Shore's award-winning vineyards were started in 1979 with the aim of producing solid table wines at a great value, and today the winery boasts one of the top two or three tasting rooms in the Finger Lakes region (indeed, in New York state), if only for sheer variety.

Owner David DeMarco bills the winery as producing "medieval wines," with his castle-like tasting room following suit, decorated with large torches, battle-axes, and all kinds of other medieval weaponry. Depending on the day you visit, the folks behind the counter might even be in medieval costume—usually around the holidays or other festive times. But all is not damsels in distress. If you like, you can opt to take in the beautiful view from a rocking chair on the winery's deck.

Wines: $–$$

White Wines
Cabernet Franc—Full bodied, medium oak, lots of tannins.
Chardonnay—Dry and smooth. No oak, no bitterness, 100% fruity. Very nice.
Gewürztraminer—Tropical fruits come through. Soft and spicy.
Reserve Chardonnay—An international-style wine fermented in oak.
Riesling—Soft with licorice and tropical fruit flavors.

Red Wines
Cabernet Sauvignon—A deep, dry red. Spicy and oaky. Nice finish.
Pinot Noir—Light body, light strawberry and perfume. Crisp!
Red Castle—Made from Baco Noir grapes. Very fruity. Low oak and tannin. Finishes nice.
Red Knight—A semisweet red with lots of fruit.

Blush Wines
Castle Blush—Bright fruit flavors. Nice.
Royal Rosé—A semisweet blush wine. Starts sweet, ends dry.

Other Wines
Moon Rise, White Castle

REVIEWS AND AWARDS
Cabernet Franc 1998—Silver medal, 2000 New York Wine and Food Classic.
Reserve Chardonnay 1998: "Best Buy."
—Beverage Testing Institute, Buying Guide to Wines of North America

HOURS AND DIRECTIONS Open year-round Mon.–Sat. 10 a.m.–5 p.m., Sun. noon–5 p.m., and by appointment. ■ From Geneva, take Rte. 14 south about 10 miles, past the intersection with Rte. 16. The winery will be immediately on your left. ■ From Watkins Glen, take Rte. 14 north approximately 22 miles. Go about 2.5 miles past the town of Dresden, past the Anthony Road Wine Company. Seneca Shore is immediately after, on your right.

Shalestone Vineyards

9681 Rte. 414, Lodi, NY 14860 • Phone 607-582-6600 • shalevin@epix.net

Among people in the know about East Coast wines, Rob Thomas is a favorite, one of those people whose wines other winemakers like to drink. Thomas built his reputation at Lamoreaux Landing Wine Cellars, and when he decided to open this small, unassuming winery with his wife Kate in 1998, it was big news, garnering a whole story in

Wine Spectator and prompting Lamoreaux to issue a statement on its website assuring patrons that Thomas would continues to serve as winemaker there, with a new assistant.

With only 5 acres planted to vines, Thomas can manage to produce only 1,000 cases of wine, and has no plans to increase his stake. He's interested in quality, not quantity, and he's interested only in reds—unusual in the Finger Lakes, where whites (especially Riesling and Gewürztraminer) are the region's signature. "I just want to keep my wine list small, with all top-quality wines," he explained to Dana Nigro of *Wine Spectator* in August 2000. He expressed the wish that more wineries in the region would focus on their craft instead of marketing what the tourists want. "If 10 or 15 wineries would do this, we could build up our reputation."

Everything here is bone dry. If you like only sweet wines, you'd better drive on, though that would be a shame.

Wines: $–$$

Red Wines

Cabernet Franc—Not tasted.

Cabernet Sauvignon—A deep, dry red.

Merlot—A soft, deep, dry red.

Pinot Noir—Not tasted.

Red Legend—Shalestone's benchmark wine. A dry red blend of Cabernet Franc, Cabernet Sauvignon, and Merlot. ♥

Blush Wines

Jem—A dry rosé in the best French tradition. ♥

HOURS AND DIRECTIONS Open May–mid-Oct. Fri.–Sun. noon–5 p.m. ■ From Watkins Glen, drive north on Rte. 414 all the way past Lodi. You'll see the small sign for Shalestone Vineyards just outside the center of town. If you come to Ovid, you've gone too far.

Silver Thread Vineyards

1401 Caywood Rd., Caywood, NY 14860 • Phone 607-582-6116 • www.silverthreadswine.com • info@silverthreadwine.com

From the naturally cooled cellars dug into the side of the hill to the watering system that uses gravity to tap a natural spring, this winery is about as organic as any winemaker can be, and is the only East Coast vinifera vineyard certified by the Northeastern Organic Farming Association.

The winery is owned by former wine writer Richard Figiel, who in 2001 told *Wine Today*, "I'm looking for a lot of ripe flavors, but holding on to a vein of acidity running through the wine. That's what we can offer in this region, not the heavy overripeness from hotter climates, but a vivid ripeness with some taut acidity that keeps the wine firm."

Silver Thread's original vines were planted in 1981, and the farming methods went organic in the late 1980s. The winery made its first wines in 1991 and now produces about 1,500 cases per year.

Wines: $–$$

White Wines

Chardonnay—Nicely balanced.

Chardonnay Reserve—Lightly oaked and full bodied.

Dry Riesling—A semisweet version of the German classic.

Good Earth White—Mostly Chardonnay blend. Light and slightly off-dry.

Red Wines
Pinot Noir—A light, dry red.

REVIEWS AND AWARDS
Chardonnay Reserve 1999: 90 points. "A breakthrough . . . with flavors of cinnamon, pears and cashews that feel custardy in the mouth. Finishes long, with tangy acids and nutty overtones. Editor's Choice"   —*Wine Enthusiast* (March 2002)

"The Finger Lakes' best Riesling."   —Dave McIntyre, *Wine Today* (April 16, 2001)

"Silver Thread's vineyard might be small but it could eventually have an enormous impact on quality throughout the region."   —*Wine Spectator* (September 1995)

HOURS AND DIRECTIONS May–Nov. Sat.–Sun. noon–5 p.m. Other times by appointment only. Call ahead. ■ From Watkins Glen, take Rte. 414 up the east shore of Lake Seneca, through Valois. When you get to Caywood, watch on your left for Caywood Rd., where you'll turn left. Silver Thread is just a little way down.

Standing Stone Vineyards

9934 Rte. 414, Hector, NY 14841 • Phone 800-803-7135 or 607-582-6051 •
Fax 607-582-6312 • www.standingstonewines.com • ssvny@standingstonewines.com

In 1991, Tom and Marti Macinski purchased historic vineyards that had been planted by Gold Seal Vineyards, crushing their first grapes in 1993 to produce a mere 800 cases, which sold out in 12 weeks. Today, Tom and Marti have become winemaking celebrities, with 30 acres that produce 6,500 cases annually and plans calling for expansion.

This is a classy wine list. Standing Stone has always been known for its outstanding Gewürztraminer, which has medaled in competitions since 1993, winning seven golds and tying four times. It is their premier wine, and possibly the region's best, anticipated by wine connoisseurs throughout the United States each year. Their Rieslings are also very nice, as are their dry reds, especially the Pinnacle and the Glen Eldridge Merlot, which sometimes get lost in all the Alsatian hype even though *Wine Spectator* awarded the 1999 bottlings a rating of 84 points.

The winery is set beautifully on a restored farm, where a renovated barn holds the tasting room and winemaking facilities. Among Finger Lakes wineries, this is a must-visit.

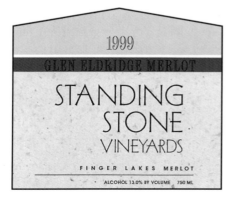

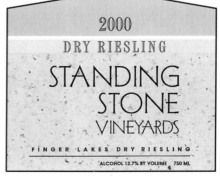

Wines: $$–$$$

White Wines

Chardonnay—Melon and vanilla flavors come through. Dry finish. Nice.

Dry Riesling—Pear and apple flavors come through. Minerally. Clean and crisp. Very nice finish. ♥ ♥ ♥

Estate White—A light, crisp white. Tropical fruits up front, but finishes clean and crisp. Very nice.

Gewürztraminer—Off-dry light white. Full of spice. Fruity but with a tart ending. Very nice. ♥ ♥

Reserve Chardonnay—Dry, full-bodied Chardonnay aged in American and French oak. Apple and melon come through. Clean and crisp.

Riesling—Off-dry Riesling. Tropical flavors come through. Clean, crisp finish. Very nice. ♥

Smokehouse Chardonnay—Not tasted.

Red Wines

Cabernet Franc—Deep, dry red with nice fruit.

Glen Eldridge Merlot—A rich, dry red. Big fruit up front but a nice, deep, dry finish. ♥

Pinnacle—A deep, dry blend of Cabernet Sauvignon, Cabernet Franc, and Merlot. Cherries and currants come through. A nice, dry finish. ♥ ♥

Pinot Noir—Light, dry red. Cherry and raspberry flavors come through. Smooth.

Dessert Wines

Late-Harvest Riesling—Crisp and well balanced. Melon, apples, and pears come through.

Vidal Ice Wine—Rich and well balanced, with honey and tropical fruit flavors.

REVIEWS AND AWARDS

"One of the Finger Lakes finest wineries, with very good Riesling, Gewürztraminer and Cabernet Franc." —*Hugh Johnson's Pocket Wine Book 2002*

"A rising star." —Karen MacNeil, *The Wine Bible*

"Standing Stone . . . raised the quality bar with Pinnacle, a superb Bordeaux blend of Cabernet Sauvignon, Merlot, and Cabernet Franc, rich in dark-cherry and blackberry flavors, with cedar accents and nicely tame tannins." —Mort Hochstein, *Food & Wine* (April 1999)

"[One of the] several top Riesling producers. . . . We began tasting an excellent dry Riesling, a soft cabernet blend . . . all of which were overshadowed by the 2000 Gewürztraminer." —Lettie Teague, *Food & Wine* (August 2002)

Reserve Chardonnay 1999: "Loads of fruit flavor in this one, along with some minerality. And the acidity makes it all sing. . . . Three stars." —*Food & Wine* magazine *Wine Guide 2002*

"[The 1999 Cabernet Franc] has a nice mix of blackberry and tobacco leaf flavors, with a focused finish. . . . 84 points." —*Wine Spectator* (July 31, 2002)

Chardonnay Finger Lakes Reserve 2000: "Score: 89." —*Wine Spectator* (April 2003)

Gewürztraminer 2000: "Intense spicy aroma, a rich, full body and a wonderfully dry finish. . . . I gushed admiration." —Lettie Teague, *Food & Wine* (April 2002)

Gewürztraminer 2001: "Five favorites . . . A crisp white from Finger Lakes New York." —Lettie Teague, *Food & Wine* (April 2002)

Gewürztraminer Finger Lakes 2001: "Score: 89." —*Wine Spectator* (April 2003)

HOURS AND DIRECTIONS Open year-round Fri. noon–5 p.m., Sat. 11 a.m.–6 p.m., and Mon., Thurs., and Sun. noon–5 p.m., or by appointment. ■ From the north, take the

N.Y. Thruway to the Geneva or Waterloo exit. From Geneva, take Rte. 96 south to Ovid, turn right onto Rte. 414, continue approximately 10 miles through the town of Lodi, and on to the vineyards, on the right. ■ From the south, take Rte. 414 north from Watkins Glen for approximately 12 miles. The winery will be on your left. ■ From the east and Ithaca, take Rte. 96 north to Trumansburg, turn left onto Rte. 227 for 0.5 mile, turn right onto the Searsburg Rd. (Rte. 1), and travel to Valois. Turn right onto Rte. 414 and travel 0.5 mile. Standing Stone Vineyards will be on your left.

Torrey Ridge Winery

2770 Rte. 14, Penn Yan, NY 14527 • Phone 315-536-1210 • Fax 315-536-1239 • www.torreyridgewinery.com • meadery@hotmail.com

The relatively new Torrey Ridge is owned and operated by John and Esther Earle, who also own the Earle Estates Winery & Meadery, just 3 miles away. While Earle focuses on mead and fruit wines, Torrey Ridge concentrates on native American grapes as well as some vinifera.

When you drive onto the property, it's hard not to be impressed with the circular driveway and the massive 1999 winery building with its giant four-columned portico. The tasting room is upstairs and lets onto spectacular views, with an ornate balcony for picnicking.

Torrey Ridge makes premium wines that suit every palate, whether your taste is sweet or dry. Be sure to take the winery tour, which is one of the most impressive in the region.

Wines: $–$$

White Wines

Cayuga White—Off-dry white that starts fruity but finishes crisp.

Chardonnay—Light, soft, buttery overtones with oak.

Delaware—Semisweet white grape wine.

Diamond—Semisweet white with a full but soft grape taste.

Niagara—Semisweet white that tastes like a grape right off the vine.

Riesling—Dry but still fruity.

Seyval—Dry white with light grape finish. Award winner.

Red Wines

Baco Noir—Oak with smoky overtones.

Bandit Red—Semisweet, full-bodied red with a soft finish.

Blue Sapphire—Semisweet, Concord-based red. Like a mouthful of red grapes.

Heritage—Smoky. Cherry overtones with oak.

Rougeon—Spicy. Smoky overtones with oak.

Torrey Ridge Red—Blend of French hybrids with a hint of oak.

Blush Wines

Bandit Blush—Semisweet blend. Hearty.

Fruit and Dessert Wines

Indigo Blush—Blend of Concord and honey wine.

Peach—A fruit wine made from fresh peaches.

Scarlet Red—Special dessert blend of raspberry, cranberry, and honey wine.

Summer Delight—A light, sweet wine that's like a mouthful of strawberry pie.

REVIEWS AND AWARDS

Blue Sapphire 1998—Gold medal, 2001 New York Wine and Food Classic.

Diamond 1999—Gold medal, 2001 New York Wine and Food Classic; gold medal, 2001 Tasters Guild International Wine Competition.

Dry Riesling 1998—Gold medal, 2001 Tasters Guild International Wine Competition.

Riesling 1998—Gold medal, 2001 Tasters Guild International Wine Competition.

HOURS AND DIRECTIONS Mon.–Sat. 10 a.m.–5:30 p.m., Sun. 11:30 a.m.–5:30 p.m., year-round. ■ From Watkins Glen, take Rte. 14 north about halfway up Seneca Lake. Pass the Rte. 5 intersection. Torrey Ridge will be on your left. ■ From Geneva, take Rte. 14 south about halfway down Lake Seneca. Pass the intersection with Rte. 26 and Prejean Winery. Torrey Ridge will be on your right.

Wagner Vineyards

9322 Rte. 414, Lodi, NY 14860 • Phone 607-582-6450 • Fax 607-582-6446 • www.wagnervineyards.com • wagwine@ptd.net

Bill Wagner is one of the great entrepreneurs of New York wine. A longtime grape grower, he played an instrumental part in pushing through the Farm Winery Act of 1976, and since then has crafted this extremely popular winery, microbrewery, and luncheon spot, which attracts locals as well as tourists.

Wagner is one of the largest of the Finger Lakes wineries in terms of volume, with 50,000 visitors every year, but the quality of its wines is the real story. Its ice wines are among some of the best in the world and have won gold medals at numerous competitions, while its reds fare just as well internationally as in the United States. Its eight-sided tasting room (of Bill's own design) remains one of the most talked-about in the Northeast.

Since opening in June 1979, Wagner has added the Ginny Lee Café, where you can sample some wonderful light fare, and the Wagner Valley Brewing Company, which makes some very nice beers, including Sugar House Maple Porter, Sled Dog Doppelbock, and Caywood Station Stout.

Wines: $–$$$

White Wines

Chardonnay—Clean, crisp, dry, and light, with flavors of pears and tropical fruits. Nice.

Gewürztraminer—A semidry white. Tropical fruits with a nice finish.

Johannisberg Riesling—A nicely balanced semisweet white. Very nice finish.

Melody—Popular and award-winning fruity white blend.

Reserve Chardonnay—Barrel fermented. Full bodied and buttery, with intense fruit and a dry finish.

Riesling—Dry light white. Apricot and peaches come through. Nice.

Seyval Blanc—A surprisingly nice Seyval prepared in the best Burgundy tradition.

Vignoles—Light, sweet white with tropical flavors and nice finish.

Red Wines

Cabernet—An award-winning blend of 73% Cabernet Sauvignon and 27% Cabernet Franc. Big fruit, deep tannins, and a dry finish. Nice.

Cabernet Franc—Smoky, with plums coming through.

Cabernet Sauvignon—A deep, dry red.

Meritage—A traditional oak-aged Bordeaux blend. Dry and deep.

Merlot—A medium-bodied red. Soft, nicely rounded.

Reserve Pinot Noir—An award-winning, medium-bodied, dry red. Nice fruit and finish.

Sparkling Wines

Brut Champagne—A *méthode champenoise* wine made from a traditional blend of Chardonnay and Pinot Noir. Dry. Nice.

Riesling Champagne, Méthode Champenoise—Semisweet Riesling bubbly.

Dessert Wines

Late-Harvest Vignoles—Honey and pineapple come through. Wonderful.

Riesling Ice Wine—Light gold, with apricots and honey. Well balanced. Nice on the palate. Rich and sweet. Who needs something from the chef? Just keep this one coming! ♥

Vidal Ice Wine—Peach, pineapple, and honey come through. Lovely.

Vignoles Ice Wine—Tropical fruits and honey come through. Very nicely balanced. Sweet, rich, and thick, without being overpowering. Very nice. ♥

REVIEWS AND AWARDS

Cabernet Sauvignon—Gold medal, 2000 Amenti del Vino statewide amateur winemakers' competition; silver medal, 2001 Tasters Guild International Wine Competition; silver medal, 2000 Indiana State Fair Indy International Wine Competition.

Reserve Pinot Noir 1999—Gold medal, 2002 Tasters Guild International Wine Competition.; silver medal, 2002 Tasters Guild International Wine Competition.

Riesling Ice Wine 1998—Gold medal/best dessert wine, 1999 New York Wine and Food Classic; gold medal, 1999 Wine Lovers Consumer Wine Competition; *Wine Spectator* rating 89; *Wine Enthusiast* rating 89.

Riesling Ice Wine 2000—"Best of the East" (Top Ten Wines), 2003 Annual Wineries Unlimited Seminar and Trade show; double gold medal, 2002 International Eastern Wine Competition; gold medal, 2002 Riverside International Wine Competition; silver medal, 2002 Finger Lakes International Wine Competition; silver medal, 2002 Tasters Guild International Wine Competition.

Vignoles Ice Wine 1999—Double gold medal, 1999 San Francisco International Wine Competition; gold medal/Best of Class/Chairman's Award, 2000 Riverside International Wine Competition; *Wine Spectator* rating 88; *Wine Enthusiast* rating 87.

"Among the Finger Lakes' most famous historic wineries."
—Karen MacNeil, *The Wine Bible*

"Consistently high-quality wines."   —*The New Sotheby's Wine Encyclopedia*

Reserve Chardonnay and Johannisberg Riesling: "Recommended."
—Ed McCarthy and Mary Ewing-Mulligan, *White Wine for Dummies*

HOURS AND DIRECTIONS Open daily 10 a.m.–5 p.m. year-round. ■ Wagner Vineyards is located 3.5 miles south of Lodi. ■ From Watkins Glen, take Rte. 414 north, past Silver Thread Vineyards on your left. Wagner Vineyards is not far up on the same side.

Woodbury Vineyards

4141 Rte. 14, Dundee, NY 14837 • Phone 888-NYS-WINE or 607-243-8925 • Fax 607-243-7837 • www.woodburyvineyards.com • wv@woodburyvineyards.com

This is the Finger Lakes branch of Fredonia, New York's Woodbury Vineyards, located near Lake Erie. See the Lake Erie region listings for more information on the winery and wines.

HOURS AND DIRECTIONS Open year-round Mon.–Sat. 10 a.m.–6 p.m., Sun. noon–6 p.m. ■ From the north, take the N.Y. Thruway (I-90) to the exit at Geneva (Rte. 14). Drive about 20 miles south on Rte. 14 to the winery. *Caution: Geneva enforces its speed limits.* We know from experience. ■ From the south, take the Southern Tier Expwy. (Rte. 17, now I-86) to the exit at Elmira Heights, to Rte. 14. Go north on Rte. 14 through Watkins Glen and about 15 miles more. The winery is on the right.

FINGER LAKES: KEUKA

Barrington Cellars / Buzzard Crest Vineyards

2690 Gray Rd., Penn Yan, NY 14527 • Phone 315-531-8923 • Fax 315 536 9686 • www.barringtoncellars.com

Barrington Cellars is a small, family-owned and -operated winery founded in 1971 by Ken and Eileen Farnan in the midst of Buzzard Crest Vineyards, where most of the grapes used to produce their wines are grown. From the beginning, their goal was to produce high-quality, award-winning labrusca (native grape) wines, a creed they've taken into the realm even of ice wines, where the grapes' sweetness makes for a different and unforgettable taste. The tasting room is housed in a 100-year-old home.

Attention New York City dwellers: Barrington Cellars wines can often be found in the Union Square farmers' market on Wednesdays.

Wines: $–$$

White Wines
Buzzard's Peach—Sweet, fruity wine made from New York State peaches.
Chardonnay—Dry, classic, oak-aged Chard. Nice nose and fruit. Nice finish.
Delaware—Semisweet, medium-bodied white.
Diamond—Off-dry, labrusca flavor. Nice fruit. Not cloying. Nice.
Gewürztraminer—Off-dry.
Riesling—Off-dry, light white. Apricots and honey. Tart finish.
Seyval—Off-dry French hybrid, done in the European style. Nice.
Vidal Blanc—Semisweet, light white. Nice balance.

Red Wines
Baco—Dry red table wine.
Cabernet Franc—Dry, red vinifera table wine. Nice fruit. Dry finish.
Concord—Sweet purple table wine.

DeChaunac—Semisweet, French hybrid red table wine.

Pink Cat—Sweet, pink Catawba wine.

Pinot Noir—Off-dry, medium-bodied table wine.

Vulture's Red—Off-dry, dark red blend of Concord, Rougeon, and Vincent grapes.

Blush Wines

Buzzard's Blush—Semisweet blend of Delaware, DeChaunac, and Cayuga.

Isabella Rosé—Semisweet, fruity blush.

Dessert Wines

Bliss—Fruity ice wine. Blend of seedless, Vidal, and Delaware grapes. Nice.

Isabella—The Buzzard's pink ice wine. Different and interesting.

Niagara—Fruity dessert ice wine. Nice fruit. Very sweet. Grapes in a glass.

REVIEWS AND AWARDS

Concord 1999—Silver medal, 2001 New York Wine and Food Classic.

Pink Cat 1999—Silver medal, 2001 New York Wine and Food Classic.

HOURS AND DIRECTIONS Open Memorial Day–Oct., Mon.–Sat. 11 a.m.–5:30 p.m., Sun. noon–5:30 p.m.; Nov.–Mar. Sat. 11 a.m.–5:30 p.m., Sun. noon–5:30; Apr.–Memorial Day, Fri.–Sat. 11 a.m.–5:30 p.m., Sun. noon–5:30 p.m. ▪ From the west via the N.Y. Thruway (I-90), take exit 44 (Canandaigua), then Rte. 332 south to Rtes. 5 and 20 east to County Rte. 5 (Post Rd.). Watch for the sign to Penn Yan on the right. Go straight through the stop sign in Hall to Rte. 14A south. Stay on 14A to Rte. 54 south (right turn at the sixth traffic light in Penn Yan). Follow Rte. 54 south 8 miles to Gray Rd. and go left. Drive 0.3 mile uphill to Barrington Cellars, on the left. ▪ From the east via the N.Y. Thruway, take Geneva exit 42, then Rte. 14 south to Rte. 54 into Penn Yan. Follow the signs for Rte. 54 south out of Penn Yan; then follow the local directions above. ▪ From Rte. 17 or I-86, take exit 38 or 39 into Bath; then follow Rte. 54 north to Hammondsport (5 miles). Go straight through the traffic light near Hammondsport on Rte. 54 north for 18 miles to Gray Rd. Turn right onto Gray Rd. and drive 0.3 mile uphill to Barrington Cellars, on the left.

Bully Hill Vineyards

8843 Greyton H. Taylor Memorial Dr., Hammondsport, NY 14840 •
Phone 607-868-3610 or 607-868 3210 • Fax 607-868-3205 • www.bullyhill.com

Bully Hill sits on the original site of the Taylor Wine Company—*the* Taylor Wine Company, which was founded by their ancestors back in 1878. In 1958, Greyton H. Taylor and Walter S. Taylor began converting the vineyards from native American grapes to French-American hybrids, and in 1970 they formally incorporated as Bully Hill Vineyards, Inc.

Here's where it gets interesting. That same year, Taylor Wine Company family members fired them from their own family's firm, and a series of now legendary court battles ensued over the use of the name, leading to beaucoup publicity for our Bully Hill Taylors. The Taylor Company sued to prevent the brothers from using the Taylor name, and at one point got a court order to mandate the transfer of all family heirlooms back to the Taylor Wine Company, as "company property." As was later reported, Walter dumped the belongings on the company steps and then took a picture of his favorite goat standing on top of the pile, saying, "They may have got my name and my heritage but they didn't get my goat."

Bully Hill Vineyards was the first small estate winery in the Keuka Lake area since Prohibition, and became the cornerstone for the growth of many wineries. Having grown from a boutique winery with few employees, it now produces over 200,000 cases of wine each year. Walter, who campaigned for French-American hybrid grape varieties and helped put New York wines before a wider public, died in June of 2001, but his spirit lingers in Bully Hill's commitment to innovation and in their funky wine names and labels.

The winery now has a nice little restaurant with wonderful views and fine Bully Hill wines. It makes over fifty different wines, including *Aurore Blanc, Banty Red, Bulldog Baco Noir, Chambourcin, Chardonnay Elise, Crystal Reserve Brut, Equinox, Estate Red, Felicity, Fish Market White, Foch, Fusion, Garnet, Goat White, Grower's Blush, Grower's Red, Grower's White, Harbor Lights, Ives, Late Harvest Vidal Blanc, Le Goat Blush, Lighthouse White, Love My Goat Red, Meat Market Red, Merlot, Miss Love White, Mother Ship over Paris, Niagara, Oh Be Joyful, Old Barnyard Red, Pinot Noir, Ravat Blanc, Riesling, Seasons, Seyval Blanc, Space Shuttle Red, Space Shuttle White, Spring Blush, Spring White, State Capital Red, Sweet Walter Red, Sweet Walter White, Verdelet Blanc,* and *Walter S. Red.*

Wines: $–$$

REVIEWS AND AWARDS

"Of all the wines, the light and refreshing estate-bottled white is a top pick.
This is the wine to try if you've never tasted a French-hybrid before."

—Karen MacNeil, *The Wine Bible*

HOURS AND DIRECTIONS Open year-round Mon.–Sat. 9 a.m.–5 p.m., Sun. noon–5 p.m. Restaurant open Mon.–Fri. 11:30 a.m.–4 p.m. and Sat.–Sun. 11:30 a.m.–5 p.m. for lunch, Fri.–Sat. 5–9 p.m. for dinner. ■ From the south, take exit 38 off Rte. 17 at Bath. Head north on Rte. 54 about 10 miles, turn left into Hammondsport, go through the village on Rte. 54A, and follow the blue and white Bully Hill Vineyards signs. ■ From the north, take exit 42 off I-90, stay on Rte. 14 south for about 30 miles, turn right in Penn Yan, follow Rte. 54 south about 22 miles, turn right into Hammondsport, and follow the local directions above.

Crooked Lake Winery

1296 Rte. 54, Hammondsport, NY 14840 • Phone 607-243-5582

Owned by Yvonne Warren, this small winery is named for Lake Keuka, which is also known as Crooked Lake. They've got more than 22 acres planted to vines. John Lebeck (also winemaker at Plymouth Colony Winery in Plymouth, Mass.) is the winemaker.

Wines: $

White Wines

Cayuga White—A delicate, semisweet white.
Chablis—An off-dry white table wine.

Red Wines

Proprietor's Red—A dry, deep table red.

Blush and Dessert Wines

Keuka Blush—A semisweet, pink blush.
Late Harvest Ravat—Golden, rich dessert wine.

HOURS AND DIRECTIONS Call for hours. ■ From Hammondsport, take Rte. 54 all the way up past the junction with Rte. 94, about 7–8 miles. The winery will be on your right, just before Keuka.

Dr. Konstantin Frank's Vinifera Wine Cellars & Chateau Frank ✪ ✪ ✪

9749 Middle Rd., Hammondsport, NY 14840 • Phone 800-320-0735 •
Fax 607-868-4888 • www.drfrankwines.com • FrankWines@aol.com

In 1951, at the age of fifty-two, Russian-born German scientist Dr. Konstantin Frank immigrated to America with his wife, his three children, and, according to legend, $50 in his pocket. Unable to speak English, he was hired at the Geneva Experiment Station to do menial work, and while there picked up enough English to kibitz with other station employees about grape-growing matters—particularly about vinifera, the doctor's passion. After arguing with American research scientists over whether or not vinifera would survive in the East, Frank was given a chance to grow vinifera at Urbana (a.k.a. Gold Seal) vineyards' nurseries by Charles Fournier, the former chief winemaker at Veuve Clicquot Ponsardin. This was in 1953. As famed wine historian Leon B. Adams wrote in his landmark book *The Wines of America*, "After countless others had failed for three centuries, [Frank] has shown dramatically that the Old World grape, the Vinifera, can be grown in the eastern wine industry." His success spawned the entire region's stupendous growth, making him one of the most important figures in all of American wine.

While I personally have nothing against French-American hybrids, Dr. Frank scoffed at them. "Frank's disdain for hybrids so enraged the wine establishment," Lettie Teague wrote in *Food & Wine* (November 2000), "that they tried to have him committed." However, Dr. Frank proved he was right. Soon after Gold Seal released its first few vinifera vintages, Dr. Frank bought his own tracts of land and began planting. He sold his first wines in 1965.

The small Vinifera Wine Cellars, founded in 1962 on Rhine-like heights over Keuka, is now one of the top wineries in the East, and is run by Dr. Frank's son Willy and grandson Wally. Willy also started Chateau Frank, located just down the road and concentrating on classic sparkling wines in the best Champagne tradition. Dr. Frank's recently started a new label, Salmon Run, to offer inexpensive, carefree varietals. We have personally liked some of these wines as much as the winery's signature Dr. Frank line (and at a great price, too!).

Wines: $–$$$

White Wines

Chardonnay—Smooth and rounded. Pears and vanilla come through. Nice. ♥ ♥

Cuvée Blanc—Dry, light white blend of Chardonnay, Johannisberg Riesling, and others. The perfect accompaniment to all dishes calling for a dry white.

Gewürztraminer—Slightly off-dry. Rich and spicy. Clean and crisp. Refreshing. ♥

Johannisberg Riesling Dry—Wonderful tropical fruits with a citrus-like quality. ♥

Johannisberg Riesling Semi-Dry—A rich, light wine with beautiful fruit notes and a lovely, refreshing aftertaste. Excellent. ♥

Rkatsiteli—Spicy, refreshing, off-dry white wine. (Pronounced ar-kat-si-TEL-ee.) It originated around Mount Ararat on the border of Armenia and Turkey, and dates back at least 5,000 years. Very nice. ♥

Salmon Run Chardonnay—A light, tropical, fruit-filled Chardonnay that finishes dry.

Salmon Run Johannisberg Riesling—
A fragrant, light white, not too sweet, with just the right amount of acidity. As lovely as it is light. ♥ ♥

Red Wines

Cabernet Sauvignon—A deep purplish wine with big fruit and a dry finish.

Fleur de Pinot Noir—A nice, light, nonvintage Pinot. Dry. ♥

Pinot Noir—Classic Burgundian-style, medium-bodied red. Nice fruit. Velvety. Nice finish.

Salmon Run Coho Red—Off-dry medium-bodied red. Nice.

Salmon Run Pinot Noir—Light, dry red. Nice fruit with soft underside and a nice, clean finish. ♥ ♥

Blush Wines

Première Blush—A blush blend of Pinot Noir and Chardonnay, with Riesling juice added for sweetness.

Dessert Wines

Johannisberg Riesling Ice Wine—Konstantin Frank was the first person in America to make late-harvest Johannisberg Riesling, back in 1962. It was the first of his wines served at the White House.

Sparkling Wines

Chateau Frank Blanc de Blanc—A dry, sparkling white. Yeasty nose followed by citrus ending.

Chateau Frank Brut Champagne—A French-style sparkling wine. Nutty, toasty, and creamy. Nice. ♥

Chateau Frank Célèbre—A sparkling Riesling. Not tasted.

Chateau Frank Célèbre Rosé—Made from Pinot Meunier. Fruity and bubbly. Refreshing. ♥

REVIEWS AND AWARDS

Cabernet Franc 1999 and *Johannisberg Riesling 2000*—"Best of the East"
  (Top Ten Wines), 2002 Wineries Unlimited Seminar and Trade Show.

Cabernet Franc 2001—Gold medal, 2003 Great Lakes Wine Competition.

Johannisberg Riesling 2002—Gold medal, 2003 Los Angeles County Fair Wine
  Competition.

Johannisberg Riesling Dry 1998—Double gold medal, "Best Riesling," 1999
  San Francisco International Wine Competition.

Johannisberg Riesling Reserve 2001—Gold medal, 2003 Great Lakes Wine Competition.

Pinot Noir Reserve 2001—Gold medal, 2003 Great Lakes Wine Competition.

Reserve Merlot 1999 and *Cabernet Sauvignon "Old Vines" 1999*—"Best of the East"
  (Top Ten Wines), 2003 Annual Wineries Unlimited Seminar and Trade Show.

Rkatsiteli 2002—Gold medal, 2003 Los Angeles County Fair Wine Competition.

"Winery of the Year" at the 2001 New York Wine and Food Classic.

"[The 1994 Chardonnay is] a real beauty. . . . Luscious, heady aromas. . . .
  It's lightly creamy, nicely balanced with good acidity and a zesty finish."
        —Debra Scoblionkov, *Philadelphia Inquirer* (August 17, 1997)

"Recommended New York Riesling."
        —Ed McCarthy and Mary Ewing-Mulligan, *White Wine for Dummies*

Johannisberg Riesling Dry 1991: "Remarkably lively, with great purity of flavor."
        —Lettie Teague, *Food & Wine* (August 2002)

Johannisberg Riesling Finger Lakes Reserve 2001: "Score: 88."
        — *Wine Spectator* (October 2002)

Pinot Noir 1999: "88 points."   —Beverage Testing Institute

"Bold peach flavors suppress a light flintiness in this full, unctuous
  [1998 Johannisberg Riesling Dry]. . . . A refined accompaniment. . . .
  87 points."   —*Wine & Spirits* (Winter 2000)

Johannisberg Riesling Dry 2000: "Few wineries in the world could create such
  an aromatic, vibrant Riesling at such a low price."   —*Food & Wine* (June 2002)

Rkatsiteli 1997: "85 points."   —*Wine Spectator* (December 1998)

"The winery produces some of the best bubblies in New York State today. . . .
  [The Chateau Frank Blanc de Blanc is] a delicious shower of light, creamy,
  gingery flavors."   —Karen MacNeil, *The Wine Bible*

HOURS AND DIRECTIONS Open daily year-round, Mon.–Sat. 9 a.m.–5 p.m., Sun. noon–
5 p.m. ■ From the south, take Rte. 17 to exit 38 or 39 in Bath and follow Rte. 54 north
6 miles to just north of Hammondsport, where you turn onto Rte. 54A into town. From
Rte. 54A take the first left past Lucy Knapp Real Estate onto County Rte. 76 and follow
the signs as described below. ■ From the north, take the N.Y. Thruway (I-90) to exit 42
and follow Rte. 14 south 7 miles through Geneva, then continue about 15 miles farther
south on Rte. 14. Take Rte. 54 west 4 miles to Penn Yan, then 54A to Branchport. From
the Branchport blinking red light, turn left to stay on Rte. 54A. Go about 9 miles and
turn right up Gibson Hill Rd. Go straight through the yield sign and turn left at the stop
sign (County Rte. 76). There is a Dr. Frank's sign there. Go about 1 mile to the next Dr.
Frank's sign and turn left. Turn right at the sign and then right again into the driveway.

Heron Hill Winery   ✪

9249 County Rte. 76, Hammondsport, NY 14840 • Phone 800-441-4241 or
607-868-4241 • Fax 607-868-4241 • www.heronhill.com • info@heronhill.com

This stunning modern winery, with its mission-like terra-cotta-and-stone masonry and silver-domed tower with heron wind vane, is the crowning achievement of John and Josephine Ingles, two University of Denver grads who met and married and in 1971 settled into a two-room back-to-nature cabin. Without benefit of running water or a bathroom, they planted a 20-acre vineyard anyway over the course of the next year, and the rest, as they say, is history.

Being located between Walter Taylor's Bully Hill Vineyards and Dr. Konstantin Frank's Vinifera Wine Cellars didn't hurt their enterprise, but some good wine vibes must have rubbed off. As the region grew, so did John and Josephine's winery, which underwent major renovations in 1999.

Wines: $–$$

White Wines

Barrel-Fermented Ingle Vineyard Chardonnay—Fermented and aged in oak barrels. Pear and butterscotch come through.

Chardonnay Reserve—Smoky, with apples and creaminess. Long finish.

Dry Riesling—Alsatian-style Riesling. Fruity yet dry finish. Clean and crisp.

Game Bird White—Semidry white with tropical fruits. Refreshing.

Ingle Vineyard Johannisberg Riesling—Semisweet, crisp, and refreshing.

Semi-Dry Riesling—Honey and apricot come through in this refreshing, light wine.

Seyval—Crisp and fresh. Pear and citrus come through. ♥

Red Wines

Baco Noir—A light, approachable dry red.

Eclipse—Classic Bordeaux-style dry red made from a blend of Cabernet Franc, Merlot, and Cabernet Sauvignon. Full bodied. Cherries come through. ♥ ♥

Game Bird Red—A dry, medium-red blend with a brilliant ruby color.

Ingle Vineyard Pinot Noir—A dry, medium-bodied red.

Blush Wines

Bluff Point Blush—Semisweet blush oozes peaches and apples.

Sparkling Wines

Brut Champagne—A *méthode champenoise* dry sparkling wine.

Dessert Wines

Late-Harvest Riesling—Thick, golden, rich dessert wine.

REVIEWS AND AWARDS

Baco Noir 1999—Gold medal, 2001 Tasters Guild International Wine Competition.

Dry Riesling 1999—Double gold medal, 2000 Tasters Guild International Wine Competition.

Eclipse 1999—Gold medal, 2001 Florida State Fair; silver medal, 2001 Tasters Guild International Wine Competition.

Semi-Dry Riesling 2002—Gold medal, 2003 Finger Lakes International Wine Competition.

Seyval 2000—Gold medal, 2001 Tasters Guild International Wine Competition; silver medal, 2001 Indiana State Fair Indy International Wine Competition.

Chardonnay 1997: "Smoky oak and citrusy aromas . . . clean and snappy. . . . 83 points."   —Beverage Testing Institute, *Buying Guide to Wines of North America*

HOURS AND DIRECTIONS
Open year-round Mon.–Sat. 10 a.m.–5 p.m., Sun. noon–5 p.m.
■ Leave Penn Yan heading south on Rte. 54A. Go past the scenic overlook and the

Sunoco station and continue to the light in Branchport. In Branchport, continue straight up Italy Hill Rd. (the Branchport Hardware Store is on your left). Go up the hill 1.8 miles and turn left on Darbys Corners Rd., where you'll see a Heron Hill Winery sign. In Pultney you come to a stop sign. Continue straight. At 6.5 miles you come to a fork in the road. Bear left, following the Heron Hill Winery signs. At 1 mile you'll come to a stop sign. Turn left and follow the winery signs 4 miles to the winery on your right. ■ From Watkins Glen, following Rte. 14 north, turn west onto Rtes. 28/23 (Mud Lake Rd.). It is 10 miles to Hammondsport. Mud Lake Rd. changes names as it heads through the towns of Tyrone and Weston. Cross Rte. 226 and Rte. 97 (this road passes between Lamoka Lake and Waneta Lake). After crossing 97, this same road will be called Fleet Rd. You'll come to a T intersection at Rte. 87 (Hammondsport-Wayne Rd.). Turn left onto Rte. 54 and follow it to Rte. 54A. Take 54A through the village of Hammondsport. Just outside the village (and just past Lucy Knapp Real Estate on your left), County Rte. 76 goes up the hill, while Rte. 54A continues along the Keuka Lake shoreline. This intersection is well marked with winery signs, as well as those for Dr. Frank, Bully Hill, and Hunt Country. Go 3 miles on County Rte. 76 to Heron Hill Winery, which will be on your left.

Hunt Country Vineyards ✧ ✧

4021 Italy Hill Rd., Branchport, NY 14418 • Phone 800-WINE-BUY • www.huntcountryvineyards.com • huntwine@eznet.net

The first time I had a Hunt Country wine was when I was working my first New York City publishing job and would go to the Wednesday farmer's market at Union Square. There, among the fruit and vegetable stalls, Hunt Country used to have a table where I'd buy an inexpensive dry red and go home a happy puppy. Ah, the salad days.

Hunt Country Vineyards is owned and operated by Art and Joyce Hunt, who moved to the property in 1973 to take over its operation. They're the sixth generation to till the soil on this farm, and live a rather Ralph Lauren–ish lifestyle with their show horses, their Bernese mountain dogs Claus and Gus, and their Great Dane, who goes by the name of Pug. But this is no Madison Avenue marketing snow job. Everything here is the real thing, including the renovated barn that houses the tasting room, which dates back to 1820.

Art and Joyce founded the winery in 1988 and have continued to grow the business since despite some up-and-down trends in the wine market. Hunt Country makes some very nice whites and reds but is primarily known these days for its two outstanding dessert wines, Vidal Blanc Ice Wine and Late-Harvest Vignoles, which are both universally applauded. The ice wine has won eight medals in the last 3 years (including four golds), and the Late-Harvest is no slouch either, earning six

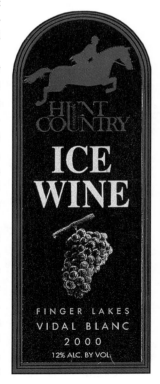

medals overall, three of them gold. One of the most fascinating things about these wines is what winemaker Tim Benedict calls "hang time." According to John Schreiner's *Ice Wine: The Complete Story*, there are two ways ice wine can be made: freeze the grapes in a commercial freezer or leave them out on the vine until they freeze. Traditionalists prefer the latter, but Hunt Country does both, leaving the grapes on the vine as late as possible, then refrigerating them until there's adequate time to complete the labor-intensive ice wine process.

The winery is located northwest of the most western tip of Lake Keuka, near Branchport. The views and the scenery are breathtaking, even by Finger Lakes standards. Rte. 54A, on which the winery is located, was chosen by British Airways' *Highlife* magazine as one of the most scenically spectacular highways in the world.

Wines: $–$$$

White Wines

Cayuga White—Semisweet, light white. Refreshing. Crisp.

Chardonnay—A full-bodied white. Tropical fruits and buttery texture. Nice.

Classic White—Not tasted.

Hunters White—Off-dry white with apples and pears. Nice. ♥

Riesling—Off-dry, with nice fruit and a tart finish.

Seyval Blanc—Made in a French style, aged in oak. Smooth and dry. ♥

Vignoles—A sweet white, but very polished. Very nice.

Red Wines

Cabernet Franc—Oak-aged red. Black cherry and raspberries come through.

Classic Red—A medium-bodied, Beaujolais-style red. Off-dry. A blend of Baco Noir, Chancellor, and DeChaunac.

Hunters Red—Slightly off-dry red. Deep fruit. Nice finish.

Sparkling Wines

Chardonnay Champagne—A sparkling wine fermented in the bottle. Just slightly off-dry.

Dessert Wines, Sherries, and Ports

Cream Sherry—Rich and nutty.

Late-Harvest Vignoles—Thick, golden, sweet, and luscious. Very nice. ♥ ♥

Ruby Port—A thick red dessert wine.

Vidal Blanc Ice Wine—Thick, rich, golden-sweet dessert wine. Real tropical flavors come through. Excellent mouth feel. Nicely balanced. Easily one of the best ice wines made, Canadian or not. Usually sells out pretty fast. ♥ ♥ ♥

REVIEWS AND AWARDS

Cabernet Franc 2001—Gold medal, 2003 Great Lakes Wine Competition.

Vidal Blanc Ice Wine 1997: "Generous earthy, honeyed melon aromas . . . tart, intense finish. . . . 85 points."
—Beverage Testing Institute, *Buying Guide to Wines of North America*

Vidal Blanc Ice Wine 1998: "Sweet, full-bodied, high acidity. From one of New York's ice wine experts comes lovely sipping, with orange and butterscotch flavors." —*Food & Wine* magazine *Wine Guide 2002*

Vidal Blanc Ice Wine 1999: "An elegant world-class wine." —Andrea Immer, *Esquire*

"[The Classic Red] delivers lovely aromatic and fruit flavors from baco noir, Chancellor and de Chaunac grapes, and a beefy body, is great for burgers, ribs and pasta." —*New York Times*

HOURS AND DIRECTIONS Open year-round Mon.–Sat. 10 a.m.–5 p.m., Sun. noon–5 p.m. (till 6 p.m. July–Oct.). ■ From the south, take Rte. 17 to exit 38 at Bath. Follow the green and white grape cluster signs to Rte. 54 north, drive 7 miles, then turn left onto Rte. 54A. Follow 54A through Hammondsport and go north 17 miles to Branchport. After leaving Hammondsport, you may instead follow the Keuka Wine Route (marked by red and white signs), which runs parallel to Rte. 54A on the upper road, above the lake. Both roads take you to Branchport and Hunt Country Vineyards. Follow Hunt Country signs to the winery. ■ From western New York, take the N.Y. Thruway (I-90) east to exit 44 (Canandaigua). Follow Rte. 332 south through Canandaigua and turn left onto Rtes. 5 and 20 east. Go about 3 miles and turn right onto Rte. 247. Follow Rte. 247 south about 10 miles. It merges with Rte. 364 east. Follow that about 5 miles east and turn right onto Guyanoga Valley Rd. (County Rte. 29). Follow Hunt Country signs 7 miles to Branchport. Turn right at the blinking light, then go 1 mile up the hill. ■ From eastern New York, take the Thruway (I-90) to exit 42 and follow Rte. 14 south 7 miles through Geneva, then continue about 15 miles farther south on Rte. 14. Take Rte. 54 west 4 miles to Penn Yan. At the intersection with the Sunoco and Mobil gas stations, take Rte. 54A west 8 miles to Branchport. Follow the Hunt Country Vineyards signs. At the blinking light go 1 mile straight up the hill to the vineyards.

Keuka Overlook Wine Cellars

5777 Old Bath Rd./Gardner Rd., Dundee, NY 14837 • Phone 607-292-6877 • www.keukaoverlook.com • TAB6877@aol.com

Bob and Terry Barrett established this lovely little winery in 1993 on one of the highest hillsides on the lake, buying their grapes from local producers and making wines that have taken prizes at some surprisingly prestigious competitions.

All the wines are affordable, and there's plenty of room to picnic at the winery. Alternatively, you can have a nice stay at the Keuka Overlook B & B across the way. The winery and inn are owned separately, but offer combined winter weekend getaway packages.

Wines: $–$$

White Wines

Blue Lake Chardonnay—Barrel-aged, off-dry white. Melon and apples.

Chardonnay Reserve—Not tasted.

Gewürztraminer—Spicy, fruity, light white. Nice.

Johannisberg Riesling—Off-dry, fruity white. Peaches and tangerines come through.

Victorian White—Alsatian-style Edelzwicker. Nice, light white.

Red Wines

Cabernet Franc—Smoky nose. Nice fruit. Vanilla.

Pinot Noir—Medium-bodied, smoky, oaked red. Cherry flavors. Very nice. ♥

Triumph—A purple blend of Cabernet Sauvignon, Cabernet Franc, and Merlot. Cherries, plums, and vanilla all come through. ♥

Victorian Red—An off-dry blend of Baco, Chambourcin, and Rougeon grapes, aged slightly in oak. Full bodied, with nice, rich fruit.

Blush Wines

Victorian Rosé—A blend of Gewürztraminer, Cayuga, Vidal, Riesling, and Colobel grapes. Light and fruity.

Dessert Wines

Blueberry—A 100% blueberry wine. Rich and sweet.

Dessert Chardonnay—Stainless steel Chard. Fruity but a tart finish. Clean. Crisp.

Dessert Riesling—Peaches, apricots, and honey come through. Nice acidity.

Red Raspberry—A 100% red raspberry wine. Mouthful of fruit. Nice finish.

HOURS AND DIRECTIONS Open daily 11 a.m.–5 p.m. spring, summer, and fall. ■ From Hammondsport, take Rte. 54 up the east side of Lake Keuka; then take Rte. 87 north. Go through Wayne, staying on 87. Keuka Overlook Wine Cellars is about 15 miles from Hammondsport, on your left.

Keuka Spring Vineyards

273 E. Lake Rd., Penn Yan, NY 14527 • Phone 315-536-3147 •
Fax 585-663-5204 • www.keukaspringwinery.com • ksvwine@frontiernet.net

This is a small winery that believes in doing wine right. Len and Judy Wiltberger planted their first vines in 1981 and sold their first vintage in 1986. However, they didn't hit real pay dirt until 1999, when their 1998 Cabernet Franc took that year's Governor's Cup and was declared New York State's best wine at the New York Wine and Food Classic, a very competitive gathering.

The understated winery is housed in a classic renovated 1840 barn located next to the couple's same-period house. Picnic tables are set up outside to enjoy the lovely views, and the gift shop is simple and tasteful. As a consequence of the winery's small size and outsize reputation, their wines are in high demand and tend to sell out quickly.

Wines: $–$$

White Wines

Cayuga White—Semidry, fruity, popular light white.

Chardonnay—Spicy. Peach and vanilla come through.

Crooked Lake White—Off-dry blend of Seyval and Vignoles.

Gewürztraminer—Spicy, with a nice finish.

Riesling—Off-dry. Nice fruit. Tart. Refreshing.

Seyval Blanc—Crisp, dry, and light. Apples and citrus come through.

Vignoles—Sweet, golden wine. Lemon and apricots come through.

Red Wines

Cabernet Franc—Dry red. Nice fruit.

Cabernet Sauvignon—Deep, rich, dry, oak-aged red. Nice fruit.

Clara's Red—A fruity, semisweet red.

Crooked Lake Red—Blend of Baco Noir and Cabernet Franc.

Epic—High-end blend of Cabernet Sauvignon, Cabernet Franc, and Merlot. Deep, rich, and fruity, but with a tart finish.

Lemberger—Dry, soft red. Nice fruit. Nice finish.

Merlot—Dry, soft red.

Pinot Noir—Medium red. Plum and raspberry come through.

Blush Wines

Harvest Blush—Semidry and crisp.

REVIEWS AND AWARDS

Cabernet Franc 1998—1999 New York Wine and Food Classic Governor's Cup, "New York State's best wine."

Cayuga 2002—Gold medal, 2003 Great Lakes Wine Competition.

Clara's Red 2002—Gold medal, 2003 Great Lakes Wine Competition.

Crooked Lake Red—Double gold, 2001 New York Wine and Food Classic.

HOURS AND DIRECTIONS Mon.–Sat. 10 a.m.–5 p.m., Sun. 11 a.m.–5 p.m., year-round. ■ Keuka Spring Vineyards is located along the east side of Keuka Lake on Rte. 54, 3 miles south of Penn Yan and 17 miles north of Hammondsport. ■ It's only 7 minutes from the west side of Seneca Lake: after you reach Penn Yan, follow the signs on Rte. 54.

McGregor Vineyards Winery

5503 Dutch St., Dundee, NY 14837 • Phone 607-292-3999 •
Fax 607-292-6929 • www.linkny.com/~mcg

In 1971, Bob and Marge McGregor established their vineyard by planting 28 acres of premium vinifera and hybrid grapes overlooking beautiful Keuka Lake. According to the McGregors, "The local wine industry [which was essentially dependent upon native American grape varieties] watched with skeptical interest."

The winery finally opened in 1980, debuting with Chardonnay, Riesling, Gewürztraminer, and Pinot Noir. Today, the McGregors take their winemaking seriously, producing a wide range of wines in small quantities, with an eye toward quality. There is no clear-cut winner in the crowd: All have won numerous awards, with many gold medals among them. Stroll the deck with the gorgeous view, walk out into the vineyards, or just hang out in the tasting room and gift shop. Very pleasant.

Wines: $–$$$

White Wines

Chardonnay—Dry and crisp, with a good balance of fruit and vanillin.

Gewürztraminer Dry—Light, Alsatian-style white. Nice.

Gewürztraminer Off-dry—A slight sweetness doesn't take away from the tartness.

Gewürztraminer Semi-Sweet Reserve—Nice light white wine. Sweet and tart. ♥

Johannisberg Riesling Semi-Sweet—Nice light white with tropical fruits and a tart finish.

Reserve Chardonnay—Barrel fermented and aged in French oak. Smooth and buttery.

Sunflower White—A nice, light, semisweet blend of Riesling, White Russian, and Chardonnay. ♥

Red Wines

Black Russian Red—Eastern European varietal blend with flavors of cherry. Nice. ♥ ♥

Cabernet Franc—Dry and soft, with nice fruit.

Highlands Red—An off-dry medium-red blend of Baco Noir and Pinot Noir. ♥

Pinot Noir—Dry, full-bodied red. Aged in oak.

Dessert Wines

Gewürztraminer Late Harvest—Rich, golden dessert wine.

REVIEWS AND AWARDS

Black Russian Red 1999—Gold medal, 2002 Finger Lakes International Wine Competition; bronze medal, 2002 Grand Harvest Awards.

Highlands Red 1999—Double gold medal, 2000 New York State Fair Wine Competition.

Late Harvest Vignoles 2001—Gold medal, 2003 Great Lakes Wine Competition.

Rob Roy Red 1999—Gold medal, 2003 Great Lakes Wine Competition.

HOURS AND DIRECTIONS Open daily Apr.–Nov. 10 a.m.–6 p.m. (to 8 p.m. Fri.–Sat. in

July–Aug.); Dec.–Mar. daily 11 a.m.–5 p.m. ■ From Penn Yan, take Rte. 54 south about 12 miles to Hyatt Hill Rd. Take Hyatt Hill about 1 mile and turn left onto Dutch St. Drive about 1 mile to the winery. ■ From Hammondsport, take Rte. 54 north about 9 miles to Hyatt Hill Rd. Turn up Hyatt Hill Rd. and follow the local directions above. ■ From Dundee, take Rte. 230, which will take you Rte. 54. Turn right onto 54 and continue to Hyatt Hill Rd., about 0.5 mile. Turn up Hyatt Hill Rd. and follow the local directions above.

Pleasant Valley Wine Company / Great Western Winery

8260 Pleasant Valley Rd., Hammondsport, NY 14840 • Phone 607-569-6111 • Fax 607-569-6112 • gwwinery@infoblvd.net

Pleasant Valley Wine Company was founded in 1860, producing a sparkling wine called Great Western Champagne, which won honorable mention in a wine-judging competition in Paris in 1867 and received a gold medal at the Vienna Exposition in 1873. The Pleasant Valley Wine Company and its Great Western label became part of Taylor Wine Company in 1962, and in 1993 they were sold again to the Canandaigua Wine Company. Pleasant Valley now operates a visitors' center in the former Taylor–Great Western–Gold Seal wine center in Hammondsport.

Wines: $–$$$

Sparkling Wines

Great Western Brut—A pale, straw-colored wine. The *cuvée* is a blend of Aurore, Delaware, Chardonnay, and Catawba. Very dry. Very good. ♥

Great Western Brut Rosé—An off-dry, blush-colored sparkling wine. The *cuvée* is blend of Aurore, Delaware, Chardonnay, Catawba, and Pinot Noir.

Great Western Chardonnay—Aged *en tirage* following secondary fermentation. Complex, toasty, nice, with a dry finish.

Great Western Extra Dry Champagne—A pale, straw-colored sparkling wine. Off-dry. The *cuvée* is a blend of Aurore, Delaware, Chardonnay, and Catawba.

Great Western Spumante—A golden-colored, semisweet sparkler. The *cuvée* is a blend of Aurore, Delaware, Chardonnay, Catawba, Muscat, and Cayuga.

Dessert Wines

Marsala—In the manner of the classic Italian dessert wine. Medium bodied. Nice. ♥

HOURS AND DIRECTIONS Open year-round Mon.–Sat. 10 a.m.–5 p.m., Sun. noon–5 p.m. ■ Take Rte. 88 south out of Hammondsport. The winery is about 1 mile out of town, on the left-hand side. If you pass Rheims, you've gone too far.

FINGER LAKES: CANANDAIGUA

Arbor Hill Grapery & Winery

6259 Hawks Rd., Naples, NY 14512 • Phone 716-374-2406 • Fax 716-374-9198 • www.thegrapery.com • js@thegrapery.com

Arbor Hill is a whole food and wine experience, a series of enchanting little New England–style buildings housing a tasting room, an extensive cheese shop, and a wide range of specialty gourmet food products, including a line of dressings and sauces made from Arbor Hill wines. Both the wines and the food offerings are award winners, entered in food competitions all across the country.

Arbor Hill hosts a series of dinners (normally one a month) with exceptional menus and a selection of their wines. It's a great taste treat.

Wines: $–$$

White Wines

Chardonnay—A nice, dry Chardonnay aged in French Nevers oak.

Johannisberg Riesling—Semisweet Riesling with tart pop.

Moores Diamond—Fresh and fruity white wine with a hint of American oak.

Traminette—Semisweet, spicy white wine. Nice.

Red Wines

Noir—Nice fruit flavors with a just-right oak balance.

Blush Wines

Very Cherry—A sweet, rosé-style wine made with the flavor of Montmorency cherries.

Fruit Wines

Very Blueberry—A sweet red wine made with wild Maine blueberries.

Sparkling Wines

Celebration—A light, fruity sparkling wine. Low in alcohol. Refreshing.

REVIEWS AND AWARDS

Noir—Bronze medal, New York State Fair Wine Competition.

Very Blueberry—Bronze medal, New York Wine and Food Classic.

Very Cherry—Bronze medal, New York Wine and Food Classic.

HOURS AND DIRECTIONS Open May–early Jan., Mon.–Sat. 10 a.m.–5 p.m., Sun. 11 a.m.–5 p.m. ■ From Rochester, take Rte. 64 south to East Bloomfield. Turn left onto Rtes. 5 and 20, then right onto Rte. 64 going south. Follow this toward Bristol Springs, where you'll see the winery signs. Arbor Hill will be on your right.

Batavia Wine Cellars

398 School St., Batavia, NY 14020 • Phone 585-344-1111 • Fax 585-344-3638

Batavia Wine Cellars is owned and operated by Canandaigua Wine Company, and specializes in producing value-priced wines bottled under many different labels, including Capri, Henri Marchant, and Vintner's Choice. Their lines include bottle-fermented champagnes, table wines, dessert wines, sparkling juice, and other specialty items. They produce about 2 million cases per year, selling primarily on the East Coast and in upper Midwest markets. No tours or tastings.

Wines: $

Canandaigua Wine Company

116 Buffalo St., Canandaigua, NY 14424 • Phone 716-394-7900 • Fax 716-394-6017 • www.cwine.com

Marvin Sands established Canandaigua Wine Company in 1945, and in the ensuing half century it has grown to become the world's second-largest wine company, with a reach extending from the Finger Lakes to California and the Pacific Northwest, and to Australia and Chile. Though they're now a division of Constellation Brands, Inc., their headquarters remain in Canandaigua, and their subsidiaries include many of the old-time wineries on the Canandaigua Wine Trail. They export to more than seventy countries, including the United Kingdom, Germany, Sweden, Japan, and Canada, and in fiscal 2002 reported net sales of $863 million.

Canandaigua Wine Company produces Almaden Bag-in-the-Box, Almaden Glass, Caywood, Chateau LaSalle, Coastal Vintners, Cribari, Deer Valley, Estate Cellars, Heritage, Inglenook, La Terre, Macaroni Grill, Nathanson Creek, Paul Masson, Taylor California Cellars, and Vendange. They also offer such California wines as Columbia, Covey Run, Dunnewood, Mystic Cliffs, Northwest, Paul Thomas, Ste. Chapelle, and Talus; nonalcoholic wines such as St. Regis; Manischewitz (the no. 1 kosher wine in the United States); sparkling wines including Chase Limogere, Cook's, Cribari Sparkling, Great Western, J. Roget, Jacques Bonet, Le Domaine, Mondoro Motif, and Taylor New York; inexpensive sweet wines including Cisco, Imperial Reserve, Red Dagger, Richards Desserts, and Wild Irish Rose; and brandies such as Paul Masson Grande Amber VS and Paul Masson Grande Amber VSOP. They import such wines as Alice White, Marcus James, and Viña Santa Carolina.

Wines: $–$$$

HOURS AND DIRECTIONS The headquarters does not offer tours, but Manischewitz and Widmer's Wine Cellars do offer tours and tastings (see below).

Casa Larga Vineyards ✪

2287 Turk Hill Rd., Fairport, NY 14450 • Phone 716-223-4210 •
Fax 716-223-8899 • www.casalarga.com • info@casalarga.com

As a young boy, Andrew Colaruotolo worked alongside his grandparents in the fields and vineyards of Gaeta, Italy, a small fishing village between Rome and Naples, and came to understand the meticulous care a vineyard needs to yield superb fruit. At the age of seventeen, just after World War II, Andrew immigrated to America, where he became an architect and eventually founded a large building company. But wine was still in his blood, and by the 1970s he had started his own vineyard, which yielded its first marketable harvest in 1978. Since then, Casa Larga—named for Mr. C's grandparents' home in Italy—has gained a reputation for reds and also boasts an excellent dessert wine, and has won more than 160 awards around the world.

Wines: $–$$$

White Wines

CLV Chardonnay—Silky. Tropical fruit and oak come through.

Gewürztraminer—A spicy, dry, Alsatian-style wine. Light. ♥

Johannisberg Riesling—A nice, light Riesling.

Lilac Hill—A light, fruity white. Blend of Muscat Ottonel and Johannisberg Riesling.

Reserve Chardonnay—Aged in Yugoslavian oak. Dry and full bodied.

Vineyard Hill Chardonnay—A light, crisp, dry Chardonnay. ♥

Red Wines

Cabernet Sauvignon—Oak aged, full bodied, and dry. Excellent with prime rib and fine meals. Multiple award winner in national competitions. ♥

Due Mille—A Meritage of three red wines: Merlot, Cabernet Sauvignon, and Cabernet Franc. Full bodied and dry, with lots of fruit and a clean finish.

Merlot—Oak-aged dry red. Berries and cherries come through.

Petite Noir—Made from 100% DeChaunac grapes. Light, dry, and fruity.

Pinot Noir—Dry, medium-bodied red aged in oak. Cherry highlights.

Tapestry—A light, dry blend of 60% Cabernet and 40% DeChaunac grapes. Nice.

Blush Wines

Blush—A semisweet blush blend. Fruity and refreshing. ♥

Sparkling Wines

Blanc de Blanc Brut—Dry and full bodied.

Dessert Wines

Fiori Delle Stelle Vidal Ice Wine—Rich, golden, delicious dessert wine with nice balance. One of the better ice wines available on the market. ♥ ♥

REVIEWS AND AWARDS

American Oak Chardonnay 2001—Double gold medal, 2003 Tasters Guild International Wine Competition.

Finger Lakes Barrel Aged Chardonnay 2001—Gold medal, 2003 Finger Lakes International Wine Competition.

New York Cab-Merlot NV—Gold medal, 2003 Finger Lakes International Wine Competition.

Due Mille: "Score: 85"　　　　　　　　　　—Beverage Testing Institute

Fiori Delle Stelle Vidal Ice Wine 2001: "Score: 87."　　—*Wine Spectator* (April 2003)

Merlot 1998: "Score: 86"　　　　　　　　　—Beverage Testing Institute

HOURS AND DIRECTIONS Open Mon.–Sat. 10 a.m.–6 p.m., Sun. noon–6 p.m. (7 p.m. in Dec.) ■ From the N.Y. Thruway, take exit 45 and follow the sign toward Victor. Turn right onto Rte. 96, then right again onto Turk Hill Rd. (fourth traffic light). Proceed 1.5 miles to Casa Larga, which will be on your left. ■ From downtown Rochester, take I-490 east to the exit at Pittsford/Palmyra (Rte. 31 east). Turn right onto Turk Hill Rd. and proceed 1 mile to Casa Larga, on your right.

Eagle Crest Vineyards, Inc.

7107 Vineyard Rd., Conesus, NY 14435 • Phone 716-346-2321 • Fax 716-346-2322

Eagle Crest Vineyards was established in 1872, which makes it one of the earliest wineries in the region. Located in the hills of Conesus high above the western shore of Hemlock Lake, the winery was originally called O-Neh-Da (the Seneca Indian name for Hemlock Lake) and made sacramental wines widely distributed to clergy in the eastern United States. It's still in the sacramental business today, making thirteen different varieties of altar wines as well as table wines for general consumption, sold under the name Eagle Crest Vineyards and made from native American grapes and other hybrids. Wines include Chablis, Cream Sherry, Mellow Burgundy, Niagara, Pink Delaware, and Rosé.

Wines: $

HOURS AND DIRECTIONS Open year-round Mon.–Fri. 9 a.m.–4 p.m. Tastings are offered during regular business hours. ■ Call for directions.

Finger Lakes Wine Center ✰ ✰ ✰

151 Charlotte St., Canandaigua, NY 14424 • Phone 585-394-4922 • Fax 585-394-2192

Located in historic Bay House at Sonnenberg Garden, the small Finger Lakes Wine Center was founded to provide information about Finger Lakes wineries, and brings many of them together under one roof. On any given day, visitors can make their tasting selections from ten to fifteen different wines. It's a great way to sample wines from houses you might not otherwise get a chance to visit.

The Wine Center represents the following wineries and their products: Arbor Hill Grapery, Arcadian Estate Vineyards, Casa Larga Vineyards, Cascata Winery, Cayuga Ridge Estate Winery, Chateau Lafayette Reneau, Dr. Frank's Vinifera Wine Cellars, Four Chimneys Farm Winery, Fox Run Vineyards, Fulkerson Winery, Glenora Wine Cellars, Goose Watch Winery, Hazlitt 1852 Vineyards, Heron Hill Winery, Hosmer Winery, Hunt Country Vineyards, Keuka Overlook Wine Cellars, Keuka Spring Vineyards, King Ferry Winery/Treleaven Wines, Knapp Vineyards Winery, Logan Ridge Estates Winery, Lucas Vineyards, McGregor Vineyards Winery, Seneca Shore Wine Cellars, Sheldrake Point Vineyard, Standing Stone Vineyards, Swedish Hill Vineyard, Thorpe Vineyard, and Wagner Vineyards.

Wines: $–$$$

HOURS AND DIRECTIONS Open daily 11 a.m.–5:30 p.m. during the garden season and 6–9 p.m. during the Festival of Lights holiday. Call to make sure which are in effect. ■ From Rochester Airport and Buffalo, take I-90 (N.Y. Thruway) east to exit 44. Follow Rte. 332 south to the city of Canandaigua. Turn left onto Rte. 21 north and follow it to Charlotte St. Turn left onto Charlotte. The large iron gate marking the entrance to Sonnenberg Garden will be a short distance ahead on your right. ■ From Syracuse and Albany, follow I-90 west to exit 43 (Manchester/Shortsville) and turn south onto Rte. 21. Follow 21 south into the city of Canandaigua to Charlotte St., and turn right. Look for the large iron Sonnenberg gate on your right.

Manischewitz Wine Company

116 Buffalo St., Canandaigua, NY 14424 • Phone 716-394-7900 • Fax 716-394-6017 • www.manischewitzwine.com

Manischewitz is a name steeped in tradition; the company operates in strict adherence to kashruth, using a 100% kosher winemaking process. Every step of the Manischewitz production is supervised by a staff of learned and reliable *mashgichim* under the strict guidance of the Union of Orthodox Jewish Congregations of America. Additionally, all Manischewitz wines are *mevushal* (boiled).

In 1933 Leo Star founded the Monarch Wine Company in New York City. In the mid-1940s, Star began producing Manischewitz after he came to an arrangement with the original company famed for its kosher food products. They let him use the Manischewitz name on his wines. Using radio, Star introduced the company tag line that would last for decades: "Man oh Manischewitz. . . . What a Wine!"

Manischewitz Wine Company was bought in 1986 by the Canandaigua Wine Company. Canandaigua is owned by prominent Jewish families who are committed to making high-quality wine within the guidelines of Rabbinical Law. The plant closes early on Friday and Erev Yom Tom (holiday eve), so the employees arrive home before candle-lighting time. The winery is also closed on the Sabbath and on Jewish holidays throughout the year.

Wines: $–$$

Traditional Wines
Blackberry—A 100% blackberry wine with the aromas and flavors of blackberry jam.
Extra Heavy Malaga—A sweetened, fruity Concord wine with a generous mouth feel.

Other Wines
Cherry, Concord Grape, Elderberry, Loganberry, Medium Dry Concord

Cream Wines
Cream Blush Concord—A pink wine with distinctive fruit aroma and flavor.
Cream Red Concord—A sweet but balanced wine with a velvety mouth feel. The distinct aroma and flavor of fresh Concord grapes, with confectionery notes.
Cream White Concord—A smooth, fruity wine with plenty of grape flavor.

Cordials
Almonetta—A dessert wine. Creamy almond, marzipan, and Amaretto flavors.
Cream Peach—A smooth, creamy, peach flavor, bursting with the taste of fresh peaches.

Other Cordials
Cream Berry, Cream Black Cherry, Pina Coconetta, Strawberry Coconetta

HOURS AND DIRECTIONS Tours and tastings are at Widmer's Wine Cellars (see below).

Widmer's Wine Cellars, Inc.

One Lake Niagara Ln., Naples, NY 14512 • Phone 800-836-5253 or 585-374-6311 • Fax 585-374-2028

Widmer's Wine Cellars had its beginnings more than 100 years ago when Swiss winemaker John Jacob Widmer immigrated from Switzerland in 1882 and bought his first plot of hillside acreage with borrowed money. He planted his first vines in early 1883, built his homestead in 1885, and sold his first wines in 1888. Over the years, Widmer's gradually enlarged, weathering Prohibition by producing unfermented grape juice, fruit and wine jellies, syrups, and a small amount of sacramental wine, which also had a medicinal use. In 1933, when Prohibition was repealed, Widmer's was among the first wineries to crank back into action.

Widmer's acquired its largest regional competitor, Maxfield Wine Cellars, in 1941. The years 1967 and 1969 saw more enlargements in facilities and storage capacity, and today the whole operation covers 860 acres (220 of which are planted), produces 75,000 gallons annually, and can hold 100,000 cases of wine. The winery produces more than fifty varieties and is owned by the Canandaigua Wine Company, Inc. Brickstone Cellars is their premium line.

Wines: $–$$$

White Wines

Chardonnay—Aged in French and American oak 8 months. Tropical fruits come through.

Dry Riesling—Floral nose and mineral flavors come through. Very nice. ♥

Semi-Dry Riesling—Peach, apricot, and melon all come through. Nice.

Red Wines

Cabernet Franc—A deep, dry red. Raspberry, violet, and cedar come through.
Aged 10 months in American and French oak.

Pinot Noir—Cherry and raspberry come through. Smoky oak too.

REVIEWS AND AWARDS

Cabernet Franc 2000—Gold medal, 2002 Finger Lakes International Wine Competition.

Dry Riesling 2000—Gold medal, 2002 Jerry Mead New World International Wine Competition.

Port Solaira—Gold medal, 2003 Great Lakes Wine Competition.

Vidal Late Harvest 2001—Gold medal, 2003 Great Lakes Wine Competition.

HOURS AND DIRECTIONS Call 800-836-5253 for seasonal hours and special event listings. ■ From Rochester, take the N.Y. Thruway to exit 44 (Canandaigua). Follow Rte. 332 south through Canandaigua. Take Rte. 21 south along the picturesque banks of Canandaigua Lake to the village of Naples. Widmer's Wine Cellars is located on the right side of the road. ■ From Syracuse, take the N.Y. Thruway to exit 43 (Manchester). Take Rte. 21 south and follow the local directions above. ■ From Binghamton and the Southern Tier Expwy., take Rte. 17 west to exit 37. Follow Rte. 53 north through Naples. Widmer's is on the left-hand side of Rte. 21.

OTHER CANANDAIGUA WINERIES

Deer Run Winery: Rte. 256 (0.5 mile south of Rte. 20A), Geneseo, NY 14454 • Phone 585-243-4497 • Noyuk@mindspring.com • Owner George Kuyon

Yates Cellars Winery: 4695 Rte. 245, Stanley, NY 14561 • Phone 716-526-5638

LAKE ERIE

Blueberry Sky Farm Winery

10243 N.E. Sherman Rd., Ripley, NY 14775 • Phone 716-252-6535 •
www.blueberryskyfarm.com • bsfw@lakeside.net

Don and Rosalind Heinert founded Blueberry Sky Farm Winery in 1998 after about 30 years of home winemaking. Like some of its colder-climate cousins farther north, Blueberry Sky concentrates mainly on fruit wines, with specialties including plum, rhubarb, apple, blackberry, dandelion, and elderberry. The Heinerts also make a line of cooking wines, including one award-winning version made from jalapeños.

The winery is truly a family-run operation, with winemaker Don still splitting time with his veterinary practice. Rosalind and their four children pick most of the fruits and vegetables. The wine is sold in an extension of the Heinert home. Almost all the wines come in sweet and dry varieties.

Wines: $–$$

Fruit Wines

Apple—Made from New York State apples. Distinctive.

Black Raspberry—The dry is thick and chewy. The sweet is a nice dessert wine.

Blackberry—Made from a mixture of wild and domestic blackberries. Nice.

Blueberry—A dry wine with an almost Merlot-like feel. Interesting.

Cherry—The dry cherry is interesting. The sweet cherry is a nice dessert-type wine.

Dandelion—One of the few wineries that makes a dandelion wine. I prefer it dry.

Elderberry—A very distinct and interesting taste.

Honey—Rich, golden honey dessert wine. Nice.

Peach—One of their most popular wines. The sweet is very nice.

Pear—Semisweet, blush-colored wine made from a combination of pears found in an old orchard. Very nice.

Plum—The sweet is very nice. The dry is something different. Worth trying.

Red Raspberry—The dry is nice; the sweet is better.

Rhubarb—Traditional wine with some Chardonnay added. Nice.

Strawberry—A deep, rich color and strong strawberry taste.

Tomato—The winery says, "An elegant appetizer with cheese and crackers." Not tasted.

REVIEWS AND AWARDS

Black Raspberry—Bronze medal, 1999 New York Wine and Grape Foundation; bronze medal, 2000 New York Wine and Grape Foundation.

Dandelion—Silver medal, 1999 New York Wine and Food Classic; silver medal, 1999 New York Wine and Grape Foundation.

Plum—Bronze medal, 1999 New York Wine and Food Classic.

"Smooth and luscious, one can taste the sun-kissed freshness of the ingredients in each sample." —Maureen Davis, *Westfield Republican* (November 5, 1998)

HOURS AND DIRECTIONS Call for hours. ■ Take I-90 to exit 12, from which you take Rte. 20 east 1 block. Turn right onto Gulf Rd. and go up the hill. At the first stop, turn left onto Kerr Rd. Go 2 miles. The farm is on the right.

Cambria Wine Cellars

4434 VanDusen Rd., Lockport, NY 14094 • Phone 716-433-8405 •
Fax 716-433-5616 • www.cambriawinecellars.com

The Smith family vineyards, which are the backbone of this winery, began in 1932 with 2 acres of vines planted at the base of the Niagara Escarpment, in a microclimate perfect for growing premium grapes. Over three generations, the vineyards have grown to 150 acres, and now the farm has a winery of its own, opened by Peter and Nancy Smith with the help of Mike and Jackie Connolly and Gary and Lori Hoover. When it recently opened its doors in the last few years, it was the first winery in Niagara County to open to the public in 20 years.

Wines: $-$$

White Wines
Blue Marlin Splash—Off-dry white with flavors of green apples. Interesting. Refreshing.
Chardonnay—An off-dry white.
Misty Niagara—Award-winning sweet white.

Red Wines
Cambria Red—Off-dry red.
Captain's Choice—An award-winning Concord wine.
Merlot—Dry, deep red.
Pinot Noir—Dry, light red.
Stearman Steuben—Semisweet red.

Blush Wines
Boxer Blush—An award-winning blush.

REVIEWS AND AWARDS
Boxer Blush 2000—Best of category (blush wine) and best of class (best blush), 2001 New York Wine and Food Classic.
Captain's Choice 2000—Bronze medal, 2001 New York Wine and Food Classic.
Captain's Choice 2001—Double gold medal, 2002 New York Wine and Food Classic Governor's Cup.
Misty Niagara 2000—Bronze medal, 2001 New York Wine and Food Classic.

HOURS AND DIRECTIONS Open Apr.–Dec. Mon.–Fri. 2–6 p.m., Sat. 10 a.m.–6 p.m., Sun. noon–6 p.m.; Jan.–Mar. Fri. 2–6 p.m., Sat.–Sun. noon–5 p.m. ■ Call for directions.

Chiappone's Cellar, Inc.

3401 Murphy Rd., Newfane, NY 14108 • Phone 716-433-9463

Chiappone's is a boutique winery that makes a wide range of award-winning wines from native grapes, French-American hybrids, and vinifera.

Wines: $-$$

REVIEWS AND AWARDS
Cleo 2002—Gold medal, 2003 Great Lakes Wine Competition.
Diamond 2002—Gold medal, 2003 Los Angeles County Fair Wine Competition; gold medal, 2003 Great Lakes Wine Competition.
Knockin' on Heaven's Door 2002—Gold Medal, 2003 Great Lakes Wine Competition.
Seyval 2000—Gold medal, 2001 Tasters Guild International Wine Competition.

HOURS AND DIRECTIONS Call for hours and directions.

Merritt Estate Winery

2264 King Rd., Forestville, NY 14062 • Phone 888-965-4800 or
716-965-4800 • Fax 716-965-4800 • www.merrittestatewinery.com •
nywines@merrittestatewinery.com

Established in 1976 by famed horticulturist James M. Merritt and his sons Bill and
James, Merritt Estate was the first farm winery organized in Chautauqua County under
regulations signed that same year by Governor Hugh Carey. The farm and house have
been in the Merritt family since the late 1800s, and today the operation is run by Bill
and his wife Christi. Their cool cellar is equipped for modern aging and production,
while the 100 acres of Triple M Farms provide the grapes, with Jason C. Merritt (Bill's
son) acting as winemaker. The annual output is somewhere around 30,000 gallons of
wines, making this one of the key wineries in the Lake Erie region.

Wines: $–$$$

White Wines

Chardonnay—Traditional, bone-dry wine with light oak and fruit overtones.
Chautauqua Niagara—Semisweet and fruity. Crisp.
Delaware—A sweet Rhine-style wine. Pleasant fruit. Clean, crisp finish.
Edelweiss—Fruity, with a flowery aroma. Refreshing.
Niagara—Inexpensive, fruity, sweet wine. Nice taste.
Seyval Blanc—Clean and dry, with a nice nose.

Red Wines

Chambourcin—Deep, dry red with berry flavors and dry finish.
Marechal Foch—A light-bodied red wine, aged in oak.

Dessert Wines

Late-Harvest Delaware—Thick and rich, with a nice balance.
Strawberry Festival—A sweet blend of grape wine and natural strawberry flavor. Nice.

REVIEWS AND AWARDS

Bella Rosa 2000—Silver medal, 2001 Finger Lakes International Wine Competition;
silver medal, 2001 Riverside International Wine Competition; silver medal,
2001 Tasters Guild International Wine Competition; bronze medal, 2001
San Diego National Wine Competition; bronze medal, 2001 Los Angeles County
Fair Wine Competition.

Late-Harvest Delaware 1999—Bronze medal, 2000 New York Wine and Food Classic.

HOURS AND DIRECTIONS Open year-round Mon.–Sat. 10 a.m.–5 p.m., Sun. noon–5
p.m. ■ From Buffalo, take I-90 to exit 58 (Silver Creek); then take Rte. 20 west to the
blinking light at Sheridan, turn left onto Center Rd., left again onto King Rd., and then
follow the signs about 1.5 miles to the winery. ■ From Erie, take I-90 to exit 59
(Dunkirk) and turn left onto Rte. 60 to Rte. 20, about 0.5 mile. Turn left onto Rte. 20,
go to the blinking light at Sheridan, turn right onto Center Rd., then left onto King
Rd. Follow the signs about 1.5 miles to the winery.

Schloss Doepken Winery

9177 Old Rte. 20, Ripley, NY 14775 • Phone 716-326-3636

This winery was founded by John Simon Watso and his wife Roxann in 1980 on 60
acres of farmland they had started planting as far back as 1972. It's all very charming

and cozy, with the tasting room located right in their house. The winery produces more than 3,000 cases per year.

Where did they get that name? Well, when they were getting ready to open, they didn't want to call it Watso Winery. So they named it after Roxann, using her maiden name Doepken. Schloss means "castle," so it's really Castle Doepken.

Wines: $–$$

White Wines
Chardonnay—Off-dry, with fruit.
Oak-Aged Chardonnay—Dry finish.
Schloss Blanc—Light white blend.

Red Wines
Cabernet Sauvignon—Dry, deep red. Not tasted.
Roxann Rouge—A Baco Noir aged in oak.

Blush Wines
Chautauquablumchen—A pink, sweet Riesling. Interesting. Try it!

HOURS AND DIRECTIONS Open daily noon–5 p.m. year-round. ■ From Buffalo or Erie, take I-90 to exit 61. Go south. Turn left onto Rte. 20, then right onto Old Rte. 20 to the winery.

Vetter Vineyards Winery

8005 Prospect Station Rd., Westfield, NY 14787 • Phone 716-326-3100

Very much a small-scale, family-run affair, 22-acre Vetter Vineyards was established in 1987 by Craig Vetter and operates out of his family's private residence: The two-car garage is the tasting room, and their basement is the wine cellar. It's all nice and homey, but as you're driving up the tree-lined driveway, you do feel like you're dropping in unexpectedly at someone's home—which, really, you are. Craig is a bit of a one-man show, but manages to produce some tasty and enjoyable wines.

Wines: $–$$

White Wines
Chardonnay—A dry, crisp, clean table white.
Gewürztraminer—An off-dry Alsatian-style Gewürz.
Riesling—Tropical flavors and a citrus ending make for an interesting white.
Seyval—A green apple white with dry finish.
Vignoles—A white wine with golden color.

Red Wines
Cabernet Sauvignon—Big berry flavors up front. Dry finish.
Chambourcin—Big berry, plum, and cherry. Dry finish.

HOURS AND DIRECTIONS Call for hours. ■ From Buffalo and Erie, take I-90 to exit 60. Turn left onto Rte. 20. Turn right onto Prospect Station Rd. and continue to the winery.

Willow Creek Winery

2627 Chapin Rd., P.O. Box 54, Sheridan, NY 14135 •
Phone 716-934-9463 • www.willowcreekwines.com

Willow Creek Winery is owned by 30-year veteran home winemaker Jim Emerson and his partner Dan Hesslinger, a 20-year veteran grape grower. In 1998 they decided to start a winery, taking as their co-conspirator Dan's 94-year-old grandmother Agnes Williams, who agreed to let the two men use her 52-acre farm. The planting began on May 30, 1999, the doors opened on July 28, 2000, and in the first year they produced 1,000 gallons of wine.

This award-winning winery offers a diverse range of wines and a number of activities for visitors. You can take guided tours, do wine tastings (of course), experience their lush and beautiful picnic groves, take out paddle boats, walk the hiking trails, use their private fishing area, and peruse their gift shop.

Wines (not tasted) include *Aunt Millie, Cabernet Franc, Cabernet Sauvignon, Catawba, Cayuga White, Chambourcin, Concord, Delaware, Marechal Foch, Merlot, Niagara, Rambo Red, Sweet Agnes*.

Wines: $–$$

HOURS AND DIRECTIONS Open May–Dec. Mon.–Fri. 11 a.m.–5 p.m., Sat.–Sun. 11 a.m.–6 p.m.; Jan.–Apr. by appointment only. ■ From Buffalo, take I-90 west to exit 58 (Silver Creek); then follow Rte. 20 west. Turn right onto Center Rd. (Rte. 79) at the caution light, then right onto Chapin Rd. ■ From Erie, take I-90 east to exit 59 (Dunkirk). Turn left onto Rte. 60 south, left again onto Rte. 20 east, and left a third time onto Center Rd. (Rte. 79), then right onto Chapin Rd.

Woodbury Vineyards

3230 S. Roberts Rd., Fredonia, NY 14063 • Phone 888-697-9463 or 716-679-9463 • Fax 716-679-9464 • www.woodburyvineyards.com • wv@woodburyvineyards.com

Gary Woodbury, a former chemistry teacher, established Woodbury Vineyards in 1979 on land his family had used for grapes since 1910. They began planting vinifera in 1966, and the company went public in 1996. Gary is now chief operating officer, with Andrew Z. Dabrowski acting as winemaker. Today the winery produces 25,000 cases per year, of a quality that's stayed high since wine historian Leon Adams wrote that he was "amazed" by their early-1970s Chardonnay. "It was equal to a true Chablis" (*The Wines of America*).

Wines: $–$$

White Wines

Barrel Fermented Chardonnay—Chardonnay aged in French oak. Well balanced, with lemon, pear, and vanilla aromas.

Dry Riesling—A full-bodied Riesling. Dry finish.

Niagara—Sweet wine made from native grapes.

Riesling—A semisweet Riesling. Intense fruit. Light. Clean.

Seaport White—A blend of Chardonnay, Seyval, and Cayuga.

Seyval—Big fruit with a pucker. Nice.

White Renard—A sweet, fruity white wine blend with a distinctive grapy flavor.

Red Wines

Glacier Ridge Red—A blend of Cabernet Sauvignon, Cabernet Franc, and Merlot. ♥

Merlot—A deep ruby-red color. Full bodied. Dry.

Red Renard—A sweet, fruity red.

Seaport Red—A soft red. Big fruit.

Blush Wines

Blush Renard—A sweet blush blend of Catawba, Delaware, and Concord.

Seaport Blush—A semisweet blush.

Sparkling Wines

Brut Champagne—A 100% Chardonnay, bottle-fermented champagne. Dry, with hint of oak. Nice fruit and bubbles.

Chautauqua Champagne—A semidry bottle-fermented blend of Chardonnay, Seyval, and Cayuga White.

Riesling Champagne—Made from 100% Riesling. Semisweet.

Fruit Wines

Cherry—Made from juice of New York State cherries. Sweet but not cloying. Tart finish. One of the best cherry wines in the Northeast. ♥

Strawberry—Made from juice of New York State strawberries.

REVIEWS AND AWARDS

Cherry—Silver medal, North American International Wine Competition.

HOURS AND DIRECTIONS Tours Mon.–Sat. 10 a.m.–4:30 p.m., Sun. noon–4:30 p.m., year-round. ■ Call for directions.

OTHER LAKE ERIE WINERIES

Roberian Vineyards Limited: 2614 King Rd., Forestville, NY 14062 • Phone 716-679-1620

Warm Lake Estate Vineyard and Winery: 3868 Lower Mountain Rd., Lockport, NY 14094 • Phone 716-877-9865 or 716-471-5108

PENNSYLVANIA

Adams County Winery

251 Peach Tree Rd., Orrtanna, PA 17353 • Phone 717-334-4631 •
Fax 717-334-4026 • www.adamscountywinery.com •
adamscountywinery@blazenet.net

Adams County Winery, a small farm with peach, apple, and pear orchards, located in Adams County (just 8 miles west of Gettysburg), began operating in 1978 under the care of founders Ron and Ruth Cooper. The present owners, John Kramb and his wife Katherine Bigler, took over in 1998. The winery operation is housed in a nineteenth-century barn and includes a gift shop selling many wine-related items.

Wines: $

White Wines

Chardonnay—Moderate oak.

Presidents Choice—Sweet white blend.

Sweet Catawba—Just the Catawba grape.

Tears of Gettysburg—Niagara blend. Light, crisp, and slightly sweet. ♥

Red Wines

Appalachian Sunset—Light, fruity wine.

Baco Noir—A dry red, medium bodied.

Chambourcin—Full-bodied, dry wine.

Rhedd Butler—A blend of Chardonnay and DeChaunac.

Blush Wines

Baron's Blush—Semidry.

Fruit Wines

Adams Apple—Spiced wine.

Other Wines

Semi-Dry Vidal, Sweet Scarlet, Three Ships to the Wind, Wisp O' the Vine

HOURS AND DIRECTIONS Open Apr.–Dec. daily, 10 a.m.–6 p.m.; open Jan.–Mar. Sat.–Sun. and holidays 10 a.m.–5 p.m. ■ From Gettysburg, proceed west on Rte. 30. After 8 miles, turn left at the blinking yellow light, toward Cashtown. There are well-marked signs for the winery at this intersection and at every turn you'll make from here. Proceed toward Cashtown. After 1 mile, the road dead-ends. Turn left. In 100 yards, turn right, following the sign to Orrtanna. In about 1 mile, you'll come to another dead end and a stop sign; turn right. You'll be facing a fork in the road. Keep to the left branch.

In less than a mile, at the bottom of the hill, turn right on Peach Tree Rd. After 0.3 mile, turn left onto the dirt road and proceed 0.3 mile to the winery.

Allegro Wines ✡

3475 Sechrist Rd., Brogue, PA 17309 • Phone 717-927-9148 •
www.allegrowines.com • info@allegrowines.com

This quaint operation enjoys a secluded setting along the bucolic lower Susquehanna River watershed, protected by mountains to the west. Early American pioneers established vineyards and wineries here in the 1830s, and in 1980 brothers Tim and John Crouch followed suit, setting out to make reasonably priced, European-style table wines. They maintain a total of 12 acres, planted mostly with Seyval and Chardonnay, and have enjoyed much critical success: Hugh Johnson awarded the winery three stars in his 2002 guide, and *The New Sotheby's Wine Encyclopedia* agreed.

Wines: $–$$

White Wines

Chardonnay—Dry, lemony, and buttery, aged in French oak. ♥

Premium White—A semidry, fruity Seyval.

Reserve Chardonnay '95—Mellow and dry, smoky and creamy. ♥

Vidal—Light, off-dry white. Intense fruit. Apricot and honey come through.

Red Wines

Cadenza '97 Reserve Cabernet Sauvignon—Deep, intense, dry red. ♥

Blush Wines

Brogue Blush—A light, fruity blush.

Fruit Wines

Apple—A light white wine made from Pennsylvania apples.

Celeste—A blend of peaches and grapes.

Cherry—Made from Pennsylvania cherries. Not too sweet. Nice.

REVIEWS AND AWARDS

Apple—Silver medal, 2002 Pennsylvania Wine Association Competition.

HOURS AND DIRECTIONS Open year-round Fri.–Sun. noon–5 p.m., other days by appointment only. ■ Take I-83 to exit 6E and go east on Rte. 74 to Brogue. Turn right on Muddy Creek Rd., go 2 miles to Sechrist Rd., and turn left. The entrance for Allegro is on the left, down the hill.

Arrowhead Wine Cellars at Mobilia Fruit Farm

12073 E. Main Rd., North East, PA 16428 • Phone 814-725-5509 •
Fax 814-725-8904 • wine@velocity.net

A young vineyard with a young team but a long history, Arrowhead Wine Cellars is a true family business. Grape growers Nick and Kathy Mobilia have been selling bulk juice to wineries for years from the Mobilia Fruit Farm, so when their son Adrian, fresh out of Penn State, expressed an interest in the business, the Mobilias simply expanded. In 1999, Adrian became manager of the Arrowhead Wine Cellars. Jeffrey Murphy, son of winery partner Pat Murphy, came aboard as winemaker in 1999 after earning a degree in food science.

Wines: $–$$

White Wines

Niagara—A light white wine. Intense grape flavors.

Riesling—A light, off-dry white wine in the best German tradition. Nice.

Red Wines

Chambourcin—Medium-bodied, ruby red wine. Dry finish. Nice oak. Cherries and currants come through.

Fredonia—Semisweet red. Fresh and fruity.

Blush Wines

Buffalo Blush—Semisweet. Berries come through. Nice.

Pink Catawba—Intense, sweet Catawba blush.

Fruit Wines

Cherry—A light, sweet-but-not-too-sweet red.

Other Wines

Apple, Apple Spice, Chardonnay, Concord, Delaware, Peach, Steuben

REVIEWS AND AWARDS

Buffalo Blush and *Pink Catawba*—Bronze medal, 2001 Pennsylvania Wine Association Competition.

Chambourcin 1999—Bronze medal, 2001 Pennsylvania Farm Show Wine Competition.

HOURS AND DIRECTIONS Open year-round Mon.–Sat. 10 a.m.–6 p.m. (8 p.m. in summer), Sun. noon–6 p.m. ■ Take I-90 to exit 12, then go west on Rte. 20 for about 0.3 mile. The winery is on the left, just past the McDonald's and 84 Lumber.

Bashore & Stoudt Country Winery

5784 Old Rte. 22, P.O. Box 167, Shartlesville, PA 19954 • Phone 610-488-9466

Bashore & Stoudt specializes in fruit wines, making more than twenty varieties from fruit grown principally on co-owner Bob L. Stoudt's farm. The winery and farm stand share a location, so jams and other fresh produce are available. It's all quite charming and fun.

Wines: $–$$

White Wines

Chardonnay—A dry, light white.

Niagara—Semisweet, with intense grape flavor.

Red Wines

Baco Noir—Off-dry, light red. Raspberry and cherry come through.

Fruit Wines

Blackberry—Inky-colored, medium-bodied, sweet wine.

Blueberry—Semisweet and medium bodied.

Nectarine—A light, sweet dessert wine. Smells like fresh-picked nectarines.

Sparkling Delicious Plum—Medium bodied, semisweet, and sparkling. Nice. ♥

Other Wines

Apple, Blue Ribbon Plum, Concord, Furmosia Plum, Methley Plum, Montmorency Cherry, Peach, Plum, Red Heart Plum, Red Raspberry, Shiro Plum, Strawberry

REVIEWS AND AWARDS

Blueberry—Silver medal, 2001 Pennsylvania Farm Show Wine Competition.

HOURS AND DIRECTIONS Open year-round Thurs.–Sun. 11 a.m.–6 p.m., or by appoint-ment. ■ From Harrisburg, take I-81 north to I-78 east to exit 8 (Shartlesville). Turn right off the exit and continue approximately 200 yards. The winery is on the right.

Big Creek Vineyards

RR 5 Box 5270, Kunkletown, PA 18058 • Phone 610-681-3959 •
www.geocities.com/NapaValley/7318/bindex.html • bigcreek@ptd.net

Set in the foothills of the Pocono Mountains, Big Creek opened in 1996 under the stewardship of Dominic Strohlein, a veterinary scientist and native of Brooklyn, N.Y. With half of his 20-plus farmland acres set up to produce grapes, Strohlein and his family produce over 5,000 gallons a year and are busily expanding production. The winery's tasting room hosts frequent parties and art openings.

Wines: $–$$

White Wines

Seyval—A light, dry white. Nice.

Red Wines

Cabernet Franc—Dry, medium-bodied red. Cherries and plums come through.

Cabernet Sauvignon—Medium-bodied red. Nice fruit. Dry finish.

Chambourcin—A dry, intense red with currant and plums.

Chambourcin Riserva—Deep, semisweet red.

Pinot Noir—Dry, light-bodied red.

Sangiovese/Dolcetto—Deep, intense, dry red. Currants and plums come through.

Sparkling and Fruit Wines

Dry Apple—Light, dry white.

Sparkling—Tart ruby sparkler. Nice.

Spiced Hard Cider—A nice, tart cider with a lingering aftertaste.

Sweet Apple—Light and semisweet. Nice.

Other Wines

Carme, Dulcinea, Vin di Pasqualia

HOURS AND DIRECTIONS Open year-round Mon.–Thurs. 1–5 p.m., Fri.–Sat. 1–7 p.m., Sun. 2–5 p.m. ■ From the south and west, take I-78 east to Rte. 22 east to Rte. 9 (Pa. Tpke. Ext.) to exit 34. Take Rte. 209 north for 10.4 miles to Rte. 534 west. Go 0.1 mile and turn left onto Beltzville Rd. Go 1.3 miles, turn left onto Keller Rd., and go 0.3 mile to a dirt lane on the left. Look for the winery's sign. ■ From the north and east, fol-low I-80 west to Rte. 209 south. Follow Rte. 209 south approximately 16 miles to Rte. 534 west, go 0.10 mile, and turn left onto Beltzville Rd. Then follow the local direc-tions above.

Blue Mountain Vineyards ✫ ✫

7627 Grape Vine Dr., New Tripoli, PA 18066 • Phone 610-298-3068 •
Fax 610-298-8616 • www.bluemountainwine.com • info@bluemountainwine.com

Blue Mountain is one of the great, secret treasures of East Coast winemaking. Like many vineyard owners, wine enthusiasts Joe and Vicki Greff thought they were just pursuing their hobby when they bought a 9-acre farm in the early 1980s and began growing grapes. By the late 1990s, however, their hobby had transformed into an 80-acre-plus business producing over 12,000 gallons of award-winning wine a year. Today,

Blue Mountain is one of the fastest-growing vineyards in Pennsylvania. Joe and Vicki are an odd combination, she dressing in business suits and he wearing jeans and sporting a ponytail, but they're both very nice, accessible, and pleasant people who make some wonderful wines.

Wines: $–$$$

White Wines

Chardonnay—A nice, dry, medium-bodied white.

Riesling—Off-dry white wine with tropical fruits and grapefruit finish.

Vidal Blanc—Crisp, light-bodied, dry white. Very nice.

Vignoles—Delicious, semisweet white with intense fruit and nice acidity. ♥ ♥

Red Wines

Blue Heron Meritage—64% Cabernet Sauvignon, 22% Cabernet Franc,
14% Merlot. Deep, inky red with flavors of black cherries and plums.
Very nice. Gives those Long Island folks a nice run for their money. ♥ ♥

Cabernet Franc—Aged in Hungarian and French oak. Medium bodied. cherry
and plum come through. ♥

Cabernet Sauvignon—Deep, red dry. Cherries and vanilla come through.

Merlot—Medium-bodied dry red. Cherries and plums come through. ♥

Pinot Noir—Bright, dry red. Intense fruity nose. Nice finish. ♥ ♥

Dessert Wines

Late Harvest Vignoles—Intense, golden, rich dessert wine. Honey and apricot
come through. Very nice. ♥

Other Wines

*Bri's Blush, Chambourcin, Mountain Breeze, Mountain Frost, Mountain Spice,
Nouveau Beaujolais*

REVIEWS AND AWARDS

Chardonnay 1999—Silver medal, 2001 Pennsylvania Farm Show Wine Competition.

Pinot Noir 1999—Gold medal, 2001 Pennsylvania Wine Association Competition.

Vignoles 1999—Gold medal, 2001 Pennsylvania Wine Association Competition.

HOURS AND DIRECTIONS Open daily 11 a.m.–6 p.m. year-round. ■ From Philadelphia and the south, take the Northeast Ext. of the Pa. Tpke. (I-476N) to the Lehigh Valley Interchange. Go west on Rte. 22 to Rte. 100 north. Take 100 north to Rte. 309 north. Take 309 north to Rte. 143. Turn left onto 143 to New Tripoli and go 0.3 mile to Madison St., at the Blue Ridge Hotel. Stay on Madison for 1 mile to Grape Vine Dr.; turn right and follow the signs.

Brookmere Farm Vineyards

RD 1 Box 53, Rte. 655, Belleville, PA 17004 • Phone 717-935-5380 •
www.brookmerewine.com • webmaster@villagehost.com

Don and Susan Chapman run 138-acre Brookmere Farm Vineyards from a gorgeous mid-1800s Victorian house in the Kishacoquilas Valley. Susan handles the finances, and Don and daughter Amy run the winery, together producing over 8,000 gallons annually. The house's Vintners Loft serves as a showcase room for local artists.

Wines: $

White Wines

Chablis—A semisweet French hybrid blend. Great nose. Nice fruit. Nicely balanced.

Chardonnay—A dry, medium-bodied white. Creamy and lemony.

Indian Summer—A semidry blend of Riesling and Chardonnay. Refreshing.

Riesling—Off-dry German-style wine. Floral nose and nice finish.

Red Wines

Autumn Red Dry—A dry red blend. Smooth.

Autumn Red Semi-Dry—Off-dry red blend. Nice acidity.

Cabernet Sauvignon—Herbaceous dry red. Deep color. Medium body. Nice finish.

Chambourcin Dry—Slightly herbaceous dry red, medium bodied.

Blush Wines

Rosé—A semisweet blush made from Chambourcin and Chelois. Very nice.

Tears of the Goose—A semisweet blush made from French hybrids. Tangy.

Other Wines

Autumn Gold, Chablis, Frog Hollow, Indian Summer, Niagara, Pinot Grigio, Shawnee Red, Valley Mist

REVIEWS AND AWARDS

Niagara—Gold medal, 2003 Pennsylvania Wine Association Competition.

HOURS AND DIRECTIONS Open year-round Mon.–Sat. 10 a.m.–5 p.m., Sun. 1–4 p.m. ■ From Harrisburg and points east, take Rte. 322 west to the Reedsville/Belleville exit. At the bottom of the ramp, turn left onto Rte. 655. The winery is 5 miles on the right. ■ From the western part of the state or Huntingdon, proceed on Rte. 22 toward Mt. Union. Take Rte. 655 north at the light. The winery is approximately 20 miles on the left, after you pass through Belleville. You will see a winery sign 5 miles from the winery.

Buckingham Valley Vineyards

1521 Rte. 413, P.O. Box 371, Buckingham, PA 18912 • Phone 215-794-7188 • www.pawine.com • comments@pawine.com

Buckingham Valley has its roots in the dorm-room dreams of its founders, Jerry Forest and Vladimir Guerrero, college classmates in the 1950s who in 1966 planted 5 acres and began making their winery dreams a reality. Since 1970 the vineyards have been owned by the Forest family, and those original 5 acres have grown to 40.

Buckingham Valley was one of the first wineries to take advantage of the state's Farm Winery Act of 1968, which allowed wineries to sell Pennsylvania-grown wine direct to the public. It's now one of the largest wineries in the state, producing over 30,000 gallons annually, with the capacity to more than double that. Despite its size, however, Buckingham Valley maintains a laid-back attitude.

Wines: $–$$

White Wines

Chardonnay—A dry white Chardonnay. Lemony and refreshing.

Riesling—Semisweet white wine with a floral nose and sweet, intense fruit. Nice.

Seyval Blanc—A medium-bodied white. Dry and refreshing.

Vidal Blanc—An off-dry, light white wine with a slight hint of sweetness and a citrus ending.

Red Wines

Chambourcin—Dry, oak-aged, full-bodied red.

Chancellor—Dry, medium-bodied red.

DeChaunac—Dry, full-bodied red.

Fruit Wines

Apple—A light, sweet white wine made from Pennsylvania apples.

Raspberry—A ruby-colored, sweet, and fruity raspberry wine. Nice tartness.

Other Wines

Cherry, Concordia, First Blush, Niagara, Nouveau, Nouvelle, Rosette, Sangria, Strawberry, White Red Sangria

HOURS AND DIRECTIONS Open year-round Tues.–Sat. 11 a.m.–6 p.m., Sun. noon–4 p.m.
- On Rte. 413, located 2 miles south of Buckingham, 2 miles south of Rte. 202.

Calvaresi Winery

107 Shartlesville Rd., Bernville, PA 19506 • Phone 610-488-7966 •
Fax 610-488-1176 • www.calvaresiwinery.com • calvaresiwinery@aol.com

Tom Calvaresi started his winery in the basement of a city row home in Reading back in 1981, producing 600 gallons of wine. Three years later, Tom and his wife Debbie upgraded to 6 acres in Bernville, and by 1988 they were producing 11,000 gallons annually, specializing in sweet wines but also making some dry whites and reds. To date, Calvaresi has won more than one hundred wine awards. Visitors can watch the processing of the wines as they taste.

Wines: $

White Wines

Cayuga—Crisp, semidry, Rhine-style white. Honeydew and apple come through.

Chardonnay—Smooth, dry white. Barrel fermented. Pear and apple come through. Citrusy.

Riesling—A tropical fruit nose and flavors with a nice, tart finish. Good! ♥

Seyval—Granny Smith apple comes through. Clean and crisp.

Red Wines

Baco Noir—Off-dry German-style red. Medium body. Cherry and plum come through.

DeChaunac—Dry, inky red. Aged in French and Slovenian oak. Smoky. Black cherry and plum flavors. Nice.

Blush Wines

Autumn Rosé—Semisweet Catawba blush wine. Floral nose. Nice fruit. Citrusy. ♥

Steuben Blush—Spicy blush. Strawberries and pineapple come through.

Other Wines

Cabernet Franc, Concord, Niagara, Pinot Gris, Raspberry, Strawberry, Sugar Plum

REVIEWS AND AWARDS

Autumn Rosé 1999—Silver medal, 2001 Pennsylvania Wine Association Competition.

Riesling—Silver medal, 2002 Finger Lakes International Wine Competition; silver medal, 2002 Pennsylvania Wine Association Competition.

HOURS AND DIRECTIONS Open year-round Thurs.–Fri. 1–6 p.m., Sat.–Sun. noon–5 p.m.
- Take Rte. 183 north from Reading. Turn right at the elementary school and go 0.5 mile to the winery, on the right.

Chaddsford Winery ✪ ✪

632 Baltimore Pike, Chaddsford, PA 19317 • Phone 610-388-6221 •
www.chaddsford.com • cfwine@chaddsford.com

Certainly one of the best and most polished wineries on the East Coast, Chaddsford opened in 1983 using fruit purchased from various regional vineyards. Today, proprietors Eric and Lee Miller have 30 acres of their own planted in northern Chester County, though they continue to buy other local grapes to satisfy their requirements—which are substantial, since Chaddsford has become the largest winery in the state and one of the most popular, with many visitors coming in from Philadelphia and New York. The Millers host many special events and festivals, including their summer outdoor concert series, and run a popular wine education program at the winery. Eric, who studied winemaking in Burgundy, is the son of Mark Miller, owner of Benmarl Vineyards & Winery in New York's Hudson Valley.

Wines: $–$$$

White Wines

Chardonnay—Light-styled Chardonnay with pear and apple flavors. Citrusy ending.

Philip Roth Vineyard Chardonnay—Classic Burgundian-style, full-bodied white. Creamy, oaky, and dry. ♥ ♥

Pinot Grigio—Smooth, light, and creamy. Peaches and apricots come through.

Red Wines

Cabernet Franc—Deep, dry red. Herbaceous. Nice.

Cabernet Sauvignon—A big, deep, classic red with flavors of currants and plums. Dry ending.

Chambourcin, Seven Valleys Vineyard—Zinfandel-like, deep red. Smoky and spicy.

Merican—A blend of Cabernet Sauvignon, Merlot, and Cabernet Franc. Nice dark fruits. Some chocolate. Nice, dry ending. ♥ ♥

Merlot—Lush, deep red. Plums and black cherry. Soft.

Pinot Noir—A nice, light-bodied red. Cherries come through. Very drinkable. ♥

Dessert Wines

Late Harvest Riesling—A nice, light, late-harvest wine. Sweet, with nice acidity. ♥ ♥

Other Wines

Cabernet/Chambourcin, Chardonnay Barrel Select, Niagara, Proprietors Reserve Red, Proprietors Reserve White, Sangri-La Sangria, Spiced Apple, Spring Wine, Sunset Blush

REVIEWS AND AWARDS

Merican 1999—Double gold medal, 2003 Tasters Guild International Wine Competition.

Chaddsford won seven silver medals, 2003 *Dallas Morning News* Wine Competition.

Merican 1999 (85 points) and Cabernet Sauvignon 2000 (84 points): Highly Recommended. —Beverage Testing Institute (March 2002)

"Wine from Pennsylvania? You bet. [The 2000 Chardonnay is] a tangy chard with crisp, clean, grapefruity flavors." —*Bon Appétit* (June 2002)

"Pennsylvania can hardly boast the tradition and breadth of New York's wine regions, but Chaddsford's [2000 Philip Roth Vineyard Chardonnay] is a shining example of the high quality that can be produced in the state." —*Wine Enthusiast* (July 2002)

"Eric and Lee Miller have turned Chaddsford into one of the rising stars of the Atlantic Northeast." —*The New Sotheby's Wine Encyclopedia*

Philip Roth Vineyard Chardonnay 2000: "Top Pick" —*American Way* magazine (July 2002)

HOURS AND DIRECTIONS Open daily noon–6 p.m. year-round. Tastings Sat. 1–5 p.m., $10 fee. ■ Located 5 miles south of Rte. 202. ■ From Philadelphia, take I-95 south to

Rte. 322; go west on 322 for 7 miles, then turn left onto U.S. 1 (Baltimore Pike). ■ From Delaware, take Rte. 52 north to U.S. 1, turn right onto it, and go about 2 miles.

Cherry Valley Vineyards

RR 5 Box 5100, Saylorsburg, PA 18353 • Phone 717-992-2255 •
Fax 570-992-5083 • www.cherryvalleyvineyards.com • cvwine@epix.com

Dominic Sorrenti grew up in the wine business in Wisconsin and dreamed of one day becoming proprietor of his own winery—a dream he began to see fulfilled in 1980, when he and his wife Mary purchased their Monroe County farm. Three years later, they planted their first grapes, and in 1986 the Cherry Valley Vineyards were open for business. Today, they produce about 20,000 gallons annually, with Mary tending to business matters and the Sorrenti children taking a hand in everything from pressing the grapes to running the tasting room.

Wines: $–$$

White Wines
Chardonnay—Well-balanced, medium-bodied, dry white.
Reserve Seyval Blanc—Dry, light white wine. Nice.
Riesling—Semidry, with a nice floral nose. Sweet on the midpalate. Tart end.

Red Wines
Baco Noir—Light-bodied, dry red. Cherries and plums. Smoky.
DeChaunac—Dry, full bodied, and hearty.
Leon Millot—Dry, medium-bodied red. Buttery vanilla comes through.
Marechal Foch—Dry, medium-bodied red.

Dessert Wines
Blush Spumante—This is something different. Very fun. Enjoy! ♥
Raspberry—A deep, tart red with big fruit. Nice.

Other Wines
Apple, Burgundy, Cayuga White, Chablis, Cherry, Cherry Valley, Cherry Valley Blush, Concord, Kittatinny Red, Lucia's Blush, Niagara, Peach, Pink, Pink Catawba, Plum, Seyval Blanc, Strawberry

REVIEWS AND AWARDS
Blackberry—Gold medal, 2002 Pennsylvania Farm Show Wine Competition.
Raspberry—Bronze medal, 2002 Pennsylvania Farm Show Wine Competition.
Marechal Foch—Bronze medal, 2002 Pennsylvania Farm Show Wine Competition.
Seyval Blanc—Bronze medal, 2002 Pennsylvania Farm Show Wine Competition.

HOURS AND DIRECTIONS Open daily 11 a.m.–5 p.m. Tours Sat.–Sun. 1–5 p.m. ■ Take Rte. 33 to the Saylorsburg exit. Take Rte. 115 south to Lower Cherry Valley Rd. The winery is located on Lower Cherry Valley Rd. in Saylorsburg.

Christian W. Klay Winery

412 Fayette Springs Rd., Chalk Hill, PA 15421 • Phone 412-439-3424 •
www.cwklaywinery.com • smklay@hotmail.com

Located in the Laurel Highlands, the Christian W. Klay Winery was just a gleam in the eye of Pittsburgh surgeon John Klay until he came upon the farm at Chalk Hill. After purchasing the property he engaged in nearly a decade of research and grape-growing experiments, finally producing his first commercial wines in 1997.

The bank barn, originally built in the 1880s and with a fine view of the 12-acre-plus vineyard, was rebuilt in recent years and now houses a tasting room and gift shop, as well as an area for special events, private parties, and weddings.

Wines: $$

White Wines

Blanc de Lafayette—Light-bodied, dry white. Citrusy end. Nice.

Fort Necessity—Brilliant, buttery, dry Chardonnay. Tart. Nice. ♥

Nemacolin Castle—Semidry white blend. Nose full of violets. Nice.

Washington Tavern White—Off-dry, light white blend.

Red Wines

Jumonville Glen Road—Medium-bodied, dry red. Black cherry comes through. Nice.

Washington Tavern Red—Fruity, light-bodied, semidry red. Not too sweet. ♥

Blush Wines

Chestnut Ridge Sunset—Semisweet blush. Cherry comes through. Nice tartness.

Other Wines

Searight's Tollhouse, White Swan Tavern

REVIEWS AND AWARDS

Fort Necessity—Silver medal, 1999 Pennsylvania Wine Association Competition.

Washington Tavern Red—Consensus gold medal, 1997 Indiana State Fair Indy International Wine Competition; gold medal, 1998 Indiana State Fair Indy International Wine Competition.

HOURS AND DIRECTIONS Open Sun.–Thurs. noon–6 p.m., Fri.–Sat. 11 a.m.–7 p.m., year-round. ■ From Rte. 40 via Uniontown, Pa., follow Rte. 40 east to Chalk Hill. Turn right onto Fayette Springs Rd. at the Christmas Shop, opposite the post office. The winery is 300 yards farther on the left. ■ From Rte. 40 via Keysers Ridge, Md., follow Rte. 40 west to Chalk Hill and then the local directions above.

Clover Hill Vineyards & Winery

9850 Newtown Rd., Breinigsville, PA 18031 • Phone 888-CLOVER-HILL or 610-395-2468 • Fax 610-366-1246 • www.cloverhillwinery.com • info@cloverhillwinery.com

Founded by John and Pat Skrip in 1975, Clover Hill opened its barn doors to the public 10 years later, in September 1985. In the intervening years, the vineyard has grown from 6 acres to over 30 (including a second vineyard in nearby Robesonia) and has increased its production from just over 1,000 gallons annually to nearly 50,000. In early 2003 the Skrips expanded even further, opening new tasting and hospitality rooms.

Wines: $–$$$

White Wines

Cayuga White—A semisweet, light white.

Chardonnay—Pear and green apple come through. Rich, velvety mouth feel. Nice. ♥

Oak Vidal Blanc—Butter and toasted wood come through. Nice, crisp, dry white.

Pinot Grigio—Delicate, dry white. Figs and citrus fruits come through.

Riesling—Peach and floral notes come through. Semisweet. Well balanced.

Vidal Blanc—Crisp, off-dry white. Grapefruit and pineapple come through.

Red Wines

Cabernet Franc—Deep, dry red. Black pepper comes through. Aged in Hungarian oak.

Cabernet Sauvignon—Plums and cherries come through. Some caramel. Nice.

Chambourcin—Intense, dry red. Rich. Ripe fruit. Nice.

Blush Wines

DeChaunac Rosé—A semisweet rosé with darker fruits. Different. Nice.

Dessert Wines

Blackberry Sparkler—Sweet, blackberry sparkling wine. Different.

Raspberry—Intense red. Nice. ♥

Spiced Apple—A sweet apple wine spiced with cinnamon and a hint of clove. Nice. ♥

Vignoles—Citrusy dessert wine. Honey and peaches come through. ♥

Other Wines

Alden, Brut, Catawba, Clover Hill Cuvée, Clover Hill Red, Clover Hill Rosé, Concord, DeChaunac, Holiday, Niagara, Turtle Rock Red

REVIEWS AND AWARDS

Chambourcin 1999—Gold medal, 2003 Pennsylvania Farm Show Wine Competition.

Chardonnay—Silver medal, 2000 Pennsylvania Wine Association Competition and 2001 Pennsylvania Farm Show Wine Competition; bronze medal, 2002 Los Angeles County Fair Wine Competition, 2002 Pennsylvania Wine Association Competition, 2002 Pennsylvania Farm Show Wine Competition, 2001 Los Angeles County Fair Wine Competition.

Concord—Gold medal, 2003 Pennsylvania Farm Show Wine Competition.

Raspberry—Silver medal, 2001 Pennsylvania Farm Show Wine Competition; bronze medal, 2001 Pennsylvania Wine Association Competition, 2002 Pennsylvania Farm Show Wine Competition.

Spiced Apple—Gold medal, 2003 Pennsylvania Farm Show Wine Competition; gold medal and Best Fruit Wine, 2000 Pennsylvania Farm Show Wine Competition; silver medal, 2001 Pennsylvania Wine Association Competition; bronze medal and Best Fruit Wine, 2001 Pennsylvania Farm Show Wine Competition.

Vignoles—Gold medal, 2002 San Francisco International Wine Competition; bronze medal, 2002 Pennsylvania Wine Association Competition, 2001 and 2002 Pennsylvania Farm Show Wine Competition, and 2001 San Francisco International Wine Competition.

HOURS AND DIRECTIONS Open year-round Mon.–Sat. 11 a.m.–5 p.m., Sun. noon–5 p.m. ■ From I-78, take exit 49A (Trexlertown). Follow Rte. 100 south to the second traffic light. Turn right onto Schantz Rd. and travel 2.8 miles to the intersection of Newtown Rd. Turn left onto Newtown. The winery is the first driveway on the right.

Conneaut Cellars Winery

U.S. 6 & Rte. 322, P.O. Box 5075, Conneaut Lake, PA 16316 •
Phone 814-382-3999 or 814-382-6151 • www.ccw-wine.com

Conneaut Cellars was founded in 1982 by Dr. Alan Wolf, who studied the winemaking business until he was able to find a perfect location—which he eventually did, building his winery on the south end of the largest natural lake in the state. When Dr. Wolf died in 1995, his son Joal, who had helped his dad make wine as a young boy in the 1960s, took over the business. Today, Conneaut Cellars makes about 10,000 cases a year using fruit grown in Erie County.

Wines: $–$$

White Wines

Gewürztraminer—An off-dry white. Apricots and grapefruit come through.

Princess Snowater—A semisweet white. Nice fruit.

Pub White—A semisweet white made from Cayuga and Pinot Gris grapes. Nice.

Riesling—A semidry white. Apples and peaches come through.

Red Wines

Cabernet Franc—A dry, hearty red. Boysenberry and cranberry come through. ♥

Cabernet Sauvignon—A dry, deep red. Chocolate, black currant, and raspberries come through.

Pinot Noir—A dry, medium-bodied Burgundian-style wine.

Blush Wines

Pymatuning Rosé—A semisweet blush wine. Named for Pymatuning Lake. Tangy.

Other Wines

Allegheny Gold, Chardonnay, Colonel Crawford, Finn Ditch Red, Hazel Park Red, Huidekoper, Ice House Misty Bubbly Pink, Ice House Misty Bubbly White, Midway Blush, Pinot Grigio, Reflections of Lake Erie, Sadsbury Red, Seyval, Snug Harbor, Summit Red, Vidal Blanc, Wolf Island

REVIEWS AND AWARDS

Cabernet Franc 1998—Gold medal, 2001 Pennsylvania Wine Association Competition; bronze medal, 2001 American Wine Society Commercial Wine Competition, 2001 Pennsylvania Farm Show Wine Competition.

Riesling—Bronze medal, 2001 American Wine Society Commercial Wine Competition.

HOURS AND DIRECTIONS Open daily 10 a.m.–6 p.m. year-round. ■ Conneaut Cellars is located approximately 80 miles north of Pittsburgh, 80 miles east of Cleveland, and 35 miles south of Erie, less than 10 minutes from I-79. ■ Take exit 147B from I-79. Proceed 6 miles west on Rte. 322 and U.S. 6 (which at this point are one and the same) to Conneaut Lake. The winery is on the left before you reach the town.

Country Creek Vineyard & Winery

133 Cressman Rd., Teleford, PA 18969 • Phone 215-723-6516

The 10-acre Country Creek Winery opened in 1978 and since the early 1990s has been run by Doug and Joy Klein and Doug's sister, Donna Killian. The winery's century-old bank barn has been spruced up during their tenure and is available for parties, weddings, and special events.

Wines: $

White Wines

Seyval Blanc—Dry, woody, and light.

Vidal—A light, off-dry white. Clean, crisp. Nice.

Red Wines

Baco Noir—A light- to medium-bodied, dry red. Smoky.

Chambourcin—A medium-bodied, dry red. Cherries and plums come through.

DeChaunac—A medium-bodied, dry red. Cherry comes through.

Fruit Wines

Country Apple—A mouthful of fresh, sweet apples. Nice.

Strawberry—A tart red dessert wine. Nice. Not cloying.

Other Wines

Cayuga, Concord, Niagara

HOURS AND DIRECTIONS Open Sat.–Sun. noon–5 p.m. year-round. ■ From Philadelphia, take I-476 north to Rte. 63 west past Harleysville and turn right onto Longmill Rd., then left onto Moyer Rd. Over the bridge at Perkiomen Creek, turn right on Cressman. The winery is on the right.

Evergreen Valley Vineyards

RR 1 Box 173D, Evergreen Rd., Luthersburg, PA 15848 •
Phone and Fax 814-583-7575 • www.evwinery.com • webmaster@evwinery.com

Nestled in a sheltered valley in the cool central highlands of Pennsylvania and producing about 2,000 gallons annually, Evergreen Valley Vineyards was the dream of proprietor Mark Gearhart, who purchased the vineyard in 1990. What makes Evergreen Valley unique is that it uses solar and wind-powered generators as its main power sources.

Wines: $

White Wines

Catawba—Light, floral, semisweet white. Tart ending.

Cayuga White—Off-dry, light white. Pear and green apple come through.

Seyval Blanc—A light, dry white. Clean. Fresh. Nice.

Vidal Blanc—Off-dry, light white. Tropical fruits come through. Clean. Crisp.

Red Wines

Baco Noir—Deep, ruby red. Nice tannic fruitiness. Plums. Smoky. Nice oak.

Leon Millot—Off-dry red. Blackberry comes through.

Marechal Foch—Medium-bodied Burgundian red. Black cherry, currant come through.

Dessert Wines

Vignoles—Rich, late-harvest dessert wine with a botrytised nectar character. Nice.

Other Wines

Aurore, Concord, Delaware, Steuben

HOURS AND DIRECTIONS Open Wed.–Sun. 10 a.m.–6 p.m. except holidays. ■ From I-80 exit 97 (old exit 16), follow Rte. 219 south through DuBois to the intersection of Rtes. 219 and 410, in Lutbersburg. From the intersection, follow 410 west exactly 2 miles, then turn sharply left at the sign on the hilltop. Proceed straight ahead 0.7 mile. The winery is on the right, just past the vineyards. ■ From I-80 exit 111 (old exit 18), follow Rte. 153 south to Rte. 322 west, arriving at the intersection of Rtes. 219 and 410. Then follow the local directions above.

Flickerwood Wine Cellars

RD 1, Flickerwood Ln., Kane, PA 16735 • Phone 814-837-7566 •
www.flickerwood.com • flicker@penn.com

Located in a peaceful and scenic country setting, Flickerwood Wine Cellars is a family-built and -operated winery, with all members of Ron and Sue Zampogna's immediate family participating in business operations. There's a gift shop and a wine tasting area, and the winery also offers personalized labels, boxes, and other items of interest. Music and entertainment events are scheduled regularly on the premises (see website for the schedule).

Wines: $

White Wines

Chardonnay Gold—A dry white with apple-citrus flavors. Clean and crisp.

Gewürztraminer—Off-dry white. Fruity, spicy flavors come through.

Seyval Blanc—Light, dry white wine. Nice.

Red Wines

Chambourcin—A medium-bodied, dry red. Herbaceous undertones. Nice balance.

DeChaunac—A light, dry red with a touch of oak.

Blush Wines

Flickerwood Sunset—Sweet, peach-colored blend. Nice tartness.

Ruby Z—A sweet pink blush from a blend of native American grapes.

Dessert Wines

Flickerberry Dew—A sweet blend of blackberry and red raspberry. Tastier than you'd think.

Moonglow—A sweet, light, crisp blend of Chardonnay and peach wines. Very nice.

Other Wines

Chantilly White, Elegance, Grandview Niagara, Pink Catawba, Pinot Grigio, Sleepy Hollow Red, Sweet Angel Red

HOURS AND DIRECTIONS Open Mon.–Sat. 11 a.m.–7 p.m., Sun. noon–6 p.m., year-round. ■ From Rte. 6 east, take Rte. 321 south past Kane High School, then take the first street on the left (School St.), which runs directly onto Flickerwood Ln. Go 0.5 mile to the winery, which is located on the right, past the Kane Area Little League ball field. ■ From Rte. 6 west, follow winery signs along Rte. 6. Turn left onto Greendale Rd., then right onto Old Smethport Rd.; continue to Flickerwood, bearing left to the winery.

Fox Ridge Vineyard & Winery

3528 E. Market St., York, PA 17402 • Phone 717-755-3384

Veterinarian Harold Neibert began growing grapes in the early 1980s as a hobby, then went pro in 1994 when he opened Fox Ridge, growing his own grapes on a little over an acre of farmland. His winery is one of the smallest in the state and has to be one of the only winemaking operations anywhere to be operated out of the basement of an animal hospital. Neibert's wife Shirley sells Harold's wine at the Spielgrund Wine Shop, located just down the street from the animal hospital.

Wines: $–$$

White Wines

Cayuga White—A light, semisweet white.

Niagara—A light, semisweet white. Nice.

Seyval Blanc—A nice, light, dry white.

Red Wines

Cabernet Sauvignon—A dry, deep red with cherries and plums.

Merlot—A medium-bodied red.

Other Wines

Apricot, Bavarian White, Cabernet Sauvignon, Chambourcin, Crimson Hills, Delaware, Dutchess, Fireside, Fox Ridge Red, Maiden's Blush, Merlot, Peach, Pear, Ridge Runner Red, Seyval Blanc, Spice, Springetts Red, Strawberry, Villard, White Nectar, White Sapphire, Winemakers Delight, Yorkshire White

HOURS AND DIRECTIONS Open Tues.–Fri. 10 a.m.–6 p.m., Sat. 10 a.m.–4 p.m., Sun. 1–4 p.m., year-round. ■ From York, go east on Rte. 462 (Market St.). The vineyard is across from the Volkswagen dealership on 462.

Franklin Hill Vineyards

7833 Franklin Hill Rd., Bangor, PA 18013 • Phone 888-887-2839 or 610-588-8708 • www.franklinhillvineyards.com • franklinhill@enter.net

Franklin Hill owner Elaine Austen planted her first French-American hybrid and vinifera wine grapes in 1976. Since then, her vineyard overlooking the Delaware River Valley has grown to 13 acres and has some of the nicest tasting rooms in the state. It's a very popular spot for special events.

In addition to the winery, Franklin Hill also operates three wine shops in Pennsylvania: The Wine Shop (Tannersville), The Grape Spot (Easton), and The Grape Arbor (Bethlehem). All sell Franklin Hill wines and wine-related products, and are popular gathering spots for wine lovers.

Wines: $–$$

White Wines

Cayuga White—An off-dry white. Easily their best wine and one of the best Cayugas you'll find. ♥

Chardonnay—A dry, oak-aged white. Apple comes through. Buttery.

Seyval Blanc—Dry, crisp, clean, and refreshing.

Vidal Blanc—A semidry white made in the Germanic style. Nice.

Vignoles—A fruity, semisweet white.

Red Wines

Cabernet Franc—A dry, oak-aged red.

Chambourcin—A nice pasta wine. Dry. Oak aged.

Pinot Noir—A medium-bodied, dry red. Berries. Nice tannins.

Sparkling Wines

Berrylicious—A semisweet sparkling white with natural raspberry flavoring.

Just Peachy—A semisweet sparkling wine with natural peach flavoring.

Strawberrylicious—A semisweet sparkling wine with natural strawberry flavoring.

Wedding Reserve—A sparkling Cayuga white brut. Interesting.

Other Wines

Country Kiss, Country Red, Country Rosé, Country White, DeChaunac, Niagara, Simply Red, White Jade, White Sangria

HOURS AND DIRECTIONS Open Mon.–Sat. 11 a.m.–4 p.m. ■ From Rte. 22, take Rte. 33 north to Rte. 191. Get off at the Stockertown exit. Follow 191 north approximately 5 miles, past Pinocchio's. Make the next right, onto Franklin Hill Rd. Stay on for 2.4 miles, then turn left onto Winery Ln. Go 1 mile to the winery.

French Creek Ridge Vineyards

200 Grove Rd., Elverson, PA 19520 • Phone 610-286-7754 • Fax 610-286-7772 • www.frenchcreekridge.com • info@frenchcreekridge.com

Sited on 6 acres of land in southeastern Pennsylvania, French Creek Ridge was founded in 1991 by Janet and Fred Maki, who reshaped the property's old farmhouse, barn, and log cabin into an elegant and charming winery. The Makis are firm in their belief that sugar is a scourge in table wines, so they take great pains to prepare their wines without, producing over 2,500 gallons annually and racking up some impressive plaudits—among them a gold medal for their 1997 Blanc de Blanc brut from the Viniales Internationales Wine Competition in Paris, where it beat out twenty-seven French champagnes. This is a very good winery, and we're looking for lots of good things from them in the future.

Wines: $$–$$$

White Wines

Barrel Fermented Chardonnay—Apples and pears come through. Vanilla. Creamy. Dry.
Viognier—An off-dry, golden white wine. Very nice. ♥

Red Wines

Cabernet Sauvignon—A deep, dry red. Plums and currants. Nice tannins.
Merlot—A deep, dry red.

Sparkling Wines

Blanc de Blanc—A nice sparkling wine. Fine bubbles. Creamy.
Brut—A bone-dry white sparkler. Pears come through. Yeasty. Creamy. Toasty. ♥
French Creek Rouge—A classic bubbly rosé. Dry and complex.

Dessert Wines

Vidal Ice Wine—A golden, sweet, rich dessert wine. Nice fruit and honey. Tart. ♥

Other Wines

Blanc de Noirs, Pinot Gris

REVIEWS AND AWARDS

Blanc de Blanc 1997—Gold medal, 2001 Viniales Internationales Wine Competition, Paris.
Merlot 1998—Bronze medal, 2001 Pennsylvania Farm Show Wine Competition.

HOURS AND DIRECTIONS Open Thurs.–Sun. noon–5 p.m. year-round. ■ From the west, take exit 22 off the Pa. Tpke. onto Rte. 23 east. After 5 miles, turn right onto Grove Rd. The winery is 0.8 mile on left. ■ From the east, take exit 23 off the Pa. Tpke. onto Rte. 100 north. Go approximately 9 miles to Rte. 23 west. After 5.5 miles, turn left onto Grove Rd. to the winery.

Galen Glen Vineyards

RD 1 Box 82-1, Winter Mountain Dr., Andreas, PA 18211 • Phone 717-386-3682 • www.galenglen.com • galenglen@eudoramail.com

Galen and Sarah Troxell opened Galen Glen in May 1999 on Galen's 32-acre farm, which had been in his family for well over a century. Galen runs the business from their hilltop house, which overlooks the vineyard, while Sarah does the actual winemaking in a potato cellar at the bottom of the hill, producing about 1,500 gallons annually.

Wines: $

White Wines

Vidal Blanc—A slightly sweet white. Crisp, clean finish.

Red Wines

Chambourcin—A medium-bodied, dry red. Cherries come through.
Winter Mountain Red—Deep, purple Concord. Sweet.

Blush Wines

Vin Gris of Chambourcin—Off-dry rosé made from Chambourcin. Nice.

Other Wines

Corkscrew Willow White, Holiday, Noah's Blush, Winter Mountain White

REVIEWS AND AWARDS

Chambourcin 1998—Bronze medal, 2001 Pennsylvania Wine Association Competition.

HOURS AND DIRECTIONS Open year-round Sat. noon–5 p.m. or by appointment. ■ From Allentown, take I-476 north to Rte. 443 going west. Turn left onto Troxell Valley Rd., then left again onto Winter Mountain Dr. The winery is on the right.

Glades Pike Winery

2706 Glades Pike, Somerset, PA 15501 • Phone 814-445-3753 • Fax 814-445-1856 • www.somersetcounty.com/winery

Steve and Karen Addleman are the majority owners of this boutique winery, located in (and named for) a pastoral setting on historic Glades Pike, 6 miles west of Somerset. They officially opened the winery in April 1995, putting winemaking operations in the hands of winemaker Mike McVicker, who buys all his grapes from other farms. The winery now produces over 9,000 gallons annually and plans to increase this production significantly. A tasting room and gift shop are housed in the winery's renovated nineteenth-century barn.

Wines: $–$$

White Wines

Chardonnay—Pears and apples come through. Buttery. Smooth and creamy.

Seyval Blanc—Granny Smith apples. Tart and dry. Clean and crisp.

Vidal Blanc—An off-dry white. Clean, crisp, and refreshing.

Red Wines

DeChaunac—Medium-bodied. Cherries and plums. Nice tannins.

Leon Millot—Deep red color. Berries and plums. Nice tannins.

Fruit Wines

Apple—Sweet white dessert wine.

Raspberry—Tart and rich.

Other Wines

Baco Noir, Bicentennial Blush, Cayuga, Cherry, Concord, Diamond, Foch, Glades Pike Red, Niagara, Sparkling Apple Cider, Spiced Apple, Steuben

REVIEWS AND AWARDS

Chardonnay—Silver medal, 2001 Pennsylvania Wine Association Competition.

Leon Millot 1994—Bronze medal, American Wine Society Commercial Wine Competition.

Seyval Blanc 1994—Silver medal, American Wine Society Commercial Wine Competition.

"[The Seyval Blanc has] good balance with nice body and a touch of oak and citrus. . . . [The Vidal Blanc is] fruity and crisp, with hints of citrus and pineapple." —Linda King, *The Working Wine Guide*

HOURS AND DIRECTIONS Open daily noon–6 p.m. year-round. ■ From Pittsburgh, take the Pa. Tpke. east to exit 9 (Donegal) and travel east on Rte. 31 for 13 miles. The winery is on the left.

Heritage Wine Cellars

12162 E. Main Rd., North East, PA 16428 • Phone 800-747-0083 or
814-725-8015 • Fax 814-725-8654 • www.heritagewine.com • bostwick@erie.net

Heritage Wine Cellars' farmland has been in owner Bob Bostwick's family since 1833, and today he and his wife Bev have a little over 100 acres set aside as a vineyard, though their production of 40,000 annual gallons means they must also buy a significant portion of their fruit from other farms. Aside from its eighteenth-century barn, the winery also boasts The Gathering, a restaurant that's open seasonally.

Wines: $–$$

White Wines

Chardonnay—Dry and crisp. Apples come through.

Seyval Blanc—Clean, crisp, and dry. Green apples come through. Nice.

Red Wines

Cabernet Franc—Medium-bodied, dry red wine. Cherries and plums.

Cabernet Sauvignon—Medium-bodied, dry red. Berries and cherries.

Dessert Wines

Bubbling Niagara—A semisweet, bubbling, *spumante*-like wine. Nice. ♥

Peach—A light, sweet dessert wine. Nice.

Other Wines

Almondiera, Apple, Bubbling Catawba, Bubbling Niagara, Cold Goose, Concord, Country Pink, Country White, Delaware, Dutch Elderberry, Gladwin, Niagara, Peach, Pink Catawba, Plum Crazy, Sangria, Solebury White, Strawberry, Sweet Fredonia, Very Berry Blackberry, White Riesling

REVIEWS AND AWARDS

Bubbling Niagara—Bronze medal, 2000 Pennsylvania Farm Show Wine Competition.

Concord—Bronze medal, 2000 Pennsylvania Farm Show Wine Competition.

Peach—Bronze medal, 2000 Pennsylvania Farm Show Wine Competition.

HOURS AND DIRECTIONS Open Mon.–Sat. 9 a.m.–6 p.m., Sun. 10 a.m.–6 p.m., year-round. ■ Take I-90 to exit 12 north. Turn left onto Rte. 20 (Main Rd.). The winery is on the right, across from McDonald's.

Hunters Valley Winery

RD 2 Box 326D, Liverpool, PA 17045 • Phone 717-444-7211 •
www.huntersvallyewines.com • dk.huntersvalley@att.net

Bill and Darlene Kvaternik established Hunters Valley in 1986 with the idea of growing grapes to use in their home winemaking and to supply other home winemakers. With just under 3 acres, they had no expectations of competing with Pennsylvania's larger commercial wineries. When they purchased a farmhouse just half a mile down the road from their vineyard, though, they realized they could indeed sell their own wines, and since then the small winery has become a popular stop for wine aficionados.

Wines: $–$$

White Wines

Chardonnay—Dry white. Apples and pears. Rich.

Riesling—Fragrant, off-dry white. Sweet midpalate. Nice.

Seyval Blanc—Crisp, off-dry white with a fruit aroma

Vidal Blanc—Off-dry white with a hint of spice.

Red Wines

Berry Mountain Red—Dry blend of oak-aged Chancellor and Baco Noir.

Cabernet Franc—Dry, deep red. Berries come through. Nice oak.

Heart of the Valley—Off-dry red blend. Very popular.

Blush Wines

Susquehanna Sunrise—Semisweet blush wine. Refreshing.

Dessert Wines

Red Raspberry—Rich red dessert wine.

Other Wines

Concord, Country Spice, Niagara, Susquehanna Crossing.

REVIEWS AND AWARDS

Cabernet Franc 1999—Bronze medal, 2001 Pennsylvania Farm Show Wine Competition, 2001 Pennsylvania Wine Association Competition.

HOURS AND DIRECTIONS Open year-round Wed., Thurs., and Sat. 11 a.m.–5 p.m., Fri. 11 a.m.–7 p.m., Sun. 1–5 p.m.; also Mon.–Tues. 11 a.m.–5 p.m. between Thanksgiving and Christmas. ■ The winery is located on the west side of the Susquehanna River 2 miles south of Liverpool, 26 miles north of Harrisburg, on Rtes. 11 and 15 at the intersection of Rte. 34.

Lancaster County Winery, Ltd.

799 Rawlinsville Rd., Willow Street, PA 17584 • Phone 717-464-3555

Lancaster County Winery is located on one of the most historic farms in Pennsylvania, dating back as far as the early eighteenth century. Its barn was built in 1815 and renovated about 100 years later, and an adjacent stone farmhouse was built in 1825, all of which gives the winery a traditional feel. The winery is also one of the oldest in the state. Todd Dickel purchased the operation in 1989, and today he and his family host many wine tastings, special events, and private parties.

Wines: $–$$

White Wines

Seyval Blanc—Dry white. Apples come though. Nice acidity.

Vidal Blanc—Dry, light, clean, and crisp. Nice.

Red Wines

Dry Red Special Reserve—Deep, dry red. Berries and plums. Nice.

Fruit Wines

Colonial Spice Apple—Sweet apple wine with cinnamon and clove. Nice.

Other Wines

Colonial Red, Colonial Sweet Pink, Colonial White, Rayon d'Or

HOURS AND DIRECTIONS Open Mon.–Sat. 10 a.m.–4 p.m., Sun. 1–4 p.m., year-round. ■ From Lancaster, take Rte. 222 south, which turns into 272 south. Turn right onto Baumgardner Rd. and go for a mile until you reach Rawlinsville Rd. Turn left; the winery is 2 miles on the left.

Lapic Winery, Ltd.

902 Tulip Dr., New Brighton, PA 15066 • Phone 724-846-2031

Paul and Josephine Lapic founded their namesake winery back in 1977 with the idea of starting small and seeing where it went from there. Where it went was to the next generation, with brothers Mike and Paul taking over the operation and cranking production up from 1,800 annual gallons to 10,000. Today, the Lapics purchase grapes and juice from outside growers to meet their production demands and put most of their emphasis on dry wines. The winery hosts many special events and weddings.

Wines: $–$$

White Wines

Riesling—Slightly off-dry white with floral nose and nice acidity.

Seyval Blanc—A nice, dry white.

Vidal Blanc—An off-dry white. Nice fruit. Clean and crisp.

Red Wines

Baco Noir—A medium- to light-bodied red. Cherries and berries. Nice tannins.

Chambourcin—A deep, dry red. Plums and berries.

Other Wines

Blush de Blanc, Cayuga, Classic Red, Concord, Diamond, Pink Catawba, Red Harvest, Steuben, Sweet Heart, Valley Red, Valley Rosé, Valley White, White Harvest

HOURS AND DIRECTIONS Open Jan.–Feb. Mon.–Sat. 10 a.m.–6:30 p.m., Sun. 1–5 p.m.; Mar.–Dec. Mon.–Fri. 10 a.m.–6 p.m., Sun. 11 a.m.–5 p.m. ■ Take I-79 north from Pittsburgh and take the exit for Rte. 68 (Zelienople). Travel west on 68 about 9 miles. Look for winery signs and turn right onto Tulip Dr. The winery is on the left.

Laurel Mountain Vineyard ✪

RD 1 Box 238, Falls Creek, PA 15840 • Phone and Fax 814-371-7022 • laurlmtn@penn.com

John and Barbara Nordberg started planting the seeds (so to speak) for Laurel Mountain in 1986, with 20 acres of farmland in northwestern Pennsylvania. Nine years later, they opened the winery that had been their dream for so long. Since then, the Nordbergs have put up a new building on the premises to house the wine tanks as well as John's ever growing museum of antique machinery. Barbara manages both the tasting room and the wine gift shop, which are located in the winery.

Wines: $–$$

White Wines

Chardonnay—Apple and melon come through. Dry and smooth.

Mountain Mist—A semisweet white blend. Nice.

Red Wines

Bella Rosa—Blend of Chancellor, DeChaunac, and Chambourcin made in a Chianti-like style. Medium tannins and nicely oaked. Tangy ending. ♥

Marechal Foch—A soft, dry red. Nice dark fruit. Nice tannins.

Blush Wines

Rattlesnake Red—A red blush with a nice bite. ♥

Dessert Wines

Ground Hog Grog—Spiced, sweet apple wine. Very fun.

Other Wines

Apple, Bucktail White, Cabernet Sauvignon, Cherry, Concord, Delaware, Laurel Blush, Niagara, Peach, Punxy Wawnic, Riesling, Ruby Red, Seyval, Treasure Lake Red, Treasure Lake White, Vidal, Vignoles

HOURS AND DIRECTIONS Open Feb.–Dec. Wed.–Sun. 10 a.m.–6 p.m. ■ Take I-80 north of DuBois to exit 16 and head north on Rte. 219 toward Brockway. Turn left at the first intersection onto Old Grade Rd. The winery is ahead on the right.

Manatawny Creek Winery

227 Levengood Rd., Douglassville, PA 19518 • Phone 610-689-9804 • Fax 610-689-9838 • www.manatawnycreekwinery.com • manatawny@aol.com

The Levengood family farm sprawls across nearly 90 acres of Lehigh Valley land, but there's something to be said for restraint: among all that yardage, only 10 acres are planted in grapes for the winery—6 acres of native and hybrid varieties including Vidal Blanc, Seyval Blanc, Foch, and Cayuga White, and an additional 4 acres that concentrate on more traditional European varieties, such as Chardonnay and Cabernet Sauvignon. With a warm and spacious tasting room, Manatawny Creek is a popular destination for wine buffs along the East Coast.

Wines: $–$$

White Wines

Chardonnay—Dry, complex white. Vanilla, butterscotch, and apples come through. ♥
Pinot Grigio—Crisp and dry light white wine. Smooth finish.
Vidal Blanc—Off-dry, German-style white. Honeysuckle, orange, and pineapple. ♥

Red Wines

Cabernet Franc—Deep, dry red. Tobacco and black currant. Nice tannins.
Dolcetto—A deep, dry red. Nice, heavy tannins. Good. ♥

Fruit and Honey Wines

Cherry—A mouthful of sour cherries. Slightly sweet and tart.
Honey—A lovely mead. Golden color. Sweet but not cloying. Nice.

Other Wines

Autumn Blush, Blackberry, Blanc de Blancs, Blueberry, Cayuga, Concord, Harvest Red, Niagara, Red Raspberry, Spiced Apple

REVIEWS AND AWARDS

Cabernet Franc NV—Gold medal, 2003 Pennsylvania Wine Association Competition.
Chardonnay 1999—Gold medal, best vinifera, 2001 Pennsylvania Farm Show Wine Competition.
Vidal Blanc 1999—Gold medal, 2001 Pennsylvania Wine Association Competition.

HOURS AND DIRECTIONS Open Fri. 10 a.m.–6 p.m., Sat. 10 a.m.–6 p.m., Sun. noon–6 p.m. ■ Located 4 miles off Rte. 422, about 30 minutes west of King of Prussia and 20 miles east of Reading ■ From Rte. 422, exit at Rte. 662 north in Douglassville and continue 3 miles. Turn right onto Blacksmith Rd., then take the first right onto Levengood Rd. The winery is 0.8 mile on the right.

Mazza Vineyards

11815 E. Lake Rd., North East, PA 16428 • Phone 800-796-9463 or 814-725-8695 • www.mazzawines.com • rmazza12@juno.com

Joseph Mazza left his vineyards in Calabria, Italy, to come to the United States in 1954, and in 1973 his sons Robert and Frank continued family tradition in the New World by opening Mazza Vineyards. Today, Robert and his wife Kathie run the show, producing about 25,000 gallons of wine each year from 9 acres of grapes. The vineyard's appearance is as Mediterranean as its name, but thanks to winemaker Helmut Kranich, a graduate of the Geisenheim enology school, its wines are actually more Germanic in style and substance. Mazza's Rieslings are among its most popular offerings.

Wines: $–$$

White Wines

Chardonnay—Dry, medium-bodied, oak-aged white. Nice.

Riesling—Floral nose and sweet midpalate. Delicate, with a tart ending. Nice. ♥

Seyval Blanc—Dry, crisp white wine. Sour apple comes through. Tart and clean.

Vidal Blanc—A semisweet, fruity white.

White Riesling—A sweeter Riesling. But still with nice acidity.

Red Wines

Cabernet Franc—Spicy, dry, dark red.

Cabernet Sauvignon—A dry, oak-aged red with good body.

Chambourcin—Dry, oak-aged, medium-bodied red.

Sherry and Fruit Wines

Cream Sherry—A nutty, creamy, smooth cream sherry. A nice surprise. ♥

Raspberry—A tart red desert wine. Smells like fresh raspberries. ♥

Other Wines

Cayuga, Champagne, Cherry, Commemorative Red, Concord, Draft Apple Cider, Holiday, Ice Wine of Vidal Blanc, Late Harvest Vidal, Pear, Pink Catawba, Reflections of Lake Erie, Riesling Vineyard Country Chablis, Spiced Apple, Strawberry, Vineyard Country Blush, Vineyard Country Gold, Vineyard Country Red, Vineyard Country Rosé

REVIEWS AND AWARDS

Cream Sherry—Gold medal, 2001 Pennsylvania Wine Association Competition.

Ice Wine of Vidal Blanc 2001—Gold medal, 2003 Pennsylvania Wine Association Competition; Governor's Cup/Best Dessert Wine/gold medal, 2003 Pennsylvania Farm Show Wine Competition.

Raspberry—Gold medal, Best Fruit Wine, 2001 Pennsylvania Farm Show Wine Competition.

Riesling 1999—Gold medal, 2001 Pennsylvania Wine Association Competition.

White Riesling 2001—Gold medal, 2003 Pennsylvania Wine Association Competition.

HOURS AND DIRECTIONS Open July–Aug. Mon.–Sat. 9 a.m.–8 p.m., Sun. 11 a.m.–4:30 p.m.; Sept.–June Mon.–Sat. 9 a.m.–5:30 p.m., Sun. 11 a.m.–4:30 p.m. ■ Located in the Lake Erie wine region of northeastern Pennsylvania. ■ From I-90, take Rte. 89 north for 3.7, then turn right onto Rte. 5, heading east, and drive 2.4 miles to Mazza Vineyards.

Mount Hope Estate & Winery

83 Mansion House Rd., Manheim, PA 17545 • Phone 717-665-7021 • royalspk@parenaissancefaire.com

The Mount Hope Estate has had more than its share of visitors over the years, but location might have something to do with that: the historic Grubb Mansion is located right on its property, and the nearby Mount Hope Memorial Day Renaissance Faire draws some 150,000 people to the area each year. The wines are the perfect memento to take away from a visit, and that's exactly what a lot of people do, to the tune of 30,000 gallons annually.

Wines: $

White Wines

Chardonnay—Dry, crisp Chardonnay, aged in oak.

Classic Vidal Blanc—Proprietor's special reserve. Aged in oak. Nice.

Riesling—Semisweet. Tropical fruits and a tart ending. Nice.

Seyval Blanc—Dry, crisp white French hybrid. Tart.

Vidal Blanc—Off-dry, fruity white French hybrid. Nice nose. Refreshing.

Vignoles—Luscious, semisweet white.

Red Wines

Cabernet Sauvignon—Dry, oak-aged, classic red. Cherries and berries. Nice tannins.

Other Wines

Burgundy, Catawba, Champagne, Cherry, Concord, Intercourse Blush, Intercourse Gold, Intercourse White, Mount Hope Red, Niagara, Nouveau, Peach, Pennsylvania Dutch Spiced Apple, Pizazz Blanc, Pizazz Cassis, Pizazz Rouge, Rosé, Sauterne, Strawberry

HOURS AND DIRECTIONS Open Mon.–Sat. 10 a.m.–5 p.m., Sun. 11 a.m.–5 p.m., year-round. ■ Take exit 20 from the Pa. Tpke. and go south on Rte. 72 for 0.5 mile. The winery is on the left.

Mount Nittany Vineyard & Winery

RD 1 Box 135, Linden Hall, PA 16828 • Phone 814-466-6373 •
Fax 814-466-3066 • www.mtnittanywinery.com •
sales@mtnittanywinery.com

In July 1990, 6 years after their first grape plantings, experienced winemakers Joe and Betty Carroll opened Mount Nittany Vineyard & Winery. Since then, the couple has grown the winery to the point where it can now store over 10,000 gallons at a time. Since only 5 acres of their 65-acre property are planted in grapes, the Carrolls must purchase grapes and juice from other regions to meet their production demands. And there is a demand: Joe, a retired professor at nearby Penn State, named the winery for that school's mascot, the Nittany Lion, which all but assures a loyal following.

Wines: $–$$

White Wines

Chardonnay—Dry and full bodied. Fermented and aged in oak.

Pinot Gris—A dry, full-bodied white. Stainless steel lovers unite! Crisp and clean. ♥

Viognier—Dry white wine. Peaches and apricots come through.

Red Wines

Cabernet Franc—A dry, dark red wine, aged in oak.

Cabernet Sauvignon—Deep, dry red. Smooth, with nice tannins.

Chambourcin—A smooth, medium-bodied, dry red. Nice fruit.

Merlot—A medium-bodied, dry red. Nice fruit.

Dessert Wines

Autumn Nectar—An ice wine. Sweet, rich, and luscious. Nice acidity. Very nice. ♥

Montmorency Cherry—Semisweet red dessert wine.

Other Wines

Bergwein, Mountain Mist, Mountain Rosé, Mt. Nittany Champagne, Nittany Mountain Blush, Nittany Mountain Red, Nittany Mountain White, Proprietor's Select Red, Proprietor's Select White, Riesling, Tailgate Red

REVIEWS AND AWARDS

Autumn Nectar 1999—Gold medal, 2000 Pennsylvania Wine Association Competition; silver medal, 2001 Pennsylvania Farm Show Wine Competition; silver medal, 2001 Pennsylvania Wine Association Competition.

Cabernet Franc 2001—Silver medal, 2002 Pennsylvania Wine Association Competition.

Pinot Gris 2000—Silver medal, 2002 Pennsylvania Farm Show Wine Competition; bronze medal, 2000 Pennsylvania Wine Association Competition.

Pinot Gris 2001—Gold medal, 2003 Pennsylvania Farm Show Wine Competition.

Vidal Blanc 2002—Gold medal, 2003 Pennsylvania Wine Association Competition.

HOURS AND DIRECTIONS Open Tues.–Fri. 1:30–5 p.m., Sat. 10 a.m.–5 p.m., Sun. 2:30–4 p.m., year-round. ■ The winery is located 3 miles east of Boalsburg, off Rte. 45. ■ From Rte. 322, turn east onto Rte. 45, pass the entrance to the Elk's Country Club on your right, and immediately turn left turn onto Linden Hall Rd. Proceed around the bend and down the hill. Turn right at the pond onto Rock Hill Rd. and go through the Village of Linden Hall. Turn left just before the church onto Brush Valley Rd. Turn right onto Houser Rd. toward the mountain, enter the woods, and continue up the lane to the winery.

Naylor Wine Cellars

4069 Vineyard Rd., Stewartstown, PA 17363 • Phone 800-292-3370 or 717-993-2431 • Fax 717-993-9460 • www.naylorwine.com • wine@naylorwine.com

Dick Naylor opened Naylor Wine Cellars in 1979 on this 10-acre farm in southeastern Pennsylvania. Back then he was just a hobbyist, producing some 1,600 gallons of wine, but today Naylor has over 30 acres planted and produces 20,000 gallons annually. Naylor has gotten his entire family into the business and hosts a number of concerts and festivals at the vineyard. The winery is known for its beautiful and innovative labels.

Wines: $–$$

White Wines

Chardonnay—Dry, full bodied, barrel fermented. Fig and citrus. Buttery.

Johannisberg Riesling—Semidry, German-style wine. Crisp and fruity.

Pinot Gris—Dry, light white wine. Crisp and clean.

Riesling—Crisp and fruity. Nice ending.

Rosé O' DeChaunac—Semisweet pink blush made from DeChaunac.

Red Wines

First Capital—Off-dry, oak-aged red. (Named for the fact that York, Pa., was the first U.S. capital.)

Seductivo—A deep, Italian-style Chambourcin. Cherries and plums. Nice tannins. ♥

Dessert Wines

Intimacy—A nice, golden Vignoles ice wine.

Rapture—A nicely balanced Delaware ice wine. ♥

Other Wines

Ambrosia's Dulce, Bubbles Galore Sparkling Niagara, Cabernet Franc, Catawba,
Chambourcin, Concord, Ekem, Fragola, Holiday Spiced, Kirse, Niagara, Old Fashioned
Apple, Peaches Plus, Pinot Noir, Rhinelander, Riesling, Vidal Perfection, York White Rosé

REVIEWS AND AWARDS

Intimacy 2001—Gold medal, 2003 Pennsylvania Wine Association Competition.

Peaches Plus—Silver medal, 2001 Pennsylvania Wine Association Competition.

Rapture 1999—Gold medal, 2001 Pennsylvania Wine Association Competition.

Seductivo 1999—Gold medal, 2001 Pennsylvania Farm Show Wine Competition.

HOURS AND DIRECTIONS Open Sun. noon–5 p.m., Mon.–Sat. 11 a.m.–6 p.m., year-round. ■ From Harrisburg, travel south on I-83 to Pa. exit 4 (Shrewsbury). Turn left onto Rte. 851 to Stewartstown, then left again onto Rte. 24 north. Drive 2 miles north of Stewartstown to Vineyard Rd., on the left. ■ From Baltimore, travel north on I-83 to Pa. exit 4 (Shrewsbury). Turn right onto Rte. 851 to Stewartstown; then follow the local directions above.

New Hope Winery

6123 Lower York Rd., New Hope, PA 18938 • Phone 800-592-9463 •
www.newhopewinery.com • info@newhopewinery.com

The New Hope Winery is a lovely vineyard that caters to the quirky, one might say. An antique bicycle museum is located in the barn loft, allowing visitors to step back to simpler times as they sip wine and take in the charming collection of boneshakers, ordinaries, and safety bicycles. Tastings are popular events here, allowing visitors to kick back in a country setting and enjoy some of the winery's twenty-five varieties. The lovely gift shop features gourmet foods, glassware, and countless wine accessories.

Wines: $–$$

White Wines

Chablis—Dry, medium-bodied wine.

Chardonnay—Dry, herbaceous white. Nice acidity and oak.

Riesling—Semisweet German-style wine. Tangerine and grapefruit. Nice.

Solebury—Light, semidry wine. Blend of Vidal Blanc and Villard Blanc. Nice.

Red Wines

Cabernet Sauvignon—Dry, oak-aged red. Deep color and nice tannins.

Chambourcin Reserve—Dry, oak aged. Plums. Soft tannins.

Chancellor—medium-bodied, dry red. Cherries and plums. Nice bite.

Dessert and Fruit Wines

Almondiera—A sweet, white, almond-flavored dessert wine with hints of vanilla.

Cherry—A sweet mouthful of tart cherries.

Dutch Apple Spice—A flavorful apple cider, tinged with cinnamon.

Other Wines

Almondiera, Blueberry, Blush, Catawba, Concord, Dutch Apple, Holiday Spice, Niagara,
Peach, Pink Red Sangria, Raspberry, Riesling, Rosé, Strawberry, White Sangria

HOURS AND DIRECTIONS Sun.–Tues. 10 a.m.–5 p.m., Thurs.–Sat. 10 a.m.–6 p.m., year-round. Call ahead to confirm hours. ■ From the New Jersey Shore, follow I-195 west. Take the exit for Rte. 29/Lambertville (stay away from Trenton exits). Follow Rte. 29 approximately 10 miles into downtown Lambertville. Turn left at the light onto Bridge

St. Cross the bridge into New Hope. At the third light (road ends), turn left. This is U.S. 202 south. The New Hope Winery is on the right, approximately 2 miles.

Nissley Vineyards

140 Vintage Dr., Bainbridge, PA 17502 • Phone 800-522-2387 (Pa. only) or 717-426-3514 • Fax 717-426-1391 • www.nissleywine.com • winery@nissleywine.com

Open since 1978, Nissley Vineyards is one of the oldest vineyards in the state, located on 300 acres in the Lancaster Valley viticulture area of western Lancaster County. Fifty acres of farmland are dedicated to fourteen varieties of grapes, which ultimately produce twenty-five wines. Built by J. Richard Nissley, the attractive, stone-arched winery is set near an eighteenth-century mill and a winding creek. Guided sampling tours and self-guided tours are available, and the summer lawn-concert series is a popular draw for both tourists and local wine lovers.

Wines: $–$$

White Wines

Seyval Blanc—A dry, lightly oaked white with a flinty, lingering flavor. Nice. ♥
Vidal Blanc—A dry, well-balanced white. Smooth. Nice fruit. Nice finish.

Red Wines

Cabernet Franc—A dry red. Big fruit up front. Nice tannins.
Chambourcin—A dry, medium-bodied red with touches of oak and a tart finish.
Valley Red—An off-dry red blend. Nice fruit. Spicy. Tart. Very popular. ♥

Blush Wines

Rosé Select—A crisp, semidry rosé made from Chambourcin. Tart.

Dessert Wines

Black Raspberry—A sweet, rich, red dessert wine. Great nose. Tart finish.

Other Wines

Apple, Bainbridge Red, Bainbridge Rosé, Bainbridge White, Belle of Donegal, Belle of the Vine, Black Raspberry, Candlelight, Classic White, Concord, Country Cherry, Fantasy, Montmorency Cherry, Naughty Marietta, Niagara, Petite Blanc, Rhapsody in Blue, Spicy Red, Topaz Select, Vignoles, Whisper White

REVIEWS AND AWARDS

Chambourcin 1999—Silver medal, 2001 Pennsylvania Farm Show Wine Competition.
Petite Rosé 2002—Gold medal, 2003 Pennsylvania Wine Association Competition.
Seyval Blanc 2000—Gold medal, 2001 Pennsylvania Wine Association Competition.

HOURS AND DIRECTIONS Open Mon.–Sat. 10 a.m.–5 p.m., Sun. 1–4 p.m., year-round. ■ From Harrisburg, take I-83 south to exit 2E (Rte. 283 east). Take Rte. 441 south to approximately 8 miles from the center of Middletown. Go past Rte. 241. Travel another mile to the next intersection. Turn left onto Stackstown Rd., heading toward Maytown. At the Y, bear right. Continue 0.5 mile to Vintage Dr.

Oak Spring Winery

RD 1 Box 612, Rte. 220N, Altoona, PA 16602 • Phone 814-946-3799 • www.oakspringwinery.com • oakspring@keyconn.net

Tucked into the splendor of central Pennsylvania's mountains, John and Sylvia Schraff's Oak Spring Winery was named for a tree and marshy spring on the spot where they'd intended to open a tiny winery back in the 1980s. That tree remains their symbol to this day, even though fate had larger plans waiting right next door in the form of a 57-acre farm perfect for a large winery operation. The Schraffs bought the property and planted 3 acres of grapes, and by fall 1987 were licensed to do business. Today, John's son Scott runs the winery, which produces 6,500 cases annually, with 10% of the fruit coming from Oak Spring's own plantings and the other 90% from other vineyards in Erie County. Since opening, the winery has won more than 150 well-deserved medals.

Wines: $–$$

White Wines
Candlelite—A semidry wine with a subtle blush. Slightly sweet with green apple.
Chardonnay—Dry white wine. Pear and tropical fruit. Smooth and creamy.

Red Wines
Chambourcin—A dry, full-bodied red. Cherry and black cherry. Nice oak.
Concord—Semisweet red/purple wine. One of the better Concord wines.
Harvest Red—Semisweet Baco Noir. Cherry comes through. Tangy. Smoky.

Blush Wines
Steuben—Made from the black Steuben grape. Floral nose. Semisweet blush. ♥
White Cin'—Semisweet blush made from Chambourcin grapes. A very popular wine.

Fruit Wines
Berry-Berry—A blend of strawberry and raspberry fruit wine. A nice dessert wine.
Peach—Sweet, clean, and fruity. ♥

Sparkling Wines
Champagne—A semidry sparkling wine. Smooth, with fine bubbles.

Other Wines
Cayuga White, Chardonnay, Classic Cherry, Gewürztraminer, Niagara, Pink Catawba, Rosé, Spiced Apple, Vidal Blanc Reserve

REVIEWS AND AWARDS
Concord 2000—Silver medal, 2001 Pennsylvania Wine Association Competition.
Peach—Bronze medal, 2001 Pennsylvania Wine Association Competition.
Steuben—Gold medal, 2001 American Wine Society Commercial Wine Competition; silver medal, 2001 Pennsylvania Farm Show Wine Competition.

HOURS AND DIRECTIONS Open daily 11 a.m.–6 p.m. year-round. ■ The winery is located 4 miles north of Altoona. Take I-99 to the Pinecroft exit and follow the signs 1 mile to the winery.

Oregon Hill Winery

840 Oregon Hill Rd., Morris, PA 16938 • Phone 717-353-2711

The experts said it couldn't be done. They said a good crop of grapes just couldn't be grown in the mountains of central Pennsylvania. But Alfred Swedrowski was a true believer, and so purchased this 100-acre farm determined to prove them wrong. As it turned out, the experts were right. Swedrowski gave it everything he had, but the area's cold winters were finally too much for the vineyard. Alfred's son Eric kept the winery going by buying grapes from local growers with more sophisticated technology, and today Oregon Hill produces some 6,000 gallons annually—which is some kind of triumph, if not the one Swedrowski, Sr., had intended.

Wines: $

White Wines

Chardonnay—A dry white. Pears and apples come through. Some citrus.

Niagara—Light, with a sweet, grapy flavor. Nice.

Seyval Blanc—Light and dry. Green apple comes through.

Red Wines

Cabernet Sauvignon—A deep, dry red. Cherries come through.

Rosen Cavalier—A semisweet red blend.

Other Wines

Baco Noir, Chardonnay Reserve, Mountain Laurel Blush, Mountain Red, Mountain White, Pinot Noir, Riesling, Steuben, Sussbeeren Tropfchen

REVIEWS AND AWARDS

Niagara—Bronze medal, 2001 Pennsylvania Wine Association Competition.

Steuben—Silver medal, 2001 Pennsylvania Farm Show Wine Competition.

HOURS AND DIRECTIONS Open daily 10 a.m.–5:30 p.m. year-round. ▪ From Williamsport, take U.S. 220 west to Rte. 287 going north. Pass through the town of English Center and turn left onto Oregon Hill Rd. The winery is on the right, about 0.5 mile.

Peace Valley Winery

300 Old Limekiln Rd., Chalfont, PA 18914 • Phone 215-249-9058 • peacevalwinery@enter.net

Way back in 1968, Susan Gross planted 3 acres with grapes and began experimenting, eventually working her way up to more than 22 acres and, with partner Robert Kolmus, trying out more than two hundred varieties. The pair opened Peace Valley Winery in 1984, and today produce about two dozen wines. All in all, it's a nice little Pennsylvania surprise.

Wines: $–$$

White Wines

Chardonnay Reserve—Dry white wine fermented in French oak.

Summer Solstice—A very sweet, light summer wine. One of their most popular.

Red Wines

Excalibur—A full-bodied, dry red aged in oak. Nice finish.

New Britain Red—A spicy, only slightly off-dry red. Nice tannins and fruit. Tangy. ♥

Sparkling Wines

Spumante—A semisweet sparkling wine made from muscat. Nice.

Other Wines

Blushing Apple, Buck's Blush, Chalfont Rouge, Fredonia, Nectarine, New Britain Rosé, New Britain White, Niagara, Nouveau, Seyval, Spiced Apple, Spicewine, Spring Fling, Winter Solstice

HOURS AND DIRECTIONS Open year-round Wed.–Sun. noon–6 p.m.; open daily in Dec., 10 a.m.–6 p.m. ▪ From the town of Chalfont (where Rte. 152, Limekiln Pike, joins U.S. 202), go north 1.6 miles on Rte. 152 and turn right onto New Galena Rd. There is a sign for Peace Valley Winery.

Penn Shore Vineyards

10225 E. Lake Rd., North East, PA 16428 • Phone 814-725-8688 •
www.pennshore.com

Penn Shore Vineyards is one of the oldest and largest wineries in the state of Pennsylvania, holding one of the first two limited winery licenses issued by the state in September 1969. By the spring of 1970, they were open for business. The winery has the capacity to store over 175,000 gallons of wine, but owner Robert Mazza (of Mazza Vineyards) keeps production at about 15,000 gallons annually. By purchasing most of his fruit from other growers, Mazza is able to focus more energy on the winemaking at this traditional vineyard.

Wines: $–$$

White Wines

Chardonnay—Medium-bodied white, finished dry with oak.

Reflections of Lake Erie—Riesling white blend. Semisweet, fruity. ♥ ♥

Seyval Blanc—Crisp, dry white with a hint of oak.

Vidal Blanc—Semidry German-style white wine.

Vignoles—Semidry white with a complex and well-balanced taste.

Red Wines

Baco Noir—Dry, red French hybrid with an oak-aged character.

Specialty Wines

Holiday Spice—Red grape wine with a spice flavor added.

Kir—Semisweet white grape with natural black currant.

Other Wines

Bianca, Blush, Burgundy, Chablis, Concord, Crystal Lake White, Diamond, Dry Red, Lambruscano, Niagara, Pink Catawba

REVIEWS AND AWARDS

Diamond—"Best American," gold medal, 2003 Pennsylvania Farm Show Wine Competition; gold medal, 2001 Pennsylvania Farm Show Wine Competition.

Reflections of Lake Erie—Bronze medal, 2001 Pennsylvania Farm Show Wine Competition.

Vidal Blanc—Bronze medal, 2001 Pennsylvania Farm Show Wine Competition.

HOURS AND DIRECTIONS Open July–Aug. Mon.–Sat. 9 a.m.–8 p.m., Sun. 11 a.m.–5 p.m.; Sept.–June Mon.–Sat. 9 a.m.–5:30 p.m., Sun. 11 a.m.–5 p.m. ■ Take I-90 to exit 11 and go north on Rte. 89. Turn left on Rte. 5 after the town of North East. Penn Shore Vineyards is on the left, 1 mile.

Philadelphia Wine Company

3061 Miller St., Philadelphia, PA 19134 • Phone 215-425-4144

For wine lovers who don't want to venture far out to Pennsylvania's vineyards to enjoy homemade wines, the Philadelphia Wine Company may be just the answer. Here, in a building once used as an icehouse, Tom Kelly has been making wines named for sections of Philly since 1992. Obviously, there are no vineyards off Miller St., but Kelly knows a thing or two about making good wines, and he has a loyal customer base. A visit here for a tasting is one of the city's best-kept secrets. Or at least is was till now.

Wines: $$

White Wines

South Philadelphia—A Pinot Grigio and Vidal Blanc blend. Light and dry. Nice.

Wissahickon Valley White—A light, dry white blend.

Red Wines

Boathouse Red—A dry, deep red blend.

Other Wines

*Appleation Port Richmond, Fishtown Red, Icehouse Crimson, Icehouse White,
    Port Richmond Red, Port Richmond White, Wissahickon Valley Red*

REVIEWS AND AWARDS

Boathouse Red—Bronze medal, 2001 Pennsylvania Wine Association Competition.

South Philadelphia 1999—Silver medal, 2001 Pennsylvania Wine Association
    Competition.

HOURS AND DIRECTIONS Open by appointment only. ■ Take I-95 north to Allegheny Ave. and turn left at the ramp. Turn left at the first light onto Richmond St., then right onto Allegheny Ave. Turn left onto Belgrade, then right onto Clearfield St. Turn left on Miller and look for the sign that says "Kensington Hygeia Ice. Co., Richmond Station," which is the winery.

Pinnacle Ridge Winery

407 Old Rte. 22, Kutztown, PA 19530 • Phone 610-756-4481 •
www.pinridge.com • pinridge@aol.com

Pinnacle Ridge was established when Brad and Dawn Knapp planted 3 acres near their 1851 bank barn, which—two years and some substantial renovation later—became their winery's home base, with a tasting room, another area for the stainless steel wine tanks, and a nearby potato cellar that's been converted into a facility for making sparkling wine. In addition to what it grows on its own acreage, Pinnacle Ridge also uses grapes grown at a nearby vineyard.

All in all, this is one of the better wineries on the East Coast, and has won enough gold medals to start an account at a Federal Reserve. Despite this, it's somewhat over-looked outside Pennsylvania—but only by those who don't know better. If you're going through Pennsylvania, it's a must visit.

Wines: $–$$

White Wines

Dry Vidal Blanc—Crisp and clean, dry white wine. Fresh fruit aromas.

Vidal Blanc—Award-winning off-dry wine. Peach and pear come through. ♥

Red Wines

Chambourcin—Deep ruby color and flavors of fruit, earth, and oak. Dry finish.
    Very nice. ♥

Pinot Noir—Award-winning dry, light red. Rich, fruity, and spicy.

Veritas—61% Cabernet Franc, 20% Cabernet Sauvignon, and 19% Merlot,
    aged 15 months in American oak barrels. Luxurious and fine. ♥

Sparkling Wines

Blanc de Blanc—A semisweet sparkling wine made from 100% Cayuga. Nice!

Brut Reserve—Fresh bread on the nose. Creamy and fine bubbles. Nice. ♥

Dessert Wines

Sweet Seduction—Port-like deep red dessert wine made from Chambourcin. Extremely nice. ♥

Other Wines

Cayuga White, Chambourcin Rosé, Cuvée Chardonnay

REVIEWS AND AWARDS

Blanc de Blanc—Gold medal, 2003 Pennsylvania Wine Association Competition; gold medal, 2000 Pennsylvania Wine Association Competition.

Brut Reserve—Gold medal, 2001 Pennsylvania Farm Show Wine Competition.

Chambourcin 1998—Gold medal, 2001 Pennsylvania Farm Show Wine Competition.

Chambourcin 1999—Gold medal, 2001 Pennsylvania Wine Association Competition.

Chambourcin 2001—Governor's Cup/Best Hybrid/gold medal, 2001 Pennsylvania Farm Show Wine Competition.

Cuvée Chardonnay 1999—Gold medal, 2001 Pennsylvania Wine Association Competition.

Veritas 1999—Gold medal, 2001 Pennsylvania Wine Association Competition.

HOURS AND DIRECTIONS Open year-round Sat. 10 a.m.–5 p.m., Sun. noon–5 p.m. Weekdays by appointment only. ▪ From Reading, take U.S. 222 north toward Kutztown. Take the Rte. 737 exit (Krumsville) and go north 6 miles to the blinking red light in Krumsville. Turn right (east) onto Old Rte. 22. The winery is located 0.8 mile ahead on the left.

Preate Winery

149 Milwaukee Ave., Old Forge, PA 18518 • Phone 800-765-5346 or 717-457-1555 • Pre8winery@aol.com

Located at the rear of 859 Main St., Preate is the Scranton area's first commercial winery, and features complimentary sampling, a small gift shop, and tours. Wines include Blush, Cabernet Sauvignon, Cayuga, Chardonnay, Concord, Marechal Foch, Merlot, Niagara, Nouveau, Port, Seyval Blanc, Strawberry, and Vidal Blanc.

Wines: $

HOURS AND DIRECTIONS Open Mon.–Sat. noon–5 p.m., Sun. noon–3 p.m., year-round. ▪ Take I-476 to exit 38, then drive south on Keyser Ave. Turn south on Milwaukee Ave. and go about 1 mile to the winery.

Presque Isle Wine Cellars

9440 Buffalo Rd., North East, PA 16428 • Phone 800-488-7492 or 814-725-1314 • Fax 814-725-2092 • www.piwine.com • prwc@erie.net

Presque Isle opened in 1964 as a supplier of juice and equipment for amateur and professional winemakers, a part of the business that owners Doug and Marlene Moorhead and Marc and Lori Boettcher continue today. From these roots, they've gone on to become one of the more famous Lake Erie wineries, producing award-winning wines and offering a beautiful day-trip experience.

Wines: $–$$

White Wines

Chardonnay—Soft, dry white, aged in oak.

Creekside White—Semisweet white blend.

Dry Riesling—Dry white. Crisp and clean. Floral nose.

Falling Waters—Bone-dry, carbonated Riesling. Light and fruity. Citrusy ending. ♥ ♥

Seyval—Dry white wine. Nice fruit. Lightly oaked.

Red Wines

Cabernet Sauvignon—Full-bodied, dry red. Cherries and plums. Nice. ♥

Merlot—Dry, smooth, and soft. Nice finish.

Syrah—Medium-bodied red. Good fruit. Plums and cherries. Nicely oaked. ♥

Other Wines

Cabernet Franc, Chambourcin, Chardonnay, Creekside Blush, Creekside Red, Creekside White, Lemberger, Muscat Ottonel, Rosé, Vignoles

REVIEWS AND AWARDS

Cabernet Sauvignon 1999—Gold medal, 2001 Pennsylvania Wine Association Competition; bronze medal, 2001 Pennsylvania Farm Show Wine Competition.

Falling Waters 1999—Gold medal, 2001 Pennsylvania Wine Association Competition; bronze medal, 2001 Pennsylvania Farm Show Wine Competition.

Merlot 1999—Gold medal, 2001 Pennsylvania Wine Association Competition.

HOURS AND DIRECTIONS Open Nov.–Aug. Mon.–Sat. 8 a.m.–5 p.m.; Sept.–Oct. Mon.–Sat. 8 a.m.–6:30 p.m., Sun. 8 a.m.–3 p.m. ■ Presque Isle Wine Cellars is located 3.5 miles west of North East and 3.5 miles east of Harborcreek (12 miles east of Erie), on U.S. 20. ■ From I-90 eastbound, take exit 10 (Rte. 531), go north 3 miles to U.S. 20, and go east 3.8 miles. ■ From I-90 westbound, take exit 12 and drive west on U.S. 20 for 7 miles. ■ From I-79 northbound, turn east onto I-90, take exit 10, and follow the eastbound directions above.

Quaker Ridge Winery

211 S. Wade Ave., Washington, PA 15301 • Phone and Fax 412-222-2914 • www.quakerridgewinery.com • info@quakerridgewinery.com

Quaker Ridge's vineyards in East Finley (south of Washington, Pa.) were originally planted in 1975 by farmer John England, a Quaker who's now buried in the Quaker cemetery on the nearby ridge road, from which the winery takes its name. The winery operation itself was begun in 1988 by John Jacobs, who sold to Bill and Barbara Verscharen two years later. The original 300–400 gallon home winemaking operation has since expanded into a several-thousand-gallon annual production facility, with further expansion plans in the works.

Wines: $

White Wines

Chablis—A dry white.

Red Wines

Burgundy—A hearty, medium-bodied red.

Chianti—An Italian-style, dry red.

Blush Wines

Blush—A semisweet pink wine. Fruity and tangy. Nice. ♥

Other Wines

Almond, Blush, Concord, Country Plum, Niagara, Raspberry, Sauterne, Spicy Apple, Vintage Red

HOURS AND DIRECTIONS Open year-round Thurs.–Fri. 11 a.m.–6 p.m., Sat.–Sun. 11 a.m.–5 p.m. Other hours by appointment. ■ From I-79, take the Laboratory exit, go west on Rte. 40 to S. Wade Ave., and turn left. The winery is on the right.

Rushland Ridge Vineyards

2665 Rushland Rd., Rushland, PA 18956 • Phone 215-598-0251 • tastingroom@rushlandridge.net

Ed Ullman opened Rushland Ridge in 1991, planting native American and French hybrid grapes on 3 acres of a 22-acre farm in Bucks County. He and wife Lisa still run the place today, and they built a new tasting room in 1999 after a fire destroyed the original.

Wines: $

White Wines

Cayuga—German-style, semisweet white wine.

Niagara—Sweet white table wine.

Seyval—Fruity but dry white table wine.

Vidal—Off dry white table wine.

Villard—Dry white table wine.

Red Wines

Chancellor—Full-bodied, spicy red.

DeChaunac—Full-bodied red table wine.

Foch—Sweet, light red table wine.

Millot—Light red table wine.

Blush Wines

Baco—Full-bodied, fruity rosé.

Rosette—A full-bodied blush.

Fruit Wines

Apple—Semisweet, light white apple wine.

HOURS AND DIRECTIONS Open Sat. noon–6 p.m., Sun. noon–4 p.m. Closed Jan. and Feb. ■ From Philadelphia, take Rte. 263 north, turn right onto Rte. 332/Almshouse Rd., then left onto Rushland Rd. The winery is on the right.

Sand Castle Winery

755 River Rd., Erwinna, PA 18920 • Phone 800-722-9463 • Fax 610-294-9174 • www.sandcastlewinery.com • winesand@epix.net

Set on the banks of the Delaware River in historic Bucks County, Sand Castle Winery was founded in 1988 by Czechoslovakia-born brothers Joseph and Paul Maxian, who have planted their 72 farmland acres exclusively with special vinifera seedlings, cloned from European stock and chosen by master winemakers. The winery produces about 40,000 gallons annually.

Wines: $–$$$

White Wines

Chardonnay Classic—Dry white with almond and butter coming through. Nice oak.

Chardonnay Private Reserve—Full-bodied, dry white. Crisp, clean, and refreshing. ♥

Johannisberg Riesling—Off-dry white. Nice tropical fruits.

Johannisberg Riesling Dry—Dry white wine with a floral nose. Crisp and clean. ♥

Johannisberg Riesling Late Harvest—An excellent balance of sweetness and acidity. ♥

Other Wines

Cayuga, Chelois, DeChaunac, Foch, Niagara, Ravat, Rosé, Rosette, Seyval, Vidal, Villard

REVIEWS AND AWARDS

"European wines from along the Delaware."

—Deborah Scoblionkov, *Philadelphia Inquirer*

"Sand Castle's well earned success plus national recognition intimates that the local wine scene has come a long way." —Ted Dziemianowicz, *Philadelphia Magazine*

HOURS AND DIRECTIONS Open Mon.–Fri. 9 a.m.–6 p.m., Sat. 10 a.m.–6 p.m., Sun. 11 a.m.–6 p.m. ■ From New York City, take the N.J. Tpke. south to exit 14 (I-78 west). Take I-78 to exit 15 (Clinton/Pittstown). At the end of ramp, go left onto Rte. 513 south and follow this for 11 miles to Frenchtown. Cross the bridge to Pennsylvania and turn left onto Rte. 32 south. The entrance to Sand Castle Winery is 2.5 miles on the right, just past the Golden Pheasant Inn.

Seven Valleys Vineyard & Winery

855 George Ct., Glen Rock, PA 17327 • Phone and Fax 717-235-6281 • www.sevenvalleys.com • lhhma@aol.com

Located in the rolling hills of southern Pennsylvania, Seven Valleys Vineyard & Winery had its beginnings in 1976, when Fred and Lynn Hunter planted 5 acres of grapevines that they tended on weekends as a therapeutic break from their careers as psychologists. They went pro with their operation in 1994, moving onto the property, restoring its century-old farmhouse, and planting about 25 of their 85 acres with grapes. Today, they produce about 2,500 gallons annually and host a number of special events throughout the year (see the website for a listing).

Wines: $–$$

White Wines

Limerick—Semisweet blend of Vidal, Seyval, Steuben, and Cayuga. Honey nose.

Seyval—Light and dry, with nice oak and fruity overtones.

Red Wines

Cabernet Sauvignon—A dry red. Cherry comes through.

Country Red—A blend of Chambourcin, Chancellor, and Cabernet Sauvignon. Spicy.

Proprietor's Reserve Chambourcin—100% Chambourcin. Dry red. Nice nose. Soft.

Blush Wines

Steuben Blush—100% Steuben. Semisweet blush wine. Tangy.

Dessert Wines

Elation—Carbonated sweet wine. Blend of Vidal, Seyval, and Cayuga. Apple comes through. Tart. Nice.

Other Wines

Cayuga, Celebration, Chardonnay, Country Red, Country White, Gewürztraminer, Late Harvest Vidal, Proprietor's White, Riesling, Seyval Blanc, Vidal, Vidal Blanc

REVIEWS AND AWARDS

Riesling 1999—Bronze medal, 2000 American Wine Society Commercial Wine Competition.

Seyval 1999—Bronze medal, 2000 American Wine Society Commercial Wine Competition.

Seyval Blanc 1999—Gold medal, 2001 Pennsylvania Wine Association Competition.

HOURS AND DIRECTIONS Open year-round Sat. noon–5 p.m., or by appointment. ■ From Baltimore, follow I-83 north into Pennsylvania and take exit 4 (Shrewsbury). At the bottom of the ramp, turn left onto Rte. 851 and continue to Main St. in Shrewsbury. ■ From York, take I-83 south to exit 4 (Shrewsbury) and follow the local directions above.

Shade Mountain Winery

RR 2 Box 204, Creek Bottom Rd., Middleburg, PA 17842 • Phone 570-873-3644 • www.shademountainwinery.com • info@shademountainwinery.com

Housed in a converted nineteenth-century barn, Shade Mountain Winery opened in 1989 on 45 acres of family farmland, and today grows all its own grapes, with room to store up to 10,000 gallons of wine. Visitors can sample the many wines offered, from dry French hybrids to fruity dessert wines, and can also rent the winery grounds for weddings and other celebrations. Unique gift boxes and custom labels are available.

Wines: $–$$

White Wines

Riesling—A crisp, semisweet wine made in the German style.

Shade Mountain White—A nice, light, semisweet blend.

Red Wines

Cabernet Franc—A robust, medium-bodied red. Dry. Nice fruit.

Chambourcin—A garnet-colored red. Cherry and black raspberry come through.

Blush Wines

Autumn Harvest Blush—A semisweet blush wine. Strawberry comes through.

Fruit Wines

Pear—A sweet wine with a pleasant aroma of autumn pears.

Plum—A semisweet wine. Nice, light, and delicious. ♥

Other Wines

Anniversary White, Blackberry, Blanc, Blueberry, Cherry, Country Spice Apple, Elderberry, Evening Blush, Jack's Mountain Red, Niagara, Peach, Proprietor's Red, Rascal Red, Raspberry, Sauvignon Chardonnay, Shade Mountain Blush, Shade Mountain Red, Strawberry

REVIEWS AND AWARDS

Cabernet Franc 1999—Silver medal, 2001 Pennsylvania Wine Association Competition.

Lemberger—Best vinifera and gold medal, 2003 Pennsylvania Farm Show Wine Competition.

Plum—Bronze medal, 2001 Pennsylvania Farm Show Wine Competition.

HOURS AND DIRECTIONS Open year-round Mon.–Thurs. and Sat. 11 a.m.–5 p.m., Fri. 11 a.m.–7 p.m., Sun. 1–5 p.m. Located in the Susquehanna Valley. ■ From Philadelphia, take the Pa. Tpke. to exit 19 and follow I-283 north to exit 19. Follow the signs toward I-81 south to exit 21 (Marysville) and exit onto to Rtes. 11/15 north, toward Selinsgrove. After Liverpool, watch for Rte. 104 north. Shade Mountain is located on Rte. 104 between Mifflinburg and Middleburg, 2.5 miles south of Penns Creek.

Slate Quarry Winery

460 Gower Rd., Nazareth, PA 18064 • Phone 610-759-0286 or 610-746-3900 •
www.slatequarrywines.com • winery@slatequarrywines.com

As is the case with so many winery stories, this one began as a hobby and then
bloomed, beginning with the first grapes Sid and Ellie Butler planted back in 1971 and
growing eventually to 13 acres planted with everything from French hybrid grapes to
Traminette. The Butlers started out selling their grapes to other winemakers, then went
into the winery trade themselves in 1989, producing more than 2,000 gallons annually and storing them in their converted bank barn, which features a large stone fireplace. It's a fine spot to sample their wide range of offerings.

Wines: $–$$

White Wines

Sauvignon Blanc—A light, dry white. Very nice.

Traminette—An off-dry, German-style blend of Traminette and Gewürztraminer.
Zesty, with a nice nose.

Red Wines

Chambourcin—Dry red dinner wine. Full bodied. Subtle tannins.

Florental—A light red. Cherry comes through.

Nouveau—A fresh red made from Florental. Fruity and zesty.

Quarry Stone Red—A light, off-dry red. Tangy.

Blush Wines

Butler's Blush—An off-dry blend of Seyval, Vidal, and Chancellor.

Ellie's Rosé—A pink blush made from muscat. Semisweet and charming. Their most
popular wine.

Sparkling Wines

Apricot—A semisweet sparkling wine. Peaches on the nose and palate. Very nice.

Other Wines

*Cabernet Franc, Chardonel, Chardonnay, Classique Brut, Kerner, Peach, Quarry Stone Red,
Sparkling Rosé, Strawberry, Vidal, Vidal Brut, Vidal Ice Wine, Vignoles*

REVIEWS AND AWARDS

Chambourcin—Silver medal, 2000 Pennsylvania Farm Show Wine Competition.

Sauvignon Blanc—Silver medal, 2000 Pennsylvania Wine Association Competition,
2000 Pennsylvania Farm Show Wine Competition.

HOURS AND DIRECTIONS Open Feb.–Oct. Fri.–Sun. 1–6 p.m.; Nov.–Dec. Wed.–Sun. 1–6
p.m. Closed Jan. ■ The winery is located northwest of Nazareth on Gower Rd. ■ From
Rte. 22, take Rte. 191 north toward Nazareth. After passing Newburg Inn on your left,
bear left at the blinking light onto Rte. 946. The next stop will be Rte. 248. Proceed
through this intersection on 946 about 0.8 mile to the first group of homes and bear
right onto Knauss Rd. Travel about 0.5 mile and look for a small winery sign, where
you'll bear right onto Gower Rd. Continue 0.3 mile to the winery; a sign marks the
entrance.

Smithbridge Cellars

159 Beaver Valley Rd., Chaddsford, PA 19317 • Phone 610-558-4703 •
www.smithbridge.com • wines@smithbridge.com

Located on a quiet country road just half a mile from busy U.S. 202, Smithbridge Cellars is a small winery that does what many Pennsylvania wineries do not, focusing on barrel-aged Chardonnay and blends of classic Bordeaux grape varieties. Geoff Harrington purchased the land in 1997 and opened Smithbridge the following year, with 7 acres planted in grape and a charming 1800s Pennsylvania bank barn that's been converted to a wine storage facility. All told, the winery produces about 3,000 gallons each year.

Wines: $–$$

White Wines

Riesling—Off-dry finish and a floral bouquet.

"Tierra" Chardonnay—Burgundy-style, dry white table wine. Nicely oaked.

Red Wines

Hearthstone Meritage—A blend of 64% Cabernet Franc, 18% Cabernet Sauvignon, and 18% Merlot. Cherries and chocolate come through. Dry and deep.

Highgate Meritage—A dry, full-bodied blend of 40% Cabernet Franc, 40% Cabernet Sauvignon, and 20% Merlot, with plum, cherries, and chocolate coming through.

Dessert Wines

Sweet Riesling—A luscious, late-harvest Riesling.

Other Wines

Apple, Chardonnay Reserve, Merlot, Northern Spy Raspberry, Pinot Noir, Sauvignon Blanc

REVIEWS AND AWARDS

Hearthstone Meritage 1998—Silver medal, 2001 Pennsylvania Wine Association Competition.

Highgate Meritage 1999—Bronze medal, 2001 Pennsylvania Wine Association Competition.

HOURS AND DIRECTIONS Open year-round Sat.–Sun. noon–6 p.m. ■ Where Rtes. 1 and 202 intersect, go south on 202 a little over 2 miles. Turn right at the light for Beaver Valley Rd. After 0.5 mile, turn right onto the gravel road, where you'll see a sign for the winery.

Stargazers Vineyard

1024 Wheatland Dr., Coatsville, PA 19350 • Phone and Fax 610-486-0422 • www.stargazersvineyard.com • stargazers@kennett.net

John and Alice Weygandt originally planted 10 acres of grapes in 1979, intending to sell them to other wineries. By 1996, though, they'd done enough of their own winemaking to feel confident, and so opened the property as a rural winery. A mix of modern and country, the winery's solar-powered building is built into the hill to ensure a constant, moderate temperature for the wines stored there in stainless steel tanks and barrels. Because Stargazers is a bit out of the way, they recently opened an outlet in nearby Kennett Square, where their loyal patrons can more easily access their wines.

Wines: $–$$

White Wines

Chardonnay—Fermented in French oak *sur lie*. Tropical fruits. Vanilla. Dry.

Muscat—A dry, aromatic white wine. Vanilla comes through.

Pinot Gris—A clean, refreshing, light white.

Red Wines

Cabernet Franc—A bright-colored red. Violets and berries come through.

Pinot Noir—Burgundy-style red. Fruity.

Sparkling Wines

Sparkling Pinot Noir Rosé—Made from Pinot Noir and Pinot Meunier.

Sparkling Pinot Noir White—Made from Pinot Noir and Pinot Meunier.

Other Wines

Domfelder, Merlot, Muscat, Sauvignon Blanc, Sparkling Riesling

HOURS AND DIRECTIONS Open year-round Sun. 10 a.m.–6 p.m. Other days by appointment only. ■ From West Chester or Unionville, going north or south on Rte. 162, turn west onto Stargazers Rd., left at the T (curve) onto Youngs Rd., right onto Laurel Rd., right onto Wheatland Dr., and continue to the top of the hill.

Stone Villa Wine Cellars

RD 1 Box 223A, Claypike Rd., Acme, PA 15610 • Phone 724-423-5604 • www.stonevilla.com • info@stonevilla.com

Stone Villa Wine Cellars is a promising new winery that opened to the public in August 2000, with 5 acres of grapes planted on a nearly 150-acre site. It's owned by Randy Paul, a construction executive who built an attractive stone-and-wood winery and tasting room next to his home. It's a beautiful and striking building, yet warm and inviting, offering a real family experience because it's run by the owner and family. Stone Villa features over twelve varieties of grapes and over fifteen varieties of wines. Production is expected to be around 4,200 gallons this year, but the facility can actually handle 20,000 gallons (10,000 cases).

Wines: $–$$

White Wines

Chardonnay—A dry white table wine.

Niagara—A light, semisweet white.

Red Wines

Cabernet Sauvignon—A deep, full-bodied red.

Chambourcin—100% Chambourcin. A dry, deep red.

Stone Villa Red—A medium-bodied red wine.

Stonegria—A sweet, sangria-style fruit wine. Nice served cold.

Dessert Wines

Cherry Dessert Wine—Deep, red, tart dessert wine. Nice.

Other Wines

Padre's Red, Padre's Rosé, Padre's White, Pink Catawba, Stone Villa Blush, Stovilli, Vistonia

HOURS AND DIRECTIONS Open year-round Tues.–Sat. 11 a.m.–6 p.m., Sun. noon–5 p.m. Closed Mon. and holidays. ■ From exit 9 of the Pa. Tpke., take Rte. 31 west 2 miles. Turn right onto Claypike Rd. (at the golf course). The winery is 5 miles on the left. ■ From Rte. 119, Mt. Pleasant exit, take Rte. 31 east through Mt. Pleasant 3 miles to Rte. 982. Turn left (Rte. 982 north) and drive 4 miles to Kecksburgh. Turn right at the stop sign. The winery is 1 mile up the hill on the right.

Stoney Acres Winery

229 Wapwallopen Rd. (Rte. 239), Nescopeck, PA 18635 •
Phone 570-379-4771 • www.stoneyacreswinery.com

Stoney Acres opened in December 1999 and has quickly established itself as an operation to watch, producing handcrafted wines using modern techniques and absolutely exceptional hard ciders balanced nicely between sweetness and acidity—if you are looking for a pleasant, refreshing alternative to beer, look no further. In its first two years of state competitions, the winery has walked away with no fewer than nine medals.

Wines: $

White Wines

Chardonnay—Cool fermented and aged in French oak. Dry and full bodied. Crisp and clean.

Vidal Blanc—A clean, off-dry, German-style white. Refreshing.

Red Wines

Leon Millot—A dry, full-bodied red, aged in French oak.

Stoney Acres Red—A lively, off-dry red blend. Fruity and tangy. Spicy. ♥

Fruit Wines

Apple-Pear—Apple and pear wine blend. Sweet and refreshing, with a clean finish.

Apple-Strawberry—A sweet and fruity blend of apple and strawberry wines.

Hard Apple Ciders

Golden—Golden, well-balanced, fragrant cider. Slightly sweeter and more appley than the traditional variety. ♥

Traditional—Bronze, well-balanced, fragrant cider. Clean, refreshing apple flavor. ♥

Other Wines

Apple, Aurore, Blueberry, Catawba, Concord, Country Blush, Niagara, Spiced Apple

REVIEWS AND AWARDS

Apple-Pear—Bronze medal, 2002 Pennsylvania Farm Show Wine Competition.

Concord—Bronze medal, 2002 Pennsylvania Farm Show Wine Competition.

Golden Hard Apple Cider—Bronze medal, 2001 and 2002 Pennsylvania Farm Show Wine Competition.

Niagara—Bronze medal, 2002 Pennsylvania Farm Show Wine Competition.

Spiced Apple—Bronze medal, 2002 Pennsylvania Farm Show Wine Competition.

Stoney Acres Red—Silver medal, 2002 Pennsylvania Farm Show Wine Competition.

Traditional Hard Apple Cider—Silver medal, 2001 Pennsylvania Farm Show Wine Competition.

Vidal Blanc—Bronze medal, 2002 Farm Show Wine Competition.

HOURS AND DIRECTIONS Open in winter Fri.–Sun. 11 a.m.–6 p.m.; in summer Thurs.–Sun. 11 a.m.–6 p.m. Call to verify hours. ■ Located in lower Luzerne County. ■ From Rte. 11 just south of Shickshinny, take Rte. 239 south across the river and follow the blue winery signs. The winery is about 8 miles from the junction of Rtes. 11 and 239 (about 3 miles past Heller's Orchard).

Susquehanna Valley Winery

802 Mount Zion Dr., Danville, PA 17821 • Phone 570-275-2364 •
mlatranyi@aol.com

Nick and Hildegarde Latranyi purchased their 200-acre farm in the hills above the Susquehanna River back in 1985, planting 3 acres from which they now produce roughly 1,000 gallons annually. They specialize in sweet wines, such as their best-selling Gluwein, a spiced red blend. Customized labels are available for special events.

Wines: $–$$

White Wines
Vidal Blanc—A light, off-dry white.

Red Wines
Baco Noir—Dry.

Specialty Wines
Gluwein—A sweet, spiced wine meant to be served hot in the German style.

Other Wines
Dry Duet, Melody, Summer Sonata, Sweet Concord, Sweet Niagara, Symphony

HOURS AND DIRECTIONS Open year-round Wed.–Sun. 1–6 p.m. ▪ Located in central Pennsylvania south of Rte. 11, a few miles east of Danville.

Twin Brook Winery

5697 Strasburg Rd., Gap, PA 17527 • Phone 717-442-4915 •
www.gabrielshill.com • gabriels@epix.net

One of the most popular wineries for aficionados visiting the Susquehanna Valley, Twin Brook was planted in 1985 by Richard and Cheryl Kaplan, two attorneys with a passion for winemaking. They opened to the public in 1990 and now produce about 10,000 gallons each year. The winery's beautiful stone manor house was built in the 1800s and stands as a reminder of the state's rich farming heritage, while a recently renovated barn houses the tasting room and storage facilities. In addition to wine, Richard and Cheryl also sell fresh fruit and grapes grown on their 30-acre spread.

Wines: $

White Wines
Chardonnay—Dry, oak-aged white wine.
Vidal Blanc—Off-dry, light white wine.
Vignoles—Fruity and sweet but with nice acidity.

Red Wines
Chancellor—Dry, oak-aged, medium-bodied red wine.

Specialty Wines
Spice Wine—A red wine with seasonal mulling spices. Very popular.

Other Wines
Blossom Blush, Cabernet Franc, Cabernet Sauvignon, Cayuga, Clocktower White,
  Consiglieri, Icebreaker Blush, Merlot, Octorara Red, Octorara Rosé, Pinot Gris,
  Spice Wine, Springhouse White, Strasburger Red

REVIEWS AND AWARDS
Cayuga—Bronze medal, 2001 Pennsylvania Farm Show Wine Competition.
Clocktower White—Bronze medal, 2001 Pennsylvania Farm Show Wine Competition.

HOURS AND DIRECTIONS Open year-round Tues.–Sat. noon–5 p.m. ▪ From Philadelphia, head west on U.S. 30, through the traffic light at Rte. 10; turn left onto Swan Rd., then right onto Strasburg Rd. Twin Brook will be on the right.

Vynecrest Winery

172 Arrowhead Ln., Breinigsville, PA 18031 • Phone 800-361-0725 or
610-398-7525 • Fax 610-398-7530 • www.vynecrest.com • landisjg@ptd.net

John and Jan Landis began growing grapes in their Breinigsville vineyard in 1974, and
in the spring of 1989 opened to the public, renovating their turn-of-the-century Swiss
bank barn to create a bottling room and a large tasting room with large windows that
let in scads of natural light. Outside, about a fifth of the farm's 30 acres is devoted to
grapes, from which Vynecrest currently produces about 2,500 gallons each year, with
the capacity to do more in the future.

Wines: $–$$

White Wines

Autumn Gold—A sweet blend of Cayuga, Vidal, and Traminette. Delightful! ♥ ♥

Seyval Blanc—A crisp, dry, French-style white wine. Refreshing.

Traminette—A dry, Alsatian-style Gewürztraminer.

Red Wines

Estate Reserve Red—A soft, off-dry red blend.

Lemberger—A dry, oak-aged wine made from an Austrian-German red varietal.

Pinot Noir—A light, dry red.

Dessert and Holiday Wines

Late Harvest Vidal—Sweet, luscious, full-bodied dessert wine. Nicely balanced.

Spiced Winter Red—Sweet holiday wine made in the German *Gluwein* tradition.

Other Wines

*Arrowhead Red, Arrowhead White, Baco Noir, Chambourcin, Vidal, Vynecrest Red,
Vynecrest White*

REVIEWS AND AWARDS

Autumn Gold—Gold medal, medal, 2003 Pennsylvania Wine Association
Competition; bronze medal, 2001 Pennsylvania Wine Association Competition.

Vignoles 2000—Silver medal, 2001 Pennsylvania Wine Association Competition.

Vignoles 2002—Gold medal, 2003 Pennsylvania Farm Show Wine Competition.

HOURS AND DIRECTIONS Open year-round Thurs.–Sun. 11 a.m.–5 p.m. ■ Located just
outside Allentown. Look for the blue Vynecrest signs within 3 miles of the winery in
all directions. ■ From I-78/U.S. 22, take exit 49A onto Rte. 100 south. Turn right onto
Schantz Rd. at the second traffic light and continue approximately 1.5 miles to Arrowhead Ln. Turn right. The winery entrance is on the left.

Westhanover Winery

7646 Old Jonestown Rd., Harrisburg, PA 17112 • Phone 717-652-3711 •
whwinery@aol.com

Like many other winemakers, former meat cutter George Kline began as something of
a hobbyist, planting vines on limited acreage and producing wines in his basement.
He's still down there now, running a small but professional winery that specializes in
semisweet varieties, with the capacity to produce about 5,000 gallons a year.

Wines: $–$$

White Wines

Aurore—A light and sweet white blend. Clean and crisp. Not cloying.

Catawba—A sweet white/pinkish sipping wine. Nice.

Chardonnay—A dry white wine.

Red Wines
Cabernet Sauvignon—A dry, medium-bodied red. Cherry comes through.

Fruit Wines
Apple—Clean and refreshing.

Other Wines
Baco Noir, Cayuga, Concord Dry, King of the North, Merlot, Niagara, Red Raspberry, Steuben, Valiant, Villard Blanc

REVIEWS AND AWARDS
Aurore—Bronze medal, 2001 Pennsylvania Farm Show Wine Competition.

Catawba—Bronze medal, 2001 Pennsylvania Farm Show Wine Competition.

HOURS AND DIRECTIONS Open year-round Tues.–Thurs. noon–6:30 p.m., Fri. noon–8:30 p.m., Sat. noon–6:30 p.m. ■ From Hershey, go north on Rte. 39 to Old Jonestown Rd. and turn left. The winery is 0.9 mile ahead on the right.

Wilhelm Winery

590 Georgetown Rd., Handley, PA 16130 • Phone 724-253-3700 • Fax 724-253-2479

Opened by Gary and Trish Shilling, Gary Rhodes, and Jackie Zingelewicz in June 2000, Wilhelm Winery currently offers fifteen different wines, some made from grapes grown at Rhodes's Fredonia home. The winery's converted 1900 barn features a large tasting room, a fireplace, and a loft.

Wines: $–$$
Red Wines
Wilhelm Red—A spicy, medium-bodied red. ♥

Blush Wines
Pink Catawba—A light, pinkish wine made from Catawba.

Fruit Wines
Blueberry—A sweet dessert wine made from fresh Pennsylvania blueberries.

Elderberry—A different kind of fruit wine. One of the few made in Pennsylvania.

Other Wines
Blackberry

HOURS AND DIRECTIONS Open year-round Thurs.–Sun. noon–6 p.m. ■ From I-79 south, take the Greenville/Sandy Lake exit. Turn left onto Rte. 358, then go north on Rte. 19 through Sheakeyville, then turn right onto Georgetown Rd. The winery is 3 miles up the road. ■ From I-79 north, take the Geneva exit. Turn left onto Rte. 19 and left onto Georgetown Rd. Go 3 miles to the winery on the right.

Windgate Vineyards

199 Hemlock Acres Rd., Smicksburg, PA 16256 • Phone 814-257-8797 • www.windgatevineyards.com • windgatewine@alltel.net

Windgate dates from 1974, when Dan and Lillian Enerson purchased a 100-acre-plus estate in northwestern Pennsylvania and began growing numerous grapes varieties as they experimented with the land. They made some wine themselves but sold the bulk of their crops to other winemakers. With 15 acres now planted, Windgate produces about 8,000 gallons annually, and plans to increase production are in the works. Due to its location in Amish Pennsylvania, the winery attracts many tourists in the summer and fall months. Their Amish Country White is among their most popular wines.

Wines: $-$$

White Wines

Niagara—Semisweet wine. Delightful, fruity palate and aroma.

Nocturne—Semidry vinifera-blend wine. Fruity palate, nice balance.

Riesling—German-style white wine. Off-dry. Fruity and aromatic.

Red Wines

Cabernet Franc—Dry red vinifera, barrel aged. Plum and cherry come through.

Eye of the Buck—A full-bodied, well-balanced, dry red. Cherry comes through.

Guyasuta Red—Also called "The Chief." Light-bodied, off-dry red. Fruity and zesty.

Blush Wines

Eye of the Shadow—A fruity, semisweet rosé. Floral nose. Refreshing. The name pays homage to Punxsutawney Phil, famous groundhog. ♥

Sparkling Wines

Sparkling Riesling—Off-dry sparkling wine with fine bubbles and nice palate.

Other Wines

Amish Blush, Amish Country Red, Amish Country White, Blueberry, Chancellor, Chardonnay, Concord, DeChaunac, Mahoning Valley Mist, Marechal Foch, Pinot Grigio, Rhapsody, Seyval Blanc, Spring Rosé, Vidal Blanc, Windgate Apple, Windgate Spiced Apple

REVIEWS AND AWARDS

Eye of the Shadow—Bronze medal, 2001 Pennsylvania Farm Show Wine Competition.

Vidal Blanc 1999—Bronze medal, 2001 Pennsylvania Farm Show Wine Competition.

HOURS AND DIRECTIONS Open daily noon–5 p.m. except Easter, Thanksgiving, Christmas, and New Year's Day. ■ From Pittsburgh, take the Rte. 28 Expwy. north beyond Kitanning. Follow signs for Rte. 28 to reach Rte. 85, where you'll turn right. Continue on 85 for 18 miles to Rte. 954 in Plumville. Turn left onto 954 and go about 10 miles to Smicksburg. Continue on Rte. 954 another 2 miles to Hemlock Acres Rd. Turn left to Windgate Vineyards. ■ From the Pa. Tpke., take exit 5 (Allegheny Valley), following signs toward Pittsburgh. Go 0.5 mile, turn right onto Rte. 910, and get onto the Rte. 28 Expwy. north, toward Kitanning; then follow the local directions above.

The Winery at Wilcox ✫✫

1867 Mefferts Run Rd., P.O. Box 39, Wilcox, PA 15870 • Phone 814-929-5598 • www.wineryatwilcox.net • carolwaw@penn.com

Located in the mountains of northwestern Pennsylvania, The Winery at Wilcox is one of the fastest-growing wineries in the state, and winemaker Mike Williams is proud of the wide variety he is able to produce, using grapes from Erie County and often naming the results for local landmarks. Williams opened the winery's doors in the summer of 1994 with an inventory of over 1,000 gallons in nearly a dozen varieties, and since then the winery has grown several times, increased production to over 25,000 gallons annually, and gained a solid reputation within the state.

Wines: $-$$

White Wines

Auxxerois—Alsatian grape. Semisweet wine. Light, with melon and citrus. Nice.♥ ♥

Chardonnay—A dry white wine with a lot of oak and a soft, vanilla aftertaste. ♥

Viognier—Crisp, off-dry white wine. Citrusy.

Red Wines

Autumn Leaves—A semidry red. Wonderful for making mulled wine at the holidays.

Cabernet Franc—A deep, dry red. Cherries and peppers come through.

Cabernet Sauvignon—A rich, dry red. Berries and plums. Nice.

Blush Wines

West Branch Sunset—Apricot-colored blush wine. Semisweet and refreshing. ♥

Dessert Wines and Ports

Peach Mist—Sparkling peach wine, excellent as an aperitif or with dessert.♥ ♥

Port of Chambourcin—A true port. Deep purple and rich, not cloying. One of the best ports on the East Coast.♥ ♥

Other Wines

Angelique, Bear-ly Blush, Blueberry Mist, Bob White, Brittany's Blush, Chambourcin, Clarion River Red, East Branch Sunset, Elk Country Red, Elk Country White, Gewürztraminer, Hunter Red, Kinzua Kiss, Leon Millot, Mefferts Run Red, Niagara, Pinot Grigio, Rasselas Rosé, Riesling, Seyval Blanc, Spiced Apple, Vidal Blanc, Vignoles, Wedding White

REVIEWS AND AWARDS

Auxxerois 2000—Bronze medal, 2001 Pennsylvania Wine Association Competition; bronze medal, 2001 Pennsylvania Farm Show Wine Competition.

Blueberry Mist—Governor's Cup/Best Sparkling Fruit Wine/gold medal, 2003 Pennsylvania Farm Show Wine Competition.

Chardonnay 1998—Silver medal, 2001 Pennsylvania Farm Show Wine Competition.

Chardonnay 1999—Silver medal, 2001 Pennsylvania Wine Association Competition.

Peach Mist—Gold medal, Governor's Cup, Best Fruit Wine, Best Sparkling Wine, "Best of Show," 1999 Pennsylvania Farm Show Wine Competition.

Port of Chambourcin 2000—Gold medal, 2001 Pennsylvania Wine Association Competition; silver medal, 2001 Pennsylvania Farm Show Wine Competition.

Schwartzbeeren NV—Gold medal, 2003 Pennsylvania Wine Association Competition.

HOURS AND DIRECTIONS Open daily 10 a.m.–6 p.m. year-round. ■ Take I-80 to exit 16 and proceed south on Rte. 219 toward Bradford. The winery is located 2 miles off Rte. 219, on Mefferts Run Rd., between Wilcox and Johnsonburg.

OTHER PENNSYLVANIA WINERIES

Folly Hill Vineyard: 700 Folly Hill Rd., Kennett Square, PA 19348 • Phone 610-388-5896

Kreutz Creek Vineyards: 533 S. Guernsey Rd., West Grove, PA 19390 • Phone 610-869-4412

Paradocx Vineyard: P. O. Box 400, Kemblesville, PA 19347 • Phone 610-255-5684 • Fax 610-255-5682 • www.paradocx.com • paradocx@brandywine.net

RHODE ISLAND

Diamond Hill Vineyards

3145 Diamond Hill Rd., Cumberland, RI 02864 • Phone 401-333-2751 or
800-752-2505 • Fax 401-333-8520 • www.favorlabel.com

Situated among 34 acres of rolling New England farmland, the 200-year-old house that Diamond Hill Vineyards calls home has been in the wine business since 1975. That's when the founders, Pete and Claire Bernston, planted their first 5 acres of Pinot Noir.

"Peter met his wife Claire while he was stationed in France with the Air Force, and she was an exchange student . . . so I probably don't have to paint you a picture of the wild and wonderful picnics they enjoyed between the vines," wrote Jonathan Alsop for *In Vino Veritas* in November 1999. "Peter and Claire resolved to have that vineyard experience close at hand always, so to speak, and today they have five acres of pinot noir vines right within easy reach of the house." Since then, they've added numerous acres of planted vinifera and hybrids. They also make wines from apples, cranberries, peaches, and blueberries.

"Bring a picnic and spread out on the broad veranda of this 200-year-old estate, then nibble on cheese and sample the popular cranberry-apple wine," said *Yankee Magazine* in an article titled "New England Uncorked." "Early autumn, when the grapes hang heavy, is a favored time to visit."

With their long-established Pinot Noir vines, Diamond Hill Vineyards uses French barrels and techniques in an effort to create an old-world Pinot Noir. The result is significant.

Wines: $–$$

White Wines
River Valley White—A blend of Chardonnay and Riesling.

Red Wines
Pinot Noir—Estate-grown, dry red.
Pinot Noir Blanc—Estate-grown, dry white.

Blush Wines
Blackstone Blush—A blend of Merlot and Chardonnay.

Fruit Wines
Blueberry (375 ml only)—Higher alcohol for a port-like finish.
Cranberry Apple—Popular blend for festive occasions.

Peach—After-dinner sweetness.

Spiced Apple—Spices added for mulling.

HOURS AND DIRECTIONS Open year-round Thurs.–Sat. noon–5 p.m., or call for an appointment. Office hours 9 a.m.–5 p.m. Tues.–Sat. ■ From I-295 north or south, take exit 11. Go north on Rte. 114 (Diamond Hill Rd.) 2 miles to the stone gates and gift shop sign on the right side of the road.

Greenvale Vineyards ✯ ✯

582 Wapping Rd., Portsmouth, RI 02871 • Phone 401-847-3777 • www.greenvale.com

Greenvale is one of those small wineries that everyone wishes they could own. The winery is anchored by a lovely, historic home. The family has been tied to the land for generations. They have grown grapes for two decades. And all is tucked away beautifully in the gorgeous Rhode Island countryside.

While we should probably start with the wine, let's leave it until last. First, let's talk about that beautiful Victorian home. It was conceived as a retirement home, a gentleman's farm, as it were. "Greenvale was built by John Barstow in 1864 and 1865. The architect for the main house and stable was John Hubbard Sturgis from Boston," say the Greenvale owners. "Sturgis and Richard Morris Hunt were friends and Hunt had just completed the Griswold House in Newport, also a Victorian Gothic structure and considered the first stick-style building in the United States." The tasting room is located in the newly restored stables. Handsomely appointed and beautifully updated, the barn, the house, and the surrounding grounds give one the feeling of Victorian New England opulence, reminiscent of nearby Newport.

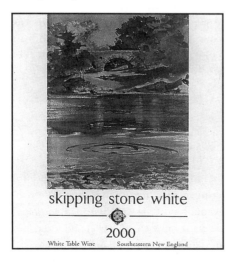

The winery is owned by the fourth generation of Parkers. "We, Cortlandt and Nancy and our four children, started on this project in 1982 in an effort to develop a productive use of our family farm located along the Sakonnet River. We began as growers for another larger winery," says the winery's literature. But now they grow the grapes and make their own wines. And they released their first wines in 1993—one a Chardonnay of only 350 cases. Since then, their wines have gone on to win acclaim and popularity throughout New England. As with other Rhode Island wineries, they remain a popular day trip destination for the summer tourists breezing through Newport and the New England coast.

At best, Michael Carmichael, the winemaker, and the winery produce no more than 5,000 cases of wine. Their average run of wines is actually quite limited in terms of volume. But their quest is, indeed, for quality. And that starts with the care they show their grapes. "They prune in the winter, then thin the vines out a bit in May," wrote Lisa Shea in her review of Greenvale for About.com in June 1999. "In late June they again thin the vines, and in August they even trim the foliage to let the most light in at the grapes. By September and October, the grapes are finally ready for picking and processing."

Wines: $–$$

White Wines

Chardonnay—A light, fresh, crisp Chardonnay. ♥

Chardonnay Select—Made from the property's oldest Chardonnay vines, the winemakers spend a little more time with this wine. More oak.

Skipping Stone White—By far their most popular wine, and rightly so. A Cayuga wine topped off with 10% Vidal Blanc. A wonderful wine with a nice summer soup or salad of arugula topped with balsamic vinegar and orange slices. ♥

Vidal Blanc—A nice, light white wine. Fruity and refreshing.

Red Wines

Cabernet Franc—A deep Cabernet Franc.

REVIEWS AND AWARDS

Skipping Stone White: "Made in a riesling style. It tasted of fruits— apricot, cherry, and green apple. It was semi-sweet and quite tasty."
—Lisa Shea, About.com (June 1999)

Skipping Stone White 1999: "Recommended Wines"
—Gerald Asher, Gourmet Magazine (August 2002)

"Greenvale Vineyards' Cabernet Franc—one of the best in New England."
—Bob Chaplin, Hartford Courant (February 10, 2002)

HOURS AND DIRECTIONS Open Mon.–Sat. 10 a.m.–5 p.m., Sun. noon–5 p.m., year-round. ▪ From Newport, take Rte. 138 north. Just past the Entering Portsmouth sign, turn right onto Braman's Ln. At the end, turn right onto Wapping Rd., then immediately left onto the vineyards' driveway, Greenvale Ln. Go to the end of the lane. ▪ From Fall River, take Rte. 24 south. Cross the Sakonnet River and take exit 1 for Rte. 138 south and the Middletown/Newport beaches. Turn right onto Rte. 138 south. Pass the state police barracks and turn left onto Sandy Point Ave. at the traffic light. Take the first right onto Wapping Rd. The vineyards' driveway is 0.9 mile on the left. Go to the end of the lane.

Newport Winery

909 E. Main Rd. (Rte. 138), Middletown, RI 02842 • Phone 401-848-5161 • Fax 401-848-5162 • info@newportvineyards.com

Located on the stunning vista of Aquidneck Island, just 10 minutes outside of beautiful Newport, the Newport Winery is a wonderful getaway for an afternoon. The winery was begun in 1977, when a retired navy captain and his wife first planted grapes on a hill over looking Newport Sound. The first plantings were of Seyval and Vidal, but the winery has since planted more classic grapes, such as Chardonnay, Cabernet Sauvignon, Merlot, Cabernet Franc, Malbec, and Landot Noir. The winery boasts well over 45 acres of planted grapes.

John and Paul Nunes bought the winery in 1995, and are responsible for its reshaping and its phenomenal growth and success. "It needed a little more energy," John Nunes told Kate Borgueta of *Newport This Week* (October 4, 2001). The Nunes brothers are from a family that has long been resident to this island, and are well tied in with the local community—so much so that local residents help harvest the crops in the fall in exchange for gift certificates. "The Nunes family has been farming on Aquidneck Island since the nineteenth century," John told Gayle Goddard-Taylor of *American Profiles* (December 17, 2000). "My father's grandfather came over from the Azores in the late 1800s, and all of his sons settled here. I'm the fourth generation."

"This portion of Rhode Island is so conducive to vineyards, Nunes said, because its proximity to the water assures a long growing season. Here, the first frost doesn't touch the grapes until mid to late November," Borgueta wrote. The brothers' ambition to create great wines has resulted in an unexpected pleasure in Newport that used to be a secret. However, their notable success has been hard to keep quiet. And it's hard not to gush about their wines.

Wines: $–$$$

White Wines
Chardonnay—A traditional, Burgundian dry white.
Great White—Semisweet light white wine. Honeydew melon and apricot come through. Nice acidity. Very refreshing. Their most popular wine. ♥ ♥
Reserve Chardonnay—100% barrel fermentation gives this dry white a full-bodied character. Nice fruit and oak.
Riesling—A traditionally styled off-dry Riesling.
Sanctuary—A barrel-fermented Seyval aged in oak. A crisp white wine with elegant floral accents.
Vidal Blanc—German-style, off-dry white. Tart.

Red Wines
Cabernet Franc—A Loire Valley–style red. Berries and spice come through. Dry.
Merlot—Currant and blackberry come through. A rich, deep, dry red.
Merlot, Vintner's Select—Aged in new French oak barrels.

Blush Wines
Rosé—A dry blend of Cabernet Sauvignon, Merlot, and Cabernet Franc grapes.

Specialty Wines
Ruby Port—A blend of vintages from 1993 through 1999.
Vidal Ice Wine—A rich, golden nectar. An excellent dessert wine. ♥
White Cap Port—A rich, sweet white port.

Other Wines
Bellevue Blush, Gemini Red, Hospitality White, Rochambeau, Seyval Blanc

Ciders
Dry "Cidre"—Handcrafted in the style of the dry ciders of northern France. Great nose. A surprisingly dry finish.
Johnny's Hard Apple Cider—Made from fresh local apples. Finished with a crisp, semidry bite. ♥

REVIEWS AND AWARDS

"A Newport Winery specialty is ice wine, made from vidal blanc grapes
(a hardy French-American hybrid) that are picked after the third hard frost
in November. ('If you try to eat frozen vidal grape, you could get slush on
your lips,' says Nunes.) The result is a fruit-flavored, deliciously sweet
dessert wine." —William A. Davis, "A Taste of Autumnal Pleasure,"
Boston Globe (October 21, 2001)

"Just planted in 1997, Newport Vineyards has an amazing selection of wines for
such a new vineyard! Great White is a crowd pleaser, and their port is smooth
and sweet. Fourteen varieties make this a great stop any time you head towards
Newport." —"Corkpops," *Wine News and Reviews, New England Wineries*

Great White: "What a treat! Full melon and apricot flavors swirled from
the wine, and the finish was long and mouth-suckingly good."
—Lisa Shea, About.com (May 1999)

Ruby Port: "This port has won medals, and it's easy to see why. Not sickly-sweet,
but with a bit of tartness to it, the port was rich, full and filling. An excellent
post-dinner lounging-by-the-water treat." —Lisa Shea, About.com (May 1999)

"The winery's Vidal Ice wine, pressed from grapes harvested after the fall's
third hard frost, was recently voted one of the 50 best wines in America
at the Thomas Jefferson Invitational Example of American Greatness."
—Kate Borgueta, *Newport This Week* (October 4, 2001)

HOURS AND DIRECTIONS Open daily Mon.–Sat. 10 a.m.–5 p.m., Sun. noon–5 p.m.,
year-round. ■ From Newport, drive east on Memorial Blvd. past Easton's Beach, then
bear left (north) on Aquidneck Ave. (Rte. 138A) to E. Main Rd. (Rte. 138). Bear right
onto Rte. 138. Newport Winery is 0.8 mile north on the right (no. 909). ■ From Providence, drive east on I-195 to Rte. 24 south. Cross the Sakonnet River Bridge. Take exit
1 to Rte. 138 and follow it south 10 minutes. The winery is on the left (no. 909).

Sakonnet Vineyards

162 W. Main Rd., Little Compton, RI 02837 •
Phone 401-635-8486 •
www.sakonnetwine.com

"Little Compton's Sakonnet Vineyards was
founded in 1975 on the premise that favorable
climate and soil conditions found along the
southeastern coast of New England were parallel to the great wine regions of the world,
including northern France," wrote *Newport This
Week* in October 2001. Sakonnet aimed to create
the best wines in New England. It would seem
that they've succeeded.

Sakonnet Vineyards has a 45-acre plot. They
also use additional grapes that are transported
from an 8-acre plot at Peckham's Vineyard. The
grapes from Peckham's allowed the winery to
increase its production to 50,000 cases of wine
in 2000.

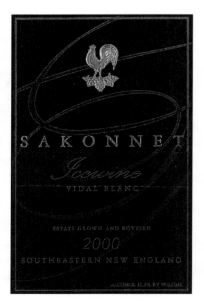

"Largest New England winery, based in Little Compton, Rhode Island," Hugh Johnson wrote in his three-star review of the winery in his *Pocket Wine Book 2002*. "Drinkable wines include Chardonnay, Vidal Blanc, dry Gewürztraminer, Cabernet Franc and Pinot Noir." And Karen Mac-Neil, author of *The Wine Bible*,

called Sakonnet "the most highly regarded and largest winery in New England" in her landmark book.

"We make wines that have a distinctive New England taste," said Susan Samson, coproprietor with her husband Earl of Sakonnet Vineyards, to William A. Davis of the *Boston Globe* (October 21, 2001). Earl Samson was a former investment banker, and Susan Samson was a former actress and an off-Broadway producer, when they bought Sakonnet from the couple who originally founded it. (Sakonnet Vineyards was originally founded in 1987 by Jim and Lolly Mitchell.) "We fell in love with Little Compton because it reminded us of the Hamptons in the 1950s when they were still surrounded by farms," Susan told Davis.

Sakonnet is a smartly run winery. The Samsons have carefully planned and established three different labels. There is the Sakonnet Vineyards Estate label, which is for the high-end varietals; the Mariner label, for medium-priced *vins de table*; and the Newport label, for the inexpensive, popularly styled wines that are a hit with summertime tourists. The winery even boasts a B & B, named The Roost. Three rooms are available in the main house of the original farm. It's a wonderful opportunity to enjoy the vineyard life, especially if you'd like to own one but don't have the capital—staying here will make you feel like a million dollars.

Easily the most impressive New England winery, Sakonnet Vineyards' greatest achievements, it seems, still lie ahead.

Wines: $–$$$

White Wines

Chardonnay—100% barrel fermented in French and American oak. Aged *sur lie* 9 months. Very nice. ♥

Fumé Vidal—100% barrel fermented in oak. Aged 9 months *sur lie*. Nice fruit. Dry. Crisp. ♥

Gewürztraminer—93% Estate Gewürztraminer, 7% Estate Vidal Blanc. Fruity and tart.

Vidal Blanc—Floral, fruity up-front nose. The finish is very dry—reminiscent of Pinot Grigio. Dry and delicious. Tart. ♥ ♥

Red Wines

Pinot Noir—Cherries come through. Jam and spice also come through. Dry finish. ♥

Rhode Island Red—100% Estate Chancellor. Berries and cherries come through. Spicy with a touch a vanilla.

Specialty Wines

Brut Cuvée—Late disgorged, full-bodied sparkling wine. Creamy, dry finish. ♥

Port—84% Estate Chancellor, 16% aged 80-proof brandy. Aged 2 years in 2-year-old American oak barrels. Sweet but not cloying.

Sirius—100% Estate Vidal. Similar to a late-harvest wine.

Vidal Ice Wine—Aromas of honey, dried apricots, and peaches. Very nice. ♥

Other Wines

America's Cup Red, America's Cup White, Eye of the Storm, Mariner Chardonnay, Mariner Merlot, Spinnaker White

REVIEWS AND AWARDS

Fumé Vidal 2000: "Recommended Wines"
—Gerald Asher, *Gourmet Magazine* (August 2002)

"Delicious sparkling Brut Cuvée." —*Hugh Johnson's Pocket Wine Book 2002*

Chardonnay 1997: "A bright attack leads a medium-bodied palate with pure citrus flavors and tart acids through the finish. Very fresh, pure style with no oak influence," 84 points
—Beverage Testing Institute, *Buying Guide to Wines of North America*

Gewürztraminer 1997: "Aromatically subdued, with clean, minerally citrus flavors in the mouth. Crisp, with vibrant audacity," 84 points
—Beverage Testing Institute, *Buying Guide to Wines of North America*

HOURS AND DIRECTIONS Open Memorial Day–Oct. 1 daily, 10 a.m.–6 p.m.; Oct. 1–Memorial Day daily, 11 a.m.–5 p.m. ■ From Boston, take I-93 south to Rte. 24 south. Exit at Tiverton/Sakonnet/Rte. 77. Go south on Rte. 77, through the traffic light at Tiverton Four Corners, and Sakonnet Vineyards will be 3 miles after the light on the left. ■ From Newport, go north on E. Main Rd. (Rte. 138) or W. Main Rd. (Rte. 114) to Rte. 24 north. Exit at Tiverton/Little Compton/Rte. 77. Go south on Rte. 77 and follow the local directions above.

OTHER RHODE ISLAND WINERIES

Prudence Island Vineyard: Prudence Island, RI 02872 • Phone 401-683-2452 •
A unique vineyard located on a beautiful island off the coast of Rhode Island.

VERMONT

L'Abeille Honey Winery ✿

638 S. Main St., Stowe, VT 05672 • Phone 802-253-2929 •
Blachere@together.net

The meadery is named L'Abeille because it is French for "The Bee." In 1996 Frenchman Bernard Blachere and his wife Diane Rice opened L'Abeille Honey Winery after operating the Bee Bee winery in Quebec, Canada, for 15 years. Located in Stowe, the 10,000-bottle winery focuses almost solely on mead. Mr. Blachere learned about making mead from a friend's grandfather in Cassis, France, near Marseilles. The meadery produces the mead in batches of 1,000 bottles. They buy the honey in large metal drums from a producer in Putnamville, as well as using honey of their own, and use Burgundy wine yeasts.

Wines: $–$$

Natural Mead—A dry white wine made from honey. Golden and excellent with fowl or fish. ♥

Other Wines

Honey Dessert Wine, Mead, Raspberry

REVIEWS AND AWARDS

"The nectar of the gods is flowing in the Green Mountain State . . . its dryish
    Natural Mead has been enthusiastically received by locals and tourists alike."
                                        —Tom Ayers, *Yankee Beer News* (August/September 1997)

"Beautiful color and aroma, but more akin to a dry white wine, and a very
    good one at that."   —Michael Moynihan, *Mead Lover's Digest* #622
                                                (December 11, 1997), ed. Dick Dunn

HOURS AND DIRECTIONS Open daily 9 a.m.–6 p.m. ■ Call for directions.

Boyden Valley Winery

70 State Rte. 104, Cambridge, VT 05444 • Phone 802-644-8151 •
Fax 802-644-8212 • www.boydenvalley.com • info@boydenvalley.com

Boyden Valley Winery is one of Vermont's most unique attractions. They make more than a dozen award-winning wines, and all the fruit wines are certified organic. They also make hard cider. The winery is part of a fourth-generation Vermont farm in the pastoral Lamoille River Valley. The family farm also produces maple syrup and other fresh products for purchase. This is a wonderful day trip or easy visit, especially during the fall foliage time of year.

Wines: $–$$

White Wines

Cayuga—A fruity, semisweet wine. Apricot comes through.

Seyval Blanc—A dry, German-style white wine. Floral nose. Crisp and clean.

Red Wines

Leon Millot—A dry, medium-bodied, Chiantiesque red.

Riverbend Red—Dry, medium-bodied red. Big berry presence. Nice tannins.

Apple Wines

Green Mountain Classic Reserve—An off-dry, medium-bodied, fruity wine.

Northern Spy Dry—Aged in French oak. Well-balanced, dry apple wine.

Vermont Maple Reserve—Dessert wine of apples and maple syrup.

Fruit Wines

Apple Raspberry—Deep and tart raspberry wine.

Cranberry—Seasonal Vermont cranberry wine. Sweet and tart.

Dessert Wines

Gold Leaf—Blend of supreme estate maple syrup and locally grown Northern Spy apples. Barrel aged like a fine white port. Excellent dessert wine.

Other Wines

Blueberry, Glogg, Pear, Rhubarb

HOURS AND DIRECTIONS Open May 31–Dec. 31 Tues.–Sun. 10 a.m.–5 p.m.; Jan. 1–May 30 Fri.–Sun. 10 a.m.–5 p.m. ■ Call for directions.

Grand View Winery

P.O. Box 91, Max Gray Rd., East Calais, VT 05650 • Phone 802-456-7012 • www.grandviewwinery.com • ptonk@plainfield.bypass.com

Getting to the Grand View Winery is difficult. At one point you find yourself on a dirt road wondering if you are going in the direction or if you are lost. One of the rewards when you get there, aside from the wine, is the awe-inspiring view of Camel's Hump, Mount Ellen, and the Worcester Range.

Owned and run by Phil Tonks and his family, this is a family affair—a house and barn turned into a winery. It is not open year-round. However, there is a tasting room in Waterbury Center, next to Cold Hollow Cider Mill, open year-round that keeps regular hours. The Tonks family created the tasting room because it's an easier retail location for people to find.

Wines: $–$$

Grape Wines

DeChaunac—A dry, light red wine. Smooth. Nice fruit. Tart.

Seyval—A fruity, light white wine.

Fruit Wines

Montmorency Cherry—Light, semisweet red wine. A tart mouthful of cherries. ♥

Raspberry-Apple—A blended fruit wine. Light, blush-type color. Light and tart. ♥

Raspberry Infusion—A deep red, dry wine made from raspberries and grapes. Surprisingly drinkable to dry red wine drinkers. Nice.

Ciders

Mac Jack Hard Cider—Off-dry, fizzy, 100% apple cider. Tart and refreshing.

Other Wines

Blueberry, Dandelion, Elderberry, Pear, Rhubarb, Riesling

REVIEWS AND AWARDS

Raspberry-Apple: "This is a great dessert wine—fresh and fruity, light, tart, on the sweet side. Very flavorful." ———Lisa Shea, About.com (May 2001)

HOURS AND DIRECTIONS Open May–Nov. Call for hours. ■ Tasting room: From I-89, take Rte. 100 north. Pass Ben & Jerry's on the left. Continue. Cold Hollow Cider Mill and the Grand View Winery Outlet Shop at The Connection are on the right. ■ Winery: Call for directions.

Green Mountain Cidery   ✪ ✪

153 Pond Ln., Middlebury, VT 05753 • Phone 802-885-2599 •
Fax 802-885-1120 • www.woodchuck.com • info@woodchuck.com

Woodchuck Draft Cider was originally made at Joseph Cerniglia Winery, but after partnering with international beer manufacturer Stroh's, it became a huge seller across the United States and Canada. Woodchuck eventually became a subsidary of Bulmers America and was moved to its new cidery. The ciders are made with champagne yeast in this massive, high-tech, gleaming facility.

Ciders: $–$$

Vermont Old Fashioned Hard Cider—A still table cider.

Woodchuck Draft Cider (Amber)—100% McIntosh. Fizzy, slightly sweet cider.

Woodchuck Draft Cider (Colonial Oak Aged)—Dark cider with a distinct vanilla smoothness to it. Made like they did before the American Revolution.

Woodchuck Draft Cider (Dark and Dry)—100% McIntosh. Added caramelized sugar adds color and caramel and apple flavor. Not as sweet as the Amber. ♥

Woodchuck Draft Cider (Granny Smith)—100% Granny Smith. Dry, fine cider. Fizzy and elegant. ♥ ♥

Woodchuck Pear Cider (Pear Essence)—A sweet pear/apple cider. More desserty. ♥ ♥

REVIEWS AND AWARDS

Woodchuck Dark and Dry—Best of Show, 2001 Albany International Beer Festival.

Woodchuck Amber: "Golden, medium light body, mild bitterness, medium sweetness, reminiscent of—apple cider, fresh herbs. Crisp and pleasant in character with a concentrated apple finish." ———Beverage Testing Institute

Woodchuck Amber: "Good balance of sweetness, fragrant fruity aroma and pleasant effervescence. A real cider but not that complex." —Denning, *Barley Corn Magazine*

Woodchuck Dark and Dry: "Tawny brown, has a medium light body, mild bitterness, mild sweetness reminiscent of apple, cinnamon, and nutmeg. Well-defined and quite tart on the palate with a mouthwatering refreshing character." ———Beverage Testing Institute

Woodchuck Dark and Dry: "Rich sweet flavor, with some sharp notes." ———Goldman, *Barley Corn Magazine*

HOURS AND DIRECTIONS Not open to the public. Products may be bought in stores across the country. ■ Green Mountain Cidery is located just off Rte. 7 in the quaint college town of Middlebury.

Joseph Cerniglia Winery

98 Winery Rd., Proctorsville, VT 05153 • Phone 800-654-6382 or
802-226-7812 • Also 37 West Rd., Bennington, VT 05201 •
Phone 802-442-3531

Set back in the woods off Rte. 103 in Proctorsville is a nice little winery. However, little though they may seem, they are world famous for their cider, known as Woodchuck Cider. Woodchuck, which is available throughout the United States, has been around since the 1980s. (The inspiration for the cider was the classic draught drawn from English pub ciders famous for centuries.) Interestingly, the success of Woodchuck drew the attention of a spirits industry giant. Stroh's bought half of Joseph Cerniglia Winery's cider operation in 1996. They immediately took 1% of the entire beer market. It was so successful other imitators followed. Woodchuck is now made at the Green Mountain Cidery. However, at the winery they also make other apple and fruit wines and ciders (including a delicious nonalcoholic version) that are not available elsewhere, so a trip to the winery is a fun and wonderful idea.

Wines: $–$$

Blueberry—A sweet dessert wine.

Pear—Light, sweet white wine made from Vermont pears.

Wassail—Spiced wine with orange peel and spices. Nice.

Other Wines

Empire, Granny Smith, McIntosh, Northern Spy, Peach, Raspberry

HOURS AND DIRECTIONS Open daily 10 a.m.–5 p.m. ▪ Call for directions.

North River Winery

P.O. Box 258, River Rd. (Rte. 112), Jacksonville, VT 05342 •
Phone 802-368-7557 • www.vtnatural.com/winery/winery.htm •
winery@vtnatural.com

North River Winery is Vermont's first bonded winery. It is located in the rolling foothills of Windham County, not far from the North River. The winery is housed in a renovated farmhouse and barn from 1850. The winery was started in 1985 by Dan Purjes and produces 16,000 gallons of wine a year, making it one of the largest wineries in all of New England (90% of the fruit is grown organically at Dwight Miller Orchards, in Vermont).

North River makes fruit wines and ciders that are served in prestigious restaurants throughout New England. Most notably, their cider is served at the Simon Pearce Restaurant, at The Mill, in Quechee. The winery has won numerous awards and is a treat to visit any time of year. It embodies New England charm and makes delicious beverages.

Wines: $

Fruit Wines

Blueberry Apple—Sweet, full-bodied dessert wine. Distinct blueberry flavor. ♥

Cranberry Apple—Tart, off-dry, seasonal favorite. Great with poultry.

Northern Spy—Dry, oak-aged apple wine. Crisp and clean white wine.

Proprietor's Reserve—Burnt Hill Farm blueberries, barrel fermented, and aged in oak.

Raspberry Apple—Semisweet, slightly tart apple-raspberry blend.

Rhubarb—A tart, off-dry, medium-bodied wine made from 100% organically grown rhubarb.

Vermont Harvest—Sherry-like dessert wine. Sweet. Made with apples, cinnamon, and 10% Vermont maple syrup. Different. Interesting. ♥

Vermont Pear—100% Vermont-grown Bartlett pears. Dry and smooth. ♥

Ciders
Metcalfe's Hard Cider—Off-dry apple thirst quencher. ♥

Other Wines
Green Mountain Apple, Vermont Blush, Woodland Red

REVIEWS AND AWARDS
Blueberry Apple—Silver medal, 1997 International Eastern Wine Competition; silver medal, 1997 Indiana State Fair Indy International Wine Competition.

Cranberry Apple—Silver medal, 1997 International Eastern Wine Competition.

Metcalfe's Hard Cider—Gold medal, International Eastern Wine Competition.

Vermont Harvest—Gold medal, Indiana State Fair Indy International Wine Competition.

Vermont Pear—Bronze medal, 1997 International Eastern Wine Competition; bronze medal, 1997 Indiana State Fair Indy International Wine Competition.

HOURS AND DIRECTIONS Open daily 10 a.m.–5 p.m. year-round. ■ North River Winery is located on Rte. 112, just south of Jacksonville. ■ The winery has a second location in Bennington (60 West Rd.). Call for hours: 802-442-9463.

Ottauquechee Valley Winery

P.O. Box 423, Quechee, VT 05059 • Phone 800-295-9463 • www.vtnatural.com/OVW/OVW.htm • winery2@vtnatural.com

Housed in the historical Dewey barn complex, Ottauquechee Valley Winery is filled with Vermont-made wines, Cabot specialty cheeses, gourmet olive oils, and other wine-related items. The cozy shop is trimmed out in natural pine and maple. It is warm and inviting. This award-winning winery in lower Vermont is as easy day trip from almost anywhere in New England and well worth the journey.

Wines: $–$$
Autumn Harvest—Apple-cherry blend. Tart, sweet, and refreshing dessert wine.

Midnight Gold—A rhubarb-honey blend. A sweet dessert wine.

Vermont Apple—Off-dry green apple wine. Tart and refreshing.

Vermont Pear—100% Bartlett pears from Vermont. Dry and smooth.

Woodstock Red—Apple-blueberry blend. Some oak. Off-dry.

Woodstock White—Apple-pear blend. A dry white wine, lightly oaked.

REVIEWS AND AWARDS
Autumn Harvest—Silver medal, 2000 Indiana State Fair Indy International Wine Competition; bronze medal, 2000 International Eastern Wine Competition.

Woodstock White—Silver medal, 2000 International Eastern Wine Competition; silver medal, 2000 Indiana State Fair Indy International Wine Competition.

HOURS AND DIRECTIONS Open daily 10 a.m.–5 p.m. year-round. ■ From I-89, take Rte. 4 south. The winery is located just east of the famous Quechee Bridge and Gorge on Rte. 4, in Quechee.

Putney Mountain Winery

71 Holland Hill Rd., Putney, VT 05346 • Phone 802-387-4610 • Putneywine@aol.com

Putney Mountain Winery is a more specialized winery. At Putney Mountain, they focus on sparkling wines made from heirloom apples. But they make still wines too. Putney Mountain can produce up to 12,000 bottles of varying kinds of ciders. It is owned by Charles and Kate Dodge, and is a wonderful little winery.

Wines: $

Fruit Wines
Blueberry Blush—Light blueberry blush wine. Semisweet and tart.
Putney Pommeau—Sweet, port-like dessert wine made from apples.
Simply Rhubarb—A tart, semisweet white wine.

Ciders
Heirloom Cuvée—A dry, champagne-like apple wine. Nice bubbles. Creamy, smooth.
Zeke's Russett—Fizzy apple cider. Named for bearded orchardist Ezekiel Goodband at Scott Farm. Cobalt blue champagne bottle.

Other Wines
Apple Brandy, *Green Mountain Mac*, *Northern Spy*, *Simply Rhubarb*, and more.

HOURS AND DIRECTIONS Call for hours and directions. You can also find their wines at the Putney General Store (Main St., Putney, VT. 05346, phone 802-387 5842).

Shelburne Vineyard

70 Pierson Dr., Shelburne, VT 05482 • Phone 802-985-2991 • kalbert5@ibm.net

Kenneth Albert, a former IBM executive, had a dream of owning a winery. In 1998 he realized that dream. He leased 2.5 acres from Shelburne Farms, located east of Lake Champlain, and established a vineyard. He plowed in January of 1998, planted vines in May, and watched them grow. With the recent addition of co-winemaker Scott Prom and vineyard manager Christine Castigren, the winery offers a range of grape and fruit wines. Albert and Shelburne Farms have a plan to expand the operations. A trip to the winery and the farm store is a wonderful day trip.

Wines: $–$$

White Wines
Cayuga White—A medium-bodied, dry wine. Crisp and citrusy. Nice.
Lake View White—Light, semisweet white wine. Blend of Riesling and Vignoles.
Riesling Ice Wine—Sweet dessert wine. Honey and apricot come through. Nice balance.

Red Wines
Merlot—A smooth, medium-bodied, dry red. Aged in French oak. Cherries come through.

Fruit Wines
Country Blue—Off-dry blueberry wine. Rich fruit. Medium bodied.
Midnight Blue—Medium-bodied, dry red wine. Berry nose. Nice oak. Nice balance.
Moonlight Blue—Sweet blueberry wine. Nice acidity. Lightly oaked.

HOURS AND DIRECTIONS Call for appointments and directions.

Snow Farm Vineyard ✡

190 W. Shore Rd., South Hero, VT 05486 • Phone and Fax 802-372-9463 • snowfarm@compuserve.com • Tasting Room: Cabot Annex/Green Mountain Chocolate Complex • Rte. 100, Waterbury, VT 05676 • Phone 802-244-7118

Yankee Magazine named Snow Farm Vineyard the "Editor's Pick" in its "Fall 2002 New England" issue. Molly and Harrison Lebowitz founded Snow Farm in 1995, with a desire to make wine and keep the land in agricultural use. The winemaker is Patrick Barrelet, who has a degree in enology from Dijon, France. Marilyn Connor (sales executive) and Roberta Courtney (tasting room manager) round out the crew.

Snow Farm has been featured in numerous publications, including *Wine Spectator*, *Appellation Magazine*, *Food & Wine*, the *Boston Globe*, the *Houston Chronicle*, and *Wine East*. It was also the subject of an essay by Tom Brookes in March 2001 on National Public Radio's *Weekend Edition*.

Wines: $-$$

White Wines

Riesling—A dry, light white. Grapefruit comes across.

Snow White—Sweet blend of Cayuga and Seyval. Light and enjoyable. ♥

Vignoles—Honey, light citrus nose. Tropical fruits. Dry, clean, crisp white.

Red Wines

Baco Noir—Smoky, medium-bodied red wine. Nice oak flavor. Cherry comes through.

Crescent Bay Red—Off-dry blend of Leon Millot, Baco Noir, and Pinot Noir. Tangy.

REVIEWS AND AWARDS

Baco Noir—Silver medal, 2001 Tasters Guild International Wine Competition.

HOURS AND DIRECTIONS Open May 1–Dec. 31 daily, 10 a.m.–5 p.m. ■ In Vermont, take exit 17 off I-89 and follow Rte. 2 about 11 miles west. Then follow winery signs from Rte. 2 or Rte. 314 in South Hero.

VIRGINIA

Abingdon Vineyard

20530 Alvardo Rd., Abingdon, VA 24211 • Phone 540-623-1255 •
Fax 276-623-0125 • www.abingdonwinery.com • info@abingdonwinery.com

Abingdon Vineyard is a small Virginia Farm Winery located on the far southwestern side of the state. It is owned and run by Janet Lee Nordin and Bob Carlson, former AT&T executives, and their Houston-based partners Richard and Cheryl Nordin. Janet and Bob, who also ran a Florida hotel successfully for some time, thought running a winery would be something to keep them healthy, active, and creative. They began planting their grapes in the late 1990s and successfully planted more than 6,000 vines on 10 acres. The entire parcel is 53 acres. Both are master gardeners, and both took extra course work at various universities to learn more about winemaking. The winery has two mascots, known as the "Winery Dogs." Sunshine, a cocker spaniel, and Lady, a Border collie, are very much employees. It's a nice little visit.

Wines: $–$$

White Wines

Chardonnay—A dry white wine aged in oak.
Misty River—A dry white table wine made from Chardonel.
Misty River II—A sweet white table wine made from Seyval.

Red Wines

Alvarado Rouge—A sweet red table wine. Different. Tangy.
Cabernet Franc—An aged-in-oak, dry red; 100% Cabernet Franc grapes.
Nouveau—An unaged, dry red table wine made from Chambourcin. Fresh. Nice.

Blush Wines

Appalachian Sunset—A semisweet blush table wine. Nice.

Other Wines

Chambourcin, Chardonel, Norton, Razzle, Riesling, Traminette, Vidal Blanc

HOURS AND DIRECTIONS Open Mar. 15–Dec. 15 Fri.–Sun. noon–6 p.m. ■ From I-81 in Virginia take exit 19. Proceed east toward Damascus on U.S. 58 for 5 miles. Turn right on Rte. 722 (Oseola Rd.), which becomes Rte. 710 (Alvarado Rd.), and proceed 2.4 miles. The winery will be just after a sharp hairpin turn; the driveway is on the right. Look for the grape cluster signs beginning at U.S. 58 and Rte. 722 to lead you in.

Afton Mountain Vineyards

234 Vineyard Ln., Afton, VA 22920 • Phone 540-456-8667 • Fax 540-456-8002 • www.virginiawines.org/wineries/afton.html • corpora@cfw.com

Tom and Shinko Corpora bought 52 acres in the Rockfish Valley that included 5 acres of vines and a small winery. Tom (who had worked for UPI and NBC News) was from Los Angeles, and Shinko was from Japan. They have since renovated this winery, expanding and updating the tasting room and improving the beautiful cellars. Tom now manages the vineyards, and Shinko is the winemaker. Together they make more than 3,000 cases of wine each year. This is a beautiful winery, and they make some tasty wines. You'll be glad you stopped by.

Wines: $–$$

White Wines

Gewürztraminer—Dry, crisp Gewürztraminer. Spicy and clean.

Mountain White—Chardonnay and Riesling blend. Semisweet white. Smooth and easy drinking.

Unwooded Chardonnay—Completely stainless steel. Tropical fruits. Clean finish.

Red Wines

Cardinal Point Cabernet Sauvignon—Big, deep red, 5–10% Cabernet Franc. Spicy Dry. ♥

Festiva Red—Medium-bodied red blend. Fruity and spicy. Clean finish.

Other Wines

Barrel Select Chardonnay, Merlot, Mountain Rose Riesling, Pinot Noir

REVIEWS AND AWARDS

Michael Shaps Cabernet Franc Monticello and *Estate Bottled Chardonnay 2001*— Gold medals, 2003 Virginia State Fair Wine Competition.

HOURS AND DIRECTIONS Open Mar.–Dec. Wed.–Mon. 10 a.m.–6 p.m. (5 p.m. Nov.–Dec.); Jan.–Feb. Fri.–Mon. 11 a.m.–5 p.m.; or by appointment. Closed Easter, Thanksgiving, Christmas, and New Year's day. ■ From Charlottesville, take I-64 west to exit 107, go west on Rte. 250 for 6 miles to Rte. 151, south 3 miles to Rte. 6, west 1.8 miles to Rte. 631, and south 1.2 miles to the vineyard entrance. ■ From Staunton, take I-64 east to exit 99, go east on Rte. 250 for 1.3 miles to Rte. 6, east 1.7 miles to Rte. 631, and south 1.2 miles to the entrance.

AmRhein Wine Cellars

9243 Patterson Dr., Bent Mountain, VA 24059 • Phone 540-387-4632 • Fax 540-387-1869 • www.roanokewine.com • jackieamrhein@att.net

AmRhein Wine Cellars is a small winery tucked into the gorgeous countryside southwest of Roanoke. This award-winning winery is run by Russ Amrhein and winemaker Steve Bolleter. They draw their grapes from three vineyards they own, from among 25,000 vines planted. The winery was begun in 1995. So far the results have been good. They have won a number of medals. And in 2002 AmRhein took the Governor's Cup with their 2001 Viognier, as well as winning three additional medals! Seems like Russ and Steve are doing things right.

Wines: $–$$

White Wines

Traminette—Light, off-dry wine. Floral nose. Citrus finish.

Vidal Blanc—A light white wine. Semisweet. Nice fruit. Smooth finish. ♥

Viognier—A complex white, fruity wine with nuances of oak. Well-balanced. Nice acidity. ♥

Red Wines

Cabernet Franc—Soft, dry red wine. Cherries and raspberries come through. Spicy.

Chambourcin—Dry, medium-bodied red wine. Plum comes through. Tart finish.

Merlot—A medium-bodied, dry wine. Cherry-plum and black currant.

Dessert Wines

Vidal Late Harvest—Golden, intense dessert wine. Tropical fruit. Nicely balanced. ♥

Other Wines

Petit Verdot, Pinot Grigio, Ruby, Virginia White Table Wine

REVIEWS AND AWARDS

Chardonnay 2001, Pinot Grigio 2001, and *Vidal Blanc 2001*—Gold medals, 2003 Virginia State Fair.

Merlot 2001—Gold medal, 2003 Virginia Wine Competition.

Vidal Blanc—Silver medal, 2002 Virginia Wine Honors; gold medal, 2001 Vinifera Wine Growers Association, Virginia Competition.

Vidal Late Harvest 2001—Governor's Cup, 2003 Virginia Governor's Cup Competition; silver medal, San Francisco International Wine Competition.

Viognier 2001—Governor's Cup, 2002 Virginia's Governor's Cup Competition.

HOURS AND DIRECTIONS Open year-round Fri.–Sun. noon–5 p.m. ■ From the Blue Ridge Pkwy. at milepost 136 (Agney Gap), exit to Rte. 221 (south), travel 0.7 mile, and turn right onto Rte. 644. Travel 1.2 miles; when the road forks, turn right on Patterson Rd. Travel 0.5 miles and turn right at the sign for AmRhein Wine Cellars.

Autumn Hill Vineyards / Blue Ridge Winery ✪

301 River Dr., Stanardsville, VA 22973 • Phone 804-985-6100 • www.autumnhillwine.com • autumnhill@mindspring.com

Ed and Avra Schwab, along with their three children, began planting the Autumn Hill vineyards in 1979. Today they have 13 acres planted. In 1986 the original winery produced 300 cases. They quickly needed to grow, and established a new winery in 1989. Currently making around 1,600 cases of wine each year, they hope to grow to 2,500. Let's hope so. Autumn Hill has won numerous awards for their wines, and deservedly so. Their motto has been: "Virginia wine with a European accent." The wine is mature, tasty, and fun. And the new deck—and the view from that deck—are spectacular.

Wines: $–$$

White Wines

Chardonnay—A flavorful, dry, Chablis-like wine. Light and fine. ♥

Chardonnay Vintners Reserve—Well-oaked Chardonnay. Melon comes through. Nice.

Riesling—Off-dry. A floral nose. Green apple comes through. Smooth, citrus finish.

Red Wines

Cabernet Franc—A medium-bodied, dry red. Cherry comes through. Soft and smooth.

Horizon Rouge—Bordeaux-style, dry red. Unfiltered blend of Cabernet Sauvignon, Merlot, and Cabernet Franc. Mellow, smooth, and very drinkable. ♥

Merlot—Medium-bodied red. Plum and black cherry.

Blush Wines

White Cabernet Sauvignon—Light pink color. Semisweet blush made from Cab. Nice.

REVIEWS AND AWARDS

Cabernet Franc 2000—Silver medal, 2001 San Diego National Wine Competition.

Cabernet Franc 1999—Bronze medal, 2000 San Diego National Wine Competition.

Cabernet Sauvignon 1998—Silver medal, 2000 Atlanta Wine Summit; silver medal, 2001 *Dallas Morning News* Wine Competition.

Horizon Rouge—Silver medal, 2001 Vinifera Wine Growers Association, Virginia Competition; bronze medal, 2000 San Francisco International Wine Competition; bronze medal, 2000 San Diego National Wine Competition; bronze medal, 2001 Atlanta Wine Summit.

Horizon Rouge 5th Edition—Gold medal, 2003 Virginia State Fair.

Cabernet Sauvignon 1995: 84 points   —Beverage Testing Institute

HOURS AND DIRECTIONS Call for hours. ■ Autumn Hill Vineyards is located 15 miles north of Charlottesville. From Charlottesville, take Rte. 29 to Rte. 33 west at Ruckersville, proceed on 33 west 2 miles to Quinque. Turn left at Rte. 633 (Amicus Rd.) and proceed 6.5 miles to where 633 ends at Rte. 603 (Bingham Mtn. Rd.). Turn left on Bingham Mtn. Rd. and proceed 1 mile to the winery, on the left.

Barboursville Vineyards   ✬ ✬

17655 Winery Rd., Barboursville, VA 22923 • Phone 540-832-3824 • Fax 540-832-7572 • www.barboursvillewine.com • bvvy@barboursvillewine.com

"Keep an eye open for Barbera and Pinot Grigio," writes Tom Stevenson in his remarks about Barboursville in *The New Sotheby's Wine Encyclopedia.*

Barboursville Vineyards is named for former Virginia governor James Barbour. The land and what was the former residence is where the winery and vineyards are now located. The house, built in 1814, was designed by Thomas Jefferson. But it burned down on Christmas 1884.

The winery is owned and operated by Giovannia Zonin, whose family has been making wine for more than 200 years in Italy. This winery is their foothold in the New World, along with winemaker Luca Paschina and vineyard manager Fernando Franco. Of the 875 magnificent acres, 175 are planted to vines. They have a delightful restaurant as well. This is a wonderful winery that makes quality wine—a must if you are going to visit Virginia wineries.

Wines: $–$$$

White Wines

Chardonnay—Stainless steel Chard. Fresh, crisp, and clean. Apple, pear, and lemon.

Pinot Grigio—Italian-style white. Apple and pear come through. Dry.

Riesling—Off-dry, well-balanced German-style white. Pear. Citrusy ending.

Sauvignon Blanc—Crisp and bright. Pear comes through. Slightly citrusy. ♥

Red Wines

Barbera Reserve—Italian-style, dry red. Raspberries and plums. Smooth, dry finish. ♥

Cabernet Franc—Dry, medium-bodied red. Berries and plums. Soft.

Cabernet Sauvignon—Dry red wine. Currant comes through. Nice oak.

Pinot Noir—Medium-bodied, dry red. Black cherry comes through. Smoky. Nice oak. ♥

Sparkling and Dessert Wines

Barboursville Brut—A dry, fine blend of Chardonnay and Pinot Noir. Pear comes through. Creamy mid- to late palate. Good. ♥

Malvaxia Reserve—Late-harvest Malvasia. Rich, opulent dessert wine. Apricot and pear notes. Some vanilla. Great depth. Very good. ♥ ♥

Phileo—Light dessert wine. Blend of Moscato, Gewürztraminer, and more. Very nice. ♥

Other Wines

Cabernet Sauvignon Reserve, Chardonnay Reserve, Merlot, Nebbiolo Reserve, Octagon IV, Sangiovese, Viognier Reserve

REVIEWS AND AWARDS

Barboursville Brut—Gold medal, 2002 Pacific Rim International Wine Competition.

Cabernet Franc 1997—Governor's Cup, 1999 Virginia Governor's Cup Wine Competition.

Cabernet Franc 2000—Gold medal, 2002 Pacific Rim International Wine Competition.

Cabernet Sauvignon 2001—Gold medal, 2003 Virginia Wine Competition.

Chardonnay Reserve 2001—Gold medal, 2003 Virginia Wine Competition.

Nebbiolo Reserve 1998—Gold medal, 2002 San Francisco International Wine Competition.

Octagon V—Double gold medal and gold medal, 2003 International Eastern Wine Competition.

Phileo—Gold medal, 2003 Virginia State Fair.

Sauvignon Blanc 2001—Best in Show, 2002 Vinifera Wine Growers Association, Virginia Competition.

Barbera Reserve: "The tight, lean, sharp smokiness of Barboursville barbera is appealingly reminiscent of the red wines of the Loire Valley."
—Karen MacNeil, *The Wine Bible*

HOURS AND DIRECTIONS Open year-round Mon.–Sat. 10 a.m.–5 p.m., Sun. 11 a.m.–5 p.m. ■ From Washington, D.C., follow I-66 west to Rte. 29 south to Ruckersville. Turn left on Rte. 33 east and go 6 miles, turn right onto Rte. 20 south, take the first left onto Rte. 678, continue 0.5 mile, turn right onto Rte. 777, and turn into the first driveway on the right. ■ From Richmond, follow I-64 west toward Charlottesville; at exit 136 (Zion Crossroads) take Rte. 15 north toward Gordonsville. In Gordonsville take Rte. 33 west, turn left onto Rte. 20 south, and follow the local directions above.

Boundary Rock Farm & Vineyard

414 Riggins Rd., Willis, VA 22973 • Phone 540-789-7098 • boundaryrock@yahoo.com

Tony Equale and Mary Risacher say that farming is a way of life for them—and that winemaking has kept them close to the earth and their 48-acre farm. Tony and Mary at one point in their lives worked and lived with poor farmers in El Salvador, Honduras, and Nicaragua during the war years of the 1980s. These are very interesting people. Their farm, Boundary Rock, is one of the smallest wineries in Virginia, with its 7 acres of vineyards being tended by the couple and their family and friends. Visit them and you won't be disappointed.

Wines: $–$$

White Wines

Autumn Dew—Semisweet white wine blend. One of their most popular wines.

Cayuga White—Fruity, off-dry white. Light and refreshing.

Chardonnay—Classic, dry-style white. Nice fruit. Tart finish.

Seyval Blanc—Soft, dry white wine. Green apples come through.

Vidal—Dry, light wine. Refreshing, crisp, and clean.

Vidal-Riesling—70% Vidal, 30% Riesling. Fruity, off-dry white.

Red Wines

Bandera Rossa—Dry, ruby blend. Cherries come through. Tangy.

Cabernet Franc—Dry, barrel-aged red dinner-table wine.

Chambourcin—Dry, Bordeaux-type red. Nice fruits. Smooth.

Highland Red—Semisweet red table wine.

Blush Wines

Summer Rain—Semisweet blush blend. One of their most popular wines.

HOURS AND DIRECTIONS By appointment only. ■ From I-81 south of Roanoke, take exit 114 and proceed eastward about 22 miles to Floyd on Rte. 8. From the stoplight in Floyd go south on Rte. 221 for 9 miles. Turn right onto Rte. 750 (Alum Ridge Rd.) and continue 1 mile. Make another right on Rte. 769 (Ferney Creek Rd.) and proceed 1 mile. Turn left onto Riggins Rd. and go 0.5 mile to the end of the road. Boundary Rock is the last farm on the road.

Breaux Vineyards

36888 Breaux Vineyards Ln., Purcellvelle, VA 20132 • Phone 540-668-6299 • Fax 540-668-6283 • www.breauxvineyards.com • breauxvin@aol.com

Since the beginning of 1997, Breaux has won more than nineteen gold medals in wine competitions across the country. This makes them one of the most decorated wineries of the last 3 years on the entire East Coast! In 1994 Paul and Alexis Breaux fell in love with a gorgeous piece of Virginia land. Along with the land they eventually got, the Breaux inherited a 3-acre vineyard planted in 1985. Dave Collins is Breaux's talented winemaker. Originally the three started making wines for themselves and family and friends. Then they decided to open a winery. New, sparkling equipment was bought, and the rest, as they say, is great wine.

Wines: $–$$

White Wines

Barrel Fermented Chardonnay—Complex, dry white. Aged *sur lie*. Lemony with a creamy, smooth finish. Butterscotch comes through. ♥

Madeleine's Chardonnay—(Madeleine Breaux is Paul and Lexi's daughter.) Stainless steel Chardonnay. Lots of fruit. Nice, dry wine with citrusy ending. Nice.

Sauvignon Blanc—Crisp. Pineapple comes through. Light and tasty. ♥

Seyval Blanc—Granny Smith apple comes through. Light and dry.

Sweet Evangeline—Light, fruity, semisweet wine.

Vidal Blanc—Pear comes through in this light, off-dry wine. Very nice. ♥

Viognier—Honeysuckle nose. Apricot and honeydew come through.

Red Wines

Cabernet Sauvignon—Raspberry comes through. Smoky and spicy. Dry.

Lafayette—Plum and dark cherry come through. Peppery too. Dry, deep. ♥

Merlot—Dark cherries and smoky plum come through. Dry finish.

Dessert Wines

Breaux Soleil—Late-harvest Vidal Blanc. Sweet and rich. Nicely balanced.

REVIEWS AND AWARDS

Barrel Fermented Chardonnay 1999—Gold medal, 2000 Virginia State Fair; gold medal, 2001 Riverside International Wine Competition.

Barrel Fermented Chardonnay 2000—Gold medal, 2001 Virginia State Fair; gold medal, 2002 Riverside International Wine Competition.

Cabernet Sauvignon 1998—Gold medal, 2000 Atlanta Wine Summit; gold medal, 2000 Virginia Governor's Cup Wine Competition; gold medal, 2000 Virginia State Fair.

Lafayette 1997—Best in Class, 1998 Virginia State Fair.

Lafayette 1998—Gold medal, 1999 Virginia State Fair.

Madeleine's Chardonnay 1997—Gold medal, 1998 Virginia State Fair.

Merlot 1998—Gold medal, 2000 Atlanta Wine Summit.

Merlot 1999—Gold medal, 2001 Virginia State Fair; gold medal, 2001 Vinifera Wine Growers Association, Virginia Competition.

Sauvignon Blanc 1999—Gold medal, 2000 Virginia State Fair.

Vidal Blanc 1997—Best in Class, 1999 Virginia State Fair.

Vidal Blanc 1998—Gold medal, 1999 *Dallas Morning News* Wine Competition.

Vidal Blanc 1999—Best in Class, 2000 Virginia State Fair; gold medal, 2000 Long Beach Grand Cru.

Vidal Blanc 2000—Gold medal, 2001 Los Angeles County Fair Wine Competition.

Barrel Fermented Chardonnay 1998: 82 points   —*Wine Enthusiast* (1999)

Madeleine's Chardonnay 1998: 84 points. "Recommended"

—Beverage Testing Institute

Merlot 1999: "Score: 83."   —*Wine Spectator* (May 2002)

HOURS AND DIRECTIONS Open Nov.–Apr. 11 a.m.–5 p.m. daily; May–Oct. 11 a.m.–6 p.m. ■ From Leesburg, take Rte. 7 west approximately 4 miles to Rte. 9 west. Go 8 miles to Hillsboro, then 2 miles to Rte. 671. Bear right onto Rte. 671 and continue 1 mile to Breaux Vineyards (on the right).

Burnley Vineyards

4500 Winery Ln., Barboursville, VA 22923 • Phone 540-832-2828 • Fax 540-832-2280 • www.burnleywines.com • dreeder@rlc.net

Burnley Vineyards' 30-acre estate is one of the oldest vineyards in the Monticello viticulture area. C. J. Reeder, a retired army colonel, is general manager. His son, Lee, is the winemaker, his son's wife, Patt, is in charge of sales, and his wife, Dawn, handles tasting and tours. The family purchased the property in 1976. In 1984, Burnleys' first vintage, 1,000 gallons of Cabernet Sauvignon and Chardonnay, was produced. In 2001, Burnley bottled approximately 5,000 cases of very nice wines. The estate also features a rentable house set within the vineyards for a romantic and wonderful weekend.

Wines: $–$$

White Wines

Chardonnay—A stainless steel, dry white. Slight touch of oak from brief aging.

Moon Mist—White and Orange Muscat and Riesling blend. Sweet and light.

Rivanna White—An off-dry Vidal Blanc. Nice, light wine.

White Cabernet Sauvignon—An off-dry, 100% Cabernet Sauvignon wine.

Red Wines

Cabernet Sauvignon—Unfiltered, dry, deep red.

Rivanna Red—A Beaujolais-style, light red. Chambourcin, Marechal Foch, and Cabernet Franc blend. Fruity yet dry. ♥

Somerset—A light, transparent red wine. Sweet. Blend of Chardonnay, Riesling, Cabernet Franc, Vidal, and Chambourcin. Interesting.

Spicy Rivanna—Rivanna Red spiced with cinnamon, clove, nutmeg, allspice, anise, orange peel, lemon peel, and residual sugar. A wonderful spiced wine. ♥ ♥

Blush Wines

Rivanna Sunset—Chambourcin semisweet blush.

Other Wines

Barrel Fermented Chardonnay, King George, Peach Fuzz, Riesling, Zinfandel

REVIEWS AND AWARDS

Cabernet Sauvignon 1998—Gold medal, 2003 Virginia State Fair.

HOURS AND DIRECTIONS Open Jan.–Mar. Fri.–Mon. 11 a.m.–5 p.m.; Apr.–Dec. daily, 11 a.m.–5 p.m. ■ From Charlottesville, take Rte. 20 north; turn left (west) onto Rte. 641. The winery is 1,700 feet away.

Chateau Morrisette Winery

P.O. Box 766, Meadows of Dan, VA 24120 • Phone 540-593-2865 • Fax 540-593-2868 • www.chateaumorrisette.com • info@chateaumorrisette.com

This is possibly one of the most beautiful wineries you will visit on the East Coast—an estate with breathtaking views. Chateau Morrisette was founded in 1978 by William, Nancy, and David Morrisette. For over 20 years, they have been producing premier wines in Virginia. (Karen MacNeil recommended the winery in *The Wine Bible*.) Many of the wines are named for their mascots—dogs (big, black, lovable Labrador retrievers). But there's not one dog on the wine list. Chateau Morrisette has a number of different wines. From the fun and fruity to the more mature, dry wines, there is something of quality for everyone. A great visit is sure to be had, good weather or bad. And say hello to Jazz, the newest Lab!

Wines: $–$$

White Wines

Black Dog Blanc—Off-dry, soft Chardonnay blend. Fruity. Tart. ♥

Chardonnay—Well-balanced, dry wine. Apple and pineapple come through.

Our Dog Blue—Semisweet Riesling blend. Characteristics of honeydew and apricot highlight this refreshing wine. A great summer fruit soup wine! Wonderful. ♥ ♥

Vidal Blanc—Off-dry, light, crisp citrus aromas of grapefruit and pineapple. ♥

Red Wines

Black Dog—Smooth, semisweet red wine. Deep, rich berry comes through.

Cabernet Franc—Dry, medium-bodied red. Blackberry, vanilla, and oak come through.

Cabernet Sauvignon—Dry, full-bodied red. Plum, spice, and oak.

Merlot—Dry, medium-bodied red. Blackberry jam. Herbaceous.

Dessert Wines

Frosty Dog—A late-harvest Riesling. Tropical, sweet, fruity, intense.

Other Wines

Blushing Dog, Pinot Noir, Red Mountain Laurel, Sweet Mountain Laurel

REVIEWS AND AWARDS

Cabernet Sauvignon 1999—Bronze medal, 2001 Vinifera Wine Growers Association, Virginia Competition.

Pinot Noir 1999—Bronze medal, 2001 Vinifera Wine Growers Association, Virginia Competition.

Virginia Chardonnay 2001—Best in Show, 2003 Virginia State Fair.

HOURS AND DIRECTIONS Open year-round Mon.–Thurs. 10 a.m.–5 p.m., Fri.–Sat. 10 a.m.–6 p.m., Sun. 11 a.m.–5 p.m. ■ From Charlotte, N.C., take I-77 north to Fancy Gap exit. Turn right onto Rte. 52 south. Follow Rte. 52; watch for the entrance sign to the Blue Ridge Pkwy. Head north on the parkway; watch for milepost 172. Approximately 0.5 mile beyond it, turn left onto Black Ridge Rd. and then immediately left onto Winery Rd. Chateau Morrisette is located approximately 300 yards down on the right. ■ From the D.C. area, take I-66 west to I-81 south to exit 114 (Floyd/Christiansburg); turn left onto Rte. 8 south and follow it approximately 22 miles into Floyd; continue through the stoplight and proceed approximately 6 miles until you see an entrance sign to the Blue Ridge Pkwy. in Tuggles Gap. Head south on the parkway; watch for milepost 171. Proceed approximately 0.5 mile past it, turn right onto Black Ridge Rd., and follow the local directions above.

Christensen Ridge

HCR 02 Box 459, Madison, VA 22727 • Phone 540-923-4800 • Fax 540-923-4900 • www.christensenridge.com

Enjoy an hour, a day, or a week on Christensen Ridge's more than 200 acres of the Blue Ridge with beautiful views of mountains, farmland, and a vineyard with some of the oldest vinifera vines in Virginia. Taste owner Larry Christensen's premium handcrafted wines. Come for the smoked trout and smoked Cornish game hen. Stay in the 1700s log cabin or modern five-bedroom manor home with pool. The winery offers light fare, sandwiches, etcetera for picnics. Wines include Cabernet Franc, Cabernet Sauvignon, Chardonnay, Merlot, and Viognier.

Wines: $–$$

REVIEWS AND AWARDS

Christensen Ridge Chardonnay 2001—Gold medal, 2003 Virginia Wine Competition.

HOURS AND DIRECTIONS Open year-round Fri.–Sun. 11 a.m.–5 p.m.; also open Tues.–Thurs. 11 a.m.–5 p.m. in Oct. Open Labor Day. ■ From the D.C. area, take I-66 west to the Gainesville exit. Follow Rte. 29 south to Madison and take the business exit to Rte. 231 at the north end of the main street; go north on Rte. 231 for 4 miles to Rte. 651. Turn left, go 2 miles, turn right onto Rte. 652, go 0.1 mile, turn left onto Rte. 698, and go 0.7 mile to the winery, passing the centuries-old farms of Madison County.

Chrysalis Vineyards

23876 Champe Ford Rd., Middleburg, VA 20117 • Phone 800-235-8804 or
540-687-8222 • Fax 540-687-8666 • www.chrysaliswine.com •
info@chrysaliswine.com

Chrysalis Vineyards is the dream come true of Jennifer McCloud. The name comes
from the idea that the grapes turn into wines like caterpillars turn into butterflies. The
winery is the chrysalis. Although relatively new, Chrysalis has made an immediate
mark. The Viognier is a smashing success, and the Chardonnay is also wonderful. On
the 209-acre farm, Jennifer has planted 51 acres to vines, many to different types of
grapes, mostly Spanish and Portuguese varieties, in order to establish different wines
from what everyone else is making. Chrysalis wines are served at the famous Inn at
Little Washington. You'll be hearing more about Jennifer and Chrysalis.

Wines: $-$$

White Wines

Alan Kinne Virginia Chardonnay—Fermented *sur lie*. Dry, rich, creamy white.

Sarah's Patio White—Off-dry white blend. Light, refreshing.

Viognier—Dry white wine. Vibrant floral nose. Apricots, peaches, and pears come
through. ♥ ♥

Red Wines

Norton-Locksley Reserve—A deep, dry red. Medium bodied but with plum. Nice.

Rubiana—A blend of Tempranillo (19%), Graciano (35%), Cabernet Sauvignon (24%),
Fer Servadou (18%), and Tannat (4%) grapes. A medium-bodied, dry red wine. ♥

Blush Wines

Mariposa—A dry, spicy rosé.

Dessert Wines

Petit Manseng—Traditionally grown in the Jurançon region of Southwest France.
Aromatic, sweet dessert wine. Golden. Honey, candied fruit, and spice.
Very nice.

REVIEWS AND AWARDS

Alan Kinne Virginia Chardonnay 1999—Gold medal, 2000 Virginia State Fair.

Alan Kinne Virginia Chardonnay 2000—Silver medal, 2001 Vinifera Wine Growers
Association, Virginia Competition.

Petit Manseng 2001—Gold medal, 2003 Virginia State Fair.

Viognier 1999—Best in Show, 2000 Virginia State Fair.

Viognier 2000—Best in Show, 2001 Vinifera Wine Growers Association, Virginia
Competition

Viognier 2001—Gold medal, 2003 Virginia State Fair; Best of Show, white wines,
2001 San Diego National Wine Competition.

"Everything is accomplished with a strict attention to detail and quality that is
required to make world-class wines."   —Guy Bell, *Potomac News* (May 31, 2000)

HOURS AND DIRECTIONS Open daily 10 a.m.–5 p.m. year-round. ■ From Washington,
D.C., take I-66 west to U.S. 50. Go west to Champe Ford Rd. (Rte. 629). A good landmark on the way is Gilbert's Corner (U.S. 50 and U.S. 15), which is 17 miles west-
northwest of I-66 and U.S. 50. From Gilbert's Corner continue west on U.S. 50 another
2.5 miles to Champe Ford Rd. (Rte. 629). Turn left (south) and go 1.3 miles to the
entrance to Chrysalis Vineyards, on your left.

Cooper Vineyards

13372 Shannon Hill Rd., Louisa, VA 23093 • Phone 540-894-5253 •
Fax 804-285-8773 • www.coopervineyards.com • gcooper@erols.com

Situated on an eroded volcanic ridgeline in the center of Louisa County, Cooper Vineyards planted their first vines in 1999. It is a small, family-owned farm winery. Everything here is done by family and friends. The feeling is that of a warm, human collective of positive people. They produce small quantities of distinctive wines and sponsor numerous events at the vineyard throughout the year—well worth the visit.

Wines: $–$$

White Wines

Rhapsody—A sweet Vidal Blanc, Chardonnay, and Chardonel blend.

Red Wines

Cabernet Sauvignon—Aged 1 year in French oak barrels. Unfiltered. Deep and dry.

Electric Harvest—Blend of 65% Chambourcin and 35% Cabernet Sauvignon.

Merlot—Red and black cherry come though. Mellow, full-bodied, dry red.

Sweet Louisa—70% Munson, 30% Chardonnay. Sweet, sangria-like in flavor.

Vin Deco—Merlot Nouveau. Bottled young, by cool carbonic maceration. Refreshing, light, and fruity.

Blush Wines

St. Stephen's Rosé—Lightly sweetened blend of Merlot, Cabernet, Chardonnay, and Vidal Blanc. Peach and strawberry come through.

HOURS AND DIRECTIONS Open year-round Sat.–Sun. 11 a.m.–5 p.m. ■ From I-95 take the Thornburg exit. Follow Rte. 606 west to Snell, then Rte. 208 west to Rte. 522 south through the town of Mineral. Approximately 3 miles past Mineral bear right onto Rte. 605, cross Rte. 33, and the winery entrance is 0.5 miles on left. If you miss it, turn right onto Rte. 522, then left onto Rte. 33. The winery is 0.5 mile on the left.

Deer Meadow Vineyard

199 Vintage Ln., Winchester, VA 22602 • Phone 800-653-6632 or
540-877-1919 • dmeadow@shentel.net

Charles and Jennifer Sarle are the owners of Deer Meadow Vineyard. One of the smaller wineries in Virginia, it's deep in the heart of the country: a tiny, rustic winery hidden in the beautiful Shenandoah Valley. Deer Meadow was a farm for 30 years before it became a winery. They make about 800 cases of wine. But if you have the time, it is a wonderful visit, with rough-hewn buildings, a beautiful pond, and farm animals—truly charming.

Wines: $–$$

White Wines

Afternoon of the Fawn—Slightly sweet, blended white. Peach comes through.

Chardonnay—Rich, buttery, full flavored, and full bodied.

Red Wines

Cabernet Sauvignon—Cherry comes through. Oaky. Nice tannins.

Chambourcin—Medium-bodied dry, spicy red wine. Peppery.

Marechal Foch—Dry and full-bodied red. Blackberry comes through.

HOURS AND DIRECTIONS Open Mar.–Dec. Wed.–Sun. 11 a.m.–5 p.m., or call for an appointment. ■ From I-81 take exit 313 (Winchester); go west on U.S. 50 for 5 miles. Turn left (south) on Rte. 608 for 6.5 miles, then left (east) on Rte. 629 (Laurel Grove) and proceed 1 mile to Vintage Ln., a driveway on the right.

Dominion Wine Cellars

1 Winery Ave., Culpeper, VA 22701 • Phone 540-825-8772 • Fax 540-829-0377 • Rob@AboutVirginiaWine.com

Originally established in 1985 as the Virginia Wineries Co-op, Dominion Wine Cellars is now owned by the Williamsburg Winery and fifteen original growers. It continues to produce award-winning and unique specialty wines, making about 5,000 cases of wine each year. While strongly linked to Williamsburg, Dominion is its own winery—large and beautiful and professionally run. It was the first winery in the country to ferment wine and fruit juices together in the Raspberry and Blackberry Merlots, for which it is well known.

Wines: $–$$$

White Wines
Lord Culpeper—Dry, barrel-aged Seyval Blanc.

Red Wines
Blackberry Merlot—Deep, soft red with mouthful of blackberries.
Filippo Mazzei Reserve—Named for the Italian viticulturist who worked for Thomas Jefferson. A Nebbiolo–Cabernet Sauvignon blend. Deep red. Dry.
Raspberry Merlot—Deep, tart red with mouthful of raspberries.

Dessert Wines
Late Harvest Vidal—A sweet, intense, golden dessert wine.

Other Wines
Blanc de Noirs, *Cabernet Rosé*, *Johannisberg Riesling*

HOURS AND DIRECTIONS Open year-round Mon.–Sat. 10 a.m.–4:30 p.m., Sun. noon–4:30 p.m. Closed Thanksgiving and Christmas. ■ From the Rte. 29 bypass, take the Culpeper exit and follow Rte. 3 west toward Culpeper. Turn right on McDevitt Dr. and continue to Winery Ave.

Dye's Vineyards

RR 2 Box 357, Honaker, VA 24260 • Phone 540-873-4659 • www.dyesvineyards.com • cleodye@yahoo.com

Dye's Vineyards is Russell County's oldest winery. Established in 1996 on a family farm tucked into the southwestern tip of the state, the winery sits on land that has been in the family for more than 200 years. Ken Dye is the proprietor, and John Dye the winemaker. Their 4-acre vineyard is located at the foot of scenic Big A Mountain, named for its size. They have a catered dinner on the third Saturday of each month (reservations required). The winery makes about 3,000 gallons of wine each year.

Wines: $–$$

White Wines
Chardonnay—An off-dry white. Stainless steel. Tart and crisp.
Seyval—A semisweet white wine. Nice fruit. Tart.

Vidal Blanc—A semidry white. Fruity flavor. Crisp and clean.

Red Wines

Cabernet Sauvignon—A dry red wine. Plums and cherries come through.

DeChaunac—An off-dry, deep red wine. Nutty. Rich.

Richlands Red—A full-bodied, semisweet red. Tart.

Villard Noir—A sweet red wine. Big berry flavor. Nice nose.

Dessert Wines

Golden Muscat—A sweet, golden dessert wine. Honey comes through.

Other Wines

Blush, Concord, DeChaunac Rosé, Pink Vidal, Russell Rosé, Russell Rouge, Sainte Marie Foch, Sainte Marie Rosé

HOURS AND DIRECTIONS Open year-round Mon.–Sat. 1 p.m.–dusk. Closed Sundays. ■ Dye's Vineyards is 0.5 mile from Rte. 80, approximately 40 miles from Break's Interstate Park, 35 miles from historical Abingdon, and just 5 miles from Honaker. ■ From U.S. 19, go west on Rte. 80. Turn left at Rte. 620.

Farfelu Vineyards

13058 Crest Hill Rd., Flint Hill, VA 22627 • Phone 540-364-2930 • www.farfeluwine.com • c-osborne@farfeluwine.com

Farfelu Vineyards was established in 1967 by former naval aviator C. J. Raney. It is the Old Dominion's first licensed winery. Upon his retirement from the navy, Chuck Raney planted his vineyard in the foothills of the Blue Ridge, flanking the rolling hills of the Rappahannock River. He named it Farfelu, an ancient French word meaning eccentric. Caroline and John Osborne, along with their children, Meryn and Cole, now run the winery; they bought it in 2000.

Wines: $–$$

White Wines

Chardonnay—Crisp elements of pineapple and citrus. Mellow oak. Vanilla.

Folly—A sweet blend of Cayuga and muscat. Nicely balanced.

Fou de Blanc—Means "crazy white." A Cayuga and Vidal blend. Light and crisp.

Vidal Blanc—Citrus nose. Velvet mouth feel. Off-dry finish.

Red Wines

Cabernet Sauvignon—Plums, chocolate, and licorice come through. Nice tannins.

Fou de Rouge—Means "crazy red." A blend of Sangiovese, DeChaunac, Chancellor, and Syrah. A light, fun red. Berries and cherries come through.

Reserve Syrah—A blend of 80% Syrah and 20% Cabernet Franc. Mellow, rich, and deep.

REVIEWS AND AWARDS

Chardonnay 2001—Gold medal, 2003 Virginia State Fair; silver medal, 2002 Virginia Governor's Cup Wine Competition; silver medal, 2002 Vinifera Wine Growers Association, Virginia Competition; silver medal, 2002 Indiana State Fair Indy International Wine Competition.

Folly 2001—Bronze medal, 2002 Virginia Governor's Cup Wine Competition; bronze medal, 2002 Vinifera Wine Growers Association, Virginia Competition; bronze medal, 2002 Indiana State Fair Indy International Wine Competition.

HOURS AND DIRECTIONS Open year-round Thurs.–Mon. 11 a.m.–5 p.m. ■ From Washington, D.C., take I-66 west. Exit at the second Marshall exit (27). Turn left at the top of the exit ramp, crossing over the highway. Turn right onto Rte. 647 (Crest Hill Rd.), and go 12 miles. Turn left into Farfelu's entrance.

First Colony Winery

1652 Harris Creek Rd., Charlottesville, VA 22902 • Phone 804-979-7105 • Fax 804-979-2303 • www.firstcolonywinery.com • firstcolonywinery@earthlink.net

Formerly known as Totier Creek Vineyard and Winery, First Colony is a wonderful new winery created by Randolph and Margaret McElroy. It is nestled in beautiful Albemarle County, the heart of Virginia wine country. Old-world traditions abound at First Colony with a fourth-generation French winemaker. The 5,000-square-foot tasting room facility includes a variety of indoor and outdoor seating areas available for picnics, group tastings, and private parties. Choose the tree-shaded deck or the sunny brick and slate patio to enjoy a glass of wine.

Wines: $–$$

White Wines

Chardonnay—French-style Chardonnay. Lemony. Butter too.

Chardonnay Reserve—Rich fruit. Nice oak. Buttery. Creamy.

Riesling—Dry, light white wine. Floral nose. Grapefruit and lime. Crisp and clean. Shocking! ♥ ♥

Vidal Blanc—Dry white wine. Apple and pear. Lemon too.

Viognier—Floral nose. Tropical and citrus notes. Long, dry finish.

Red Wines

Cabernet Franc Reserve—Beaujolais-style red. Cherries and berries. Spicy, peppery.

Claret—A blend of Cabernet Sauvignon, Cabernet Franc, and Merlot. Black cherry and plum. Dry.

Dessert Wines

Late Harvest Vidal Blanc—An ice wine. Incredibly sweet. Honey and apricot. Nice.

Other Wines

Blush, Riesling (Off-Dry)

REVIEWS AND AWARDS

Cabernet Franc Reserve 2001—Gold medal, 2002 Virginia Wine Competition.

Chardonnay 2001—Gold medal, 2003 Virginia State Fair; gold medal, 2002 Virginia State Fair; silver medal, 2002 Tasters Guild International Wine Competition; silver medal, 2002 Virginia Governor's Cup Wine Competition.

Chardonnay Reserve 2001—Gold medal, 2003 Virginia State Fair; gold medal, 2002 Virginia State Fair; silver medal, 2002 Virginia Governor's Cup Wine Competition.

HOURS AND DIRECTIONS Open year-round daily, 11 a.m.–5 p.m. ■ The winery is located 15 miles from downtown Charlottesville just south of Monticello. ■ From I-64 take exit 121 (Rte. 20 south) toward Scottsville. Continue 10 miles past the Monticello Visitors Center to a right turn on Rte. 720. The winery is 1 mile farther, at end of road.

Gabriele Rausse Winery

P.O. Box 3956, Charlottesville, VA 22903 • Phone and Fax 804-296-5328

This is what every wine fanatic looks to find—a small gem, hidden away, that is little known. Gabriele Rausse Winery is named for its talented and accomplished winemaker-owner. It is located near Monticello—a good thing, since Gabriele is associate director of gardens and grounds there. A native Italian, he began making wine for the Zonin family in the early 1980s at Barboursville Vineyards. He then became a consultant, working with many winemakers throughout Virginia. His wines are surprisingly complex and well worth the ride to his little winery—except that it's not open to the public! However, the wines are available in some local stores and sell quickly. Call Gabriele to find out which stores. You'd better go now; the secret's already out.

Wines: $-$$

White Wines

Chardonnay—Dry white wine. Nice fruit. Nice finish.

Red Wines

Cabernet Sauvignon—A nice, medium-bodied red with black cherry. Dry finish.

Cabernet Sauvignon Reserve—Plum and blackberries come through. Nice oak. Deep and dry. A lovely red. ♥ ♥

Rosso—A young, light red made from Cabernet Sauvignon and Sangiovese. Black cherry and strawberry come through. Tart ending. ♥

HOURS AND DIRECTIONS Not open to the public.

Gray Ghost

14706 Lee Hwy., Amissville, VA 20106 • Phone 540-937-4869 •
Fax 540-937-4869 • www.tricountyi.net/~nstultz/grayghos.htm

Gray Ghost is located in Amissville. It's an easy place to miss, but if you see the Amissville Fire Department on one side of the road, immediately look across the road. It's over there! The winery is owned by Cheryl and Al Kellert. Its gray and white dormered building and the beautiful vineyards make it a lovely day trip. The Kellerts grow 11 acres of vines and also buy some fruit to make their wines. The name Gray Ghost invokes the heroes of the Civil War. It's a popular historical spot for those interested in John Singleton Mosby. Civil War fans will find lots to love here, and good wine too!

Wines: $-$$

White Wines

Reserve Chardonnay—Vanilla, pear, and spice come through. Nice.

Seyval Blanc—Tart, light white wine. Green apple finish.

Victorian White—A stainless steel Chardonnay. Off-dry. Lemony with a slight sweetness.

Vidal Blanc—A Vidal Blanc/Riesling blend. Crisp. Fruity. Honeydew comes through.

Red Wines

Cabernet Franc—Cherry and raspberry come through. Spicy.

Cabernet Sauvignon—Black cherry and plum come through. Nice tannins. Good.

Reserve Cabernet Sauvignon—Dark and intense. Smooth. Dry. Nice finish.

Dessert Wines

Adieu—Muscat dessert wine. Peach comes through. Very nice. ♥

REVIEWS AND AWARDS

Adieu 2000—Silver medal, San Francisco International Wine Competition; silver medal, Long Beach Grand Cru; silver medal, Amenti del Vino International

Wine Competition; silver medal, Tasters Guild International Wine Competition; silver medal, Indiana State Fair Indy International Wine Competition; silver medal, Wine Lovers Consumer Wine Competition; bronze medal, Los Angeles County Fair Wine Competition.

Adieu 2002—"Best of the East" (Top Ten Wines), 2003 Annual Wineries Unlimited Seminar and Trade Show; gold medal, 2003 Virginia Wine Competition.

Cabernet Franc 2000—Silver medal, Tasters Guild International Wine Competition.

Seyval Blanc 2000—Gold medal, Tasters Guild International Wine Competition.

Vidal Blanc 2000—Gold medal, Tasters Guild International Wine Competition.

HOURS AND DIRECTIONS Open Jan.–Feb. Sat.–Sun. 11 a.m.–5 p.m.; Mar.–Dec. Fri.–Sun. 11 a.m.–5 p.m. ■ From Washington, D.C., go west on I-66 to the Gainesville exit, then west on Rte. 29 to the Warrenton exit (Rte. 29/211). Continue west on Rte. 211 for 11.5 miles to Amissville. Gray Ghost is on left, across from the Amissville Fire Department. ■ From Richmond, take I-95 north to Rte. 17 north to exit 133 (Rte. 29 north). At the first Warrenton exit (Business Rte.) go west on Rte. 211 and follow the local directions above.

Grayhaven Winery

4675 E. Grey Fox Circle, Gum Spring, VA 23065 • Phone and Fax 804-556-3917 • VA-Grayhaven@AllAmericanWineries.com

Charles and Lyn Peple named their winery after Grayhavens in J.R.R. Tolkien's Ring trilogy, where people can live peaceful and successful lives. The entire Peple family pitches in at this vineyard tending the grapes, making wine, and constructing new buildings. The winery was established in 1978. As they like to say, "If we're home, we're open."

Wines: $–$$

White Wines

Chardonnay—An elegant, dry Chardonnay. Nice fruit. Nice finish.

Fumé Blanc—The winery's signature wine. Sauvignon Blanc. Dry, light, and citrusy.

Riesling—An off-dry, grapefruity white wine.

Seyval—A crisp, dry Seyval. Light and refreshing. Tart.

Vidal Blanc—A dry, light, clean, refreshing white wine.

Red Wines

Marechal Foch—A dry, medium-bodied red.

HOURS AND DIRECTIONS Open year-round Sat.–Sun. 10 a.m.–6 p.m. Weekdays, please call ahead. ■ From Richmond, take I-64 west to exit 159 (Gum Springs). Go south 0.3 mile to U.S. 250, turn right onto Providence Three Chopt Rd. for 2.8 miles, then turn right onto New Line Rd. to a right on Shepherd Spring Rd., then bear left onto Fox Chase Run to a right on E. Grey Fox Circle, to the Grayhaven Winery entrance on your right. ■ From Charlottesville, take I-64 east to exit 159 and follow the directions above.

Guilford Ridge Vineyard

328 Running Pine Rd., Luray, VA 22835 • Phone 540-778-3853

Guilford Ridge Vineyard is located on Guilford Ridge, west of the Blue Ridge. The vineyard was established in 1971, but the winery was not established until 1983. Co-owners John Gerba and Harland Baker planted the vineyard in the early 1970s—

4 acres of vines on the 80-acre farm. If you go, get ready for a rustic experience. The tastings are alfresco, rain or shine, and assorted visitors may include llamas, peacocks, goats, sheep, and a potbellied pig. Hey, they were their first!

Wines: $–$$

White Wines

Pinnacles—A crisp, white blend of Seyval, Rayon d'Or, and a touch of Chardonnay. Dry, light, and refreshing. ♥

Red Wines

Page Valley Red—Full-bodied, dry, deep red wine. Blend of Chambourcin, Chelois, and Cabernet Sauvignon. Currants come through. Nice finish.

et Delilah—A light red wine. Beaujolais-style blend of Chambourcin and Chelois. Fruity and tart.

Other Wines

Bel Canto, Caboose

HOURS AND DIRECTIONS Open for tastings federal holiday weekends May–Nov. at 2 and 3 p.m. Reservations required; minimum party 8 adults. Fee $3/person. ■ From the traffic light at the intersection of U.S. 340 and U.S. 211 Business in Luray, go south 4 miles on U.S. 340 Business and west 1 mile on Rte. 632.

Hartwood Winery

345 Hartwood Rd., Fredericksburg, VA 22406 • Phone and Fax 540-752-4893 • jdliving@erols.com

Hartwood Winery is owned by Jim and Beverly Livingston, along with partner David Barber. They grow the grapes and make the wines. The first vineyards were planted in 1984. The winery is named for the deer that are so prevalent in the area. Indeed, a stag's head is the winery's icon. This is a beautiful little spot of the earth, any time of year. Enjoy award-winning wines in a warm and friendly atmosphere. Special events and dinners are held throughout the year. Picnic on the front deck overlooking lovely flowers and the vineyard.

Wines: $–$$

White Wines

Chardonnay—A dry, fruity Chardonnay. Nutty.

DeWeese—A semisweet Vidal Blanc. Nice fruit. Slightly sweet.

Hartwood Station White—A light, fruity, off-dry white. Spicy. A Chardonnay, Seyval Blanc, and Sauvignon Blanc blend. Stainless steel. Tart.

Rappahannock White—A medium-dry white, 50/50 blend of Seyval Blanc and Vidal Blanc. Citrusy.

Seyval Blanc—Nice fruit. Hint of oak. Tart, crisp, and clean.

Red Wines

Claret—A light-bodied wine made from Cabernet Sauvignon grapes. Dry. Cherry comes through.

Rappahannock Red—A light, stainless steel, blended red, Beaujolais style.

HOURS AND DIRECTIONS Open year-round Wed.–Fri. 11 a.m.–5 p.m., Sat.–Sun. 11 a.m.–6 p.m. Closed Thanksgiving, Christmas, and New Year's Day. ■ From the intersection of Rte. 17 and I-95 go 6 miles north on Rte. 17. Turn right on Rte. 612. Go 2 miles; the winery is on the left.

Hickory Hill Vineyards

1722 Hickory Cove Ln., Moneta, VA 24121 • Phone 540-296-1393 •
www.hickoryhillvineyards.com • info@hickoryhillvineyards.com

Owners Roger and Judy Furrow's Hickory Hill Vineyards is located at beautiful Smith Mountain Lake in Bedford County, 15 minutes from the National D-Day Memorial. The small, family-owned winery opened in June 2002 in a renovated 1923 farmhouse that has Virginia country charm. The dining room is converted into a cozy tasting room, and is decorated with artifacts and memorabilia found during the renovation. A screened porch and shade trees provide a relaxing setting for tasting wine and cheese or for a picnic overlooking the vineyard. Wines include Cabernet Sauvignon, Chardonnay, Smith Mountain Lake Red, Smith Mountain Lake White, and Vidal Blanc.

Wines: $–$$

HOURS AND DIRECTIONS Fri.–Mon. 11 a.m.–5 p.m. from spring opening through Oct. Other times call for hours. ■ From Roanoke, take Rte. 24 east to Rte. 122. Turn right on Rte. 122. Just south of Moneta, turn left on Rte. 655, drive 2 miles, and turn right on Rte. 654 (Hickory Cove Ln.). The winery is 0.7 mile on the left.

Hidden Brook Winery

43301 Spinks Ferry Rd., Leesburg, VA 20176 • Phone 703-737-3935 •
www.hiddenbrookwine.com • hiddenbrookwine@aol.com

This is one of Virginia's newest wineries, opened in September 2002 and owned by Eric and Deborah Hauck. Sip wine in their early-American-style log winery. Guests are invited to relax by a cozy fireplace or on the deck overlooking the vineyards and mountains. Wines include Cabernet Sauvignon, Chardonnay, Merlot, and Vidal Blanc.

Wines: $–$$

HOURS AND DIRECTIONS Open year-round Sat.–Sun. 10 a.m.–5 p.m. Closed Easter, Thanksgiving, Christmas, and New Year's Day. ■ Hidden Brook is located 7 miles north of historic Leesburg, off Rte. 15. ■ From Washington, D.C., take I-66 west to Rte. 267 (Dulles access) to the Greenway (Rte. 267.) Take the Rte. 15 north exit and proceed approximately 7.5 miles. Turn right onto Rte. 657 (Spinks Ferry Rd.) and proceed 2.1 miles to the winery on right.

Highlands Harvest Vineyard and Farm Winery

Rte. 1, Box 321, Castlewood, VA 24224 • Fax 540-762-9561 •
buffalo@cablenet-va.com

A crofter's cottage houses this family-owned winery located on a working Virginia Century Farm in Russell County. Opened in 2002, Highlands Harvest features a small but select initial offering of wines exclusively from their vineyard. This winery offers a fun experience. Wines include Chambourcin, Norton, Seyval Blanc, and Vidal Blanc.

Wines: $

HOURS AND DIRECTIONS Call for hours. ■ Scenic country road: From I-81 (Abingdon) take Rte. 19 north/Rte. 58 west to Hansonville. Turn left onto Rte. 614. Turn right on Rte. 71, then almost immediately left onto Rte. 614. After crossing the Clinch River bear left to the top of the hill. Turn left onto Rte. 628 and go approximately 2 miles to winery.

Hill Top Berry Farm & Winery

2800 Berry Hill Rd., Nellysford, VA 22958 • Phone 804-361-1266 •
hilltop1@intelos.net

Hill Top Berry Farm & Winery is a small, family-owned farm and winery nestled at the foot of the Blue Ridge Mountains. Owners and sisters Marilyn and Sue Allen's motto is that they make wines that are "true to the fruit." Their specialty wine selections include blackberry, raspberry, apple, peach, and plum. Moreover, Hill Top is a working farm, and it features many U-pick opportunities that give families a great opportunity for a something-for-everyone kind of outing.

Wines: $–$$

Grape Wines

Virginia Blush—A Concord and Niagara semisweet pink blend. A grape-only wine.

Fruit Wines

Cranberry—Medium-bodied red cranberry wine. Nice fruit. Very tart. Good. ♥
Virginia Blackberry Dry—A dark red, dry wine. Nice, deep fruit. A nice surprise.
Virginia Peach—A delicate, light white wine. Smells like a fresh peach pie. ♥

Other Wines

Apple, Pear, Plum and Blackberry (sweet and semisweet), *Raspberry*.

HOURS AND DIRECTIONS Open Apr. 16–July 3 Wed.–Sun. 11 a.m.–5 p.m.; July 4–Sept. 5 daily, 9 a.m.–6 p.m.; Sept. 6–Jan. 15 Wed.–Sun. 11 a.m.–5 p.m. Closed Jan. 15–Apr. 15. ■ From Charlottesville, follow I-64 west to Crozet (exit 107), go left onto U.S. 250 west, left on Rte. 151 south, and proceed approximately 10 miles to a left turn on Rte. 612 (Berry Hill Rd.) at the Tuckahoe Antique Mall. Proceed approximately 1 mile on Berry Hill Rd., across the bridge and up the hill to the Hill Top Berry Farm & Winery on your left.

Horton Vineyards / Montdomaine Cellars ✿ ✿ ✿

6399 Spotswood Trail, Gordonsville, VA 22942 •
Phone 800-829-4633 or 540-832-7440 • Fax 540-832-7187 •
www.hvwine.com • vawinee@aol.com

"Dennis Horton is Virginia's lone Rhone Ranger and he is performing brilliantly," writes Tom Stevenson in *The New Sotheby's Wine Encyclopedia*, "but with vineyards planted between 1989 and 1990, the best is yet to come." Dennis Horton is certainly one of the darlings of the wine world, and rightfully so. He is the man who almost single-handedly saved Norton (as a varietal wine), introduced one of the best Viogniers in the United States, and Rkatsiteli too!

Lauded in *Wine Spectator, Wine Enthusiast*, and numerous other magazines, Horton's place in the wine world is secure. But he's looking to improve it—luckily for us. He began making wine with a small home vineyard in Madison County in 1983. In 1988, Dennis and longtime business partner Joan Bieda acquired 55 acres for the beginning of Horton Vineyards. Dennis's wife Sharon is the vineyard manager. Dennis and Joan then took over management of Montdomaine Cellars. They produce classic Chardonnay- and Cabernet-style wines, which complement Dennis's own Rhôneish tendencies.

Horton Cellars has garnered excellent reviews and is one of the most decorated U.S. wineries anywhere, having won more than one hundred medals in 1999 alone! You cannot say you've tasted Virginia wine unless you've tasted Horton!

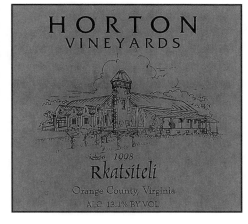

Wines: $–$$$

White Wines

Chardonnay (Floral Dry)—a touch of Viognier adds something to this. Very nice.

Dom Virginion—A sparkling Viognier. Brut. Nice fruit. Creamy. Dry finish.

Rkatsiteli—Orange peels come through. Citrus too. Dry, long finish. Excellent. ♥ ♥

Vidal Blanc (Semi-Dry White)—Ripe fruit. Slight lemon finish. Light and good.

Viognier—A spicy, aromatic wine. Peach and vanilla. ♥

Red Wines

Cabernet Franc—Bordeaux-style blend. Cherry comes through. Dry. ♥

Dionysus—A dry, Portuguese-style blend. 76% Touriga Nacional, 13% Tinta Cao, 8% Petite Verdot, and 3% Tannat. Intense, complex, elegant, and rich.

Mourvedre—Intense, spicy, dry red. Blackberry comes through. Smoky.

Stonecastle Red (Monster Red)—A blend of more than ten grapes. Ripe berry comes through. Deep, smooth, and dry.

Dessert Wines

Vidal Late Harvest—Tropical fruits and spice. Golden, sweet, and well balanced.

Fruit Wines

Blueberry—86% Blueberry, 14% Nebbiolo. Semisweet. Aromatic, full bodied.

Raspberry—86% Raspberry, 14% Tinta Cao. Off-dry, highly aromatic, full bodied.

Other Wines

Apricot, Cotes d'Orange, Eclipse Red, Eclipse White, Iberia, Ivy Creek Vineyard, Late Harvest Viognier, Malbec, Marsanne, Nebbiolo, Norton, Peach, Pear and Blackberry, Pear Port, Plum, Reserve Horton Chardonnay, Route 33 Red, Route 33 White, Spotswood Trail Chardonnay, Stonecastle Rosé, Stonecastle White, Syrah, Tannat, Vintage Port

REVIEWS AND AWARDS

Spotswood Trail Tannat 2000—Gold medal, 2003 Virginia State Fair.

Stonecastle Red Bin 2000—Gold medal, 2002 Vinifera Wine Growers Association, Virginia Competition.

Viognier 2000—Gold medal, 2000 Virginia State Fair.

"Dennis Horton has won national recognition for his work with Viognier. . . . This melony, layered, dry-but-wonderfully-fruity wine shows the elegant touch of a master." —Richard Nalley, *Food & Wine* (May 2002)

Viognier: "Would blow almost every California Viognier off the table." —Michael Dressor, *Baltimore Sun*

Viognier: "It ranks among the top viogniers made in the United States . . .
elegant and sophisticated."   —Karen MacNeil, *The Wine Bible*

"Horton's Norton would make any red-wine drinker gleeful. . . . the wine's
mouthfilling black cherry flavor bursts on the scene like a thunderstorm."
—Karen MacNeil, *The Wine Bible*

Vidal Blanc: 89 points. "Best Buy"
—Beverage Testing Institute, *Buying Guide to Wines of North America*

HOURS AND DIRECTIONS Open year-round daily, 10 a.m.–5 p.m. ■ From Washington, D.C., go south on I-95. At Fredericksburg, take Rte. 3 west to Rte. 20 south to Orange. Turn left onto Rte. 15 south to Gordonsville; at the circle take Rte. 33 west. The winery is 4 miles on the right. (An alternative is to go west on I-66 to the Gainesville exit, take Rte. 29 south to Ruckersville, then turn left onto Rte. 33 east; the winery will be 8 miles on the left.) ■ From Richmond, go west on I-64 to Rte. 15 north. At the Gordonsville circle, get onto Rte. 33 west. The winery is 4 miles on the right.

Ingleside Plantation Vineyards   ✪

5872 Leedstown Rd., Oak Grove, VA 22443 •
Phone 804-224-8687 • Fax 804-224-8573 • www.ipwine.com •
sales@ipwine.com

Virginia's Northern Neck is a peninsula formed by the Rappahannock and Potomac Rivers, both breathtaking in their beauty. With 70 acres of vineyards, Ingleside makes lots of fine wine. The winery is housed in the plantation's former dairy barns. The first wines were produced in 1980. "Ingleside produced Virginia's first sparkling wine in the early 1980s," writes Tom Stevenson in *The New Sotheby's Wine Encyclopedia*, "but its Chardonnay and Cabernet Sauvignon are of more interest."

Ingleside Plantation Vineyards is one of the oldest and largest wineries in Virginia. It is part of a 3,000-acre estate that has been owned by the Flemer family for over 100 years. Charles H. Flemer purchased Ingleside in 1890, and today one of his great-great-grandsons is proprietor of Ingleside Winery.

Wines: $–$$

White Wines

Chardonnay "Special Reserve"—Vanilla, apples, honey. Smooth. Nice oak.

Chesapeake Blue Crab Blanc—Chardonnay and Seyval Blanc blend. Apple, lemon, and honey come through. Light and fruity. ♥

Pinot Gris—A dry white. Citrus and peach come through.

Viognier—Medium-bodied white. Tropical fruit and spice come through.

Red Wines

Cabernet Franc—A well-balanced, dry red. Nice fruit. Clean, dry finish. ♥

Cabernet Sauvignon—A full-bodied red. Black cherries come through. Nice tannins.

Chesapeake Blue Crab Red—Medium-bodied, off-dry red. Spicy. Strawberry, cherry. ♥

Specialty Wines

Brut Champagne—Made *méthode champenoise*. Crisp, clean. Nice mouth feel. And a touch of sweetness. Nice.

October Harvest—Tangerine and melon. Honey and pears. Rich, well-balanced dessert wine. ♥ ♥

Other Wines

Chardonnay, Chesapeake Blanc, Chesapeake Blue Crab Blush, Chesapeake Claret,
Colonial Rosé, Merlot

REVIEWS AND AWARDS

Cabernet Sauvignon 1999—Gold medal, 2003 Virginia State Fair; bronze medal,
2002 Virginia Governor's Cup Wine Competition.

Chardonnay 2000—Silver medal, 2002 Virginia Governor's Cup Wine Competition.

Chardonnay "Special Reserve" 2000—Gold medal, 2002 Virginia Governor's Cup Wine
Competition.

Merlot 1999—Silver medal, 2002 Virginia Governor's Cup Wine Competition.

October Harvest—Bronze medal, 2002 Virginia Governor's Cup Wine Competition.

Viognier 2000—Bronze medal, 2002 Virginia Governor's Cup Wine Competition.

Viognier Reserve 2000—Bronze medal, 2002 Virginia Governor's Cup Wine
Competition.

Merlot 1997: 86 points   —Beverage Testing Institute

Cabernet Sauvignon 1994: 86 points   —Beverage Testing Institute

HOURS AND DIRECTIONS Open year-round Mon.–Sat. 10 a.m.–5 p.m., Sun. noon–5 p.m.
■ From Washington, D.C., take I-95 south to Rte. 3 at Fredericksburg. Travel on Rte. 3
east 32 miles until Oak Grove. Turn right on Leedstown Rd. (Rte. 638). ■ From Richmond, take I-95 north to the U.S. 301/Carmel Church exit. Follow U.S. 301 north 10
miles to Oak Grove. Turn right on Leedstown Rd. (Rte. 638).

James River Wine Cellars

11008 Washington Hwy., Glen Allen, VA 23059 • Phone 804-550-7516 •
Fax 804-550-1869 • winecellars@jrgm.com

Located in historic Hanover County, 10 minutes north of Richmond, James River
Wine Cellars is the closest winery to the Virginia capital. James River is owned by
Ray Lazarchic. James Batterson and Ann Kiernan manage the winery. James River
opened in 2001. The gift shop offers wine tastings, tours, and light gourmet fare.
A landscaped picnic area is also available. Visit the gift shop or bring a picnic
lunch.

Wines: $–$$

White Wines

Chardonel—A light, off-dry white wine.

Chardonnay—A light white wine. Apples and pears.

Gewürztraminer—A semisweet, light white wine. Tropical fruits. Citrus ending.

Red Wines

Cabernet Sauvignon—A medium-bodied red wine.

Merlot—A soft, medium-bodied, dry red.

Other Wines

Hanover Red

HOURS AND DIRECTIONS Open Mar. 15–Dec. 23 Wed.–Sun. 11 a.m.–5 p.m.; tour and
tasting $1 or $3 with souvenir glass. Closed Dec. 24–Mar. 14. ■ From I-95, take exit 86
(Atlee/Elmont) west to Rte. 1 north. The winery entrance is 1.2 miles on the right,
immediately after the driving range.

Jefferson Vineyards

1353 Thomas Jefferson Pkwy., Charlottesville, VA 22902 •
Phone 800-272-3024 or 804-977-3042 • Fax 804-977-5459 •
www.jeffersonvineyards.com • info@jeffersonvineyards.com

In 1774, Thomas Jefferson convinced Italian winemaker Filippo Mazzei to move to Virginia to grow and make vinifera wines. In 1981, on the same land where Mazzei first planted his vines, Jefferson Vineyards was established. Today, Jefferson Vineyards produces numerous award-winning wines on 650 acres of historic land high atop the Monticello Appellation. The visit is a mixture of history and gastronomy.

Frenchman Frantz Ventre started as a Jefferson Vineyards intern in 1997 and ended up being the winery's winemaker by 2001. Since then he has also worked at Dr. Frank's Vinifera Wine Cellars and Pellegrini Vineyards, both in New York, as well as in Bordeaux. He's doing wonderful things with Virginia grapes these days—go and see.

Wines: $$–$$$

White Wines
Capriccio—Fruity blend of Chardonnay and Riesling. Light and refreshing. ♥
Chardonnay Reserve—Aged *sur lie*. Apple, spice come through. Nutty. Nice.
Johannisberg Riesling—Acidity and sweetness are well balanced.
Pinot Gris—Peach, apricot, honey come through. Nutty too. Nice.

Red Wines
Cabernet Franc—Raspberry and black cherry. Spicy. Full-bodied, dry red.
Cabernet Sauvignon—Full-bodied, dry red. Cherry, cassis, oak, and spice.
Meritage—Deep, dry blend of Merlot (48%), Cabernet Sauvignon (26%), Cabernet Franc (13%), Petit Verdot (9%), and Malbec (4%). Cherry, currant, raspberry. Smooth.
Merlot—Currants and cherry come through. Nice tannins. Dry and deep.

Dessert Wines
Late Harvest Vidal Blanc—Tangerine and honey. Peach too. Rich. Sweet. Nice acidity.

Other Wines
Chardonnay Fantaisie Sauvage, Estate Reserve, Klevner, Vinland Estate Cabernet Sauvignon

REVIEWS AND AWARDS
Chardonnay Fantaisie Sauvage 2001—Gold medal, 2003 *Dallas Morning News* Wine Competition.

Chardonnay Fantaisie Sauvage 1997: 86 points	—Beverage Testing Institute
Meritage 1997: 86 points	—Beverage Testing Institute
Merlot 1997: 88 points	—Beverage Testing Institute

HOURS AND DIRECTIONS Open year-round daily, 11 a.m.–5 p.m. ■ From Washington, D.C., take I-66 west to Rte. 29 south to Charlottesville. In Charlottesville take the Rte. 250 west bypass to I-64 east toward Richmond. Take exit 121A off I-64 (Rte. 20 south toward Scottsville). Immediately past the first traffic light, turn left onto Rte. 53. Jefferson Vineyards is 3 miles on the right. ■ From Richmond, follow I-64 to Charlottesville and take exit 121A (Rte. 20 south toward Scottsville), then follow the local directions above.

The Kluge Estate Winery & Vineyard

3740 Blenheim Rd., Charlottesville, VA 22902 • Phone 804-977-3895 •
Fax 804-977-0606 • www.klugeestate.com • info@klugeestate.com

The Kluge Estate Winery & Vineyard was established in the fall of 2002 by Patricia Kluge. It is situated in the heart of historic Albemarle County, near Jefferson's Monticello, where Virginia's winemaking history began. The vineyards are tucked into the beautiful foothills of the Blue Ridge Mountains. The winery echoes the magnificent eighteenth-century architecture of the Kluge family's home and chapel. Also located on the estate grounds is a dazzling 18-hole golf course designed by Arnold Palmer.

Wines: $$-$$$

New World Red—A deep, dry red. Blackberry and cherries.

Virginia Champagne—A rich, full-bodied champagne. Pears and apples come through. Smooth and creamy. Fine bubbles.

HOURS AND DIRECTIONS Call for hours. ■ From Charlottesville traveling south on Rte. 20, turn left onto Rte. 627 and follow it to Blenheim Rd. Turn right onto Blenheim and right onto Grand Cru Dr. (to the winery); vineyards will be on the right.

Lake Anna Winery

5621 Courthouse Rd., Spotsylvania, VA 22553 • Phone 540-895-5085 • Fax 540-895-9749 • www.lawinery.com • LakeAnnaWinery@cs.com

Ann and Bill Heidig planted their first vines in 1983, after returning from a trip to France. They continued growing grapes and expanding their vineyards in subsequent years, to 10 planted acres today. Ann and Bill decided to go from growers to winemakers and built a winery in 1990, which was great news for those of us who like good wine.

Wines: $-$$

White Wines

Chardonnay—Golden, dry white. Buttery oak flavors.

Chardonnay Barrel Select—Full-bodied, well-oaked, dry white wine with a creamy middle and a clean aftertaste.

Gewürztraminer—Fruity, semisweet white. Spicy finish.

Seyval Blanc—Light, fruity, dry white. Green apples and oak. Refreshing.

Red Wines

Cabernet Sauvignon—Dry, full-bodied red. Cherry comes through. Nice.

Lake Side Red—Off-dry to semisweet, fruity red.

Merlot—Full-bodied red. Berries come through. Dry finish.

Spotsylvania Claret—Italian-style, lighter-bodied, off-dry red. Tangy. ♥

Blush Wines

Lake Side Sunset—Fruity, berry-flavored, semisweet blush.

Other Wines (Historic Fredrickson labels)

Caroline Street White, Monroe Chardonnay, Old Town Blush Table Wine, Washington Merlot, William Street Red

REVIEWS AND AWARDS

Chardonnay Barrel Select 1999—Gold medal, 2001 Vinifera Wine Growers Association, Virginia Competition; gold medal, Wine Guild of America Wine Lovers Consumer Wine Competition; silver medal, 2001 Virginia Governor's Cup Wine Competition.

Chardonnay Barrel Select 2000—Silver medal, 2002 Vinifera Wine Growers Association, Virginia Competition.

Merlot 2000—Silver medal, 2002 Wine Guild of America Wine Lovers Consumer Wine Competition.

Spotsylvania Claret 2000—Silver medal, 2001 Wine Guild of America Wine Lovers Consumer Wine Competition.

HOURS AND DIRECTIONS Open year-round Wed.–Sat. 11 a.m.–5 p.m., Sun. 1–5 p.m. ■ From Washington, D.C., go south on 1-95 to the Thornburg exit. Go west on Rte. 606 to Snell. Cross the intersection at Snell; Rte. 606 becomes Rte. 208 (Courthouse Rd). Continue on Rte. 208, turning left at Post Oak. Go 7 miles to the winery; the entrance is on the left. ■ From Fredericksburg, take the Rte. 1 bypass south to Four Mile Fork. Turn right on Rte. 208 (Courthouse Rd) and follow local directions above.

Landwirt Vineyard

8223 Simmers Valley Rd., Harrisonburg, VA 22802 • Phone and Fax 540-833-6000 • www.valleyva.com/landwirt/ • landwirt@shentel.net

Landwirt Vineyard was established in 1982 by Charles Byers and Gary Simmers. Charles, a longtime member of the Vinifera Wine Growers Association, brought the experience, and Gary provided the perfect site, an expansive 100-acre former dairy farm. The 14-acre vineyard's 1,400-foot elevation, steep hillside location, and southern exposure have made this winery what it is today. It's a rustic, fun stop in scenic Virginia.

Wines: $–$$

White Wines

Chardonnay—Dry white. Aged *sur lie*. Nice fruit and oak.

Riesling—Semisweet, German-style white. A hint of sweetness with tropical fruit aromas.

Red Wines

Cabernet Sauvignon—Dry, full-bodied red. Rich.

Cabernet Franc—An intense, dry red. Aged in oak 2 years. Vanilla comes through.

Pinot Noir—A soft, dry red. Medium bodied. Nice fruit. Spicy. Nice tannins.

REVIEWS AND AWARDS

Chardonnay 1995—Gold medal, 1996 Virginia State Fair; gold medal, 1997 Virginia Governor's Cup Wine Competition; silver medal, 1997 Grand Harvest Awards; bronze medal, 1996 Town Point Virginia Wine Competition.

Riesling 1995—Silver medal, 1996 Town Point Virginia Wine Competition; silver medal, 1997 Vinifera Wine Growers Association, Virginia Competition; bronze medal, 1996 Virginia State Fair; bronze medal, 1997 Grand Harvest Awards.

HOURS AND DIRECTIONS Open year-round Sat.–Sun. 1–5 p.m.; other times by appointment. ■ From I-81, take exit 251. Go north on Rte. 11 for 5 miles, left on Rte. 806 for 2.5 miles, and straight at the intersection of Rtes. 806 and 619 for 0.5 mile; the winery is on the right.

Linden Vineyards

3708 Harrels Corner Rd., Linden, VA 22642 • Phone 540-364-1997 • Fax 540-364-3894 • www.lindenvineyards.com • linden@crosslink.net

The winery sits on a high mountain ridge surrounded by vineyards. Linden Vineyards grows grapes at four different sites on the Blue Ridge. The combination of a cool mountain microclimate and well-drained mineral soils makes for excellent fruit. At Linden Vineyards they are constantly fine-tuning the vines. Owner James M. Law believes in pruning, thinning, leaf pulling, tying, hedging, and yield reduction—all are vineyard techniques used to enhance wine flavor, aroma, and concentration. After you taste their wines, you'll be a believer too.

Wines: $–$$

White Wines

Avenius Chardonnay—Melon and honeysuckle. Tart finish.

Glen Manor Chardonnay—Melon and pear. Creamy mouth feel. Toasty finish.

Red Wines

Glen Manor Red—Herbaceous. Raspberries. Full bodied. Soft tannins.

Hardscrabble Red—Plums and cherries come through. Dry, deep red. Peppery.

Dessert Wines

Late Harvest—Vidal and Riesling blend. Pear and honey come through. Rich, sweet.

Other Wines

Chardonnay, Red, Sauvignon Blanc, Seyval

REVIEWS AND AWARDS

Glen Manor Red 1994: 88 points   —Beverage Testing Institute

Riesling-Vidal 1998: 83 points   —Beverage Testing Institute

HOURS AND DIRECTIONS Open Apr.–Nov. Wed.–Sun. 11 a.m.–5 p.m., also Mon. on Memorial Day, Labor Day, and Columbus Day; Dec.–Mar. weekends only, 11 a.m.–5 p.m. Closed Easter, Thanksgiving, and Christmas. ▪ The winery is one hour from the Washington, D.C., Beltway. ▪ From I-66 traveling east or west, take exit 13 and go east on Rte. 55 for 1 mile. Turn right on Rte. 638 and go 2 miles; the winery on the right.

Lost Creek Winery

43227 Spinks Ferry Rd., Leesburg, VA 20176 • Phone 703-443-9836 • www.lostcreekwinery.com • winery@lostcreekwinery.com

Lost Creek is one of the newest wineries in Virginia, opened July 2002. Owners Bob and Carol Hauk built the winery on a hill overlooking the vineyards and northern Virginia horse country. It has spacious tasting rooms with areas inside and outside to relax and enjoy the views and the wine. Wines include Cabernet Sauvignon, Chambourcin, Chardonnay, Merlot, and Vidal.

Wines: $–$$

HOURS AND DIRECTIONS Open year-round Sat.–Sun. 11 a.m.–5 p.m., weekdays by appointment. ▪ From Leesburg, go north on Rte. 15 for 5 miles. Turn east onto Rte. 657 and continue 1.5 miles until the road becomes gravel; then continue another 0.5 mile to the second driveway on the right.

Loudoun Valley Vineyards

38638 Old Wheatland Rd., Waterford, VA 20197 • Phone 540-882-3375 • wine@loudounvalleyvineyards.com

Loudoun Valley is an estate winery of more than 32 acres located near the northern tip of Virginia. They have been growing their own vines since 1978 at their estate grapevine nursery. They also offer a full selection of gourmet foods including imported cheeses, fresh-baked baguettes, and several varieties of pâtés that complement their wines. The winery enjoys a large glass-walled tasting room and wraparound decks.

Wines: $-$$

White Wines

"Limited Edition" Virginia Oak Native Yeast Chardonnay—Barrel fermented and native yeast fermentation. Excellent oak. Rich, buttery. ♥ ♥

Monte Bianco—An Italian-like blend of Chardonnay, Sauvignon Blanc, and Muscato. Nice fruit. Citrus and honey and oak.

Sauvignon Blanc—Fumé-style, barrel-aged Sauvignon Blanc. Nutty. Dry, clean. ♥

Vinifera White—Chardonnay and Riesling blend. Slightly off-dry. Clean, crisp, spicy. ♥

Red Wines

Cabernet Franc—Big, deep, dry red. Currants and berries. Dry finish.

Cabernet Sauvignon—Cabernet Sauvignon (80%) and Cabernet Franc (20%). Cassis and blackberry. Peppery. Spicy. Nice.

Pinot Noir—Medium-bodied red. Berries come through.

Other Wines

Blush-Zinfandel, Classic White, Dynasty, Gamay, Late Harvest Gewürztraminer, Poire, Reserve Chardonnay, Rosé, Sangiovese, Vinifera White, "Vintner Select" Chardonnay, Zinfandel

HOURS AND DIRECTIONS Jan.–Mar. Sat.–Sun. 11 a.m.–5 p.m.; Apr.–Dec. Fri.–Sun. 11 a.m.–5 p.m. Wed. and Thurs. by appointment only. Open Mon. holidays 11 a.m.–5 p.m. Closed Easter, Thanksgiving, Christmas, and New Year's Day. ■ From Washington, D.C., take Rte. 7 west or the Dulles Greenway to Leesburg. Continue on Rte. 7 west past Leesburg 2 miles to Rte. 9 west toward Harper's Ferry. Continue 4 miles on Rte. 9 (Old Wheatland Rd.) to the winery entrance on the right.

Misty Mountain Vineyards

SR 2 Box 458, Madison, VA 22727 • Phone 540-923-4738

Owned and operated by Dr. Michael and Aline V. Cerceo, Misty Mountain Vineyards is comprised of 13 acres in Madison, in central Virginia. They make award-winning, traditionally made wines of classic elegance and structure. They have taken part in the Taste of the Mountains Festival.

Wines: $-$$

White Wines

Chardonnay—Pears and apples come through. A traditional white table wine.

Riesling—A semisweet, light Riesling. Nice fruit. A citrusy ending.

Red Wines

Cabernet Sauvignon—A medium-bodied red. Plums and cherries. Nice tannins.

Merlot—A medium-bodied, dry red. Cherries come through.

HOURS AND DIRECTIONS Open Feb.–Dec. Thurs.–Tues. 11 a.m.–4 p.m. Closed Wed. Tours by appointment only in Jan. ■ Misty Mountain Vineyards is located on Rte. 652 in Madison. From Rte. 29, go north on Rte. 231; at Madison, turn left onto Rte. 651, right onto Rte. 652, and follow the winery signs.

Mountain Cove Vineyards

1362 Fortunes Cove Ln., Lovingston, VA 22949 • Phone 800-489-5392 or 804-263-5392 • Fax 804-263-8540 • www.mountaincovevineyards.com • aweed1@juno.com

Mountain Cove Vineyards was founded in 1973 by Al and Emily Weed. It is Virginia's oldest continuously operating winery. Al and Emily, still the sole regular staff, welcome you when you visit. They replanted their mature vineyard in 1997, and the 8 acres will be back in full production by 2004. The fully modern winery is housed in a fieldstone building. A rustic salesroom offers a wide variety of wines and gift items. Surrounded by hills, the welcoming lawn invites you to picnic and enjoy the farm.

Wines: $

White Wines

Dry White—Vouvray-style, off-dry, spritzy.

Silver Creek Chardonnay—Dry, barrel fermented.

Red Wines

Tinto—A dry Cabernet Franc–Petit Verdot blend.

Fruit Wines

Blackberry—A sweet mouthful of blackberries. A nice dessert wine.

Ginger Gold Apple—A sweet apple wine from locally grown fruit.

HOURS AND DIRECTIONS Open year-round Wed.–Sun. noon–6 p.m. and on Mon. of federal holiday weekends. Closed Thanksgiving and Christmas. ■ The winery is located 3.5 miles off U.S. 29 just north of Lovingston in central Virginia. Take Mountain Cove Rd. (Rte. 718) west from U.S. 29 and follow the "grape" signs.

Naked Mountain Vineyards

2747 Leeds Manor Rd., Markham, VA 22643 • Phone 540-364-1609 • Fax 540-364-4870 • www.nakedmtn.com • pgharper@erols.com

Naked Mountain Vineyards owners Bob and Phoebe Harper fondly refer to their start in the winemaking business as a hobby that got out of hand. As amateur winemakers, the first grapes they planted in the spring of 1976 were Chardonnay, Riesling, Sauvignon Blanc, Cabernet Sauvignon, and Cabernet Franc. They continued to expand their vineyard until it was producing at a level that they could open a winery in 1981. Today, 75% of their production is dedicated to Chardonnay, very much in the tradition of the wine houses of France.

Wines: $$

White Wines

Chardonnay—Crisp, dry white wine. Made in the style of a classic French Meursault. Aged in French barrels. Nice fruit. Toasty vanilla, butterscotch, ripe fig come through.

Riesling—German-style white. Peaches, apricots, and apple come through.

Sauvignon Blanc—A dry, light white wine. Clean and crisp.

Red Wines

Cabernet Franc—A dry red wine. Cherry, toasty oak come through. Soft tannins.

Cabernet Sauvignon—A dry red wine made in the Médoc style. Aged in French oak.

REVIEWS AND AWARDS

Raptor Red 2000—Gold medal, 2003 Virginia State Fair.

Riesling 2000—Gold medal, 2003 Virginia State Fair.

Chardonnay 1997: 82 points   —Beverage Testing Institute

HOURS AND DIRECTIONS Open daily year-round, 11 a.m.–5 p.m. ■ From Washington, D.C., take I-66 west to exit 18 (Markham). Turn north off the exit ramp onto Rte. 688 (Leeds Manor Rd.). Naked Mountain Vineyards is about 2 miles ahead on the right.

North Mountain Vineyard & Winery

4374 Swartz Rd., Maurertown, VA 22644 • Phone 540-436-9463 • www.northmountainvineyard.com • wine@northmountainvineyard.com

North Mountain Vineyard & Winery's distinctive winery building was modeled after a European-style farmhouse and constructed in 1989. It is one of the more striking of such buildings in the region and is featured on the winery's label. The cellar produces some 3,000 gallons of premium table wine per year from 10 acres of vines. The cozy tasting room and gift shop offers free tastings of each of their wines.

Wines: $–$$

White Wines

Chardonnay—Apple, melon, and pineapple come through. Nice oak. Good. ♥
Vidal-Riesling—An off-dry, light white wine, 80% Vidal and 20% Riesling. Refreshing.♥

Red Wines

Cabernet Sauvignon—Intense, dry red wine. Nice fruit. Smooth tannins.
Chambourcin—A full-bodied, dry red. Cherry comes through. Soft tannins.
Virginia Claret—An off-dry, smooth, light-bodied red. In the English style, fruity nose, a touch of sweetness. Crisp finish.

Blush Wines

Caroline's Blush—A semisweet white wine tinted with Chambourcin. Fresh and spicy.
Mountain Sunset—Apple and Riesling blend. A touch of cinnamon.

Fruit Wines

Pippin—White wine made with Golden Delicious, Winesap, and Stayman apples. Mulled spices have been added. ♥

REVIEWS AND AWARDS

Chardonnay 1999—Gold medal, 2000 Virginia State Fair.
Riesling 1999—Silver medal, 2000 Virginia State Fair.

HOURS AND DIRECTIONS Open Mar.–Nov. Wed.–Sun. and most federal holidays 11 a.m.–5 p.m.; Dec.–Feb. Sat.–Sun. 11 a.m.–5 p.m. Closed Christmas and New Year's Day. ■ From Washington, D.C., take I-66 west to I-81 south, go 10 miles to exit 291 (Tom's Brook), west 1.5 mi. on Rte. 651 to Mt. Olive, left on Rte. 623 for 2 miles, left on Rte. 655 for 0.3 mile, and right on Swartz Rd. Follow the signs to the winery 0.3 mile on the left.

Oak Crest Vineyard and Winery

8215 Oak Crest Dr., King George, VA 22485. • Phone 540-663-2813 • oakcrest@crosslink.com

Conrad Brandts is the manager of Oak Crest Vineyard and Winery. The vineyard is planted with Cabernet Franc, Cabernet Sauvignon, Merlot, and Symphony. The rootstock was planted in 1986. The winery didn't begin construction until 1999. Their goal is to create exceptional Bordeaux-style reds and Rhine-style whites. Opened in mid-summer 2002, the winery features old-world atmosphere, especially in the post-and-beam tasting room, art/antique gallery, and wine cellar. Wines include Cabernet Franc, Cabernet Sauvignon, Merlot, and Symphony (dry and sweet).

HOURS AND DIRECTIONS Open June 1–Sept. 30 and Dec. 1–24 Fri.–Sun. 10 a.m.–6 p.m. Call to confirm hours. ■ Oak Crest Winery is 3 miles off Rte. 201, halfway between Washington, D.C., and Richmond. ■ At 4 miles south of the Rte. 301 Potomac River Bridge, turn southeast on Rte. 218. Proceed 2.5 miles to Belle Isle Rd. on the right (Rte. 613 on the left). Proceed on Belle Isle Rd. 200 feet, turn left on Oak Crest Dr., and proceed to the winery entrance on the left.

Oakencroft Vineyards & Winery

1486 Oakencroft Ln., Charlottesville, VA 22901 • Phone 804-296-4188 • Fax 804-293-6631 • www.oakencroft.com • mail@oakencroft.com

Oakencroft Vineyards & Winery was founded by Felicia Warburg Rogan and licensed in 1983. The first vineyard plantings were made in 1980. Oakencroft's first vintage, the 1983 Seyval Blanc, won medals in the International Eastern Wine Competition and the Virginia Governor's Cup Wine Competition, a major coup! Presidents Ronald Reagan and Bill Clinton both drank Oakencroft. Michael T. Shaps is the winemaker and Philip Ponton is the vineyard manager. Oakencroft has been reviewed in the *New York Times*, the *Wall St. Journal*, *Saveur* magazine, and *Cooking Light*. They're writing nice things about Oakencroft—go see why.

Wines: $$

White Wines

Chardonnay—Fresh white wine. Apples and pears. Citrus too.

Chardonnay Reserve—Rich, full, creamy texture. Vanilla overtones. ♥

Countryside White—Semisweet, light white blend. Viognier is the secret ingredient. Citrusy and crisp. ♥

Red Wines

Cabernet Franc—Nice fruit. Soft but firm tannins. Dry finish.

Cabernet Sauvignon—Dry red wine. Nice berry flavors. Smooth finish. Nice.

Jefferson Claret—A blend of Chambourcin, Cabernet Sauvignon, and Merlot. Good! ♥

NV Countryside Red—A fruity, off-dry red. Cherries come through. Soft tannins.

Fruit Wines

Sweet Virginia—A sweet dessert wine. Hint of honeysuckle in the aroma. Good balance.

REVIEWS AND AWARDS

Cabernet Sauvignon Reserve 2001—Gold medal, 2003 Virginia Wine Competition; gold medal, 2003 International Eastern Wine Competition.

Chardonnay Reserve 1999—Bronze medal, 2001 Vinifera Wine Growers Association, Virginia Competition.

VC-Classic 2001—Gold medal, 2003 Virginia State Fair.

Merlot 1996: Score: 88   —*Wine Spectator*

Cabernet Sauvignon 1995: 86 points   —Beverage Testing Institute

Cabernet Sauvignon 1993: Top Ten   —"Tasting Panel Report," *Bon Appétit*

HOURS AND DIRECTIONS Open Apr.–Dec. daily, 11 a.m.–4:30 p.m.; Mar. weekends only, 11 a.m.–4:30 p.m. ■ From Washington, D.C., take I-66 west to Rte. 29 south. Turn right at the exit marked 250 Bypass. Take the first exit, marked Barracks Rd., and turn right at the light. The winery is 3 miles ahead on left. ■ From Richmond, take I-64 west and get off at Charlottesville exit 118B onto the Rte. 250/29 Bypass. Take the third exit, Barracks Rd. (Rte. 654), turn left, and follow the grape logo signs.

Oasis Winery

14141 Hume Rd., Hume, VA 22639 • Phone 800-304-7656 or 540-635-7627 • Fax 540-635-4653 • www.oasiswine.com • oasiswine@aol.com

Owned by Tareq Salahi and his wife Michaele Holt, Oasis Winery, with its 100 acres of planted vines, is one of the oldest wineries in the state. Oasis is a combination of University of California, Davis, graduates and vinifera vines that date back to 1977, some of the first of those varieties. The winery is recommended by Karen MacNeil, who wrote *The Wine Bible*. The winery has a capacity of 100,000 gallons. Numerous open house events are held throughout the year when new wine releases are featured. Lunch is available at the Oasis Café, with a wonderful selection of gourmet food in a casual atmosphere. In addition, Oasis is a Davidoff Grand Reserve Recipient offering premium Davidoff cigars.

Wines: $$–$$$

White Wines

Barrel Select Chardonnay—A light, dry white wine. Pears and apples. Citrusy ending. Gold medal winner from the San Francisco International Wine Competition sponsored by *Bon Appétit* magazine, outscoring over 2,800 other wines in the world!

Dogwood Chardonnay—Floral nose. Buttery. Creamy texture.

Gewürztraminer—Floral nose. Tropical fruits. Grapefruit ending.

Riesling—An off-dry white wine. Tropical fruits. Citrusy ending.

Red Wines

Cabernet Sauvignon Reserve—Tinged with Merlot and Cabernet Franc. Plums and currants. Dry finish.

Dogwood Cabernet—Cherries and plums. More tannic.

Meritage—A Bordeaux-style, dry red blend. Deep and complex.

Merlot—Cherries come through. Soft and smooth.

Blush Wines

Dogwood Blush—An off-dry rosé. A blend of two finished wines, Riesling and Cabernet Sauvignon.

Sparkling Wines

Brut—Nutty. Pear and fresh-cut apple aromas. Smooth, creamy, with small, delicate, spiraling bubbles! Very nice.♥

Celebration Brut Cuvée—Fresh bread nose. Apples and toasty almonds. Creamy.♥

Cuvée d'Or—Flaxen-colored wine. Fine bubbles. Creamy and smooth.

REVIEWS AND AWARDS

Brut: 88 points	—Beverage Testing Institute
Cabernet Sauvignon Reserve: 91 points	—*Wine & Spirits*
Celebration Brut Cuvée: "Highly Recommended"	—*Wine Enthusiast*
Celebration Brut Cuvée: 86 points	—Beverage Testing Institute

Cuvée d'Or: "Virginia boasts a small number of very good sparkling wines, among them Oasis brut. This is a crisp, light sparkler with hints of vanilla."
—Karen MacNeil, *The Wine Bible*

Riesling 1997: 88 points   —Beverage Testing Institute

HOURS AND DIRECTIONS Open year-round daily, 10 a.m.–5 p.m. ■ From Washington, D.C., take I-66 west to exit 27. Turn left at the exit, then immediately right on Rte. 647 for 4 miles, and right on Rte. 635 for 10 miles. The winery is on the left; follow the state highway Tours signs. ■ From Richmond, take I-95 north and U.S. 17 into Warrenton. Turn left onto U.S. 211 and proceed for 18 miles, then right on Rte. 522 north for 8 miles, and right on Rte. 635 for 1 mile. Oasis is on the right; follow the state highway Tours signs.

Old House Vineyards

18351 Corky's Ln., Culpeper, VA 22701 • Phone 540-423-1032 • Fax 703-938-2744 • zuk1994@aol.com

Nestled in the country close to historic Culpeper, Old House Vineyards is a 75-acre farm with 24 acres of vineyards. The winery was opened in June 2002 in a renovated 1820s farmhouse. Enjoy owners Allyson and Patrick Kearney's beautiful mountain views while touring the vineyards. The grounds are available for private parties, weddings, and receptions. Wines include Cabernet Franc, Cabernet Sauvignon, Chardonnay, Merlot, and Vidal Blanc.

Wines: $-$$

HOURS AND DIRECTIONS Open Sat. 11 a.m.–5 p.m., Sun. 1–5 p.m. year-round. All other times please call for appointment. Closed Thanksgiving, Christmas, and New Year's Day. ■ From Rte. 29 south toward Culpeper, turn left at Brandy Station and left at the stop sign (Brandy Rd.). Go over railroad tracks and turn right on Mount Dumpling Rd., which veers left to become Stevensburg Rd. (Rte. 663). Follow Stevensburg Rd. 3 miles; turn right at the vineyard sign. ■ From Culpeper, take Rte. 3 east approximately 7 miles to Stevensburg. Turn left on Stevensburg Rd. (Rte. 633), go 1.1 miles, and turn left at the vineyard sign.

Peaks of Otter Winery

2122 Sheep Creek Rd., Bedford, VA 24523 • Phone 800-742-6877 or 540-586-3707 • Fax 540-586-4792 • www.peaksofotterwinery.com • DJohnson@peaksofotterwinery.com

Johnson's Orchards is a family farm, established in 1919. Peaks of Otter Winery was established there in 1996. They are located in the Blue Ridge mountains of Virginia and the foothills of the Peaks of Otter in Bedford County. The orchards are comprised of two hundred varieties of apples, peaches, plums, and nectarines The winery is versatile too, producing over twenty-five different wines, among them some very tasty drinking wines and some wonderful cooking wine. Owners Nancy and Danny Johnson also offer a wide range of jellies, jams, butters, and cider.

Wines: $-$$

Red Wines

Cabernet Sauvignon—Fruity, off-dry red wine. Only a hint of sweetness. Tangy.

Pinot Noir—A medium-bodied, light red wine. Soft tannins.

Fruit Wines

Almost Nun—Semisweet white apple wine. Light and crisp.

Apple Cinnamon—A spiced apple wine. Sweet and light.

Apple Elderberry—A sweet, light wine. Not cloying. Nicely balanced.

Apple Pepper—95% apple wine and 5% chili pepper wine. Tastes like pepper jelly.

Cherry—A deep, dark, Shiraz-like, dry red. Interesting!

Crabapple—Tart, sweet, sake-like. With a little touch of ginger.

Dry Apple—A light white wine with a whiff of fresh-cut apples.

Dry Plum—Merlot taste with touch of caramel. Off-dry. Clove too.

Fig—Sweet pink wine, with a slight smoky taste. Like a dry fig.

Peach—White and yellow peaches. A sweet, light wine.

Ras Mas Tas Raspberry—An apple-raspberry wine.

Sweet Peach—Like a frozen, slushy peach. Very nice.

Other Wines

Apple-Apricot, Apple-Cranberry, Apple-Mulberry, Blackberry Cobbler, Blueberry Muffin,
Cherry Cheese Cake, Pear, Spiced Honey Wine, Strawberry Cream, Sweet Concord Grape,
Sweet Plum

Cooking Wines

Apple Peanut, Chili Pepper, Roasted Peanut

HOURS AND DIRECTIONS Open Aug.–Nov. 8 a.m.–5 p.m.; Dec.–July by appointment only. ■ From Bedford, take Rte. 460 west 1 mile; turn right on Rte. 680 north (Patterson Mill Rd.) and go 4 miles. Continue on Rte. 680 (Sheep Creek Rd.) 1 mile to the Peaks of Otter sign on the left. ■ From the Blue Ridge Pkwy., exit at milepost 86 onto Rte. 43 south. Go approximately 4 miles and turn right on Rte. 682 west (Kelso Mill Rd.) for 3.5 miles. Turn right at Rte. 680 (Sheep Creek Rd.) for 1 mile to the Peaks of Otter sign on the left. From August through October, follow the Yellow Apple signs.

Piedmont Vineyards and Winery

2546 Halfway Rd. #D, The Plains, VA 20198 • Phone 540-687-5528 •
Fax 540-687-5777 • www.piedmontwines.com • info@piedmontwines.com

Elizabeth Furness convinced her husband to purchase this beautiful home and what was then a dairy in 1943. Thirty years later she planted Chardonnay, with the intent of starting a winery. She was 75 years old, and there was no stopping her. "Mrs. Furness proved to be one of Virginia's best winemakers and reveled in her new job until her death in 1986," writes Tom Stevenson in his rave review in *The New Sotheby's Wine Encyclopedia*. Piedmont is owned now by three German businessmen; the winemaker and viticulturist is John Fitter, who does an amazing job. It's a beautiful spot in the middle of Virginia horse country. This is a nice stop any day, any time of year.

Wines: $$

White Wines

Hunt Country Chardonnay—70% stainless steel. Aged in French and American oak. A medium-bodied white. Nice fruit. Citrus ending.

Semillon—100% stainless steel Semillon. Nice fruit. Crisp and clean.

Special Reserve Chardonnay—Barrel fermented in French oak and aged *sur lie*. Unfiltered. Full bodied, complex.

Red Wines

Cabernet Sauvignon—16% Cabernet Franc. Berries comes through. Dry. Nice tannins.

REVIEWS AND AWARDS

Hunt Country Chardonnay 1999—Bronze medal, 2001 International Wine and Spirits Competition, London.

Special Reserve Chardonnay 1999—Silver medal, 2001 International Wine and Spirits Competition, London.

Special Reserve Chardonnay 1993: "Score: 91"   —*Wine Spectator*

HOURS AND DIRECTIONS Open Apr.–Oct. Mon.–Sat. 10 a.m.–6 p.m., Sun. 11 a.m.–6 p.m.; Nov.–Dec. Mon.–Sat. 10 a.m.–5 p.m., Sun. 11 a.m.–5 p.m.; Jan.–Mar. Mon.–Tues. and Wed.–Sun. 11 a.m.–5 p.m. ■ From Washington, D.C., take I-66 to U.S. 50 west at exit 57. Stay on U.S. 50 approximately 22 miles to Middleburg. Go straight through the light in Middleburg; turn left on The Plains Rd. (Rte. 626 south) 2 blocks west of the light. The winery is 3 miles south on 626, on the right.

Prince Michel Vineyards / Rapidan River Vineyards   ✠ ✠

Rte. 29 S., Leon, VA 22725 • Phone 800-869-8242 or 540-547-3707 • Fax 540-547-3088 • www.princemichel.com • info@princemichel.com

Prince Michel Vineyards is also known as Prince Michel de Virginia. Founded in 1983, Prince Michel today includes over 115 planted acres dedicated exclusively to vinifera grapes. Prince Michel de Virginia produces award-winning wines under three distinct labels: Prince Michel de Virginia, Prince Michel's Madison Series, and Rapidan River Vineyards. Much of the success of Prince Michel can be credited to consulting enologist Jacques Boissenot and the hard work of winemaker Brad Hansen.

Wines: $$–$$$

White Wines

Barrel Select Chardonnay—A rich, yeasty nose. Pear and vanilla bean. Butter and oak. ♥

Madison Chardonnay—Well balanced. Crisp and fruity. Pear and apple.

Madison Sweet Reserve White—A light, sweet dessert wine blend. ♥

Rapidan River Dry Riesling—Alsatian-style white. Crisp, fruity, with citrusy ending.

Rapidan River Gewürztraminer—Off-dry. Fruit and spice comes through. Nicely balanced. ♥

Rapidan River Semi-Dry Riesling—Apricot, pear, and green apple. Clean and crisp.

Red Wines

Cabernet Sauvignon, Cask 99—Deep, rich red. Plum, cherry, and cedar. Dry.

Madison Cabernet Sauvignon—Deep, dry red. Berries come through. Smooth.

Madison Sweet Reserve Red—Sweet red wine with a fruity nose. Intense cherry and plum.

Merlot, Cask 99—10% Cabernet Sauvignon; 4% Cabernet Franc. Deep and tasty. ♥

Merlot Cabernet Virginia Reserve—Blackberry and raspberry. Roasted coffee bean.

Blush Wines

Madison Classic Rosé—An off-dry blush. Strawberries and apricot. Nice.

Sparkling Wines

Virginia Brut—60% Chardonnay; 40% Pinot Noir. Classic fruit and toasty, yeasty characteristics. Fine bubbles.

Other Wines

Chardonnay, Rapidan River Harmony, Wayside Merlot

REVIEWS AND AWARDS

Barrel Select Chardonnay 2000—Gold medal, 2002 Virginia Governor's Cup Wine Competition.

Barrel Select Chardonnay 1997: 88 points	—Beverage Testing Institute
Barrel Select Chardonnay 1999: "Score: 82."	—*Wine Spectator* (May 2002)
Merlot Cabernet Virginia Reserve 1999: "Score: 82."	—*Wine Spectator* (May 2002)
Rapidan River Gewürztraminer 1997: 82 points	—Beverage Testing Institute
Rapidan River Gewürztraminer 1999: "Score: 80."	—*Wine Spectator* (May 2002)

HOURS AND DIRECTIONS Open daily year-round, 10 a.m.–5 p.m. Closed major holidays. ■ From Washington, D.C., take I-66 west to Rte. 29 south (exit 43, toward Gainesville). Remain on Rte. 29 about 45 miles. Prince Michel is located directly on Rte. 29 on the right side, about 10 miles past Culpeper.

Rappahannock Cellars ✧ ✧

14437 Hume Rd., Huntly, VA 22630 • Phone 540-635-9398 • Fax 540-635-8720 • winery@rappahannockcellars.com

It is refreshing to run across a winery that makes fewer than ten different wines. In fact, Rappahannock Cellars makes only a handful. And all are drinkable and tasty. But they are new. The winery planted its vines in 1998, and more wines are just shy of being introduced. Regardless, they should all come out incredible.

Originally, this was going to be called Glenway Winery, but the name was changed to Rappahannock. It is owned by John and Sue Delmare, who moved from a Santa Cruz, Calif., vineyard to raise their family in Virginia. Who's to argue? This is a wonderful operation. And the wine will not disappoint. In fact, we are expecting great things from Rappahannock.

Wines: $$

White Wines

Chardonnay—Fermented in French oak. Honeysuckle nose. Tropical flavors. ♥
Vidal Blanc—Soft. Ripe pear comes across. Light, off-dry white. ♥
Viognier—Honey and melon come through. Light and just slightly off-dry. ♥ ♥

Red Wines

Cabernet Franc—Dark ruby color. Black cherry and plum come through. Peppery. ♥
Cabernet Sauvignon—Not tasted.

REVIEWS AND AWARDS

Cabernet Franc 2000—Gold medal, 2002 Vinifera Wine Growers Association, Virginia Competition.

Chardonnay 2001—Gold medal, 2003 Virginia State Fair; gold medal, 2002 Vinifera Wine Growers Association, Virginia Competition.

Seyval 2001—Gold medal, 2002 Vinifera Wine Growers Association, Virginia Competition.

Veramar Chardonnay 2001—Gold medal, 2003 Virginia State Fair.

HOURS AND DIRECTIONS Open Mar.–Dec. Wed.–Mon. 11:30 a.m.–5 p.m. and an hour later on Sat. (6 p.m.); open Jan.–Feb. Fri.–Mon. 11:30 a.m.–5 p.m. ■ From Washington, D.C., take I-66 west to exit 27. Turn left at the exit, then immediately right on Rte. 647 for 4 miles, then right on Rte. 635 for 11 miles. The winery is on the right; follow the state highway Tours signs.

Rebec Vineyards

2229 N. Amherst Hwy., Amherst, VA 24521 • Phone 804-946-5168 •
www.rebecwinery.com • rebecwinery@hotmail.com

Rebec Vineyards is a charming and rustic little winery owned by Richard Hanson. It is located on the historic Mountain View property in northern Amherst County. The two-story wood frame home is listed on the National Register of Historic Places. Richard first planted the vineyards in 1980, with 8 acres of noble *Vitis vinifera* grapes. By 1987, Rebec Vineyards began selling under the Rebec label.

The winery features rich, weathered chestnut siding and exposed beams from a 200-year-old tobacco barn originally located on the property. This structure was designed and built under the direction of Richard and his son-in-law Mark Magruder. Bulgarian winemaker Svetlozar Kanev makes some interesting wines, including several handsome styles from his homeland.

Wines: $–$$

White Wines

Chardonnay—A dry, classic, complex white. Aged in oak. Rich.

Gewürztraminer—A dry, spicy, light white. Intense fruit. Nice finish.

Landmark White—A dry, golden, vinifera blend. Slightly oaked.

Riesling—An off-dry, crisp, Alsatian-style wine. Floral nose. Nicely sweet.

Viognier—A dry, North Rhône Valley–style white. ♥

Red Wines

Cabernet Sauvignon—A dry, full-bodied, deep garnet red wine. Aged in oak.

Merlot—A medium-bodied, off-dry red. Nice fruit. Soft tannins. Tangy.

Pinot Noir Dry—Classic, medium-bodied, Burgundy-style red wine. Slight sweetness.

Blush Wines

Autumn Glow Sweet—Riesling and Pinot Noir blend. Distinctive, sweet taste.

Sweet Briar Rose—Semisweet vinifera blend. Fruity, clean taste.

Dessert Wines

Landmark Sweet—A balanced blend of light fruit and vanilla.

Sweet Sofia—An herbal-flavored, Bulgarian-style, sweet wine. ♥ ♥

HOURS AND DIRECTIONS Open daily 10 a.m.–5 p.m. year-round. ■ Rebec is located 5 miles north of the town of Amherst on U.S. 29.

Rockbridge Vineyard

30 Hillview Ln., Raphine, VA 24472 • Phone and Fax 888-511-9463 or
540-377-6204 • www.rockbridgevineyard.com • rocwine@cfw.com

Rockbridge Vineyard is owned by Shepherd and Jane Rouse. In 1978 Shepherd moved to California and earned a master's degree in enology at the University of California, Davis. He then worked at Schramsberg, Chateau St. Jean, and Carneros Creek Wineries. He returned to Virginia in 1986 and began working at Montdomaine Cellars (his 1990 Cabernet Sauvignon won the 1993 Virginia Governor's Cup). In 1988 Rouse purchased a farm in northern Rockbridge County, in the Shenandoah Valley at higher elevation than most Virginia vineyards, and planted 5 acres of grapes. It still looks like a dairy farm, with its massive red barn and two grain silos. But the vines are a dead giveaway. Taste what Shepherd is up to these days as he and Jane make their award-winning wines.

Wines: $–$$

White Wines
Chardonnay—A dry, barrel-fermented, full-bodied white. Nice fruit.

Chardonnay Reserve—A dry, French-oak-fermented, full-bodied white. Buttery. Creamy. ♥

Dashiell Chardonnay—A dry white. The reserve without heavy oak and little malolactic fermentation. Very nice.

St. Mary's Blanc—A dry, barrel-fermented, *sur lie* Vidal Blanc. Smooth and toasty. ♥

Traminette—Off-dry, light wine. Floral nose. Nice finish.

Vignoles—Off-dry, light white. Tropical fruit. Green apple finish.

Vin de Pomme—An off-dry apple wine fermented in American oak. Spicy.

Red Wines
Cabernet—Cherry and cassis come through. Dry red wine with nice tannins.

Chambourcin—A dry and fruity red. Soft tannins. Smooth.

DeChiel Merlot—Dry red. Rich body. Smooth and elegant.

DeChiel Pinot Noir—A dry, light red wine. Fruity. Cherry and black pepper. Spicy. ♥

Blush Wines
Jeremiah's—Semisweet rosé of Concord. Fruity.

Dessert Wines
V d'Or—Vidal Blanc ice wine. Oranges and honey come through on this golden, rich dessert wine. Very nice balance of sweetness and tart finish. ♥

REVIEWS AND AWARDS
Chardonnay 1998—Gold medal, 2001 Virginia State Fair.

Chardonnay Reserve 1998—Silver medal, 2000 Vinifera Wine Growers Association, Virginia Competition; silver medal, 2000 Jefferson Cup; bronze medal, 2000 Virginia Governor's Cup Wine Competition; bronze medal, 2001 Vinifera Wine Growers Association, Virginia Competition.

DeChiel Merlot 1999—Gold medal, 2003 Virginia State Fair.

Red Wine, Bordeaux Blend 1998—Gold medal, 2001 Vinifera Wine Growers Association, Virginia Competition.

V d'Or 2000—Gold medal, 2001 Vinifera Wine Growers Association, Virginia Competition.

V d'Or 2001—Gold medal, 2003 Virginia State Fair.

Vignoles 1999—Silver medal, 2000 Vinifera Wine Growers Association, Virginia Competition; silver medal, 2000 Jefferson Cup.

White Riesling 2000—Silver medal, 2001 Vinifera Wine Growers Association, Virginia Competition.

HOURS AND DIRECTIONS Open year-round Wed.–Sun. 11 a.m.–5 p.m. ■ From I-81, take exit 205 to Rte. 606. Go west; the winery is 1 mile on the right.

Rose Bower Vineyards & Winery

P.O. Box 126, Hampden-Sydney, VA 23943 • Phone 804-223-8209 • Fax 804-223-3508

Rose Bower is a small winery located almost in the center of Virginia, about 90 minutes east of Lynchburg. You can find bottles of Rose Bower Chardonnay at Ye Old Dominion Wine Shoppe in Occoquan, Virginia (phone 703-494-1622).

Wines: $–$$

Virginia Chardonnay—A dry, elegant Chardonnay. Nice fruit. Citrusy ending.

HOURS AND DIRECTIONS Open Mar.–Dec. Tues.–Sun. noon–5 p.m., by appointment only. ■ Call for directions.

Rose River Vineyards

Rte. 648, P.O. Box 186, Syria, VA 22743 • Phone 540-923-4050 • Fax 540-923-4564 • www.roseriverwine.com • ken@roseriverwine.com

A rustic, lovely little stop for wine lovers, Rose River Vineyards is owned by Dr. Ken McCoy, Sr., and Ken McCoy, Jr. The McCoy family planted 3 acres of vines in 1976 on their 170-acre farm. There are now 2,000 vines across the property. They also grow mountain apples, peaches, and honey. The winery does not use paper labels; instead, every bottle has a logo silk-screened directly onto the glass. They also offer gourmet bottles of healthful grapeseed oil for your culinary pleasure. Most surprising, from September through November and March through June (call for exact dates), visitors can fish the Rose River Trout Farm ponds for rainbow trout raised in the springwaters. A day at Rose River is a wonderful day for the whole family. Bring a picnic and enjoy!

Wines: $–$$

White Wines

Chardonnay—Light gold. Medium bodied. Nicely balanced acidity. Soft.

Riesling—Light golden. Dried herbs. Nice fruit.

Red Wines

Cabernet Sauvignon—Bright ruby red. Medium bodied. Red fruit. Mildly tannic.

Specialty Wines

Mountain Blush—Light bodied. Tart berry middle. Delicate finish.

Mountain Peach—Light amber. Full bodied. Spicy, full fruit flavors.

Rosé—Bright cherry red. Light effervescence. Well-balanced acidity. Zesty!

HOURS AND DIRECTIONS Open Apr.–Dec. Sat.–Sun. 11 a.m.–5 p.m. Other times by appointment only ■ From Washington, D.C., take I-66 west to Gainesville; exit onto Rte. 29 south to Madison; turn right on Rte. 231 to Banco, then left on Rte. 670; after passing Graves Mountain Lodge, turn left on Rte. 648 to Rose River Vineyards on the right.

Sharp Rock Winery & Vineyards

5 Sharp Rock Rd., Sperryville, VA 22740 • Phone 540-987-9700 • Fax 540-987-9031 • www.sharprock.com/sharprock/ • darmor@sharprockvineyards.com

The white clapboard buildings of Sharp Rock Vineyards are warm and inviting. David and Marilyn Armor's winery is located on the Hughes River in an unspoiled valley at the foot of Old Rag Mountain, and they produce wine in limited lots from carefully grown and hand-selected grapes. The vineyards were planted in 1992, and the first vintage was bottled in 1997 and sold in 1998. They make award-winning wines and are especially known for their Chardonnay. The Armors also have a B & B right there on the farm. You can't stay in a nicer part of the world, on a nice weekend, any time of year.

Wines: $$

White Wines

Chardonnay—Fruity white wine. Dry, medium bodied. Clean finish.

Chardonnay Reserve—Pears and other tropical fruits. Buttery. Creamy texture. Nice finish.

Sauvignon Blanc—A light, zesty white wine.

Red Wines

Cabernet Franc—Wonderful color, rich aromas, and deep berry flavors. Good.

Other Wines

Malbec

REVIEWS AND AWARDS

Cabernet Franc 2000—Bronze medal, 2001 International Eastern Wine Competition.

Chardonnay Reserve 2000—Bronze medal, 2001 Indiana State Fair Indy International Wine Competition; silver medal, 2001 Virginia Governor's Cup Wine Competition; gold medal, 2001 Virginia State Fair.

HOURS AND DIRECTIONS Open every Fri. 1–5 p.m., Sat. noon–5 p.m., and Sun. 1–5 p.m. ■ From the D.C. area, take I-66 west to the Gainesville exit; follow Rte. 29 south to Warrenton. Exit at Business Rte. 29 to Warrenton; follow signs to Rte. 211. Take Rte. 211 west 28 miles to Sperryville; turn left on Rte. 522 into town. Stay on 522 and follow signs to Rte. 231. Go 0.5 mile, turn right on Rte. 231, go 8 miles to Rte. 601, turn right, and go 1+ mile to the intersection with Rte. 707. Sharp Rock is on the right and across the Hughes River bridge at the intersection.

Shenandoah Vineyards

3659 S. Ox Rd., Edinburg, VA 22824 • Phone 540-984-8699 • Fax 540-984-9463 • www.shentel.net/shenvine/ • shenvine@shentel.net

Shenandoah Vineyards is the fourth oldest in the state, founded in 1976 by Jim and Emma Randel, and the oldest in the historic Shenandoah Valley of Virginia. Emma now runs the 26 acres of vineyards and winery with the help of her children, their friends, and others. Rick Burroughs is the winemaker. It's a lovely little place filled with family and attention to detail. If you are fortunate enough to meet Emma, that will make your trip all the more enjoyable.

Wines: $–$$

White Wines

Chardonnay—Abundant fruit. Nicely oaked. Very drinkable.

Founders Reserve Chardonnay—Pear and vanilla. Smooth. Nice oak. Excellent! ♥ ♥

Johannisberg Riesling—Medium-bodied, off-dry wine with lovely floral aroma.

Shenandoah Blanc—Proprietor's white blend. Distinctive fruity taste. Nice.

Red Wines

Cabernet Sauvignon—A smooth, medium-bodied red. Light berry fruit. Unfiltered.

Shenandoah Ruby—Plummy fruit with hints of oak. Off-dry red. Smooth.

Blush Wines

Blushing Belle—Fruity, medium-dry blush.

Other Wines

Fiesta, Founders Reserve Chambourcin, Raspberry Serenade, Sweet Serenade

REVIEWS AND AWARDS

Founder's Reserve Chardonnay 1999—Gold medal, 2001 Vinifera Wine Growers Association, Virginia Competition

Johannisberg Riesling 1999—Silver medal, 2001 Vinifera Wine Growers Association, Virginia Competition.

HOURS AND DIRECTIONS Open daily year-round, 10 a.m.–6 p.m. ■ The winery is 2 minutes from I-81. ■ Take I-81 northbound or southbound to exit 279 at Edinburg. Go west on Rte. 675 (Stoney Creek Rd.) and take the first right onto S. Ox Rd. Go 1.5 miles; you'll see the Shenandoah sign and vineyard on the left. The winery is a red barn with white trim, nestled amid the grapevines.

Smokehouse Winery

10 Ashby Rd., Sperryville, VA 22740 • Phone 540-987-3194 • Fax 540-987-8189 • www.smokehousewinerybnb.com • smokehouse@tidalwave.net

At the Smokehouse Winery you can taste unusual and unique wines underneath the thatched roof of the tasting house. Located in idyllic, rural Rappahannock County among the Blue Ridge Mountain foothills, the winery specializes in the production and cellaring of traditional and nontraditional mead (honey wine): "Man's First Fermented Drink" (so say the winery's owners). In addition, they produce seasonal, one-of-a-kind, English-style, cask-served hard ciders and unusual old-world historic beverages. Also located on the premises is a mid-nineteenth-century log cabin that functions as a B & B.

Wines: $–$$

Meads

Braggot—Made from honey, malt, and hops. "The drink of choice in fourteenth- and fifteenth-century England that still rings true today; 6% alcohol."

Cassis Melomel—An off-dry mead. Fermented with black and red cassis currants.

Crapple Cyser—Cider-like apple mead with a tart, off-dry finish. Made from crab apples and antique varietal apples.

Honeysuckle Metheglin—Fermented with handpicked honeysuckle blossoms. Floral nose and delicate honey flavors.

Juniper Berry Metheglin—A wintertime Metheglin (spiced mead). Steeped with juniper berries and their growing tips. Piney hints of a Scotch ale.

Three Berry Melomel—Wineberries, mulberries, and blackberries. A dry mead.

Traditional Mead—Semisweet, made with champagne yeast. Nice.

Ciders

Old English Style Hard Cider—Their "seasonal" hard cider blended from old-time apple varietals such as Albemarle Pippin, Ashmead Colonel, Spitzenburg, and Virginia crab apples. Cask-served at their tasting house! 4% alcohol. ♥

HOURS AND DIRECTIONS Open Feb.–Dec. Sat.–Sun. noon–6 p.m. All other times please call for appointment. Closed Thanksgiving, Christmas, and New Year's Day. ■ From the Charlottesville/Richmond area, take I-64 west to Rte. 29 north to Madison. At Madison turn left onto Scenic Byway Rte. 231 north toward Sperryville. Go about 20 miles and turn left onto Rte. 608; proceed 0.8 mile to the winery on the left.

Spotted Tavern Winery

P.O. Box 175, Hartwood, VA 22471 • Phone 540-752-4453 • VA-SpottedTavern@AllAmericanWineries.com

Spotted Tavern is Virginia's only combination winery and cidery. Cathy and John Harris opened it in 1995, and it houses an antique cider press that was purchased at a county fair by the owner's great-grandfather. A part of old Virginia with a colorful history, the historic Dodd Brothers Cider Mill is on display; call for operating hours.

Wines: $

White Wines

Stonehouse White—An off-dry varietal blend.

Hard Ciders

MoonBeam Virginia Hard Cider—A fresh appley nose. Nice bubble. Not too sweet. Nice. ♥

Ciders

Dodd Brothers Sparkling Cider—A nonalcoholic sparkling apple cider.

Fresh Apple Cider—Available seasonally. Nonalcoholic.

HOURS AND DIRECTIONS Open Apr.–Dec. Sat.–Sun. noon–4 p.m. Closed Thanksgiving and Christmas. Closed Jan.–Mar., with tours available by appointment only. ■ From Fredericksburg, go north on I-95 to exit 133 (U.S. 17). Proceed north on U.S. 17 for 5 miles to Rte. 612 (Hartwood Rd.). Turn right onto Rte. 612 and proceed 4 miles north to the white stucco building on the left side of the road.

Stone Mountain Vineyards

1376 Wyatt Mountain Rd., Dyke, VA 22935 • Phone 804-990-9463 • www.stonemountainvineyards.com • info@stonemountainvineyards.com

Stone Mountain Vineyards is situated atop the Blue Ridge Mountains in Greene County, Virginia (elevation approximately 1,700 feet). Established in 1995 by Al and Chris Breiner, the winery had its first pressing in 1998. Gabriele Rausse is the consulting winemaker, which helps to account for this young winery's very drinkable dry reds. You can come relax on the mountain and partake of panoramic views while enjoying their fine wines. A picnic area is available. Be sure to visit the wine cave, where aging at nature's own temperature takes place.

Wines: $$

White Wines

Bacon Hollow Revenuers' Select White—A sweet white wine. Different. Nice. ♥

Chardonnay—An all-steel Chardonnay. A little sweetness up front. Citrus ending. Clean.

Chardonnay Reserve—Peach aromas. Aged in oak. Creamy, smooth finish.

Chasselas Dore—A Swiss varietal. Soft and neutral white. Pucker at end. Refreshing.

Pinot Grigio—Stainless steel fermentation, aged in oak. Clean and crisp.

Red Wines

Cabernet Franc Reserve—Medium-bodied red. Nice oak and tannins. Cherries and plums. Dry and drinkable. ♥

Cabernet Sauvignon Reserve—Deep red. Big dark fruit. Soft tannins. Dry finish. ♥

REVIEWS AND AWARDS

Cabernet Franc Reserve 2000—Silver medal, 2002 Vinifera Wine Growers Association, Virginia Competition.

Cabernet Sauvignon Reserve 2000—Bronze medal, 2002 Vinifera Wine Growers Association, Virginia Competition.

Chardonnay 2000—Bronze medal, 2002 Vinifera Wine Growers Association, Virginia
   Competition

Chardonnay Reserve 1999—Bronze medal, 2001 Vinifera Wine Growers Association,
   Virginia Competition.

Chardonnay Reserve 2000—Bronze medal, 2002 Vinifera Wine Growers Association,
   Virginia Competition.

HOURS AND DIRECTIONS Open Mar.–Dec. Sat.–Sun. 11 a.m.–5 p.m. Closed Jan.–Feb. ■
From Charlottesville, take Rte. 29 north to Ruckersville, then Rte. 33 west to Stanardsville. Turn left onto Rte. 810 (Dyke Rd.) to Dyke. Turn right onto Rte. 627 (Bacon
Hollow Rd.) and proceed 3.6 miles. Turn left onto Rte. 632 (Wyatt Mountain Rd., gravel)
and proceed up Wyatt Mountain 2 miles to the entrance of Stone Mountain Vineyards.

Stonewall Vineyard

RR 2 Box 107A, Concord, VA 24538 • Phone 804-993-2185 •
Fax 804-993-3975 • stonewallwine@juno.com

Founded in 1983, Stonewall now produces over 5,000 cases of wine each year.
Stonewall's fine hybrid and vinifera grapes are grown on the 200-acre farm, on leased
vineyards, and by growers throughout the state. Larry and Sterry Davis bought the
winery in 1990. Bart Davis, Larry and Sterry's son, has been the winemaker and viticulturist since 1991.

Wines: $–$$

White Wines

Cayuga—Crisp, refreshing, off-dry, light white. Nice nose.

Chardonnay—Aged in French oak. Dry, crisp, and clean, with a balanced fruitiness.

Mist—A semisweet white blend.

Regiment—A semidry blend of Vidal and Riesling. Light. Good. ♥

Vidal Blanc—A crisp, dry white. Citrusy ending.

Red Wines

Brigade—A light, off-dry red. Low tannins.

Cabernet Sauvignon—Rich and full-bodied red. Nice fruit. Nice, dry ending.

Chambourcin—Light and dry red. Lightly oaked.

Merlot—Berries come through. Nicely oaked. Smooth.

Other Wines

Cabernet Blanc, Claret, Mirage, Pyment

HOURS AND DIRECTIONS Open Mar.–Dec. Wed.–Sun. 11 a.m.–4 p.m., or by appointment. ■ From Lynchburg, drive 12 miles east on Rte. 460. At the Concord light, go
north 5 miles on Rte. 608 and left 100 yards on Rte. 721. Stonewall is on your left.

Swedenburg Estate Vineyard

23595 Winery Ln., Middleburg, VA 20117 • Phone 540-687-5219 •
www.swedenburgwines.com

This is the Washington area's most easily accessible winery, with 15 acres of beautifully
maintained vineyards and breathtaking views on 130-acre Valley View Farm (circa
1762). Just one mile away is Middleburg, a designated National Historic District and a
mecca for tourists and shoppers with many boutiques, antique shops, inns, and restaurants. Wayne A. Swedenburg and family produce fine Continental-style wines.

Wines: $–$$

White Wines

Chantilly—100% Seyval, made French Chablis–style. Off-dry. Citrusy.

Chardonnay—Barrel fermented in French oak. Dry, medium bodied.

Great Falls Vidal Blanc—A lively, off-dry white wine. Tart, crisp, clean.

Riesling—An off-dry Alsatian-style Riesling. Peach and apple come through.

Red Wines

Cabernet Sauvignon—Aged in oak. Unfiltered. Rich. Berries. Dry finish.

Pinot Noir—A light-bodied, Burgundy-style red. Berry. Spicy.

Blush Wines

C'est La Vie Rosé—An off-dry pink wine. Nice fruit.

REVIEWS AND AWARDS

C'est La Vie Rosé 1999—Gold medal, 2000 Virginia State Fair.

Great Falls Vidal Blanc 1999—Bronze medal, 2000 Virginia State Fair.

Pinot Noir 1999—Bronze medal, 2000 Virginia State Fair.

HOURS AND DIRECTIONS Open year-round, 10 a.m.–4 p.m. Closed July 4, Thanksgiving, and Christmas. ■ From the D.C. area, take I-66 west to U.S. 50 west. Proceed 21 miles to Valley View Farm; the winery is on the left. ■ From Middleburg, take U.S. 50 east 1 mile to Valley View Farm; the winery is on the right.

Tarara Vineyards & Winery

13648 Tarara Ln., Leesburg, VA 20176 • Phone 703-771-7100 • Fax 703-771-8443 • www.tarara.com

"Located so close to Leesburg, and yet it feels like you're so far away." That's Tarara's tag line—and it's true! Owned by Whitie and Margaret Hubert, Tarara makes some wonderful wines on this idyllic 375-acre farm, which they bought in 1985. Tour the winery and visit the underground wine cellars—or just sit on the deck, admiring the view and wondering what all those poor folks who are working at that moment are doing. It's a respite more urban dwellers should take advantage of.

Wines: $$–$$$

White Wines

Chardonnay—Oak-barrel-aged, estate-grown Chardonnay. Dry and well balanced.

Pinot Gris—A light, dry white wine. Fruity and citrusy. Crisp.

Viognier—Apple blossom and honeysuckle nose. Melon and tropical fruit.

Red Wines

Cabernet Franc—Medium-bodied red. Dark fruit. Spicy.

Cabernet Sauvignon—Full-bodied, dry red wine. Plums come through. Dry finish.

Meritage—Bordeaux-style blend. Aged 18 months. Plums, berries. Dry finish. ♥

Lost Corner Wines

Cameo, Charval, Terra Rouge, Wild River Red

Other Wines

Chambourcin, Merlot

REVIEWS AND AWARDS

Cabernet Franc 1999—Silver medal, 2001 Vinifera Wine Growers Association, Virginia Competition.

Merlot 1999—Silver medal, 2001 Vinifera Wine Growers Association, Virginia Competition.

Tarara Viognier 2002—Gold medal, 2003 Virginia Wine Competition.

HOURS AND DIRECTIONS Open Feb.–Dec. daily, 11 a.m.–5 p.m. Jan. weekends only, 11 a.m.–5 p.m. ▪ From Washington, D.C., take the Dulles Toll Rd. (Rte. 267) to Leesburg. Go north on U.S. 15 toward Frederick, Md., and travel 8 miles to the small town of Lucketts. Turn right on Rte. 662. Proceed 3 miles until you see the entrance to the winery on the left. Follow signs to the winery parking.

Tomahawk Mill Winery

9221 Anderson Mill Rd., Chatham, VA 24531 • Phone 804-432-1063 • Fax 804-432-2037 • Tomahawk@gamewood.net

Corky and Nancy Medaglia purchased the historic water-powered mill on Tomahawk Creek that was built by James Anderson in 1888. Walter Crider, Anderson's descendant, had planted a small vineyard in 1988 and opened a winery. He sold the winery, the mill, and a small plot of land to Corky and Nancy in 1996. Since then the winery has continued to grow, and there is no stopping them now. It's a magical-looking place: it looks like a movie set. Go and experience some of the magic.

Wines: $–$$

White Wines

Chardonnay—A dry Chardonnay aged in French oak barrels and stainless steel.

Johannisberg Riesling—A dry Riesling, complex and well balanced.

Vidal Blanc—An off-dry, light white wine.

Red Wines

Cabernet Sauvignon—A lighter Cabernet, well balanced, aged in French oak.

Tobacco Road Blues—Smooth, dry, proprietary red blend with slight spice nose.

Specialty Wines

Apple—A light, sweet fruit wine from crushed red apples.

Mead—A sweet honey-based wine.

Other Wines

Conco Road, Estate Concord

HOURS AND DIRECTIONS Open Mar. 15–Dec. 15 Tues.–Sat. 11 a.m.–5 p.m., closed Sun. and Mon. ▪ From Lynchburg, go south on U.S. 29 approximately 35 miles to a right turn on Rte. 649 (Anderson Mill Rd). Proceed 10 miles west, remaining on 649; follow the grape signs to the winery on the left.

Unicorn Winery

487 Old Bridge Rd., Amissville, VA 20106 • Phone 540-347-7069 • www.unicornwinery.com • info@unicornwinery.com

Taste a new breed of wines in the Blue Ridge foothills. At Unicorn Winery you can picnic pondside on the deck, stroll down to the Rappahannock River, or play horseshoes in the "Unicornshoe Pit." Opened in June 2000, this new winery has already made a splash. Dave Whittaker is the owner, and Chris Pearmund is the winemaker. Together, they have turned out some tasty wine. Keep an eye out for this pair.

Wines: $–$$

White Wines

Chardonnay—Classic sweet taste with fig, tangerine, and melon. Toasty vanilla too.

Pearmund Chardonnay—From Chris Pearmund's 15-year-old vineyard. Very nice.

Seyval—Bright, dry, crisp white with citrus notes of ripe lemon and Asian pear.

Vidal—Light, bright white wine. Off-dry and tart.

Viognier—Light white wine. Fruity, crisp, and clean.

Red Wines

Cabernet Sauvignon—Big berry flavors. Smoky.

Cabernet Sauvignon Reserve—Dark fruit. Cassis. Nice oak and tannins.

Merlot—Cherry and plums. Medium-bodied, dry red.

Blush Wines

Slightly Embarrassed—Semisweet blush blend.

REVIEWS AND AWARDS

Viognier 2001—Gold medal, 2003 Virginia State Fair.

HOURS AND DIRECTIONS Open Sat., Sun., and some Mon. federal holidays. Nov.–Mar. 11 a.m.–5 p.m., Apr.–Oct. 11 a.m.–6 p.m. Closed major holidays. ■ From Washington, D.C., head west on I-66 to the Gainesville exit. Go west on Rte. 29 to the Warrenton exit (Rtes. 29/211). Follow Rte. 211 west approximately 7 miles toward Amissville. Turn right onto Rte. 622 (Old Bridge Rd.); the Unicorn Winery entrance will be on the right.

Valhalla Vineyards ✪ ✪ ✪

6700 Mt. Chestnut Rd., Roanoke, VA 24018 • Phone 540-725-9463 •
Fax 540-772-7858 • www.valhallawines.com • valhalla@aol.com

If you are a red wine drinker, you've just hit the jackpot. Valhalla Vineyards makes some of the best reds on the entire East Coast. These don't smell or taste like East Coast wines. Long Island has nothing on these folks! And their whites are good too.

Jim and Debra Vascik began planting at Valhalla in 1995 atop their 2,000-foot granite mountain. Since then the wines have tasted as if they had come from heaven (Valhalla is the Viking heaven). Valhalla was conceived as a vineyard and winery to allow Jim and Debra to strive for perfection. Is there an endpoint? We hope not. Unfortunately, it can't get that much better—it's hard to improve on perfection.

Wines: $$–$$$

White Wines

Chardonnay—A classic, French-style white. Lemony, with a touch oak.

Viognier—A fruity, light white wine. ♥ ♥

Red Wines

Alicante Bouschet—Dark and inky. Red and dark fruit. Big, dry, and long lasting. ♥ ♥

Cabernet Sauvignon—Dark fruit and coffee come through. Smooth and dry.

Gotterdammerung—75% Cabernet Franc, 25% Merlot. Smooth, full bodied, dry. ♥ ♥

Sangiovese—Cherry and strawberry on the nose and palate. Dry.

Syrah—Deep fruit, peppery, dry red. Spicy.

Valkyrie—Dark fruits and layers of spice and vanilla. Smooth and dry.

REVIEWS AND AWARDS

Alicante Bouschet—Silver medal, 2000 Indiana State Fair Indy International Wine Competition; gold medal, 2000 Vinifera Wine Growers Association, Virginia Competition.

Cabernet Sauvignon 1998—Gold medal, 2001 Vinifera Wine Growers Association, Virginia Competition.

Gotterdammerung—Gold medal, 2000 International Eastern Wine Competition; gold medal, 2000 Wines of the Americas Competition; gold medal, 2000 Los Angeles County Fair Wine Competition; gold medal, 2000 Virginia Governor's Cup Wine Competition; gold medal, 2000 InterVin International; gold medal, 2000 Indiana State Fair Indy International Wine Competition; gold medal, 2001 *Dallas Morning News* Wine Competition.

Syrah 1998—Gold medal, 2000 Virginia Governor's Cup Wine Competition.

Alicante Bouschet 2000: "Score: 81."　　　　　　*—Wine Spectator* (May 2002)

Gotterdammerung 2000: "Score: 85."　　　　　*—Wine Spectator* (May 2002)

Syrah 1999: "Score: 86."　　　　　　　　　*—Wine Spectator* (May 2002)

Viognier 2000: "Score: 83."　　　　　　　　*—Wine Spectator* (May 2002)

HOURS AND DIRECTIONS Open for tours, tastings, and picnicking Apr. 4–Dec 21, Sat. noon–5 p.m. and Sun. 1–5 p.m. ■ From Roanoke, take Rte. 419 west to Rte. 221 at Brambleton Ave. Turn right onto 221 and proceed to the second traffic light. Turn right onto Roselawn Rd. and go 2.3 miles to a stop sign. Turn left onto Mt. Chestnut Rd.; proceed 0.8 mile to the Valhalla Vineyards gate on the left.

Veramar Vineyard

905 Quarry Rd., Berryville, VA 22611 • Phone 540-955-5510 • Fax 540-955-0404 • www.veramar.com • veramar1@msn.com

Veramar Vineyard is located on a private, 100-acre estate in the heart of Hunt County at the base of the Blue Ridge Mountains along the Shenandoah River. James and Della Bogaty's small, family-run winery is dedicated to producing naturally dry, full-bodied wines. Opened in May 2002, one vineyard is on-site with a second vineyard on Hume Rd. in Huntly. At the winery's restaurant, you can order from a light, casual, gourmet bill of fare (catering is available for groups of fifty or more). If you are in the mood for romance or to enjoy fine wines, or simply want a picnic outing in the country, or a hike on the Blue Ridge Mountain trails, go and visit Veramar Vineyard. Wines include Cabernet Sauvignon, Chambourcin, Chardonnay, Norton, and Riesling.

Wines: $–$$

HOURS AND DIRECTIONS Open May–Dec. Fri.–Sun. 11:30 a.m.–5 p.m. Special events 7 days a week by appointment. ■ From the Washington, D.C., area, follow Rte. 267 (Dulles Toll Rd.) to Leesburg, then Rte. 7 west. After crossing the Shenandoah River, turn left onto Rte. 612 (Quarry Rd.). Veramar Vineyard will be on the left.

Veritas Vineyards & Winery

245 Saddleback Farm Rd., Afton, VA 22920 • Phone 540-456-8000 • Fax 540-456-8483 • www.veritaswines.com • veritaswines@aol.com

Veritas Winery, which opened in June 2002, is nestled in the foothills of the Blue Ridge Mountains. The recently planted 20-acre vineyard is ideally located on southeast-facing slopes. Owners Andrew and Patricia Hodson's new wines are from young vines and are made by combining the intimate relationship between wine grower and winemaker. The vineyard has plantings of Cabernet Franc, Cabernet Sauvignon, Chardonnay, Merlot, Petit Verdot, Tannat, and Traminette. Sit on the winery deck and enjoy the true spirit and enthusiasm of Veritas: "In Vino Veritas" (Pliny the Elder). Wines include Cabernet Franc, Chardonnay, Merlot, Traminette, and others.

Wines: $–$$

REVIEWS AND AWARDS

Cabernet Franc "Flying Fox" 2001—Gold medal, 2003 International Eastern Wine Competition.

HOURS AND DIRECTIONS Open Mar.–Dec. Wed.–Mon. 10 a.m.–6 p.m. (5 p.m. Nov. and Dec.); Jan.–Feb. Fri.–Mon. 11 a.m.–5 p.m.; or by appointment. Closed Easter, Thanksgiving, Christmas, and New Year's Day. ■ From Charlottesville, take I-64 west to exit 107. Go west on Rte. 250 for 6 miles to Rte. 151, south 3 miles to Rte. 6, and west 1.3 miles to Saddleback Farm Rd. Turn right; the winery entrance will be on your right.

Villa Appalachia Winery

752 Rock Castle Gorge Rd., Floyd, VA 24091 • Phone 540-593-3100 • www.villaappalaccia.com • chianti@villaappalaccia.com

Villa Appalachia is the answer to a red wine drinker's prayers. While they make a stunning Pinot Grigio and Simpatico, their trio of Italian-style reds were some of the first wines my wife and I drank as soon as we got home from the 2001 Virginia Wine Festival. We couldn't wait.

Owners Stephen Haskill and Susanne Becker farm 12 acres of Italian varietals and make 3,000–4,000 cases of excellent wine annually. Villa Appalachia was constructed between 1999 and 2002 by Susanne and Stephen to integrate the concept of a Virginia Farm Winery with the northern Italian wine and food experience. The Italian-style villa where the wine is made is quite picturesque. On a hot dusty day, when you drive up, you might think you're in Italy. Enjoy the trip—a must if you're drinking Virginia wine.

Wines: $$–$$$

White Wines

Lirico—Vidal Blanc, Italian-style. Dry but well balanced. Clean and crisp.

Pinot Grigio—A rich, full-bodied, and very complex dry wine. Crisp. ♥ ♥

Simpatico—A dry, intensely fruity, and aromatic table wine. Slightly sweet and spicy. ♥

Red Wines

Francesco—91% Cabernet Franc, 9% Merlot. Ripe cherry and raspberry. Smoky. Dry finish. ♥ ♥

Sangiovese—Chianti-style dry red. Touched with Malvasia and Trebbiano. A smooth, light-bodied red wine of intense aroma and mouth feel. ♥ ♥

Toscanello—"Super-Tuscan"–style, dry red wine, 25% Sangiovese and 75% Cabernet Franc. Raspberry and cherry come through. Peppery. ♥ ♥

REVIEWS AND AWARDS

Cabernet Franc 1999—Silver medal, 2001 Vinifera Wine Growers Association, Virginia Competition.

Cabernet Franc 2000—Gold medal, 2003 Virginia Wine Competition.

Pinot Grigio 2000—Silver medal, 2001 Vinifera Wine Growers Association, Virginia Competition.

Francesco: "world class" red wine

—*Washington Post*

Pinot Grigio 2000: "Score: 82." — *Wine Spectator* (May 2002)

HOURS AND DIRECTIONS Open year-round Thurs.–Sat. and holidays 11 a.m.–5 p.m., Sun. noon–4 p.m. ■ From I-81 south, take the second Christiansburg exit to Rte. 8 east; go through Floyd and 6 miles farther to the Blue Ridge Pkwy. Go south on the parkway 5.2 miles to Rte. 720 on the left (immediately after milepost 170). Follow the gravel road to the winery entrance.

White Hall Vineyards

5184 Sugar Ridge Rd., White Hall, VA 22987 • Phone 804-823-8615 • Fax 804-823-7491 • www.whitehallvineyards.com • tastingroom@whitehallvineyards.com

Welcome to wonderful fun! White Hall, named for the town it resides in, at one point won the coveted Governor's Cup two years in a row—in 1996 and 1997. Established in 1991 with 6 acres of vines, which have since grown to 25 acres, the winery produced its first vintage in 1993 and opened a new state-of-the-art wine-tasting facility in 1996.

Former New Yorkers, owners Antony and Edith Champ moved from the big city to the country in 1988 and slowly decided to follow their dreams. The winery buildings have an Italianate style. Brad McCarthy is the winemaker, doing wonderful things with the grapes that vineyard manager Scott Cruden hands him. They make some delightful wines, highly rated by the Beverage Testing Institute and other wine aficionados. Go and see what all the fuss is about.

Wines: $$–$$$

White Wines

Chardonnay—Apple and pears come through. Clean, crisp, and nice oak. ♥

Pinot Gris—Fermented in oak *sur lie*. Floral nose. Apples and pears. Hazelnuts. ♥

Reserve Chardonnay—Vanilla and buttered toast. Mineral and sweet spicy oak. ♥ ♥

Soliterre—Riesling. Spicy aromas. Mangos, papayas, and passion fruit. Clean and crisp.

Sugar Ridge White—Honey and peach nose. Apples and raspberries. Tart.

Red Wines

Cabernet Franc—Spicy. Berries come through. Smooth and nice tannins. ♥

Cabernet Sauvignon—Black cherries and currants come through. Dry, deep wine. ♥

Merlot—Spicy nose. Nice oak. Dark fruits. Cherries and cranberries. Bold, rich, and full-bodied palate with supple tannins and gobs of ripe cherry and cranberry fruit. ♥

REVIEWS AND AWARDS

Cabernet Franc 2000—Silver medal, 2002 Virginia Governor's Cup Wine Competition.

Chardonnay 2000—Silver medal, 2002 Grand Harvest Awards; bronze medal, 2002 San Francisco International Wine Competition.

Merlot 2000—Bronze medal, 2002 Virginia Governor's Cup Wine Competition.

Pinot Gris 2001—Gold medal, 2003 International Eastern Wine Competition.

Soliterre 2001—Gold medal, 2002 Virginia Governor's Cup Wine Competition.

Cabernet Franc 1997: 84 points — Beverage Testing Institute

Reserve Chardonnay 1997: 89 points. "Highly Recommended"
— Beverage Testing Institute

HOURS AND DIRECTIONS Open Mar. 1–Dec. 15 Wed.–Sun. 11 a.m.–5 p.m. Closed Dec. 15–Mar. 1 and major holidays. ■ From Rte. 29 in Charlottesville, head west on Barracks/Garth Rd. to the town of White Hall. Veer right on Rte. 810 north (Brown's Gap

Tpke.). Turn left on Rte. 674 (Break Heart Rd.). Continue straight when the road becomes Sugar Ridge Rd. White Hall Vineyards is 1.5 miles on the right.

Williamsburg Winery ✪ ✪

5800 Wessex Hundred, Williamsburg, VA 23185 • Phone 757-229-0999 • Fax 757-229-0911 • www.williamsburgwinery.com • wine@wmbgwine.com

Wessex Hundred, a 320-acre farm, is the home of the Williamsburg Winery. The farm dates back to the colonial era. It appears in the 1781 maps of the Revolutionary War as being owned by the Reverend William Bland. In 1983, interested in commemorating the efforts of the early settlers, Patrick and Peggy Duffeler were encouraged by the Virginia Department of Agriculture to consider planting vines and making wines. Today, there are 44 acres planted to vines. Now, the Duffelers own 25% of the winery; the rest is owned by some forty shareholders. The Duffelers planted the first vines in 1985. The first harvest was in 1988, when the seventeenth- and eighteenth-century style winery began construction. In their first year, the winery produced 2,700. Now they make more than 65,000 cases. Their goal is to make 100,000 cases per year. It seems like a lot, but there are plenty of takers.

Wines: $$–$$$

White Wines

Governor's White—A fruity, off-dry white blend. Light and refreshing.

James River White—A citrusy, off-dry Seyval. Light and crisp.

John Adlum Chardonnay—A crisp, dry white table wine. Nice fruit. Well balanced.

Vintage Reserve Chardonnay—Rich fruit. Nicely oaked. Creamy. Long, smooth finish.

Red Wines

Cabernet Sauvignon—Rich and ample fruit character. Balanced. Nice tannins. ♥

Gabriel Archer Reserve—A premium dry red wine. Bordeaux-style. Dark fruits. Nice tannins and long finish. ♥

Merlot Reserve—A well-balanced, dry red. Cherries, cedar, and spice come through. ♥

Dessert Wines

Blackberry Merlot—Merlot and blackberry, blended and fortified. Rich, dark, and tart. ♥

Late Harvest Vidal—Golden, elegant dessert wine. Honey and tropical fruit. ♥ ♥

Raspberry Merlot—Merlot and raspberry, blended and fortified. Rich, dark, and tart. ♥

Other Wines

Acte12 Chardonnay, Arundell Cabernet-Sauvignon, Cabernet Sauvignon Reserve, J. Andrews Merlot, Merlot Reserve, Plantation Blush, Susan Constant Red, Two Shilling Red

REVIEWS AND AWARDS

Gabriel Archer Reserve 1997—Gold medal, Virginia State Fair.

Governor's White 1998—Gold medal, Mid-Atlantic Wine Festival.

Late Harvest Vidal 1997—Gold medal, Town Point Virginia Wine Competition.

Ratcliff Chardonnay 1997—Gold medal, Town Point Virginia Wine Competition.

Gabriel Archer Reserve 1993: 85 points. "Recommended."—Beverage Testing Institute

Merlot Reserve 1998: "Best of Class" —Virginia State Fair

HOURS AND DIRECTIONS Open year-round Mon.–Sat. 10 a.m.–5:30 p.m., Sun. noon–5:30 p.m. ■ From Richmond, take I-64 south to exit 234 (Lightfoot/Rte. 199). Go 0.2 mile and turn right onto Rte. 199. After 8.3 miles turn right onto Brookwood Dr. (the third traffic light after exiting I-64). After a very quick 0.1 mile, at a four-way stop, turn left onto Rte. 617 (Lake Powell Rd.). Go 0.9 mile, turn left onto Wessex Hundred Rd., go 0.5 mile, and look for the sign at the winery entrance. ■ From Colonial Williamsburg, travel on Rte. 132 south (North Henry St.) through the historic area to the junction with Rte. 199. Turn right onto 199 west, left at the next traffic light onto Lake Powell Rd., and follow the directions above.

Willowcroft Farm Vineyards ✦

38906 Mt. Gilead Rd., Leesburg, VA 22175 • Phone 703-777-8161 •
Fax 703-777-8157 • www.willowcroftwine.com • willowine@aol.com

"After seeing Willowcroft, you'll want to pack your bags, move to the country and make wine," claimed the *Washington Post*. The vineyards at Willowcroft are located high atop the Catoctin Ridge, with panoramic views of the Loudoun Valley. In the 1800s the slopes were recognized for their potential and were planted to orchards. Lew Parker purchased the 30-acre farm in 1979. Today the vineyards, which have replaced the fruit trees, yield superior grapes. The winery has tremendous rustic beauty, including an old red bard and—of course—the award-winning wines.

Wines: $$

White Wines
Cold Steel Chardonnay—Pears and apples come through. Lemony. Crisp, clean finish.
Reserve Chardonnay—Butter and toasted oak. Creamy. Crisp finish.
Riesling-Muscat Ottonel—58% Riesling, 42% Muscat Ottonel. Fragrant. Off-dry.
Seyval—Stainless fermented and finished in oak. Green apples. Very dry and crisp. ♥
Traminette—Spicy, aromatic, off-dry white wine. Nicely balanced.
Willowcroft Vidal—Off-dry white. Pear comes through. Crisp finish.

Red Wines
Cabernet Franc—Dark cherries come through in this medium-bodied, dry red wine. ♥
Cabernet Sauvignon—A deep, dark red wine. Dry, with dark fruits and good tannins.
Merlot—Light-bodied Merlot. Cherries come through.

Specialty Wines
Applause—Off-dry apple wine. Mouthful of apples. Refreshing.
Cabernet Blanc—100% Cabernet Sauvignon rosé. Melon comes through. Refreshing.

REVIEWS AND AWARDS
Cabernet Franc 1999—Silver medal, 2001 Pacific Rim International Wine Competition; silver medal, 2001 American Wine Society Commercial Wine Competition; bronze medal, 2001 International Eastern Wine Competition; bronze medal, 2001 Vinifera Wine Growers Association, Virginia Competition.
Cabernet Sauvignon 1999—Silver medal, 2001 Virginia Governor's Cup Wine Competition; bronze medal, 2001 Virginia State Fair.
Riesling-Muscat Ottonel 2001—Silver medal, 2002 International Eastern Wine Competition.
Riesling-Muscat Ottonel 2002—Double gold medal, 2003 International Eastern Wine Competition.
Traminette 2001—Silver medal, 2002 Virginia State Fair; bronze medal, 2002 San Diego National Wine Competition; bronze medal, 2002 International Eastern Wine Competition.

HOURS AND DIRECTIONS Open Mar.–Dec. Fri.–Sun. 11 a.m.–5 p.m. Call ahead Jan. and Feb. ■ From Leesburg take Rte. 15 south for 3 miles. Turn right onto Rte. 704 (Harmony Church Rd.) and immediately left onto Rte. 797 (Mt. Gilead Rd.). Go 3.1 miles to the winery on the right.

Windham Winery

14727 Mountain Rd., Hillsboro, VA 20132 • Phone 540-668-6464 or 703-759-7860 • Fax 703-291-5659 • www.windham.com • windhamwinery@hotmail.com

This is a beautiful 300-acre farm owned by Dr. George and Nicki Bazacos. They have produced only about 700 cases of wine annually in past years, but plans are in the works to raise that level to more than 2,000 cases very soon. A new tasting room is now open to visitors, and it's well appointed and inviting—a very enchanting winery.

Wines: $–$$

White Wines

Chardonnay—Barrel fermented. Malolactic fermentation. Pears. Creamy and clean.

Fumé Blanc—Clean and dry Sauvignon Blanc white wine. Light and refreshing.

Riesling—Alsatian-style, full-bodied white. Crisp. Floral nose.

Short Hill Mountain White—Gewürztraminer and Riesling blend.

Red Wines

Cabernet Franc—A dry, medium-bodied red. Peppery. Nice fruit and oak.

Cabernet Sauvignon Reserve—Currant overtones. Nice oak.

Merlot—Red berry comes through. Some vanilla. Smooth, deep, and dry.

Red Blend Vintners Reserve—Cabernet Sauvignon, Merlot, and Cabernet Franc. Deep, rich red.

REVIEWS AND AWARDS

Cabernet Sauvignon Reserve 1998—Bronze medal, 2001 Vinifera Wine Growers Association, Virginia Competition.

Fumé Blanc 2002—Gold medal, 2003 Virginia Wine Competition.

Merlot 2001—Silver medal, 2002 Virginia Wine Festival.

Red Blend Vintner's Reserve 1998—Bronze medal, 2001 Vinifera Wine Growers Association, Virginia Competition.

Red Blend Vintner's Reserve 2000—Gold medal and Virginia Wine Honors, 2002 Virginia Governor's Cup Wine Competition.

HOURS AND DIRECTIONS Open Mar.–Dec. Sat. noon–6 p.m., Sun. 2–6 p.m. Closed Jan.–Feb. ■ From Washington, D.C., take I-66 west to Rte. 267 (Dulles Toll Rd.) and follow it to the Greenway. Take the Rte. 7 west exit and proceed to the Rte. 9 exit (Hillsboro). After 7.3 miles, turn right onto Mountain Rd. (Rte. 690 north). Proceed 1 mile to Windham Farm on the left. ■ From Manassas, follow I-66 west to Rte. 15 north to Leesburg and exit to Rte. 7 west. Proceed to the Rte. 9 exit (Hillsboro) and follow the local directions above.

Windy River Winery

20268 Teman Rd., Beaverdam, VA 23015 • Phone 804-449-6996 • Fax 804-449-6138 • www.windyriverwinery.com • sales@windyriverwinery.com

Windy River Winery is a beautiful and historic Hanover County farm located on the shores of the North Anna River. In 1990, Judith Rocchiccioli purchased 70 acres of farmland. In the spring of 1994, the family planted their first vines. On April 3, 1997, the Rocchicciolis poured their wine for the first time at the Virginia Governor's Cup Wine Competition in Richmond. Windy River Winery is a family business. Kathryn Rocchiccioli manages the vineyard and markets the wine. Her husband Eric helps out as well. Stop by and soak up what a small, home-farm winery is. And taste The Wolf!

Wines: $$

White Wines

Cayuga—Off-dry white. Lemon and grapefruit. Touch of sweetness at the end.

Chardonnay—Barrel aged and lightly oaked. Apples, melons, pears, and vanilla. Creamy.

Viognier—A dry, full-bodied white. Floral nose. Peach and apricots.

Wolf Blanc—Off-dry, well-balanced white. Citrus, melons, and apricots.

Red Wines

Cabernet Sauvignon—Black cherries and raspberries come through. Dry. Smooth.

Merlot—100% fermented on the skins *sur lie*. Intense color, flavor, and character. Aged in oak.

Roué—A semisweet wine tasting of raspberries.

The Wolf—60% Cabernet Franc, 40% Cabernet Sauvignon. Black cherries and black pepper on the finish. Dry. ♥

Blush Wines

Ruby Blush—Fruity, off-dry wine tasting of strawberries.

HOURS AND DIRECTIONS Open year-round Sat. noon–5 p.m., Sun. 1–5 p.m. Other times by appointment. Closed major holidays. ■ From I-95 southbound take the Ladysmith exit. Turn right onto Rte. 639; follow it 6 miles to Rte. 738 (Teman Rd.). Turn left; the winery is 4 miles on the left.

Wintergreen Vineyards & Winery ✪

P.O. Box 702, Nellysford, VA 22958 • Phone 804-361-2519 • Fax 804-361-1510 • www.wintergreenwinery.com

Wintergreen is owned Jeff and Tamara Stone, who purchased the existing winery and vineyards in 1999. Jeff is originally from the Finger Lakes. Wintergreen was established by Mike and Kathy Riddick in 1989, when they planted their first vines. It is located in the beautiful Rockfish Valley of Nelson County, on the eastern slope of the Blue Ridge Mountains. Nestled inside a nineteenth-century farm building are the state-of-the-art winery operation, a comfortable tasting room, and a lovely gift shop chock-full of all kinds of things. A scenic picnic area is near the South Fork of the Rockfish River. Light gourmet picnic fare is available for purchase.

Wines: $–$$$

White Wines

Black Rock Chardonnay—Tropical nose. Creamy palette. Nice oak. Crisp acidity. ♥

Monticello Chardonnay—Fermented in stainless steel. A dry, crisp wine. Tropical and citrus fruits.

Riesling—Off-dry. Fruity and floral with a spicy finish. Nice acidity.

Thomas Nelson White—Semisweet Riesling. Lively.

Three Ridges White—Chablis-style blend of Seyval, Vidal, and barrel-fermented Chardonnay.

Red Wines

Brent's Mountain Merlot—Medium-bodied, dry red. Blackberry and spice. Good
tannins.

Cabernet Franc—Bright cherry comes through. Spicy. Medium-bodied.

Cabernet Sauvignon—Black currant, smoke. Spicy. Full-bodied, dry red. Good tannins.

Three Ridges Red—Beaujolais-style blend. Light bodied. Lots of fruit but dry finish.

Fruit Wines

Mill Hill Apple—Semisweet apple wine with slight tartness.

Raspberry—Sweet, dessert-style wine with fresh raspberry taste. Tart and well
balanced. One of the better dessert wines. ♥ ♥ ♥

REVIEWS AND AWARDS

Black Rock Chardonnay Reserve 2001—Double gold medal and gold medal,
2003 International Eastern Wine Competition; gold medal, 2003 Virginia Wine
Competition; gold medal, 2003 Finger Lakes International Wine Competition.

Raspberry: 84 points   —Beverage Testing Institute

HOURS AND DIRECTIONS Open daily, Apr.–Oct. 10 a.m.–6 p.m.; Nov.–Mar. 10 a.m.–
5 p.m. ■ From I-64 west, take exit 107 (Crozet). Turn left onto U.S. 250 west, go 6
miles to a left turn onto Rte. 151 south, 14 miles to a right turn onto Rte. 664 west,
and 0.5 mile to the winery entrance on the right.

Ye Old Dominion Wine Shoppe   ✿ ✿ ✿

408 Mill St., Historic Occoquan, Virginia 22125 • Phone 703-494-1622 •
Fax 703-339-0869

This little shop features wines from across the state of Virginia—a truly unique store
in the state, owned by Janet Carper and Mari Spragins. It's nicely appointed and is a
one-stop shop for all the state's award-winning wines. If you can't make it to some of
the wineries you'd like to visit because they are so spread out, this is an excellent place
to stop. Come sample the gourmet items including jellies, special crackers and nuts,
dips, cheeses, and wine snacks. Special wine accessories are also available for home use
or gift giving.

Wines include Afton Mountain Vineyards, Autumn Hill Vineyards, Breaux Vine-
yards, Burnley Vineyards, Chateau Morrisette Winery, Chrysalis Vineyards, Gabriele
Rausse Winery, Gray Ghost, Horton Vineyards, Ingleside Plantation Vineyards, Jeffer-
son Vineyards, Lady Caroline's Blush of North Mountain, Lake Anna Winery, Linden
Vineyards, Loudoun Valley Vineyards, Naked Mountain Vineyards, North Mountain
Vineyards, Oakencroft Vineyards, Oasis Winery, Piedmont Vineyards, Prince Michel
Vineyards, Rockbridge Vineyard, Rose Bower Vineyards, Shenandoah Vineyards, Stone
Mountain Vineyards, Stonewall Vineyard, Tarara Vineyards, Unicorn Winery, Valhalla
Vineyards, Villa Appalachia Winery, Williamsburg Winery, and Windy River Winery.
They also carry five Virginia sparkling wines, port, and nonalcoholic cider from Le
Mousseux.

Wines: $–$$$

HOURS AND DIRECTIONS Open Mon.–Sat. 10:30 a.m.–5:30 p.m., Sun. 1–5 p.m. ■ From
Richmond, take I-95 to exit 160 B; at the fourth light turn left onto Commerce St.; Mill
St. is the main street that follows parallel to the Occoquan River. ■ From Washington,

D.C., take I-95 to exit 160; at the third light turn left onto Commerce St.; see the directions above for Mill St. ▪ The shop is located on the upstream end of the town near the museum and the old Rockledge Manor.

OTHER VIRGINIA WINERIES

Blenheim Vineyards: 31 Blenheim Farm Rd., Charlottesville, VA 22902 • Phone 434-242-5473 • Fax 434-984-1448 • brad@blenheimvineyards.com • www.blenheimvineyards.com

House of Marquis: 1017 Thomas Jefferson Pkwy., Charlottesville, VA 22902 • Phone 804-979-2965 • Owners John and Mary Marquis • Wines: Chardonnay • Not open to the public.

Keswick Vineyards: 1575 Keswick Winery Dr., Keswick, VA 22947 • Phone 434-244-3341 • www.keswickvineyards.com

King Family Vineyards: 6550 Roseland Farm, Crozer, VA 22932 • Phone 434-823-7800 • Fax 434-823-7801 • www.kingfamilyvineyards.com

WEST VIRGINIA

A-T Gift Company Farm Winery / West Virginia Farm Winery

Rte. 3, Box 802, Harper's Ferry, WV 25425 • Phone 304-876-6680

Frank and Angie Gift had to start making wine. Angie needed to get Frank from underfoot once he had retired from the construction business. Their hobby turned into business in 1986, after the couple had refined their craft with the help of family and friend "testers." Their cherry wine was named the official wine of the Mayor's International Taste of Washington, D.C., at the 2002 Cherry Blossom Festival. Their fruity dessert wines are made from fruit raised by the Gifts and from growers in the surrounding area. (The law in West Virginia states: "25% of the fruit used to make West Virginia Farm Wine must be raised by the wine maker.") Located in historic Harper's Ferry, they are a welcome stop.

Fruit Wines: $

Cherry—A bright-colored mouthful of cherries. Very tasty.

Other Wines

Blueberry, *Strawberry*, and others

HOURS AND DIRECTIONS Call for hours and directions.

Daniel Vineyards ✪

200 Twin Oaks Rd., Crab Orchard, WV 25827 •
P.O. Box 888, Beckley, WV 25801 • Phone 304-252-9750 •
Fax 304-252-6011 • www.danielvineyards.com • dvine@cwv.net

Daniel Vineyards was established in 1990 by Dr. C. Richard Daniel. It is located on the former Twin Oaks Golf Course near Beckley. After evaluating the 190-acre tract, the retired radiologist decided that the best use of the rolling, verdant land was to apply his scientific skills and love of fine wine to the art of winemaking. Daniel Vineyards offers a complete line of West Virginia wines made from French hybrid, Swenson hybrid, and American varietal grapes. Dr. Daniel began his dream by planting eighty-six varieties of grapes, on more than 10,000 vines! The grape varieties that Daniel cultivates include those that will survive the region's sometimes harsh winters. Master

Italian winemaker Marco Bertaccini joined Dr. Daniel in November 2000. His impact was immediate. These wines are a hole in one!

Wines: $$–$$$

White Wines

Aurore—Off-dry, light white wine. Distinct flowery nose and rich taste.

Cayuga White—A fine, fruity, light white wine.

Chardonel—French-American hybrid. Medium-bodied white.

Seyval—A medium-bodied table white. Nice fruit and nose, good body.

St. Pepin—100% St. Pepin, a hardy Northern Swenson hybrid. Distinct rich, spicy wine.

Vidal Blanc—Off-dry white. Forward fruit due to aging in stainless steel. Crisp. ♥

Vignoles—Off-dry, light white. Spicy.

Red Wines

Baco Noir—Dark red, dry wine. Rich, cassis taste.

Marechal Foch—Medium-bodied red. Smooth finish and cassis taste.

Norton—Hardy, medium-bodied, dry red wine.

St. Vincent—100% St. Vincent (a hardy Midwestern variety). Merlot-like taste. Medium-bodied, dark red, dry wine.

Fruit Wines

Blackberry—Sweet, rich, and fun to drink.

REVIEWS AND AWARDS

Baco Noir 1998—Bronze medal, 2000 Atlanta Wine Summit.

Blackberry—Silver medal, 2000 Atlanta Wine Summit.

Chardonel 1998—Silver medal, 2000 Atlanta Wine Summit.

Vidal Blanc 1997: (rating 3 glasses out of 4): "A restrained nose of apples and melon leads to delightful fruity flavors that turn to a crisp and clean citrus-y finish . . . this wine is crisp and refreshing."   —Travelenvoy.com

HOURS AND DIRECTIONS Open year-round Mon.–Sat. 10 a.m.–6 p.m., Sun. 1–6 p.m. ■ From I-77 and I-64 (W. Va. Tpke.), take exit 42 (Robert C. Byrd Dr./Mabscott). Follow Rte. 16 south 1.4 miles to the second stoplight, turn right, and go 1 block to a BP gas station. Turn left onto Old Rte. 54 (Glen View Rd.) and go 1.4 miles to Daniel Vineyards on the left.

Fisher Ridge Winery

Quarrier St., Suite 201, Charleston, WV 25301 • Phone 304-342-8702 • wewbonbin@citynet.net

Wilson Ward's Fisher Ridge Winery was West Virginia's first Farm Winery. It was established in 1977 by Dr. William E. Ward and his wife Louise Pearson. Located in the Kanawha River Valley, Fisher Ridge Winery cultivates 7 acres to produce 1,200 cases per year. Their specialty is wines produced from French-American grapes. Wines include Aurore, Cabernet Sauvignon, Chardonnay, Rayon d'Or, Riesling, Seyval, Vidal, and others.

Wines: $–$$

HOURS AND DIRECTIONS Tastings and tours by appointment. Call for hours and directions.

Forks of Cheat Winery

2811 Stewartstown Rd., Morgantown, WV 26508 • Phone 877-989-4637 or
304-598-2019 • Fax 304-598-2019 • www.wvwines.com • winemogul@labs.net

This is a nice little family-run winery offering more than twenty varietals. Susan and Dr. Jerry Deal, along with their two cats, founded Forks of Cheat Winery. It is the first in West Virginia to produce a port wine, called Black Jewel Port. The Deals use a variety of fruits and berries for their splendid wines; they spend 75% of their time growing and harvesting their fruits. Susan and Jerry have more than 15 acres under vines, including new plantings of Merlot and Cabernet Sauvignon. It's a lovely spot. One of the nice things to do during visits in warm months is to enjoy a few sips of their wine while sitting by their koi pond!

Wines: $–$$

White Wines

Seyval Blanc—A dry, tart white wine with a light taste.

Vidal Blanc—A semidry white wine with a light citrus taste. ♥

Vin Gris—A light, off-dry blush blend wine with a foxy aroma.

Red Wines

Baco Noir—A dry, hearty red wine with light oak aging.

Chambourcin—A dry red wine with a light oak taste.

Leon Millot—A dry, oak-aged red wine with an earthy aroma.

Marechal Foch—A dry red wine with a light oak aging.

Fruit Wines

Black Jewel Port—Made from aged red wine and distilled grape spirits. ♥

Blackberry—An aromatic wine with the full taste of blackberries. ♥

Pear—A light wine with a subtle flavor.

Plum—An aromatic wine with a full fruit taste.

Spiced Apple—An apple wine spiced with cinnamon.

Other Wines

Apple, Blueberry, Cabernet Sauvignon (new), *DeChaunac, Merlot* (new), *Niagara, Raspberry, Schwarze Bär, Spice, Strawberry, Van Buren, Villard Blanc*

REVIEWS AND AWARDS

Black Jewel Port—Gold medal and Best of Show, 2000 West Virginia Wineries Competition; bronze medal, 2000 San Diego National Wine Competition.

Blackberry—Gold medal, 2000 West Virginia Wineries Competition; gold medal, 2000 Indiana State Fair Indy International Wine Competition.

DeChaunac—Gold medal, 2000 West Virginia Wineries Competition.

Plum—Silver medal, 2000 West Virginia Wineries Competition.

Vidal Blanc—Gold medal, 2000 West Virginia Wineries Competition; gold medal, 2000 Wine on the Beach Competition; gold medal, 2000 Mid-Atlantic Wine Festival.

Vin Gris—Silver medal, 2000 West Virginia Wineries Competition.

HOURS AND DIRECTIONS Open year-round Mon.–Sat. 10 a.m.–5 p.m., Sun. 1–5 p.m. Other hours by appointment. ■ From I-79, take exit 148 onto I-68 east. From I-68 at exit 7, turn left (right if heading west on I-68) and proceed through three lights approximately 3.5 miles on Point Marion Rd. (also known as Rte. 119). Turn right at the winery sign onto Stewartstown Rd. and go 2 miles; the winery is on the left.

Jones Cabin Run Vineyards

HC 71 Box 129F, Tanner, WV, 26137 • Phone 304-462-4446 •
Fax 304-462-5450 • jcrv@rtol.net

Owned by Alan Wolfe, Jones Cabin Run Vineyards offers a wide range of award-winning wines.

Wines: $-$$

White Wines
Seyval—A bright, crisp, medium-bodied white wine.
Vignoles—A fruit-forward, light, off-dry white.

Red Wines
Chambourcin—Medium-bodied, garnet-colored wine.

Blush Wines
Chambourcin Rosé—Off-dry blush wine made from Chambourcin.

Sparkling Wines
Apple (Méthode Champenoise)—Sparkling off-dry apple wine. ♥

Other Wines
*Black Currant, Blanc de Blanc (Méthode Champenoise), Blanc de Noir
(Chambourcin Méthode Champenoise), Elderberry, Norton (Cynthiana)*

REVIEWS AND AWARDS
Apple 2001—Bronze medal, 2000 Indiana State Fair Indy International Wine
Competition.
Chambourcin 2001—Silver medal, 2000 Indiana State Fair Indy International Wine
Competition.
Norton 2001—Bronze medal, 2000 Indiana State Fair Indy International Wine
Competition.
Vignoles 2001—Bronze medal, Indiana State Fair Indy International Wine Competition.

HOURS AND DIRECTIONS Call for hours and directions.

Kirkwood Winery

1350 Phillips Run Rd., Summersville, WV 26651 • Phone 888-498-9463 or
304-872-2134 • www.kirkwood-wine.com • kirkwood@geoweb.net

Since 1984, Rodney Facemire has been lovingly cultivating Kirkwood's vineyard. The old family oak press featured on their label has been used since trial production began almost two decades ago. With his two sons, Rodney planted his vineyards in the spring of 1984, only to lose the vines due to harsh weather. Determined to succeed, the vineyards were replanted in the following years and now consist of over 6 acres that produce 40 tons of grapes annually. That makes 4,000 gallons of wine annually, from which more than thirty different wines are produced. Kirkwood is the only winery to offer Appalachian Ramp Wine—a garlic-onion cooking wine! And they have a yearly grape stomping!

Wines: $-$$

White Wines
Chardonnay—A medium-bodied white wine that has a unique flavor.
Seyval—A fresh, delicate wine with a unique taste.

Red Wines

Baco Noir—A Burgundy-style wine. Delicate, spicy aroma.

Cabernet Sauvignon—Burgundy-style wine with a firm, easy, distinguished flavor.

Chianti—A dark red wine with a well-balanced bouquet.

Merlot—A rich, well-balanced, full fruit character wine with a hint of oak.

Fruit Wines

Black Satin Blackberry—A rich, pleasant, fruity aroma with a pronounced berry flavor.

Moonglow Pear—A distinguished, light white wine that has a slight taste of oak.

Superior Plum—A full-flavored wine with a strong, pleasant character.

Winesap—Dessert wine with a soft, fruity flavor and a light hint of oak.

Yellow Transparent—A crisp, dry white wine with a light taste of oak.

Specialty Wines

Appalachian Ramp—Ramps are a type of local wild onion. This garlic-onion wine is great for cooking.

Ginseng—Made with Harding's Ginseng Farm 100% ginseng. High potency.

Seyval Mead—A unique, fresh wine with a delicate honey flavor.

Other Wines

Cayuga, Chancellor, The Concord Stomp, Elderberry, Foch, Mountain Blueberry, Native Niagara, Ray of Gold, Red Currant, Red Raspberry, Ripple Blush, Swiss Chard Rhubarb, Wild Grapple, and more

HOURS AND DIRECTIONS Open Apr.–Oct. 9–6 p.m., Sun. 1–6 p.m.; Nov.–Mar. 9–5 p.m., Sun. 1–5 p.m. ■ From Charleston, take I-79 north to U.S. 19 (exit 57). Take U.S. 19 south to Summersville. At Summersville, turn left onto Phillips Run Rd. and follow the signs to the winery.

Lambert's Vintage Wines

Rte. 1, Box 332-1, Weston, WV 26452 • Phone 304-269-4903 • Fax 304-269-3973

Lambert's Vintage Wines is one of West Virginia's newest wineries. Founded and still owned by James and Debbie Lambert, it offers twenty-two varieties of wines. Lambert's Vintage Wines is located in Weston, approximately 15 miles from Buckhannon. Jim and Debbie Lambert, who are also avid motorcyclists, offer wonderful vintage wines, tours, and tastings. The winery features a beautiful waterfall. And the gift shop offers herbs and blends, jellies, and jams, and other assorted goodies.

Wines: $–$$

Grape Wines

Catawba—An off-dry, native American grape varietal wine.

Fredonia—A semisweet white wine.

Fruit Wines

Blackberry—100% blackberries. A mouthful of blackberries.

Other Wines

Chardonnay, Seyval, and many others

HOURS AND DIRECTIONS Call for hours and directions.

Little Hungary Farm Winery

Rte. 6, Box 323, Buckhannon, WV 26201 • Phone 304-472-6634 • http://home.earthlink.net/~homebrewinbeer/Home/Melomel.html

Ferenc (Frank) Androczi, even in his mid-eighties, practices organic farming principles at Little Hungary Farm Winery. Ferenc Androczi learned the practice of winemaking from his father in Hungary in the 1920s. He grew up in Budapest, gaining his Ph.D. in law and social sciences, and was a Hungarian freedom fighter fighting against the Communist takeover. Imprisoned in a forced-labor camp after World War II, he and another made a perilous but successful escape from the Communist regime. Frank first settled in the Buffalo, N.Y., area and attended Syracuse University. He later fell in love with the foothills of West Virginia, settling here and became a professor of library sciences at West Virginia Wesleyan College. He retired in 1981, and Little Hungary Farm Winery was born.

Wines: $$

Melomel—The only old-fashioned, traditional European-style honey mead produced in the state of West Virginia, and some say the best in the world. Made from honey, grapes, apples, and pears. Nice. Try it! ♥

Pink—Semisweet blush wine.

Red—Off-dry red blend. Tangy.

White—Off-dry white blend.

REVIEWS AND AWARDS

"The organic-made Melomel is unique, not just to West Virginia and the USA, but maybe the world!" *—American Wine Association Magazine*

"One of the best melomels in the U.S." *—Meadmaker's Journal*

"This is just to tell you of a wonderful tour and time I just had at the Little Hungary Farm Winery in Buckhannon, West Virginia." *—Mark Cassells, Mead Lover's Digest #650, ed. Dick Dunn*

"My wife and I took the tour at Little Hungary Farm winery last year and really enjoyed it. After talking for an hour or more after the tour and tasting all of his melomels we bought three more bottles." *—Marc Shapiro, Mead Lover's Digest #650, ed. Dick Dunn*

HOURS AND DIRECTIONS Call for an appointment. ■ From Buckhannon, take U.S. 33 east (about 3 miles) toward Elkins. Turn left on Kesling Mills Rd. and go approximately 5 miles (you will pass a winery sign at the sharp turn with the large mirror). After passing the large rock that seems to be jutting out into the road, start looking for the second winery sign, which is rather small and on the right-hand side of the road. At this sign, turn left up the dirt road (go about 2 miles). There will be a large Little Hungary Winery sign on the right. Please pull into driveway and honk your horn several times.

Potomac Highland Winery

Rte. 1, Box 247-A, Keyser, WV 26726 • Phone 304-788-3066 • www.potomac-highland-winery.com • ptc00579@mail.wvnet.edu

Charles and Rebecca Whitehill, the owners of Potomac Highland, began planting grapes in 1979. But the winery was not founded until 1992. The Whitehills' winery has enjoyed a reputation for producing numerous award-winning wines. In 1997 they won four gold medals in one competition! Located in the Eastern Panhandle of West Virginia, the terrain provides an idyllic setting as well as an advantageous microclimate for grape growing.

Wines: $–$$

White Wines

Aurore—German Riesling–style white. Semisweet. Fruity and elegant.

Chardonnay—Crisp, dry white. Smooth. Nice oak aging.

Riesling—Semisweet, German-style white. Crisp. Nice aroma and flavor.

Seyval Blanc—Full-bodied, off-dry wine. Further enhanced by oak aging.

Red Wines

Chambourcin—A full-bodied, robust red. Nice character. Rich oak.

Chancellor—Full bodied, slightly off-dry. Nice fruit. Oak aged.

Meritage—A medium-bodied, dry red blend of Cabernet Sauvignon, Cabernet Franc, and Merlot. Forward fruit. Nice oak. Nice tannins.

Pinot Noir—A light-bodied red. Berry comes through. Oak aged.

Seyval Blush—Semisweet blush. Nice.

REVIEWS AND AWARDS

Chancellor 1996—Gold medal and Best of Show, West Virginia Wineries Competition

HOURS AND DIRECTIONS Call for an appointment. ■ From Keyser, take Rte. 46 east 3.8 miles, turn right on Knobley Rd. 0.8 mile, bear left on Fountain-Headsville Rd. 1.2 miles, turn right on Fried Meat Ridge Rd. 1.5 miles, and look for the vineyard and sign on the left. ■ From Burlington, take Dry Run Rd. (1 mile west of Burlington on Rte. 50) 1.8 miles, bear right on Fried Meat Ridge Rd. 2.9 miles, and watch for the vineyard and sign on the right.

Roane Vineyards

1585 Reedyville Rd., Spencer, WV 25276 • Phone 304-927-1939 • www.roanevineyards.com • paul@roanevineyards.com

The idea for Roane Vineyards dawned on owners Paul and Anna-Neale Taylor when, in 1995 while clearing a part of their farm, they discovered a tangle of wild grapes growing along the hillside. And so, in 1996 Paul and Anna-Neale planted their first test grapes and began planting their main vineyard in 1997. Roane Vineyards became an official West Virginia winery in April 2000 when the Taylors received their Federal Bonded Winery Permit and state license. Roane Vineyards wine can be found for purchase in Tamarack Capital Market in Charleston, and Main Street Wine in Ravenswood, as well as several restaurants in the state. Try the award-winning Elderberry wine when you visit—and smile.

Wines: $–$$

White Wines

Country Lane—Sweet Niagara wine. Grapy. A nice dessert wine.

Seyval Blanc—Dry white wine. Crisp and clean with a hint of grapefruit flavor.

Red Wines

Billings Point—Semisweet red blend of French-American hybrids. Rich and full bodied.

Chambourcin—Dry, ruby-colored wine. Slightly herbaceous flavor and aroma.

Tuckers Run—Off-dry, medium-bodied blend. Light oak balanced with fruit.

Blush Wines

Blush—Semisweet blush blend.

Noble Ridge—Semisweet French-American hybrid with a tart, citrus taste.

Summer Mist—Semisweet Catawba blush.

Fruit Wines

Elderberry—Sweet and tart wine made from elderberries. One of the winery's more popular wines, and for good reason. Very nice.

Other Wines

Melomel, Plum, Raspberry

HOURS AND DIRECTIONS Open daily year-round, 10 a.m.–6 p.m. ■ From Spencer, take U.S. 14 (Parkersburg Rd.) from the Go-Mart/Traders Bank/Monarch intersection approximately 6.5 miles to Billings. Take Reedyville/Golf Course Rd. left off U.S. 14 and go 1 mile to the vineyard on the right.

Robert F. Pliska and Company Winery

101 Piterra Pl., Purgitsville, WV 26852 • Phone 304-289-3493

Robert F. Pliska Winery was founded in 1975 by Robert F. Pliska and R. Elizabeth Haley-Pliska. Robert was a management philosophy professor and held a master's in enology, while Elizabeth had been a healthcare professional. Together they decided to found a winery with a distinctively Mediterranean style. According to *The New Sotheby's Wine Encyclopedia*, Pliska has "shown the most potential" among West Virginia wineries. The popular award-winning 160-acre winery is actively involved with handicapped individuals. A portion of its proceeds benefit Homes for the Mentally Handicapped. And its wines have been served in the American Embassy in Paris, France!

Wines: $

White Wines

Aurore—A semisweet, light white wine. Grapy. Nice.

Ridgerunner Gold—Off-dry white table wine.

Red Wines

Foch—Medium-bodied, classic red. Nice fruit. Good finish.

Ridgerunner Red—Off-dry, medium-bodied red.

Fruit Wines

Mountain Mama—Semisweet, golden apple wine. Good aroma and taste. Nice.

HOURS AND DIRECTIONS Open May–Oct. Tastings are held the third Sun. of each month. Call for hours and directions.

West-Whitehill Winery, Ltd.

HC 85 Box 153, Moorefield, WV 26836 • Phone 304-538-2605

West-Whitehill Winery is located in the South Branch Valley. In *The New Sotheby's Wine Encyclopedia* by Tom Stevenson, West-Whitehill is noted along with Robert F. Pliska as having "shown the most potential" in West Virginia. This winery produces a variety of fine wines including a wonderful West Virginia Rosé and Red. The best time for visitors to make the trek is weekend afternoons, when things are really humming. The winery takes part in many regional fairs, and their wines are worth the trip wherever you find them.

Wines: $–$$

White Wines

Aurore—A semisweet, light white wine. Grapy.

Seyval Blanc—Light white wine. Green apples come through.

Vidal Blanc—Classic, light white varietal.

Red Wines

West Virginia Red—A solid table red. Off-dry but with a tanginess.

Blush Wines

West Virginia Rosé—A semisweet, salmon-colored blush wine.

HOURS AND DIRECTIONS Open year-round Sat.–Sun. 1–5 p.m. ■ Call for directions.

ABOUT THE AUTHOR

CARLO DE VITO is currently Associate Publisher at Running Press Book Publishers. He has published several extremely successful books, including *Strange Fruit* by *Vanity Fair* editor David Margolick, which was chosen by the *New York Times* as a Notable Book of 2000, *My Soul Has Grown Deep* by John Edgar Wideman, which was picked as one of the best African-American books of the year by both *Ebony* and *Essence*, *Voices of Ireland* by Malachy McCourt, and *On the Shoulders of Giants*, an international hit by Stephen Hawking. He is a former editor from Macmillan, Simon & Schuster, and McGraw-Hill.

He has also edited numerous wine books such as *Making Sense of Wine* (revised and updated) by Matt Kramer as well as the award-winning *Wine Chronicles* by Greg Moore. He is also the author of *The Everything Beer Book*. He lives in Freehold, New Jersey, with his wife, two sons, and one Calico Oranda goldfish.